# The Law of State Succession

# The Law of State Succession

*Principles and Practice*

ARMAN SARVARIAN

# OXFORD
UNIVERSITY PRESS

Great Clarendon Street, Oxford, OX2 6DP,
United Kingdom

Oxford University Press is a department of the University of Oxford.
It furthers the University's objective of excellence in research, scholarship,
and education by publishing worldwide. Oxford is a registered trade mark of
Oxford University Press in the UK and in certain other countries

© Arman Sarvarian 2025

The moral rights of the author have been asserted

All rights reserved. No part of this publication may be reproduced, stored in a retrieval system, transmitted, used for text and data mining, or used for training artificial intelligence, in any form or by any means, without the prior permission in writing of Oxford University Press, or as expressly permitted by law, by licence or under terms agreed with the appropriate reprographics rights organization. Enquiries concerning reproduction outside the scope of the above should be sent to the Rights Department, Oxford University Press, at the address above.

You must not circulate this work in any other form
and you must impose this same condition on any acquirer

Public sector information reproduced under Open Government Licence v3.0
(https://www.nationalarchives.gov.uk/doc/open-government-licence)

Published in the United States of America by Oxford University Press
198 Madison Avenue, New York, NY 10016, United States of America

British Library Cataloguing in Publication Data
Data available

Library of Congress Control Number: 2024949657

ISBN 978–0–19–881795–6

DOI: 10.1093/oso/9780198817956.001.0001

Printed and bound by
CPI Group (UK) Ltd., Croydon, CR0 4YY

The manufacturer's authorised representative in the EU for product safety is Oxford University Press España S.A. of El Parque Empresarial San Fernando de Henares, Avenida de Castilla, 2 – 28830 Madrid
(www.oup.es/en or product.safety@oup.com). OUP España S.A. also acts as importer into Spain of products made by the manufacturer.

*Իմ նախահայրերի եւ զաւակների համար:*
*Fyrir fallega ylfuna mína.*
*Pro Deos et Jure.*

King Henry IV:
Canst thou, O partial sleep, give thy repose
To the wet sea-boy in an hour so rude,
And in the calmest and most stillest night,
With all appliances and means to boot,
Deny it to a king? Then happy low, lie down!
Uneasy lies the head that wears a crown.
*Enter WARWICK and SURREY*
[...]
Warwick:
There is a history in all men's lives,
Figuring the nature of the times deceased;
The which observed, a man may prophesy,
With a near aim, of the main chance of things
As yet not come to life, which in their seeds
And weak beginnings lie intreasured.
Such things become the hatch and brood of time.
King Henry IV:
Are these things then necessities?
Then let us meet them like necessities.

*King Henry IV*, Act II, Scene III

# Foreword

The law of State succession has been termed a particularly controversial one, and rightly so. The controversies start with defining what should be understood by State succession: whether it is the replacement of sovereignty over territory by successively existing States or the 'replacement of one State by another in the responsibility for the international relations of territory' as defined in the two Vienna Conventions on State succession. States have perished and been replaced by other States throughout history. The ways in which these changes in sovereignty over territory have been described vary and one of the perplexing insights of students of this field of law is that there are hardly any reliable criteria distinguishing between different forms of State succession. One only needs to be reminded of the fairly recent cases of the 'breakups' of the former Soviet Union and former Yugoslavia, which, in spite of similarities, have been quite differently assessed by the international community: a continuation of the USSR through the Russian Federation implying that other parts of the USSR separated from a State that remained in existence, on the one hand, and a true and full *dismembratio* in the case of the former Yugoslavia, which ceased to exist and was replaced by a number of successor States, on the other hand.

But the issue is not only the lack of reliable legal criteria to make the distinction between full and partial State succession. What is even worse is that fundamental legal consequences in cases of State succession remain uncertain. State practice and *opinio juris* seem to firmly establish that localized or territorial treaties automatically pass to the respective territorial successor States, on the one extreme, and that political treaties and those forming constituent agreements of international organizations automatically lapse, on the other. However, treaties 'in between', that is, those not falling under these specific categories (and that means the great majority of treaties), are subject to an undetermined fate. It is true that the past 40 to 50 years seem to indicate a practice in favour of presuming that successor States continue to be bound by the treaties of their predecessors. However, even that presumption is not fully clear and is contested by adherents to clean slate or *tabula rasa* approaches.

In light of all these uncertainties, it is particularly valuable that this monograph by Arman Sarvarian deeply dives into actual State practice and analyses in detail the vast field of instances of State succession and how the ensuing legal questions have been addressed. These questions cover succession into treaties, but also address the practice of States in regard to assets and liabilities or, in the words of the second Vienna Convention, succession into State property and State debts.

Sarvarian also analyses how the issue of private rights, including acquired rights, has been dealt with by successor States, how State responsibility may be affected by State succession, and similar matters. The study is a highly valuable, detailed assessment of actual practice that will contribute to a field that has often been dominated by theoretical generalizations which may derive from analogies to domestic inheritance law or from presumptions of non-succession deriving from an emphasis on State sovereignty. In addition, this book is particularly helpful because it shows how national courts (as well as international courts and tribunals) have reacted to the many instances of State succession. Sarvarian thereby provides a refreshing bottom-up analysis of actual State judicial practice trying to cope with State succession.

August Reinsch
Vienna
November 2024

# Preface

International law has been described as 'not only an intellectual discipline whose roots are grounded in philosophy but also a practical adjunct of diplomacy ... so that while its systematic elaboration is a matter of juristic reasoning its practical content must correspond to the realities of international life and intercourse'.[1] A rule of positive international law derives from the practice of States according to an empirical system of identification and interpretation. Its progressive development rests upon normative considerations of equity and justice.

Apart from pending territorial disputes, the scope for States to acquire original title to territory in the modern world is nugatory. If history is any guide, the acquisition of derivative title is inevitable because the international community of States has never remained completely static in its territorial composition for more than a few decades. The rules of international law concerning to the effects of such a transfer are consequently of perpetual relevance.

The genesis of this book was an essay that I contributed seven years ago to the *European Journal of International Law* reflecting upon the experiences of the International Law Commission in codifying the law of State succession.[2] It occurred to me that the last treatise by a single author on the entire subject remained the classical work of DP O'Connell published in 1967. After consulting with senior international lawyers, I proposed to Oxford University Press an attempt to provide a modern account of the law.

Though inspired by the great work of O'Connell, this book differs from it in significant respects. A draft chapter analysing in detail the theories of State succession ('universal succession', 'popular continuity', 'organic substitution', etc.) developed by scholars since the late nineteenth century[3] has been omitted. This was for three reasons: first, none of the grand theories won general acceptance in State practice as authoritative descriptions of the phenomenon; second, priority was given to digesting more of the abundant State practice in the book; and third, preceding works have comprehensively analysed the doctrinal history of the field.[4] While scholarship has been widely consulted and cited for this book, its principal focus is

---

[1] DP O'Connell, *State Succession in Municipal Law and International Law* vol 1 (CUP 1967) v.
[2] Arman Sarvarian, 'Codifying the Law of State Succession: A Futile Endeavour?' (2016) 27(3) EJIL 789.
[3] See Chapter 2.
[4] E.g. – Matthew Craven, *The Decolonization of International Law: State Succession and the Law of Treaties* (OUP 2007).

X PREFACE

not a doctrinal study of the views of commentators but rather the digestion of State practice and jurisprudence to extrapolate and to interpret the positive law.

Whereas O'Connell espoused an approach that combined the empirical interpretation of State practice with normative considerations of ethics, this book omits the personal views of its author concerning the merits or demerits of a given rule against a normative standard. Rather, his role is that of a reporter and interpreter of State practice to synthesize the sources digested and to articulate the law. Methodological choices are made that necessitate a distinction between the pronouncement of a conclusion on the existence of a rule of law and the posing of an argument with respect to its interpretation. For example, the rules of succession proposed in Chapter 8 with respect to nationality are derived from State practice as an empirical conclusion and the interpretation of that practice to distil general principles of law is a methodological choice. The essential point is that a conclusion concerning a given question of law is based upon State practice and jurisprudence, as interpreted by the author according to orthodox principles on the sources of general international law.

The scope of this book is confined to the rules of State succession applicable in international law. In contrast to the work of O'Connell, it does not investigate the legal effects of State succession on the legal system (e.g.—constitutions), judicial system (e.g.—proceedings pending at the date of succession), and public administration (e.g.—taxation) of transferred territories.[5] Due to its potential importance to the question of the effects of a succession on nationality and the high degree of coherence and consistency in national practice, the one exception is the general principle of law concerning the provisional retention in force of the legislation of the predecessor applied to the transferred territory.[6] Whereas the rules of international law can be applied in the internal legal systems of those States that permit it, those rules of internal law not regulated by international law remain their prerogative.[7]

Taking account of the great diversity of original languages in the cited sources, the two key considerations are the accuracy of the source and convenience for the reader. Unless a significant difference exists between an authentic linguistic version and a translation into English, an English-language version is cited whenever practicable. For sources lacking an English version, the applicable language of the cited document is indicated. Full citations are provided in the tables with their original titles while shortened translations into English are provided in footnotes.

When available, judgments and awards are cited in specialist reports of international law that are published for an international readership (e.g.—International

---

[5] O'Connell (n 1) 101–98.
[6] See Chapter 2.
[7] On the complexities of this dynamics, see Chapter 1.

PREFACE xi

Law Reports,[8] Reports of International Arbitral Awards, and Commonwealth International Law Cases). Multiple citations of the relevant judgment or award, such as reports from national jurisdiction, are provided in the table.

This work is the fruit of eight years' labour, including some two years under various restrictions arising from the global COVID-19 pandemic. Such have been its scale and logistics that my debts of gratitude are many and profound. I thank the School of Law of the University of Surrey, and in particular Professor Alexander Sarch and Professor Bebhinn Donnelly-Lazarov, for its financial and logistical support to enable me to pursue the project. I also thank my doctoral research assistants who have ably helped with research, translation, and editing tasks: Dr Miriam Sheikh, Mr Shashi Kant Yadav, Mr Jason De Mink, Dr Daniel Peixoto Murata, and Mr Juan Diego Dimate Gomez.

While I am grateful to the benefactors and staff of the many university and other libraries for their preservation for posterity of the priceless volumes necessary for this research, I express my especial gratitude to the Bodleian Law Library and the Institute of Advanced Legal Studies, where I most frequently profited from their valuable collections. As lines of investigation frequently reached junctures requiring detours to search for obscure materials, I am grateful to the many archivists, librarians, and other colleagues who have allowed me access to their collections and assisted in locating documents:

- Centre des Archives diplomatiques, Ministère de l'Europe et des Affaires étrangères de la République française (M Alain Peyrot and his team, particularly M Guillaume Frantzwa (Conservateur du patrimonie, Chef du pôle des Traités));
- Hamilton Library of the University of Hawai'i (Ms Eleanor Kleiber, Librarian, Pacific Collection);
- Instituto Diplomático de la República Portuguesa (Sra Benita Ferreira, Arquivista. Técnica Superior, Divisão de Arquivo e Biblioteca and her team);
- International Monetary Fund Archives (Ms Zoe Dickinson, Archives Officer);
- Legal Directorate of the Foreign, Commonwealth and Development Office of the United Kingdom (Ms Sally Langrish (Legal Adviser and Director General, Legal Directorate) and Mr Iain Macleod (former Director Legal Adviser and Director General) and their teams);
- Library of the International Telecommunication Union ($M^{me}$ Guylaine Thioulouse);
- Ministry of Foreign Affairs for the Kingdom of the Netherlands (Mr Rieks Boekholt (Legal Officer, Treaties Division));

---

[8] Originally published under the title 'Annual Digest of Public International Law Cases', the series is cited for simplicity as the 'International Law Reports' according to a continuous numbering system.

xii  PREFACE

- Ministry of Foreign Affairs for the Kingdom of Norway (Mr Gro Aaserød, Unit for Treaties and Documentation);
- Ministry of Foreign Affairs for the Republic of Slovenia (Ms Tadeja Marinič, International Law Department and Mr Boštjan Pucelj, Minister Plenipotentiary (Department for Boundaries and Succession));
- Ministry of Foreign Affairs for the State of Israel (Ms Naomi Elimelech, Director of Treaties Department);
- Ministry of Justice for the Republic of Namibia (Mr Cecil John Jossob, Law Reform and Development Commission, NamibLII Project);
- Nationaal Archief of the Kingdom of the Netherlands (Mr Diederik van Romont, Medewerker Dienstverlening);
- Rigsarkivet of the Kingdom of Denmark (Mr Tyge Krogh (Seniorforsker, Brugerservice);
- Stanford University Library (Mr James R Jacobs);
- State Department for the United States of America (Mr Mike Mattler, Treaty Office);
- Supreme Court of New South Wales (Mr Nathan Storos, Senior Courts Clerk);
- Tribunal fédéral suisse (Central Registry);
- United Nations Archives (New York & Geneva);
- United Nations Dag Hammarskjöld Library;
- United Nations Office of Legal Affairs (Mr Arnold Pronto, Principal Legal Officer, Codification Division); and
- World Bank Archives (Ms Bertha F Wilson, Archivist).

I likewise express my gratitude to the many colleagues and friends for their good offices and valuable assistance to execute the research:

- Dr Athanasia Hadjigeorgiou (University of Central Lancashire, Cyprus);
- Dr Joshua Andresen (University of Surrey);
- Dr Filippo Fontanelli (University of Edinburgh);
- Professor Todd Buchwald (George Washington University Law School);
- Dr Maria Louca (University of Leicester);
- Professor Chiara Giorgetti (University of Richmond);
- Professor Roger Skalbeck (University of Richmond);
- Professor Duncan Hollis (Temple University);
- Professor Shotaro Hamamoto (University of Kyoto);
- Professor Kanstantsin Dzehtsiarou (University of Liverpool);
- Mr Steven Sengayen (President, International Law Association (Mauritius Branch)); and
- Professor Marko Milanović (University of Reading).

I thank colleagues who have provided encouragement and robust scrutiny, whether in discussing the project or criticizing written drafts:

- Dr Daniel Costelloe (International Court of Justice);
- Dr James Devaney (University of Glasgow);
- Professor Patrick Dumberry (University of Ottowa);
- Professor Dr Andreas Kulick (Johannes Gutenberg University Mainz);
- Professor Mārtiņš Paparinskis (University College London; International Law Commission);
- Professor Dr August Reinisch (University of Vienna; International Law Commission);
- Professor Christian Tams (University of Glasgow);
- Dr Jamie Trinidad KC (University of Cambridge); and
- Professor Dr Michael Waibel (University of Vienna).

Any errors in the book are my sole responsibility. The cut-off date for the practice and jurisprudence digested is 31 August 2024.

Arman Sarvarian
Oxford, 2024

# Contents

| | |
|---|---|
| *Table of Cases* | xix |
| *Table of Legislation* | xliii |
| *Table of Treaties and other International Instruments* | lvii |
| *List of Abbreviations* | lxxxi |

| | | |
|---|---|---|
| 1. | Introduction | 1 |
| 2. | The Nature of State Succession | 15 |
| | 2.1 Introduction | 15 |
| | 2.2 The Concept of State Succession in International Law | 18 |
| | 2.2.1 The Definition of the International Law Commission | 20 |
| | 2.2.2 A Transfer of Territorial Title | 31 |
| | 2.3 A General Law of State Succession | 35 |
| | 2.3.1 The Prohibition of Conquest | 37 |
| | 2.3.2 The Question of Legal Personality | 37 |
| | 2.3.3 The Date of Succession | 40 |
| | 2.3.4 The Provisional Continuity of Internal Law | 41 |
| | 2.4 A Typology of State Succession | 43 |
| | 2.4.1 Merger | 45 |
| | 2.4.2 Absorption | 45 |
| | 2.4.3 Dismemberment | 45 |
| | 2.4.4 Cession | 46 |
| | 2.4.5 Secession | 47 |
| | 2.4.6 Accession to Independence | 47 |
| | 2.5 The Interpretation of State Practice | 51 |
| | 2.5.1 The Identification of Customary International Law | 52 |
| | 2.5.2 The Transposition of General Principles of Law | 55 |
| | 2.5.3 The Persuasive Authority of International Courts and Tribunals | 58 |
| | 2.6 Conclusions | 59 |
| 3. | Succession to Territorial Rights and Obligations | 61 |
| | 3.1 Introduction | 61 |
| | 3.2 Territorial Rights | 63 |
| | 3.2.1 Territorial Claims | 63 |
| | 3.2.2 Boundaries | 66 |
| | 3.3 Territorial Obligations | 77 |
| | 3.3.1 Leases | 78 |
| | 3.3.2 Neutralization | 82 |
| | 3.3.3 Customs Restrictions | 82 |

| | | |
|---|---|---|
| | 3.3.4 Rights of Passage | 83 |
| | 3.3.5 Navigation and Water Rights | 84 |
| | 3.3.6 Fishing and Grazing Rights | 86 |
| 3.4 | The Process of Succession | 87 |
| | 3.4.1 Territorial Treaties | 88 |
| | 3.4.2 Persistent Objection | 94 |
| | 3.4.3 Acquiescence | 98 |
| | 3.4.4 Estoppel | 99 |
| 3.5 | Conclusions | 100 |
| **4.** | **Succession to State Property and Debt** | **102** |
| 4.1 | Introduction | 102 |
| 4.2 | The General Principle of Automaticity | 104 |
| | 4.2.1 Territoriality | 105 |
| | 4.2.2 Equitable Apportionment | 106 |
| | 4.2.3 State Property | 107 |
| | 4.2.4 State Debt | 115 |
| 4.3 | Application to the Classes of Succession | 122 |
| | 4.3.1 Merger | 123 |
| | 4.3.2 Absorption | 124 |
| | 4.3.3 Dismemberment | 126 |
| | 4.3.4 Cession | 129 |
| | 4.3.5 Secession | 132 |
| | 4.3.6 Accession to Independence | 140 |
| 4.4 | Conclusions | 143 |
| **5.** | **Succession to Treaties** | **145** |
| 5.1 | Introduction | 145 |
| 5.2 | The General Principle of Consent | 146 |
| | 5.2.1 Eligibility to Succeed to a Treaty | 148 |
| | 5.2.2 Multilateral Treaties | 155 |
| | 5.2.3 Bilateral Treaties | 162 |
| 5.3 | Application to the Classes of Succession | 168 |
| | 5.3.1 Merger | 169 |
| | 5.3.2 Absorption | 170 |
| | 5.3.3 Dismemberment | 172 |
| | 5.3.4 Cession | 175 |
| | 5.3.5 Secession | 176 |
| | 5.3.6 Accession to Independence | 178 |
| 5.4 | The Process of Succession | 179 |
| | 5.4.1 Formalities | 180 |
| | 5.4.2 General Agreements on Succession | 183 |
| | 5.4.3 General Declarations on Succession | 188 |
| | 5.4.4 The Interpretation of Silence | 191 |
| 5.5 | Conclusions | 194 |

CONTENTS    xvii

6. Succession to International Claims and Responsibility    197
   6.1  Introduction    197
   6.2  The General Principle of Automaticity    202
        6.2.1  International Claims and Responsibility    205
        6.2.2  Territoriality    207
        6.2.3  Equitable Apportionment    208
   6.3  Application to the Classes of Succession    209
        6.3.1  Merger    210
        6.3.2  Absorption    213
        6.3.3  Dismemberment    217
        6.3.4  Cession    222
        6.3.5  Secession    225
        6.3.6  Accession to Independence    231
   6.4  The Process of Succession    234
        6.4.1  Succession Agreements    235
        6.4.2  Adoption    237
        6.4.3  Diplomatic Protection    238
   6.5  Conclusions    239

7. Succession and Nationality    242
   7.1  Introduction    242
   7.2  The General Principle of Automaticity    245
        7.2.1  The Affected Body of Nationals    248
        7.2.2  The Principle of Territoriality    250
        7.2.3  The Right of Option    254
        7.2.4  Legal Persons    257
   7.3  Application to the Classes of Succession    258
        7.3.1  Merger    259
        7.3.2  Absorption    261
        7.3.3  Dismemberment    262
        7.3.4  Cession    264
        7.3.5  Secession    268
        7.3.6  Accession to Independence    284
   7.4  Conclusions    288

8. Succession and Private Property    291
   8.1  Introduction    291
   8.2  The International Minimum Standard of Treatment    294
        8.2.1  Property    305
        8.2.2  Concessions    308
        8.2.3  Nationality    315
   8.3  The Criteria for Lawful Expropriation    316
        8.3.1  Prescribed Law    317
        8.3.2  Public Interest    318

xviii CONTENTS

| | | |
|---|---|---|
| | 8.3.3 Discrimination | 318 |
| | 8.3.4 Compensation | 318 |
| 8.4 | The Principles of Reparation | 320 |
| 8.5 | Conclusions | 325 |
| 9. | Conclusion: The Future of State Succession | 327 |

| | |
|---|---|
| *Illustrative List of Successions* | 337 |
| *Primary Bibliography* | 359 |
| *Index* | 383 |

# Table of Cases

(arranged by jurisdiction in alphabetical order)

## AFRICAN COMMISSION ON HUMAN AND PEOPLES' RIGHTS

*CEMIRIDE and Minority Rights Group International on behalf of Endorois Welfare Council v Kenya (Endorois Case)* African Commission on Human and Peoples' Rights (4 February 2010) ACHPR 27th Activity Report, Annex 5; **142 ILR 1** ...... 304

## AFRICAN COMMITTEE OF EXPERTS ON THE RIGHTS AND WELFARE OF THE CHILD

Decision No 002/2018 on the Communication submitted by the African Centre of Justice and Peace Studies (ACJPS) and People's Legal Aid Centre (PLACE) against the Government of Republic of Sudan, African Committee of Experts on the Rights and Welfare of the Child (May 2018) <https://cadmus.eui.eu/bitstr eam/handle/1814/74634/RSC_GLOBALCIT_CR_2022_05.pdf?sequence= 1&isAllowed=y> accessed 31 January 2025 ................................... 281

## CLAIMS COMMISSIONS

*Administrative Decision No V*, US-German Mixed Claims Commission (31 October 1924) **7 RIAA 1** .................................................... 235–36
*Atlantic and Hope Insurance Companies v Ecuador (The Mechanic)* (Opinion) Claims Commissioner Hassaurek (8 January 1865) **29 RIAA 108**. ..................... 215
*Civilians Claims: Eritrea's Claims 15, 16, 23 & 27-32* (Partial Award) Eritrea-Ethiopia Claims Commission (17 December 2004) <https://pcacases.com/web/sendAtt ach/755> accessed 5 February 2024. ....................................... 9–10
'Commission mixte (du 1[er] janvier 1952 – 31 décembre 1955)' France Archives, Série E, Carton 81, Dossier 5 ................................................ 129
'Commission mixte (du 1[er] janvier 1952 – 31 décembre 1955)' France Archives, Série E, Carton 81, Dossier 5, 31 ........................................... 129
*Consolidated Debt of New Grenada Cases*, US-Colombian Claims Commission (1864) **IV Moore 3612**. ...........................................126–29, 215
*Delimitation of the Border between Eritrea and Ethiopia* (Award of 13 April 2002) Eritrea-Ethiopia Boundary Commission (13 April 2002) **25 RIAA 83** ......... 47, 100
'Inde française : questions judiciaires et nationalité (1 décembre 1949 – 28 février 1950)' **France Archives, Série E, Carton 81, Dossier 7B**. ...................... 129
*Lusitania Cases* (Opinion) German-American Claims Commission (1 November 1923) **7 RIAA 32**. ..................................................... 55–56
*Pablo Nájera (of the Lebanon) Case (France v Mexico)* France-Mexico Claims Commission (19 October 1928) 4 ILR 393, **V RIAA 466 (French)** ............ 235–36
*Pensions: Eritrea's Claims 15, 19 & 23* (Final Award) (19 December 2005) Eritrea-Ethiopia Claims Commission ......................................... 9, 138–39
*Sarah Campbell and W. Ackers Cage*, Anglo-Venezuelan Mixed Claims Commission (1 October 1869) **II Recueil des arbitrages internationaux (1923) 552** .......... 106

XX    TABLE OF CASES

*Texas Bond Cases* (Award) British-American Claims Commission
(29 November 1854) **IV Moore 3591**....................................... 124

## COMMERCIAL ARBITRAL TRIBUNALS

*BP Exploration Co. Ltd v Libya* (Award) Arbitral Tribunal (1 August 1974)
**53 ILR 297**........................................................... 315–16
*Compagnie d'Enterprises CFE SA. v Republic of Yemen* ICC Case No 77489/BGD/
OLG, Memorandum Opinion of the United States District Court for the
District of Columbia (30 May 2001)................................117–18, 210, 310
*The Ditta Luigi Gallotti v The Somali Government* (Award) Arbitral Tribunal
(5 December 1964) **40 ILR 158**........................................ 209, 309
*Kuwait v Aminoil* (Award) Arbitral Tribunal (24 March 1982) **66 ILR 518** ............ 309

## CONCILIATION COMMISSIONS

*Collas & Michel Claim*, Franco-Italian Conciliation Commission (21 January 1953)
4 Recueil des Décisions 134; 13 RIAA 298; **20 ILR 628** ....................... 306–7
*Différend relatif à la répartition des biens des collectivités locales (Italie c. France)*
Commission France-Italie, Décision n° 163 (9 octobre 1953) **XIII RIAA 503** ... 112–14
*Flegenheimer Case* (Decision No 182) Italian-United States Conciliation
Commission (20 September 1958) **XIV RIAA 327** .......................... 235–36
*Frontier (Local Authorities) Award*, Franco-Italian Conciliation Commission
(1 December 1953) Part IV Recueil des Décisions 213; **20 ILR 63** ............. 307–8
*L'affaire du F. OABV (Maroc c. France)* Commission de conciliation (1958)
**4 AFDI 282** ......................................................156–58, 184
*Partition of Property of Local Communities (Italy v France)* (Decision No 163)
Franco-Italian Conciliation Commission (9 October 1953) **XIII RIAA 503**.... 112–14
*Raibl Claim*, Anglo-Italian Conciliation Commission (19 June 1964) **40 ILR 260**.... 306–7

## EUROPEAN COURT OF HUMAN RIGHTS

*Ališić and others v Bosnia and Herzegovina, Croatia, Serbia, Slovenia and the
Former Yugoslav Republic of Macedonia* App No 60642/08, European Court
of Human Rights, Grand Chamber (16 July 2014) .......................10, 114–15
*Bijelić v Montenegro and Serbia* No 11890/05, European Court of Human Rights
(28 April 2009) **142 ILR 146**............................... 203, 204, 227, 228, 238
*Ilić v Serbia* App No 30132/04 European Court of Human Rights (9 January 2008) .... 225
*Kovačić and others v Slovenia* Nos 44574/98, 45133/98 & 48316/99, European
Court of Human Rights (3 October 2008) .................................... 127
*Lakićević and Others v Montenegro and Serbia*, App Nos 27458/06, 37205/06,
37207/06 and 33604/07 European Court of Human Rights (13 December 2011).... 226
*Mandić v Montenegro, Serbia and Bosnia and Herzegovina* App No 32557/05
European Court of Human Rights (12 June 2012) ........................... 226
*Matijašević v Serbia* App No 23037/04 European Court of Human Rights
(19 December 2006) 48 EHRR (2009) 876 ............................... 204, 225
*Milić v Montenegro and Serbia* App No 28359/05 European Court of Human Rights
(11 December 2012) ...................................................... 226
*Si Amer v France* No 29137/06 European Court of Human Rights (29 October 2009)..... 118
*Slovenia v Croatia* No 54155/16, European Court of Human Rights
(16 December 2020) ...................................................... 127
*Tomić v Serbia* App No 25959/06 European Court of Human Rights (26 June 2007).... 225

TABLE OF CASES    xxi

*von Maltzan and Others, von Zitzewitz and Others, and Ferrostaal and Stiftung v Germany*, App Nos 71916/01, 71917/01 & 10260/02 European Court of Human Rights (Grand Chamber) (2 March 2005) ............................. 213

## EUROPEAN COURT OF JUSTICE

*Belgium v Banque Indosuez and Another* Case C-177/96 Court of Justice of the European Union, Sixth Chamber (16 October 1997) [1997] ECR I-05659 ........ 115

*Mario Vicente Micheletti and Others v Delegación del Gobierno en Cantabria* Case C-369/90 Court of Justice of the European Union (7 July 1992) .............. 242–43

*Micheletti v Delegación del Gobierno en Cantabria* Case C-369/90 Court of Justice of the European Union (7 July 1992) ...................................... 242–43

## INTER-STATE ARBITRAL TRIBUNALS

*Acquisition of Polish Nationality (Germany v Poland)* Arbitrator Kaeckenbeeck (10 July 1924) **I RIAA 403**............................................... 252–53

*Adolph G. Studer Claim (United States v Great Britain)* British-American Claims Arbitral Tribunal (1925) **6 RIAA 149**........................................ 304

*Affaire de la Dette Publique Ottomane (Bulgarie, Irak, Palestine, Transjordanie, Grèce, Italie et Turauie)* Arbitre (Eugène Borel) (18 avril 1925) **1 RIAA 529**....... 107

*Affaire de l'île de Clipperton (Mexique c. France)* (Award) Arbitre (S.M. Victor-Emmanuel III) (28 janvier 1931) **2 RIAA 1105** .................................65

*Affaire des biens britanniques au Maroc Espagnol (Espagne contre Royaume-Uni)* (Sentence) Arbitre (Max Huber) (1er mai 1925) **2 RIAA 615** .....................49

*Affaire des chemins de fer zeltweg-Wolfsberg (Autriche c. Yougoslavie)* Tribunal d'arbitrage (12 mai 1934) **3 RIAA 1795** .................................... 306–7

*Affaire des Frontières (Colombie c. Vénézuéla)*, Arbitre (Conseil fédéral suisse) (24 mars 1922) **1 RIAA 223** .............................................. 72–73

*Affaire des réparations allemandes selon l'article 260 du traité de Versailles Réparation (Allemagne c. Commission des Réparations)* Arbitre (M. Beichmann) (3 septembre 1924) **1 RIAA 429**........................................126–29, 306

*Affaire du chemin de fer Sopron-Koszeg (Compagnie du chemin de fer vicinal de Sopron-Köszeg c. Autriche et Hongrie)* Tribunal d'arbitrage (18 juin 1929) **2 RIAA 961** ......................................................... 306–7

*Affaire relative à l'acquisition de la nationalité polonaise (Allemagne c. Pologne)* (Sentence) Arbitre Kaeckenbeeck (10 juillet 1924) **1 RIAA 403** .............. 251–52

*Affaire relative à la concession des phares de l'Empire Ottoman (Grèce c. France)* Cour Permanente d'Arbitrage (24/27 juillet 1956) **12 RIAA 165** ................. 222

*Arbitral Award of 31 July 1989 (Guinea-Bissau v Senegal)* ad hoc Arbitral Tribunal (31 July 1989) in *Case Concerning the Arbitral Award of 31 July 1989 (Guinea-Bissau v Senegal)* (Application) Annex; 83 ILR 1 ........ 22–23, 100, 176–78

*Arbitral Award relating to the boundaries between Brazil and French Guiana* (1 December 1900) **28 RIAA 349** ...............................................66

*Arbitration between Guyana and Suriname* (Award) PCA Case No 2004-04 (17 September 2007) **30 RIAA 1** ................................... 66–76, 176–77

*Chemins de fer Barcs-Pakrac (Hongrie c. Yougoslavie)* (Arrêt) Tribunal d'arbitrage (5 octobre 1934) **3 RIAA 1569**............................................ 306–7

*Beagle Channel Arbitration (Argentina v Chile)* ad hoc Arbitral Tribunal (18 February 1977), 17(5) ILM 1198, XXI RIAA 53, **52 ILR 93** ................ 72–73

*Bering Fur Seals (United States v United Kingdom)* (Award) ad hoc Arbitral Tribunal (15 August 1893) **28 RIAA 263**...................................... 66–76

xxii  TABLE OF CASES

*Boundaries Case (Colombia v Venezuela)* (Award) Arbitral Tribunal
  (24 March 1922) **1 RIAA 223**. . . . . . . . . . . . . . . . . . . . . . . . . . . . . . . . . . . . . . . . . . . 72–73
*Boundaries of the Island of Timor (Netherlands v Portugal)* Permanent Court of
  Arbitration (Arbitrator Lardy) Award (25 June 1914) in Wilson, *The Hague
  Arbitration Cases* (1915) 380 . . . . . . . . . . . . . . . . . . . . . . . . . . . . . . . . . . . . . . . . . . 70–72
*Boundary between the Colony of British Guiana and Venezuela (United Kingdom v
  Venezuela)* (Award) Arbitral Tribunal (3 October 1899) **28 RIAA 331**. . . . . . . . . . . . . .97
*Boundary Case between Bolivia and Peru* Arbitrator (J. Figeuroa Alcorta,
  President of the Argentine Republic) (9 July 1909) **11 RIAA 133**. . . . . . . . . . . . . . . 72–73
*Boundary Case between Costa Rica and Panama* Arbitrator (E. Douglass White,
  Chief Justice of the United States) (12 September 1914) **11 RIAA 519** . . . . . . . . . 72–73
*Chagos Marine Protected Area Arbitration (Mauritius v United Kingdom)* (Award)
  Permanent Court of Arbitration (18 March 2015) . . . . . . . . . . . . . . . . . . . . . . . . .46, 78–79
*Claim of Finnish Shipowners against Great Britain in respect of the Use of Certain
  Finnish Vessels During the War (Finland v United Kingdom)* (Award) Sole
  Arbitrator (Dr Bagge) (9 May 1934) **3 RIAA 1479** . . . . . . . . . . . . . . . . . . . . . . . . . . . . 236
*F.H. Redward and others (Great Britain) v United States* (Award) *ad hoc* Arbitral
  Tribunal (10 November 1925) Nielsen 160; (1926) 20 AJIL 382; 3 ILR 80;
  **6 RIAA 157** . . . . . . . . . . . . . . . . . . . . . . . . . . . . . . . . . . . . . . . . . . . . . . . . . . . . . . . . . . 213
*German Reparations under Article 260 of the Treaty of Versailles (Germany v
  Reparations Commission)* (Award) Arbitral Tribunal (3 September 1924)
  1 RIAA 429. . . . . . . . . . . . . . . . . . . . . . . . . . . . . . . . . . . . . . . . . . . . . . . . . . . . . . . . 126–29
*Goldenberg (Romania v Germany)* (Award) Sole Arbitrator Robert Fazy
  (27 September 1928) 2 RIAA 903 . . . . . . . . . . . . . . . . . . . . . . . . . . . . . . . . . . . . . . . . . . 291
*Guiana Boundary Case (Brazil v Great Britain)* (Arbitral Award) (6 June 1905)
  11 RIAA 21. . . . . . . . . . . . . . . . . . . . . . . . . . . . . . . . . . . . . . . . . . . . . . . . . . . . . . . . . . . .69
*Guinea – Guinea-Bissau Maritime Delimitation Case* (Award) *ad hoc* Arbitral
  Tribunal (14 February 1985) 19 RIAA 149; **77 ILR 636**. . . . . . . . . . . . . . . . . . .100, 176–78
*Gulf of Piran Arbitration (Croatia v Slovenia)* (Final Award) Permanent Court of
  Arbitration Case No 2012-04 (29 June 2017) . . . . . . . . . . . . . . . . . . . 32–33, 70–72, 74–75
*Honduras Borders (Guatemala v Honduras)* (Award) *ad hoc* Arbitral Tribunal
  (16 July 1930) 2 RIAA 1307 . . . . . . . . . . . . . . . . . . . . . . . . . . . . . . . . . . . . . . . . . . . . 72–73
*Indo-Pakistan Western Boundary (Rann of Kutch) Case (India v Pakistan)* (Award)
  *ad hoc* Arbitral Tribunal (19 February 1968) 17 RIAA 1; **50 ILR 2** . . . . . . . . . . . . . 65, 98
*Iron Rhine Arbitration (Belgium v Netherlands)* (Award) Arbitral Tribunal
  (24 May 2005) 140 ILR 131; **27 RIAA 41**. . . . . . . . . . . . . . . . . . . . . . . . . . . . . . . . . . . .83
*Isaac M. Brower Case (United States v Great Britain)* British-American Claims
  Arbitral Tribunal (1923) 6 RIAA 109 . . . . . . . . . . . . . . . . . . . . . . . . . . . . . . . . . . . . . . . 304
*Island of Palmas (or Miangas)* (Award) Permanent Court of Arbitration (Arbitrator
  Max Huber) (4 April 1928) 22 AJIL (1928) 867; II RIAA 829, 128 BFSP 863,
  **4 ILR 103** . . . . . . . . . . . . . . . . . . . . . . . . . . . . . . . . . . . . . . . . . . . . . . . . . . . . 65, 66–76
*Italy v Libya*, UN Tribunal for Libya (3 July 1954) 25 ILR 13. . . . . . . . . . . . . . . . . . . . 303–4
*Italy v Libya*, UN Tribunal for Libya (27 June 1955) 22 ILR 103. . . . . . . . 108, 255–56, 303–4
*Italy v United Kingdom and Libya*, UN Tribunal for Libya
  (31 January 1953) 25 ILR 2. . . . . . . . . . . . . . . . . . . . . . . . . . . . . . . . . . . . . . . . . . . . . 303–4
*Maritime Delimitation Arbitration (Eritrea v Yemen)* (Second Stage) 12 RIAA 335 . . . 70–72
*North Atlantic Coast Fisheries Case (Great Britain v United States)* (Award)
  Arbitral Tribunal (7 September 1910) 11 RIAA 167 . . . . . . . . . . . . . . . . . . . . . . . . . . . .77
*Norwegian Shipowners Claims (Norway v United States)* (Award) Arbitral
  Tribunal (13 October 1922) 1 RIAA 307 . . . . . . . . . . . . . . . . . . . . . . . . . . . . . . . . . . . . 313
*Robert E. Brown Claim (United States v Great Britain)* British-American Arbitral
  Tribunal (23 November 1923) Nielsen 187; VI RIAA 120; **2 ILR 66**. . . . . . .213–16, 238

TABLE OF CASES xxiii

*Sentence arbitrale relative à la question des frontières du Brésil et de la Guyane*
*française*, Tribunal arbitral (Gouvernement de la Confédération suisse)
(1 décembre 1900) 28 RIAA 349 ............................................................68
*The Sopron-Köszeg Local Railway Company Case*, Arbitral Tribunal (Council of the League
of Nations) (18 June 1929) LNOJ (1929) 1359; 24 AJIL (1930) 164; **5 ILR 57**..........309–10
*Spanish Zone of Morocco Claims (Great Britain v Spain)* Rapporteur Max Huber
(23 October 1924) Rapports 170; **2 ILR 19**..................................... 49–50
*Tacna-Arica Question (Chile v Peru)* (Award) Arbitrator Calvin Coolidge
(4 March 1925) 2 RIAA 921 ................................................................83
*Territorial Sovereignty and Scope of the Dispute (Eritrea v Yemen)* Arbitral Tribunal
(Permanent Court of Arbitration) (9 October 1998) 22 RIAA 211 ............. 30, 65
*Watercourses in Katanga Case (Compagnie du Katanga v Colony of the Belgian*
*Congo)* (Award) Arbitral Tribunal in JG Wetter and SM Schwebel, 'Some
Little-Known Cases on Concessions' (1964) 40 BYIL 183................... 309–10
*Webster Claim (United States v Great Britain)* British-American Claims Arbitral
Tribunal (1925) 6 RIAA 166............................................................ 304

## INTRA-STATE ARBITRAL TRIBUNALS

*Delimiting Abyei Area (Sudan v Sudan People's Liberation Movement/Army)*
(Final Award) PCA Case No 2008-07 (22 July 2009) ............................76
*Dubai-Sharjah Border Arbitration* (Award) *ad hoc* Court of Arbitration
(19 October 1981) 91 ILR 543 ............................................................76

## INTERNATIONAL COURT OF JUSTICE

*Ahmadou Sadio Diallo (Guinea v Democratic Republic of the Congo)* (Merits)
(Judgment of 30 November 2010) [2010] ICJ Rep 639...........................292
*Ahmadou Sadio Diallo (Guinea v Democratic Republic of the Congo)*
(Compensation) (Judgment of 19 June 2012) [2012] ICJ Rep 324 ................292
*Ahmadou Sadio Diallo (Guinea v Democratic Republic of the Congo)* (Preliminary
Objections) (Judgment of 25 May 2007) [2007] ICJ Rep 582 ....................292
*Application of the Convention on the Prevention and Punishment of the Crime*
*of Genocide (Bosnia and Herzegovina v Serbia and Montenegro)* (Merits)
(Judgment of 26 February 2007) [2007] ICJ Rep 43 ............................40
*Application of the Convention on the Prevention and Punishment of the Crime of*
*Genocide (Croatia v Serbia)* (Merits) (Judgment of 3 February 2015)
[2015] ICJ Rep 3...................................................................... 217
*Barcelona Traction, Light and Power Company, Limited (Belgium v Spain)*
(Second Phase) (Judgment of 5 February 1970) [1970] ICJ Rep 3..... 235–36, 255–56
*Certain Phosphate Lands in Nauru (Nauru v Australia)* (Preliminary Objections)
(Judgment of 26 June 1992) [1992] ICJ Rep 240 ................ 30, 206, 229, 320–25
*Compagnie du Port, des Quais et des Entrepôts de Beyrouth and the Société Radio-*
*Orient (France v Lebanon)* (Order of 31 August 1960) [1960] ICJ Rep 186 ..... 308–14
*Convention on the Prevention and Punishment of the Crime of Genocide*
*(Bosnia and Herzegovina v Yugoslavia)* (Preliminary Objections)
(Judgment of 11 July 1996) [1996] ICJ Rep 595......................... 40, 155, 225
*Convention for the Prevention and Punishment of the Crime of Genocide*
*(Croatia v Serbia)* (Preliminary Objections) (Judgment of 18 November
2008) [2008] ICJ Rep 412 ........................................54, 156–57, 225
*Delimitation of the Gulf of Maine Area (Canada v United States of America)*
(Judgment of 12 October 1984) [1984] ICJ Rep 305........................... 190

xxiv  TABLE OF CASES

*Delimitation of the Maritime Boundary in the Gulf of Maine Area (Canada v United States of America)* (Judgment of 12 October 1984) [1984] ICJ Rep 305 ........... 190

*Électricité de Beyrouth Company Case (France v Lebanon)* (Order of 29 July 1954) [1954] ICJ Rep 107 ..................................................... 308–14

*Frontier Dispute (Benin v Niger)* (Judgment of 12 July 2005) [2005] ICJ Rep 90 ......... .73

*Frontier Dispute (Burkina Faso v Mali)* (Judgment of 22 December 1986) [1986] ICJ Rep 554 ..................................................... .73

*Frontier Dispute (Burkina Faso v Niger)* (Judgment of 16 April 2013) [2013] ICJ Rep 44 ..................................................... .73

*Gabčikovo-Nagymaros Project (Hungary v Slovakia)* (Judgment of 25 September 1997) [1997] ICJ Rep 7 .................. 55–56, 92, 172, 199, 205, 215, 216, 234, 235

*International Status of South West Africa* (Advisory Opinion of 11 July 1950) [1950] ICJ Rep 128 ..................................................... .50

*Kasikili/Sedudu Island (Botswana v Namibia)* (Judgment of 13 December 1999) [1999] ICJ Rep 1045 ..................................................... 65, 93

*Land, Island and Maritime Frontier Dispute (El Salvador v Honduras)* (Application to Intervene) (Order of 28 February 1990) [1990] ICJ Rep 92 .... 191–92

*Land, Island and Maritime Frontier Dispute (El Salvador v Honduras, Nicaragua Intervening)* (Judgment of 11 September 1992) [1992] ICJ Rep 351 ............ 72–73

*Land and Maritime Boundary (Cameroon v Nigeria, Equatorial Guinea intervening)* (Judgment of 10 October 2002) [2002] ICJ Rep 303 .......... 49–50, 100

*Legal Consequences of the Separation of the Chagos Archipelago from Mauritius in 1965* (Advisory Opinion of 25 February 2019) [2019] ICJ Rep 95 .....27–28, 73–74

*Maritime Delimitation in the Caribbean Sea and the Pacific Ocean (Costa Rica v Nicaragua) and Land Boundary in the Northern Part of the Isla Portillos (Costa Rica v Nicaragua)* (Judgment of 2 February 2018) [2018] ICJ Rep 139 ....... .32

*Maritime Delimitation and Territorial Questions (Qatar v Bahrain)* (Judgment of 16 March 2001) [2001] ICJ Rep 40 ..................................... 70–72

*Maritime Dispute (Peru v Chile)* (Judgment of 27 January 2014) [2014] ICJ Rep 3 ....... .83

*North Sea Continental Shelf Cases (Germany v Denmark; Germany v Netherlands)* (Judgment of 20 February 1969) [1969] ICJ Rep 3 ........................... 55–56

*Nottebohm Case (Liechtenstein v Guatemala)* (Second Phase) (Judgment of 6 April 1955) [1955] ICJ Rep 4 ..................................... .235–36, 243

*Nuclear Tests (Australia v France)* (Judgment of 20 December 1974) [1974] ICJ Rep 253 ............................................. 99–100, 191–92

*Rights of Nationals of the United States of America in Morocco (France v United States of America)* (Judgment of 27 August 1952) [1952] ICJ Rep 176 ........ .49–50, 146, 229

*Rights of Passage over Indian Territory (Portugal v India)* (Merits) (Judgment of 12 April 1960) [1960] ICJ Rep 6 ........................................... 29, 83

*Sovereignty over Certain Frontier Land (Belgium v Netherlands)* (Judgment of 20 June 1959) [1959] ICJ Rep 209 ...................................... 72–73

*Sovereignty over Pedra Branca/Pulau Batu Puteh, Middle Rocks and South Ledge (Malaysia v Singapore)* (Judgment of 23 May 2008) [2008] ICJ Rep 12 ....... 100, 190

*Sovereignty over Pulau Ligitan and Pulau Sipadan (Indonesia v Malaysia)* (Application by the Philippines to Intervene) (Judgment of 23 October 2001) [2001] ICJ Rep 575 ..................................................... .65

*Sovereignty over Pulau Ligitan and Pulau Sipadan (Indonesia v Malaysia)* (Merits) (Judgment of 17 December 2002) [2002] ICJ Rep 625 ........................ 65–66

*Temple of Preah Vihear (Cambodia v Thailand)* (Merits) (Judgment of 15 June 1962) [1962] ICJ Rep 6 ..................................... .55–56, 90, 98, 190

*Temple of Preah Vihear (Cambodia v Thailand)* (Preliminary Objections) (Judgment of 26 May 1961) [1961] ICJ Rep 17 ............. 49, 89–90, 146, 160, 184

*Territorial Dispute (Libya v Chad)* (Judgment of 3 February 1994) [1994] ICJ Rep 6 ... 100

# INTERNATIONAL CRIMINAL TRIBUNAL FOR THE FORMER YUGOSLAVIA

Case No. IT-96-21-T *Prosecutor v Zejnil Delalić*, ICTY Trial Chamber
(16 November 1998) *Judicial Reports* (1998) 1031 . . . . . . . . . . . . . . . . . . . . . .242–45, 261

# INTERNATIONAL TRIBUNAL FOR THE LAW OF THE SEA

*Delimitation of the Maritime Boundary in the Bay of Bengal (Bangladesh v Myanmar)* (Judgment of 14 March 2012) [2012] ITLOS Rep 4. . . . . . . . . . . . . . . . . . .89

# INVESTOR-STATE ARBITRAL TRIBUNALS

*Achmea B.V (formerly known as "Eureko B.V") v Slovak Republic* (Final Award)
PCA Case No 2008-13 (7 December 2012). . . . . . . . . . . . . . . . . . . . . . . . . . . . . . . . 303
*Active Partners Group Limited v South Sudan* (Final Award) PCA Case No 2013/4
(27 January 2015). . . . . . . . . . . . . . . . . . . . . . . . . . . . . . . . . . . . . . . . . . . . . . . . . . . 310
*Asian Agricultural Products Ltd (APPL) v Sri Lanka* (Award) ICSID Case
No ARB/87/3 (27 June 1990) 30 ILM 557. . . . . . . . . . . . . . . . . . . . . . . . . . . . . . . . 292
*Binder v Czech Republic* (Final Award) UNCITRAL *ad hoc* Arbitration (15 July 2011)
<https://investmentpolicy.unctad.org/investment-dispute-settlement/cases/
194/binder-v-czech-republic> accessed 31 January 2025. . . . . . . . . . . . . . . . . . . . . . 303
*Caratube International Oil Co. LLP and Mr Devincci Salah Hourani v Kazakhstan*
(Award) ICSID Case No ARB/13/13 (27 September 2017) . . . . . . . . . . . . . . . . . . 315–16
*CME Czech Republic B.V (The Netherlands) v Czech Republic* (Final Award)
UNCITRAL *ad hoc* Arbitral Tribunal (14 March 2003) 9 ICSID Reports 412. . . . . 317
*Compañia de aguas del Aconquija S.A. and Vivendi Universal S.A. v Argentina*
(Award) ICSID Case No ARB/97/3 (20 August 2007) . . . . . . . . . . . . . . . . . . . . . . . . 316
*Edmond Khudyan and Arin Capital & Investment v Armenia* (Award) ICSID Case
No ARB/17/36 (15 December 2021) (not published). . . . . . . . . . . . . . . 2, 9, 242–45, 246,
248–49, 277–78, 331
*European American Investment Bank AG (Austria) v The Slovak Republic*
(Award on Jurisdiction) PCA Case No 2010-17 (22 October 2012) . . . . . . . . . . . . . 155
*Frontier Petroleum Services Ltd v Czech Republic* (Final Award) PCA Case
No 45035 (12 November 2010). . . . . . . . . . . . . . . . . . . . . . . . . . . . . . . . . . . . . . . . . . . 303
*Gold Pool v Kazakhstan* (Award) PCA Case No 2016-23 (30 July 2020)
(UNCITRAL) (not published) . . . . . . . . . . . . . . . . . . . . . . . . . . . . . . . . . . . . . . . . 164–65
*Government of Kuwait v American Independent Oil Company (Aminoil) ad hoc*
Arbitral Tribunal (24 March 1982) 66 ILR 518 . . . . . . . . . . . . . . . . . . . . . . . . . 309, 317
*Haakon Korsguard v Croatia* (Award) UNCITRAL *ad hoc* Arbitral Tribunal
(7 November 2022) (not published). . . . . . . . . . . . . . . . . . . . . . . . . . . . . . . . . . .2, 126–27
*InterTrade Holding GmbH (Germany) v Czech Republic* (Final Award) PCA
Case No 2009-12 (29 May 2012). . . . . . . . . . . . . . . . . . . . . . . . . . . . . . . . . . . . . . . . . 303
*Medusa Oil and Gas Limited v Montenegro* (Award on Jurisdiction) PCA Case
No 2015-39 (UNCITRAL) (17 July 2019) (not published). . . . . . . . . . . . . . . . . . . . . 181
*MNSS B.V and Recupero Credito Acciaio N.V v Montenegro* (Award) ICSID Case
No ARB(AF)/12/8 (4 May 2016). . . . . . . . . . . . . . . . . . . . . . . . . . . . . . . . . . . . . . . . . 303
*Mytilineos Holdings SA v State Union of Serbia & Montenegro and Republic of
Serbia* (Partial Award on Jurisdiction) Arbitral Tribunal (UNCITRAL)
(8 September 2006) <https://www.italaw.com/cases/documents/726>
accessed 10 September 2019 . . . . . . . . . . . . . . . . . . . . . . . . . . . . . . . . . . . . . . . . 225, 230
*Oleg Vladimirovich Deripaska v Montenegro* (Award of 25 October 2019)
PCA Case No. 2017-07 (not published). . . . . . . . . . . . . . . . . . . . . 2, 9, 162–68, 191, 192

xxvi TABLE OF CASES

*Sanum Investments Limited v Laos* (Award) PCA Case No 2013-13
(6 August 2019)..................................2, 9, 149–50, 152, 163, 176, 184
*Sudapet v South Sudan* (Award) ICSID Case No ARB/12/26
(30 September 2016) ..........................2, 9, 108, 109, 110, 139, 141, 331
*Voecklinghaus v Czech Republic* (Final Award) UNCITRAL *ad hoc* Arbitration
(19 September 2011) <https://investmentpolicy.unctad.org/investment-dispute-set
tlement/cases/301/v-cklinghaus-v-czech-republic> accessed 31 January 2025 ....... 303
*World Wide Minerals v Kazakhstan (2)* (Award on Jurisdiction) UNCITRAL
*ad hoc* Arbitral Tribunal (15 October 2015) (not published)..................9, 164–65

## MIXED ARBITRAL TRIBUNALS

*Burt (George Rodney) Case*, British-American Claims Arbitral Tribunal (26 October
1923) Nielsen 588; VI RIAA 93; **2 ILR 78**..................................... 304
*Falla-Nataf and Brothers v Germany*, Franco-German Mixed Arbitral Tribunal
(30 December 1927) VII Recueil 642; **4 ILR 44**............................. 49–50
*Grzesik v Polish State*, Upper Silesian Arbitral Tribunal (4 March 1935) V Amtliche
Sammlung von Entscheidungen des Schiedsgerichts für Oberschlesien 186;
**8 ILR 136**........................................................118–19
*Hausen v Polish State*, Upper Silesian Arbitral Tribunal (16 November 1934) V
Schiedsgericht für Oberschlesien Trybunał Rozjemczy dla Górnego Śląska
(1935) 21; **7 ILR 102** ...................................................... 292
*Katz and Klump v Yugoslavia*, Germano-Yugoslav Mixed Arbitral Tribunal (30
September 1925) V Recueil des décisions 963; **3 ILR 33** ...................... 150
*Municipal Trust Company Limited c. État hongrois* (Décision) Tribunal arbitral
mixte hungaro-britannique (26 juillet 1923) III des décisions 248 ............ 126–29
*National Bank of Egypt v Austro-Hungarian Bank*, Anglo-Austrian Mixed Arbitral
Tribunal (13 July 1923) III Recueil des décisions 236; **2 ILR 23**.............. 255, 282
*National Bank of Egypt v German Government and Bank für Handel und Industrie*,
Anglo-German Mixed Arbitral Tribunal (31 May 1924) IV Recueil des décisions
233; **2 ILR 21**........................................................ 282
*Office Français v Office Allemand (Zinc de Silésie)* French-German Mixed Arbitral
Tribunal (9 April 1926) VI Recueil des décisions 278; **3 ILR 108**................ 292
*Parounak and Bedros Parounakian v Turkish Government*, Anglo-Turkish Mixed
Arbitral Tribunal (16 December 1929) IX Recueil des décisions 748; **5 ILR 25**.....262–64
*Ul Ltd. v Polish State*, Upper Silesian Arbitral Tribunal (21 July 1932) III(2/3)
Schiedsgericht für Oberschlesien , Amtliche Sammlung von Entscheidungen
118; **6 ILR 70**........................................................118–19
*Victor Rubens c. État autrichien* (Decision) Anglo-Austrian Mixed Arbitral
Tribunal (2 May 1923) III Recueil des décisions 38 ........................ 126–29

## PERMANENT COURT OF INTERNATIONAL JUSTICE

*Acquisition of Polish Nationality* (Advisory Opinion of 15 September 1923)
PCIJ Rep Series B, No 7...........................................252–53
*Certain German Interests in Upper Silesia (Poland v Germany)* (Merits)
(Judgment of 25 May 1926) PCIJ Rep Series A No 7.....................58, 108, 292
*Factory at Chórzow (Germany v Poland)* (Jurisdiction) (Judgment of 26 July
1927) PCIJ Rep Series A No 7 ............................................ 292
*Free Zones of Upper Savoy and the District of Gex (France v Switzerland)* (Judgment
of 7 June 1932) PCIJ Rep Series A/B No 46...............................82–83
*Mavrommatis Jerusalem Concessions (Greece v Great Britain)* (Judgment of
26 March 1925) PCIJ Rep Series A No 5 .....................................50

TABLE OF CASES  xxvii

*Mavrommatis Palestine Concessions (Greece v Great Britain)* (Preliminary
 Objections) (Judgment of 30 August 1924) PCIJ Rep Series A No 2 .... 55–56, 242–43
*Nationality Decrees Issued in Tunis and Morocco (French Zone) on November 8, 1921*
 (Advisory Opinion of 7 February 1923) PCIJ Rep Series B, No 4 ...... 49–50, 243, 284
*Oscar Chinn Case (United Kingdom v Belgium)* (Judgment of 12 December 1934)
 PCIJ Rep Series A/B No 63. .................................................................. 84
*Panevezys-Saldutiskis Railway Case (Estonia v Lithuania)* (Preliminary
 Objections) (Judgment of 28 February 1939) PCIJ Rep Series A/B No 76 ........ 239
*S.S. "Wimbledon" (United Kingdom et al. v Germany)* (Judgment of 17 August
 1923) PCIJ Rep Series A No 1 .............................................................. 77, 83

## UN HUMAN RIGHTS COMMITTEE

*Wan Kuok Koi v Portugal* No 925/2000, UN Human Rights Committee (8 February
 2002) ORIL IHRL 1726 (UNHRC 2001); UN Doc CCPR/C/73/D/925/2000 .... 149

## NATIONAL COURTS

### Algeria

*SONAREM v Genebrier and Others*, Court of Annaba (Algeria)(26 December
 1968) **41 ILR 384** ................................................................. 255, 274, 300

### Argentina

*Manuata v Embassy of Russian Federation*, Supreme Court of Argentina (22 December
 1994) Clunet (1996) 413; La Ley (1 September 1995); **113 ILR 429** ................. 138

### Australia

*Clunies-Ross v Commonwealth of Australia and Others*, High Court of Australia
 (25 October 1984) 55 ALR (1984) 609; **118 ILR 311**. ........................... 296
*J. Tokic v Government of Yugoslavia* Case No S14790/91 Supreme Court of New South
 Wales (12 December 1991) 9-10 (unpublished) (on file with author) ....... 2–3, 217–22
*Ure v Australia*, Federal Court of Australia (4 February 2016) 236 FCR 458;
 329 ALR 45; 150 ALD 202; **173 ILR 623** ......................................... 52
*Wong Man On v The Commonwealth*, High Court of Australia (6 June 1952)
 86 C.L.R. 125; **19 ILR 327**. ............................................................. 283–84

### Austria

*Case No 2Ob69/92*, Supreme Court of Austria (16 December 1992) (German) ........ 186
*Case No 7Ob573/93*, Supreme Court of Austria (6 October 1993)
 (German). .................................................................. 91, 171, 184, 186
*Croatia et al. v Girocredit Bank A.G. der Sparkassen*, Supreme Court of Austria
 (17 December 1996) 36 ILM 1520 ...................................................... 109
*Effects of State Succession on Real Property Abroad: The Soviet Embassy Building in
 Vienna*, Supreme Court of Austria (9 November 2004) Case No OGH 5
 Ob 152/04w, RPfl SlgG 2004 No. 2908, 18-29, 27-28, **9 ARIEL (2004) 231** ........ 138
*German Railways (Austria) Case*, Court of Appeal (Landesgericht) of Vienna
 (16 August 1949) 4 Ö.J.Z. No 690 (1949) 623; **16 ILR 61** ....................... 311
*Kleihs v Republic of Austria*, Supreme Court of Austria (24 January 1948) 15 ILR 51.... 311
*Schäcke and another v Austria*, Supreme Restitution Commission of Austria
 (23 September 1950) 17 ILR 34. .......................................................... 311

xxviii   TABLE OF CASES

*Schleiffer v Directorate of Finance for Vienna, Lower Austria and Burgenland*,
    Administrative Court of Austria (23 May 1958) Vw GH No 1834 (F) 299;
    Zl. 2040/57; **26 ILR 609** ...................................................... 311
*State Succession (Gold Bonds) Case*, Supreme Court in Civil Matters of Austria
    (5 March 1929) XI Entscheidungen des Obersten Gerichtshofs in Zivilsachen
    (1929) 160; **5 ILR 65** ...................................................... 126–29
*Tax Legislation (Austria) Case*, Administrative Court of Austria (4 February 1949)
    Vw.G.H. (F) 4 (1949) 6; **16 ILR 66** .......................................... 311

### Bahamas

*United States v Bowe*, Judicial Committee of the Privy Council (4 August 1989)
    [1990] 1 AC 500; **85 ILR 128** ............................................... 161

### Bangladesh

*Bangladesh Enemy Property Management Board and Others v Md. Abdul Majid*,
    Supreme Court of Bangladesh (1975) 27 DLR (1975) 52........................ 135
*Bangladesh (substituted in place of the Province of East Pakistan) v Naziruddin
    Ahmed*, High Court of Bangladesh (15 December 1972) I DLR (1973) 1.......... 120
*Benoy Bhusan v Sub-Divisional Officer, Brahmanbaria and another*, Supreme
    Court of Bangladesh (29 November 1977) 30 DLR (1978) 139 ...........135, 298–99
*Governor, Bangladesh Bank and others v Shamsul Huda Khan and others*, Supreme
    Court of Bangladesh (1975) 27 DLR (1975) 71 ............................... 311
*Mirza Shahab Ispahani v Bangladesh*, Supreme Court of Bangladesh (1988)
    40 DLR (AD) 87 .......................................................... 275
*Md. Sadaqat Hossain Khan (Fakku) and Others v Chief Election Commissioner*, Supreme
    Court of Bangladesh (2008) 60 DLR (HCD) 407 (WP No. 10129 of 2007).......... 275
*Mokhtar Ahmed v Government of Bangladesh*, Supreme Court of Bangladesh
    (7 June 1979) (1982) 34 DLR (HCD) 29 ...................................... 275

### Belgium

*Azov Shipping Company v Werf-en Vlasnatie NV*, Hof van beroep Antwerpen (19 March
    2001) (2001) Antwerp Maritime L Rep 318; **ORIL ILDC 43 (BE 2001)** ...............156
*Baugnet-Hock c. État Belge*, Cour d'Appel de Bruxelles (4 December 1962)
    (1965) 1 RBDI 513 ....................................................... 135
*« Chimique du Congo c. Coelho »*, Cour de Cassation (4 June 1964) (1966)
    2(2) RBDI 546 (French) .................................................. 134–35
*Creplet c. Etat belge et Soc. Des Forces Hydro-Electriques de la colonie*, Tribunal
    civil de Bruxelles (30 janvier 1962) (1965) 1 RBDI 514 (French)................. 135
*De Keer Maurice v État Belge*, Court of First Instance of Ghent (9 December 1963);
    *Demol v État Belge, Ministre des Finances*, Court of First Instance of Brussels
    (23 September 1964) 3(4) ILM 666; (1965) 1 RBDI 520; (1964) Journal des
    tribunaux 600; **47 ILR 75** ................................................. 135
*Dupont c. Etat Belge*, Cour de Cassation (8 février 1968) (1970) 6(2) RBDI 684........ 135
*État Belge v Dumont*, Cour d'appel de Bruxelles (4 December 1963) II Pasicrisie
    belge (1964) 308; **48 ILR 8** ............................................... 134–35
*État Belge v Dumont; Pittacos v État Belge*, Cour de cassation du Belgique
    (26 May 1966) I Pasicrisie belge (1966) 1221; **48 ILR 20** ..................... 135
*Kepp and Associates v Belgian State*, Court of Cassation of Belgium
    (22 May 1925) I Pasicrisie belge (1925) 253; **3 ILR 120** ...................... 65–66
*Met den Ancxt c. État Belge*, Cour d'appel de Bruxelles (9 January 1968)
    (1970) 6(2) RBDI 687 (French).............................................. 118–19

TABLE OF CASES    xxix

*Myncke v Van de Weghe et Neerinckx*, Belgium Court of Assizes(2 October 1967)
  (1970) 6(2) RBDI 718 . . . . . . . . . . . . . . . . . . . . . . . . . . . . . . . . . . . . . . . . . . . . . . . 149
*Pittacos v État Belge, Ministre des Affaires Étrangères, Ministre du Commerce Extérieur*
  *et de l'Assistance Technique and Ministre des Finances*, Court of Appeal of
  Brussels (1 December 1964) II Pasicrisie Belge (1965) 263; **45 ILR 24**. . . . . . . . . . . 120
*Procureur général Dumont*, Tribunal civil de Bruxelles (26 December 1961)
  (1965) 1(1) RBDI 509 . . . . . . . . . . . . . . . . . . . . . . . . . . . . . . . . . . . . . . . . . . . . . . 134–35
*Schumacher v Office des séquestres*, Court of Cassation of Belgium (16 January
  1954) I Pasicrisie belge (1954) 409; **21 ILR 177** . . . . . . . . . . . . . . . . . . . . . . . . . . . . 265
*Société de personnes à responsabilité limitée « Chimique du Congo c. Coelho »*,
  Cour de Cassation (4 June 1964) (1966) 2(2) RBDI 546 (French). . . . . . . . . . . . . 134–35
*Stoffels*, Court of Cassation of Belgium, *In re* (9 March 1936) I Pasicrisie Belge (1936)
  184; **9 ILR 339**. . . . . . . . . . . . . . . . . . . . . . . . . . . . . . . . . . . . . . . . . . . . . . . . . . . . . . 265
*United Nations v B.*, Civil Tribunal of Brussels (27 March 1952) III Pasicrisie belge
  (1953) 65; **19 ILR 490** . . . . . . . . . . . . . . . . . . . . . . . . . . . . . . . . . . . . . . . . . . . . . 10–11

### Canada

*Charles R. Bell Ltd v Canadian National Railways*, Newfoundland Supreme
  Court (21 February 1951) 2 D.L.R. 346. . . . . . . . . . . . . . . . . . . . . . . . . . . . . . . . . . . 129
*Edwards v The Queen*, Federal Court of Appeal of Ontario (14 October 2003)
  [2003] FCA 378. . . . . . . . . . . . . . . . . . . . . . . . . . . . . . . . . . . . . . . . . . . . . . . . . . . . . . 152
*Reference by the Governor in Council concerning Certain Questions relating to the*
  *Secession of Quebec from Canada*, Supreme Court of Canada (20 August 1998)
  [1998] 2 SCR 217 . . . . . . . . . . . . . . . . . . . . . . . . . . . . . . . . . . . . . . . . . . . . . . . . . . . . .47

### Czech Republic

*Acquisition of Czech citizenship by Slovak citizens – the right of option of citizens*
  *of the expired Czechoslovak Republic* Case No Pl. ÚS 9/94 Constitutional
  Court of the Czech Republic (13 September 1994) (Czecho-Slovak). . . . . . . . . . 261–62
*Succession of States and Individuals Case*, Constitutional Court of the Czech
  Republic (30 January 2001) Constitutional Court's Collection of
  Judgments and Rulings No N 21/21 SbNU 183; **142 ILR 175**. . . . . . . . . . . . . . . . 126–29
*VJ v Czech Social Security Administration*, Supreme Administrative Court of
  Czechia (28 November 2008) 6 Ads 42/2007; **ORIL ILDC 1405 (CZ 2008)** . . . 186–87

### Cyprus

*Yemen v Compagnie d'Enterprises CFE SA*. Case No 9757 Supreme Court
  of Cyprus (28 June 2002) (2002) 1(1) Cyprus Law Reports 1;
  **ORIL ILDC 630 (CY 2002)** . . . . . . . . . . . . . . . . . . . . . . . . . . . . . . . . . . . . . .117–18, 210, 310

### Egypt

*Agapios v Sanitary and Quarantine Council of Egypt*, Egypt Mixed Court
  of Appeal (21 January 1920) (1920) Gazette des Tribunaux Mixtes
  d'Egypte 49; **1 ILR 201** . . . . . . . . . . . . . . . . . . . . . . . . . . . . . . . . . . . . . . . . . . . . .262–64
*Algiers Land and Warehouse Company Ltd.*, Conseil d'État, *Re* (13 July 1967)
  Recueil (1967) 320; **48 ILR 58**. . . . . . . . . . . . . . . . . . . . . . . . . . . . . . . . . . . . . . . . . . 303
*Compagnie des Eaux d'Hanoi*, Conseil d'État of France, *Re* (19 June 1963)
  Recueil (1963) 375; **44 ILR 37**. . . . . . . . . . . . . . . . . . . . . . . . . . . . . . . . . . . . . . . . . . 311
*Hamou Ben Brahim Ben Mohamed, otherwise Paci*, Conseil d'État, *Re* (18 March
  1955) Revue juridique et politique de l'Union française (1955) 405; **22 ILR 60** . . . . 284

XXX    TABLE OF CASES

*Job*, Administrative Tribunal of Paris, *Re* (31 January 1967) Recueil (1967) 550;
    **48 ILR 59** . . . . . . . . . . . . . . . . . . . . . . . . . . . . . . . . . . . . . . . . . . . . . . . . . . . . . . . 310
*Marchi*, Administrative Court of Paris, *Re* (22 June 1965) Recueil (1965) 754;
    Annuaire français de droit international (1966) 869; **47 ILR 83**. . . . . . . . . . . . . . 133–34
*Messih v Minister of the Interior*, Conseil d'État of Egypt (26 December 1950)
    Revue Egyptienne de Droit International (1953) 140; **28 ILR 291** . . . . . . . . . . . 262–64
*Rothschild & Sons v Egyptian Government*, Egypt Mixed Court of Appeal (29 March
    1926) Gazette des Tribunaux Mistes (August 1925); Journal des Tribunaux
    Mixtes (6 May 1926); 53 Clunet (1926) 754; **3 ILR 21** . . . . . . . . . . . . . . . . . . . . . . . 214

### France

*Agent Judiciaire du Trésor Public v Labeunie*, Court of Cassation of France
    (15 June 1971) Clunet (1972) 812; **72 ILR 53**. . . . . . . . . . . . . . . . . . . . . . . . . . . . . . 120
*Bakalian and Hadjithomas v Ottoman Bank*, Court of Appeal of Paris
    (19 March 1965) Clunet (1966) 118; **47 ILR 216**. . . . . . . . . . . . . . . . . . . . . . . . . . . . 255
*Banque Nationale pour le Commerce et l'Industrie Afrique v Narbonne*,
    Court of Appeal of Aix-en-Provence (2 December 1965) Clunet (1966) 108;
    **47 ILR 120** . . . . . . . . . . . . . . . . . . . . . . . . . . . . . . . . . . . . . . . . . . . . . . . . . . . . . . 297, 314
*Bounouala*, Conseil d'État of France (25 May 1970) 72 ILR 56. . . . . . . . . . . . . . . . . . . 121
*Caisse centrale de Réassurance des Mutuelles agricoles v Mutuelle Centrale
    d'Assurance et de Réassurance*, Court of Cassation of France (30 March 1971)
    I Bull. Cass. (1971) 92; 2 Gaz. Pal. (1971) 470; Clunet (1972) 834 ;
    Revue critique (1971) 451; RGDIP (1972) 588; **72 ILR 565** . . . . . . . . . . . . . . . . . . . . 255
*Cie. Française de Crédit et de Banque v Atard*, Court of Cassation of France
    (23 April 1969) Revue critique (1969) 718; **52 ILR 8** . . . . . . . . . . . . . . . . . . . . . . . 314
*Cohen v Crédit du Nord*, Court of Appeal of Paris (14 March 1967) II J.C.P. (1967)
    15083; Annuaire français de droit international (1968) 835; **48 ILR 82** . . . . . . . 297, 314
*Crédit du Nord v Ribes-Brossette*, Court of Appeal of Aix (12 July 1966)
    Clunet (1966) 838; (1967) Annuaire français de droit international 837;
    **47 ILR 60** . . . . . . . . . . . . . . . . . . . . . . . . . . . . . . . . . . . . . . . . . . . . . . . . . . . . . . . 297, 314
*El Glaoui v Grilhé and Fongrave*, Tribunal Correctionel de la Seine
    (8 February 1934) Gazette des Tribunaux (23 juin 1934); **7 ILR 31** . . . . . . . . . . . 49–50
*Grilhe v Hadj Thami el Glaoui; Babin v Hadj Thami el Glaoui*, Court of Cassation of
    France (27 June 1936) Gazette du Palais (29 October 1936); Revue critique de
    droit international (1937) 494 ; Recueil Général Part 3 (1937) 12; **8 ILR 94** . . . . . 49–50
*MacKinnon c. Air-France*, Tribunal de premiere instance de la Seine (10 avril 1964)
    **(1965) 11 AFDI 949** (French). . . . . . . . . . . . . . . . . . . . . . . . . . . . . . . . . . . . . . . . . . 181
*Ministre du budget v N'guyen Van Gio*, Conseil d'État of France (27 February 1987)
    Recueil Lebon (1987) 77; **106 ILR 224** . . . . . . . . . . . . . . . . . . . . . . . . . . . . . . . . . 118–20
*Nguyen Kim Hai*, Conseil d'État of France, *In re* (8 July 1966) Recueil des arrêts
    du Conseil d'État (1966) 457; **47 ILR 97** . . . . . . . . . . . . . . . . . . . . . . . . . . . . . . . . 242–43
*Orsini v Ferrovecchio*, Cour of Cassation of France (28 July 1925) I Sirey (1925) 303;
    54 Clunet (1927) 719; **3 ILR 39 (note)**. . . . . . . . . . . . . . . . . . . . . . . . . . . . . . . . . . . 49–50
*Procureur de la République v Gova*, Court of Appeal of Paris (13 April 1972) Clunet
    (1972) 817; **73 ILR 565** . . . . . . . . . . . . . . . . . . . . . . . . . . . . . . . . . . . . . . . . . . . . . . . 273
*Rekhou*, Conseil d'État de France (29 May 1981) Recueil Lebon (1981) 220;
    **106 ILR 222**. . . . . . . . . . . . . . . . . . . . . . . . . . . . . . . . . . . . . . . . . . . . . . . . . . . . . . . . . 118
*Sadok*, Conseil d'État de France (15 March 1972) Recueil des décisions du Conseil
    d'État (1972) 213; **73 ILR 36** . . . . . . . . . . . . . . . . . . . . . . . . . . . . . . . . . . . . . . . . . . 118
*Société Anonyme Ballande-Vanuatu c. République Française* No 49300, Conseil
    d'État of France (27 September 1985) (French). . . . . . . . . . . . . . . . . . . . . . . . . . . . . 118

TABLE OF CASES xxxi

*Société d'Assurances la Nationale*, Conseil d'État of France, *Re* (12 April
1967) 48 ILR 61 .......................................................... 120
*Société de personnes à responsabilité limitée « Chimique du Congo c. Coelho »*,
Cour de Cassation (4 June 1964) **2(2) RBDI (1966) 546** (French) ............ 134–35
*Société des Transports en Commun de la Région d'Hanoi*, Conseil d'État of France,
*In re* (28 June 1967) Recueil des arrêts du Conseil d'État (1967) 279; (1968)
Annuaire français de droit international 861; **52 ILR 5** ......................... 311

## Gabon

*Re Draft Ordinance Modifying Law 6/61 Governing Expropriation* Case
No 59 Supreme Court of Gabon (14 August 1970) **48 ILR 151**. ................... 295

## Germany*

*Compulsory Acquisition of Nationality Case*, Court of Appeal of Cologne
(16 May 1960) 15 MDR (1961) 770; **32 ILR 166** ............................... 245
*Eastern Treaties Constitutionality Case*, Federal Constitutional Court of Germany
(7 July 1975) 40 BVerfGE 141; Fontes Iuris Gentium Series A, Sectio II,
Tomus 7 (1971-1975) 455; **78 ILR 177**. .................................. 261, 296
*Former Syrian Ambassador to the German Democratic Republic*, Federal
Constitutional Court of Germany (10 June 1997) 96 BVerfGE 68;
**115 ILR 596**. ........................................................ 170–72
*German Railway Station at Basle Case*, District Court of Karlsruhe (22 June 1928)
238 Arbeitsrechtssprechung (1928) 369; **4 ILR 136** ......................... 82–83
*Germany-Poland Border Treaty Constitutionality Case*, Federal Constitutional Court
of Germany (5 June 1992) EuGRZ (1992) 306; NJW (1992) 3222; **108 ILR 657** .....72
*International Registration of Trade-Mark (Germany) Case*, Federal Supreme Court
of Germany (18 December 1959) 31 BGHZ 374; 13 NJW (1960) 1102; 14 MDR
(1960) 472; **28 ILR 82** ...................................................... 313
*Jorgic Case, J (A Bosnian Serb)* Constitutional Court of Germany (12 December
2000) 2 BvR 1290/99; **ORIL ILDC 132 (DE 2000)**. ......................... 170–72
*N.V Verenigde Deli-Maatschappijen and N.V Senembah Maatschappij v Deutsch-
Indonesische tabak-Handelsgesellschaft m.b.H.*, Court of Appeal of Bremen (21
August 1959) Hanseatisches Oberlandesgericht Bremen I U 159/1959; **28 ILR 16**......296
*Personal Injuries (Upper Silesia) Case*, Court of Appeal of Cologne (10 December
1951) 5 NJW (1952) 1300; **18 ILR 67**. ..................................... 221
*Single German Nationality (Teso) Case*, Federal Constitutional Court of Germany
(21 October 1987) **91 ILR 211**. ........................................... 261
*South-West Africa (Succession) Case*, Reichsgericht of Germany (3 April 1930)
XLIII Z.I. (1930) 402; **5 ILR 60** ......................................... 119–20
*Tanganyika Succession Case*, German *Reichsgericht* in Civil Matters (10 October
1922) 1 ILR 61. ........................................................ 118
*Unification Treaty Constitutionality Case (Merits)* Federal Constitutional
Court (23 April 1991) 84 BVerfGE 90; NJW (1991) 1597; **94 ILR 42** ....... 213, 303–4

## Greece

*Samos (Liability for Torts) Case*, Court of the Aegean Islands (Greece) (1924)
35 Thémis 294; **2 ILR 70**. ................................................. 222

---

\* Includes courts of the Federal Republic of Germany ('West Germany'), the German Democratic
Republic ('East Germany') and Berlin.

xxxii  TABLE OF CASES

## Jamaica

*R v Commissioner of Correctional Services, ex parte Fitz Henry*, Supreme Court of
  Jamaica (1 October 1976) 14 J.L.R. (1976) 288; **72 ILR 63** ...................... 161
*R v DPP, ex parte Schwartz*, Supreme Court of Jamaica (1 December 1976)
  (1976) 24 WIR 491; **73 ILR 44**..........................................161, 165–66

## India

*Ahmadunnissa Begum v Union of India*, High Court of Anhra Pradesh
  (29 January 1968) [1969] AIR (A.P.) 423; **4 CILC 463** ....................108, 118–19
*Central Bank of India Ltd v Ram Narain*, Supreme Court of India (12 October 1954)
  M.W.N. (S.C.) (1954) 999; **21 ILR 92** ......................................... 269
*Cipriano Negredo v Union of India through the Administrator of Goa, Daman and*
  *Diu Government*, Judicial Commissioner's Court of Goa, Daman and Diu
  (13 January 1969) [1969] AIR (Goa) 76, **8 CILC 299** ........................... 129
*Damodhar Bapu, Laxman Bapu and Another v Central Provinces and Berar*, High
  Court of Nagpur (7 April 1955) [1956] AIR (Nag.) 59; **3 CILC 475** .............. 303
*D. Gobalousamy v Union Territory of Pondicherry*, High Court of Madras
  (6 April 1966) [1968] AIR (Mad.) 298; **8 CILC 212** ........................... 129
*Firm Bansidar Premsukhdas v State of Rajasthan*, Supreme Court of India
  (29 March 1966) [1967] AIR (S.C.) 40; **4 CILC 453** ........................... 303
*Gosalia v Agarwal and Others*, Supreme Court of India (26 August 1981) AIR (1981)
  SC 1946; **118 ILR 429** ................................................... 29, 310
*Gudder Singh and Another v The State*, High Court of Punjab (12 August 1953)
  I.L.R. [1954] VII Punjab 649; **20 ILR 145** ......................................73
*Gwalior Rayon Silk Manufacturing Weaving Co. Ltd. v Union of India and Others*,
  High Court of Madhya Pradesh (30 April 1960) [1960] AIR (M.P.) 330;
  **4 CILC 172** ............................................................. 118
*Indumati v State of Saurashtra*, High Court of Saurashtra (7 February 1955) AIR
  (1956) Saurashtra 32; **23 ILR 109**........................................ 54–55
*Izhar Ahmad Khan, Syed Abrahul Hassan, Habib Hidayatullah v Union of India and*
  *Others*, Supreme Court of India (16 February 1962) [1962] 3 SCR (Supp.) 235;
  **16 CILC 379** ............................................................. 269
*Na'Oroji Bera'mji v Henry Roberts and Others, trading in Bombay and Puna as*
  *Rogers and Co.*, High Court of Bombay (1 August 1867) (1867) 4 Bom.
  H.C.R. 1; **7 CILC 142** ..................................................... 304
*Nazirambai v State*, High Court of Masdhya Bharat (7 May 1957) [1957] AIR
  (M.B.) 1; **16 CILC 285** .................................................. 276–77
*Rajasthan and Another v Sawai Tejsinghi Maharaja of Alwar*, High Court of
  Rajasthan (29 April 1968) **5 CILC 464.**...................................... 304
*Rev Mons. Sebastiao Francesco Xavier dos Remedios Monteiro v State of Goa*,
  Supreme Court of India (26 March 1969) [1970] 1 SCR. 87; **8 CILC 306** ......... 265
*Sagoon Jayaidee Dhond and Others v Sociedade Civil e Particular Dos Taris of Volvoi,*
  *Ponda Conchelhe and Others*, Judicial Commissioner's Court of Goa (29 April
  1966) [1966] AIR (Goa) 38; **8 CILC 225**..................................... 129
*Scindia Steam Navigation Co. Ltd. v Union of India*, Supreme Court of India
  (31 August 1961) [1962] 3 S.C.R. 412; **4 CILC 216** ......................... 117–18
*Shripatrao Patwardhan v State of Bombay*, High Court at Bombay (14 December
  1960) I.L.R. (1961) Bombay 100; AIR (1961) Bombay 11; **49 ILR 468**............ 303
*Shri Shubhlaxmi Mills Ltd. v Union of India and Another*, Supreme Court of India
  (2 September 1966) [1967] AIR (S.C.) 750; **4 CILC 459** ...................... 42–43

TABLE OF CASES    xxxiii

*S. Masthan Sahib v Chief Commissioner Pondicherry*, Supreme Court of India (28 April
1961; 8 December 1961) [1963] AIR (SC) 533, [1962] AIR (SC) 797; **8 CILC 172** . . . . . . . 129
*SM. Sau. Indumati v State of Saurashtra*, High Court of Saurashtra (2 July 1955)
[1956] AIR (Sau.) 32; 27 ILR 109; **4 CILC 3** . . . . . . . . . . . . . . . . . . . . . . . . . . . . . . . . . 54–55
*Sree Rajendra Mills Ltd. and Others v Income-Tax Officer*, High Court of Madras
(10 April 1957) 45 AIR (1958) Madras 220; **26 ILR 100**. . . . . . . . . . . . . . . . . . . . . . . . 107
*State of Andhra Pradesh v Abdul Khader* [1961] 1 S.C.R. 737; **16 CILC 343**. . . . . . . . . . . 269
*State v Ghoraishi (Qureshi) Sayed Mahomed*, High Court of Bombay (24 July 1963)
[1964] AIR (Bom.) 235; **16 CILC 451** . . . . . . . . . . . . . . . . . . . . . . . . . . . . . . . . . . . . . 269
*State of Gujarat v Vora Fiddali Badruddin Mithibarwala*, Supreme Court of India
(30 January 1964) [1965] 6 S.C.R. 461; **4 CILC 308** . . . . . . . . . . . . . . . . . . . . . . . . . 54–55
*State of Rajasthan and Another v Sawai Tejsinghi Maharaja of Alwar*, High Court
of Rajasthan (29 April 1968) **5 CILC 464** . . . . . . . . . . . . . . . . . . . . . . . . . . . . . . . . . . 304
*State v Sharifbhai Jamalbhai*, High Court of Bombay (23 April 1958) [1959] AIR
(Bom.) 192, **16 CILC 299**. . . . . . . . . . . . . . . . . . . . . . . . . . . . . . . . . . . . . . . . . . . . . . 269
*State of Tripura v Province of East Bengal*, Supreme Court of India
(4 December 1950) [1951] SCR. 1; **3 CILC 274**. . . . . . . . . . . . . . . . . . . . . . . . . . . . . . . 107
*State of West Bengal v Serajuddin Batley*, Supreme Court of India (24 November
1953) **[1954] AIR (SC) 406** . . . . . . . . . . . . . . . . . . . . . . . . . . . . . . . . . . . . . . . . . . . . 118
*Union of India v Manmul Jain and Others*, High Court of Calcutta
(11 August 1954) **[1954] AIR (Cal) 615**. . . . . . . . . . . . . . . . . . . . . . . . . . . . . . . . . . . 107
*Union of India and Others v Sukumar Sengupta and Others*, Supreme Court of
India (3 May 1990) 3 SA (1986) 107 (ZS); 2 ZLR (1985) 358; **92 ILR 554** . . . . . . . . . . .64
*Virendra Singh and Others v State of Uttar Pradesh*, Supreme Court of India
(29 April 1954) S.C.R. (1955) 415; **22 ILR 131**. . . . . . . . . . . . . . . . . . . . . . . . . . . . . . 54–55

## Israel

*A.B. v M.B.*, District Court of Tel Aviv (6 April 1950) 3 Pesakim Mehoziim
(1950–1951) 263; **17 ILR 110** . . . . . . . . . . . . . . . . . . . . . . . . . . . . . . . . . . . . . . . . . . 265
*Attorney-General v Levitan*, Supreme Court of Israel (3 May 1954) 3 Pesakim
Mehoziim (1950-1951) 195; 8 Piskei-Din (1954) 627; 15 Pesakim Elyonim
(1954) 385; **18 ILR 64**
*Custodian of Absentee Property v Samra*, Supreme Court of Tel-Aviv (12 December
1956) 10 Pesakim Mehoziim (1955) 335; 10 Piskei-Din (1956) 1825;
26 Pesakim Elyonim (1957) 209; **22 ILR 5** . . . . . . . . . . . . . . . . . . . . . . . . . . . . . . . . 107
*Diamond v 1) Minister of Finance; 2) Custodian of Enemy Property*, Supreme
Court of Israel (20 April 1950) 4 Piskei Din (1950) 164; **17 ILR 113**. . . . . . . . . . . . . . 108
*Hussein v Governor of Acre Prison*, Supreme Court of Israel (6 November 1952)
3 Pesakim Mehoziim (1950-1951) 263; **17 ILR 111** . . . . . . . . . . . . . . . . . . . . . . . . . 284
*Khayat v Attorney-General*, District Court of Haifa (27 April 1954) 9 Pesakim
Mehoziim (1954) 378; **22 ILR 123** . . . . . . . . . . . . . . . . . . . . . . . . . . . . . . . . . . . . . . 111
*Naqara v Minister of the Interior*, Supreme Court of Israel (sitting as the High Court
of Justice) (16 October 1953) 7 Piskei-Din (1953) 955; 14 Pesakim Elyonim
(1954) 35; **20 ILR 49** . . . . . . . . . . . . . . . . . . . . . . . . . . . . . . . . . . . . . . . . . . . . . . . . 284
*Pales v Ministry of Transport*, Supreme Court of Israel (sitting as the Court of Civil
Appeals) (17 March 1955) 9 Piskei-Din (1955) 436; 18 Pesakim Elyonim
(1955) 304; **22 ILR 113** . . . . . . . . . . . . . . . . . . . . . . . . . . . . . . . . . . . . . . . . . 120, 310
*Richuk v The State of Israel*, Supreme Court of Israel (11 June 1959) 21 Pesakim
Mehoziim (1959) 99; **28 ILR 442** . . . . . . . . . . . . . . . . . . . . . . . . . . . . . . . . . . . . . . 140
*Shimshon Palestine Portland Cement Factory Ltd v Attorney-General*, Supreme
Court of Israel (12 April 1950) 4 Piskei-Din (1950) 143; 9 Pesakim
Elyonim (1951) 16; **17 ILR 72** . . . . . . . . . . . . . . . . . . . . . . . . . . . . . . . . . . . .54–55, 140

xxxiv    TABLE OF CASES

*Sifri v Attorney-General*, Supreme Court of Israel (20 July 1950) 4 Piskei-Din
    (1950) 613; 5 Pesakim Elyonim (1951-1952) 197; **17 ILR 92** .................... 311
*Tyre Shipping Co. Ltd v Attorney-General*, Admiralty Court of Israel (22 June 1950)
    4 Piskei-Din (1950) 288; 5 Pesakim Elyonim (1951-1952) 55; **17 ILR 107** ........ 108

## Italy

*Antona-Traversi c. Ministero delle finanze*, Corte di cassazione di Torino
    (19 febbraio 1881) II Giurisprudenza 1144 (Italian) .......................... 124
*Bottali*, Court of Appeal of Rome, *Re* (17 October 1980) 64 RDI (1981) 883;
    **78 ILR 105** ........................................................ 155, 177
*Comune di Belgioioso c. Ministeri delle finanze*, Tribunale di Pavia (16 maggio
    1879) Giurisprudenza 944 (Italian) ....................................... 306-7
*Comune di Bramans c. Comune di Ferrera*, Corte di cassazione di Torino
    (23 aprile 1880) I Giruisprudenza 1054 (Italian). .......................... 306-7
*Jadranko*, Court of Cassation of Italy (6 July 1995) in *Mauritius v Nandanee* .......... 165
*Lorra and Tonya v Società Industria Armamenti*, Court of Appeal of Genoa
    (26 June 1971) 71 ILR 48. ................................................ 160
*Mauritius c. Soornack Nandanee* No 14237-17 Corte di Cassazione
    (3 February 2017) (Italian) (on file with author). .................146, 166–68, 189
*Ministry of Home Affairs v Kemali*, Court of Cassation of Italy (1 February 1962)
    16 Rivista di diritto internazionale (1962) 262; 87 Foro italiano Part I (1962)
    190; **40 ILR 191.** ...................................................... 272
*Società Anonima Principe di Paternò Moncada v INPS*, Court of Appeal of
    Palermo (18 June 1966) 71 ILR 219 ....................................... 303-4

## Malaysia

*Lim Lian Geok v Minister of the Interior, Federation of Malaya*, Judicial
    Committee of the Privy Council (23 March 1964) [1964] 1 W.L.R. 554;
    108 Sol. Jo. 296; **8 BILC 444**. ....................................... 270-71
*Public Prosecutor v Oie Hee Koi and Others*, Judicial Committee of the Privy
    Council (4 December 1967) [1968] AC 829; **9 BILC 235** .................... 270-71
*Tunku Mahmoud bin Sultan Ali et al. v Tunku Ali bin Tunku Allum et al.*, Straits Settlements
    Court of Appeal (23 December 1897) (1897) 5 S.S.L.R. 96; **7 CILC 429**. ................304

## Lebanon

*Cie d'assurances « La Baloise » c. Cie Air France, Cie Air Liban*, Tribunal civil de
    Beirut (3 octobre 1958) (1960) 14 RFDA 92. ................................ 177

## Malawi

*Lufazema v Malawi*, Malawi Supreme Court of Appeal (12 June 1967)
    SCA Cr App No 40 of 1967; **ALR Mal. 415** ............................... 42-43
*Murphy v Liquidating Agency*, High Court of Malawi (1 July 1966) (1966-1968)
    ALR Mal. 15. ........................................................... 118
*Mwakawanga and Others v Malawi*, Supreme Court of Appeal (23 October 1968)
    (1968-1970) ALR Mal. 14 ............................................... 254-56
*R v Amihiya*, High Court of Malawi (3 December 1964) (1964-1966) ALR Mal. 157 .... 42-43

## Mauritius

*Ex parte Deprez and Fontaine*, Supreme Court of Mauritius (29 January 1976) 73
    DLR (1991) 420; 75 OR (1990) 1331; **87 ILR 311** ......................... 166
*Heeralall v Commissioner of Prisons; France v Heeralall & Attorney-General*,
    Supreme Court of Mauritius (30 March 1992) [1992] MR 70; **107 ILR 168** ....... 166

TABLE OF CASES XXXV

*La Compagnie Sucrière de Bel Ombre Ltée and Others v Mauritius*, Judicial
Committee of the Privy Council (13 December 1995) [1995] MR 223 . . . . . . . . . . . . 303
*Panjanadum v Prime Minister of Mauritius*, Supreme Court of Mauritius
(19 July 1995) [1995] MR 93; **248 SCJ (1995) 93** . . . . . . . . . . . . . . . . . . . . . . . . . . . 266–67
*Société United Docks v Mauritius & Desmarais Brothers Ltd and Others v Mauritius*,
Supreme Court of Mauritius (7 December 1981) (1981) MR 500 . . . . . . . . . . . . . . . 303

## Micronesia

*Sproat*, Supreme Court of Micronesia, *In re* (6 February 1985) **2 FSM Intrm. 1** . . . . . . . . 286

## Morocco

*Biria v Kiardo* Judgment No 251 Supreme Court of Morocco (5 July 1967) **45 ILR 53** . . . . 177
*Ecoffard (Widow) v Cie Air France*, Court of First Instance of Rabat
(29 April 1964) Revue Marocaine de Droit (1964) 354; **39 ILR 453** . . . . . . . . . . . 156–58

## Myanmar ('Burma')

*Hasan Ali & Meher Ali v Secretary, Ministry of Immigration and National Registration
and Another*, Supreme Court of Burma (4 November 1959) [1959] BLR 187 . . . . . . 270
*Karam Singh and Others v Controller of Immigration*, Supreme Court of Burma
(25 June 1956) [1956] BLR 25 . . . . . . . . . . . . . . . . . . . . . . . . . . . . . . . . . . . . . . . . . . . . 269
*Ko Mya Din and Another v Koby Bin Nga*, High Court of Burma (29 November
1951) [1951] BLR 240 . . . . . . . . . . . . . . . . . . . . . . . . . . . . . . . . . . . . . . . . . . . . . . . 269–70
*Maung Ko Gyi v Union of Burma*, High Court of Burma (10 September 1959)
[1959] BLR 268 . . . . . . . . . . . . . . . . . . . . . . . . . . . . . . . . . . . . . . . . . . . . . . . . . . . . . . 269
*Saw Chain Poon v Union of Burma*, Supreme Court of Burma (1 March 1949)
[1949] BLR 408 . . . . . . . . . . . . . . . . . . . . . . . . . . . . . . . . . . . . . . . . . . . . . . . . . . . . . . 270
*U Kyaw Myint and U Kyaw Thein v Union of Burma*, High Court of Burma
(25 July 1955) [1956] BLR 175 . . . . . . . . . . . . . . . . . . . . . . . . . . . . . . . . . . . . . . . . 142–43
*Union of Burma v Ebrahim Suleman Variava*, High Court of Burma
(19 November 1951) [1952] BLR 6 . . . . . . . . . . . . . . . . . . . . . . . . . . . . . . . . . . . . . . . . 270
*Union of Burma v U Ah Tun*, Supreme Court of Burma (8 June 1949)
[1949] BLR 541 . . . . . . . . . . . . . . . . . . . . . . . . . . . . . . . . . . . . . . . . . . . . . . . . . . . . 269–70
*U Tha Din v The Secretary, Ministry of Co-Operative and Commodity Distribution*,
Supreme Court of Burma (30 October 1959) [1959] BLR 94 . . . . . . . . . . . . . . . . . 118–19
*U Tun Hla and One v Daw Sein*, High Court of Burma (18 March 1959)
[1959] BLR 95 . . . . . . . . . . . . . . . . . . . . . . . . . . . . . . . . . . . . . . . . . . . . . . . . . . . . . . . 303
*Vrajlal Narandas and One v Collector of Rangoon*, Supreme Court of Burma
(21 July 1952) [1952] BLR 118 . . . . . . . . . . . . . . . . . . . . . . . . . . . . . . . . . . . . . . . . . . . 303

## Namibia

*Courtney-Clarke v Bassingthwaighte*, High Court of Namibia (7 September 1990)
[1990] NR 89 (HC) . . . . . . . . . . . . . . . . . . . . . . . . . . . . . . . . . . . . . . . . . . . . . . . . . . . . 311
*De Roeck v Campbell and Others (1)* High Court of Namibia (15 June 1990) [1990]
NR 28 (HC) . . . . . . . . . . . . . . . . . . . . . . . . . . . . . . . . . . . . . . . . . . . . . . . . . . . . . . . . 300–1
*De Roeck v Campbell and Others (2)* High Court of Namibia (14 September 1990)
[1990] NR 126 (HC) . . . . . . . . . . . . . . . . . . . . . . . . . . . . . . . . . . . . . . . . . . . . . . . . . 300–1
*Government of the Republic of Namibia and Another v Cultura 2000 and Another*,
Supreme Court of Namibia (15 October 1993) [1993] 3 LRC 175; **103 ILR 104** . . . . 300–1
*Minister of Defence, Namibia v Mwandinghi*, Supreme Court of Namibia
(25 October 1991) 91 ILR 341 . . . . . . . . . . . . . . . . . . . . . . . . . . . . . . . . . . . . . . . 142, 311
*Namibian Broadcasting Corporation v Kruger and Others*, Supreme Court of
Namibia (12 June 2009) [2009] (1) NR 196 (SC) . . . . . . . . . . . . . . . . . . . . . . . . . . . . . 311

xxxvi  TABLE OF CASES

*S v Malumo* (CC 32-2001) High Court of Namibia (7-14 September 2015)
 [2015] NAHCMD 213. . . . . . . . . . . . . . . . . . . . . . . . . . . . . . . . . . . . . . . . . . . . . . . . . . . . . . .93
*Simon v Administrator-General, South West Africa*, High Court of Namibia
 (3 April 1991) [1991] NR 151 (HC) . . . . . . . . . . . . . . . . . . . . . . . . . . . . . . . . . . . . . . . . 303

### The Netherlands

*Amato Narodni Podnik v Julius Keilwerth Musikinstrumentenfabrik*, District Court
 of The Hague (11 December 1956) IV Netherlands International Law Review
 (1957) 428; **24 ILR 435** . . . . . . . . . . . . . . . . . . . . . . . . . . . . . . . . . . . . . . . . . . . . . . . . 265
*Aponno et al. v The State of the Netherlands (Amboinese Soldiers' Case)* Supreme
 Court of the Netherlands (2 March 1952) N.J. (1951) No 217; **17 ILR 199** . . . . . . . . 272
*D.C. v Public Prosecutor*, Supreme Court of the Netherlands (31 August 1972) NYIL
 (1973) 391; N.J. (1972) No 4; **73 ILR 38**. . . . . . . . . . . . . . . . . . . . . . . . . . . . . . . . . . . . 152
*Hehanussa*, Court of Appeal of The Hague, *In re* (6 November 1952) N.J. (1953)
 No 59; **19 ILR 337** . . . . . . . . . . . . . . . . . . . . . . . . . . . . . . . . . . . . . . . . . . . . . . . . . . . . . 272
*Nederlands Beheers-Instituut v Handels-Vereeniging Amsterdam*, Court of Appeal of
 The Hague (20 November 1957) N.J. (1958) No 508; **24 ILR 60** . . . . . . . . . . . . . . . . 108
*Pamanoekan & Tjiasemlanden and Anglo-Dutch Plantations of Java, Ltd v State of
 the Netherlands*, District Court of The Hague (3 April 1952) N.J. (1954) No 84;
 **19 ILR 116** . . . . . . . . . . . . . . . . . . . . . . . . . . . . . . . . . . . . . . . . . . . . . . . . . . . . . . . . . . . . 115
*Poldermans v State of the Netherlands*, Supreme Court (15 June 1956) N.J. (1959)
 No 7; *UN Materials on Succession of States* UN Doc ST/LEG/SER.B/14
 (1967) 114; **24 ILR 69** . . . . . . . . . . . . . . . . . . . . . . . . . . . . . . . . . . . . . . . . . . . . . . . . . . 120
*R*, Court of Appeal of The Hague, *In re* (6 July 1976) 8 Netherlands Yearbook of
 International Law (1977) 253; **74 ILR 115** . . . . . . . . . . . . . . . . . . . . . . . . . . . . . . . . . . 189
*Stichting tot Opeising Militaire Inkomsten van Krijgsgevangen v State of the Netherlands*,
 Court of Appeal of The Hague, Judgment (30 November 1955) N.J. 1956 No. 121, III
 *Nederlands Tijdschrift voor Internationaal Recht* (1956) 406; **UN Materials on
 Succession of States UN Doc ST/LEG/SER.B/14 (1967) 113** . . . . . . . . . . . . . . . . . 118
*Ter K. v State of the Netherlands, Surinam and Indonesia*, District Court of
 The Hague (28 May 1951) N.J. (1952) No 472; **18 ILR 223** . . . . . . . . . . . . . . . . . . . . 118
*Van Os v State of the Netherlands*, Court of Appeal of The Hague (7 April 1954)
 21 ILR 77 . . . . . . . . . . . . . . . . . . . . . . . . . . . . . . . . . . . . . . . . . . . . . . . . . . . . . . . . . . . . . . . 120
*Weber v Nederlands Beheer-Instituut*, Council for the Restoration of Legal Rights
 in The Hague (4 July 1955) X No 55/486 Rechtsherstel 1215; **24 ILR 431** . . . . . . . . 265
*Mrs W v T.S.*, Court of First Instance of Amsterdam (8 April 1954) in *UN Materials
 on Succession of States* UN Doc ST/LEG/SER.B/14 (1967) 112. . . . . . . . . . . . . . . . . 170

### New Zealand

*Levave v Immigration Department*, Court of Appeal of New Zealand (20 July, 31 August
 1979) [1972] 2 N.Z.L.R. 74; **16 CILC 141** . . . . . . . . . . . . . . . . . . . . . . . . . . . . . . . . . . . 284

### Pakistan

*Yangtze (London) Ltd v Barles Bros (Pakistan) Ltd*, Supreme Court of Pakistan
 in International Law Association, *The Effect of Independence on Treaties*
 (1965) 6 (note 5). . . . . . . . . . . . . . . . . . . . . . . . . . . . . . . . . . . . . . . . . . . . . . . . . . . . . . . . . 146

### Palestine (Mandatory)

*Shehadeh et al. v Commissioner of Prisons, Jerusalem*, Supreme Court of Palestine
 (31 October 1947) 14 P.L.R. (1947) 461; **14 ILR 42**. . . . . . . . . . . . . . . . . . . . . . . . . . . 177

## Philippines

*José Tan Chong v Secretary of Labor*, GR No 47616, Supreme Court of the
Philippines (16 September 1947) . . . . . . . . . . . . . . . . . . . . . . . . . . . . . . . . . . . . . . . . . . . 269

## Poland

*Bartholomeus T.*, District Court of Cracow, *Re* (Poland) (21 December 1970)
1 S.A. (1969) 153; **52 ILR 28** . . . . . . . . . . . . . . . . . . . . . . . . . . . . . . . . . . . . . . . . . . .285–86
*Company X v Tax Chamber*, Supreme Administrative Court of Poland (16 July
2003) III SA 3042/01; **ORIL ILDC 277 (PL 2003)**. . . . . . . . . . . . . . . . . . . . . . . . . 152
*Poland v Stanek*, Supreme Court of Poland (17 December 1924) IV O.S.P. No 331;
**2 ILR 103** . . . . . . . . . . . . . . . . . . . . . . . . . . . . . . . . . . . . . . . . . . . . . . . . . . . . . . . . . . . .82–83
*Polish State Treasury v Deutsche Mittelstandkasse*, Supreme Court of Poland
(4 April 1929) III Zb.O.S.N.C. (1929) No 26; **5 ILR 55**. . . . . . . . . . . . . . . . . . . . . . 107
*Polish State Treasury v Paduchowa and Others*, Supreme Court of Poland
(20 March 1927) P.P.A. (1927) 310; **4 ILR 74** . . . . . . . . . . . . . . . . . . . . . . . . . . . . . . . 107
*Polish State Treasury v Skibniewska*, Supreme Court of Poland (24 January
1928) P.P.A. (1928) 284; **4 ILR 73** . . . . . . . . . . . . . . . . . . . . . . . . . . . . . . . . . . . . . . . . . 108
*Polish State Treasury v Von Bismarck*, Supreme Court of Poland (28 April 1923)
II O.S.P. No 498; **2 ILR 80** . . . . . . . . . . . . . . . . . . . . . . . . . . . . . . . . . . . . . . . . . . . . . . . . 292

## South Africa

*Alexkor Ltd and Government of the Republic of South Africa v Richtersveld
Community and Others*, Constitutional Court of South Africa
(14 October 2003) 5 SA (2004) 460; **127 ILR 501** . . . . . . . . . . . . . . . . . . . . . . . . . . . 152
*Nederlandsche Zuid Africaansche Spoorweg Maatschappij v Douglas Colliery Ltd.
and the Central South African Railways*, Supreme Court of the Transvaal
(14, 23 June 1905) [1905] T.S. 374; **8 CILC 18** . . . . . . . . . . . . . . . . . . . . . . . . . . . . . . . 108
*Postmaster-General v Taute, Treasurer-General v Van Vuren, Postmaster-General v
Parsons, Master of the Supreme Court v Roth*, Supreme Court of the
Transvaal (22 August & 22 September 1905) [1905] T.S. 582; **3 CILC 92**. . . . . . . . . 124
*Rimpelt v Clarkson*, Transvaal Provincial Division (1947) 14 ILR 32. . . . . . . . . . . . . 246, 285
*S v Bull*, Transvaal Provincial Division (11 November 1966) 2 S.A. (1967) 636 (T);
**52 ILR 84** . . . . . . . . . . . . . . . . . . . . . . . . . . . . . . . . . . . . . . . . . . . . . . . . . . . . . . . . . . . . . . 165
*S. v Eliasov*, Supreme Court of South Africa (Appellate Division) (28 September
1967) 2 S.A. (1967) 770 (T); **52 ILR 408** . . . . . . . . . . . . . . . . . . . . . . . . . . . . . . . . . . . 165
*Westphal et uxor v Conducting Officer of Southern Rhodesia*, Cape Provincial Division
of the Union of South Africa (24 January 1948) II Sirey (1949) 41; **15 ILR 211** . . . . 285

## Singapore

*Laos v Sanum Investments Ltd*, Singapore High Court (20 January 2015)
[2015] SGHC 15 . . . . . . . . . . . . . . . . . . . . . . . . . . . . . . . . . . . . . . . . . . . . . . . . . . . . . . . . . 152
*Sanum Investments Ltd v Laos*, Singapore Court of Appeal (29 September 2016)
[2016] SGCA 57 . . . . . . . . . . . . . . . . . . . . . . . . . . . . . . . . . . . . . . . . . . . . . . . . 9, 152, 163, 184
*Westerling*, High Court of the Colony of Singapore, *Re* (15 August 1950)
2 S.A.L.R. (1950) 265; **17 ILR 82**. . . . . . . . . . . . . . . . . . . . . . . . . . . . . . . . . . . . . . . . 165–66

## Spain

*Comercial F SA v Council of Ministers* Case No 516 Supreme Court of Spain
(6 February 1987) Repertorio de Jurisprudencia (1987) No 516; 40(2)
REDI (1988) 176; **88 ILR 691** . . . . . . . . . . . . . . . . . . . . . . . . . . . . . . . . . . . . . . . . . .297–98

xxxviii    TABLE OF CASES

### Sri Lanka

*Asary et al. v Vanden Dreesen (Inspector of Police)* Supreme Court of Ceylon
(22 February 1962) (1952) 54 NLR 66; **16 CILC 183** . . . . . . . . . . . . . . . . . . . . . . . . . . . . 251
*Mudanayake et al v Sivagnanasunderam,* Supreme Court of Ceylon (28 September
1951) (1951) 53 NLR 25; **16 CILC 163** . . . . . . . . . . . . . . . . . . . . . . . . . . . . . . . . . . . . . 251

### Sudan

*Ramadan v Ministry of Interior* Case No 223/2017 Supreme Court of the Sudan
(7 September 2017) <https://www.refworld.org/cases,SDN_SC,59bfc5654.html>
accessed 31 December 2023 . . . . . . . . . . . . . . . . . . . . . . . . . . . . . . . . . . . . . . . . . . . . . . . 281

### Switzerland

*Dvoriantschikov et autres c. Office federal de la police (extradition à l'Ukraine)*
Case No 1A/249/1995, Federal Supreme Court of Switzerland (16 January
1996) (French) (on file with author) . . . . . . . . . . . . . . . . . . . . . . . . . . . . . . . . . . . . . . 192
*K v Socialist Republic of Vietnam,* Court of Appeal of the Canton of Berne
(20 January 1981) Annuaire suisse de droit international (1984) 138;
Revue de la Société des jurists bernois (1983) 253; **75 ILR 122** . . . . . . . . . . . . . . . . . 123
*M v Federal Department of Justice and Police,* Federal Tribunal of Switzerland
(21 September 1979) BGE 105 Ib 286; Annuaire Suisse de droit
international (1980) 204; **75 ILR 107** . . . . . . . . . . . . . . . . . . . . . . . . . . . . . . . . . . 161, 164
*X and Y v Government of the Canton of Zurich,* Federal Supreme Court of
Switzerland (22 November 2005) ATF 132 II 65; **ORIL ILDC 340 (CH 2005)** . . . . 181

### Timor-Leste

*Gaspar de Oliveira Amaral Sarmento and Gaspar Sarmento v Maria Lígia A.
Sarmento,* Case No AC-10-03-2010-P-12-CIV-09-TR Court of Appeal of
Timor-Leste (3 October 2010) (Portuguese) . . . . . . . . . . . . . . . . . . . . . . . . . . . . . 276, 303
*Norberta Belo v Libert Soares and Clara Ana Augusta Freitas,* Case No AC-10-03-
2010-P-23-CIV-01-TR, Court of Appeal of Timor-Leste (3 October 2010)
(Portuguese) . . . . . . . . . . . . . . . . . . . . . . . . . . . . . . . . . . . . . . . . . . . . . . . . . . . . . . . . 276, 303

### Trinidad and Tobago

*Saroop v Maharaj and Others,* Court of Appeal of Trinidad and Tobago (16 May,
26 July 1995) 3 LRC [1996] 1 . . . . . . . . . . . . . . . . . . . . . . . . . . . . . . . . . . . . . . . . . . . . . 164

### Uganda

*Attorney-General v Godfrey Katondwaki,* High Court of Uganda (10 January
1963) [1963] East Africa Law Reports 323; **51 ILR 1.** . . . . . . . . . . . . . . . . . . . . . . . . 311

### United Kingdom*

*Asrar Ahmed v Durgah Committee, Ajmer,* Judicial Committee of the Privy
Council (29 July 1946) [1947] AIR (PC) 1; **8 CILC 112.** . . . . . . . . . . . . . . . . . . . . . . . 303

---

* Includes all sub-national jurisdictions (e.g. – Scotland, England and Wales) and the Judicial
Committee of the Privy Council as imperial court of final appeal. Judgments of colonial courts of the
British Empire are listed under the successor in whose territory they were rendered. Judgments of the
Judicial Committee of the Privy Council in overseas jurisdiction are listed under the Commonwealth
jurisdiction concerned.

TABLE OF CASES   xxxix

*Assicurazioni Generali v Selim Cotran*, Judicial Committee of the Privy Council
(27 November 1931) [1932] AC 268; **6 BILC 695** .............................. 255
*Bulmer v Attorney-General*, Chancery Division (21 June 1955) [1955] Ch. 558,
[1955] 3 W.L.R. 197; [1955] 2 All E.R. 718; 99 Sol. Jo. 472; 105 L. Jo. 441;
220 L.T. Jo. 241; **7 BILC 979** ............................................... 269
*Coreck Maritime GmbH v Sevrybokholodfloti*, Court of Session of Scotland
(19 March 1993) [1994] SLT 893; **107 ILR 659** ............................... 138
*Croatia v Serbia*, High Court of England (2 July 2009) [1009] EWHC 1559 (Ch); [2010]
Ch. 200; [2009] 7 WLUK 55; [2010] 1 P.&C.R. 5; [2010] WLR 555; **164 ILR 429**........128
*Doss v Secretary of State for India* Judicial Committee of the Privy Council
(1875) LR 19 Eq 509......................................................... 291
*Emperor v Jagardeo*, Supreme Court of Bombay (18 June 1925) [1925] AIR (Bom.)
489; **15 CILC 190**........................................................ 272
*Ex-Rajah of Coorg (Veer Rajunder Wadeer) v East India Company*, Court of
Chancery (13-14 November, 8 December 1860) 29 Beav 300; 54 E.R. 642;
30 L.J. (Ch.) 226; 7 Jur. (N.S.) 350; 9 W.R. 247; **1 BILC 571** ..................... 304
*Gold Pool JV Limited v Republic of Kazakhstan*, High Court of Justice
(15 December 2021) [2021] EWHC 3422 (Comm) ....2, 11, 51, 161, 164–65, 194, 331
*Groedel v Administrator of Hungarian Property*, High Court of Justice of
England (10 November 1927) 44 T.L.R. 65; **4 ILR 304**......................... 214
*Jabbour v Custodian of Israeli Absentee Property*, Queen's Bench Division
(27 November 1953) [1954] 1 WLR 139; [1954] 1 All E.R. 145; [1953] 2
Lloyd's Rep. 760; 98 Sol. J. 45; 104 L. Jo. 58; 217 L.T. Jo. 35; **7 BILC 219**....... 108, 294
*Keyu and Others v Secretary of State for Foreign and Commonwealth Affairs*,
Supreme Court of the United Kingdom (25 November 2015) [2015] UKSC 69.... 120
*Madzimbamuto v Lardner-Burke*, Judicial Committee of the Privy Council
(23 July 1968) [1969] AC 645; **39 ILR 61**...................................... 213
*In the Matter of Mangold's Patent*, High Court of Justice (9 October 1950)
68 R.P.C. 1; **18 ILR 244** ..................................................... 260
*Motala v Attorney-General*, House of Lords (7 November 1991) [1992] 1 AC 281...... 269
*Mutua v Foreign and Commonwealth Office*, High Court of England (21 July
2011 & 5 October 2012) [2012] EWHC 2678 (QB); [2012] 10 WLUK 204;
(2012) 162 N.L.J. 1291; **156 ILR 629**........................................ 120
*Rahimtoola v Nizam of Hyderabad*, House of Lords (7 November 1957)
[1958] AC 379; [1957] 3 W.L.R. 884; [1957] 3 All E.R. 441; 101 Sol. Jo.
901; 7 BILC 844; **24 ILR 175** ............................................. 108, 124
*Ram v Secretary of State in Council of India*, Judicial Committee of the Privy
Council (1872) LR Ind App Suppl 119.......................................... 291
*R. v Secretary of State for the Home Department, ex parte Thakrar*, Court of Appeal
of England (4 February 1974) [1974] 1 Q.B. 684; 59 ILR 450 ................... 269
*R (on the application of Hassan and others) v Secretary of State for the Home
Department*, High Court of England and Wales (Administrative Court)
(24 May 2019) [2019] EWHC 1288 (Admin).................................... 271
*R (on the application of Nooh) v Secretary of State for the Home Department*, High
Court of England and Wales (27 June 2018) [2018] WHC 1572 (Admin)......... 271
*Rothschild v Administrator of Austrian Property*, High Court of Justice of England
(31 July 1923) [1923] L.R. 2 Ch. 542; **2 ILR 237**.............................. 214
*Salaman v Secretary of State in Council for India*, Court of Appeal (20, 21, 27
February 1906) [1906] 1 K.B. 613; 75 L.J. (K.B.) 418; 94 L.T. 858; **1 BILC 594**..... 304
*Secretary of State in Council of India v Kamachee Boye Sahaba*, Judicial Committee
of the Privy Council (9 July 1859) 7 Moo.Ind.App. 476; 19 E.R. 388;
13 Moo.P.C.C. 22; 15 E.R. 9; 7 W.R. 722; **1 BILC 543** .......................... 304

xl  TABLE OF CASES

*Secretary of State for India v Bai Rajbai* (1915) L.R. 42 Ind. App. 229; **2 BILC 631** ...... 291
*Secretary of State for India v Sardar Rustam Khan*, Judicial Committee of the Privy
  Council (28 April 1941) (1941) 4 Printed Cases in Indian and Colonial Appeals;
  2 BILC 626; **8 CILC 66** ...................................................... 291
*Serbia v Ganić*, City of Westminster Magistrates' Court (27 July 2010) (2010)
  81 BYIL 395 .......................................................... 171–72
*Serbia v ImageSat International NV*, High Court of England (16 November 2009)
  [2010] 2 All ER (Comm) 571; [2010] 1 Lloyd's Rep 324; **142 ILR 644** ......... 226–27
*Sirdar Bhagwan Singh v Secretary of State for India in Council*, Judicial Committee of
  the Privy Council (12 November 1874) (1874) L.R. 2 Ind. App. 38; **2 BILC 582** ..... 291
*Vajesingji Joravarsingji and Others v Secretary of State for India in Council*, Judicial
  Committee of the Privy Council (26 June 1924) (1924) L.R. 51 Ind. App. 357,
  **2 BILC 642**. ....................................................... 291
*West Rand Central Gold Mining Company Limited v The King*, Divisional Court
  of England and Wales (1905) [1905] 2 K.B. 391, **2 BILC 238** .................... 213

**United States of America***

*Ahmed v Goldberg* Civil Action No 00-0005, Civil Case No 99-0046 (D.N. Mar. I.)
  US District Court for the Northern Mariana Islands (11 May 2001)
  (on file with author). ................................................... 151
*Arnbjornsdottir-Mendler v United States*, Ninth Circuit Court of Appeals
  (8 December 1983) 721 F. 2d 679 (1983); **96 ILR 105**. ................... 160, 165, 186
*Artukovic v Rison*, US Ninth Circuit Court of Appeals (1 February 1986)
  628 F. Supp. (1986) 1370; **79 ILR 383**. ....................................... 152
*Belgrade v Sidex Intern. Furniture*, US Southern District Court of New York
  (31 March 1998) 2 F Supp 2d 407 (SDNY 1998) .............................. 108
*Can and Others v United States*, US Second Circuit Court of Appeals
  (13 January 1994) 14 F. 3d 160 (1994); **107 ILR 255**. .......................... 123
*Canter v The American Insurance Co,* Supreme Court of the United States
  (1 January 1828) 1 Peters 511. ............................................... 246
*Del Guercio v Gabot*, US Ninth Circuit Court of Appeals (13 May 1947) 161 F. 2d.
  559; **14 ILR 20**. ........................................................ 269
*Elijah Ephraim Jhirad v Thomas E. Ferrandina*, Southern District Court of New York
  (23 January 1973) 355 F Supp 1155 (SDNY 1973); **22 AILC (1969-1978) 261**..... 160, 164
*Extradition of Cheung*, US Second Circuit Court of Appeals (23 May 2000)
  [2001] SC 143; [2001] SCCR 296; [2001] SLT 507; **122 ILR 659** ................ 152
*Extradition of Platko*, US Southern District Court for California (26 July 2002)
  **213 F Supp 2d 1229 (2002)** .......................................... 164, 189
*Extradition of Sacirbegovic*, US Southern District Court for New York (18 January
  2005) **No 03 Crim Misc 01 Page 19 (SDNY 18 Jan 2005)**. ...................... 164
*Extradition of Tuttle*, US Ninth Circuit Court of Appeals (12 June 1992) 966 F. 2d
  1316; **96 ILR 110** ....................................................... 163
*Extradition of Zwagendaba Jère*, District Court for the District of Columbia
  (29 March 1966) in O'Connell, *State Succession in Municipal Law and*
  *International Law* vol I (OUP 1968) 115 (note 1) .....................2–3, 165, 189
*Federal Republic of Germany v Elicofon (Grand Duchess of Saxony-Weimar*
  *intervening) and Kunstsammlungen Zu Weimar v Elicofon*, United States
  Second Circuit Court of Appeals (25 April 1973) 678 F. 2d 1150
  (2d Cir. 1982) 390; **61 ILR 143** ........................................ 108, 303

* Includes all federal and sub-national jurisdictions.

TABLE OF CASES xli

*Government v Diaz*, US District Court for the Canal Zone (31 January 1924)
  3 C.Z. 465; **2 ILR 95** . . . . . . . . . . . . . . . . . . . . . . . . . . . . . . . . . . . . . . . . . . . . . . 46, 78–79
*Harcourt v Gaillard*, United States Supreme Court (3 March 1827) 25 US
  (12 Wheat) 523 (1827); **2 AILC 389** . . . . . . . . . . . . . . . . . . . . . . . . . . . . . . . . . . . . . . .64
*Ivancevic v Artukovic*, US Ninth Circuit Court of Appeals (19 February 1954)
  211 F. 2d 565; 348 U.S. 818; **21 ILR 66** . . . . . . . . . . . . . . . . . . . . . . . . . . . . . . . . . . 150
*Kasterova v United States*, US Eleventh Circuit Court of Appeals (8 April 2004)
  **365 F 3d 980** . . . . . . . . . . . . . . . . . . . . . . . . . . . . . . . . . . . . . . . . . . . . . . . . . . . . . . . . 189
*Kuntstsammlungen zu Weimar and Others v Elicofon*, US Second Circuit Court
  of Appeals (5 May 1982) 678 F. 2d 1150 (1982); **94 ILR 135** . . . . . . . . . . . . . . . . 108, 303
*In the Matter of Ameyund*, Surrogate's Court of Kings County (23 November 1951)
  201 Misc 547; 108 NYS 2d 326 (Surr Ct, 1951); **1 AILC 94** . . . . . . . . . . . . . . . . . . . 271–72
*Morgan Guaranty Trust Company of New York and Others v Republic of Palau*,
  US Second Circuit Court of Appeals (4 February 1991) 924 F. 2d 1237
  (2nd Cir 1991); **87 ILR 591** . . . . . . . . . . . . . . . . . . . . . . . . . . . . . . . . . . . . . . . . . . . 172
*Republic of Vietnam v Pfizer Inc and Others*, US Eighth Circuit Court of Appeals
  (15 June 1977) 556 F 2d 892 (8th Cir 1977); I AILC, Second Series (1979-1986)
  68; **94 ILR 199** . . . . . . . . . . . . . . . . . . . . . . . . . . . . . . . . . . . . . . . . . . . . . . . . . . . . . 123
*Rupali Bank v Provident National Bank*, US Eastern District Court (22 September
  1975) 403 F. Supp. 1285 (1975); **66 ILR 192** . . . . . . . . . . . . . . . . . . . . . . . . . . . . . . 298
*Sabatier v Dabrowski*, US First Circuit Court of Appeals (15 November 1978)
  **586 F 2d 866 (1978)** . . . . . . . . . . . . . . . . . . . . . . . . . . . . . . . . . . . . . . . . . . . . . . . . . 164
*Suspine et al. v Compañía Transatlantica CentroAmericana, S.A., et al.*, US District
  Court for the Southern District (New York) (13 February 1941) 37 F. Supp. 268;
  **9 ILR 38** . . . . . . . . . . . . . . . . . . . . . . . . . . . . . . . . . . . . . . . . . . . . . . . . . . . . . . . . . . 269
*Then v Melendez*, US Ninth Circuit Court of Appeals (7 August 1996)
  **92 F 3d 851** . . . . . . . . . . . . . . . . . . . . . . . . . . . . . . . . . . . . . . . . . . . . . . . . . .163, 172–75
*United Bank Ltd et al. v Cosmic International, Inc.*, US Southern District Court
  of New York (31 March 1975) 392 F Supp 262 (SDNY 1975); **22 AILC 279** . . . . . . . 298
*United States v Fullard-Leo et al.*, US Ninth Circuit Court of Appeals (23 May 1946)
  156 F. 2d. 756; **13 ILR 35** . . . . . . . . . . . . . . . . . . . . . . . . . . . . . . . . . . . . . . . . . . . . . .64
*United States v Lui Kin-Hong*, US First Circuit Court of Appeals (20 March 1997)
  110 F. 3d 103 (1997); **114 ILR 606** . . . . . . . . . . . . . . . . . . . . . . . . . . . . . . . . . . . . . 149
*United States et al. v Rodiek*, United States Circuit Court of Appeals (17 February
  1941) 117 F. (2d) 588; **10 ILR 279** . . . . . . . . . . . . . . . . . . . . . . . . . . . . . . . . . . 246, 260
*United States ex rel. d'Esquiva v Uhl, District Director of Immigration*, US Second
  Circuit Court of Appeals (18 August 1943) 137 F. 2d 903; **11 ILR 23** . . . . . . . . . . . . 124
*United States ex rel Saroop v Garcia*, US Third Circuit Court of Appeals (21 March
  1997) **109 F 3d 165 (3d Cir 1997)** . . . . . . . . . . . . . . . . . . . . . . . . . . . . . . . . . . . . . 165
*United States ex rel. Schwarzkopf v Uhl, District Director of Immigration*, US Second
  Circuit Court of Appeals (18 August 1943) 137 F. 2d 898; **12 ILR 188** . . . . . 56, 245, 260
*Yucyco, Ltd. v Slovenia*, US Southern District Court of New York (18 November
  1997) **984 F Supp 209 (SDNY 1997)** . . . . . . . . . . . . . . . . . . . . . . . . . . . . . . . . . . . . 303

**Zambia**

*Shipanga v Attorney-General*, Supreme Court of Zambia (21 September 1976,
  20 January 1977 and 5 January 1978) [1976] Zambia Reports 224; **79 ILR 18** . . . .285–86

.

# Table of Legislation

(arranged by jurisdiction in alphabetical order)

## ALGERIA

Constitution of Algeria (10 September 1963) in AJ Peaslee and DX Peaslee, *Constitutions of Nations* (Martinus Hijhoff 1965) 559 . . . . . . . . . . . . . . . .297

Law No 62-157 [Loi No 62-157] 2 Journal officiel (11 January 1963) (French) . . . . . . . . . . . . . . . . . . . . 42–43

## ARMENIA

Armenia Law on Citizenship (28 November 1995) <https://www. refworld.org/pdfid/51b770884. pdf> accessed 1 October 2024. . . . . . . . . . . . . . . . . . . . 76, 277–78

Armenia Law on Ownership (31 October 1990) in JN Hazard and Vratislav Pechota (eds) Russia and the Republics: Legal Materials (Juris 1993) . . . . . . . . . . . .301

Armenia Law No ZR-265 on the Frontier (17 December 2001) in *CIS Legislation Database* <https://cis-legislation.com/> accessed 1 January 2024 . . . . . . . . . . .76

Constitution of the Republic of Armenia (5 July 1995) in European Commission for Democracy through Law ('Venice Commission') Opinion No 313/2004 (29 November 2004). . . . . 277

Declaration on Independence of Armenia (23 August 1990) in *CIS Legislation Database* <https:// cis-legislation.com/> accessed 1 January 2024. . . . . . . . . . . . . . . . . . .76

## AUSTRALIA

Cocos (Keeling) Islands Act 1955 (Australia) <https://www.legislat ion.gov.au/C1955A00034/latest/ versions> accessed 17 February 2024 . . . . . . . . . . . . . . .296

## AZERBAIJAN

Constitution of Azerbaijan (12 November 1995) in *World Constitutions Illustrated Database* <https://home.heinonl ine.org/content/world-constituti ons-illustrated/> accessed 9 January 2024 (Russian) . . . .76, 99–100

Law No 13 on the State Border (9 December 1991) in JN Hazard and Vratislav Pechota (eds) *Russia and the Republics: Legal Materials* (1993) binder 1 . . . . . . . . . . . . .76, 99–100

## BANGLADESH

Bangladesh Citizenship (Temporary Provisions) Order, 1972, 25 DLR (1973) Bangladesh Statutes 1973, 57 . . . . . . . . . . . . . . . . .275

Bangladesh Collaborators (Special Tribunal) Order, 24 DLR (1972) Bangladesh Statutes 1971-72 . . . . . . . . . . . . . 298–99

Bangladesh (Legal Proceedings) Order 1972, 24 DLR (1972) Bangladesh Statutes 1971-72, 28 . . . . . . . . . . 135–36

Bangladesh Local Councils and Municipal Committees (Dissolution and Administration) Order 1972, 24 DLR (1972) Bangladesh Statutes 1971-72, 14. . . . . . . . . . . . . . . . . 135–36

Bangladesh Public Servants' (Retirement) Order 1972, 24 DLR (1972) Bangladesh Statutes 1971-72 . . . . . . . . . . . . . . . . .311

xliv    TABLE OF LEGISLATION

Bangladesh (Restoration of Evacuee
Property) Order 1972, 24 DLR
(1972) Bangladesh Statutes
1971-72, 30. . . . . . . . . . . . . . . . . 298–99
Bangladesh (Taking over Control and
Management of Industrial and
Commercial Concerns) Order
1972, 24 DLR (1972) Bangladesh
Statutes 1971-72, 8 . . . . . . . . . . . 298–99
Finance (1971-72) Order 1972 BGE
(24 May 1972) 921 . . . . . . . . . . . . . . .135
High Court of Bangladesh Order
1972, 24 DLR (1972) Bangladesh
Statutes 1971-72, 12 . . . . . . . . . . 135–36
Law Continuance Enforcement
Order, 24 DLR (1972) 1. . . . . . . . . . .311
Proclamation of Independence (10 April
1971) 24 DLR (1972) Bangladesh
Statutes 1971-72, 1. . . . . . . . . . . . . 135, 275
Provisional Constitution of Bangladesh
Order 1972 (11 January 1972) 24
DLR (1972) Bangladesh Statutes
1971-72, 29. . . . . . . . . . . . . . 135, 275, 298

## BELARUS

Law on Citizenship (adopted 18
October 1991, entered into force
12 November 1991) in JN Hazard
and Vratislav Pechota (eds)
Russia and the Republics: Legal
Materials binder 1 (Juris 1993) . . . . 277

## BELGIUM

Law on the Government of the
Belgian Congo [Loi sur le
gouvernement du Congo belge]
(18 October 1908) 265 Pasin.
(1908); **101 BFSP 733** (French) . . . .86

## BOSNIA-HERZEGOVINA

Constitution of Bosnia and Herzegovina
(14 December 1995) <http://www.
ccbh.ba/public/down/USTAV_B
OSNE_I_HERCEGOVINE_engl.
pdf> accessed 17 February 2024. . . . . 261
Law on Citizenship (6 October
1992) <https://www.refworld.
org/docid/3ae6b4d828.html>
accessed 9 January 2024 . . . . . . . . . .261

## BRAZIL

Draft Constitution for the Empire of
Brazil [Projet de Constitution pour
l'Empire du Brésil] (25 March
1826) 13 BFSP 936 (French). . . . . . . 269

## CAMBODIA

Civil Code (1 July 1920) in UN
Legislative Series, *Laws Concerning
Nationality* (1954) 67 (French). . . . . . 272
Decree No 913-NS [Krâm No 913-
NS] (30 November 1954) in UN
Legislative Series, *Supplement to
the Laws Concerning Nationality*
(1959) 13 (French). . . . . . . . . . . . . . .272

## CANADA

Canadian Citizenship Act 1946
10 Geo. VI c.15 . . . . . . . . . . . . . . . . .269

## CHINA

Basic Law of the Hong Kong Special
Administrative Region (May
2021 edition) <https://www.
basiclaw.gov.hk/filemanager/
content/en/files/basiclawtext/
basiclaw_full_text.pdf> accessed
31 December 2023 . . . . . . .242–43, 311
Basic Law of the Macao Special
Administrative Region (31
March 1993) <https://bo.io.gov.
mo/bo/i/1999/leibasica/index.
asp> accessed 31 December 2023
(Portuguese) . . . . . . . . . . . . . . . . . . . .243
Clarifications by the Standing
Committee of the National
People's Congress on the
application of the Nationality
Law in the Macao Special
Administrative Region, Sixth
Session of the Standing Committee
of the 9th National People's
Congress (29 December 1998)
(Portuguese) <https://bo.io.gov.
mo/bo/i/1999/01/aviso05.asp#7>
accessed 17 February 2024 . . . . . . . . . 265
Explanations of the Implementation
of the Nationality Law in the

Hong Kong SAR, Standing
Committee of the 8th National
People's Congress, 19th Session
(15 May 1996) <https://www.
immd.gov.hk/eng/residents/
immigration/chinese/law.html>
accessed 17 February 2024 . . . . . . . .265
Immigration Ordinance of the Hong
Kong Special Administrative
Region Cap. 115 (1 April 1972)
L.N. 62 of 1972 <https://www.
elegislation.gov.hk/hk/cap115>
accessed 17 February 2024 . . . . . . . .265
Law No 7/1999 on Nationality
Requirements for Residents of
the Macao SAR, <https://bo.io.
gov.mo/bo/i/1999/01/lei07.
asp> accessed 31 December 2023
(Portuguese) . . . . . . . . . . . . . . . . . . . .265
Nationality Law (10 September 1980)
<https://www.immd.gov.hk/
eng/residents/immigration/chin
ese/law.html> accessed
31 December 2023 . . . . . . . . . . . 242–43

## CROATIA

Law No 53 on Citizenship (8 October
1991) in *Nationality & Statelessness:
A Collection of Nationality Laws*
vol I (Independent Bureau for
Humanitarian Issues 1996) 275;
**UNHCR, 'Citizenship and
Prevention of Statelessness Linked
to the Disintegration of the SFRY'
(1997) 3(1) European Series** . . . . . . . .261

## CZECHIA ('CZECH REPUBLIC')

Act No 40/1992 (1 January 1993)
<https://www.refworld.org/
docid/3ae6b51a8.html> accessed
31 December 2023 . . . . . . . . . . . 261–62
Constitutional Act No 542/1992 Coll.
(25 November 1992)
Coll. Zákony Prolidi
(13 November 1992)
(Czecho-Slovak). . . . . . .32–33, 126–29

Constitutional Act No 624/1992 Coll.
Zákony Prolidi (17 December
1992) (Czecho-Slovak) . . . . . . . 126–29
Constitutional Law No 4/1993 Coll.
Zákony Prolidi (15 December
1992) (Czecho-Slovak) . . . . . . . . . .302

## CZECHO-SLOVAKIA

Act on the Succession of the
Agreements of the former
Yugoslavia with the former Czech
and Slovak Federal Republics
(Slovenia-Czechia) 35/1994
Uradni list RS (Slovenian) . . . . . . . . 172
Constitution of Slovakia (1 September
1992) No 460/1992 Coll Pravne
Predpisy (Czecho-Slovak) . . . . . . .302
Constitutional Act No 541/1992 Coll.
Zákony Prolidi (13 November
1992) (Czecho-Slovak) . . . . . . . . . .107
Constitutional Act No 624/1992
Zákony Prolidi Coll. (17
December 1992); **UN Doc A/47/
848 (31 December 1992)** . . . . . 126–29
Constitutional Law No 4/1993 Coll
Zákony Prolidi (15 December
1992) (Czecho-Slovak) . . . . . . . . . .302

## DEMOCRATIC REPUBLIC OF THE CONGO*

Basic Law on the Structures of the
Congo (19 May 1960) Moniteur
Congolais (27 May 1960) 1535-
83; TM Franck, John Carey and
LM Tondel, *Legal Aspects of the
United Nations Action in the
Congo* (Oceana Publications,
1963) . . . . . . . . . . . . . . . . . . . . 35, 274–75
Constitution of the Congo
(Leopoldville) (30 May 1964)
in AJ Peaslee and DX Peaslee,
*Constitutions of Nations* (Martinus
Hijhoff 1965) 98 . . . . . . . . 35, 274–75, 296
Decree cancelling Belgian Companies'
Rights to Grant Mining
Concessions (29 November 1954)
4(2) ILM 232 . . . . . . . . . . . . . . . . 35, 296

* Including the Congo Free State.

xlvi TABLE OF LEGISLATION

Investment Code (30 August 1965)
19 Moniteur congolais (15
October 1965); CRISP, *Congo
1965: Political Documents of a
Developing Nation* (Princeton
University Press 1967) 252
(French) . . . . . . . . . . . . . . . . . . . . . . .296
Nationality Law 04/024 (12
November 2004) in Franck
Kamunga, 'Report on
Citizenship Law: Democratic
Republic of Congo', EUI Country
Report 2022/1 (2022) 10 . . . . . . 274–75
Nationality Law 1972-002 [Loi n°
1972-002 du 5 janvier 1972
relative à la nationalité zaïroise]
(5 January 1972) JOZ (15
January 1972) (French) . . . . . . . 274–75
Nationality Law 1981-002 [Loi no
1981-002 du 29 juin 1981 sur la
nationalité zaïroise] 13 JOZ (1
July 1981) (French) . . . . . . . . . . 274–75
Ordinance-Law No 66-341 on the
Head Offices and Administrative
Offices of Companies for which
the Principal Site of Operations
is in the Congo, I Moniteur
Congolais (15 August 1966) 523
(French) . . . . . . . . . . . . . . . . . . . . . . .297
Ordinance-Law No 66-343
guaranteeing to the Democratic
Republic of the Congo
its Proprietary Rights in
Sovereignty for the Concession
of Real Estate, Forestry and
Mines throughout its Territory
[Ordonnance-loi n° 66-343
du 7 juin 1966 assurant à la
République Démocratique du
Congo la plénitude de ses droits
de propriété sur son domaine] I
Moniteur Congolais (15 August
1966) 560 (French) . . . . . . . . . . . . .297
Ordinance-Law No 67-01 on the
Revocation of Approval of the
Constitution of the S.C.A.R.L.
and Union Minière du Haut-
Katanga I Moniteur Congolais
(1967) 28 (French). . . . . . . . . . . . . .297
Ordinance-Law No 67-01bis
transferring to the Democratic
Republic of the Congo the

Movable and Immovable
Property of the Union Minière
du Haut-Katanga and its
Affiliates, I Moniteur Congolais
(1967) 29 (French). . . . . . . . . . . . . .297
Ordinance-Law No 67-55 relating to
the Devolution of Ownership
of the Properties and Holdings
of Union Minière du Haut-
Katanga on the Democratic
Republic of the Congo and to the
Prohibition of Union Minière
du Haut-Katanga from Carrying
on any Activity in the Territory
of the Republic of the Congo (28
January 1967) 6(5) ILM 915. . . . . . .297
Ordinance-Law No 71-020 on
the Acquisition of Congolese
Nationality by Persons
originating in Rwanda-Urundi
and established in the Congo on
30 June 1960 [Ordonnance-loi n°
71-020 du 26 mars 1971 relative
à l'acquisition de la nationalité
congolaise par les personnes
originaires du Rwanda–Urundi
établies au Congo à la date du
30 juin 1960] <https://citizens
hiprightsafrica.org/rdc-ord
onnance-loi-n-71-020-du-26-
mars-1971-relative-a-lacquisit
ion-de-la-nationalite-congola
ise-par-les-personnes-originai
res-du-rwanda-urundi-etablies-
au-congo-a-l/?lang=fr> accessed
17 February 2024 (French). . . . 274–75

### DENMARK

Law providing for the Union of
Denmark and Iceland (30
November 1918) 111 BFSP 703. . . . . .56

### EGYPT ('UNITED ARAB REPUBLIC')

Law No 82 (1958) in **Dalia Malek,
'Report on Citizenship Law:
Egypt', EUI Country Report
2021/16 (July 2021) 5,** Eugene
Cotran, 'Some Legal Aspects of
the Formation of the United Arab

Republic and the United Arab States' (1959) 8(2) ICLQ 346, 380 . . . . . . . . . . . . . . . . . . . . . . . 268–84
Provisional Constitution of the United Arab Republic (5 March 1958) in Eugene Cotran, 'Some Legal Aspects of the Formation of the United Arab Republic and the United Arab States' (1959) 8(2) ICLQ 346 . . . 123–24, 259–61, 295

### EQUATORIAL GUINEA

Constitution of Equatorial Guinea Decree No 2467 (9 October 1968) BOGE (24 July 1968) (Spanish) . . . . . . . . . . . . . . . . . . . . . . .132

### ERITREA

Investment Law (31 December 1991) Proclamation No 18/1991 4 Gazette of Eritrean Laws (1991) . . . 302
Investment Proclamation (24 August 1994) No 59/1994 4 Gazette of Eritrean Laws (1994) . . . . . . . . . . 303–4
Nationality Proclamation No 21/ 1992 (6 April 1992) <https:// www.refworld.org/legal/legislat ion/natlegbod/1992/en/14094> accessed 17 February 2024 . . . . . . . .278
Referendum Proclamation No 22/1992 (7 April 1992) <https://www.loc. gov/item/eritrean-proc-22-1992/> accessed 17 February 2024 . . . . . . . . 278
Transitional Administration of Justice Proclamation No 1/1991 (15 September 1991) <https://www. loc.gov/item/eritrean-proc-1- 1991/> accessed 17 February 2024 (Tigrinya) . . . . . . . . . . . . . . 42–43

### FRANCE

Constitution of the Fourth Republic (27 October 1946) <https:// www.elysee.fr/la-presidence/ la-constitution-du-27-octobre- 1946> accessed 30 December 2023 . . . . . . . . . . . . . . .272
Decree No 53-161 on the Application of the Nationality Code in the Overseas Territories [Décret no 53-161 du 24 février 1953 déterminant les modalités d'application du code de la nationalité française dans les territoires d'outre-mer] JORF (27 February 1953) 1984 (French) . . . .272
Decree No 69-283 (24 March 1969) 101 JORF (30 March 1969) 3180 (French) . . . . . . . . . . . . . . . . . . . 118–19
Decree on the Reorganisation of the Justice Service in the Government of Western Africa [Décret du 10 novembre 1903 portant réorganisation du service de la justice dans les colonies relevant du gouvernement général de l'Afrique occidentale] 309 JORF (24 November 1903) 7094 (French) . . . . . . . . . . . . . . . . . . .272
Nationality Code [Ordonnances n° 45-2441 du 19 octobre 1945 portant code de la nationalité française] (19 October 1945) 247 JORF (20 October 1945) 6700 (French) . . . . . . . . . . . . . . . . . . . . . . .272

### GABON

Constitution of Gabon (21 February 1961) in Peaslee and Peaslee, *Constitutions of Nations* vol I (Springer 1965) 191 . . . . . . . . . . . . . .295

### GEORGIA

Constitution of Georgia (24 August 1995) in *World Constitutions Illustrated Database* <https:// home.heinonline.org/content/ world-constitutions-illustrated/> accessed 9 January 2024 . . . . . . . . .277
Law on Citizenship (25 March 1993) <https://www.legislationline. org/documents/id/5498> accessed 9 January 2024 . . . . . . . . .277
Law on Principles of Entrepreneurial Activity (25 July 1991) in JN Hazard and Vratislav Pechota (eds) Russia and the Republics: Legal Materials (Juris 1993) (note 110) binder 1 . . . . . . . . . . . . . .301

xlviii    TABLE OF LEGISLATION

## GERMANY*

Law on the Reunion of the Sudeten
German Districts with the
German Reich (21 November
1938) 142 BFSP 585 . . . . . . . . . . . . . .265

## GUINEA

Constitution of the Republic of
Guinea (10 November 1958)
in AJ Peaslee and DX Peaslee,
*Constitutions of Nations*
(Martinus Hijhoff 1965) 229 . . . 272–73
Ordinance No 11 [Ordonnance N°
11] (1 March 1960) in Faciala
Keita, 'Guinea' *International
Encyclopaedia of Comparative
Law Online* vol 1 (1979) . . . . . . 272–73

## INDIA

Citizenship Act 1955 23 GIE (2 May
1955) <https://www.refworld.
org/legal/legislation/natlegbod/
1955/en/19544> accessed 16
February 2024 . . . . . . . . . . . . . . . . . .265
Constitution of the Sovereign
Democratic Republic of India
(26 November 1949) 157 BFSP
34 . . . . . . . . . . . . . . . . . . . . . . . . 124, 269
Dadra and Nagar Haveli Act No 35
1961 <https://www.indiacode.
nic.in/bitstream/123456789/
1640/2/A1961-35.pdf> accessed
30 December 2023 . . . . . . . 29, 129, 220
Goa, Daman and Diu
(Administration) Act 1962
<https://www.indiacode.nic.
in/bitstream/123456789/1369/
2/A1962-01.pdf> accessed 30
December 2023 . . . . . . . . . . . . . 29, 220
Goa, Daman and Diu (Citizenship)
Order (28 March 1962) <https://
www.refworld.org/docid/3ae
6b51d1c.html> accessed 30
December 2023 . . . . . . . . . . . . . . . .265
Goa, Daman and Diu Mining
Concessions (Abolition and
Declaration as Mining Leases) Act
No 16 of 1987 <https://www.indiac

ode.nic.in/handle/123456789/
1884?view_type=browse&sam
_handle=123456789/1362>
accessed 30 December 2023 . . . . . . . . 310
Mines and Minerals (Regulation and
Development) Act No 67 1957
<https://ibm.gov.in/writereadd
ata/files/07102014115602M
MDR%20Act%201957_10052012.
pdf> accessed 30 December 2023 . . . 310

## INDONESIA ('NETHERLANDS EAST INDIES')

Act No 3 concerning Citizens and
Residents of Indonesia (10 April
1946) in UN Legislative Series,
*Laws Concerning Nationality*
(1954) 230 . . . . . . . . . . . . . . . . . . 271–72
Act regulating the Nationality of the
Dutch East Indies, 296 Staatsblad
van Nederlandsch-Indië
(1 March 1910) (Dutch) . . . . . . 271–72
Act regulating the Nationality of the
Dutch East Indies [Nederlandsch
Onderdaanschap wet van den
10den Februari 1910, houdende
regeling van het Nederlandsche
onderdaanschap van de
bevolking van Nederlandsch-
Indië] 296 Staatsblad van
Nederlandsch-Indië (1 March
1910) (Dutch) . . . . . . . . . . . . . . 271–72
Nationalization of Dutch Enterprises
Act No 86 (31 December 1958)
(1959) 6 NTIR 291 . . . . . . . . . . . . . .296
Provisional Constitution of the
Republic of Indonesia Act No 7
(15 August 1950) 37 Gazette of
Indonesia (1950); **AJ Peaslee,
*Constitutions of Nations* vol 2
(Martinus Nijhoff 1956) 368** . . . . .296

## ISRAEL

Absentee Property Law 1950 IV Israel
Laws 68 . . . . . . . . . . . . . . . . . . . . . . . .294
Law and Administration Ordinance
No 5708-1948, I Laws of the
State of Israel 7 . . . . . . . . . . 43, 140, 284

---

* Including Prussia and the German Democratic Republic.

Law of Return No 5710-1950 (5 July
1950) V Israel Laws 114. . . . . . . . . . .284
Nationality Law No 5712-1952 VI
Israel Laws 50
Registration of Inhabitants
Ordinance No 5709-1949
(3 February 1949) II Laws of the
State of Israel 103 . . . . . . . . . . . . . . . .284
State Property Law No 5711-1951 V
Laws of the State of Israel 45 . . . 43, 284

## KAZAKHSTAN

Law on Citizenship (20 December
1991) art 3 in JN Hazard and
Vratislav Pechota (eds) Russia
and the Republics: Legal
Materials (Juris 1993) (note 369)
binder 1; <https://www.legislat
ionline.org/download/id/6559/
file/Kazakh_Citizenship_law_
1991_am2013_en.pdf> accessed
9 January 2024. . . . . . . . . . . . . . 276–77

## KYRGYZSTAN

Law No 130 on Citizenship (18
December 1993) <https://www.
refworld.org/docid/40fe4f3e4.
html> accessed
17 February 2024 . . . . . . . . . . . 276–77
Law on General Principles of
Entrepreneurship in JN Hazard
and Vratislav Pechota (eds)
Russia and the Republics: Legal
Materials binder 1 (1993) . . . . . . . .301

## LAOS

Constitution of the Kingdom of Laos
(11 May 1947) in AJ Peaslee and
DX Peaslee, Constitutions of
Nations (Martinus Hijhoff
1965) 624 . . . . . . . . . . . . . . . . . . . . . .272
Law No 138 on the Acquisition and
Loss of Laotian Nationality [Loi
No 138 sur l'acquisition ou la
perte de la nationalité laotienne]
(6 April 1953) UN Legislative
Series, Laws Concerning
Nationality (1954) 283 (French) . . . 272

## LEBANON

Decision No 2825 (30 August 1924)
in UN Legislative Series, Laws
Concerning Nationality (1954)
284 (French) . . . . . . . . . . . . . . . . . . . .284
Decree No 15/S on Lebanese
Nationality [Arrêté N° 15/S
relatif à la nationalité libanaise]
(19 January 1925) UN Legislative
Series, Laws Concerning
Nationality (1954) 285 (French). . .284

## LIBYA

Constitution of Libya (7 October
1951) UN Legislative Series, Laws
Concerning Nationality (1954) 293. . . .272

## MADAGASCAR

Constitution of the Republic of
Madagascar (29 April 1959)
in AJ Peaslee and DX Peaslee,
Constitutions of Nations
(Martinus Hijhoff 1965) 453 . . . . . .296
Convention on Establishment
(adopted 27 June 1960, entered
into force on 18 July 1960) 820
UNTS 364 . . . . . . . . . . . . . . . . . . . . .296
Ordinance No 60-064 [Ordonnance
N° 60-064] (22 July 1960) 111
JORM (30 July 1960) 1305;
**(1960) UNYBHR 227** . . . . . . . . . . .273

## MARSHALL ISLANDS

Constitution of the Republic of the
Marshall Islands (1 May 1979)
<http://paclii.org/mh/legis/con
sol_act/cotrotmi490/> accessed
31 December 2023 . . . . . . . . . . . . . . .286

## MICRONESIA

Constitution of the Federated States
of Micronesia (adopted 1
October 1978, entered into force
10 May 1979) in BM Turcott,
'The Beginnings of the Federated
States of Micronesia Supreme
Court' (1983) 5 UHLR 361. . . . . . . .286

## TABLE OF LEGISLATION

Federated States of Micronesia
Annotated Code 2014, Title 7
('Citizenship') Ch 2, PL 17-54 . . . . .286

### MOLDOVA

Law on Nationality (5 June 1991) in
UNHCR, 'Nationality Laws of
the Former Soviet Republics' (1
July 1993) <https://www.refwo
rld.org/docid/3ae6b31db3.html>
accessed 9 January 2024 . . . . . . . .276–77
Law on Property (22 January 1991) in
JN Hazard and Vratislav Pechota
(eds) Russia and the Republics:
Legal Materials binder 2 (Juris
1993) . . . . . . . . . . . . . . . . . . . . . . . . . . .301

### MONTENEGRO

Declaration of Independence of
Montenegro (3 June 2006) in Jure
Vidmar, 'Montenegro's Path to
Independence: A Study of Self-
Determination, Statehood and
Recognition' (2007) 3(1) HLR 73 . . . 280
Foreign Investment Law (25 March
2011) <https://investmentpol
icy.unctad.org/investment-laws/
laws/121/montenegro-foreign-
investment-law> accessed 31
December 2023 . . . . . . . . . . . . . . . . .302
Law on State-Legal Status of the
Republic of Montenegro,
<http://www.rtcg.org/referen
dum/regulativa/zakon_o_refe
rendumu.pdf#search=%22za
kon%20o%20referendumu%>
accessed 9 January 2024 . . . . . . . . . .280
Montenegrin Citizenship Act No 13/
08 2008 Crne Gore (26 February
2008) 46 (Montenegrin) . . . . . . . . . .280

### MOZAMBIQUE

'Alto Comissão Moçambique',
Portugal Archives Box 40603
(Portuguese) . . . . 132, 224–25, 309–10
'Finances – Current Accounts with the
Metropole' ['Finanças – Contas
Correntes com a Metropole']
Portugal Archives [Arquivo da
Repartição de Gabinete] Box
55344 Pasta J/11-l, J/9-a J/5-aJ3
(Portuguese) . . . . . . . . . . . . . . . . .133–34

### MOROCCO

Constitution of Morocco (14
December 1962) in AJ Peaslee
and DX Peaslee, *Constitutions of
Nations* (Martinus Hijhoff 1965)
563 . . . . . . . . . . . . . . . . . . . . . . . . . . . . .296
Decree No 1-06-14 promulgating
Law No 42-05 rescinding
certain measures on agricultural
property transferred to the
State [Dahir no 1-06-14 du 15
moharrem 1427 (14 février 2006)
portant promulgation de la loi no
42-05 édicant certaines mesures
relatives aux immeubles agricoles
ou à vocation agricole dont la
propriété est transférée à l'Etat]
(14 February 2006) 5400 BORM
(2 March 2006) 347 (French) . . . . . .296
Decree No 1-58-250 on the Moroccan
Nationality Code [Dahir n°
1-58-250 du 21 safar 1378 (6
septembre 1958) portant code
de la nationalité morocaine] (6
September 1958) 2394 BORM
(12 September 1958) 1492
(French) . . . . . . . . . . . . . . . . . . . . . . . .285
Decree No 1-63-289 setting the
Conditions for the Recovery
by the State of Colonisation
Lots [Dahir no 1-63-289 du
7 joumada I 1383 fixant les
conditions de la reprise par l'Etat
des lots de colonisation] (26
September 1963) 2657 BORM
(27 September 1963) 1527
(French) . . . . . . . . . . . . . . . . . . . . . . . .296
Joint Ordinance No 500-63 of
26 September 1963 on Real
Property Transferred to the State,
2657 BORM (27 September
1963) 1528 (French) . . . . . . . . . . . . .296
Law No 1-73-213 on the Transfer to
the State of Agricultural Estates
(2 March 1973) 3149 BORM (7
March 1973) (7 March 1973) 391
(French) . . . . . . . . . . . . . . . . . . . . . . . .296

Law No 70-632 [Loi N° 70-632] (15
July 1970) & Decree on the
Determination and Valuation of
Compensable Properties located
in Morocco [Décret du 21 avril
1971 relatif à la détermination
et à l'évaluation des biens
indemnisables situés au Maroc]
(21 April 1971) in Administrative
Court of Appeal of Lyon Case
Nos 96LY02491 (6 November
1998) 93LY00210 (29 June 1994)
& 92LY00730 (16 March 1994)
(French) . . . . . . . . . . . . . . . . . . . . . . .320

### MYANMAR ('BURMA')

Burma Transfer of Immoveable
Property (Restriction) Act No 86
(31 December 1947) <https://
www.burmalibrary.org/en/
government-of-the-union-of-
burma-law-no-861947-the-trans
fer-of-immoveable-property-rest
riction-act> accessed 12 January
2024 . . . . . . . . . . . . . . . . . . . . . . . . . .296
Constitution of the Union of Burma
(24 September 1947, entered into
force 4 January 1948) in Maung
Maung, *Burma's Constitution*
(Springer 1961) 258 . . . . . . . . . 132, 296
Land Nationalization Act No LX 1948
(Superintendent, Government
Printing and Stationery, Burma
1950) . . . . . . . . . . . . . . . . . . . . . . . . .296
Union Citizenship Act No LXVI 1948
<https://www.mlis.gov.mm/
mLsView.do;jsessionid=8AA79
74B82F6039DAFFFA1B4379C7
424?lawordSn=660> accessed 16
February 2024 . . . . . . . . . . . . . . . . . .270

### NAMIBIA ('SOUTH WEST AFRICA')

Constitution of Namibia
(21 March 1990) UN Doc
S/10967/Add.2 . . . . . . . . . . . . . .96–97,
142, 265, 300–1, 311
Namibian Citizenship Act No 14 1990
Government Gazette 65 . . . . . . 285–86

### NETHERLANDS

Indonesia Civil Service Personnel
Guarantee Act [Garantiewet
Burgerlijk Overheidspersoneel
Indonesië] (11 May 1950) 268
Staatsblad (1950) Wet No K 268 . . . 314

### NORTH MACEDONIA (THE FORMER YUGOSLAV REPUBLIC OF MACEDONIA')

Constitutional law on the entry into
force of the Constitution of
Macedonia (25 November 1991)
in Foreign Broadcast Information
Service, *JPRS Report: East Europe
Recent Legislation* (US Department
of Commerce, 10 February 1992) . . . 171
Law on Citizenship (adopted 27
October 1992, entered into force
12 November 1992) in UNHCR,
'Citizenship and Prevention
of Statelessness Linked to the
Disintegration of the Socialist
Federal Republic of Yugoslavia'
(1997) 3(1) European Series 40 . . . .261

### PAKISTAN

Pakistan Citizenship Act No 2 of
1951 158 BFSP 609 . . . . . . . . . . . . . .269
Pakistan Citizenship (Amendment)
Ordinance 1978 in Hoque, 'Report
on Citizenship Law: Bangladesh',
EUI Country Report No 2016/14
(December 2016) 10 . . . . . . . . . . . . .275

### PALAU

Constitution of the Republic of Palau
(adopted 2 April 1979, entered into
force 1 January 1981) <http://paclii.
org/pw/constitution.html> accessed
31 December 2023 . . . . . . . . . . . . . . .286

### PALESTINE (MANDATORY TERRITORY OF)

Palestinian Citizenship Order
(24 July 1925) Official Gazette
(16 September 1925) . . . . . . . . . . . . .284

## PHILIPPINES

Constitution of the Philippines (8 February 1935) 17 *International Conciliation* (1936) 137; **AJ Peaslee, *Constitutions of Nations* (Martinus Nijhoff 1950) 789** .....269
Proclamation of Philippine Independence (4 July 1946) 146 BFSP 899 .................. 41, 269

## POLAND

Decree on the Administration of the Recovered Territories [Dekret z dnia 13 listopada 1945 r. o zarządzie Ziem Odzyskanych] (13 November 1945) 51 Dziennik Ustaw 295 .............296

## PORTUGAL

Decree-Law No 308-A/75 (24 June 1975) 143 Diário Series I 862 (Portuguese) ................ 275–76
Nationality Law No 37/81 (3 October 1981) 228 Diário da República Series I (Portuguese); <https://www.refworld.org/docid/3ae6b52e4.html> accessed 31 December 2023 .........................265

## RUSSIAN FEDERATION ('UNION OF SOVIET SOCIALIST REPUBLICS')

Constitution of Russia (12 December 1993) in *CIS Legislation Database* <https://cis-legislation.com/> accessed 1 January 2024 .........75–76
Law on Citizenship of the RSFSR (28 November 1991) 19(3) RCEEL (1993) 293 .....................280
Law No 4730-1 (1 April 1993) *CIS Legislation Database* <https://cis-legislation.com/> accessed 1 January 2024 ................ 276–77
USSR Citizenship Law 1990 in George Ginsburgs, 'From the 1990 Law on the Citizenship of the USSR to the Citizenship Laws of the Successor Republics (Part I) (1992) 18 RCEEL 1 ...........276

## SERBIA ('FEDERAL REPUBLIC OF YUGOSLAVIA')

Citizenship Act of the Federal Republic of Yugoslavia (accessed 16 July 1996, entered into force 1 January 1997) <https://www.refworld.org/docid/3ae6b4d44.html> accessed 9 January 2024 ...................... 261, 280
Constitutional Charter of the State Union of Serbia and Montenegro (2003) 70(2) Rivista di studi politici internazionali 292.... 138, 280
Law on Citizenship of the Republic of Serbia, 135/04 Службени гласник (February 2008) <https://www.refworld.org/pdfid/4b56d0542.pdf> accessed 31 December 2023 ..............280

## SINGAPORE

Constitution of Singapore (9 August 1965) <https://sso.agc.gov.sg/Act/CONS1963> accessed 9 January 2024............... 81, 268

## SLOVAKIA

Constitution of the Slovak Republic (1 September 1992) 460/1992 Coll. Pravne Predpisy (Czecho-Slovak) ..................... 125–26
Law No 40 (19 January 1993) <https://www.legislationline.org/documents/action/popup/id/3848> accessed 31 December 2023..........................284

## SLOVENIA

Act on the Inheritance of the Agreements of the former Yugoslavia with Japan 8/1994 Uradni list RS (Slovenian) .... 172–75
Constitution of Slovenia (23 December 1991) in *World Constitutions Illustrated Database* <https://home.heinonline.org/content/world-constitutions-illustrated/> accessed 9 January 2024

Slovene Citizenship Act, No 1/91 Uradni
list (25 June 1991) (Slovene) ......... 261

## SOMALIA*

Law No 5 (31 January 1961) 2 Official
Bulletin of the Somali Republic
(1961) ................ 123, 168, 209
Law of Union between Somaliland
and Somalia (27 June 1960) 164
BFSP 697 ............... 95, 123, 259
Somali Citizenship Law No 28 (22
December 1962) Official Bulletin
of the Somali Republic Supplement
No 4 to No 12 (1962) .............. 259

## SOUTH AFRICA

Citizenship at Attainment of
Independence by Namibia
Regulation Act No 74 of 1990,
300 SAGG (29 June 1990) 2 ... 285–86
Recognition of the Independence of
Namibia Act, 20 March 1990, 297
GG (20 March 1990) .......... 96–97
Transfer of Walvis Bay to Namibia Act
No 203 of 1993 (South Africa)
33 ILM 1573 ................... .265
Walvis Bay and Offshore Islands Act
No 1 of 1994, 28 SAGG
(28 February 1994). .............. .265

## SOUTH SUDAN

Transitional Constitution of South
Sudan 2011 <https://www.
ilo.org/dyn/natlex/natlex4.
detail?p_lang=en&p_isn=
90704&p_classification=01>
accessed 3 January 2024 ......... 303

## SPAIN

Decree 1.748-68 submitting to
Referendum the Text of the
Constitution written by the
Constitutional Conference
[Decreto de 27 de julio de 1968,
núm. 1.748-68 sometiendo
a referéndum el texto de

Constitución elaborado por la
Conferencia Constitucional] 181
BOE (29 July 1968) (Spanish) ..... .275
Decree 1347/1969 on the Nationality
Option provided in the Treaty
on the Retrocession of Ifni
[Decreto 1347/1969 por el
que se reglamenta la opción
de nacionalidad prevista en el
Tratado sobre retrocesión del
territorio de Ifni] 158 BOE (3
July 1969) 10445 (Spanish). ....... .265
DGRN Resolutions [Resoluciónes
DGRN] (28 January 1989 & 18
May 1989) 41(2) REDI (1989)
276 (Spanish) ................... .275
Fundamental Law No 191/1963
[Ley de Bases] (20 December
1963) 312 BOE (30 December
1963) in 'Declaration on the
Granting of Independence
to Colonial Countries and
Peoples: information on
the implementation of the
Declaration', UN Doc A/AC.109/
71 (6 May 1964) Annex ........... .275
Law No 49-68 authorising the
Government to Grant
Independence to Equatorial
Guinea [Ley 49-68 autorizando
al Gobierno para conceder
la independencia a Guinea
Ecuatorial] (27 July 1968) 181
BOE (29 July 1968) (Spanish) ..... .275

## SOUTH SUDAN

South Sudan Nationality Act 2011
<https://www.refworld.org/coun
try,LEGAL,NATLEGBOD,LEGI
SLATION,SSD,,4e94318f2,0.html>
accessed 31 December 2023 ......... .281

## SUDAN

Sudanese Nationality Act 1994/5/17 (17
May 1994) <https://www.refwo
rld.org/docid/503492892.html>
accessed 31 December 2023. ........ 281

---

* Including the Republic of Somaliland.

liv TABLE OF LEGISLATION

Sudanese Nationality Act (Amendment) 2018 <https://www.refworld.org/docid/503492892.html> accessed 31 December 2023 ................ 281

## SYRIA*

Decision No 2825 [Arrêté N° 2825] (30 August 1924) UN Legislative Series, *Laws Concerning Nationality* (1954) 284 (French) ... 284
Legislative Decree No 67 (31 October 1961) (1961) JOS 1090 (Arabic) ............... 268–84

## TANZANIA**

Acts of Union of Tanganyika and Zanzibar Government Notice No 243 (1 May 1964); **3(4) ILM 763**.... 123
Citizenship Act 1961 (CAP52) <https://data.globalcit.eu/NationalDB/docs/Tanganyika-Citizenship-Act-1961_1.pdf> accessed 17 February 2024........259
Extension and Amendment of Laws Decree No 5 1964, GN No 652 (13 November 1964) .............259

## TIMOR-LESTE ('EAST TIMOR')

Constitution of Timor-Leste (adopted 22 March 2002, entered into force 25 May 2002) <http://timor-leste.gov.tl/wp-content/uploads/2010/03/Constitution_RDTL_ENG.pdf> accessed 31 December 2023......... 138, 139, 311
Decree-Law No 308-A/75 (24 June 1975) 143 Diário da República, Series I 862 (Portuguese & Tetum).........275–76
Law on Real Estate Property No 1/2003 Jornal da República Series I (Portuguese & Tetum)....... 138, 303
Nationality Law No 37/81 228 Diário da República, Series I (Oct. 3, 1981) (Portuguese & Tetum) ................265, 275–76

## TURKMENISTAN

Law on Citizenship (30 September 1992) Turkmenskaya Iskra (11 October 1992) <https://www.legislationline.org/documents/action/popup/id/7023> accessed 9 January 2024 ................ 276–77

## UKRAINE

Law on Citizenship (October 1991) in Václav Mikulka, 'Second report on State Succession and its impact on the nationality of natural and legal persons', UN Doc A/CN.4/474 (17 April 1996).....................276–77
Law on Legal Succession of Ukraine No 1543-XII (12 September 1991) in JN Hazard and Vratislav Pechota (eds) *Russia and the Republics: Legal Materials* binder 2 (Juris 1993)................ 276–77
Law on Property (7 February 1991) in JN Hazard and Vratislav Pechota (eds) Russia and the Republics: Legal Materials binder 2 (Juris 1993)..........................301
Law on the Protection of Foreign Investments in Ukraine (10 September 1991) in JN Hazard and Vratislav Pechota (eds) Russia and the Republics: Legal Materials binder 2 (Juris 1993) ....301

## UNITED KINGDOM

Aden, Parim and Kuria Muria Islands Act 1967 (Appointed Day) Order SI 1967/1761 ....................132
Aden, Perim and Kuria Muria Islands Act 1967, 15 & 16 Eliz. 2 c.71.... 132, 271
British Nationality Act 1948, 11 & 12 Geo 6 c 56......................269
British Nationality Act 1981 c 61, s 15 .... 265
British Nationality (Hong Kong) Act 1990 c 34.......................265
British Nationality (Hong Kong) Act 1997 c 20.......................265

* Including the Mandatory Territory for Syria and the Lebanon.
** Including Tanganyika and Zanzibar.

British Nationality (People's Republic of Southern Yemen) Order SI 1968/1310 .....................271

British Nationality and Status of Aliens Act 1914 4 & 5 Geo c 17 ....269

British North America Act 1949 (23 March 1949) 153 BFSP 130...... 32–33, 129, 262

British Protectorates, Protected States and Protected Persons Order in Council, SI 1949 No 140..........269

Burma Independence Act 1947 (10 December 1947) 11 Geo 6 c 3 .....132

Cocos Islands Order in Council 1955 (United Kingdom) (adopted 28 October 1955, entered into force 23 November 1955) SI 2435.......296

Constitution of Malaysia 1963, in Agreement concluded between the United Kingdom and the Federation of Malaya, Cmd 2094 (July 1963) 89-91, annex A ... 129, 221

Federation of Malaya Independence Act 1957, 5 & 6 Eliz. II c.60; *UN Materials on Succession of States*, UN Doc ST/LEG/SER.B/14 (1967) 76 .......................132

Federation of Rhodesia and Nyasaland (Dissolution) Order in Council 1963 No 2085 ..... 126–27

Government of India Act 1935 26 Geo 5 ch 2........................ 38–39

Independence of Somaliland Order-in-Council (26 June 1960) SI 1960/1060, annex ('Constitution of Somaliland') ..................248

India (Adaptation of Existing Laws) Order 1947 (14 August 1947) G.G.O. 16, Gazette of India Extraordinary (14 August 1947)...................126–29, 294

Indian Independence Act 1947, 10 & 11 Geo 6 ch 30........... 95–96, 294

Indian Independence (International Arrangements) Order 1947, 3 CILC 144 ................ 38–39, 183

Indian Independence (Rights, Property and Liabilities) Order, G.G.O. 18 of 1947 (14 August 1947) 2 Reserve Bank of India Bulletin (1948) 72; (24-31 January 1948) Kiesing's

Contemporary Archives 9066; **3 CILC 134**...........126–29, 225, 294

India (Provisional Constitution) Order 1947, 3 CILC 134 ......126–29, 225, 294

Malaysia Act 1963 c 35................265

Mauritius Independence Act 1968, 16 & 17 Eliz II c 8 ........ 132, 266–67

Mauritius Independence Order 1968, Government Notice No 54 (6 March 1968) ......132, 266–67, 311

Order in Council regarding the establishment of the Federation of Malaya (26 January 1948) 150 BFSP 30; *UN Materials on Succession of States*, **UN Doc ST/LEG/SER.B/14 (1967) 81** ..... 132, 265

Palestine Act 1948 (11 & 12 Geo. 6) c 27.............. 140, 284

Tanganyika (Constitution) Order in Council 1961, SI. 1961 No 2274............ 123, 285

Tanganyika Independence Act 1961 c 1........................285

Tanganyika Order in Council 1920, SI 1920/1583 ....................285

Uganda Independence Act 1962, 10 & 11 Eliz II, c 57..............269

## UNITED STATES OF AMERICA

Act of the Congress of the United States of America to provide for the Independence of the Philippines Islands (24 March 1934) 137 BFSP 690..............132

Covenant to Establish a Commonwealth of the Northern Mariana Islands in Political Union with the United States of America, Public Law 94-241, 90 Stat. 263 (24 March 1976); **14 ILM 344**......151, 286

Department of Interior Secretarial Order No 3039 (25 April 1979) ....142

Joint Resolution annexing the Hawaiian Islands (7 July 1898) 90 BFSP 1250 ......................124

Organic Act of 30 April 1900, 31 United States Stat 141, 8 U.S.C.A ........... 260

Proclamation 5564 (3 November 1986) 51 Federal Register 40339, Title One .................120

lvi TABLE OF LEGISLATION

Proclamation 6826 (27 September
    1994) 108 Stat 5631 . . . . . . . . . . . . . .142
Public Law 94-241 (24 March
    1976) 90 Stat 263. . . . . . . . 151, 286, 303

### UZBEKISTAN

Law on Citizenship Law No 632-XII
    (2 July 1992) 9 Gazette of the
    Supreme Council of the Republic
    of Uzbekistan 338 . . . . . . . . . . . . 276–77
Law on Ownership (31 October
    1990) in JN Hazard and Vratislav
    Pechota (eds) Russia and the
    Republics: Legal Materials
    binder 2 (Juris 1993) . . . . . . . . . . . . .301

### VIET NAM*

Civil Code of Tonkin 1931 [Code
    civil du Tonkin] UN Legislative
    Series, *Supplement to the Laws
    Concerning Nationality* (1959)
    549 (French) . . . . . . . . . . . . . . . . . . .272
Constitution of the Democratic
    Republic of Vietnam (31
    December 1959) <http://vbpl.
    vn/TW/Pages/vbpq-toanvan.
    aspx?ItemID=889> accessed 9
    January 2024 (Vietnamese) . . . . . . .296
Constitution of the Republic of
    Vietnam (26 October 1956) 162
    BFSP 1056 . . . . . . . . . . . . . . . . . . . . .296
Constitution of the Socialist Republic
    of Viet Nam (18 December 1980)
    <https://vbpl.vn/TW/Pages/
    vbpq-toanvan.aspx?ItemID=
    1534> accessed 16 February
    2024 (Vietnamese). . . . . . . . . . . 30, 259
Democratic Republic of Viet Nam
    Law No 29 (10 September 1945)
    <http://vbpl.vn/TW/Pages/
    vbpq-toanvan.aspx?ItemID=
    804> accessed 12 January 2024,
    art 2 (Vietnamese) . . . . . . . . . . . . . .296

Democratic Republic of Viet Nam
    Law No 48 (9 October 1945)
    <http://vbpl.vn/TW/Pages/
    vbpq-toanvan.aspx?ItemID=
    804> accessed 12 January 2024,
    art 1 (Vietnamese) . . . . . . . . . . . . . .296
Democratic Republic of Viet Nam
    Law on Land Reform (4
    December 1953) <http://vbpl.
    vn/TW/Pages/vbpq-toanvan.
    aspx?ItemID=535> accessed
    12 January 2024, arts 1-2
    (Vietnamese). . . . . . . . . . . . . . . . . . .296
Law No 208/2016/QH13 on Treaties
    (on file with author). . . . . . . . . . . 73–74
Provisional Act constituting the
    Republic in South Vietnam (26
    October 1955) 161 BFSP 539 . . . . . .272
Resolution of the National Assembly
    of the Socialist Republic of
    Vietnam on the Organization
    and Operation of the State (2
    July 1976) (on file with author)
    (Vietnamese). . . . . . . . . . . . . . . . . . .123
Resolution No 52/2005/QH11
    (29 November 2005) on the
    Ratification of the Treaty
    (on file with author)
    (Vietnamese). . . . . . . . . . . . . . . . 73–74
Socialist Republic of Viet Nam Law
    on Vietnamese Nationality 1988
    (1988) 15(3) RSL 287. . . . . . . . . . . .259

### YEMEN**

Constitution of the Republic of
    Yemen (22 May 1990) (1992)
    7(1) ALQ 70. . . . . . . . . . . . . . . 259, 300
People's Republic of Southern Yemen
    Law of Nationality No 4 (1968)
    Ch. 2 . . . . . . . . . . . . . . . . . . . . . . . . .271
Republic of Yemen Law No 22 of 1991
    in Abdulla Maktari and John
    McHugo, *Business Laws of
    Yemen* (1995) 37 . . . .300, 303, 313, 317

---

\* Including the Democratic Republic of Viet Nam ('North Viet Nam') and the Republic of Viet Nam
('South Viet Nam').
\*\* Including the Arab Republic of Yemen ('North Yemen') and the People's Democratic Republic of
Yemen ('South Yemen').

# Table of Treaties and other International Instruments

(bilateral treaties arranged by successor* in alphabetical order)

## OPEN MULTILATERAL TREATIES

Additional Protocol to the Geneva Conventions of 12 August 1949 (adopted 8 June 1977, entered into force 7 December 1978) 1125 UNTS 3 . . . . . . . . . . . . . . . 151–54

Agreement on the Establishment of the 'Intersputnik' International System and Organization of Space Communications (adopted 15 November 197112 July 1972) 862 UNTS 4 . . . . . . . 170–72

Agreement on German External Debts (adopted 27 February 1953, entered into force 16 September 1953) 333 UNTS 3 . . . . .158

Agreement relating to Refugee Seamen (adopted 23 November 1957, entered into force 27 December 1961) 506 UNTS 125. . . . . . . . . . . . . . 171–72

Charter of the United Nations (adopted 26 June 1945, entered into force 24 October 1945) <https://treatiesun. org/pages/ViewDetailsaspx?src= IND&mtdsg_no=I-1&chap ter=1&clang=_en> accessed 25 January 2025 . . . . . . . . . . . . . . . . . . 24, 179

Convention (I) for the Amelioration of the Condition of the Wounded and Sick in Armed Forces in the Field (adopted 12 August 1949, entered into force 21 October 1950) 75 UNTS 31 . . . . . . . . . . . . . . .157

Convention on Assistance in the Case of a Nuclear Accident or Radiological Emergency (adopted 26 September 1986, entered into force 26 February 1987) 1457 UNTS 133. . . . . . . . 171–72

Convention concerning the Protection of World Natural and Cultural Heritage (adopted 16 November 1972, entered into force 17 December 1975) 1037 UNTS 151 . . . . . . . . . . . . . . . . . . . . . .113–14

Convention on the Elimination of All Forms of Racial Discrimination (adopted 7 March 1966, entered into force 4 January 1969) 660 UNTS 195 . . . . . . . . . . . . . . . . . . . . . .251

Convention establishing a Customs Co-Operation Council (adopted 15 December 1950, entered into force 4 November 1952) 157 UNTS 129 . . . . . . . . . . . . . . . . . . . . . .149

Convention on International Civil Aviation (adopted 7 December 1944, entered into force 4 April 1947) 15 UNTS 295 . . . . . . . . . . 148–49

Convention for Limiting the Manufacture and Regulating the Distribution of Narcotic Drugs (adopted 13 July 1931 & 11 December 1946, entered into force 21 November 1947) 139 LNTS 301. . . . . . . . . . . . . . 150, 157–58

---

* Arranged by predecessor for: Syria and the Lebanon; the Trust Territory for the Pacific Islands (Northern Mariana Islands, Micronesia, Palau and the Marshall Islands); the Union of Soviet Socialist Republics (Armenia, Azerbaijan, Belarus, Georgia, Moldova, Kazakhstan, Tajikstan, Uzbekistan, Kyrgyzstan and the Ukraine); French Indochina (Laos, Cambodia and South Viet Nam); and the Socialist Federal Republic of Yugoslavia (Slovenia, Croatia, Bosnia-Herzegovina, Northern Macedonia and the Federal Republic of Yugoslavia (Serbia-Montenegro)).

## lviii TABLE OF TREATIES AND OTHER INTERNATIONAL INSTRUMENTS

Convention on the Nationality of
Married Women (adopted 20
February 1957, entered into force
11 August 1958) 309 UNTS 65.....247
Convention on Offences and certain
other Acts committed on board
Aircraft (adopted 14 September
1963, entered into force 4
December 1969)
704 UNTS 219...........158, 171–72
Convention on the Prevention of
Marine Pollution by Dumping of
Wastes and other Matter, London
(adopted 29 December 1972,
entered into force 30 August
1975) 2046 UNTS 120........ 171–72
Convention on the Prohibition of the
Use, Stockpiling, Production
and Transfer of Anti-Personnel
Mines and on their Destruction
(adopted 18 September 1997,
entered into force 1 March 1999)
2056 UNTS 211 .................192
Convention for the Protection of
Cultural Property in the Event of
Armed Conflict (adopted 14 May
1955, entered into force 7 August
1956) 249 UNTS 240......... 113–14
Convention (III) relative to the
Treatment of Prisoners of
War (adopted 12 August 1949,
entered into force 21 October
1950) 75 UNTS 135.......... 171–72
International Convention on the
Prohibition of the Use of White
(Yellow) Phosphorus in the
Match Industry (adopted 26
September 1906, entered into
force 1 January 1912) <https://
www.fedlex.admin.ch/eli/cc/
24/70_72_69/fr> accessed 25
January 2025 (French) ....... 159–60
International Convention for the
Unification of Certain Rules
relating to Bills of Lading (25
August 1924) 1412 UNTS 121.....154
International Opium Convention
(adopted 23 January 1912,
entered into force 28 June 1919)
8 LNTS 187, 187 UNTS 8.........177
International Telecommunication
Convention (adopted 2 October

1947, entered into force
1 January 1949) 193
UNTS 188 .....................150
International Telecommunication
Convention (12 November 1965)
91 <https://search.itu.int/hist
ory/HistoryDigitalCollectio
nDocLibrary/5.9.61.en.100.pdf>
accessed 25 January 2025 ..... 149–50
Protocol on the Accession to the
Convention for the Pacific
Settlement of International
Disputes of 19 July 1899 (14
June 1907) Netherlands Treaty
Database No 03308 ..............154
Protocol amending the Agreements,
Conventions and Protocols of
Narcotic Drugs (11 December
1946) 12 UNTS 179.......... 157–58
Protocol of Signature relating to the
Statute of the Permanent Court
of International Justice (16
December 1920) 6 LNTS 380.... 55–56
Statute of the International Court
of Justice (24 October 1945)
<https://treaties.un.org/pages/
ViewDetails.aspx?src=TRE
ATY&mtdsg_no=I-3&chapter=
1&clang=_en> accessed
25 January 2025...................58
Treaty on the Non-Proliferation of
Nuclear Weapons (adopted 1 July
1968, entered into force 5 March
1970) 729 UNTS 161......... 171–72

### PLURILATERAL ('CLOSED MULTILATERAL') TREATIES

Act regarding Navigation and
Economic Co-operation
between the States of the Niger
Basin (Cameroon, Ivory Coast,
Dahomey, Guinea, Upper Volta,
Mali, Niger, Nigeria, Chad)
(adopted 26 October 1963,
entered into force 1 February
1966) 587 UNTS 10...............84
Additional Protocol to the
Convention regarding the
Regime of Navigation on the
Danube (26 March 1998) 19(II)
BGBl (1999)....................149

## TABLE OF TREATIES AND OTHER INTERNATIONAL INSTRUMENTS  lix

Agreement on the Repatriation of Prisoners of War and Civilian Internees (Bangladesh-India-Pakistan) (9 April 1974) 13 ILM 501 .......... 275

Convention regarding the Regime of Navigation on the Danube (adopted 18 August 1948, entered into force 11 May 1949) 33 UNTS 181....................149

Convention respecting the Free Navigation of the Suez Maritime Canal (adopted 29 October 1888, entered into force 22 December 1888) 15 MNRG (2nd Series) 557; *UN Materials on Succession of States* (1967) UN Doc ST/LEG/SER.B/14, 158; **79 BFSP 18** (French)...........86, 89

Traité de Berlin du 13 juillet 1878, 3 MNRG 2nd Series 449 ..........86, 89

Peace Treaty between the Allied and Associated Powers and Austria (adopted 10 September 1919, entered into force 16 July 1920) (1919) 226 CTS 8 ............45–46, 126–29, 214, 246–47

Peace Treaty of Lausanne (adopted 24 July 1923, entered into force 6 August 1924) 28 LNTS 11 .......222

Peace Treaty of Neuilly-sur-Seine (adopted 27 November 1919, entered into force 9 August 1920) 226 CTS 332 ............... 246–47

Peace Treaty of Versailles (adopted 28 June 1919, entered into force 10 January 1920) 225 CTS 188 .........78–79, 221, 285

Peace Treaty with Hungary (adopted 10 February 1947, entered into force 15 September 1947) 48 UNTS 168 .................. 113–14

Peace Treaty with Italy (adopted 10 February 1947, entered into force 15 September 1947) 49 UNTS (1950) 3..................... 113–14

Protocol to the Soviet-American Treaty on Strategic Offensive Arms (adopted 23 May 1992, entered into force 5 December 1994) (1992) 96 RGDIP 1030 .....160

### BILATERAL TREATIES*

Aspects of Maritime Delimitation (Egypt-Saudi Arabia) (adopted 8 April 2016, entered into force 2 July 2017) UNTS I-5477..........32

Treaty for the Adjustment of the Border (Belgium-Netherlands) (adopted 28 November 2016, entered into force 1 January 2018) UNTS I-55014 .......32

Treaty concerning the Encouragement and Reciprocal Protection of Investment (Argentina-United States) (adopted 14 November 1991, entered into force 20 October 1994) UNTS I-54935..... 303

### ALGERIA

Accord concernant certaines questions financières (France-Algérie) (23 décembre 1966) France Archives No TRA19660023 (on file with author)......................... 132

Convention concerning the State Frontier Line (Morocco-Algeria) (adopted 15 June 1972, entered into force 14 May 1989) 2189 UNTS 87 ....94

Declarations drawn up in Common Agreement at Evian (France-Algerian National Liberation Front) (18 March 1962) 507 UNTS 25; 57 AJIL 1963 716; JORF (mars 1962) 301; **1(2) ILM 214** ........ 51–52, 132, 274, 297

Protocol on the Application and Execution of the 1845 Treaty in South-West Algeria (France-Morocco) (20 July 1901) 101 BFSP 428 ..........94

Treaty concluded between the Emperor of the French and the Emperor of Morocco (18 mars 1845) 34 BFSP 1287 (French) ......94

### ANGOLA

Agreement with regard to certain Angolan and Northern Rhodesian natives living on the Kwando River (United Kingdom-Portugal) (18 November 1954) 161 BFSP 167.......87

---

* Includes plurilateral treaties of specific application to a succession.

## AUSTRALIA

Treaty concerning Sovereignty and Maritime Boundaries in the Area between the Two Countries (Australia-Papua New Guinea) (adopted 18 December 1978, entered into force 15 February 1985) 1429 UNTS 207............73

Treaty for the Mutual Surrender of Fugitive Criminals (Yugoslavia-United Kingdom) (adopted 23 November & 6 December 1900, entered into force 13 August 1901) Australia Treaty Database (19 February 2003)......... 146, 160

## AUSTRIA

Convention regulating Payments between Austria and Italy [Convention concernant le règlement des paiements entre le pays d'Autriche et l'Italie] (Germany-Italy) (28 May 1938) 39 MNRG 302...................124

## BANGLADESH

Agreement on the Assumption of Debt Liabilities (Switzerland-Bangladesh) (adopted 4 December 1974, entered into force on 10 October 1975) 1127 UNTS 318 .....................135–36

Agreement concerning the Demarcation of the Land Boundary (India-Bangladesh) (16 May 1974) India Treaties Database No BG74B2547..........64

Agreement concerning Outstanding Debts (Bangladesh-United Kingdom) (20 September 1979) 1197 UNTS 187 ..................64

Protocol to the Agreement concerning the Demarcation of the Land Boundary (Bangladesh-India) (6 September 2011) in *India & Bangladesh: Land Boundary Agreement* (Ministry of External Affairs (Government of India) 2012); **India Treaty Database No BG11B0578**.....................64

## BELGIUM

Germany-Belgium, Arrangement relating to Option, and Final Protocol, Aix-la-Chapelle (11 September 1922) 41 LNTS 141................... 252–53

## BOTSWANA

Special Agreement to submit to the International Court of Justice the dispute existing between the two States concerning the boundary around the Kasiliki/Sedudu Island and the legal status of the Island' (15 May 1996) <https:// www.icj-cij.org/public/files/ case-related/98/7185.pdf> accessed 25 January 2025 .........265

## BURUNDI

Agreement respecting the Boundary between Tanganyika Territory and the Belgian Mandated Territory of Ruanda-Urundi (5 August 1924) Treaty Series No 6 (1927); Cmd 2812; **123 BFSP 462**...............99

Arrangement extending to the Belgian Congo and to Ruanda-Urundi the provisions of the above-mentioned arrangement (Belgium-Pakistan) (9 September 1952 & 28 July 1953) 173 UNTS 408.............149

Convention with a view to facilitating Belgian Traffic through the Territories of East Africa (Belgium-United Kingdom) (15 March 1921) 114 BFSP 182; **5 LNTS 319**................... 79–80

## CHILE

Treaty of Peace and Friendship (Chile-Peru) (adopted 20 October 1883, entered into force 28 March 1884) Colección de Actos Internacionales Celebrados por la Républica del Peru (1915) 1; **74 BFSP 349**......221

## TABLE OF TREATIES AND OTHER INTERNATIONAL INSTRUMENTS  lxi

### CHINA

Joint Declaration on the Question
of Hong Kong (China-United
Kingdom) (adopted 19 December
1984, entered into force 27 May
1985) (1984) ILM 1366; **1399
UNTS 33**. . . . . . . . . . . . 30, 129, 265, 302
Joint Declaration on the Question
of Macao (China-Portugal)
(adopted 13 April 1987, entered
into force 15 January 1988) 1498
UNTS 228 . . . . . .33, 129, 265, 302, 311

### CONGO (REPUBLIC OF)

Agreement relating to the continued
Application of Certain Treaties
(Congo (Brazzaville)-United States)
(12 May & 5 August 1961)
603 UNTS 19. . . . . . . . . . . . . . . . . . . .164

### CONGO (DEMOCRATIC REPUBLIC OF)*

Agreement modifying the Agreement
relating to the Spheres of
Influence of Great Britain and
the Independent State of the
Congo in East and Central Africa
(Congo-United Kingdom) (9
May 1906) 99 BFSP 173. . . . . . . . . . .86
Agreement concerning the
Indemnification of Zaireanized
Property belonging to Belgian
Natural Persons (Belgium-Zaire)
(adopted 28 March 1976, entered
into force 16 July 1976) in Weston,
Lillich and Bederman, International
Claims: Their Settlement by Lump
Sum Agreements, 1975-1995
(1999) 229. . . . . . . . . . . . . . . . . . . . . . .300
Arrangement extending to the
Belgian Congo and to Ruanda-
Urundi the Provisions of the
above-mentioned Arrangement
(Belgium-Pakistan) (9
September 1952 & 28 July 1953)
173 UNTS 408. . . . . . . . . . . . . . . . . .149
Convention for the Settlement of
Questions relating to the Public

Debt and Portfolio of the Belgian
Congo Colony (Belgium-Congo)
(adopted 6 February 1965,
entered into force 11 May 1965)
540 UNTS 227. . . . . . . . . . . . . . . . . .134
Convention with a view to facilitating
Belgian Traffic through the
Territories of East Africa
(Belgium-United Kingdom) (15
March 1921) 114 BFSP 182; **5
LNTS 319**. . . . . . . . . . . . . . . . . . . 79–80
Traité de cession de l'Etat
Indépendant du Congo à la
Belgique (Congo-Belgique)
(signé le 28 novembre 1907 et
approuvé le 18 octobre 1908)
265 Pasin (1908); 2 MNRG (3rd
Series) 101; **100 BFSP 705
(French)**. . . . . . . . . . . . . . . . . . . . . . . .86

### CYPRUS

Treaty concerning the Establishment
of the Republic of Cyprus
(Cyprus-Greece-Turkey-United
Kingdom) (16 August 1960) 382
UNTS 8. . . . . . . . . . . . . . . . 132, 182–83

### CZECHO-SLOVAKIA (1993)

Act on the Succession of the
Agreements of the former
Yugoslavia with the former
Czech and Slovak Federal
Republics (Slovenia-Czechia)
35/1994 Uradni list RS
(Slovenian) . . . . . . . . . . . . . . . . 172–75
Aerial Transport Convention
[Convenio sobre transporte
aéreo] (Mexico-Czechoslovakia)
(adopted 14 August 1990,
entered into force 4 February
1991) Mexico Treaty Database
(Spanish) . . . . . . . . . . . . . . . . . . . . . . .172
Agreement for the Cession by
Czechoslovakia to Germany
of Sudeten German Territory
(Munich Agreement) (Germany-
France-Italy-United Kingdom)
(29/30 September 1938) 142
BFSP 438 . . . . . . . . . . . . . . . . . . . . . .265

* Includes the absorption of the Independent State of the Congo (1908) and the secession of the Democratic State of the Congo (1960).

lxii TABLE OF TREATIES AND OTHER INTERNATIONAL INSTRUMENTS

Agreement on the Common State
Border (Poland-Slovakia)
(adopted 6 July 1995, entered
into force 16 February 1996)
UNTS No 55060 . . . . . . . . . . . . . 70–72

Agreement on the General
Delimitation of Common State
Borders [Smoulvy o generálním
vymezení společných státních
hranic] (Czechia-Slovakia) (29
October 1992 & 2 May 1993)
229/1993 Coll. Zákony Prolidi . . . . .73

Agreement on Good Neighbourliness,
Friendly Relations and
Cooperation (Ukraine-Slovakia)
(adopted 29 June 1993, entered into
force 16 June 1994) Resolution No
4022-XII of the Verkhovna Rada of
the Ukraine (24 February 1994);
42 Zakon (1 November 2006) 192
(Ukrainian). . . . . . . . . . . . . . . . . . . . .70–72

Agreement on Sucession to Bilateral
Treaties [Acuerdo sobre
la sucesion a los tratados
bilaterales] (Colombia-Czechia)
(17 & 24 February 1997)
Colombia Treaty Database No
043/97 (Spanish & Czecho-
Slovak) . . . . . . . . . . . . . . . . . . . . . . . .172

Agreement on Succession to Treaties
[Accord sur la succession par
la République tchèque des
traités conclus entre la France
et la Tchécoslovaquie] (France-
Czechia) (19 June 1995)
France Treaty Database No
TRA19950270 (French) . . . . . . . . .172

Bilateral Agreements in Force [Die
zwischen geltended bilateralen
Verträge] (Austria-Czechia) 123
BGBl. (31 July 1997) (German). . . . .91

Convention relative to Legal
Proceedings in Civil and
Commercial Matters
(Czechoslovakia-United
Kingdom) (adopted 11 November
1924, entered into force 9
November 1933) [1933] ATS 2;
**Australia Treaty Database**. . . . . . . . 172

Exchange of Letters regarding
the Continuation of Bilateral
Treaties (Netherlands-Czechia)

[Handelsverdrag tussen het
Koninkrijk der Nederlanden en
de Tsjechoslowaakse Republiek,
met Protocol en Bijlagen]
(8 & 9 December 1994) 27
Tractatenblad (1995) (Dutch &
English) . . . . . . . . . . . . . . . . . . . . . . . .172

Exchange of Notes ((换文) (China-
Czechia) (10 August 1994) China
Treaty Database (Chinese). . . . . . . .172

Exchange of Notes on Bilateral
Treaties [Intercambio de Cartas
sobre los Tratados bilaterales
concluidos entre España y
Checoslovaquia] (Spain-
Czechia) (21 March 1994 & 2
February 1995) 142 BOE (15
June 1995) 17846 (Spanish) . . . . . . .172

Exchange of Notes [Notenwechsel
zwischen der Österreich und der
Slowakei] (Austria-Slovakia)
(22 December 1993 & 14
January 1994) 1046 BGBl. (28
December 1994) (German &
Czechoslovak) . . . . . . . . . . . . . . 91, 155

Exchange of Notes regarding the
Validity of Bilateral Agreements
(Switzerland-Slovakia) (25
November 1994) Switzerland
Treaty Database No 99990915
(unpublished) . . . . . . . . . . . . . . . . . . .172

Exchange of Notes on Treaties
concluded with Czecho-Slovakia
[Notas sobre los tratados
firmados con la Republica de
Checoslovaquia] (Argentina-
Eslovaquia) (13 July 1995)
Argentina Treaty Database No
5671. . . . . . . . . . . . . . . . . . . . . . . . . . . .172

Exchange of Notes (United
Kingdom-Czechia) (29 August
& 16 September 1996) Treaty
Series No 96 (1996) Cmd 3528
(January 1997) 8 . . . . . . . . . . . . . . . .172

Protocol concerning Bilateral
Treaties [Protokoll om bilaterale
traktater] (Norway-Slovakia) (16
September 1994) Norway Treaty
Database No 16-09-1994 No 1
Bilateral (Norwegian) . . . . . . . . . . .172

Protocol on the Inventory of
Bilateral Treaties Протокол

TABLE OF TREATIES AND OTHER INTERNATIONAL INSTRUMENTS  lxiii

(Россия-Словакия) (Russia-Slovakia) (31 October 1995 & 3 July 1996) (1997) 4 Бюллетень международных договоров [Bulletin of International Treaties] 28; **Russia Treaty Database No 1995082**............172

Protocol on the Romanian-Czechoslovak Agreements [Protocolul privind acordurile româno-cehoslovace] (Romania-Czechia) (26 May 1995 & 3 March 1997) 339 Monitorul Oficial (11 November 1996) (Romanian).....................172

Treaty concerning the Common Frontier (Czechia-Germany) (adopted 3 November 1994, entered into force 1 September 1997) 266/1997 Coll Zákony Prolidi; **2292 UNTS 379**....... 70–72

Treaty regarding Nationality and Option Questions (Germany-Czechoslovakia) (adopted 20 November 1938, entered into force 26 November 1938) 142 BFSP 525 ......................265

## DJIBOUTI

Protocols respecting the Delimitation of the French and Italian Possessions on the Coast of the Red Sea and the Gulf of Aden (France-Italy) (24 January 1900 & 10 July 1901) 94 BFSP 588 .......82

## EQUATORIAL GUINEA

Convention for the Delimitation of the French and Spanish Possessions on the Coast of the Sahara and on the Coast of the Gulf of Guinea (France-Spain) (27 June 1900) 92 BFSP 1014.......93

Convention establishing a Transitional Regime [Convenio de 12 de octubre de 1968 se establece en regimen transitorio Spain-Equatorial Guinea] (adopted 12 October 1968, entered into force 14 February

1972) 50 BOE (28 February 1972) 3511 (Spanish).............132

Treaty of Friendship and Co-operation (Spain-Equatorial Guinea) (adopted 23 October 1980, entered into force 14 April 1982) 1322 UNTS 66......... 297–98

## ERITREA

Agreement relating to Certain Matters connected with the Withdrawal of British Military Administration from the Territories designated as the Reserved Area and the Ogaden (Ethiopia-United Kingdom) (29 November 1954) 161 BFSP 93......35

Agreement regarding Financial Arrangements on the Establishment of the Federation (Ethiopia-United Kingdom) (5 & 6 September 1952) 149 UNTS 57 ......................304

Agreement for the Settlement of Displaced Persons (Eritrea-Ethiopia) (12 December 2000) 2138 UNTS 93.......100, 235–36, 279

Protocols respecting the Delimitation of the French and Italian Possessions on the Coast of the Red Sea and the Gulf of Aden (France-Italy) (24 January 1900 & 10 July 1901) 94 BFSP 588 ... 82–83

## ESWATINI ('SWAZILAND')

Agreement Continuing in Force the Extradition Treaty of December 22, 1931 (47 Stat. 2122) between the United States and the United Kingdom (United States-Swaziland) (13 May & 28 July 1970) 756 UNTS 103.............192

## FINLAND

Convention respecting the Aaland Islands (Russia-France-United Kingdom) (adopted 30 March 1856, entered into force 27 April 1856) 46 BFSP 23 .................77

## FRANCE

Peace Convention (France-Thailand) (adopted 9 May 1941, entered into force 5 July 1941) 144 BFSP 805 (French)........................265
Settlement Agreement (France-Siam) (17 November 1946) 344 UNTS 59 ................... 285–86

## GABON

Convention for the Delimitation of the French and Spanish Possessions on the Coast of the Sahara and on the Coast of the Gulf of Guinea (France-Spain) (27 June 1900) 92 BFSP 1014.......93

## GERMANY*

Agreement on the Settlement of Financial Questions and Questions relating to the Law of Property (Finland-German Democratic Republic) (adopted 3 October 1984, entered into force 26 December 1984) 1392 UNTS 502 ......................117–18
Agreement on the Termination of the Activities of the Joint Organization 'Petrobaltik' [Соглашение о прекращении деятельности совместной организации «Петробалтик»] (USSR-Poland-German Democratic Republic) (12 July 1990) Russia Treaty Database No 19900084 (Russian)....... 170–72
Protocol concerning the Consequences of the Reunification of Germany for their Bilateral Treaty Relations (Germany-Netherlands) (adopted 25 January 1994, entered into force 19 July 1994) 2441 UNTS 135 ................152
Report of Tripartite Conference of Berlin (United States–United Kingdom-USSR) (1945) 39 AJIL 245 ....................296

Supplementary Agreement to the Transfer Agreement of 1 July 1938 [Accord additionnel à l'Accord de transfert du 1er juillet 1938] (Germany-United Kingdom) (13 August 1938) 36 MNRG 379 (French) ..........124
Transfer Agreement (Germany-United Kingdom) (1 July 1938) Cmd 5788; **36 MNRG 370** .......124
Treaty on the Basis of Intra-German Relations (German Democratic Republic-Federal Republic of Germany) (21 December 1973) 12 ILM 16.................... 303–4
Treaty concerning the Common Frontier (Czechia-Germany) (adopted 3 November 1994, entered into force 1 September 1997) 266/1997 Coll Zákony Prolidi; **2292 UNTS 379**....... 70–72
Treaty concerning the Demarcation of the established and existing Polish-German State Frontier (Poland-Germany) (14 November 1990) 1708 UNTS 383...........70–72
Treaty on the Establishment of German Unity (Federal Republic of Germany-German Democratic Republic) (adopted 30 August 1990, entered into force 3 October 1990) 30 ILM 463 .....32–33, 124, 170, 211, 261, 300

## GHANA

Agreement on continued Application to Ghana of Certain Treaties (Ghana-United States) (4 September 1957, 21 December 1957 & 12 February 1958) TIAS (1963) 4966; 13 United States Treaties and Other International Agreements 240; 442 UNTS 175... 179

## GUINEA

Agreement relative to the Settlement of Financial Claims [Accord relative au règlement du contentieux

* Includes the cession of the Sudetenland, secession of East Germany and absorption of East Germany.

TABLE OF TREATIES AND OTHER INTERNATIONAL INSTRUMENTS  lxv

financier] (Guinea-France)
(adopted 26 January 1977,
entered into force 14 February
1978) JORF (14 February 1978)
711 (French)................. 134, 296

### GUYANA

Agreement to Resolve the
Controversy over the Frontier
between Venezuela and British
Guiana (Venezuela-United
Kingdom) (17 February 1966)
561 UNTS 322.....................97
Treaty for the Settlement of the
Boundary between British
Guiana and Brazil (Brazil-
United Kingdom) (adopted 22
April 1926, entered into force 16
April 1929) 123 BFSP 468..........69

### INDIA*

Agreement on certain outstanding
Financial Issues (Pakistan-India)
(adopted 12 June 1955, entered
into force 4 October 1955) 228
UNTS 211 ......................41
Agreement concerning the Future
of the French Establishments
(France-India (21 October 1954)
161 BFSP 533............... 220, 296
Air Services Agreement (France-India)
(16 July 1947) 27 UNTS 325.......150
Boundary Agreement (India-Burma)
(adopted 10 March 1967, entered
into force 30 May 1967) India
Treaty Database No MM67B1503...73
Convention between Great
Britain and Thibet (adopted 7
September 1904, entered into
force 27 April 1906) 98 BFSP 148 ...96
Convention respecting Tibet (China-
United Kingdom) (adopted 27
April 1906, entered into force 23
July 1906) 99 BFSP 171 ............96
Exchange of Notes on the Tibet-
Sikkim and Sino-Indian Border
Dispute (India-China) (12 & 16
September 1965) 168 BFSP 220.....96

Financial Agreement (United
Kingdom-India) (14 August
1947) 147 BFSP 865........... 126–29
Joint Communique regarding the
Sino-Indian Border Dispute
(India-China) (25 April 1960)
164 BFSP 584.....................96
Trade Agreement (Thailand-India)
(13 December 1968)
656 UNTS 3.............. 89–90, 163
Treaty ceding the French
Establishments of Pondicherry,
Karikal, Mahe and Yanam to
India (France-India) (adopted
28 May 1956, entered into
force 16 August 1962)
162 BFSP 848.......... 129, 265, 296
Treaty of Cession of the Free Town of
Chandernagore (France-India)
(adopted 2 February 1951,
entered into force on 9 June
1952) 158 BFSP 599..... 129, 220, 265
Treaty on Recognition of India's
Sovereignty over Goa, Daman,
Diu, Dadra and Nagar Haveli
(Portugal-India) (adopted
31 December 1974, entered
into force 3 June 1975)
982 UNTS 153.......29, 129, 220, 265

### INDOCHINA (FRENCH)

Agreement on Financial Disputes
[Accord sur le règlement du
contentieux financier] (France-
South Viet Nam) (24 March
1960) France Treaty Database
No TRA19600378 (on file with
author) (French)............. 118–20
Agreement for a *modus vivendi*
(France-South Viet-Nam)
(adopted 14 September 1946,
entered into force 30 October
1946) 149 BFSP 659.............296
Agreement relating to the Exchange of
Official Publications (Australia-
South Viet Nam) (28 September
1954 & 20 December 1956)
Australia Treaty Database;
**201 UNTS 349** .................244

---

* Includes the secession of India and the cessions of French India and Portuguese India.

lxvi   TABLE OF TREATIES AND OTHER INTERNATIONAL INSTRUMENTS

Agreement on the Resolution of
  Financial Disputes (France-
  South Viet Nam) (24 March
  1960) France Treaty Database
  No TRA19600378 (on file with
  author) (French)............ 118–20
Agreement on the Settlement of the
  Question of Public Property
  (France-South Viet Nam) (24
  March 1960) 728 UNTS 271....118–20
Convention annexed to the
  Treaty between France and
  Cambodia of 8 November 1949
  on Economic and Financial
  Matters [Convention annex
  au traité entre la France et le
  Cambodge conclu le 8 novembre
  1949 relative aux questions
  économiques et financières]
  (Indochina-Cambodia) (27 May
  1946) France Treaty Database
  No TRA9460073 (French)........132
Convention between France and
  Viet-Nam (under the Presidency
  of M. Ho Chi Minh) recognising
  the Independence of Viet-Nam
  (6 March 1946) 149 BFSP 657
  (French)........................296
Convention on the Delimitation of
  the Frontier between China and
  Tonkin [Convention relative à la
  Delimitation de la Frontère entre
  la Chine et le Tonkin] (France-
  China) (26 June 1887) 85 BFSP
  748 (French) ....................96
Convention on the Transfer of
  Judicial and Police Powers
  and Services [Convention de
  transfert des compétences et
  services en matière judiciaire et
  de police et sûreté entre la France
  et le Viet-Nam] (15 September
  1954) JORF (3 May 1959) 4762
  (French)........................272
Financial Convention annexed to
  the General Convention of 19
  July 1949 [Convention annexe
  financière à la Convention
  Générale du 19 Juillet 1949]
  (France-Laos) France Treaty
  Database No TRA19500158
  (French)........................132

Judicial Convention [Convention
  judiciaire] (France-Laos) (22
  October 1953) JORF (3 May
  1959) 4768.............. 182–83, 272
Nationality Convention [Convention
  sur la nationalité] (France-South
  Viet Nam) (17 August 1965)
  JORF (3 May 1959) 4767; UN
  Materials on Succession of
  States (1967) UN Doc ST/LEG/
  SER.B/14, 446...................272
Protocol No 2 on the Apportionment
  of the Property and Debt in
  the Liquidation of the former
  Indochina Treasury [Protocole
  N° 2 relatif à la répartition des
  éléments d'actif et de passif
  de la liquidation de l'ancien
  Trésor Indochinois et la clôture
  des opérations de la Caisse
  Autonome de Gestion et
  d'Amortissement de la dette]
  (Cambodia-Laos-Vietnam)
  Documentation française, Notes
  et Études Documentaires Doc
  No 1973 (1955) 17 (French)... 126–29
Protocol on Financial Disputes
  [Protocole relative aux
  contentieux financier] (France-
  South Viet Nam) (14 November
  1959) France Treaty Database
  No TRA19590339 (on file with
  author) (French)................132
Protocol on State Property (France-
  South Viet-Nam) (14 November
  1959) France Treaty Database
  No TRA19590338 (on file with
  author) ........................132
Protocol on the Transfer of Judicial
  Powers [Protocole de transfert
  au Gouvernement royal du
  Cambodge des compétences
  judiciaires exercées par la France
  sur le territoire du royaume]
  (France-Cambodia) (29 August
  & 9 September 1953) JORF
  (3 May 1959) 4758 ;
France Treaty Database Doc
  TRA19500158 (French).........132
Treaty of Friendship and Association
  (France-Laos) (22 October 1953)
  155 BFSP 658............... 182–83

## INDONESIA

Agreement concerning outstanding Financial Problems (Indonesia-Netherlands) (adopted 7 September 1966, entered into force on 21 May 1969) 686 UNTS 122 . . . . . . . . . . . . . . . . . . . . .296

Agreement concerning the Transfer of Claims against Netherlands Nationals (Indonesia-Netherlands) (11 August 1954) 241 UNTS 134. . . . . . . . . . . . . . . . .108

Agreement concerning West New Guinea (West Irian) (Indonesia-Netherlands) (15 August 1962) 1(2) ILM 231; **437 UNTS 273** . . . . .296

Air Services Agreement (United Kingdom-Indonesia) (23 November 1960) Indonesia Treaty Database No GBR-1960-0001 . . . . . . 150

Economic Agreement (Indonesia-Netherlands) (11 February 1952) 165 UNTS 77. . . . . . . . . . . . . . . . . . .132

Round-Table Conference Agreements (Netherlands-Indonesia) (adopted 2 November 1949, entered into force 27 December 1949) 69 UNTS 200 . . . . . . . . . . . . . .225, 263–64, 271–72

## IRAQ ('MESOPOTAMIA')

Boundary Treaty (Iraq-Iran) (4 July 1937) 190 LNTS 256 . . . . . . . . . . . . . .84

Treaty of Alliance (Iraq-United Kingdom) (adopted 10 October 1922, entered into force 19 December 1924) 119 BFSP 389; **35 LNTS 14**. . . . . . . . . . . . . . . . . . . .182

## ISRAEL

Agreement of Good Neighbourly Relations concluded on behalf of the Territories of Palestine, on the one part, and on behalf of Syria and Great Lebanon, on the other part (France-United Kingdom) (2 February 1926) 56 LNTS 79 . . . . . . . . 85

Agreement respecting the Boundary Line between Syria and Palestine from the Mediterranean to

El Hammé (France-United Kingdom) (7 March 1923) 22 LNTS 363. . . . . . . . . . . . . . . . . . . . . .85

Agreement for the Settlement of Financial Matters outstanding as a Result of the Termination of the Mandate for Palestine (United Kingdom-Israel) (30 March 1950) 86 UNTS 231 . . . . . . . . . . . . . .140

Agreements on the Settlement of Outstanding Financial Matters (United Kingdom-Israel) (15 April 1965) 551 UNTS 19 . . . . . . . .311

Convention on certain points connected with the Mandates for Syria and the Lebanon, Palestine and Mesopotamia (France-United Kingdom) (23 December 1920) 113 BFSP 355; 22 LNTS 353. . . . . . . . . .85

Convention regulating various questions arising from the Unification of Savoy and Nice with France [Convention destinée à régler diverses questions auxquelles a donné lieu la réunion de la Savoie et de l'arrondissement de Nice à la France] (France-Sardinia) (adopted 23 August 1860, entered into force 4 October 1860) 17(2) MNRG (2nd Series) 22 (French). . . . . . . . . . . . . . . .291, 306–7

Extradition Convention (France-Israel) (adopted 12 November 1958, entered into force 14 November 1971) 805 UNTS 251. . .163

General Armistice Agreement (Syria-Israel) (20 July 1949) 42 UNTS 327 . . . . . . . . . . . . . . . . . . . 68–69

Maritime Boundary Agreement (Jordan-Israel) (adopted 18 January 1996, entered into force 7 February 1996) Israel Treaty Database. . . . . . . . . . . . . . . . . . . . . 70–72

Peace Treaty (Egypt-Israel) (26 March 1979) 18 ILM 362 . . . . . . . . . .72

## ITALY

Peace Treaty [Traité de Paix] (Autriche-Italie) (adopted 3 October 1866, entered into force 12 October 1866) 56 BFSP 700 . . . . . . . . . 29, 306–7

lxviii  TABLE OF TREATIES AND OTHER INTERNATIONAL INSTRUMENTS

## JAMAICA

Continued Application of certain
Agreements to Scheduled Services
(United States-Jamaica)
(25 October & 29 November
1962) TIAS 5244................186

## JORDAN

Convention on certain points
connected with the Mandates for
Syria and the Lebanon, Palestine
and Mesopotamia (France-United
Kingdom) (23 December 1920)
113 BFSP 355; **22 LNTS 353** ........85
Maritime Boundary Agreement (Israel-
Jordan) (adopted 18 January 1996,
entered into force 7 February 1996)
Israel Treaty Database ..........70–72
Treaty of Alliance (Transjordan-
United Kingdom) (adopted 22
March 1946, entered into force
17 June 1946) 6 UNTS 143........182

## KIRIBATI

Treaty of Friendship (Kiribati-United
States) (adopted 20 September
1979, entered into force 23
September 1983) 1643 UNTS 239 .....94

## KUWAIT

Agreed Minutes regarding the
Restoration of Friendly Relations
(Kuwait-Iraq) (4 October 1963)
485 UNTS 321....................69

## LIBYA

Agreement concerning the Disposal
of Italian Private Property in
Cyrenaica and Tripolitania
(United Kingdom-Italy) (28 June
1951) 118 UNTS 115.......... 303–4
Agreement on Economic Cooperation
and Settlement of Issues arising
from Resolution 388(V) of 15
December 1950 (Italy-Libya)
(adopted 2 October 1956, entered
into force 7 December 1957)
2328 UNTS 1 ................ 303–4

## MADAGASCAR

Agreement on Co-operation in
Monetary, Economic and
Financial Matters (France-
Madagascar) (adopted 27 June
1960, entered into force 18 July
1960) 820 UNTS 248............132
Agreement intended to Settle the
Financial Consequences
of Nationalization and
Expropriation Measures taken
between 1975 and 1978 by the
Government of Madagascar
relating to Properties and
Interests belonging to French
Companies or Private Individuals
(France-Madagascar) (1 October
1998) 2179 UNTS 43......... 255, 296
Convention concerning State
Property Matters (France-
Madagascar) (adopted 4 June
1973, entered into force 19
March 1975) 978 UNTS 368 ......108
Convention on Establishment
(France–Madagascar) (adopted
27 June 1960, entered into force
18 July 1960) 820 UNTS 364 ......296
Property Agreement [Protocole
d'Accord Domanial] (France-
Madagascar) (18 October
1961) France Archives No
TRA19610006 (French) ..........108

## MALAWI ('NYASALAND')

Agreement regarding continued
Application to Malawi of certain
Treaties concluded between the
United States and the United
Kingdom (United States-Malawi)
(adopted 17 December 1966 & 6
January 1967, entered into force 4
April 1967) 692 UNTS 191......186–87
Exchange of Notes on the
Preservation in force of the
Anglo-Swiss Extradition
Treaty of 26 November 1880
(Switzerland-Malawi) (6
January 1967 & 16 December
1967) RO 1968 168, Switzerland
Treaty Database No 0.353.953.2
(French, German, Italian) ........186

TABLE OF TREATIES AND OTHER INTERNATIONAL INSTRUMENTS    lxix

Extradition Agreement (Malawi-South
Africa) (25 February 1972) 81 South
Africa Government Gazette
(24 March 1972) 3424 . . . . . . . . . . . .165

## MALAYSIA*

Agreement concerning Succession to
Rights and Obligations arising
from International Instruments
(Malaya-United Kingdom)
(12 September 1957)
279 UNTS 287. . . . . . . . . . . .51, 182–83
Agreement for the Establishment of
the Federation of Malaya as an
Independent Sovereign Country
within the Commonwealth
(Malaya-United Kingdom)
(5 August 1957) 163 BFSP 46 in
*UN Materials on Succession of
States* (1967) UN Doc ST/LEG/
SER.B/14, 72 . . . . . . . . . . . . . . . . . . .132
Agreement on Extension of the Franco-
Malaysian Transport Agreement
of 30 December 1961 to Singapore,
Sarawak and Sabah (France-
Malaysia) (13 June 1964) France
Treaty Database No TRA19640251
(French, not published) . . . . . . . . . . . 152
Agreement on the Extension to the
Territories of Singapore, Sarawak
and Sabah of the Franco-
Malaysian Transport Agreement
of 30 December 1961 (France-
Malaysia) (adopted 13 June &
4 July 1964, entered into force 1
September 1964) in Pinto and
Rollet, *Recueil général des Traités
de la France* (1976) 427 (French) . .152
Agreement on External Defence and
Mutual Assistance (Malaya-
United Kingdom) (12 October
1957) 285 UNTS 59 . . . . . . . . . . . . . .81
Agreement on the Independence
of the Federation of Malaya (5
August 1957) 163 BFSP 46 . . . . . . . .132
Agreement relative to the Sulu
Archipelago (Sulu-United States)
(20 August 1899) 92 BFSP 1323. . . . .79

Agreement concluded between
the United Kingdom and the
Federation of Malaya, Cmd
2094 (July 1963) . . . . . . . 129, 221, 265
Convention regarding the Boundary
between the Philippine
Archipelago and the State of
North Borneo (United States-
United Kingdom) (adopted
2 January 1930 & 6 July 1932,
entered into force 13 December
1932) Treaty Series No 2 (1933);
**Cmd 4241** . . . . . . . . . . . . . . . . . 93, 308
Exchange of Notes regarding
Extradition Treaty (Thailand-
Malaya) (27 October 1959)
Thailand Treaty Database. . . . . . . . .186
Public Officers Agreement (Malaya-
United Kingdom) (27 July 1959)
374 UNTS 22. . . . . . . . . . . . . . . 118–19

## MALTA

Agreement relative to the Inheritance
of International Rights and
Obligations (Malta-United
Kingdom) (31 December 1964)
525 UNTS 221. . . . . . . . . . . . . . . . . .149
Convention for the Mutual Extradition
of Malefactors (Italy-United
Kingdom) (adopted 4 January
1873, entered into force 18 March
1873) Italian Treaty Database No
BILMT011 (Italian). . . . . . . . . . . . . . 162

## MAURITIUS

Agreement concerning Public
Officers' Pensions (United
Kingdom-Mauritius) (adopted
3 July 1975, entered into force 31
July 1975) 1018 UNTS 133 . . . . 118–20
Agreement on Mutual Defence and
Assistance (Mauritius-United
Kingdom) (12 March 1968) 648
UNTS 3. . . . . . . . . . . . . . . . . . . 111, 311
Public Officers Agreement (United
Kingdom-Mauritius) (12 March
1968) 648 UNTS 44 . . . . . . . . . 111, 311

---

* Includes the secession of Malaya and the cession of North Borneo, Singapore and Sarawak (1963).

## MEMEL TERRITORY

Convention concerning the Territory of Memel (France, Italy, Japan, Lithuania, United Kingdom) (adopted 8 May 1924, entered into force 27 September 1924) 29 LNTS 86 .....................169

## MONTENEGRO

Agreement on the Application of Certain Treaties [Ulkoasiainministeriön ilmoitus eräiden Suomen ja Serbia ja Montenegron välisten sopimusten soveltamisesta Suomen ja Montenegron välisissä suhteissa] (Finland-Montenegro) (18 April 2007) 45 Sähköinen sopimussarja (2007) 456 (Finnish) ...........162–63

Agreement on the Regulation of Membership in International Financial Organizations and Division of Financial Rights and Liabilities (Serbia-Montenegro) (10 July 2006) 45(6) Službeni list Crne Gore 17....................138

Agreement on the State Border (Montenegro-Bosnia) (adopted 26 August 2015, entered into force 20 April 2016) I-55488 UNTS................ 70–72

Agreement on Succession to Bilateral Treaties [Accord relatif à la succession en matière de traités bilateraux] (France-Montenegro) (30 September 2010 & 13 June 2011) 105 JORF (4 May 2012) 7895 (French).......163

Council Decision No 2008/784/EC establishing a Separate Liability of Montenegro (2 October 2008) L 269/8 OJEU (10 October 2008) ........... 117–18

## MOROCCO

Agreement concerning Compensation for the Lands recovered by the Moroccan State under the Dahir of 2 March 1973 (Morocco-Spain) (8 November 1979) 1410 UNTS 195... 296

Agreement on Monetary and Financial Matters [Accord relatif aux domaines monétaire et financier] (France-Morocco) (2 March 1956) France Archives Doc TRA19560203 (French).......................141

Agreement concerning the Settlement of the Financial Consequences resulting from the Transfer to the Moroccan State of Agricultural Estates (Morocco-Switzerland) (adopted 6 June 1978, entered into force 5 February 1981) 1226 UNTS 120 .....................296

Agreement on the Reciprocal Cession of Military Real Estate [Accord relatif à la cession récriproque de biens immobiliers militaires] (Morocco-France) (21 June 1958) France Archives Doc TRA19580211 (French) ..........141

Agreement for the Settlement of the Financial Consequences of Measures taken by the Moroccan Government with respect to Agricultural Property owned by French Nationals (Morocco-France) (2 August 1974) 962 UNTS 49 .....................296

Agreement on the Transfer of Property of the Spanish State in the former Northern Zone (Morocco-Spain) (10 July 1978) 1120 UNTS 383 ................141

Agreement on Transfer of Responsibility of Tetuan and Nador Airports (Spain-Morocco) (16 March 1967) 1 SPTI 340 (Spanish)........ 89, 176

Agreement on the Withdrawal of the Peseta (Morocco-Spain) (adopted 7 July 1957, entered into force 7 July 1970) 1353 UNTS 287 .....................141

Diplomatic Accord (France-Morocco) (28 May 1956) (1957) 51 AJIL 679 ..............81, 182–83

Diplomatic Convention (Spain-Morocco) (11 February 1957) 63 BOE (4 March 1957) 1387 (Spanish) .....................175

Exchange of Letters on the Pension Regime of French Agents [Échange des lettres relative à la prise en charge des pensions principales concédées par la Caisse marocaine des Retraites à des fonctionnaires français des ex-cadres chérifiens] (Morocco-France) (17 October 1964) 101 JORF (30 March 1969) 3180 (French)..................118–19

Final Declaration and Annexed Protocol of the International Conference of Tangier (United States-Belgium-France-Italy-Morocco-Netherlands-Portugal-Spain-United Kingdom) (29 October 1956) **(1957) 51(2) AJIL 460**; 263 UNTS 165 .... 141, 304

Joint Declaration on Moroccan Independence (Morocco-France) (2 March 1956) 162 BFSP 958 (French).......... 141, 296

Joint Declaration on Moroccan Independence (Morocco-Spain) (7 April 1956) 162 BFSP 1017 .....296

Treaty between the Emperor of the French and the Emperor of Morocco [Traité conclu entre l'Empereur des Français et l'Empereur de Maroc] (18 March 1845) 34 BFSP 1287 (French) ......94

Treaty on the Establishment of a Regular Regime [Traité pour l'Établissement d'un Régime régulier] (France-Morocco) (30 March 1912) 106 BFSP 1023 (French).................. 49–50, 94

Treaty on the Retrocession of Ifni [Tratado sobre retrocesión de Ifni] (Spain-Morocco) (adopted 4 January 1969, entered into forcé 9 January 1971) BOE (5 June 1969) 8805 (Spanish) ..........175, 265, 296

### MOZAMBIQUE

Agreement with regard to the Nyasaland-Mozambique Frontier (Portugal-United Kingdom) (18 November 1954) Portugal Archives, Ministério do Ultramar, Delegação Portuguesa de Delimitação de Fronteiras Moçambique-Niassalãndia (1956)....99

Agreement regulating the Use of the Kunene River (South Africa-Portugal) (adopted 1 July 1926, entered into force 14 February 1928) 70 LNTS 315 ...............86

Treaty between Great Britain and Ethiopia (14 May 1897) 89 BFSP 31......................87

### MYANMAR ('BURMA')

Agreement annexed to the Boundary Treaty (China-Burma) (adopted 1 October 1960, entered into force on 4 January 1961) 1010 UNTS 144 ....................79, 93

Agreement on the Construction, Ownership, Operation, Management and Maintenance of the Friendship Bridge crossing the Moei/Thaungyin River (Thailand-Myanmar) (17 October 1994) Thailand Treaty Database.........89–90

Agreement on the Demarcation of a Fixed Boundary in the Naaf River (Burma-Pakistan) (9 May 1966) 1014 UNTS 3 ...............73

Boundary Agreement (India-Burma) (adopted 10 March 1967, entered into force 30 May 1967) India Treaty Database No MM67B1503....73

Boundary Treaty (China-Burma) (adopted 1 October 1960, entered into force 4 January 1961) 1010 UNTS 111..........79, 93

Exchange of Notes (Burma-United Kingdom) (17 October 1947) 70 UNTS 196 .....................296

Exchange of Notes regarding the Boundary between Burma (Tenasserim) and Siam (United Kingdom-Siam) (1 June 1934) Treaty Series No 19 (1934) Cmd 4671.................... 89–90

Treaty regarding the Recognition of Burmese Independence and Related Matters (Burma-United Kingdom) (adopted 17 October 1947, entered into force 4 January 1948) 70 UNTS 183.... 132, 182, 269, 296

## NEWFOUNDLAND

Agreement relating to the Use by Civil Aircraft of certain Air Bases in Newfoundland (United States-Canada) (4 June 1949) 200 UNTS 201 .................. 80–81

Agreement regarding Leased Naval and Air Bases (United States-United Kingdom) (27 March 1951) 204 LNTS 15 ........... 80–81

## NAMIBIA

Agreement respecting Zanzibar, Heligoland, and the Spheres of Influence of the two Countries in Africa (Germany-United Kingdom) (1 July 1890) 82 BFSP 35 .............. 97

Special Agreement to submit to the International Court of Justice the dispute existing between the two States concerning the boundary around the Kasikili/Sedudu Island and the legal status of the Island' (15 May 1996) <https://www.icj-cij.org/public/files/case-related/98/7185.pdf> accessed 25 January 2025 .......... 93

## NAURU

Note on the State of the Treaties of Nauru (4 April 1973) Argentina Treaty Database No 7353 (Spanish) ...................... 189

## NIGERIA

Agreement relative to the Inheritance of International Rights and Obligations (Nigeria-United Kingdom) (1 October 1960) 384 UNTS 207 ...................... 79

## PACIFIC ISLANDS (TRUST TERRITORY OF)

Trusteeship Agreement for the Former Japanese Mandated Islands, approved by the Security Council (2 April 1947) 8 UNTS 189 ..... 34, 286

## PAKISTAN

Agreement on the Boundary between China's Sinkiang and the Contiguous Areas (China-Pakistan) (2 March 1963) 3 PTS 230; **China Treaty Database** .................. 64

Agreement on certain outstanding Financial Issues (Pakistan-India) (adopted 12 June 1955, entered into force 4 October 1955) 228 UNTS 211 ...................... 41

Agreement on the Demarcation of a Fixed Boundary in the Naaf River (Burma-Pakistan) (9 May 1966) 1014 UNTS 3 ............... 73

Financial Agreement (United Kingdom-India) (14 August 1947) 147 BFSP 865 .......... 126–29

Treaty establishing Friendly and Commercial Relations (United Kingdom-Afghanistan) (adopted 22 November 1921, entered into force 6 February 1922) 114 BFSP 174 ........ 86, 95–96

## PAPUA NEW GUINEA

Agreement on the Exchange of Planting Material (Malaya-Papua New Guinea) (26 November 1962) 453 UNTS 161 .............. 177

Treaty concerning Sovereignty and Maritime Boundaries in the Area between the Two Countries (Australia-Papua New Guinea) (adopted 18 December 1978, entered into force 15 February 1985) 1429 UNTS 207 ...................... 73

## PERU

Treaty of Peace and Friendship (Chile-Peru) (adopted 20 October 1883, entered into force 28 March 1884) Colección de Actos Internacionales Celebrados por la Républica del Peru (1915) 1; **74 BFSP 349** ............ 221

## PHILIPPINES

Agreement relative to the Sovereignty, Trade, &c., of the Sulu Archipelago (United States-Sulu) (20 August 1899) 92 BFSP 1323.....79

Agreement for the Sale of Surplus War Property (11 September 1946) 43 UNTS 232 ......................111

Convention regarding the Boundary between the Philippine Archipelago and the State of North Borneo (United States-United Kingdom) (adopted 2 January 1930 & 6 July 1932, entered into force 13 December 1932) Treaty Series No 2 (1933); **Cmd 4241** ................. 93, 308

Exchange of Notes regarding the Transfer of the Administration of the Turtle and Mangsee Islands to the Philippine Republic (United Kingdom-Philippines) (19 September 1946; 7 July, 24 September, 11 October & 16 December 1947; 20 April 1948) Treaty Series No 58 (1951); **Cmd 8320** ............ 93

Treaty of General Relations and Protocol (Philippines-United States) (adopted 4 July 1946, entered into force 22 October 1946) 7 UNTS 3 ............ 41, 132, 269, 294–316

## POLAND

Agreement providing for the Settlement of French Claims for Compensation due to Nationalisation in Poland (France-Poland) (19 March 1948) 152 BFSP 369 ......... 296, 319

Convention concerning Questions of Option and Nationality (Germany-Poland) (adopted 30 August 1924, entered into force 31 January 1925) 32 LNTS 333....................251–52

Convention on the Upper Silesia [Convention concernant la Haute-Silésie] (15 May 1922) 16 MNRG 645 (French).....118–19, 292

Exchange of Notes concerning Compensation for British Interests affected by the Polish Nationalisation Law of 3rd January, 1946 (Poland-United Kingdom) (24 January 1948) 151 BFSP 67 .......296

## RWANDA

Agreement respecting the Boundary between Tanganyika Territory and the Belgian Mandated Territory of Ruanda-Urundi (5 August 1924) Treaty Series No 6 (1927); Cmd 2812; **123 BFSP 462** .................99

Arrangement extending to the Belgian Congo and to Ruanda-Urundi the Provisions of the above-mentioned Arrangement (Belgium-Pakistan) (9 September 1952 & 28 July 1953) 173 UNTS 408 .................... 149

Convention with a view to facilitating Belgian Traffic through the Territories of East Africa (Belgium-United Kingdom) (15 March 1921) 114 BFSP 182; **5 LNTS 319**.................... 79–80

## SAAR TERRITORY

Treaty for the Settlement of the Question of the Saar (France-Federal Republic of Germany) (adopted 27 October 1956, entered into force 1 January 1957) 1053 UNTS 3 ..............170

## SINGAPORE

Agreement relating to the Separation of Singapore from Malaysia (Singapore-Malaysia) (adopted 7 August 1965, entered into force 9 August 1965) 4 ILM 928; **563 UNTS 89** ......81, 132, 182–83, 225, 268, 309

## SOMALIA

Agreement (Italy-Somalia) (1 July 1960) 148 Gazzetta Ufficiale della Repubblica Italiana Serie Generale (13 June 1962) ...... 182–83

## SOUTH AFRICA

Agreement respecting Zanzibar, Heligoland, and the Spheres of Influence of the two Countries in Africa (Germany-United Kingdom) (1 July 1890) 82 BFSP 35 . . . . . . . . . . . . . . . . . . 96–97

## SOUTH SUDAN

Agreement on Certain Economic Matters (Sudan-South Sudan) (adopted 27 September 2012, entered into force 17 October 2012) <https://www.peaceagreeme nts.org/view/857/Agreement%20 between%20Sudan%20and%20So uth%20Sudan%20on%20Cert ain%20Economic%20Matters> accessed 25 January 2025 . . . . . . . . . . . 105

## SUDAN

Agreement for the Full Utilization of the Nile Waters (Sudan-United Arab Republic) (adopted 8 November 1959, entered into force 12 December 1959) 453 UNTS 63 . . . . . . .85
Agreement modifying the Agreement signed at Brussels relating to the Spheres of Influence of Great Britain and the Independent State of the Congo in East and Central Africa (Congo-United Kingdom) (adopted 12 May 1894, entered into force 9 May 1906) 99 BFSP 173 . . . . . . . . . . . . . .310
Exchange of Notes in regard to the Use of the Waters of the River Nile for Irrigation Purposes (Egypt-United Kingdom) (7 May 1929) 130 BFSP 104 . . . . . . . . . . . . . . .85

## SURINAME

Convention to Delimit the Border between the Colonies of French Guiana and Suriname (adopted

30 September 1915, entered into force 16 September 1916) 110 BFSP 872 . . . . . . . . . . . . . . . . . . . . 70–72

## SYRIA AND LEBANON*

Agreement concerning Monetary and Financial Relations (Lebanon-France) (adopted 24 January 1948, entered into force 16 February 1949) 173 UNTS 99 . . . . . . . . . . . . . .141, 308–14
Agreement of Good Neighbourly Relations concluded on behalf of the Territories of Palestine, on the one part, and on behalf of Syria and Great Lebanon, on the other part (France-United Kingdom) (2 February 1926) 56 LNTS 80 . . . . . . . . . . . . . . . . . . . . . . . .85
Agreement respecting the Boundary Line between Syria and Palestine from the Mediterranean to El Hammé (France-United Kingdom) (7 March 1923) 22 LNTS 363 . . . . . . . . . . . . . . . . . . . . .85
Convention on the Liquidation of the Bank of Syria and the Lebanon [Convention de Liquidation des avoirs syriens en francs de la Banque de Syrie et du Liban] (Syria-France) (adopted 7 February 1949, entered into force 6 March 1950) 60 JORF (10 March 1950) 2697 (French) . . . . . . .140
General Armistice Agreement (Israel-Syria) (20 July 1949) 42 UNTS 327 . . . . . . . . . . . . . . . . . . . . .68

## TANZANIA**

Agreement maintaining in force the 1922 Franco-British Convention on Civil Procedure and the 1936 Convention on Legal Assistance (France-Tanganyika) (29 November 1963 & 3 February 1964) France Treaty Database No TRA19630209 (French) . . . . . . .150

---

\* Includes the accessions to independence of Syria and the Lebanon (1944) and the secession of Syria (1961).
\*\* Includes the secessions of Tanganyika and Zanzibar and their merger.

## TABLE OF TREATIES AND OTHER INTERNATIONAL INSTRUMENTS  lxxv

Agreement respecting the Boundary between Tanganyika Territory and the Belgian Mandated Territory of Ruanda-Urundi (5 August 1924) Treaty Series No 6 (1927); Cmd 2812; 123 BFSP 462 ... 99

Agreement respecting Zanzibar, Heligoland, and the Spheres of Influence of the two Countries in Africa (Germany-United Kingdom) (1 July 1890) 82 BFSP 35 ........... 96–97

Convention with a view to facilitating Belgian Traffic through the Territories of East Africa (Belgium-United Kingdom) (15 March 1921) 114 BFSP 182; **5 LNTS 319**.................... 79–80

Exchange of Notes concerning the preservation in force of the 1880 Anglo-Swiss Extradition Treaty (2 August & 28 September 1967) (Switzerland-Tanzania) Switzerland Treaty Database No 19670196 (French & Italian) .. 162–63

Memorandum: Germans in the Mandated Territory of South-West Africa (23 October 1923) 28 LNTS 418......................285

Trusteeship Agreement for the Territory of Tanganyika, as approved by the General Assembly (13 December 1946) Cmd 7015......................285

### TIMOR-LESTE

Agreement concerning the continued Operation of the Treaty between Australia and Indonesia on the Zone of Cooperation (UNTAET-Australia) (10 February 2000) 9 ATS [2000]; **29 ILM 469** .........311

Agreement regarding the Modalities for the Population Consultation of the East Timorese through a Direct Ballot (United Nations-Indonesia-Portugal) (5 May 1999) 2062 UNTS 39............276

Agreement relating to the Unitisation of the Sunrise Troubadour Fields (Australia-Timor-Leste) (adopted 6 March 2003, entered into force 23 February 2007) 2483 UNTS 317 .................311

Convention relative to Commerce (Trade in Fire-arms, &c.) Navigation, Boundaries, and mutual right of Pre-emption as regards their respective Possessions in the Timor and Solor Archipelago (Portugal-Netherlands) (adopted 10 June 1893, entered into force 31 January 1894) 85 BFSP 394 (French)......70–72

Convention for the Settlement of the Boundary between their Possessions in the Island of Timor (Netherlands-Portugal) (adopted 1 October 1904, entered into force 29 October 1908) 101 BFSP 497 (French) .......................70–72

Provisional Agreement on the Land Boundary (Indonesia-Timor-Leste) (adopted 8 April 2005, entered into force 7 May 2005) Indonesia Treaty Database..... 70–72

Timor Sea Treaty (Australia-Timor-Leste) (adopted 20 May 2002, entered into force 2 April 2003) 2258 UNTS 3....................311

Treaty regulating the Limits of the Netherlands and Portuguese Possessions in the Archipelago of Timor and Solor (Netherlands-Portugal) (adopted 28 April 1859, entered into force 21 August 1860) 50 BFSP 1116 (French)..........70–72

### TRINIDAD AND TOBAGO

Air Transport Agreement (United States-Trinidad and Tobago) (23 May 1990) 2207 UNTS 229....186

### TURKEY

Exchange of Notes (France-Turkey) (23 June 1939) 143 BFSP 484......265

Arrangement for the Settlement of Territorial Questions between Turkey and Syria (France-Turkey) (adopted 23 June 1939, entered into force 13 July 1939) 143 BFSP 477 (French)...........265

## UNION OF SOVIET SOCIALIST REPUBLICS

Additional Protocol to the Frontier Treaty concerning the Line to be taken by the New Frontier (USSR-Iran) (adopted 7 May 1970, entered into force 11 May 1971) 787 UNTS 356 . . . . . . . . . . . . . .98

Agreement on Basic Intergovernmental Relations (Kyrgyzstan-Tajikistan) (adopted 12 July 1996, entered into force 16 October 1997) 2015 UNTS 139 . . . . . . . . . . . . . . . . . . 75–76

Agreement concerning the Settlement of Frontier and Financial Questions (USSR-Iran) (adopted 2 December 1954, entered into force 20 May 1955) 451 UNTS 227 . . . . . . . . . . . . . . .98

Agreement on the continued Validity of the German-Soviet Treaties (Germany-Georgia) (19 May & 9 September 1992) II BGBl (1992) 1128 (German) . . . . . . . . . . . . . . . . . .164

Agreement on the Division of all Property of the former USSR abroad (6 July 1992) 2380 UNTS 69 . . . . . 70–72, 91–92, 107, 183

Agreement establishing the Commonwealth of Independent States (Belarus-Ukraine-Russia) (8 December 1991) 31 ILM 143 . . . . .75

Agreement on Good Neighbourliness, Friendly Relations and Cooperation (Ukraine-Slovakia) (adopted 29 June 1993, entered into force 16 June 1994) Resolution No 4022-XII of the Verkhovna Rada of the Ukraine (24 February 1994); 42 Zakon (1 November 2006) 192 (Ukrainian) . . . . . . . . . . . . . . . . . . . . . .70–72

Agreement on the maintenance in force of the 1985 Franco-Soviet Finance Treaty (France-Turkmenistan) (28 April 1994) No TRA1994069 (French) . . . . . . . .163

Agreement on the State Border (China-Tajikstan) (adopted 13 August 1999, entered into force 7 April 2000) China Treaty Database (Chinese, Tajik, Russian)

Boundary Agreement [中华人民共和国和哈萨克斯坦共和国关于中哈国界的协定] (Kazakhstan-China) (adopted 26 April 1994, entered into force 11 September 1995) (Kazakh, Russian, Chinese) China Treaty Database (Chinese) . . . . . . . . . . . . . . . . . . . . 70–72

Boundary Agreement [中华人民共和国和塔吉克斯坦共和国关于中塔国界的协定] (China-Tajikistan) (adopted 13 August 1999, entered into force 4 July 2000) (Chinese, Tajik, Russian) China Treaty Database (Chinese) . . . . . . . . . . . . . . . . . . . . 70–72

Boundary Agreement (Ukraine-Poland) (adopted 12 January 1993, entered into force 21 December 1993) UNTS No I-57046 . . . . . . . . . . . . . . . . . . . 70–72

Boundary Treaty (Belarus-Ukraine) (adopted 12 May 1997, entered into force 18 June 2013) 3018 UNTS I-52468 . . . . . . . . . . . . . . . . . . . .75

Boundary Treaty (Kazakhstan-Kyrgyzstan) (adopted 15 December 2001, entered into force 5 August 2008) <https://adilet.zan.kz/rus/docs/Z0300004 59_#z1> accessed 25 January 2025 (Kazakh). . . . . . . . . . . . . . . . . . . . .75

Boundary Treaty (Moldova-Ukraine) (18 August 1999) 34 Tratate Internationale No 332 . . . . . . . . . . . . .75

Convention on the Legal Status of the Caspian Sea (Russia-Iran-Kazakhstan-Azerbaijan-Turkmenistan) (12 August 2018) (not in force) Russia Treaty Database No 20180068 . . . . . . . . 91–92

Delimitation Agreement (Turkmenistan-Uzbekistan) (21 September 2000) cited in Agreement on the Area of the Joint Point of the State Borders of the Three States (Kazakhstan-Turkmenistan-Uzbekistan) (10 November 2017) <https://adilet.zan.kz/rus/docs/Z1800000190> accessed 25 January 2025 (Kazakh) . . . . . . . . . . . . . . . . . . . . . .75

Memorandum on Security Assurances in connection with Ukraine's Accession to the Treaty on the Non-Proliferation of Nuclear Weapons (Ukraine-Russia-United Kingdom-United States) (5 December 1994) UNTS No I-52241 . . . . . . . . . . . . 75–76

Memorandum of Understanding concerning Legal Succession concerning the Agreements of the former USSR which are of Mutual Interest (6 July 1992) (1993) 26 RBDI 627 . . . . . 70–72, 91–92

Protocol to the Agreement establishing the Commonwealth of Independent States (21 December 1991) (1992) 31 ILM 147 . . . . . . . . . . . 75

Protocol concerning the Validity of Treaties (Germany-Azerbaijan) (2 July 1996) 2420 UNTS 114. . . . . .163

Succession Agreement on the External Public Debt and Assets of the former USSR (Russia-Moldova) (adopted 19 October 1993, entered into force 9 April 1997) Russia Treaty Database No 19930121 (Russian). . . . . . . . . . .138

Supplementary Treaty to the Treaty of Peace (Germany-Russia-Austria-Hungary-Bulgaria-Turkey) [Traité additionel au Traité de paix] (29 March 1918) 10 MNRG (3rd series) 797 (German)

Treaty concerning the Regime of the Soviet-Iranian Frontier (USSR-Iran) (adopted 14 May 1957, entered into force 20 December 1962) 457 UNTS 161. . . . . . . . . . . . . .98

Treaty concerning the Trans-Carpathian Ukraine (Czechoslovakia-USSR) (adopted 29 June 1945, entered into force 30 January 1946) 504 UNTS 310 . . . . . . . . . . . . . . . . . . . . .293

Treaty of Friendship, Good-Neighbourliness and Cooperation (Belarus-Ukraine) (adopted 17

July 1995, entered into force 6 August 1997) 1993 UNTS 108. . . . . . . 75

Treaty on Inter-State Relations (Belarus-Ukraine) (adopted 29 December 1990, entered into force 31 August 1991) 1669 UNTS 3. . . . . . . .75

## UNITED ARAB REPUBLIC*

Agreement amending the Agreement between Egypt and Greece for the Establishment of Scheduled Air Services (Greece-UAR) (29 November 1962 & 6 May 1963) 533 UNTS 324. . . . . . . . . . . . . . . . . . .186

Air Transport Services Agreement (Egypt-Syria) (adopted 3 July 1955, entered into force 11 March 1956) 393 UNTS 5652. . . . . . . . 162–63

## UNITED STATES OF AMERICA**

Treaty between the United States and Russia (30 March 1867) II Malloy 1521; **24 BFSP 1269.** . . . . . . . . . . . . . .254

Treaty of Peace, Friendship, Limits and Settlement (Mexico-United States) (2 February 1848) 102 CTS 29. . . . .260

## VIET NAM***

Agreement concerning the Settlement of Certain Property Claims (Vietnam–United States) (28 January 1995) 34 ILM 685 . . . . . . .210

Agreement on the Delimitation of the Territorial Seas, Exclusive Economic Zones and Continental Shelves in the Beibu Gulf (China-Vietnam) (adopted 25 December 2000, entered into force 30 June 2004) in Zou, 'The Sino-Vietnamese Agreement on Maritime Boundary Delimitation in the Gulf of Tonkin' (2005) 36(1) Ocean Development and International Law 13. . . . . . . . . . . . . . .96

---

* Including the merger of Egypt with Syria (1958) and the secession of Syria (1961).
** Includes the absorption of Texas as well as cessions of territory by Mexico, Russia and Denmark.
*** Includes the secessions of North Viet Nam and South Viet Nam from France and the merger of North Viet Nam with South Viet Nam.

## YEMEN

Administrative Arrangement concerning the project 'Temporary Support Office Shabwah' (Netherlands-Yemen) (1 February 1994) 131 Tractenblad [1994] 17; **Netherlands Treaty Database No 005384** .......................... 244

Agreement proclaiming the Republic of Yemen (Yemen Arab Republic-People's Democratic Republic of Yemen (adopted 22 April 1990, entered into force 22 May 1990) 2373 UNTS 131 ...... .32–33, 95, 259

Agreement regarding Relations between the United Kingdom and Yemen (20 January 1951) 101 UNTS 39.....................91

Boundary Agreement (Oman-Yemen) (adopted 1 October 1992, entered into force 25 December 1992) 1709 UNTS 409.............95

Boundary Treaty (Yemen-Saudi Arabia) (adopted 12 June 2000, entered into force 4 July 2000) 2389 UNTS 203 ..................91

Memorandum of Agreed Points relating to Independence for South Arabia (29 November 1967) 169 BFSP 136.....95, 132, 183–87, 273

Memorandum of Understanding (adopted 26 February 1995, entered into force 15 May 1995) 2389 UNTS 193 ..................91

Treaty of Islamic Friendship and Arab Brotherhood (Yemen-Saudi Arabia) (adopted 20 May 1934, entered into force 22 June 1934) 2389 UNTS 231 ..................91

## YUGOSLAVIA* (SOCIALIST FEDERAL REPUBLIC OF)

Accord on the Delimitation of the Continental Shelf (adopted 8 January 1968, entered into force 21 January 1970) Italy Treaty Database No BILHRV031 (Italian); **7(3) ILM (1968)** 547 ....70–72

Agreement on certain Yugoslav-Austrian Treaties (Slovenia-Austria) (adopted 16 October 1992, entered into force 24 September 1993) 14/93 Uradni list RS (Slovenian); **714/1993 BGBl (German)**............. 172–75

Agreement on the Encouragement and Reciprocal Protection of Investments [Accord sur l'encouragement et protection réciproques des investissements] (Slovenia-France) (11 February 1998) France Treaty Database No TRA19980010 (French).......186

Agreement regarding continuation of Treaties (FRY-Norway) (29 May 2003) Norway Treaty Database No 29-05-2003 Nr 23 Bilateral (Norwegian) ....................146

Agreement on the Residence and Employment of Yugoslav Citizens in Australia (SFRY- Australia) (adopted 12 February 1970, entered into force 20 May 1970) Australia Treaty Database.......172–75

Agreement on Succession to the Agreements of the former Yugoslavia with New Zealand (Slovenia-New Zealand) (13 March 2003) 13/04 Uradni List RS (2004) (Slovenian)........ 172–75

Agreement on Succession to Treaties between the former Yugoslavia and Canada (Slovenia-Canada) (23 June 1997) 34/1997 Uradni list RS (Slovenian) ........... 171–72

Agreement on Succession (FRY-Egypt) (23 November 2005) 12 Службени гласник Србије и Црне Горе међународни уговори [Official Gazette of Serbia and Montenegro International Treaties] (May 2006) 32.........172–75

---

\* Includes the absorption of the Yugoslavia and the dismemberment of the Socialist Federal Republic of Yugoslavia.

## TABLE OF TREATIES AND OTHER INTERNATIONAL INSTRUMENTS lxxix

Agreement on Succession (FRY-
Portugal) (3 November 2003)
101 Diário dq República I-A (29
April 2004) (Portuguese) ..... 172–75
Agreement on Succession Issues
between the Five Successor States
of the former State of Yugoslavia
(adopted 29 June 2001, entered
into force 2 June 2004) 41 ILM 3;
**2262 UNTS 251**.... 19, 126, 217–22, 301
Agreement on the Succession of
Serbia and Montenegro (FRY-
France) (26 March 2003) 2239
UNTS 325 ............... 22, 172–75
Agreement on Succession to Treaties
(Bosnia-Norway) (20 August
2008) Norway Treaty Database
No 20-08-2008 Nr 20 Bilateral
(Norwegian) ........ 162–63, 172–75
Arrangement on Succession to
Bilateral Treaties (Slovenia-
United Kingdom) (28 May & 3
June 1998) 43/1998 Uradni list
RS (Slovenian); **Treaty Series
No 39 (1998) Cmd 4046**...... 172–75
Boundary Treaty (Croatia-Bosnia)
(30 July 1999) <https://www.
un.org/depts/los/LEGISLA
TIONANDTREATIES/PDFFI
LES/TREATIES/HRV-BIH199
9SB.PDF> accessed 25 January
2025......................... 74–75
Boundary Treaty (SFRY-Italy)
(adopted 10 November 1975,
entered into force 3 April 1977)
1466 UNTS 25................ 32–33
Convention for the Maintenance of
the State Border (Slovenia-Italy)
(7 March 2007) 61 Uradni list RS
(16 June 2008) 1593 (Slovenian);
**Italy Treaty Database No
BILSVN029 (Italian)** ......... 70–72
Exchange of Letters (Croatia-China)
(27 August 1996) China Treaty
Database (Chinese) .......... 172–75
Exchange of Notes (Bosnia-United
Kingdom) (1 October 1997 & 4
May 1998) Treaty Series No 135
(2000); **Cmd 5028** ........... 162–63
Exchange of Notes (North
Macedonia-Netherlands) (27

June & 11 July 1994) Netherlands
Treaty Database No 011806
(Dutch)..................... 172–75
Exchange of Notes regarding the
validity of certain Bilateral
Agreements (North Macedonia-
Switzerland) (21 May 1997)
Switzerland Treaty Database
No 99990739 (not published)
(German)................... 172–75
Exchange of Notes on Succession
to Bilateral Treaties (Slovenia-
Spain) (5 February & 9
September 1996) 8/1996
Uradni list RS (Slovenian);
**32 BOE (6 February 1997)
3750 (Spanish)**.............. 172–75
Exchange of Notes on Succession to
Treaties (Slovenia-Italy)
(31 July & 8 September 1992)
Italy Treaty Database No
BILSVN049 (French) ........ 172–75
Extradition Treaty (Serbia-United
States) (12 & 25 October 1901)
94 BFSP 727....................152
Investment Agreement (Slovenia-
France) (11 February 1998)
France Treaty Database No
TRA19980010 (French,
Slovenian) ......................186
Joint Declaration on Bilateral
Treaty Relations (Slovenia-
Netherlands) (18 March & 21
April 1992) 98 Tractatenblad
(19 April 1995); **Netherlands
Treaty Database No 011806
(Dutch)** ................... 172–75
Protocol on Succession (Croatia-
Romania) (adopted 5 March
2004, entered into force 20
August 2004) Romania Treaty
Database.................... 172–75
Protocol on the Principles of
Identification-determination of
the Border Line (Croatia-FRY)
(23 April 2002) Croatia Treaty
List (Serbo-Croatian) (not
published) ......................75
Trade Agreement (SFRY-Mexico)
(adopted 17 March 1950,
entered into force 25 September

1953) Mexico Treaty Database
(Spanish) .................. 172–75

Treaty for the Mutual Surrender of
Fugitive Criminals (Serbia-
United Kingdom) (23 November
& 6 December 1900) Australia
Treaty Database ................146

## ZAMBIA ('NORTHERN RHODESIA')

Agreement with regard to certain
Angolan and Northern Rhodesian
natives living on the Kwando River
(United Kingdom-Portugal) (18
November 1954) 161 BFSP 167 .......99

# Abbreviations

| | |
|---|---|
| ADI | Anuario de derecho internacional |
| AFDI | Annuaire française de droit international |
| AILC | American International Law Cases |
| AIR (SC) | All India Reports (Supreme Court) |
| AJCL | American Journal of Comparative Law |
| AJIL | American Journal of International Law |
| AJPIL | Austrian Journal of Public and International Law |
| ALR | African Law Reports |
| ALQ | Arab Law Quarterly |
| ARIEL | Austrian Reports of International and European Law |
| ASDI | Annuaire suisse de droit international |
| ATS | Australia Treaty Series |
| AYIL | Australian Yearbook of International Law |
| BGBl | Bundesgesetzblatt [Official Gazette of the Federal Republic of Germany] |
| BGE | Bangladesh Gazette Extraordinary |
| BILC | British International Law Cases |
| BIN | Bulletin of International News |
| BJILIR | Belarus Journal of International Law and International Relations |
| BLR | Burma Law Reports |
| BOE | Boletín official del España [Official Gazette of the Kingdom of Spain] |
| BOGE | Boletín oficial de la Guinea Ecuatorial [Official Gazette of the Republic of Equatorial Guinea] |
| BORL | Bulletin Officiel du Royaume de Laos [Official Gazette of the Kingdom of Laos] |
| BORM | Bulletin Officiel du Royaume du Maroc [Official Gazette of the Kingdom of Morocco] |
| BYIL | British Year Book of International Law |
| CCFB | Reports of the Council of the Corporation of Foreign Bondholders |
| CDT | Cuadernos de Derecho Transnacional |
| CETS | Council of Europe Treaty Series |
| CILC | Commonwealth International Law Cases |
| CLR | California Law Review |
| Col LR | Columbia Law Review |
| Crne Gore | Službeni list Crne Gore [Official Gazette of the Republic of Montenegro] |

lxxxii ABBREVIATIONS

| | |
|---|---|
| CRTC | Canada Reports of Transport Commissioners |
| CTC | Canadian Tax Cases |
| C.T.S. | Canada Treaty Series |
| CTS | Consolidated Treaty Series |
| CYIL | Canadian Yearbook of International Law |
| Diário | Diário da República [Official Gazette of Timor-Leste] |
| DIL | Digest of International Law |
| D.L.R. | Dominion Law Reports |
| DLR | Dhaka Law Reports |
| Dziennik Ustaw | Dziennik Ustaw Rzezypospolitej Polskiej [Journal of Laws of the Republic of Poland] |
| ECR | European Court Reports |
| EWHC | Judgments of the England and Wales High Court |
| FBPC | Reports of the Foreign Bondholders Protective Council |
| FCA | Reports of the Federal Court of Appeal |
| Federal Rep | Federal Reports |
| France Archives | Archives diplomatiques du Ministère de l'Europe et des Affaires Étrangères de la République Française |
| FRUS | Foreign Relations of the United States |
| FSM Intrm. | Federated States of Micronesia Reports |
| GAOR | General Assembly Official Records |
| Gazzetta Ufficiale | Gazzetta Ufficiale della Repubblica Italiana Serie Generale [Official Gazette of the Republic of Italy] |
| GIE | Gazette of India Extraordinary |
| Giurisprudenza | La Giurisprudenza italiana di diritto internazionale |
| GJICL | Georgia Journal of International and Comparative Law |
| HJIL | Heidelberg Journal of International Law [Zeitschrift für ausländisches öffentliches Recht und Völkerrecht] |
| HLR | Hanse Law Review |
| ICJ | Rep Reports of the International Court of Justice |
| ICSID Rep | Reports of the International Centre for the Settlement of Investment Disputes |
| IJIL | Indian Journal of International Law |
| ILC Yearbook | Yearbook of the International Law Commission |
| ILM | International Legal Materials |
| ILP | International Legal Perspectives |
| ILR | International Law Reports [Annual Digest of Public International Law Cases] |
| IRRC | International Review of the Red Cross |
| Israel Laws | Laws of the State of Israel |
| ITLOS Rep | Reports of the International Tribunal for the Law of the Sea |
| JAE | Journal of African Elections |
| JAH | Journal of African History |
| JCLIL | Journal of Comparative Legislation and International Law |
| JDI | Journal du Droit International |

| | |
|---|---|
| JdR | Jornal da República [Official Gazette of the Republic of Timor-Leste] |
| JIANL | Journal of Immigration, Asylum and Nationality Law |
| JCLIL | Journal of Comparative Legislation and International Law |
| JORF | Journal Officiel de la République Française [Official Gazette of the French Republic] |
| JOS | Journal Officiel du Syrie [Official Gazette of the Arab Republic of Syria] |
| JOZ | Journal Officiel du Zaïre [Official Gazette of the Republic of Zaire] |
| JYIL | Jewish Yearbook of International Law |
| KB | King's Bench |
| LNOJ | League of Nations Official Journal |
| LR | Law Reports (England and Wales) |
| LRC | Law Reports of the Courts |
| Malloy | Malloy, *Treaties, Conventions, International Acts, Protocols and Agreements between the United States of America and Other Powers, 1776–1909*, 2 vols (1910) |
| MAS | Modern Asian Studies |
| Mayers | WM Mayers, *Treaties between the Empire of China and Foreign Powers* (4th edn, North-China Herald Office 1902) |
| MJIL | Melbourne Journal of International Law |
| Moniteur Belge | Official Gazette of the Kingdom of Belgium |
| Monitorul Oficial | Official Gazette of the Republic of Romania |
| Moore | JB Moore, *History and Digest of the International Arbitrations to which the United States Has Been a Party* (Government Printing Office 1898) |
| MPEPIL | Max Planck Encyclopaedia of Public International Law |
| MR | Mauritius Reports |
| NCJIL | North Carolina Journal of International Law & Commercial Regulation |
| NILR | Netherlands International Law Review |
| NTIR | Nederlands Tijdschrift voor Internationale Recht |
| NJIL | Nordic Journal of International Law |
| NR | Namibian Reports |
| NZG | New Zealand Gazette |
| ODIL | Ocean Development and International Law |
| OJEU | Official Journal of the European Union |
| ORIL | Oxford Reports of International Law |
| PCIJ Rep | Reports of the Permanent Court of International Justice |
| Peters | Peters' United States Supreme Court Reports |
| Portugal Archives | Instituto Diplomático Divisão de Arquivo e Biblioteca [Archives of the Ministry of Foreign Affairs and Overseas Ministry of the Republic of Portugal] |
| Pravne Predpisy | Collection of Laws of the Slovak Republic |

lxxxiv ABBREVIATIONS

| | |
|---|---|
| PTS | Pakistan Treaty Series |
| RBDI | Revue belge de droit international |
| RBIB | Reserve Bank of India Bulletin |
| RCEEL | Review of Central and East European Law |
| RdC | Recueil des Cours [Collected Courses of the Hague Academy of International Law] |
| RDSPI | Rivista di studi politici internazionali |
| Recueil des décisions | Recueil des décisions des tribunaux arbitraux mixtes |
| Recueil des traités | Recueil des traités conclus par la France en extrême-orient (1684–1902) |
| Recueil général | Pinto and Rollet, Recueil général des Traités de la France (1976) |
| REDI | Revista española del derecho internacional |
| RFDA | Revue française de droit aérien |
| RGBl | Reichsgesetzblatt [Official Gazette of the German Reich] |
| RHDI | Revue hellénique du droit international |
| RIAA | Reports of International Arbitral Awards |
| RSL | Review of Socialist Law |
| RSPI | Rivista di studi politici internazionali |
| SAGG | South African Government Gazette |
| SALJ | South African Law Journal |
| Sähköinen sopimussarja | Official Gazette of the Republic of Finland |
| Sbírka zákonů | Sbírka zákonů nařízení republiky Československé [Collection of Laws and Regulations of the Czechoslovak Republic] |
| SC | Reports of the Supreme Court of India |
| SCOR | UN Security Council Official Records |
| SCR | Supreme Court Reports |
| SGCA | Singapore Court of Appeal Reports |
| SGHC | Singapore High Court Reports |
| SPSQ | Southwestern Political Science Quarterly |
| SPTI | Censo de Tratados Internacionales Suscritos por España |
| Staatsblad | Official Gazette of the Netherlands |
| SUP | Stanford University Press |
| TIAS | Treaties and other International Acts Series |
| Tractatenblad | Official Gazette of the Kingdom of the Netherlands |
| UBLJ | University of Botswana Law Journal |
| UCDLR | University of California Davis Law Review |
| UHLR | University of Hawai'i Law Review |
| UKSC | Judgments of the United Kingdom Supreme Court |
| UMLR | University of Malaya Law Review |
| UNJY | United Nations Juridical Yearbook |
| UNYBHR | United Nations Year Book on Human Rights |
| Uradni list | Official Gazette of the Republic of Slovenia |
| US | United States Reports |
| VCSSP | 1983 Vienna Convention on Succession of States in respect of State Property, Archives and Debts |

| | |
|---|---|
| VCSST | 1978 Vienna Convention on Succession of States in respect of Treaties |
| Večernji List | Official Gazette of the Republic of Croatia |
| VJIL | Virginia Journal of International Law |
| Wall | Wallace's Reports |
| YJWPO | Yale Journal of World Public Order |
| YLN | Yearbook of the League of Nations |
| Службени гласник | Службени гласник Србије и Црне Горе међународни уговори Official Gazette of Serbia and Montenegro International Agreements |
| Sbírka zákonů | Sbírka zákonů nařízení republiky Československé [Collection of Laws of the Czechoslovak Republic] |
| Zakon | Official Gazette of the Ukraine |
| Zákony Prolidi | Collection of Laws of the Czech Republic |

# 1

# Introduction

State succession has been described as a 'transfer of territory from one national community to another [, giving] rise to legal problems of a difficult and complex character ... frequent in modern history, and often drastic in their extent and consequences'.[1] Such has been the polarizing nature of debate concerning its content over the 140 years of its intellectual existence that its status as a neutral field of general international law—as opposed to one of 'political' character—has been shrouded in doubt.[2] Amidst ongoing practical interest due to at least five investor-State arbitrations turning on State succession questions in the past decade, one recent commentary has observed:

> The legal framework under general international law relating to State succession is unsettled and highly controversial, with one approach favoring, as a matter of international law and policy, continuity of treaty obligations and one departing from the principle that new States should start from a clean slate; in addition, State practice in respect of State succession is characterized by what has been described as situation-specific 'diplomatic bricolage'. One major attempt at codification, the 1978 Vienna Convention on Succession of States in Respect of Treaties, was largely unsuccessful, and only in part reflects customary international law. Much will therefore depend on the circumstances of the succession in question.[3]

Paradoxically, this tendency towards doubt as to the existence and content of general rules has been reinforced by the 'largely unsuccessful' nature of the four attempts of the International Law Commission ('ILC') to codify or to progressively develop such rules for the law of succession—more than in any other field of general international law.[4]

---

[1] DP O'Connell, *State Succession in Municipal Law and International Law* vol I (CUP 1967) 1.

[2] For examples of divergent views on the field during the decolonization period, see: Erik Castrén, 'Aspects récents de la succession d'états' (1951-I) 78 RdC 379; Karl Zemanek, 'State succession after decolonization', (1965-III) 116 RdC 181; Mohammed Bedjaoui, 'Problèmes récents de succession d'états dans les états nouveaux' (1970-II) 130 RdC 454; DP O'Connell, 'Recent Problems of State Succession in Relation to New States' (1970-II) 130 RdC 95. In this book, 'general international law' refers to the fundamental areas of international law that apply across the discipline – Rüdiger Wolfrum, 'General International Law (Principles, Rules, and Standards) *Max Planck Encyclopaedia of Public International Law* (December 2010).

[3] Stephan W Schill, 'Article 25(1)' in Stephan W Schill et al. (eds) *Schreur's Commentary on the ICSID Convention* (CUP 2022) 80, 302–03.

[4] The topic was also partially considered on a fifth occasion in the scope of the 'reservations to treaties' project. For an overview, see: Václav Mikulka, 'First report on State succession and its impact

---

*The Law of State Succession.* Arman Sarvarian, Oxford University Press. © Arman Sarvarian 2025.
DOI: 10.1093/oso/9780198817956.003.0001

## 2  INTRODUCTION

Whereas intellectual interest in the topic has waned since the turn of the twenty-first century with the seeming completion of the successions associated with the collapse of the 'second world' of socialist States aligned to the Union of Soviet Socialist Republics ('desovietization'), it remains an area of practical concern. Even as the most recent case of succession was the secession of South Sudan in 2011, the tendency to produce delayed effects has seen succession problems regularly arise in recent years with respect to earlier cases—particularly in the field of investor-State arbitration.[5] As the polarizing tendency of the debates that took place during the decolonization and desovietization periods has largely[6] subsided, the jurisprudence of national and international courts and tribunals has fluctuated between the identification of positive rules of succession[7] and the application of alternative solutions without engaging with them.[8] Since the scope for the acquisition by States of original title to territory by means other than the delimitation of borders has diminished,[9] the law of succession will be of perpetual relevance in international affairs to regulate the obtainment of derivative title by secession, cession, or other means.[10]

Despite the large number of successions to have occurred in the Charter era, a recurrent theme has been the inadequacy of empirical information available to identify general or 'default' rules on succession matters. State practice on succession matters is frequently difficult to identify, collate, and analyse.[11] Logistical

---

on the nationality of natural and legal persons' (17 April 1995) UN Doc A/CN.4/467, paras 1–14; Pavel Šturma, 'First report on succession of States in respect of State responsibility' (31 May 2017) UN Doc. A/CN.4/708, paras 8–18. For the original list of topics compiled by Hersch Lauterpacht, see: 'Survey of international law in relation to the work of codification of the International Law Commission' (5 November 1948) UN Doc A/CN.4/1.

[5] E.g. – *Oleg Deripaska v Montenegro* (Award) PCA Case No 2017-07 (25 October 2019) (not published) reported in Vladislav Djanić, 'Revealed: Reasons Surface for Tribunal's Decision that Montenegro was not bound by the Russia-Yugoslavia BIT' IA Reporter (3 July 2020); *Khudyan v Armenia*, ICSID Case No. ARB/17/36, Award of 15 December 2021 (not published) reported in Lisa Bohmer, 'Analysis: ICSID tribunal examines citizenship of individual investor in state succession context' (21 December 2021) IAReporter < https://www.iareporter.com/articles/analysis-icsid-tribunal-examines-citizenship-of-individual-investor-in-state-succession-context-and-sees-insuffici ent-proof-that-corporate-co-claimant-made-an-investment/> accessed 26 December 2023; *Haakon Korsguard v Croatia* (Award) UNCITRAL *ad hoc* Arbitral Tribunal (7 November 2022) (not published) reported in Vladislav Djanić, 'Croatia claims victory in under-the-radar treaty arbitration' (10 November 2022) <https://www.iareporter.com/articles/croatia-claims-victory-in-under-the-radar-tre aty-arbitration/> accessed 26 December 2023.

[6] E.g. – Šturma (n 4) paras 30–64.

[7] E.g. – *Sudapet v South Sudan*, ICSID Case No. ARB/12/26, Award of 30 September 2016, paras 440–541; *Gold Pool JV Limited v Kazakhstan* [2021] EWHC 3422 (Comm) paras 7–8, 111–14.

[8] E.g. – *Sanum Investments Limited v Laos* (Award) UNCITRAL *ad hoc* Arbitration (6 August 2019) paras 178–250; *Ališić and others v Bosnia and Herzegovina, Croatia, Serbia, Slovenia and Macedonia*, App No 60642/08 European Court of Human Rights (16 July 2014) paras 98–122.

[9] MG Kohen, 'Introduction' in MG Kohen (ed.) *Territoriality and International Law* (Elgar 2016) xvii, xx.

[10] See Chapter 2.

[11] For example, the studies of State practice produced for the two ILC codification projects during the desovietization era, alongside the considerable scholarship, generally omitted the cases of Namibia and Eritrea.

barriers include: long delays for the resolution of a succession matter;[12] inexistence of official records;[13] inaccessibility of documents held only in physical form in archives around the world; security classification and confidentiality;[14] publication;[15] and language.[16] Information on cases of succession has often been sporadic and fragmentary, including when a case was not yet complete at the time of study; for example, when negotiations for a succession agreement[17] or the settlement of a dispute were pending or had not yet arisen at the date of succession.[18]

When the ILC undertook its first two projects on succession, two different methodologies were adopted by the respective Special Rapporteurs.[19] While Sir Humphrey Waldock primarily followed an empirical approach based on State practice, Mohammed Bedjaoui prioritized normative considerations of policy or 'international ethics' to promote the perceived objectives of decolonization over 'traditional' methods of codification. As Rapporteur of the International Law Association Committee on State Succession in the 1960s, O'Connell was sceptical of the suitability of State succession for codification; though favouring an empirical approach, he emphasized its historical context and proposed solutions based on ethics in the absence of coherence in State practice.[20] These methodological differences had important implications for the inclusion and interpretation of State practice in the ILC projects.

For the project on succession to treaties led by Waldock,[21] the UN Secretariat furnished extensive information—much of which was provided by States—in the

---

[12] The claim of Somalia to the Ogaden region of Ethiopia, for example, was asserted in 1960 and abandoned in 1983: see Chapter 3.

[13] For instance, the judgment of the United States District Court for the District of Columbia on the succession of Zambia to the the 1931 Anglo-American Extradition Treaty is not published and judgment is no longer held by the District Court, the National Archives Records Administration, or the law firm of record – *Extradition of Zwagendaba Jère*, District Court for the District of Columbia (29 March 1966) summarized in O'Connell (n 1) vol II, 115 (n 1).

[14] A large number of documents of the various archives cited in this book were declassified decades after the successions to which they pertain (e.g. – under the 'twenty year rule' of the International Monetary Fund). Some documents were declassified on the application of the author.

[15] For example, the judgment of the Supreme Court of New South Wales has not been published and a digitized copy was procured by application of the author to the Court – *J. Tokic v Government of Yugoslavia* Case No S14790/91 Supreme Court of New South Wales (12 December 1991) 9–10 (unpublished) (on file with author). As a large number of archival documents are not digitized, printed copies were consulted, or they were digitized on application of the author.

[16] Translation software, professional translation, and research assistance were used for the languages not spoken by this author.

[17] On the definition of a succession agreement, see Chapter 2.

[18] For an example of scholarly work undertaken prior to the ILC projects that acknowledged these problems in examining contemporary State practice to determine whether a rule of customary international law exists, see: Karl Zemanek, 'State Succession after Decolonization' (1965-III) 116 RdC 186, 187–88.

[19] Arman Sarvarian, 'Codifying the Law of State Succession: A Futile Endeavour?' (2016) 27(3) EJIL 789, 799–800.

[20] Ibid, 794–95, 797–98. See also, e.g. – DP O'Connell, 'Reflections on the State Succession Convention' (1979) 39 ZaöRV 725; The United Nations (ed.) *Seventy Years of the International Law Commission: Drawing a Balance for the Future* (Brill Nijhoff 2021).

[21] See Chapter 5.

4  INTRODUCTION

form of 12 studies, 2 memoranda, and a volume of materials with a supplement.[22] However, the timing of the project meant that information concerning practice arising from many successions in the decolonization era was often fragmentary or unavailable.[23] Though grounded in empirical studies of State practice, the adoption of the 1978 Vienna Convention on the Succession of States with respect to Treaties ('VCSST')[24] necessarily preceded the practice to emerge from the decolonization era and the new successions of the desovietization era. Besides the low level of participation in that treaty, the cleavage between its provisions and the approaches taken in the desovietization practice in the 1990s was generally observed by commentators.[25] To date, it has never been directly applied as treaty law to a case of succession as it was designed.[26]

Due to the weight given to policy considerations as progressive development over 'traditional' methods of codification in the methodology of Bedjaoui[27] and logistical constraints between 1970 and 1972, the empirical contribution of the Secretariat to the project on succession to State property, archives, and debt comprised but a single volume of materials that was received by the ILC in 1978.[28] While State practice was also considered by the Special Rapporteur, the scope of its study was often selective and the 'traditional' rules to be derived from such practice could be disregarded if conflicting with the new international public policy stated to derive from decolonization.[29] Consequently, the scope of the State practice included by Bedjaoui in his reports not only frequently omitted recent successions arising from decolonization but also tended to disregard 'agreements concluded between the former metropolitan country and the former colony' as 'texts which have fallen into disuse ... [or] remained a dead letter'[30].

Whereas Bedjaoui noted the occurrence of challenges by some decolonized successors to succession agreements that they had concluded with predecessors,[31] the

[22] 'Report of the International Law Commission: Twenty-Sixth Session (6 May–26 July 1974)' UN Doc A/9610/Rev.1, para. 44.

[23] In executing the first of its three tasks 'to collect every scrap of practice relating to treaty succession in connection with decolonisation' through 'field work on a broad scale, consulting all of the governments of the newly-independent States, at Cabinet level, as well as those of older States and particularly the international organizations [through] a systematic survey', the International Law Association ('ILA') Committee on State Succession (1961–73) with O'Connell as its Rapporteur acknowledged this constraint – ILA Committee on State Succession: Final Report (1973) (on file with author) paras 4–15.

[24] Vienna Convention on the Succession of States with respect to Treaties 1978 (adopted 23 August 1978, entered into force 6 November 1996) 1946 UNTS 3 ('VCSST').

[25] E.g. – Matthew Craven, *The Decolonization of International Law: State Succession and the Law of Treaties* (OUP 2007) 1–3, 7–16.

[26] VCSST (n 24) art 7. See further Chapter 5.

[27] Mohamed Bedjaoui, 'First report on succession of States in respect of rights and duties resulting from sources other than treaties' (5 April 1968) UN Doc A/CN.4/204 ('First Bedjaoui Report') paras 27–35.

[28] 'Report of the International Law Commission: Twenty-Sixth Session (6 May–26 July 1974)' UN Doc A/9610/Rev.1, paras 33–47.

[29] First Bedjaoui Report (n 27) paras 30–34. See further Chapter 4.

[30] Ibid, para 33.

[31] Ibid, para 34.

methodology of the project meant that the complete history of such cases was infrequently covered in his reports. In many cases, for example, the 'actual practice' resulting from such challenges resulted in a settlement (often modified) with the predecessor. Adopted not by consensus but rather by a split vote that largely reflected geopolitical divisions, the 1983 Vienna Convention on Succession of States in respect of State Property, Archives and Debts ('VCSSP')[32] has yet to attract enough ratifications to enter into force. In the face of the practical problems arising from desovietization, commentators frequently criticized the treaty for its 'heavy reliance throughout on equity ... making it too vague for application to specific situations'.[33]

These methodological problems prompted considerable doubt as to whether the VCSST and VCSSP accurately reflected the intricate and fragmentary practice analysed by the ILC and the Contracting States. As O'Connell wrote, invoking his own experience in 'advising ten newly independent governments, some at least of which would classify themselves as Third World countries', on the occasion of the adoption of the VCSST:

> Savigny said: 'The call for codes arose from indolence and dereliction of duty on the part of the legal profession, which, instead of mastering the materials of the law, was overpowered and hurried headlong by their overwhelming mass.' I found that apt ... for the purpose of criticising the proposal to codify the law of State succession instead of leaving it to evolve as common law, and I find it even more apt for the purpose of criticising the result of this effort at codification. For what the draft of the ILC has done has been to force the topic within the constraints of inflexible dogmas that are at once over-simple and insufficiently comprehensive.
>
> [...]
>
> I am told that the ILC was constrained politically to reach the conclusions it did reach. No other scheme would, it thought, be acceptable to a conference. That may well be so and it may well exonerate the Commission from blame for an analysis that is far from scientific. But this only reveals the unsuitability [of] State succession for codification. For it is inevitable that a political conference could not grapple with concepts that are so various, subtle and jurisprudentially complex as those concerned with State succession.
>
> Because the State Succession Convention is so obviously legislative in character, and unlikely to become universal unless its rules come to influence customary law, it is clearly important that the underlying doctrine of State succession

---

[32] Vienna Convention on Succession of States in respect of State Property, Archives and Debts 1983 (adopted 8 April 1983, not in force) 22 ILM 306.

[33] E.g. – Anthony Aust, 'Vienna Convention on the Succession of States in respect of State Property, Archives and Debts', UN Audiovisual Library of International Law (2009).

6   INTRODUCTION

be critically examined. The tendency is for jurists to abandon this task on the supposition that codification has rendered it unnecessary, whereas I would argue that the opposite is the case.[34]

In spite of the contemporary criticisms made by international lawyers of the VCSST and VCSSP, their accessibility in the context of the logistical difficulties in obtaining and digesting State practice means that they have since been the focus of scholarly attention by either testing their provisions against subsequent State practice[35] or analysing the causes of their weaknesses as codification projects.[36]

In the rare cases before the International Court of Justice ('ICJ') to feature issues of State succession, the arguments of counsel to the disputing parties have likewise focused on the authority of provisions of the VCSST as customary international law rather than an independent examination of State practice to identify a general rule.[37] In 2002, the ILA adopted a report and resolution based upon 'available data that are incomplete ... [due to] the impossibility of surveying the totality of cases for which the process is still largely pending' in which it assessed the status of provisions of the VCSST against State practice in desovietization.[38] In 2001, the

[34] O'Connell (n 20) 733–34.

[35] Covering the period 1989 to 1995 and confined to the cases of Germany, the Union of Soviet Socialist Republics, the Socialist Federal Republic of Yugoslavia, and Czecho-Slovakia, the Pilot Project on State Practice regarding State Succession and Issues of Recognition of the *Ad Hoc* Commtitee of Legal Advisers on Public International Law (CAHDI) of the Council of Europe reported in 1998 that 'both the scope and the origins of submitted practice [from 16 Member States] diverged widely' – Jan Klabbers, Martti Koskenniemi, Olivier Ribbelink, and Andreas Zimmermann (eds) *State Practice regarding State Succession and Issues of Recognition* (Kluwer 1999) 16. In the extensive study of The Hague Academy of International Law, seven pages of analysis in the report of the francophone section provided incisive commentary on succession to treaties and six pages to 'territorial regimes' while two pages were spent on succession to State property and debt (described as 'une alchimie particulièrement obscure') with no conclusions presented on other fields: Pierre Michel Eisemann, 'Rapport du directeur d'études de la section de langue française du Centre' in Pierre Eisemann and Martti Koskenniemi (eds) *State Succession: Codification Tested against the Facts* (Martinus Nijhoff 2000) 1, 9-48-62. Similarly, 27 pages were dedicated in the report of the anglophone section to treaties (including membership in international organizations), 6 pages to State property and debt, 1 page to private rights, and 1 page to nationality in Martti Koskenniemi, 'Report of the Director of Studies of the English-speaking Section of the Centre' in Eisemann and Koskenniemi, ibid., 65, 69-96, 106-08, 112-19. An article-by-article commentary has been produced solely on the VCSST: Giovanni Distefano, Gloria Gaggioli, and Aymeric Hêche, 'Introduction' in Giovanni Distefano, Gloria Gaggioli, and Aymeric Hêche (eds) *La Convention de Vienne de 1978 sur la succession d'États en matière de traités* (Bruylant 2016) 1, 2–4.

[36] E.g. – Craven (n 25) 1–6.

[37] See Chapter 5. For a general survey of the pronouncements of the Court, see Andreas Zimmermann, 'The International Court of Justice and State Succession to Treaties: Avoiding Principled Answers to Questions of Principle' in Christian Tams and James Sloan (eds) *The Development of International Law by the International Court of Justice* (OUP 2013) 53-70, 60.

[38] International Law Association Committee: Aspects of the Law of State Succession, Final Report, Seventieth Conference, New Delhi (2002) 70 ILA Reports 575 (author's translation from original French).

INTRODUCTION 7

Institut de droit international ('IDI') completed a similar exercise with respect to the VCSSP;[39] the ILA followed suit in 2008.[40]

Amidst the unfolding problems arising from the successions connected to desovietization, the ILC undertook a third project from 1993 to 1999 on the effects of a succession on the nationality of natural persons.[41] A dearth of information on State practice in the reports of the Secretariat or responses from States to requests[42] was one reason for the approach of the Special Rapporteur, Professor Václav Mikulka, to treat nationality as governed by internal law but restricted by international law with particular respect to considerations of statelessness and human rights.[43] Principally an exercise in progressive development, the Sixth Committee (Legal) of the UN General Assembly did not reach consensus on the proposal of the ILC——to adopt the 1999 ILC Articles on Nationality of Natural Persons in relation to the Succession of States ('ILC Articles')[44] as a declaration. Rather, it took the unprecedented step of recommending that the General Assembly merely 'take note of the Articles' and annex the text to its resolution.[45] Unlike the 2001 Articles on the Responsibility of States for Internationally Wrongful Acts,[46] this action had not been recommended by the ILC and arguably reflected the limited appetite of States to legislate without a strong basis of practice.[47]

Though briefly examined in scholarship dealing with desovietization practice[48] and inspiring one regional treaty,[49] there is scant evidence of the application of the ILC Articles in State practice (notably, the secessions of Montenegro

---

[39] Institut de droit international, 'State Succession in Matters of Property and Debts', Seventh Commission, Report and Resolution (2001) 69 IDI Annuaire 119 (French).

[40] International Law Association Committee: Aspects of the Law on State Succession, Final Report, Seventy-Third Conference, Rio de Janeiro (2008) 73 ILA Reports 250; ILA Resolution No 3/2008, 'Aspects of the Law on State Succession', (2008) 73 ILA Reports 40.

[41] See Chapter 7.

[42] ILC, 'Summary Record of the 2385th meeting' (17 May 1995) UN Doc A/CN.4/SR.2385, para 51 (Special Rapporteur); 'Report of the International Law Commission on the work of its forty-ninth session (12 May–18 July 1997)', UN Doc A/52/10, para 202. See also: ILC, 2488th meeting (5 June 1997) UN Doc A/CN.4/2488, paras 23, 33–34, 36, 40–41, 43, 49.

[43] Václav Mikulka, 'Introductory Note: Articles on Nationality of Natural Persons in relation to the Succession of States', UN Audiovisual Library of International Law <https://legal.un.org/avl/ha/annp rss/annprss html> accessed 9 January 2024. See also: 'Report of the International Law Commission on the work of its forty-seventh session, 2 May–21 July 1995', UN Doc A/CN.4/472/Add.1 (10 January 1996) paras 188–91.

[44] ILC, Draft Articles on Nationality of Natural Persons in relation to the Succession of States with commentaries, (1999) ILC Yearbook vol II Part Two, 42. See also: First Mikulka Report (n 4) paras 1–14.

[45] UNGA Res 55/153 (12 December 2000).

[46] 'Report of the International Law Commission: Fifty-Third Session (2001)' UN Doc A/56/10, paras 72–73.

[47] This episode sparked a trend in subsequent years of the ILC proposing similar action for other products – Mikulka, 'Introductory Note' (n 43).

[48] E.g. – Koskenniemi (n 35) 112–13; Andreas Zimmermann, 'State Succession and the Nationality of Natural Persons – Facts and Possible Codification' in Eisemann and Koskennimi (n 35) 611.

[49] Convention on the Avoidance of Statelessness in relation to State Succession (adopted 19 May 2006, entered into force 1 May 2009) CETS No 200.

8   INTRODUCTION

in 2006 and South Sudan in 2011) or the jurisprudence of courts and tribunals.[50] As general interest in State succession waned in the new millennium, some scholars—notably, Professor Marcelo Kohen and Professor Patrick Dumberry—took up the question of succession to State responsibility,[51] which had been implicitly omitted by the ILC from the 2001 Articles on the Responsibility of States for Internationally Wrongful Acts.[52] After eight years of work, the IDI adopted its Resolution on State Succession and State Responsibility ('IDI Resolution') in August 2015.[53] Its methodology was 'not limited to the examination of the practice followed by States' but also 'proposed ... solutions that logically seem[ed] to be most appropriate in a number of situations where State practice is scarce or when it is contradictory'.[54]

Inspired by the recently adopted IDI Resolution, the ILC added this topic to its programme of work in 2017 and appointed Professor Pavel Šturma as Special Rapporteur.[55] In acknowledging a 'dearth' of State practice that 'made it difficult to identify customary rules', he proposed a set of draft articles with commentaries on the basis of such practice as was available and scholarly opinion on the normative issues.[56] Amidst division in the ILC concerning a binary proposition on a 'basic rule of succession or non-succession to responsibility', the ILC decided in 2022 to change the format of the product to 'draft guidelines' after the proposed draft articles with commentaries met with considerable scepticism at first reading from States in the Sixth Committee.[57] A recurring point of methodological criticism was the degree to which the Special Rapporteur and the ILC were perceived to have relied on the work of the IDI and scholarly opinion.[58]

At its seventy-fifth session in 2024, a working group under the chairmanship of Professor August Reinisch[59] recommended that the ILC establish a working group for the purpose of drafting a concluding report in its seventy-sixth session in 2025 that 'would contain a summary of the difficulties that the Commission would face if it were to continue its work on the topic and explain the reasons for the

---

[50]   Mikulka, 'Introductory Note' (n 43).

[51]   Patrick Dumberry, *State Succession to International Responsibility* (Martinus Nijhoff 2007) 8–11.

[52]   James Crawford, *State Responsibility: The General Part* (2013) 436–37.

[53]   Institut de droit international, 'State Succession in Matters of State Responsibility', Fourteenth Commission, Final Report & Resolution (2015) 76 IDI Annuaire 511 in Marcelo Kohen and Patrick Dumberry, *The Institute of International Law's Resolution on State Succession and State Responsibility: Introduction, Text and Commentaries* (CUP 2019) 141.

[54]   Ibid, 9.

[55]   ILC, 'Provisional summary record of the 3354th meeting' (9 May 2017) UN Doc A/CN.4/SR.3354 (2 June 2017) 10.

[56]   ILC, 'Provisional summary record of the 3374th meeting' (13 July 2017) UN Doc A/CN.4/SR.3374 (14 August 2017) 10.

[57]   ILC, 'Provisional summary record of the 3583rd meeting' (17 May 2022) UN Doc A/CN.4/3583 (16 June 2022) 3–8.

[58]   See Chapter 7.

[59]   ILC, 'Report on the work of the seventy-fourth session (2023)' UN Doc A/78/10 (September 2023) paras 235–46.

discontinuance of such work'.[60] Difficulties identified by the Working Group included the sufficiency of State practice to enable identification of customary international law, a distinction between a transfer of rights arising from international responsibility and obligations arising therefrom, the applicability of a potential parallel with rules governing State debt, and identification of underlying policy justifications as progressive development.[61]

Alongside this effort to progressively develop the law of State succession with respect to State responsibility, the attention of general international lawyers working in international investment law—notably, Christian Tams[62] and Patrick Dumberry[63]—has also been sustained by succession issues to have come before investor-State arbitral tribunals as well as national courts in set-aside proceedings. Principally engaging with 'threshold' issues of jurisdiction and admissibility, these arbitrations have addressed succession to bilateral investment treaties, State property, and the nationality of natural persons.[64] In dealing with issues arising from State practice concerning Macao, Montenegro, Croatia, South Sudan, and Armenia, investor-State arbitral tribunals and national courts have relied on provisions of the VCSST[65] and VCSSP[66] only insofar as the disputing parties have expressly agreed them to reflect customary international law.[67]

Absent such agreement, national and international courts and tribunals have not sought to postulate a general rule of succession but rather to forensically deduce the intentions of the States concerned from their conduct. Amidst a lack of information on State practice to identify such general rules, they have also rejected

---

[60] ILC, 'Succession of States in respect of State responsibility' UN Doc A/CN.4/L.1003 (12 July 2024) para 23.

[61] Ibid, paras 4–7.

[62] CJ Tams, 'State Succession to Investment Treaties: Mapping the Issues' (2016) 31(2) ICSID Review 314.

[63] Patrick Dumberry, *A Guide to State Succession in International Investment Law* (Elgar 2018).

[64] Arman Sarvarian, 'The Protection of Foreign Investment in the Law of State Succession' in Andreas Kulick and Michael Waibel (eds) *Commentary on General International Law in International Investment Law* (OUP 2024) 443; Arman Sarvarian, 'The Procedure for Succession to Bilateral Investment Treaties' in Kulick and Waibel, ibid, 416; James Devaney and CJ Tams, 'Succession in respect of cession, unification and separation of States' in Kulick and Waibel, ibid, 428.

[65] *Sanum Investments Ltd v Laos* (Award on Jurisdiction) PCA Case No 2013-13 (13 December 2013) paras 212, 219–24, 264–69; *Sanum Investments Ltd v Laos*, Singapore Court of Appeal (29 September 2016) [2016] SGCA 57, paras 36–122; *Gold Pool JV Limited v Kazakhstan*, High Court of Justice of England and Wales (15 December 2021) [2021] EWHC 3422 (Comm) paras 7–9, 33–42, 47–50, 55–60, 69–81, 84–96, 111–14. On these decisions and the unpublished awards of *World Wide Minerals v Kazakhstan* and *Deripaska v Montenegro*, see Chapter 5.

[66] *Sudapet v South Sudan* (Award) ICSID Case No ARB/12/26 (30 September 2016) paras 427–540. See further Chapter 6.

[67] In the absence of agreement by the disputing parties, the Arbitral Tribunal also reportedly rejected the relevance of the ILC Articles in *Khudyan v Armenia* while the Eritrea–Ethiopia Claims Commission made no reference to that text in its award of 17 December 2004 on the nationality of persons of Eritrean origin resident in Ethiopia – *Pensions: Eritrea's Claims 15, 19 & 23* (Final Award) Eritrea–Ethiopia Claims Commission (19 December 2005). See Chapter 7.

10  INTRODUCTION

claims that were based on succession[68] or decided succession issues on other grounds (e.g.—an obligation to negotiate in good faith).[69] Even as they have refrained from treating the products of the ILC as authoritative statements of general international law,[70] the problem has been to identify general rules while lacking a robust foundation of State practice.

The fruit of eight years of labour, this book seeks to identify a general law of State succession on the basis of empirical evidence of State practice and the doctrinal interpretations of jurisprudence and scholarship. It builds upon the contemporary literature that has followed the classical treatise of O'Connell, such as the work of Brigitte Stern,[71] Andreas Zimmermann,[72] and Photini Pazartzis[73] on succession to treaties; August Reinisch and Gerhard Hafner on succession to State debt;[74] and Patrick Dumberry on succession to State responsibility[75] and investment treaties.[76] It also examines the collective studies of international lawyers, notably in the ILA,[77] IDI,[78] Council of Europe,[79] and The Hague Academy of International Law.[80]

The book investigates neither the constitutional organization of the transferred territory by the successor in its internal law, succession of governments in which no transfer of territory occurs,[81] nor succession with respect to an international organization.[82] It does not deal with the law of belligerent occupation, which applies

[68] E.g. – *Civilians Claims: Eritrea's Claims 15, 16, 23 & 27–32* (Partial Award) Eritrea–Ethiopia Claims Commission (17 December 2004) paras 41–42.

[69] E.g. – *Ališić and others v Bosnia and Herzegovina, Croatia, Serbia, Slovenia and the Former Yugoslav Republic of Macedonia* App No 60642/08, 16 July 2014, paras 9–11, 60, 98–125. Though not cited by the Court, the notion of 'equitable proportion' appears to be based on Article 41 of the VCSSP.

[70] On the few occasions when the International Court of Justice has encountered a question of succession to treaties, it has generally refrained from making a pronouncement on general international law – see Zimmermann (n 37). See Chapters 5 and 6.

[71] Brigitte Stern, 'La succession d'États' (1996) 262 RdC 9.

[72] Andreas Zimmermann, *Staatennachfolge in völkerrechtliche Verträge* (Springer 2000).

[73] Photini Pazartzis, *La succession d'Etats aux traités multilatéraux* (Pedone 2002).

[74] August Reinisch and Gerhard Hafner, *Staatensukzession und Schuldenübernahme beim "Zerfall" der Sowjetunion* (Service Fachverlag 1995).

[75] Note 51.

[76] Note 63.

[77] International Law Association Committee: Aspects of the Law of State Succession, Final Report, Seventy-Third Conference, Rio de Janeiro (2008).

[78] Institut de droit international, 'State Succession in Matters of Property and Debts', Seventh Commission, Vancouver, Resolution (2001) 69 IDI Annuaire 711; Kohen and Dumberry (n 53).

[79] Klabbers (n 35).

[80] Eisemann and Koskenniemi (n 35).

[81] For example, the extensive jurisprudence concerning the debt of Imperial Russia after its repudiation by the Union of Soviet Socialist Republics. For early, theoretical discussion of the distinction, see, e.g. – Henry Wheaton, *Elements of International Law* vol I (Little 1857) 48; GF de Martens, *Précis du droit des gens moderne de l'Europe* (1858) 110–12; Robert Phillimore, *Commentaries on International Law* (Butterworths 1879) 94–157.

[82] E.g. – *United Nations v B.* (Civil Tribunal of Brussels) (27 March 1952) 19 ILR 490, 491. See also: UNGA Sixth Committee, 1317th Meeting (29 September 1972) UN General Assembly Official Records: Twenty-Seventh Session, paras 16–17. The ILC were aware of this issue during the codification process (for example, with respect to the then live issue of direct UN administration following the revocation of the Mandate of South West Africa). e.g. – ILC, Summary Record of 1158th Meeting (15 May 1972) 135 (para 78); Humphrey Waldock, 'Fifth report on succession in respect of treaties', UN Doc A/CN.4/256 (10 April, 29 May and 8, 16, and 28 June 1972) ILC Yearbook (1972) vol II, 19 (para 5); James Crawford, *The Creation of States in International Law* (OUP 2006) 236–40, 503–64.

to a territory over which a State exercises effective control without a transfer of territorial title.[83] Even if the occupier considers itself to have received title from the predecessor and so purports to apply the law of succession to the occupied territory, the general principle of law *ex injuria jus non oritur* requires that such practice (e.g.—the ostensible 'absorptions' by Italy of Abyssinia (Ethiopia) in 1937 and Albania in 1939) be disregarded because no 'succession' occurs.[84]

In contrast, the practice generated by a succession to have received general and contemporaneous recognition may be taken into account to identify the law, even if the succession be subsequently annulled with retroactive effect.[85] This is because the contemporary practice and *opiniones juris* resulting from the succession reflect the genuine views of States concerning the law of succession. Conversely, practice arising from a premature annexation may be examined only if retroactively validated so as to affirm the lawfulness of the succession itself.[86]

The book investigates the existence and content of the general rules of the law of succession, which perform three functions in succession practice:

1. to guide States and other relevant parties (e.g.—representatives of a secessionist territory) in the negotiation of succession agreements;
2. to interpret provisions of succession agreements that are ambiguous or incomplete; and
3. to resolve disputes concerning issues in default of a provision in a succession agreement.

Its scope embraces State practice from the secession of the United States of America in 1784 to the secession of South Sudan in 2011. In researching 'historical' successions, it offers new information on cases of succession concerning which data has been incomplete or unknown to scholarship (e.g.—Eritrea, Mozambique, India, and Pakistan). Due to space constraints, its scope is limited to a representative selection of the mass of data held by the author on succession practice.

From these analyses, the book argues that general rules of customary international law can be identified in the following fields that are each examined in a substantive chapter:

1. territorial rights and obligations;
2. State property (including State archives) and debt;

---

[83] See Chapter 2.

[84] On the purported 'absorption' of Czecho-Slovakia by Germany in 1939, see: 'Comments and observations of Governments on the draft articles on succession of States in respect of matters other than treaties', UN Doc A/CN.4/338 and Add.1-4, ILC Yearbook (1981) vol II, Part Two, para 7.

[85] For example, the absorption of Austria by Germany in 1938 and the cession of the Sudetenland by Czecho-Slovakia in 1938.

[86] For example, the annexation by India of Portuguese India in 1961 and 1962 retroactively validated by the treaty of cession concluded with Portugal in 1974.

## 12 INTRODUCTION

3. treaties, including those constituting international organisations;
4. international claims and responsibility;
5. nationality of natural and legal persons; and
6. private property.

This sequence is ordered according to the nature of the rights and obligations and the degree of automaticity in the governing principle for respective field. In a crude analogy with 'proprietary' rights and obligations, territorial rights and obligations are intrinsic to the very definition of State succession while automatic rules apply to succession to State property and debt in the absence of specific agreement to the contrary. For 'personal' rights and duties, a general principle of consent regulates succession to treaties and default rules of succession only apply to certain classes of succession for international claims and responsibility. For the effects of a succession on private persons, default rules for nationality do not yet have general acceptance while the general principle concerning private property is not one of the law of succession but rather the application to successions of the international minimum standard of treatment as a broader rule of general international law.

While the structure of each chapter varies according to its substance, they are generally framed on the following lines. After posing the key issues in doctrine and (as relevant) the codification projects of the ILC and IDI, they state the overarching principle that governs the relevant field (e.g.—the principle of consent for succession to treaties). In elaborating upon the basic principle, they set out the system of rules supported by State practice with an evaluation of the relevant rule elaborated by the ILC or IDI. The application of the principles to the various classes of succession (e.g.—a merger of two States versus the absorption of one State by another) is then explained with the relevant State practice digested. In the chapters on territorial rights and obligations, treaties, and international claims and responsibility, an additional section describes the process by which a succession can be achieved. Finally, the chapters offer the conclusions reached on the key doctrinal problems identified in the introduction with reflections on the current trends in practice and likely issues to arise in future.

While the book concludes that customary international law does not regulate the effects of State succession on the nationality of natural and legal persons, it proposes general principles of law to determine those matters.[87] It engages with theoretical questions concerning definitions of basic concepts of succession[88] but does not rely upon a general theory of succession or—unlike the approach of O'Connell—normative arguments to resolve questions of succession according to ethical considerations that are independent of State policy. Concerning the nature

---

[87] Ibid.
[88] See Chapter 2.

of State succession, however, it makes two arguments deriving from interpretation of State practice that depart from the received literature:

1. a succession of States is defined in customary international law not as the 're-placement of one State by another in the responsibility for international relations of a territory' but rather as a transfer of territorial title (i.e.—territorial rights of jurisdiction and ownership) from one State to another;[89] and
2. the class of 'newly independent State' is confined to territories having limited international legal personality prior to the succession (i.e.—Mandatory Territories, Trusteeship Territories, protected States and international protectorates) so that most cases of 'decolonization' are to be classified as 'secessions' from the parent State.[90]

As these arguments are confined to the character of successions in international law, they are compatible with political and constitutional law narratives that emphasize the will of the successor to effect a succession in a case of decolonization independent of the parent State.

While the focus of this work is not the creation or continuity of the legal identity of a State, the question of identity precedes the determination of the legal effects of a succession when the character of the succession is itself contested.[91] Examples of such situations include:

- the ambiguity concerning the status of the Saar Territory as an anomalous international protectorate under the protection of France between 1947 and 1957, as opposed to an occupied territory of Germany;
- the claim of the Federal Republic of Yugoslavia to continue the legal personality of the Socialist Federal Republic of Yugoslavia between 1991 and 1999 before accepting the status of successor; and
- the successful claim of Russia to continue the legal personality of the Union of Soviet Socialist Republics from 1991.

Succession practice has been generated in such cases amidst the ongoing dispute concerning legal identity, yet the nature of such practice is not clarified until the definitive resolution of the character of the succession itself.

The typology of succession practice is key to compare like cases with like for the identification of general rules. This book accordingly engages with this question by identifying the classes of succession from common characteristics shared by cases in practice and assigning succession practice from case studies to the respective

---

[89] See Chapter 1.
[90] See Chapter 2.
[91] See Chapter 1.

14 INTRODUCTION

classes of succession. This is a question of interpretation to classify cases that have been interpreted in multiple ways, such as:

- the concurrent secessions of India and Pakistan from the United Kingdom in 1947, rather than the hypothesis that India continued an international legal personality of British India from which Pakistan seceded;
- the secession of Syria from the United Arab Republic in 1958, rather than a resumption of the legal personality that existed prior to its merger with Egypt; and
- the absorption of the German Democratic Republic by the Federal Republic of Germany in 1990, as opposed to their merger to create a new State.

In examining a wide range of case studies from 1784 to 2024, this book analyses succession practice that is widespread, representative, and diverse from the standpoint of geography, language, and legal system. To distil and synthesize that practice in the interest of comprehensibility, it focuses upon key examples to illustrate doctrinal rules with supplementary examples cited briefly in footnotes.

The analytical structure of the book identifies a general rule of international law on the basis of digested State practice before comparing that rule with an applicable provision of an ILC text.[92] While a particular provision might partially or wholly reflect the general rule, it might also not yet be accepted by States. Consequently, the principal question is not on the success or failure of the codification projects but rather the identification of the general law on the basis of original data on State practice.

---

[92] In its project focusing on State property, archives, and debt, the ILC 'had felt that other topics such as succession in respect of legislation and the problems of nationality did not fall entirely under public international law' – 40th Meeting of the Committee of the Whole (30 March 1983) *United Nations Conference on Succession of States in respect of State Property: Official Records* (vol I) 253 (para 57).

# 2

# The Nature of State Succession

## 2.1 Introduction

From the sixteenth to the eighteenth century, neither State practice nor international lawyers systematically addressed the legal consequences of a loss of territory by a State for treaties, private property, State property, or other matters.[1] As international law and finance grew increasingly sophisticated over the course of the nineteenth century,[2] States became interested not only in the regulation of such territory changes (e.g.—treaties of cession) but also in their implications for their interests in the territory concerned. As scholarly interest in the subject grew, the phrase 'a succession of States' was coined in 1868[3] in an analogy with the Roman law of inheritance.[4]

---

[1] E.g. – Francisco de Vitoria, *Francisco de Vitoria and his Law of Nations* (tr. J.P. Bate) (Clarendon Press 1532/1934); Francisco Suárez, *Selections from Three Works of Francisco Suárez, S.J.* (tr. GL Williams, A Brown, and J Waldron) (Clarendon Press 1612/1613/1621/1944); Alberto Gentili, *De iure belli libri tres* (tr. JC Rolfe) (Clarendon Press 1612/1933); Hugo Grotius, *De jure belli ac pacis libri tres by Hugo Grotius* (tr. CFW Kelsey) (Clarendon Press 1625/1925); Richard Zouche, *Juris et Judicii Fecialis, sive, Juris inter Gentes et Quæstionum de Eodem Explicatio* (tr. JL Brierly) Carnegie Institution 1650/1911); JW Textor, *Synopsis juris gentium* (tr. JP Bate) (Carnegie Institution 1680/1916); Samuel von Pufendorf, *De jure naturae et gentium libri octo* (tr. CH Oldfather and WA Oldfather) (Clarendon Press 1688/1934); Cornelius van Bynkershoek, *Quæstionum juris publici libri duo* (tr. T Frank) (Clarendon Press 1737/1930); Emmanuel de Vattel, *Le droit des gens, ou principes de la loi naturelle* (tr. CG Fenwick) (Carnegie Institution 1758/1916).

[2] E.g. – Johann-Ludwig Klüber, *Droit des gens modern de l'Europe* (Aillaud 1831) 38–57; Henry Wheaton, *Elements of International Law* (6th ed) (Little, Brown, & Co. 1857) 32–45; GF de Martens, *Précis du droit des gens moderne de l'Europe* (3rd ed) (Guillaumin 1858) 103–06, 173–75; Robert Phillimore, *Commentaries on International Law* (3rd ed) (Butterworths, 1879) 202–12, 369–87; FH Heffter, *Das Europäische Völkerrecht der Gegenwart* (Schroeder 1881) 193–98, 284–99; JJ Moser, *Grundsätze Des Jetzt-üblichen Europäischen Völker-rechts In Friedenszeiten* (Hanau 1750/2017) 380–81.

[3] The first essay to use the term was by JC Bluntschli, *Das moderne Völkerrecht der civilisirten Staten als Rechstbuch Dargestellt* (Beck 1868). See also, e.g. – CF Gabbà, 'Successione di Stato a Stato' in *Questioni di diritto civile* (Mascarelli 1882) 375–92; Pasquale Fiore, *Nouveau droit international public* (2nd ed.) vol I (Pedone-Lauriel 1885) 260–69, 309–22; ibid, vol II, 140–57, 417–18; vol III, 659–80; Léon Larivière, *Des Conséquences des transformations territoriales des États sur les traités antérieures* (1892) 75–90; Charles Calvo, *Le droit international* (5th ed) (Rousseau 1896) vol I, 246–63; ibid, vol II, 125–30; ibid, vol IV, 394–401; ibid, vol V, 370–72; Karl Gareis, *Institutionen des Völkerrechts* (Emil Roth 1901) 63–70; John Westlake, *International Law* vol I (CUP 1904) 59–83; Lassa Oppenheim, *International Law* vol I (Longman, Green, and Co. 1905) 114–40, 268–74, 290–92, 553, 556–57; Frantz Despagnet, *Cours de droit international public* (3rd ed) (Larose & Forcel 1905) 98–118, 126–45, 443–54, 714–19; AS Hershey, 'The Succession of States' (1911) 5(2) AJIL 285–97; Henry Bonfils, *Manuel de droit international public* (7th ed) (Rousseau 1912) 130–39, 204–08, 1084–85; Gaston Jèze, 'La Répartition des Dettes publiques entre États au cas de démembrement du territoire' (1921) 19 Revue de science et de législation financières 59–90; Frantz von Holtzendorff, *Handbuch des Völkerrechts* vol II (Richter 1887) 33–43; WE Hall, *International Law* (8th ed) (Clarendon Press 1924) 114–23.

[4] Hersch Lauterpacht, *Private Law Sources and Analogies of International Law* (Longman, Green and Co., 1927) 125–43.

---

*The Law of State Succession*. Arman Sarvarian, Oxford University Press. © Arman Sarvarian 2025.
DOI: 10.1093/oso/9780198817956.003.0002

## 16 THE NATURE OF STATE SUCCESSION

Amidst an explosion of scholarly interest from the mid-nineteenth to the early twentieth centuries, many international lawyers attempted to construct a general theory of succession to define the event and to prescribe the legal consequences flowing from such definition. In this intellectual debate, the following general theories were proposed:

- 'universal succession', in a private law analogy from the Roman law of inheritance whereby a successor inherits the entirety of the rights and obligations of the 'deceased' predecessor by operation of law;[5]
- rejecting a private law analogy, 'popular continuity', as a public law analogy by which a successor 'continues' the rights and obligations of the predecessor through a 'total or partial transfer of people and land';[6]
- rejecting the notion of transfer, 'organic substitution', whereby a State establishes its own 'sovereignty' over the territory and its inhabitants to replace that of the predecessor and may acquire rights and obligations attached to it;[7] and
- rejecting the existence of a general law, 'contractual succession', whereby a predecessor abandons sovereignty over a territory and a replacing successor may choose by a positive act of will ('novation') to adopt specific rights and their corresponding obligations.[8]

These theories came to be grouped into 'two traditions (or perhaps tendencies of thought)', which 'have subsequently come to delimit the intellectual domain of state succession in a profound way'.[9] These two tendencies were presented in doctrine as the continuity or 'universal succession' tendency and the discontinuity or 'clean slate' (*tabula rasa*) tendency whereby *all* rights and obligations of predecessors either automatically transferred to successors or not.[10] Even as none of the grand theories won general acceptance,[11] international lawyers also digested State

---

[5] E.g. – Gentili (n 1) 308; Grotius (n 1) 319; Zouche (n 1) 130; Textor (n 1) 307; van Bykershoek, ibid, Book II, Chapter XXV; von Pufendorf (n 1) 1313–14; de Vattel (n 1) 260.

[6] E.g. – Bluntschli (n 3) 75–82; Gabbà (n 3) 379–82; Henri Appleton, *Des effets des annexions de territoires sur les dettes de l'État démembré ou annexé* (Larose 1895) 28–29; Gilbert Gidel, *Des effets de l'Annexion sur les Concessions* (Libraire de la Société du recueil général des lois et des arrêts 1904) 80–97.

[7] Max Huber, *Die Staatensuccession* (Duncker & Humblot 1898) 18–25; Westlake (n 3) 69, 74–83.

[8] E.g. – von Holtzendorff (n 3) 33; Gareis (n 3) 61; Albert Zorn, *Grundzüge des Völkerrechts* (2nd ed) (Weber 1903) 150–54; AB Keith, *The Theory of State Succession with Special Reference to English and Colonial Law* (Stevens and Sons 1907) 1–7, 49–52; Georg Jellinek, *Allgemeine Staatslehre* (O. Häring 1905) 259–79, 364–730.

[9] Matthew Craven, *The Decolonization of International Law: State Succession and the Law of Treaties* (OUP 2007) 36.

[10] E.g. – Brigitte Stern, 'La succession d'États' (1996) 262 RdC 9, 120.

[11] Craven (n 9) 36–39.

practice to identify rules of customary international law on succession to treaties, State property, and other matters.[12]

When the International Law Commission ('ILC') first examined the topic of 'Succession of States and Governments' over the course of seven days in 1963, it decided to forego a general debate on fundamental questions and instead to divide it into two projects with two Special Rapporteurs to replace Manfred Lachs on his election to the International Court of Justice ('ICJ') in 1966.[13] In 1968, it appointed 'Sir Humphrey Waldock, Special Rapporteur on the law of treaties, who was particularly well-qualified ... [s]ince a United Nations Conference on the Law of Treaties was to be convened at Vienna in 1968 and 1969, the Commission decided that the succession of States in respect of treaties should be given priority'.[14] It also appointed Mr Mohammed Bedjaoui to the second project ('succession in respect of rights and duties resulting from sources other than treaties') and requested him to undertake a 'preparatory study' on this 'diverse and complex' topic.[15]

In elaborating the texts that would become the 1978 Vienna Convention on Succession of States in respect of Treaties ('VCSST')[16] and 1983 Vienna Convention on Succession of States in respect of State Property, Archives and Debt ('VCSSP'),[17] these two projects were led by Special Rapporteurs with differing methodologies.[18] Whereas Waldock primarily followed an empirical approach that emphasized the practice and policies of States, he viewed succession to treaties as a doctrinal branch of the law of treaties rather than a part of a general law of succession 'on the premise that neither the prevalent theories nor the existing practice offered a unified approach'.[19] In contrast, Bedjaoui espoused a normative approach for the 'progressive development' of a 'new' law of succession that would prioritize the political and economic 'sovereignty' of decolonized States over 'the codification of traditional rules which already seem obsolete' and 'in whose formulation most existing States took no part'.[20]

---

[12] E.g. – JB Moore, *A Digest of International Law* vol I (US Government Printing Office 1906) vol I, 270, 290–91, 302, 339–42, 347–51, 385–90, 396, 484, 553–54; EH Feilchenfeld, *Public Debts and State Succession* (Macmillan 1931) 35–56, 79–95, 119–70, 191–246, 287–93, 361, 371–78.

[13] Arman Sarvarian, 'Codifying the Law of State Succession: A Futile Endeavour?' (2016) 27(3) EJIL 789, 796.

[14] Mohammed Bedjaoui, 'First report on succession of States in respect of rights and duties resulting from sources other than treaties' UN Doc A/CN.4/204 (5 April 1968) 94 ('First Bedjaoui Report') para. 14.

[15] Ibid, para. 15.

[16] Vienna Convention on the Succession of States with respect to Treaties 1978 (adopted 23 August 1978, entered into force 6 November 1996) 1946 UNTS 3 ('VCSST').

[17] Vienna Convention on Succession of States in respect of State Property, Archives and Debts 1983 (adopted 8 April 1983, not in force) 22 ILM 306 ('VCSSP').

[18] Sarvarian (n 13) 706–801.

[19] Ibid, 799.

[20] Ibid, 798; First Bedjaoui Report (n 14) paras 29–30.

18  THE NATURE OF STATE SUCCESSION

Due to this lack of a cohesive conceptual foundation, the ILC and the Contracting States at the two UN Diplomatic Conferences encountered recurring difficulty on essential questions. The most significant were the following:

1. definition of 'a succession of States' as a factual or legal phenomenon;
2. existence of a general law of succession as a cohesive field;
3. construction of a cohesive typology of classes of succession; and
4. interpretation of State practice for the identification of general rules.

In this chapter, it is contended that State practice provides an empirical basis for the identification of a general law of State succession. This relies not on normative arguments to further policy objectives (e.g.—O'Connell, Bedjaoui) but on the distillation of States' common positions according to positivist methodology. It also does not treat State succession as a sub-branch or annexe of other fields of general international law (e.g.—Waldock) but rather as an integral field of law in its own right. The general failure of the VCSST, VCSSP, and other ILC codification projects to influence subsequent State practice is a consequence of conceptual weaknesses in the understanding of State succession as a legal phenomenon and the treatment of State practice.

## 2.2  The Concept of State Succession in International Law

Whereas none of the grand theories propounded around the turn of the twentieth century won general acceptance to define the phenomenon of State succession, the theoretical debate produced two doctrinal distinctions that have been accepted in the conceptual construction of the field.[21] The first was between a change of government that left the 'sovereignty' of a State over its territory intact ('governmental succession') and a change in that 'sovereignty' whereby one State replaced another in a territory ('State succession').[22] The second was between a 'belligerent occupation' of territory by a State and an 'annexation' of territory whereby sovereignty changed to another State.[23]

Although these two distinctions provided some of the contours of the subject, doctrinal definitions of 'State succession' in the twentieth century

ranged from those that tie the issue to the 'transfer' of territory from one State to another, to those that speak about it in terms of the 'replacement' or 'substitution' of one legal subject by another in legal relations ... [s]ome have been content to

---

[21]  Craven (n 9) 38–39.
[22]  On the 'Tsarist debt controversy', for example, see: Feilchenfeld (n 12) 538–42.
[23]  Craven (n 9) 38–39.

THE CONCEPT OF STATE SUCCESSION IN INTERNATIONAL LAW   19

limit the concept to territorial change while others have emphasized the importance of the change as being one that affects territorial *sovereignty* ... [o]thers still
have preferred the language of 'responsibility' seeking to avoid, in the process any
mention of the contested idea of sovereignty.[24]

Those scholars employing an empirical approach to identify doctrinal rules on
the basis of digestion of State practice (e.g.—Sack;[25] Wilkinson;[26] Feilchenfeld;[27]
Zemanek[28]) were 'almost unanimous'[29] in employing definitions with the language of 'transfer of territory' or 'change in sovereignty in a territory'.[30]

It is proposed that State practice provides for a definition of State succession in
customary international law as a transfer of territorial title—rights and obligations
of jurisdiction and ownership appurtenant to territory—from one State to another.
As Mohammed Bedjaoui explained:

> The problems of State succession arise, by definition, from a change of sover-
> eignty over a territory. The main purpose of succession is therefore the transfer
> of a territory from the predecessor State to the successor State. All the other prob-
> lems of succession—enforceability of treaties, devolution of property ... are, so
> to speak, only secondary effects granted on to the main effect: *the transfer of the
> territory and of the sovereignty over that territory*.[31]

This definition appeared in his first, exploratory report surveying the field as a
whole that preceded a radical shift in his second report on the topic of acquired
rights to an understanding of State succession as a 'substitution of sovereignties',
thus entitling a successor to deny recognition to the private property of aliens.[32] As
a 'succession' is never defined expressly in State practice,[33] its definition is a matter
of interpretation of the implicit effects of that practice. This proposed definition
thus accords with the traditional understanding of doctrine that was dominant before the new definition adopted by the ILC in its codification projects.

---

[24] Ibid, 56.

[25] AN Sack, 'La succession aux dettes publiques d'État' (1928-III) 23 RdC 145, 150.

[26] HA Wilkinson, *The American Doctrine of State Succession* (Johns Hopkins 1934) 16.

[27] Feilchenfeld (n 12) 2.

[28] Karl Zemanek, 'State Succession after Decolonization' (1965-III) 116 RdC 181, 189.

[29] Lorenzo Gradoni, 'Article 2' in Giovanni Distefano, Gloria Gaggioli and Aymeric Hêche (eds)
*La Convention de Vienne de 1978 sur la succession d'États en matière de traités*, vol 1 (Bruylant, 2016)
87, 101.

[30] Referring both to a 'transfer of territory' and 'the factual situation ... of substitution', O'Connell
opined that one could reject the notion of transfer of sovereignty and yet accept transfer of rights and
obligations 'because international law so directs' - DP O'Connell, *State Succession in Municipal Law
and International Law* vol I (CUP 1967) 3, 32.

[31] First Bedjaoui Report (n 14) para 117 (emphasis in original).

[32] n 162.

[33] E.g. – Agreement on Succession Issues between the Five Successor States of the former State of
Yugoslavia (adopted 29 June 2001, entered into force 2 June 2004) 2262 UNTS 251, art 7.

## 2.2.1 The Definition of the International Law Commission

When the ILC first examined State succession in 1963, it abandoned its theoretical debate on its nature.[34] Taking up the question of definition in his first report, Waldock remarked the 'ambiguity surrounding the expression' as 'truly succession by operation of law or merely a voluntary arrangement of the States concerned'.[35] Observing that the question 'whether and how far the law recognizes any cases of 'succession' in the strict, municipal law sense of the transfer of rights or obligations by operation of law ... will only become clear ... [on] a full examination of the subject', he considered it desirable 'for working purposes ... to use the term "succession" exclusively as referring to the *fact* of the replacement of one State by another in the possession of the competence to conclude treaties with respect to a given territory'.[36]

In 1968, Bedjaoui posed the question whether a general definition of State succession should be elaborated and, if so, which of the Special Rapporteurs should do so.[37] Considering a general definition to be theoretical and abstract, most ILC members opined that 'many of the difficulties might prove easier to dispose of ... [in] specific rules to deal with concrete issues'[38] while a minority regarded a definition as 'essential'.[39] In his second report, Waldock proposed the following: '"Succession" means the replacement of one State by another in the sovereignty of territory or in the competence to conclude treaties with respect to territory'.[40]

Noting that 'the word "succession" ... is certainly ambiguous since it may denote either the mere fact of a change of sovereignty or both a change of sovereignty and a transmission of rights and obligations as a legal incident of that change', Waldock added the word 'sovereignty' to the draft to reflect 'the feeling of some members that change of "sovereignty" should find mention in the formulation' while retaining 'competence to conclude treaties' to cover 'special cases', such as mandates and protectorates.[41] Although some members of the Commission supported the notion of 'the passing of sovereignty over a territory from one State to another',[42] others objected to the term on the ground that 'the effect of ... Article 73 of the United Nations Charter ... [was] that the Charter had brought into being a new international legal order by virtue of which the colonial status was automatically

---

[34] Craven (n 9) 96–105.

[35] Humphrey Waldock, 'First report on succession of States and Governments in respect of treaties' ILC Yearbook (1968) vol II Part One 91 ('First Waldock Report').

[36] Ibid.

[37] ILC 962nd Meeting (26 June 1968) UN Doc A/CN.4/204, para 1.

[38] Ibid, paras 41 (Albónico), 60 (Ruda), 64 (Ago).

[39] Ibid, para 51 (Tsuruoka), 75 (Bartoš).

[40] First Waldock Report (n 35) 50.

[41] Ibid, 51.

[42] ILC, Summary Record of the 1156th Meeting (11 May 1972) ILC Yearbook (1972) vol I, para 54 (Sette Câmara). See also: ibid, paras 61 (Tammes), 63–64 (Ago).

THE CONCEPT OF STATE SUCCESSION IN INTERNATIONAL LAW   21

abolished ... the former colonies had ceased to be subject to the sovereignty of the metropolitan Powers concerned.[43] Still others considered it to be 'inadvisable to say anything about the source of sovereignty, which might have been usurped or exercised in a manner incompatible with the principles now in force.'[44]

Summing up the debate, the Special Rapporteur commented that his draft text was not an expression of the 'traditional doctrine':

> Considerable stress had been laid during the discussion on the principle of self-determination. It went without saying that the present topic should be considered in the light of all the principles of international law, of which the principle of self-determination was particularly relevant. Nevertheless, it should be remembered that it was an autonomous principle, just as the law of treaties and the law of succession were autonomous. It was also necessary to be cautious about the principle of self-determination, because if it was carried too far it would make it impossible to adopt what he understood to be the Commission's view on the question of localized or territorial treaties.[45]

As a 'neutral' compromise, a modified version was agreed in the Drafting Committee: '[A] succession of States is the replacement of one State by another in the responsibility for the international relations of territory.'[46] It was agreed to leave aside 'from the definition all questions of the rights and obligations as a legal incident of that change.'[47]

After expressing an early preference for the term 'sovereignty' over 'jurisdiction' to exclude belligerent occupation,[48] Bedjaoui proposed a definition that deviated from the text that had been adopted by the Drafting Committee: '"Succession of States" means the replacement of one sovereignty by another with regard to its practical effects on the rights and obligations of each for the territory affected by the change of sovereignty.'[49] Considering that 'it would have been impossible to work out a single definition' valid for both drafts, he explained:

> In turning from succession in respect of treaties to succession in respect of matters other than treaties, one passes from the *fact* of the simple replacement of one

---

[43] ILC, Summary Record of the 1157th Meeting (12 May 1972) ILC Yearbook (1972) vol I, para 32 (Alcívar). See also: ibid, para 4 (Bartoš).

[44] Ibid, para 27 (Yasseen). See also: ILC, 1156th Meeting (n 42) para 42 (Thiam). See further: Gradoni (n 29) 101, 102.

[45] ILC, Summary Record of the 1158th Meeting (11 May 1972) ILC Yearbook (1972) vol I, para 10 (Waldock).

[46] VCSST (n 16) art 2(1)(b); VCSSP (n 17) art 2(1)(a). The definition survived the criticism of the term 'responsibility' as a confusion with 'competence' or 'jurisdiction' – Gradoni (n 29) 104–09.

[47] ILC Yearbook (1972) vol II, 226 (para 30).

[48] ILC, 1158th Meeting (n 45) para 6.

[49] Mohammed Bedjaoui, 'Sixth report on succession in respect of matters other than treaties' (20 May 1973) UN Doc A/CN.4/267 ILC Yearbook (1973) vol II, 9 (draft art 3(1)).

## 22 THE NATURE OF STATE SUCCESSION

State by another in the responsibility for the international relations of a territory to the problem of the concrete content of the rights and obligations transferred *as a result of that fact* to the successor State in the various fields relating to public property, public debts, the status of the inhabitants and so forth. But in so doing, one must not completely lose sight of the original fact of the replacement of sovereignty which occasioned the transfer or exercise of given rights and obligations. This is the very thing which complicates the problems relating to succession of States.[50]

In the plenary debate, multiple members noted that the proposed definition embraced not only 'property' as defined by internal law but also territorial rights in international law (e.g.—the continental shelf).[51] However, several members favoured a single definition for both projects and objected to the term 'sovereignty'.[52]

The debate shows that the decision of the ILC in 1963 to divide the topic of State succession had created difficulty both on substance and draftsmanship. As Bedjaoui observed, the ILC had decided in 1968 that there was no need for a general definition before becoming convinced of the need 'to avoid having several different definitions for one and the same topic. Nevertheless, the mere fact that State succession had been divided into three topics showed that each had its own characteristics, and that might militate in favour of different definitions'.[53] Observing that '[t]he attachment of ... Waldock's topic to the general law of treaties showed the difference between the two topics', he 'noted that the two definitions proposed did not conflict but complemented one another'.[54] After putting the draft article on definitions to one side,[55] the definition that the ILC had agreed for the succession to treaties project was duplicated verbatim for the succession to State property, archives and debts project by the Drafting Committee without explanation.[56]

Adopted in the VCSST[57] and the VCSSP,[58] this definition was reproduced in the 1999 ILC Articles on Nationality of Natural Persons in relation to the Succession of States ('ILC Articles').[59] It has also been followed by the Institut de droit

---

[50] Ibid, 15 (para 4). See also: ILC, 1219th Meeting (4 June 1973) UN Doc. A/CN.4/226, ILC Yearbook (1973) vol I, 87 (para 14, Bedjaoui).

[51] ILC, 1219th Meeting (n 50) 88 (para 29, Reuter).

[52] ILC, 1220th Meeting (5 June 1973) UN Doc A/Cn.4/SR.1220, 91 (para 31, Kearney), 91 (para 34, Ushakov), 92 (para 40, Ago), 93 (para 48, Tsuruoka); ILC, 1221st Meeting (6 June 1973) UN Doc A/CN.4/SR.1221, 94 (para 15, Martínez Moreno), 95–96 (para 33, Quentin-Baxter), 96 (para 39), 97 (para 49, Yasseen),

[53] ILC, 1222nd Meeting (7 June 1973) UN Doc A/CN.4/SR.1222, 99 (para 16, Bedjaoui).

[54] Ibid, 100 (para 17, Bedjaoui).

[55] Ibid, 103 (para 55).

[56] ILC, 1230th Meeting (20 June 1973) UN Doc A/CN.4/SR.1230, 143 (paras 9–10, Yasseen).

[57] VCSST (n 16) art 2(1)(b). See also: Paolo Gaeta and Sâ Benjamin Traoré, 'Article 1' in Distefano et al (n 29) 67–69 (paras 6–9).

[58] VCSSP (n 17) art 2(1)(a).

[59] ILC, Draft Articles on Nationality of Natural Persons in relation to the Succession of States with commentaries, vol II, Part Two, ILC Yearbook (1999) 26 (para 2). Alternative proposals were

THE CONCEPT OF STATE SUCCESSION IN INTERNATIONAL LAW    23

international ('IDI')[60] and the International Law Association ('ILA').[61] While there exists a general consensus insofar as doctrinal scholarship and the opinions of advisory bodies are concerned,[62] this is not the case for State practice: the VCSST has never been applied to a succession,[63] the VCSSP has yet to enter into force, and there are very few examples of the application of the ILC definition.[64]

The formulation proposed by Waldock of 'replacement of one State by another in the sovereignty of territory' was not based on a general theory, such as organic substitution,[65] but rather was a working definition. While the term 'sovereignty' has 'a long and troubled history, and a variety of meanings' in international law, its most common meaning is 'plenary competence ... the totality of powers that States may have in international law'.[66] Variegated meanings have been attributed to it for the law of State succession, such as to deny the existence of general international law to 'bind' decolonized States,[67] to reject rules providing for automatic transfer of legal *obligations* (e.g.—State debt) in the absence of specific consent of the successor[68] or to advance normative arguments for the 'progressive development' of the law to account for the 'economic and social realities' of decolonization.[69]

In formulating the ILC definition, however, the objections to the use of the term were not based on doctrine but rather on political perceptions of decolonization:

The classical doctrine was that succession, in other words, continuity, occurred even in cases of the emancipation of colonies. But since the establishment of the United Nations and the appearance of the phenomenon of decolonization, a new

considered and rejected – ILC, 'Summary record of the 2388th meeting' (24 May 1995) UN Doc A/CN.4/SR.2388, paras 24, 33, 40; ILC, 'Summary record of the 2389th meeting' (24 May 1995) UN Doc A/CN.4/SR.2389, paras 16–18.

[60] Institut de droit international, 'State Succession in Matters of Property and Debts', Seventh Commission, Vancouver Resolution (2001) art 1; Marcelo Kohen and Patrick Dumberry, *The Institute of International Law's Resolution on State Succession and State Responsibility: Introduction, Text and Commentaries* (CUP 2019) art 1(a).

[61] International Law Association Committee: Aspects of the Law of State Succession, Final Report & Resolution, Seventy-Third Conference, Rio de Janeiro (2008) 73 ILA Reports 250, Annex, para 1.

[62] E.g. – Conference on Yugoslavia, Arbitration Commission, Opinion No. 1 (29 November 1991), 92 I.L.R. 162, 165; Alain Pellet, 'Note sur la Commission d'arbitrage de la Conférence européenne pour la paix en Yougoslavie' (1991) 37 AFDI 329, 338.

[63] See Chapter 5.

[64] E.g. – *Arbitral Award of 31 July 1989 (Guinea-Bissau v Senegal)* (Award) Arbitral Tribunal (31 July 1989) 83 ILR 1.

[65] n 7.

[66] James Crawford, *The Creation of States in International Law* (OUP 2006) 32 32. See also: Samantha Besson, 'Sovereignty' MPEPIL (April 2011) paras 1, 150; Jean Bodin, *The Six Books of a Commonweale* (HUP 1962)A15-A-16, 84–113.

[67] E.g. – n 20 (Bedjaoui).

[68] Mohammed Bedjaoui, 'Ninth report on succession of States in respect of matters other than treaties', UN Doc A/CN.4/301 (13 and 20 April 1977) paras 249–50; Mohammed Bedjaoui, 'Problèmes récents de succession d'états dans les États nouveaux' (1970) 130 RdC 457, 468–70.

[69] E.g. – Mohammed Bedjaoui, *Towards a New International Economic Order* (UNESCO 1979) 99; First Bedjaoui Report (n 14) paras 6, 12, 28, 31–32, 38, 43–44, 69, 72–73.

## 24 THE NATURE OF STATE SUCCESSION

doctrine had come into being, according to which States born of decolonization did not automatically assume the rights and obligations of the former colonial Power.

Excepting the case of the former British colonies and possessions, such as India, whose independence had been recognized by an act of internal law providing for devolution of sovereignty, the States which had issued from decolonization considered that they had obtained their independence by their own will and that the consent of the former 'holder' of the territory, which they regarded as a usurper, had no part in the creation of the new State. In the eyes of those States there could be no continuity of sovereignty or, consequently, of rights and obligations, unless they agreed to it.

The Commission was thus faced with a choice: either it must fully support the Special Rapporteur's proposals and adhere to the old 'classical' doctrine dear to certain States, or it must adopt the new revolutionary doctrine, which many States did not accept. The difference was more political than technical.[70]

It is contended that the departure of the ILC from received doctrine was based upon a mischaracterization of the principle of self-determination under the law of the UN Charter and does not reflect State practice showing a succession to entail a transfer of territorial title. Leaving aside the problem that the ILC definition applies not only to 'newly independent States' but also to all other classes of succession in the VCSST and VCSSP,[71] it is not supported by the resolutions of the General Assembly and State practice concerning decolonization.

### (a) The Law of Decolonization

In 1945, the United Nations had created a new international trusteeship system in Chapter XII of the UN Charter for three specified types of territory[72] whose basic objectives included the 'progressive development [of the Trust Territories] towards self-government or independence as may be appropriate to the particular circumstances of each territory and its peoples and the freely expressed wishes of the peoples concerned, and as may be provided by the terms of each trusteeship agreement.'[73] While a right of external self-determination to decide the question of the international status of a Trust Territory was vested in its people, it was to be exercised according to each trusteeship agreement.[74]

---

[70] ILC, 1157th Meeting (n 43) 37–38 (para 2, Bartoš). See also: ILC, 1156th Meeting (n 51) 32 (para 16, Ushakov), 39–40 (para 27, Yaseen) 40 (paras 33–34, Alcívar). For contrary views, see ibid, 37 (para 63, Ago), 41 (para 39, Rossides).

[71] As discussed below, the degree to which decolonization shaped the definition of 'a succession of States' is also shown by the drafting history of the definition of 'a newly independent State'.

[72] Charter of the United Nations, 26 June 1945 (entered into force 24 October 1945) 892 UNTS 119, art 77(1).

[73] Ibid, art 76(b).

[74] UN Charter (n 72) art 76(b); Dietrich Rauschning, 'Article 76' in Bruno Simma et al (eds) *The Charter of the United Nations: A Commentary* (OUP 2012) 1849, 1855–59; Maurice Glele-Ahanhanzo,

In contrast, Chapter XI of the UN Charter ('Declaration regarding Non-Self-Governing Territories') provides, *inter alia*, for a duty of UN Member States with 'responsibilities for the administration of territories whose peoples have not yet attained a full measure of self-government' to 'develop self-government, to take due account of the political aspirations of the peoples, and to assist them in the progressive development of their free political institutions, according to the particular circumstances of each territory and its peoples and their varying stages of development'.[75] A *right* of external self-determination was not expressly vested in the peoples of Non-Self-Governing Territories in 1945, with the United Kingdom and France 'only willing to accept self-government of colonies as an objective—which, depending on the circumstances, did not exclude the possibility of also granting independence'.[76] There was also no agreed method or criteria to designate 'non-self-governing' territories.[77]

In 1953, the UN General Assembly resolved 'that the validity of any form of association between a Non-Self-Governing Territory and a metropolitan or any other country essentially depends on the freely expressed will of the people at the time of the taking of the decision'.[78] It also considered 'that the manner in which [Non-Self-Governing] Territories ... can become fully self-governing is primarily through the attainment of independence, although it is recognized that self-government can also be achieved by association with another State or group of States if this is done freely and on the basis of absolute equality'.[79] It recommended a list of 36 'factors indicative of the attainment of independence or of other separate systems of self-government' to determine the attainment of 'a full measure of self-government' according to the three recognized outcomes of independence, self-government, or free association.[80]

In 1960, the General Assembly adopted the 'Declaration on the Granting of Independence to Colonial Countries and Peoples', in which it welcomed 'the emergence in recent years of a large number of dependent territories into freedom and independence' and recognized 'the increasingly powerful trends towards freedom in such territories which have not yet attained independence'.[81] Proclaiming 'the necessity of bringing [colonialism] to a speedy and unconditional end', it declared, *inter alia*: 'All peoples have the right to self-determination; by virtue of that right

---

'Article 76' in JP Cot and A Pellet (eds) *La Charte des Nations-Unies* vol II (Economica 2005) 1798, 1803–05.

[75] UN Charter (ote 72) art 73(b).
[76] Ulrich Fastenrath, 'Article 73' in Simma (n 74) 1829, 1831; Mohammed Bedjaoui, 'Article 73' in Cot and Pellet (n 74) 1753, 1754–55.
[77] UNGA Res 66 (I) (14 December 1946) preamble.
[78] UNGA Res 742 (VIII) (27 November 1953) para 5.
[79] Ibid, para 6.
[80] Ibid, paras 2, 7–8, annex.
[81] UNGA Res 1514(XV) preamble.

# 26 THE NATURE OF STATE SUCCESSION

they freely determine their political status.'[82] It also declared: 'Immediate steps shall be taken in Trust and Non-Self-Governing Territories or all other territories which had not yet attained independence, to transfer all powers to the peoples of those territories ... in order to enable them to enjoy complete independence and freedom.'[83]

Bearing in mind the list of factors that it had recommended in 1953, the General Assembly also approved 12 guiding principles to determine whether a territory was 'non-self-governing'.[84] Principle VI states: 'A Non-Self-Governing Territory can be said to have reached a full measure of self-government by: (a) emergence as a sovereign independent State; (b) free association with an independent State; or (c) integration with an independent State.' The General Assembly created the Special Committee on Decolonization ('Committee of 24'),[85] which adopted a 'preliminary list' of 60 Non-Self-Governing Territories.[86]

In 1970, the General Assembly adopted the Friendly Relations Declaration, for which 'deep ideological divisions between East and West ... strongly impeded the formulation of the Declaration ... consensus concerning controversial points could often only be achieved by vague and generalizing wording'.[87] It states in relevant part:

> The territory of a colony or other Non-Self-Governing Territory has, under the Charter, a status separate and distinct from the territory of the State administering it; and such separate and distinct status under the Charter shall exist until the people of the colony or Non-Self-Governing Territory have exercised their right of self-determination in accordance with the Charter, and particularly its purposes and principles.[88]

The clause 'separate and distinct' has never been interpreted by an international court or tribunal.[89] However, its linking to the right of self-determination shows that it pertains to the exercise of that right rather than the invalidity of the title of the 'administering' State.[90]

There exists no unitary definition of 'decolonization' in the law of the UN Charter but rather 'each individual case was to be judged [by the General Assembly] according to the respective circumstances'.[91] The interpretation of Chapter XI by the

---

[82] Ibid, para 2.

[83] Ibid, para 5.

[84] UNGA Res 1541(XV) (15 December 1960) preamble, annexe.

[85] UNGA Res 1654 (XVI) (27 November 1961) para 4.

[86] 'Report of the Special Committee on the Situation with regard to the Implementation of the Declaration on the Granding of Independence to Colonial Countries and Peoples' UN Doc A/5446/Rev.1 (30 October 1963) annex I.

[87] Helen Keller, 'Friendly Relations Declaration (1970)' MPEPIL (June 2021) para 3.

[88] UNGA Res 2625 (XXV) UN Doc A/8082 (1970) 121.

[89] E.g. – *Western Sahara (Advisory Opinion)* [1975] ICJ Rep 12, para 58; Keller (n 87) paras 33–35.

[90] Fastenrath (n 76) 1835–36; Bedjaoui (n 76) 1754.

[91] Ibid, 1834–35; Bedjaoui, ibid, 1755.

General Assembly shows that it considered the peoples of designated Non-Self-Governing Territories to have the right of external self-determination to determine their international status by freely choosing amongst three outcomes of autonomy or independence. Whereas Trust Territories were recognized as having an international legal personality distinct from the administering State, the Non-Self-Governing Territories (as opposed to their 'peoples') lacked such personality.[92] Designation as a Non-Self-Governing Territory did not entail a declaration of invalidity of territorial title by an administering State.[93]

In this context, the law of the UN Charter recognizes the right of external self-determination of Trust Territories and Non-Self-Governing Territories.[94] Contrary to the assertions of certain ILC Members, however, the General Assembly did not declare the Charter to have voided the territorial titles held by States to 'colonies' but rather asserted the right of the peoples of territories so designated to freely choose their international status. In recognizing this right, the General Assembly did not define the transition to independence of a Non-Self-Governing Territory as a *factual* event due to the invalidity of territorial title of the metropolitan State.[95]

While the great majority of the successions to have occurred in decolonization were handled between a metropolitan State and a colonial territory, the General Assembly was directly involved in the secession of Libya from Italy in 1951.[96] Not only did it decide that Libya would succeed to a range of legal rights (e.g.—State property) but it made no pronouncement of invalidity of the Italian title to the Colony in deciding that 'Libya ... be constituted an independent and sovereign State'.[97] For example, it decided to retain the international boundaries of the colony that had been delimited by Italy with neighbouring States.[98]

The distinction between the right of external self-determination in the law of decolonization and the validity of the title of the predecessor is also implicit in the *Chagos Islands* advisory proceedings.[99] In answering the first question posed by the General Assembly 'that, having regard to international law, the process of

---

[92] Crawford (n 66) 574, 613–15, 617–19.

[93] E.g. – *Western Sahara Advisory Opinion* (n 89) para 43. See further: Jamie Trinidad, Self-Determination in Disputed Colonial Territories (CUP 2018) 21–69; Malcolm Shaw, International Law (CUP 2021) 92–144.

[94] E.g. – Quincy Wright, Mandates under the League of Nations (University of Chicago 1930) 286–332, 368–435, 445–61; Ralph Wilde, International Territorial Administration (OUP 2008) 99–105, 161–67.

[95] There is no suggestion that the metropolitan States of the 17 Non-Self-Governing Territories today lack title to those territories. On New Caledonia, for example, see: UNGA Special Committee on the Situation with regard to the Implementation of the Declaration on the Granting of Independence to Colonial Countries and Peoples, 'New Caledonia: Working paper prepared by the Secretariat' UN Doc A/AC.109/2023/11 (28 March 2023) paras 1–23.

[96] UNGA Res 387(V) (17 November 1950); UNGA Res 995(X) (14 December 1955).

[97] UNGA Res 289 (IV)(A) (21 November 1949) para 1.

[98] UNGA Res 391 (V) (15 December 1950) para 1(a).

[99] *Legal Consequences of the Separation of the Chagos Archipelago from Mauritius in 1965* (Advisory Opinion of 25 February 2019) [2019] ICJ Rep 95.

## 28 THE NATURE OF STATE SUCCESSION

decolonization of Mauritius was not lawfully completed when that country acceded to independence in 1968',[100] the ICJ advised that the Friendly Relations Declaration, though 'formally a recommendation ... has a declaratory character with regard to the right to self-determination as a customary norm'.[101] Mauritius made no argument that the United Kingdom had lacked title to the Crown Colony of Mauritius and the ICJ noted its 'authority' over the Colony after its cession by France in 1814 in finding that the agreement of the Colony to the detachment of the Chagos Islands 'was not based on the free and genuine expression of the will of the people concerned'.[102]

### (b) State Practice

This interpretation is fortified by the legal positions concerning succession to territorial rights that have since been taken, particularly those of decolonized States that had been designated Non-Self-Governing Territories.[103] On the one hand, rare challenges to the validity of the *legal* title of a State to a colony were not accepted by third States. On the other hand, States have consistently asserted succession to territorial claims made by colonial States without any prior formality (e.g.—a specific declaration of succession) being required. Had metropolitan States lacked title to the colonial territories so that the succession was a 'factual replacement' according to the ILC definition, then the successors would not have asserted succession to the 'titles' of the colonial States.[104]

When Portugal used force to suppress rebellions in its overseas territories of Angola, Mozambique, and Portuguese India, for example, the General Assembly did not condemn it.[105] As Crawford explained:

> It is consistent with the primary emphasis in Article 2 paragraph 4 [of the UN Charter] on prevention of direct military force against the territory of another State. The principle of self-determination does not deprive an administering State of its sovereignty with respect to a self-determination territory, but, rather, requires administration of the territory in furtherance of and in preparation for an act of self-determination. The use of force by a metropolitan power against a self-determination unit is not a use of force against the territorial integrity and

---

[100] Ibid, para 183.

[101] Ibid, para 152.

[102] Ibid, paras 27, 160, 172; 'Written Statement of the Republic of Mauritius' (1 March 2018) vol 1, paras 2.6–2.15; Oral Hearings, CR 2018/20 (3 September 2018) 27, 45–49 (Mauritius).

[103] See Chapter 3.

[104] This notion of the 'clean slate' would thus accord with the 'contractual succession' theory (n 8) to explain how a successor can simultaneously be a factual replacement of the predecessor and yet arrogate territorial claims asserted by a predecessor before the date of succession.

[105] E.g. – UNGA Res 1699 (XVI) (19 December 1961) para 1; UNGA Res 1807 (XVII) (14 December 1962) paras 2–4.

THE CONCEPT OF STATE SUCCESSION IN INTERNATIONAL LAW    29

political independence of a State, though it will be in another manner inconsistent with the purposes of the United Nations.[106]

In 1961, a majority of the Security Council took the view that the use of force by India to occupy Portuguese India was unlawful notwithstanding its argument that Portuguese India was 'historically and legally Indian territory' as 'a colonial question, in the sense that part of [India] is illegally occupied by right of conquest by the Portuguese'.[107] After annexing Portuguese India in 1961[108] and 1962,[109] India nevertheless concluded a succession agreement with Portugal in 1974 in which Portugal 'recognize[d] the full sovereignty of India over these territories with effect from the dates when they became parts of India'.[110] While this formula was ambiguous, the fact that India departed from its initial legal position to conclude a succession agreement entailing a 'recognition' by Portugal means that the better construction is that the parties agreed to a retroactive cession of Portuguese India from the dates of annexation rather than an implicit recognition by Portugal of the original Indian thesis.[111]

When West Pakistan used force to suppress a rebellion in East Pakistan in 1971, the armed intervention of India 'was decisive in effecting the emergence of Bangladesh' as a State with effect from the recognition by Pakistan on 22 February 1974.[112] East Pakistan, which was geographically separate from West Pakistan and predominately inhabited by a people speaking a different language, met several of the 'factors' and 'principles' elaborated by the General Assembly for designation as a 'Non-Self-Governing Territory'.[113] While India described East Pakistan as being 'in reality' a Non-Self-Governing Territory and East Pakistan 'clearly qualified as a non-self-governing territory in 1971 ... it was not designated as such a territory at the time nor treated as one by the General Assembly'.[114] Even India made no suggestion that West Pakistan had lacked title to East Pakistan before its recognition in 1974 with retroactive effect to its declaration of independence in 1971.

---

[106] Crawford (n 92) 137.

[107] Ibid, 138. See further: UNSC 987th Meeting (17 December 1961) SCOR (18 December 1961) paras 37–47 (India); UNSC 988th Meeting (18 December 1961) SCOR (18 December 1961) paras 74, 79–85; *Rights of Passage over Indian Territory (Portugal v India)* (Merits) [1960] ICJ Rep 6, 39.

[108] Dadra and Nagar Haveli Act No 35 1961 <https://www.indiacode.nic.in/bitstream/123456789/1640/2/A1961-35.pdf> accessed 30 December 2023, ss 6–8.

[109] Goa, Daman and Diu (Administration) Act 1962 <https://www.indiacode.nic.in/bitstream/123456789/1369/2/A1962-01.pdf> accessed 30 December 2023, ss 4–5.

[110] Treaty on Recognition of India's Sovereignty over Goa, Daman, Diu, Dadra and Nagar Haveli (adopted 31 December 1974, entered into force 3 June 1975) 982 UNTS 153, art I.

[111] In a case concerning a concession granted by Portugal, the Supreme Court of India stated that 'the territories comprised in Goma, Daman and Diu under the Portuguese rule were annexed by ... India by conquest ... [t]hese territories became a part of India' – *Gosalia v Agarwal and Others*, Supreme Court of India (26 August 1981) 118 ILR 429, 443.

[112] Crawford (n 92) 141.

[113] UNGA Res 742 (n 78); UNGA Res 1541 (n 84).

[114] Ibid, 142, 393.

## 30 THE NATURE OF STATE SUCCESSION

These examples show that the lawfulness of territorial title is distinct from the political legitimacy of its acquisition. While a successor may challenge legitimacy,[115] it may also invoke rights of international law devolving upon it.[116] Apart from the conceptual problems in the ILC definition as a misinterpretation of the law of decolonization with an intrinsic tension between the notion of 'replacement' and the source of the legal rights devolving upon a successor, the definition has not been positively confirmed by the subsequent practice of States (particularly decolonized States) concerning territorial rights. Still less is there any example of a decolonized State asserting a claim for reparation against a metropolitan State on the theory that the metropolitan State had unlawfully extracted natural resources due to its lack of ownership over the territory of the colony.[117]

Not only have successors asserted the status of 'successor-in-interest' or 'successor-in-title' in dispute settlement without any prior declaration but no disputing State has objected to their status. In the Red Sea islands dispute between Eritrea and Yemen, for example, Eritrea based its claim on a 'chain of title' through succession to Ethiopia and Italy.[118] Had Italy lacked title to the Colony of Eritrea due to having been a mere 'holder' of the territory, then Yemen could have argued that no transfer of a territorial claim to the Red Sea Islands to Ethiopia on its acquisition of Eritrea in 1950 could have occurred in law without a specific act of succession to that claim.[119] It might even have alleged that no territorial claim by Ethiopia was admissible in the absence of a specific act of succession by Eritrea because Ethiopia had become a 'colonial power' and 'holder' of Eritrea after it abolished its federal autonomy in 1962.[120] Not only was admissibility not at issue but the Arbitral Tribunal examined the merits of Eritrean claim in detail before concluding that Italy had not established its claim while the legal acts of Ethiopia did 'not indicate whether the islands referred to' were those in dispute.[121]

Consequently, neither the key resolutions and decisions of the UN General Assembly nor the practice of States—in particular, decolonized States—supports

---

[115] E.g. – Constitution of the Socialist Republic of Viet Nam (18 December 1980) <https://vbpl.vn/TW/Pages/vbpq-toanvan.aspx?ItemID=1534> accessed 16 February 2024 (Vietnamese) preamble. On the territorial claims of Viet Nam in succession to South Viet Nam and France, see Chapter 3.

[116] For example, the English version of the succession agreement on Hong Kong refers to its 'handing over' while the Chinese version describes its 'return' – Joint Declaration on the Question of Hong Kong (China-United Kingdom) (19 December 1984) 1399 UNTS 33, paras 1–2; Trinidad (n 93) 110. The agreement on Walvis Bay states its 'incorporation/reintegration' into Namibia – Agreement with respect to Walvis Bay (Namibia-South Africa) (adopted 28 February 1994, entered into force 1 March 1994) 2548 UNTS 17, art 2.

[117] E.g. – *Certain Phosphate Lands in Nauru (Nauru v Australia)* (Preliminary Objections) [1992] ICJ Rep 240, Memorial of Nauru vol 1 (April 1990) para 419. See further: Christopher Weeramantry, *Nauru: Environmental Damage under International Trusteeship* (OUP 1992) 77–153, 320–22.

[118] *Territorial Sovereignty (Eritrea v Yemen)* (Award) Permanent Court of Arbitration (9 October 1998) XXII RIAA 211, paras 13, 91.

[119] UNGA Res 390 (V)(A) (2 December 1950) para 1. See also: UNGA Res 530 (VI) (29 January 1952).

[120] Raymond Goy, 'L'indépendance de l'Érythrée' (1993) 39 AFDI 337, 341.

[121] *Eritrea v Yemen* (n 118) paras 149–99, 448, 450.

the 'revolutionary' doctrine advanced by certain ILC Members that 'colonial' States (however defined) did not possess title to the territories that became independent through decolonization. It has since come to be widely accepted that the most significant cause of the lack of application of the VCSST and VCSSP was their treatment of decolonization. In 1999, the anglophone section of the Hague Academy of International Law observed that the VCSST had an 'apparently obsessive focus on decolonization'[122] while the francophone section concluded that State succession and its typology, including a definition of 'newly independent State', was intrinsically a 'political phenomenon' rather than a neutral exercise.[123]

## 2.2.2 A Transfer of Territorial Title

Whereas the rules governing the transfer of rights and obligations arising from a succession of States form a discrete field of general international law, the definition of a succession is connected to the international law of territory.[124] This concerns the acquisition by a State of the international rights of jurisdiction and ownership to land, sea, air, or space.[125] Though primarily a question of relations between States, it also concerns other international legal persons in myriad contexts, such as territorial jurisdiction or concessions for the exploitation of natural resources.[126] In the international law of territory, territorial title is the 'preferred' term to refer generally 'to the acts or facts that constitute the legal foundation for the establishment of a right over territory ... the source of a right or competence over territory'.[127]

A private law analogy,[128] territorial title encompasses both authority or jurisdiction (*imperium*) and profit or use (*dominium*).[129] Excepting rare cases such as *condominia*,[130] territorial title is vested in a single State to the exclusion of others. Although the utility of the analogy is limited,[131] it denotes the concept of transferability ('alienability') of 'real' rights and obligations independent of an underlying agreement of transfer (e.g.—a 'territorial treaty').[132]

---

[122] Martti Koskenniemi, 'Report of the Director of Studies of the English-speaking Section of the Centre' in Pierre Eisemann and Martti Koskenniemi (eds) *State Succession: Codification Tested against the Facts* (Martinus Nijhoff 2000) 65, 71–72.

[123] Pierre Michel Eisemann, 'Rapport du directeur d'études de la section de langue française du Centre' in Eisemann and Koskenniemi (n 122) 1, 33. On the notion of succession as a factual event without necessarily generating legal effects, see: Stern (n 10) 89–98.

[124] Shaw (n 93) 418. See, however: ibid, 834, 836.

[125] Ibid, 420.

[126] Ibid.

[127] MG Kohen and Mamadou Hébié, 'Territory, Acquisition' MPEPIL (November 2021) para 3.

[128] Hersch Lauterpacht, *Private Law Sources and Analogies of International Law* (Longman, Green and Co., 1927) 125–43.

[129] See Chapter 3.

[130] n 231.

[131] Crawford (n 92) 717.

[132] n 45. See further Chapter 3.

## 32  THE NATURE OF STATE SUCCESSION

The modes of acquisition of territory by a State are traditionally divided into 'original title' for territories belonging to no State and 'derivative title' for territories already belonging to another State.[133] For derivative title, the 'validity of the transfer will depend on whether the previous sovereign possessed a lawful title over the territory purportedly ceded.'[134] While the variegated meanings that have been attributed to the term 'sovereignty' have tended to confuse and to polarize doctrinal debate,[135] the term 'territorial sovereignty'[136] can be equated to the preferred term of territorial title to denote the territorial rights of jurisdiction and ownership of States in international law.[137] In defining State succession according to the traditional doctrine of a transfer of territorial title, two complexities arise: (1) the notion of 'transfer'; and (2) the limited sense of 'title' when the territorial rights of a predecessor are not 'plenary'.

### (a)  The Notion of 'Transfer'

A transfer of title can occur in various ways.[138] State practice and doctrine agree that it excludes an abandonment of a territorial claim in favour of another,[139] a settlement of a territorial dispute,[140] a restitution of occupied territory,[141] a border delimitation,[142] and an adjustment of an existing border.[143] Although the verb 'to transfer' can be construed to imply a *conveyance* of title by the predecessor akin to the ownership of land in internal law, there is no evidence in State practice of any formality requirement.[144]

Even as predecessors and successors have effected a succession by means of a treaty or statute,[145] there have been many examples of successions realized by a

---

[133]  Kohen and Hébié (n 127) para 7.

[134]  Ibid, para 8.

[135]  On the 'new mythology about State succession' of 'a Third World practice ... opposed to succession' in contrast to 'older, established States [that] are conservative and hence in favour of succession', see: DP O'Connell, 'Reflections on the State Succession Convention' (1979) 39 ZaöRV 725, 726.

[136]  E.g. – Zemanke (n 28). See also: ILC, 1156th Meeting (n 51) 36 (para 42, Thiam) 36 (para 63, Ago).

[137]  E.g. – Shaw (n 93) 419. See also: Malcolm Shaw, Title to Territory in Africa (OUP 1986) 11–26.

[138]  ILC Draft articles on Succession of States in respect of State Property, Archives and Debts with commentaries 1981, ILC Yearbook (1981) vol II, Part Two 20, para 4; *United Nations Conference on Succession of States in respect of State Property, Archives and Debts: Official Records* UN Doc A/CONF.117/16 vol II, paras 51–54.

[139]  E.g. – Treaty of Peace and Amity (France–Netherlands) (11 April 1713) 28 CTS 37, arts VII, IX, XI, XXIII.

[140]  E.g. – *Maritime Delimitation in the Caribbean Sea and the Pacific Ocean (Costa Rica v Nicaragua) and Land Boundary in the Northern Part of the Isla Portillos (Costa Rica v Nicaragua)* (Judgment) [2018] ICJ Rep 139, para 59.

[141]  E.g. – Convention between Austria, Great Britain, Prussia and Russia, and France (9 October 1818) 69 CTS 283, arts I–IV (French).

[142]  E.g. – Maritime Delimitation (Egypt–Saudi Arabia) (adopted 8 April 2016, entered into force 2 July 2017) UNTS I-5477, art I.

[143]  E.g. – Treaty for the Adjustment of the Border (Belgium–Netherlands) (adopted 28 November 2016, entered into force 1 January 2018) UNTS I-55014, arts 1–3.

[144]  Shaw (n 93) 417–18.

[145]  E.g. – British North America Act 1949, 153 BFSP 130, ss 1–2, sch ('Terms of Union of Newfoundland with Canada'); Agreement proclaiming the Republic of Yemen (North

THE CONCEPT OF STATE SUCCESSION IN INTERNATIONAL LAW    33

simple act of recognition or without formality.[146] Notwithstanding that the dismemberment of the Socialist Federal Republic of Yugoslavia ('SFRY') was achieved by a variety of legal acts from the declarations of independence of Croatia and Slovenia on 25 June 1991[147] to the declaration of succession of the Federal Republic of Yugoslavia ('FRY') on 27 October 2000 with retroactive effect to 27 April 1992,[148] the successors received title to their respective territories without any formal act of transfer.[149] Consequently, a transfer of territorial title is an objective question of substance rather than a subjective one of form.

The term 'cession' has a dual meaning in international law.[150] In the law of territory, it signifies a transfer of a territorial unit from one State to another as an acquisition of derivative title.[151] This pertains to the *source* of the title of the successor. As all classes of succession entail a transfer of title, they come collectively within the meaning of 'cession' for the law of territory because a successor acquires derivative rather than original title.[152] In the law of succession, it also has a narrower meaning as a transfer by one existing State of title to a part of its territory to another existing State, such as the retrocession of Macao by Portugal to China in 1999.[153] In this respect, it refers to one of the classes of succession for which reason the verb 'to transfer' is used instead of 'to cede' in the definition of State succession.

## (b) Jurisdiction and Ownership

In general, a predecessor transfers 'plenary' title that is comprehensive, exclusive and perpetual: international law vests a State with authority to regulate, use and

---

Yemen–South Yemen) (adopted 22 April 1990, entered into force 22 May 1990) 2373 UNTS 131; Treaty on the Establishment of German Unity (Federal Republic of Germany–German Democratic Republic) (adopted 30 August 1990, entered into force 3 October 1990) 30 ILM 463, art 1; Czechia Constitutional Act No 542/1992 Zákony Prolidi Coll (25 November 1992) arts 1–2, 6, 8 (Czecho-Slovak).

[146] On the 'old Dominions', see: Crawford (n 92) 358–66; O'Connell (n 30) vol I, 36–57; PJN Baker, *The Present Juridical Status of the British Dominions in International Law* (Longmans, Green & Co 1929) 35–63, 130–212, 250–57, 343–72.

[147] Daniel Bethlehem and Marc Weller, *The Yugoslav Crisis* (Cambridge University Press 1997) xxvii–xxx.

[148] Daniel Bethlehem and Marc Weller, *The Yugoslav Crisis* (1997) xxvii–xxx.

[149] For example, the successors accepted the legal presumption of automatic succession to the international borders of the SFRY delimiting their respective territories. On Trieste, for example, see: Delimitation Treaty (Italy–SFRY) (adopted 10 November 1975, entered into force 3 April 1977) 1466 UNTS 25, arts 1–2. See also: *Gulf of Piran Arbitration (Croatia v Slovenia)* (Final Award) Permanent Court of Arbitration Case No 2012-04 (29 June 2017) paras 9, 685.

[150] Oliver Dörr, 'Cession', *Max Planck Encyclopaedia of Public International Law* (April 2006) para 1.

[151] Shaw (n 93) 423.

[152] On the theoretical connection made by Hyde and Jennings between the law of territory and the law of succession, see, e.g. – JG Starke, 'The Acquisition of Title to Territory by Newly Emerged States' (1965–66) 41 BYIL 411.

[153] Joint Declaration on Macao (Portugal–China) (adopted 13 April 1987, entered into force 15 January 1988) 1498 UNTS 228, art 1; Protocol, Treaty, Convention and Agreement (Portugal–China) (26 March 1887) 78 BFSP 521, art II. Though not stated in the Joint Declaration, it has been suggested that Portugal agreed in 1987 to the thesis of China that it lacked plenary title to Macao – Trinidad (n 93) 119–20. If so, then the case was one of 'administrative cession' of a lease.

34  THE NATURE OF STATE SUCCESSION

profit from its territory to the exclusion of other States.[154] In 'special cases',[155] a State lacks general title to a territory that it administers:

1. leases;
2. Mandatory and Trust Territories;
3. protected States; and
4. international protectorates.

While the scope of legal authority exercised by the administering State over the territory varies according to the specific arrangement, they share the common feature that its authority is limited rather than plenary. According to the general principle of law whereby a State may transfer no more rights than it possess,[156] a succession to a limited title entails the transfer of the territorial rights of the predecessor without prejudice to those of another State.[157]

Although a transfer of general title encompasses not only rights of jurisdiction but also ownership of territory, a 'clear distinction must be maintained between the acquisition of private rights over a given territory and the acquisition of sovereignty over that territory ... [which] does not prejudice the ownership rights that individuals or even States may possess in the same territory'.[158] The concept of territorial ownership has evolved into the principle of permanent sovereignty over natural resources, which 'embodies the right of States and peoples to freely dispose of their natural resources'.[159] While this principle was advanced by some proponents during decolonization as 'a legal shield against infringements of their economic sovereignty as a result of property rights or contractual rights claimed by other States or foreign companies',[160] its meaning in the definition of State succession refers to the economic rights of use and profit with respect to the territory as a whole rather than specific assets therein.[161]

In proposing that the ILC take up the question of State succession and acquired rights in his second report, Mohammed Bedjaoui changed his position to assert that 'there is not a *transfer* of one sovereignty, but a *substitution* of sovereignties by the extinction of one and the creation of another'.[162] This contention was made on the basis of a 'relationship between the two ideas of a transfer of sovereignty and the imposition of an international obligation on the successor State' in order

---

[154] Kohen and Hébié (n 127) para 5.
[155] First Waldock Report (n 41).
[156] Kohen and Hébié (n 127) para 8.
[157] E.g. – Trusteeship Agreement for the Former Japanese Mandated Islands (2 April 1947) 8 UNTS 189, art 3.
[158] Kohen and Hébié (n 127) para 2.
[159] Nico Schrijver, 'Permanent Sovereignty over Natural Resources' MPEPIL (June 2008)para 2.
[160] Ibid, para 1.
[161] See Chapter 10.
[162] Second Bedjaoui Report (n 22) para 29.

to refute the notion that a successor assumes 'a *derived* obligation imposed upon it by the will of the predecessor'.[163] Made for the purpose of denying an obligation to respect private property rather than territorial rights of ownership,[164] the hypothesis conflated the discrete questions of defining State succession as a transfer of *territorial* rights and the *other* rights and obligations resulting from that transfer.

State practice on succession illustrates this distinction between the transfer of territorial rights of ownership to the successor and the consequential question of a legal obligation to respect private property acquired before the succession. When the Colony of Belgian Congo seceded from Belgium in 1960 as the Democratic Republic of the Congo ('DRC') under a constitution elaborated at the Round Table Conference, it received the right to determine, *inter alia*, the granting of concessions and leases on the land, mines, minerals, mineral oils, water resources, forests, and other public property.[165] In a dispute with three Belgian charter companies concerning the existence of a duty to respect concessions granted by the Colony in the vital minerals sector, the DRC accepted that it had 'taken over' the rights of use and profit from Belgium in arguing that the charter companies had been public companies of the Belgian State rather than private companies.[166] Though denying the validity of the titles granted by the Congo Free State,[167] the DRC accepted and claimed the rights of ownership of the Belgian State after the creation of the Colony in 1908.

## 2.3 A General Law of State Succession

While 'a common fault of writers is to classify issues primarily as "succession" and consequently to consider particular issues in isolation from the matrix of rules governing the subject-matter ... for example, the law of treaties',[168] doctrine traditionally regarded the law of State succession as an integral area of law.[169] In his *magnum opus* published in the months preceding the commencement of the ILC projects, O'Connell saw the existence of a 'body of law known as "State succession"' to be so evident that he did not consider it to be necessary to justify its unitary character.[170]

---

[163] Ibid, paras 19, 25–26, 33, 35.

[164] ILC 960th Meeting, UN Doc A/CN.4/204 (24 June 1968) para 22 (Bedjaoui).

[165] Basic Law of the Congo (19 May 1960) in TM Franck, John Carey and LM Tondel, *Legal Aspects of the United Nations Action in the Congo* (Oceana Publications, 1963) 108–16 (arts 2, 189, 263); Constitution of the Congo (Leopoldville) (30 May 1964) in AJ Peaslee and DX Peaslee, *Constitutions of Nations* (Martinus Hijhoff 1965) art 195.

[166] Congo Decree cancelling Belgian companies' rights to grant mining concessions (29 November 1954) (1965) 4(2) ILM 232, Explanatory Statement (paras 9, 11–13).

[167] Ibid, para 6.

[168] James Crawford, *Brownlie's Principles of Public International Law* (OUP 2012) 438–39.

[169] E.g. – RWG de Muralt, *The Problem of State Succession with regard to Treaties* (vam Stockum 1954) 13–19; Feilchenfeld (n 21) 1–11.

[170] O'Connell (n 30) vol I, 3.

36 THE NATURE OF STATE SUCCESSION

Rejecting 'a universal touchstone of succession or non-succession', he neverthe-less espoused a general 'presumption of continuity which concrete analysis may rebut ... in relation to specific issues.'[171]

The ILC departed from this doctrinal assumption of a holistic body of general international law. From the outset, Waldock had proposed to approach the question of succession 'from the point of view of the law of treaties ... as a sequel to the draft articles on the law of treaties rather than as one section of a single comprehensive codification of the several branches of the law application to succession of States.'[172] This was because 'the diversity in the actual practice is in itself a legal phenomenon which can hardly be disregarded or subordinated to a particular theory of succession in order to achieve ... formulation of the rules governing succession in respect of treaties.'[173] While Bedjaoui did not expressly address the question, he implicitly considered succession to State property, archives, and debts to be a branch of a wider law of succession.[174]

Having divided the original topic of State succession into two projects for reasons of expediency, the received doctrine was also challenged in the course of debate on the definition. Some members opined, for example, that the two projects should be kept separate because 'any action ... to integrate the two aspects of succession, namely, treaties and matters other than treaties, such as credits, debits and contracts ... would cause complete confusion.'[175] Starting from its decision to discard the definition of 'succession of States' proposed by Bedjaoui, the ILC nevertheless charted a course of drafting consistency between the two texts for substantive concepts that were considered to be common to both:

- the definitions of 'predecessor State' and 'successor State';
- the definition of the 'date of succession'; and
- the requirement of 'a succession of States occurring in conformity with international law and, in particular, with the principles of international law embodied in the Charter of the United Nations.'[176]

The ILC also pursued consistency in the development of a common system of classification of successions. Though adopted principally for drafting reasons, the ILC acknowledged the common nature of these substantive questions arising out of

---

[171] Ibid, 35.

[172] First Waldock Report (n 41) 89, paras 10–11.

[173] Ibid, para 10.

[174] First Bedjaoui Report (n 14) para 22; Second Bedjaoui Report (n 22) para 3; ILC 960th Meeting (n 164) para 27 (Bedjaoui).

[175] ILC 1158th Meeting (n 45) para 37 (Nagendra Singh).

[176] ILC 'Draft articles on Succession of States in respect of Treaties with commentaries' (1974) ILC Yearbook vol II, part I 174, 175 (draft art 2), 181 (draft art 6); ILC Draft articles on Succession of States in respect of State Property and Debt (n 138) 21 (draft art 2), 22 (draft art 3).

State practice showing a succession of States to be a singular event with consequences for various fields of activity.

### 2.3.1 The Prohibition of Conquest

The prohibition of the acquisition of territory by conquest is implicit in the general prohibition of the use of force in Article 2(4) of the UN Charter and customary international law.[177] This rule has been claimed to be a peremptory norm of general international law.[178] As accurately expressed in the VCSST and VCSSP,[179] the effect of the prohibition of conquest is to deny its application of the law of State succession to an unlawful annexation of territory.[180] An annexation is composed of three elements: (1) a use of force; (2) effective control over the occupied territory; and (3) intention to permanently incorporate the territory.[181]

While this rule can be conceived to be a corollary of the definition of State succession, the better view is that the unlawfulness of an annexation denies legal effect according to the general principle of law *ex injuria jus non oritur*.[182] Though a treaty concluded under State coercion is void,[183] State practice shows that an agreement freely concluded by an occupied State to cede the occupied territory can effect a succession with retroactive effect to the date of annexation.[184] Otherwise, the law of belligerent occupation applies to the occupied territory instead of the law of State succession (e.g.—for private property rights).

### 2.3.2 The Question of Legal Personality

While there exists no conclusive legal definition of Statehood,[185] the classical attributes of a State are an independent government with a populated territory.[186]

---

[177] UN Charter (n 72) art 2(4). See further: Sharon Korman, *The Right of Conquest* (Clarendon Press 1996); Dire Tladi, 'Third report on peremptory norms of general international law (jus cogens)' (12 February 2018) UN Doc A/CN.4/714, paras 103–11.

[178] Dire Tladi, 'Fifth report on peremptory norms of general international law (*jus cogens*)' (24 January 2022) UN Doc A/CN.4/747, paras 215–25. See also: *East Timor (Portugal v Australia)* (Judgment) [1995] ICJ Rep 90, 94–95, 98, 99.

[179] VCSST (n 16) art 6; VCSSP (n 17) art 3.

[180] E.g. – Lauri Mälksoo, Illegal Annexation and State Continuity (BRILL 2022).

[181] E.g. – Hersch Lauterpacht (ed.) *Oppenheim's International Law* (OUP 1948) vol I, 519; Korman (n 177) 98–99.

[182] E.g. – Patrick Dumberry, *A Guide to State Succession in International Investment Law* (Elgar 2018) 201, 240–41.

[183] Vienna Convention on the Law of Treaties, 23 May 1969 (entered into force 27 January 1980) 1155 UNTS 331 ('VCLT') art 31(3)(c) art 52. See also: Olivier Corten, 'Article 52 1969 Vienna Convention' in Corten and Klein (n 309) 1217, 1217–20.

[184] On Portuguese India, for example, see: n 111.

[185] Crawford (n 92) 31, 37.

[186] Ibid, 45–95.

38   THE NATURE OF STATE SUCCESSION

These characteristics, though common to all States, are loose: where formal and actual independence diverge, for example, factors such as the presence of widespread recognition by the international community of States can be decisive.[187] The relationship between the question of legal personality and State succession was explained by James Crawford:

> There is then a clear distinction in principle between the legal personality of the State and its government for the time being. This serves to distinguish in turn the field of State personality (which includes the topics of identity and continuity of States) and that of State succession. State succession depends upon the conclusion reached as to State personality ... Views taken of particular State succession situations may illuminate related problems of personality. In some areas, at least, the principles and policy considerations involved are similar ... Nonetheless the concepts of continuity and succession remain distinct, and blurring them serves no useful goal.[188]

As territory is one of the attributes of a State, for example, the extinction of a State necessarily prompts the question of succession to its territorial title even as a succession can occur (e.g.—cession) that does not entail a creation or termination of legal personality.

The answer to the preceding question of legal personality determines the class of the succession. When a predecessor continues to exist, a 'partial succession' arises whereby it transfers title to a unit of its territory to the successor. When a predecessor becomes extinct, a 'total succession' occurs through which title to the entirety of its territory is transferred to one or more successors. This distinction is critical, not only to enable comparison of like cases of State practice with like in order to accurately identify the general rules of State succession but also to determine the States, rights, and obligations that are involved in a particular case.

An example of misclassification is the case of British India. When India and Pakistan became independent in 1947, the question arose as to the nature of that event due to the membership of 'India'[189] in the League of Nations. The relevant legislation provided for the sole 'devolution' to India of the rights and obligations of British India only insofar as membership in international organizations was concerned.[190] In the admission process to UN membership, the Secretariat issued a legal opinion in which it considered 'the existing State of India [to have] become

---

[187]  Ibid, 88–89.

[188]  Ibid, 35–36. See also: Krystyna Marek, *Identity and Continuity of States in International Law* (Droz 1968) 9–10; O'Connell (n 30) 5; Lauri Mälksoo, 'International Law and the 2020 Amendments to the Russian Constitution' (2021) 115(1) AJIL 78, 83–84.

[189]  Government of India Act 1935 26 Geo 5 ch 2, s 311(1); White Paper on Indian States (Government of India, July 1948) 3 (paras 2–3) 169 (app VIII) 173 (app IX) 274–82.

[190]  Indian Independence (International Arrangements) Order 1947 3 CILC 144, arts 2(b), 3.

a Dominion' with 'no change in [its] international status' as 'an original member state' so that 'the situation is one in which a part of an existing state breaks off and becomes a new state'; consequently, Pakistan 'would have to apply for admission' for membership.[191]

While the opinion was controversial in the Security Council and the General Assembly, India was accredited as an original member and Pakistan was admitted as a new member.[192] However, it failed to acknowledge the fact that membership in the League of Nations had been open not only to a State but also to a 'Dominion or Colony'.[193] While British India was a Member of the League of Nations, it was not a Dominion but 'in all respects subordinate to the British Cabinet and Parliament' and was a 'part of another State accorded by membership in a political international organization a distinct status for essentially political reasons'.[194]

As the premise of the opinion that British India had been 'an existing State' was wrong, so too was its classification of the situation as a secession of Pakistan from British India 'analogous to the separation of the Irish Free State from Great Britain, and of Belgium from the Netherlands'.[195] Rather, the case was a rare example of the simultaneous secessions of two new States that had belonged to a single territorial unit of the predecessor.[196] The ILC has nevertheless followed the legal opinion of the Secretariat, which has resulted in the misclassification of the case in its codification projects.[197]

While customary international law provides no fixed criteria for legal identity and continuity,[198] a test of independence has been advanced that is difficult to apply in practice due to the complexities of formal versus actual independence.[199] A protected State, for example, remains 'independent' in spite of the considerable control frequently exercised by the protecting State.[200] The voluntariness of a termination of Statehood, as opposed to the presence of an unlawful threat or use of force,[201] is a critical factor.

---

[191] O'Connell (n 30) vol II, 184–85.

[192] Ibid, 186–87.

[193] Covenant of the League of Nations (28 June 1919) 108 LNTS 188, art 1(2).

[194] Crawford (n 92) 366–67.

[195] O'Connell (n 30) vol II, 184.

[196] MM Whiteman, *Digest of International Law* vol II (Government Printing Office 1964) 800–01; DP O'Connell, 'The British Commonwealth and State Succession after the Second World War' (1949) 26 BYIL 454, 455–56.

[197] ILC Draft Articles on Succession of States in respect of Treaties (n 176) 178 (para 2), 200 (para 15), 234 (para 5), 242 (para 4), 264 (para 17), 266 (para 27); ILC Draft Articles on Succession of States in respect of State Property and Debt (n 138) 41 (para 20), 45 (para 5), 46 (para 12), 94–95 (para 15); Václav Šturma, 'Third Report on Succession of States in respect of State Responsibility' UN Doc A/CN.4/731 (2 May 2019) para 55. The case was not examined in the project on nationality of natural persons.

[198] O'Connell (n 30) vol II, 7–9, 700–01, 715–17.

[199] Ibid, 62–89, 161–89.

[200] Marek (n 188) 180 (n 3); Crawford (n 92) 88.

[201] Mohammed Bedjaoui, 'Fourth report on succession in respect of matters other than treaties' (2 and 19 April 1971) ILC Yearbook (1971) vol II, Part One 160, 162–67.

## 40 THE NATURE OF STATE SUCCESSION

The most fraught and complex cases have featured the alleged presence of an unlawful use of force in a contested case of State continuity. For example, recognition of one entity claiming to continue the identity of the predecessor impacts upon the validity of the claims to secession from that State of another entity due to the customary rule requiring the consent of the parent State to effect a secession. In the absence of determinative criteria and machinery, a contested case of State continuity (e.g.—the claim of the FRY between 27 April 1992 and 27 October 2000 to continue the personality of the SFRY[202]) impacts upon a succession, such as jurisdictional objections connected to the temporal existence of the disputing parties.[203]

### 2.3.3 The Date of Succession

The date of succession is the date on which the transfer of territorial title takes place, as designated by the parties to the succession.[204] Unless they adopt a different date for the purposes of a particular succession matter, such as a treaty[205] or an asset,[206] the default date of succession applies in general. It is a critical issue affecting various matters, such as the valuation of assets or the application of a treaty the day before the succession.[207]

In the *Bosnia Genocide Case*, for example, the seventh preliminary objection was that the Applicant's notification of succession to the 1948 Genocide Convention, dated 29 December 1992, was 'not ... operative between the parties prior to 29 December 1992' so that 'the Applicant's claims pertaining to the alleged acts or facts which occurred prior to 29 December 1992 [did] not fall within the jurisdiction of the Court'.[208] The ICJ found it to be unnecessary to decide whether Bosnia had automatically succeeded from its independence on 6 March 1992 but held that its notification of succession provided the Court with jurisdiction *ratione temporis* over the dispute from the beginning of the armed conflict in Bosnia because the terms of the Convention permitted such retroactive effect.[209] Had the objection been upheld, then most of the claims would have been temporally inadmissible.[210]

---

[202] Crawford (n 92) 707–14.

[203] E.g. – *Croatia Genocide Case* (n 327) paras 57–91, 120–29.

[204] E.g. – Arthur Watts, 'State Succession: Some Recent Practical Legal Problems' in Volkmar Götz, Peter Selmer, and Rüdiger Wolfrum (eds) *Liber amicorum Günther Jaenicke* (Springer 1998) 397, 411.

[205] E.g. – IAEA, Convention on Nuclear Material, Status List (21 September 2020) note 1.

[206] E.g. – Agreement on Succession Issues (n 33) annex B (arts 3–4), appendix. See further Watts (n 204).

[207] E.g. – 'Succession of States in respect of bilateral treaties: study prepared by the Secretariat', UN Doc A/CN.4/229 (28 May 1970) paras 94–96.

[208] *Convention on the Prevention and Punishment of the Crime of Genocide (Bosnia and Herzegovina v Yugoslavia)* (Preliminary Objections) [1996] ICJ Rep 595, paras 1, 7.

[209] Ibid, paras 20, 23, 34, 47.

[210] *Convention on the Prevention and Punishment of the Crime of Genocide (Bosnia and Herzegovina v Yugoslavia)* (Merits) [2007] ICJ Rep 43, paras 246, 250, 252–75.

The ILC adopted a definition of 'the date upon which the successor State replaced the predecessor State in the responsibility for the international relations of the territory to which the succession of States relates'.[211] Allowing for the difference in this definition according to the aforementioned concept of transfer of territorial title, it reflects customary international law. In State practice, the notion of a single date that determines the temporal point of transfer from a predecessor to a successor is widespread.

The date of succession is a question of fact to be identified with reference to the agreement of the parties,[212] whether expressed in a verbal agreement[213] or implied by their conduct. Negotiated successions offer the advantage of flexibility in date selection: for example, a different date may be used for a particular asset[214] or treaty.[215] For successions occurring in chaotic circumstances, the determination of the date of succession can be a key factual issue in dispute settlement.[216]

### 2.3.4 The Provisional Continuity of Internal Law

Prior to the ILC codification projects, the question of the effect of a succession on legislation in force in the transferred territory was a matter of doctrinal interest.[217] In his first report, Mohammed Bedjaoui observed:

> The free formulation of municipal law is the unmistakable mark of a country's internal sovereignty. Thus, just as the demands of economic sovereignty impose non-succession, those of political sovereignty, which are here brought into play, call for a break with the former juridical order. But in this sphere, even more than in others, there is a wide divergence between principle and practice.
>
> ...
>
> It may be said that the principle of non-succession to the municipal law of the predecessor State is incontestable, but that in practice the principle of continuity remains in force for a period whose duration varies according to the country, the

---

[211] VCSST (n 16) art 2(1)(e). See further: Gradoni (n 29) 105–06.

[212] E.g. – Malcolm Shaw, 'State Succession Revisited' (1994) 5 FYBIL 34, 59–60.

[213] E.g. – Proclamation of Philippine Independence (4 July 1946) 146 BFSP 899; Treaty of General Relations (Philippines–United States) (adopted 4 July 1946, entered into force 22 October 1946) 7 UNTS 3, art I.

[214] E.g. – Financial Agreement (Pakistan–India) (adopted 12 June 1955, entered into force 4 October 1955) 228 UNTS 211.

[215] E.g. – ILC, 'Succession of States to multilateral treaties; seventh study prepared by the Secretariat', UN Doc A/CN.4/225 (24 April 1970) ILC Yearbook (1970) vol II, para 72.

[216] E.g. – 'International Conference on the former Yugoslavia Arbitration Commission – Opinion No. 11' in BG Ramcharan (ed), *The International Conference on the Former Yugoslavia: Official Papers* (Kluwer 1997) vol 2, 1290–93.

[217] E.g. – O'Connell (n 30) vol 1, 10141.

## 42 THE NATURE OF STATE SUCCESSION

era and the sectors of juridical life involved. This comment seems applicable both to traditional State succession and to that arising from decolonization.

...

However extensive and general continuity in the matter of legislation may be in practice, it does not affect the undisputed principle of non-succession ... [i]f, having regard to the widespread practice of succession in this sphere, the International Law Commission were to sanction it by deciding that a rule of continuity truly exists, that action would deprive the successor State of the right to amend or revoke inherited legislation.[218]

In assuming a rule of succession to be automatic and definitive, this conclusion overlooked the possibility of a presumption that can be displaced by a successor through legislative action. In positing that the practice of 'succession' to legislation was widespread but excluding the topic from further study, it did not acknowledge the potential for nuance in the treatment of legislation by successors.

At a basic level, the assertion that successors have widely retained the legislation of the predecessor in force in the transferred territory was correct. Such examples were widespread and consistent in the nineteenth[219] and twentieth[220] centuries. It is suggested that State practice in the form of constitutional provisions and other legislation is coherent and consistent to support the existence of a general principle of law 'common to the various legal systems of the world'.[221] A critical feature of the practice is that it is essentially 'internal' in addressing the status of national legislation, albeit with implications for international rights and obligations (e.g.—administrative debt). As the principle has functioned on the national plane, its proposed status as a general principle of law rather than customary international law has less to do with its operation as a rule (e.g.—the inapplicability of persistent objection) than the character of the State practice (i.e.—national legislation and jurisprudence) underpinning it.

According to this general principle, the laws[222] of the predecessor applied to the transferred territory at the date of succession are automatically preserved in force by the successor until amended or repealed, which can be done expressly[223] or implicitly.[224] While successors have expressly addressed legislation in most cases, the

---

[218] First Bedjaoui Report (n 14) paras 105–06, 113. See also Dumberry (n 182) 8.

[219] See, e.g. – Moore (n 12).

[220] E.g. – RR Ludwickowski, 'Constitution Making in the Countries of Former Soviet Dominance: Current Development' (1993) 23(2) GJICL 155, 167–90.

[221] Note 352.

[222] The meaning of 'laws' is determined by the successor; e.g. – *Shri Shubhlaxmi Mills Ltd. v India and Another*, Supreme Court of India (2 September 1966) 4 CILC 459. For example, it can include judicial precedent – *Lufazema v Malawi*, Malawi Supreme Court of Appeal (12 June 1967) ALR Mal 415, 417–18.

[223] E.g. – Walvis Bay and Offshore Islands Act No 1 1994, 28 Government Gazette (28 February 1994).

[224] For example, French laws were retained by Algeria unless contrary to national sovereignty, discriminatory, or colonialist – Law No 62-157, 2 Journel officiel (11 January 1963) (French). Whether the applicable legislation on independence enacted by the predecessor or successor intended to repeal the

general principle can find application when a law is overlooked[225] or a successor is unable to address it for logistical, political, or other reasons.[226]

This issue is particularly important in the field of nationality, which is principally regulated by the nationality laws of the States concerned with general rules of international law applying in default.[227] In acceding to independence on 14 May 1948, for example, Israel provisionally retained the laws of Mandatory Palestine in force.[228] This included the 1925 Palestine Citizenship Orders, which were not repealed until the enactment of the 1952 nationality law of Israel.[229] From 1948 to the entry into force of the nationality law in 1952, nationals of Mandatory Palestine automatically acquired the nationality of Israel and persons qualifying for nationality under the Orders could acquire Israeli nationality while the 1952 nationality law regulated the acquisition of nationality from its entry into force.[230]

## 2.4 A Typology of State Succession

A fundamental feature of the general law of State succession is the assortment of successions into a system of classification. Though each succession is unique in factual terms, the construction of a typology necessarily assumes the existence of a sufficient degree of commonality and difference. The handling of the transfer of Newfoundland by the United Kingdom to Canada in 1949, for example, was comparable to the handover of Ifni by Spain to Morocco in 1969 because no question of legal identity arose for any of the States or the territories concerned. In contrast, it differed in many respects to the issues raised by the breaking of Czecho-Slovakia in 1993 in which the legal personality of Czecho-Slovakia was terminated with two new States replacing it.

A doctrinal distinction is drawn between a 'total succession' and a 'partial succession' according to the continuation or termination of the international legal personality of the predecessor(s). A total succession results from the extinction of one or more States whereby title to the totality of its territory is transferred to one

---

law is a question of interpretation; e.g. – *R v Amihiya*, High Court of Malawi (3 December 1964) (1964–1966) ALR Mal 157, 166–68.

[225] On the omission of persons naturalized in the Province of Burma from the nationality laws of Burma, for example, see Chapter 6.
[226] Eritrea, for example, did not legislate on the general status of the Ethiopian laws applied to its territory from 1959 – Goy (n 120) 341. In 1991, Eritrea enacted eight transitional laws on specific areas; e.g. – Transitional Administration of Justice Proclamation No 1/1991 (15 September 1991) <https://www.loc.gov/item/eritrean-proc-1-1991/> accessed 17 February 2024, art 1 (Tigrinya). The provisional government began work on a draft constitution in 1991, which was not enacted until 1997 – BH Selassie, 'Creating a Constitution for Eritrea' (1998) 9(2) Journal of Democracy 164, 164–65.
[227] See Chapter 7.
[228] Law and Administration Ordinance 5708-1948, I Laws of the State of Israel 7, ss 11, 15, 17, 21.
[229] Nationality Law 5712-1952 VI Israel Laws 50, ss 2–9.
[230] See Chapter 7.

# 44 THE NATURE OF STATE SUCCESSION

or more successors. A partial succession results from a transfer by a State of a part of its territory by which it retains the remainder of its territory and its international legal personality.[231]

The typology adopted in the VCSST and VCSSP do not 'fully correspond with international practice', such as its combination of the distinct classes of merger and absorption in a single class of 'a uniting of States'.[232] Done to avoid drafting redundancy, its premise that the doctrinal rules governing both classes were identical was based on a survey of State practice that was entirely composed of mergers.[233] It has since acknowledged the difference—demonstrated by the absorption of East Germany by West Germany in 1990—in its subsequent projects.[234]

Whereas the other categories largely correspond to State practice, the most troublesome is the class of 'newly independent State'. Whereas Waldock had intended it to cover the 'special cases ... of mandates or protectorates',[235] the ILC widened it to include colonies, colonial protectorates, overseas territories, and other 'colonial' territories. The vagueness of the definition blurred its distinction from a 'separation of a part of the territory of a State', enabling an extremely wide range of successors to claim the status of 'newly independent State'.[236]

While the provisions of the VCSST and VCSSP drafted by the ILC on newly independent States have rarely been invoked in subsequent practice, the ILC subsequently decided to omit the category from the ILC Articles.[237] However, it is argued that States have distinguished in their practice between protected States and Territories having limited international legal personality and other dependent territories (e.g.—Non-Self-Governing Territories) that do not. Consequently, the category of newly independent State should be retained in doctrine with a clear definition to distinguish such cases from secessions.

---

[231] Rarely, there can be multiple predecessors, as in the case of a condominium – Alain Coret, Le Condominium (Pichon & Durand-Auzias 1960) 133–236, 307–13; DP O'Connell, 'The Condominium of the New Hebrides' (1968–1969) 43 BYIL 71, 141–43; FAA Taha, 'Some Legal Aspects of the Anglo-Egyptian Condominium over the Sudan, 1899–1954' (2005) 76 BYIL 337, 347–53, 361–82; de Muralt (n 169) 22–26.

[232] ILA Committee Resolution (n 61) annex (paras 2–3); ILC, 'Provisional summary record of the 3377th meeting' (19 July 2017) UN Doc A/CN.4/SR.3377, 7.

[233] See Chapters 4 and 5.

[234] ILC Articles on Nationality (n 59) art 21; Václav Mikulka, 'First report on State succession and its impact on the nationality of natural and legal persons' (17 April 1995) UN Doc A/CN.4/467, para. 93; ILC, 2388th meeting (n 59) para 30.

[235] First Waldock Report (n 41).

[236] For example, Montenegro succeeded to the VCSST in 2006 and did not apply Article 34 on separation of States but rather Article 22 on newly independent States even though it had not been a colony – 2390 UNTS (2006) 228, A-33356; Multilateral Treaties Deposited with the Secretary-General, UN Doc ST/LEG/SER.E/26 (1 April 2009) vol I, xxxii (n 1).

[237] ILC, 'Report on the work of its forty-ninth session (12 May-18 July 1997)' UN Doc A/52/10, ILC Yearbook, vol II, Part Two.

### 2.4.1 Merger

A merger (also called a 'union') occurs when two or more States create a new State to which they transfer title to their territories.[238] Its distinctive feature is the extinction of the predecessors' legal personalities, which can coincide with the creation by the successor of regional governments in their former territories. Whereas the 'Southern (Egypt) Region' and the 'Northern (Syria) Region' of the United Arab Republic were granted a high degree of financial autonomy and the treaties of Egypt and Syria remained in force only in their respective regions, for example, the *international* legal personalities of the predecessors were nonetheless terminated.[239]

### 2.4.2 Absorption

An absorption (also known as an 'incorporation') takes place when one State consents to become part of the territory of another State, thereby terminating its legal personality. As the subjugation of a State through the use of force (*deballatio*) and State coercion are unlawful, an absorption is based upon the free consent of the States concerned.[240] Whereas an absorbing State might apply different terms in its internal law to describe the event,[241] the legal test is whether one of the States concerned retains its international legal personality after the event.

### 2.4.3 Dismemberment

A dismemberment (also known as 'dissolution' or 'disintegration') is the extinction of a State from which multiple States succeed to title to its territories. While the two modern cases of the SFRY in 1991–92 and Czecho-Slovakia in 1993 only featured the creation of new States from the respective dismemberments, it is also possible for an existing State to incorporate a part of the territory of the predecessor.[242] An example of this from classical practice is the dismemberment of Austria-Hungary in 1920 whereby Yugoslavia and Romania incorporated parts of its territory alongside the creations of Austria, Hungary, and Czecho-Slovakia.[243] Due to the priority

---

[238] E.g. – Kohen and Dumberry (n 46) art 13.

[239] Eugene Cotran, 'Some Legal Aspects of the Formation of the United Arab Republic and the United Arab States' (1959) 8(2) ICLQ 346, 367–68, 374–80.

[240] On the creations of the German Empire and the Kingdom of Italy by successive absorptions, for example, see: Moore (n 12) vol V, 344–46, 353–55.

[241] E.g. – Treaty on the Establishment of German Unity (n 145) preamble, art 1.

[242] ILC Articles on Nationality (n 59) 43 (para 2).

[243] The description of the event ('whereas the former Austro-Hungarian Monarchy has now ceased to exist, and has been replaced in Austria by a republican government') was ambiguous – Treaty of Saint-Germain-en-Laye, 10 September 1919 (16 July 1920) (1919) 226 CTS 8, preamble; Treaty of

# 46 THE NATURE OF STATE SUCCESSION

of the question of personality, a contested claim to continuity of Statehood by an entity delays the resolution of succession issues until the dispute over identity be resolved.[244]

## 2.4.4 Cession

A cession is the transfer by one existing State of title to a part of its territory to another existing State.[245] The simpler form is the cession of general title over a defined unit, such as an island.[246] More complicated is the cession of a lease, which is an agreement by which a State grants another State the right to use and exercise control over part of the territory of the former.[247] The hallmark of a lease is that 'ultimate title' remains with the lessor and is divorced from jurisdiction, which is granted to the lessee (normally for a fee). As there is no general international law of leasehold, the rights of 'jurisdiction' granted to the lessee and the other terms (e.g.—duration and alienability[248]) are governed by each agreement.

Due to this division between the ultimate title of the lessor and the limited title of the lessee, this is described as an 'administrative cession'.[249] Intended to underscore the limited nature of the transferred title, it remains a (rare) type of cession because the territorial rights of one State as lessee are ceded to another State. The most prominent example was the cession by Russia to Japan of its lease over Port Arthur and Talien ('Kwantung') in 1905 with the consent of China as holder of ultimate title to the territories.[250]

Trianon, 4 June 1920 (26 July 1921) 3 Malloy 3539, preamble. Though heavily debated as a dismemberment or multiple secessions in contemporary doctrine, the case is one of dismemberment because neither Austria nor Hungary accepted continuity of the legal personality of the Dual Monarchy while the Allied Powers treated them as successors to the Empire of Austria (*Cisleithania*) and the Kingdom of Hungary (*Transleithania*) rather than the Dual Monarchy in the peace treaties and implementing practice – Marek (n 188) 208–26.

[244] Crawford (n 92) 706–14. On the two-month Federation of Mali, see: Rosalyn Cohen, 'Legal Problems Arising from the Dissolution of the Mali Federation' (1960) 36 BYIL 375, 376–80.

[245] Dörr (n 150) para 1.

[246] E.g. – Joint Declaration on Hong Kong (n 116) art 2.

[247] Yaël Ronen, 'Lease Territory' MPEPIL (July 2008) para 1. On the cession of general title that is subject to a lease, see Chapter 3.

[248] E.g. – *Chagos Marine Protected Area Arbitration (Mauritius v United Kingdom)* (Award) Permanent Court of Arbitration (18 March 2015) paras 69–87; Convention for the Construction of a Ship Canal (Panama-United States) (adopted 18 November 1903, entered into force 25 February 1904) 96 BFSP 553, arts II-III; *Government v Diaz*, US District Court for the Canal Zone (31 January 1924) 2 ILR 95, 96.

[249] Dörr (n 150) para 3.

[250] Treaty of Peace (Japan–Russia) 23 August and 6 September 1905 (entered into force 15 October 1905) 98 BFSP 735, arts V–VI (French). See further: CW Young, *The International Legal Status of the Kwantung Leased Territory* (OUP 1931) 1–37, 50–73, 97–152.

## 2.4.5 Secession

A secession (also known as 'separation') is the creation of a new State from a territorial unit of a parent State with its consent.[251] While this can occur through a planned process of independence or violent insurrection, customary international law in either case requires the consent of the parent State.[252] Violation of a peremptory norm of international law, such as an unlawful threat or use of force[253] or self-determination,[254] can be ineffective through a general denial of recognition by the international community of States.[255]

In creating a new State by secession, the recognition of the parent State necessarily entails a transfer of territorial title. Though the transfer need only include title to some territory, it might also involve the delimitation of a new border.[256] In the great majority of cases, secessions entail the creation of a single State from a territory transferred by the parent State. Rarely, however, multiple States can be created concurrently by secession from a territorial unit of the predecessor.[257]

## 2.4.6 Accession to Independence

Derived from the ILC definition of 'a succession of States' that was based on the aforementioned misconception of the law of decolonization as invalidating the territorial title of the colonial State over colonies and other Non-Self-Governing Territories, the definition of 'newly independent State' was the following: 'a successor State the territory of which immediately before the date of the succession of States was a dependent territory for the international relations of which the predecessor State was responsible.'[258] The ILC intended it to comprise 'any case of emergence to independence of any former dependent territories whatever its particular type may be' to encompass colonies, trusteeships, mandates, and protectorates, but not 'cases concerning the emergence of a new State as a result of a separation of part of an existing State, or of a uniting of two or more existing States.'[259]

Sir Humphrey Waldock originally termed the 'new State' and defined it as 'a State which has arisen from a succession where a territory which previously formed part of an existing State has become an independent State ... [t]his includes

---

[251] *Reference by the Governor in Council concerning Certain Questions relating to the Secession of Quebec from Canada*, Supreme Court of Canada (20 August 1998) [1998] 2 SCR 217, paras 83, 111–12.

[252] Crawford (n 92) 390; O'Connell (n 30) vol II, 88, 100.

[253] Ibid, 131–34.

[254] Ibid, 341–48.

[255] Ibid, 128–31, 140–43.

[256] E.g.– *Delimitation of the Border between Eritrea and Ethiopia* (Award of 13 April 2002) Eritrea-Ethiopia Boundary Commission (13 April 2002) 25 RIAA 83, paras 1.2, 2.112.14.

[257] On British India, for example, see notes 191–196.

[258] VCSST (n 16) art 2(f); VCSSP (n 17) art 2(e).

[259] ILC Draft Articles on Succession of States in respect of Treaties (n 176) 176 (paras 6–8).

## 48   THE NATURE OF STATE SUCCESSION

a secession of part of the metropolitan territory of an existing State and the secession or emergence to independence of a colony.[260] His intention was to distinguish between the various types of 'colonies' (e.g.—colonial protectorates) over which the metropolitan State had 'sovereignty' and the 'special cases' of Mandatory Territories, Trusteeship Territories, and protectorates over which it had not.[261] An early draft article 18 entitled 'former protected States, trusteeships and other dependencies' provided for a rule of continuity both for treaties existing prior to the protectorate and treaties concluded during the protectorate 'in its own name and by its own will'.[262] Following considerable debate,[263] he acquiesced to the view of a clear majority that neither principle nor practice supported differentiation between protected States and colonies (including colonial protectorates) and accordingly discarded draft article 18.[264]

The decision of the ILC to broaden the category of newly independent State to include 'colonies' led to a significant number of cases in which State practice was inconsistently classified.[265] For example, Bangladesh was designated a 'separation' while Algeria was named a 'newly independent State'; in applying the ILC criterion of 'colonial' status, neither French Algeria nor East Pakistan had been designated a 'Non-Self-Governing Territory'.[266] This typological vagueness resulted in two problems: (1) an elaboration of substantive rules on succession that was based on a distinction between 'separations' and 'newly independent States' that lacked a *legal* rationale; and (2) a failure to recognize the application in State practice of a rule of continuity for protected States and territories in certain circumstances. This mischaracterization led the ILC to wrongly regard the 'extremely rich' decolonization practice as a unique and self-contained historical epoch without implications for cases of secession that would take place in future.[267]

While the criticisms made of the ILC methodology for the class of newly independent State are well-founded,[268] State practice supports the existence of a distinct class of succession for protected States and territories possessing limited international legal personality. This legal rationale distinguishes the accession to independence of a newly independent State from the secession of a dependent territory. Three types have occurred in practice:

---

[260] Humphrey Waldock, 'Third report on succession in respect of treaties' (22 April and 27 May 1970) UN Doc A/CN.4/224, 28, para 9.

[261] Note 41.

[262] Humphrey Waldock, 'Fifth Report on succession in respect of treaties' UN Doc A/CN.4/256 (10 April 1972) 3 (draft art 18).

[263] ILC Yearbook (1972) vol I, 133–41, 145–49.

[264] Fifth Waldock Report (n 262) 9–10 (para 22) 231 (para 6).

[265] E.g. – ILC Draft Articles on Succession of States in respect of Treaties (n 176) 211, 219, 222–25, 228–29, 234–35, 237–38; ILC Articles on Succession of States in respect of State Property and Debt (n 138) 38–39, 41–42, 45, 62–65, 91–98.

[266] E.g. – ILC Articles on Succession to State Property and Debt (n 265) 38, 45, 62, 97–98, 109.

[267] 'Report of the International Law Commission on the work of its twenty-fourth session, 2 May–7 July 1972' ILC Yearbook (1972) Vol II Ch 2, para 26.

[268] E.g. – ILA Committee Resolution (n 61) 252, 331–33, 362–63, 369, 372; ILA Committee Resolution, ibid, paras 2, 14, 18, 20–21.

A TYPOLOGY OF STATE SUCCESSION   49

1. a protectorate vested by a protected State in a protecting State;
2. a Mandate or Trusteeship vested by the international community of States in a protecting State over a Mandatory or Trusteeship Territory; and
3. an international protectorate vested in a protecting State by the international community of States over a protected Territory.[269]

State practice thus supports the original position of Waldock rather than that of the ILC majority, such as the rule of continuity for certain rights and obligations under the protectorate following the accession to independence of the protected State of Morocco in 1956.[270]

## (a) Protected States

A protected State vests limited title to exercise specific powers (e.g.—to conduct its external affairs) over some or all of its territory in a protecting State while retaining its international legal personality.[271] Rooted in the classical idea of a 'vassal' or 'half-sovereign' State with limited international legal personality, a distinction was drawn between protected States and colonial protectorates according to whether the territory had formal Statehood.[272] The authority that might be granted to a protecting State includes the power to legislate or to contract public debt. Due to the potential application of the rule of continuity to a protected State, such as participation in a treaty,[273] this distinction has been important in dispute settlement.[274]

A protectorate can be created by an existing State (e.g.—Morocco[275] and Tunisia[276]) or a new State upon seceding from the metropolitan State

---

[269] E.g. – Carsten Stahn, *The Law and Practice of International Territorial Administration* (CUP 2008) 544–78; Wilde (n 94) 107–90.

[270] E.g. – *Rights of Nationals of the United States* (n 275) (Pleadings) vol I, 235, vol II, 431–34; ibid (Judgment) 179, 185. See also: *British Interests in Spanish Morocco (Spain v Great Britain)* (Award) Arbitrator (Max Huber) (1 May 1925) 2 RIAA 615, 648–49 (French); ILC, Articles on the Responsibility of States for Internationally Wrongful Acts with Commentaries, ILC Yearbook (2001) vol II, Part Two (ARSIWA) art 17.

[271] Crawford (n 92) 296.

[272] Ibid, 286–87. See also: Fifth Waldock Report (n 262) para 4; International Law Association, *The Effect of Independence on Treaties* (Stevens & Sons 1965) 368–69; de Muralt (n 169) 59–77.

[273] E.g. – *Temple of Preah Vihear (Cambodia v Thailand)* (Preliminary Objections) (Observations du Cambodge) (22 July 1960) 164–66 (paras 30–34); (Pleadings, Oral Arguments, Documents) Vol II, 77–79, 83 (French); *Temple of Preah Vihear (Cambodia v Thailand) (Preliminary Objections)* (Judgment) [1961] ICJ Rep 17, 38.

[274] E.g. – *Rights of Nationals of the United States* (Judgment) (n 275) 188.

[275] Treaty for the Establishment of a Regular Regime (France–Morocco) (30 March 1912) 106 BFSP 1023, arts I–V. See further, e.g. – *Spanish Zone of Morocco Claims (Great Britain v Spain)* Max Huber (Rapporteur) 2 ILR 19, 21; *Grilhe v Hadj Thami el Glaoui; Babin v Hadj Thami el Glaoui*, Court of Cassation of France (27 June 1936) 8 ILR 94, 94–96; *Rights of Nationals of the United States of America in Morocco (France v United States of America)* (Judgment) [1952] ICJ Rep 176, 179, 185; ibid (Pleadings) vol I 235, vol II 431–34.

[276] Treaty of Friendship (France–Tunis) (12 May 1881) 72 BFSP 247, arts I–VII. See further, e.g. – *Orsini v Ferrovecchio*, Court of Cassation of France (28 July 1925) 3 ILR 39 (note); *Falla-Nataf and Brothers v Germany*, Franco-German Mixed Arbitral Tribunal (30 December 1927) 4 ILR 44; *Nationality Decrees Issued in Tunis and Morocco (French Zone) on November 8, 1921* (Advisory Opinion) PCIJ Series B No 4.

50 THE NATURE OF STATE SUCCESSION

(e.g.—Egypt[277] and Iceland[278]). Whereas protected States had largely disappeared by the 1970s,[279] the ILC nevertheless included the category within the class of newly independent States.[280] Though obsolete in modern practice, the protected State retains residual significance under for disputes engaging with historical periods in which a protectorate applied.[281]

## (b) Mandatory and Trusteeship Territories

The Mandate system was created by the League of Nations to encourage the well-being and development of the peoples of the designated territories of the former German and Ottoman Empires as a sacred trust, thus excluding their cession to the Mandatories.[282] Employing the term 'tutelage', Article 22 of the Covenant of the League implicitly envisaged their progressive development towards self-government or independence.[283] Despite a 'baffling' doctrinal debate concerning the location of 'sovereignty',[284] the creation of the Mandates involved the creation of a limited title of jurisdiction for the Mandatory with limited international legal personality for the Mandatory Territory (e.g.—a separate nationality).[285] Though differing in their administration and regulation, the UN Trusteeship system shared the same fundamental approach.[286] In State practice, a rule of continuity has applied to those rights and obligations vested in a Mandatory or Trust Territory[287] while rules of succession have applied to the rights and obligations of the predecessor exercised within the scope of their administrative titles.[288]

---

[277] Circular Despatch stating the decision of His Majesty's Government to terminate the Protectorate and to recognise Egypt as an independent sovereign States (15 March 1922) 116 BFSP 84.

[278] Danish Law providing for the Union of Denmark and Iceland (30 November 1918) 111 BFSP 703, ss 1, 7, 19.

[279] On the United Arab Emirates, for example, see: General Agreement on Tariffs and Trade (30 October 1947) Depositary Notification (18 July 1995) UN Doc C.N.154.1995.TREATIES-7.

[280] Fifth Waldock Report (n 262) paras 1–2.

[281] E.g. – *Land and Maritime Boundary between Cameroon and Nigeria (Cameroon v Nigeria, Equatorial Guinea Intervening)* (Judgment of 10 October 2002) [2002] ICJ Rep 303, paras 37, 203–08.

[282] Covenant of the League of Nations (n 193) 108 LNTS 188, art 22; UN Charter (n 72) art 76(b); *International Status of South West Africa* (Advisory Opinion) [1950] ICJ Rep 128, 131.

[283] Crawford (n 92) 566.

[284] Ibid, 568–69. See also, e.g. – Giulio Diena, 'Les mandats internationaux' (1924-IV) 5 RdC 211, 229–60; Norman Bentwich, 'Le système des mandats' (1929-IV) 29 RdC 115, 129–32.

[285] E.g. – *Mavrommatis Jerusalem Concessions (Greece v United Kingdom)* (Judgment) PCIJ Series A No 5, 38–39; *International Status of South West Africa* (n 282) 133. For an overview, e.g. – Nicolas Veïcopoulos, *Traité des Territoires Dépendants* vol I (Larcier 1960) 59–70, 138–49, 439–41; ibid vol III, 1400–30; Albert Millot, *Les Mandats Internationaux* (Larose 1924) 87–121.

[286] HD Hall, Mandates, Dependencies and Trusteeship (Stevens & Sons Limited 1948) 56–65, 91–106, 259–92; Giuseppe Vedovato, 'Les accords de tutelle' (1950-I) 76 RdC 609, 614–21.

[287] E.g. – *Certain Phosphate Lands* (n 117) (Memorial of Nauru) vol 1 (April 1990).

[288] O'Connell (n 30) vol II, 150–63.

## (c) International Protectorates

International protectorates are created by the international community of States with limited title vested in a State over a territorial unit.[289] A rarity, the principal examples are the Memel Territory (1920–23),[290] the Free City of Danzig (1920–45),[291] and the Saar Territory (1947–57).[292] Though similar to Mandatory and Trusteeship Territories insofar as the protectorate may be vested either in an international organization or a State on its behalf, the distinguishing feature of international protectorates is their creation on an ad hoc basis.[293] However, they share the common feature of the creation of limited legal personality for the protected Territory, notwithstanding the exercise of (at times, extensive) powers by the protecting State.

## 2.5 The Interpretation of State Practice

Typically, the parties to a succession adopt specific rules by agreement to govern succession matters.[294] Such a 'succession agreement' can be a single instrument to address succession matters in a comprehensive manner[295] or to regulate a specific succession issue (e.g.—succession to treaties)[296] as well as multiple instruments dealing with various questions arising from a succession (e.g.—on State property and debt).[297] Succession agreements are made between predecessors, successors, or third States[298] and can take the form of a treaty, national law,[299] or other instrument.[300]

According to the general principle of law that a special law displaces general laws (*lex specialis derogat lege generali*),[301] the specific provisions of a succession agreement will apply to the extent that they regulate a succession issue. However,

---

[289] Méir Ydit, *Internationalised Territories* (AW Sythoff 1961) 22–50.

[290] Treaty of Versailles (n 250) art 99; 'The Status of the Memel Territory' (1924) 5 LNOJ 121, 122–23.

[291] Malcolm Lewis, 'The Free City of Danzig' (1924) 5 BYIL 89, 93–95.

[292] Whiteman (n 196) 406–09.

[293] UN Charter (n 72) arts 86–87.

[294] While a succession agreement must be interpreted in light of the parties' subsequent conduct, this does not render it immaterial as a form of practice. *Contra*: First Bedjaoui Report (n 14) para 33.

[295] Treaty on the Establishment of German Unity (n 145).

[296] E.g. – Succession Agreement (United Kingdom–Malaya) (12 September 1957) 279 UNTS 288.

[297] E.g. – Agreement on Succession Issues (n 33).

[298] E.g. – Agreement between France and Serbia and Montenegro concerning succession to bilateral treaties (26 March 2003) 2239 UNTS 325. For an example of an oral treaty, see: *UN Materials on Succession of States* (1967) UN Doc ST/LEG/SER.B/14, 211-213; Agreement on Treaties (Ghana-United States) (4 September and 21 December 1957) (adopted 12 February 1958, entered into force 12 September 1958) 442 UNTS 175.

[299] E.g. – Indian Independence (International Arrangements) Order (n 190).

[300] E.g. – *Gold Pool JV Limited v Kazakhstan*, High Court of Justice (15 December 2021) [2021] EWHC 3422 (Comm) paras 49–50.

[301] Marcelo Vázquez-Bermúdez, 'Third report on general principles of law' UN Doc A/CN.4/753 (18 April 2022) paras 95–107 ('Third Vázquez-Bermúdez Report').

## 52 THE NATURE OF STATE SUCCESSION

'[t]he application of the special law does not normally extinguish the relevant general law ... [which] will remain valid and applicable and will, in accordance with the principle of harmonization ... continue to give direction for the interpretation and application of the relevant special law and will become fully applicable in situations not provided for by the latter.'[302] A general rule of succession can perform three functions in relation to a special rule contained in a succession agreement:

1. to guide States and other relevant parties (e.g.—representatives of a secessionist territory[303]) in their negotiations;[304]
2. to interpret provisions that are ambiguous;[305] and
3. to regulate issues in default of an applicable provision.[306]

The *lex specialis* rule is reflected in the primacy given to specific agreement by parties to a succession in the VCSST and VCSSP.[307] There is no example in State practice of a peremptory norm rendering a succession agreement void.[308]

### 2.5.1 The Identification of Customary International Law

Customary international law comprises rules that are formed by a general practice of States accepted by them as law (*opinio juris*).[309] For the identification of State practice as the 'material' or 'objective' element, a wide range of conduct may be taken into account, such as:

- diplomatic acts and correspondence;
- conduct in connection with resolutions adopted by an international organization or an international conference;
- conduct in connection with treaties;
- executive conduct;

---

[302] Ibid, para 96.

[303] E.g. – Declarations drawn up in Common Agreement at Evian (France-Algerian National Liberation Front) (18 March 1962) 1(2) ILM 214.

[304] This can apply to decisions taken to derogate from the general rule. On the secession of Libya, for example, see: UNGA Res 388(V)(A) (15 December 1950) arts I–IV, VI(1), IX(1).

[305] E.g. – VCLT (n 183) art 31(3)(c).

[306] Martti Koskenniemi, 'Report of the Study Group of the International Law Commission: Fragmentation of International Law' (13 April 2006)UN Doc A/CN.4/L.682; ILC, 'Conclusions of the Work of the Study Group', ILC Yearbook (2006) vol II, Part Two, 177–84.

[307] E.g. – VCSST (n 16) art 10(3) ('unless the treaty otherwise provides or it is otherwise agreed').

[308] VCLT (n 183) art 53. See further, e.g. – Olivier Corten and Pierre Klein (eds) *The Vienna Convention on the Law of Treaties: A Commentary* (OUP 2011); Oliver Dörr and Kirsten Schmalenbach, *Vienna Convention on the Law of Treaties: A Commentary* (Springer 2018).

[309] ILC, 'Draft Conclusions on Identification of Customary International Law' in 'Report of the International Law Commission: Seventieth Session (30 April–1 June and 2 July–10 August 2018)' UN Doc A/73/10, conclusion 2. See also, e.g. – *Ure v Australia*, Federal Court of Australia (4 February 2016) 173 ILR 623, 635–76.

THE INTERPRETATION OF STATE PRACTICE    53

- legislative and administrative acts; and
- decisions of national courts.[310]

'Conduct' may include physical and verbal acts as well as deliberate inaction.[311]

## (a)  State Practice

A wide range of State practice may be taken into account.[312] There must exist a general practice consistently affirmed by States, with the views of those 'specially affected' by that practice given particular weight.[313] Sources of State practice to evince general rules of succession principally comprise the following:

1. succession agreements;
2. decisions on succession issues taken by competent bodies, such as the UN General Assembly;[314]
3. national legislation (including executive orders or other instruments) addressing succession matters; and
4. decisions of national courts on succession disputes.

There is no hierarchy among these sources of practice.[315] Rather, the quality of the practice concerned determines its evidentiary value; in particular, the extent to which it is consistent with other practice to support the existence of a general rule as opposed to an isolated approach or a special rule consciously adopted as an exception to the general rule.[316] Whereas agreements concluded before the date of succession between a metropolitan State and the representatives of a colonial territory must be interpreted (like other succession agreements) in light of the subsequent practice of the counterparties and agreements not based on the free consent of the colonial territory (whether its local government or a secessionist organization representing its interests in independence negotiations) can breach the law of decolonization,[317] these considerations do not obviate the value of such agreements as a source of State practice.[318] Rather, the question is whether the successor affirms[319] or rejects[320] a succession agreement after the date of succession that had been concluded before the date of succession.

---

[310]  Ibid, conclusion 6(2).

[311]  Ibid, conclusion 6(1). See further, e.g. – Michael Wood, 'Second report on identification of customary international law' UN Doc A/CN.4/672 (22 May 2014) paras 32–59.

[312]  Ibid, conclusion 6.

[313]  Ibid, conclusion 8.

[314]  E.g. – UNGA Res 392 (V) (15 December 1950).

[315]  ILC Conclusions (n 310) conclusion 6(3).

[316]  Ibid, conclusion 7.

[317]  E.g. – *Chagos Islands* (n 102).

[318]  *Contra*: First Bedjaoui Report (n 14) para 33.

[319]  On the examples of Algeria and South Sudan, see Chapter 4.

[320]  On the examples of Indonesia and the DRC, see Chapters 4 and 8.

## 54 THE NATURE OF STATE SUCCESSION

While succession agreements can displace general rules, they also collectively comprise a source of evidence for the identification a general rule.[321] This exercise is, however, complicated by the fact that succession agreements are necessarily tailored to the particular circumstances: their various provisions may or may not reflect a general trend. Moreover, the mere existence of a single treaty providing for a certain rule does not evince the customary status of that rule; rather, *subsequent* affirmation of that rule by States is required. The question is therefore whether a consistent pattern of practice can be discerned from succession agreements to evince a general rule.

Judgments rendered by national courts on succession matters have been a significant source of State practice.[322] On the one hand, they can be in themselves a source of practice and *opiniones juris* for the identification of customary international law;[323] on the other hand, they can evince the contemporary state of the law through interpretation of preceding State practice. Unlike an international court or tribunal, a national court can not only express a judicial view on the applicable rules of succession but also potentially express the position of the State to which it belongs as one of its organs.[324]

### (b) Opinio Juris

In addition to the objective element of State practice, customary international law requires the 'acceptance as international law' by States (*opinio juris*) of a positive rule of international law as the 'psychological' or 'subjective' element.[325] For the law of succession, the identification of *opinio juris* can be a subtle exercise insofar as States often manifest their views on the general rule of law implicitly. Dispute settlement, particularly adjudication or arbitration, tends however to prompt express statements from disputing parties on the pertinent succession practice and general rules of succession.[326]

In contrast, the *opiniones juris* of counterparties to succession agreements and other instruments resulting from negotiation must typically be deduced from textual analysis and negotiating records.[327] Regardless of the source, contradictory State practice that is exceptional to the prevailing trend can inversely prove the general rule; for example, when a conscious exception is made for political reasons.[328] Similarly, a judgment of a national court disposing of a succession matter on

---

[321] ILC Conclusions (n 310) conclusion 11.

[322] E.g. – n 330.

[323] On national courts and treaties, for example, see: Chapter 4.

[324] Ibid.

[325] ILC Conclusions (n 322) conclusion 9. See further, e.g. – Wood (n 312) paras 60–80.

[326] E.g. – *Convention for the Prevention and Punishment of the Crime of Genocide (Croatia v Serbia)* (Preliminary Objections) [2008] ICJ Rep 412, paras 105–10, 114–19.

[327] E.g. – 'Former Italian Colonies, Economic and Financial Provisions Relating to Libya: Report of the Ad Hoc Political Committee' (14 December 1950) UN Doc A/1726, 9.

[328] Ibid.

procedural grounds (e.g.—the 'act of State doctrine'[329]) while admitting the existence of a general rule of succession in international law can constitute an *opinio juris* of that State in support of the general rule.[330] While the statements made by States on the ILC projects[331] potentially manifest *opiniones juris* statements, statements made concurrently with their own practice are generally the more precise and credible.

### (c) Persistent Objection

While a State may 'persistently object' to a customary rule, the evidentiary standard is a high one[332] and there are relatively few examples of persistent objections being made in the law of succession.[333] Despite the controversial nature of the private property owned by foreign nationals in the territories of decolonized States,[334] for example, those successors expropriating such property (e.g.—the DRC) did not challenge the existence of a legal duty to respect the private property of foreign nationals nor object to its application to their particular succession.[335] Nevertheless, persistent objection is a key feature distinguishing customary international law from general principles of law.[336]

## 2.5.2  The Transposition of General Principles of Law

The rationale for general principles of law[337] was to fill gaps in treaty law and customary law.[338] Doctrinal views differed, however, concerning whether they were merely principles found in national legal systems or could also be in the international legal system. As international courts and tribunals have only infrequently invoked general principles of law, methodological difficulties have

---

[329] On the abundant jurisprudence concerning British India, for example, see, e.g. – *Virendra Singh and Others v Uttar Pradesh*, Supreme Court of India (29 April 1954) 22 ILR 131, 137–38; *SM. Sau. Indumati v Saurashtra*, High Court of Saurashtra (2 July 1955) 4 CILC 3; *Gujarat v Vora Fiddali Badruddin Mithibarwala*, Supreme Court of India (30 January 1964) 4 CILC 308, 309–11.

[330] E.g. – *Shimshon Palestine Portland Cement Factory Ltd v Attorney-General*, Supreme Court of Israel (12 April 1950) 17 ILR 72, 75–78.

[331] E.g. – 'Observations of Member States on the draft articles on succession of States in respect of treaties adopted by the Commission at its twenty-fourth session', UN Doc A/CN.4/275 ILC Yearbook (1974) vol II, 313–30; *United Nations Conference on Succession of States in respect of Treaties: Official Records* (1978) UN Doc A/CONF.80/16/Add.1.

[332] ILC Conclusions (n 322) conclusion 15.

[333] On the preservation of boundaries, for example, see Chapter 3.

[334] Second Bedjaoui Report (n 22).

[335] n 166. See Chapter 8.

[336] E.g. – JA Green, *The Persistent Objector Rule in International Law* (OUP 2016) 3–9, 88–90.

[337] Protocol of Signature relating to the Statute of the Permanent Court of International Justice (16 December 1920) 6 LNTS 380, art 38(1)(c).

[338] Giorgio Gaja, 'General Principles of Law' MPEPIL (2013); Bin Cheng, *General Principles of Law as Applied by International Courts and Tribunals* (Stevens & Sons Ltd, 1953).

56  THE NATURE OF STATE SUCCESSION

included the criteria for the selection from national legal systems[339] and the justification for principles of law identified independently from their status in internal law. Nevertheless, general principles of law that can apply in succession disputes include acquiescence,[340] estoppel,[341] intertemporal law[342] and *ex injuria jus non oritur.*[343]

Based on the recognition of the ILC of the category of general principles of law derived from national legal systems, the Special Rapporteur for the pending ILC project has proposed a two-step methodology for their identification.[344] This entails the establishment of: (1) recognition of principles common to the principal legal systems of the world; and (2) the transposition of those principles to the international legal system.[345] Whereas national legislation and decisions of national courts can also comprise State practice for the identification of customary international law, it must be accompanied by the subjective element of acceptance of a rule of *international* law.[346] This subjective element is not required for recognition as a general principle of law: 'what is relevant is how national legislations and courts regulate and solve essentially domestic matters.'[347]

Based on a thesis first advanced by Ian Brownlie,[348] it is proposed in this book that this category of general principles of law forms the legal basis for the identification of general rules concerning the effects of a succession of States on the nationality of natural and legal persons.[349] While there have been a few cases in which national courts have recognized customary international law,[350] the field is a quintessential example of national legal systems addressing the effects of an international phenomenon through the elaboration and application of internal laws concerning nationality.

---

[339] *Lusitania Cases* (Opinion) German–American Claims Commission (1 November 1923) 7 RIAA 32. *Contra: Mavrommatis Palestine Concessions (Greece v Great Britain)* (Preliminary Objections) PCIJ Rep Series A No 2, 10.

[340] E.g. – *Temple of Preah Vihear Case (Thailand v Cambodia)* (Merits) [1962] ICJ Rep 6, 16, 23, 32–33.

[341] E.g. – *North Sea Continental Shelf Cases (Germany v Denmark; Germany v Netherlands)* (Judgment) [1969] ICJ Rep 3, para 30.

[342] ILC Articles on State Responsibility (n 270) art 13.

[343] E.g. – *Gabčikovo-Nagymaros Project (Hungary v Slovakia)* (Judgment) [1997] ICJ Rep 7, para 133.

[344] Marcelo Vázquez-Bermúdez, 'Second report on general principles of law' UN Doc A/CN.4/741 (9 April 2020) paras 2, 16.

[345] Ibid, paras 19–22.

[346] Ibid, para 110.

[347] Ibid.

[348] Ian Brownlie, 'The Relations of Nationality in Public International Law' (1963) 39 BYIL 284, 314–26.

[349] See Chapter 7.

[350] E.g. – *Schwarzkopf v Uhl*, US Second Circuit Court of Appeals, 12 ILR 188, 194.

## THE INTERPRETATION OF STATE PRACTICE   57

### (a)  Principles Common to the Principal Legal Systems of the World

To identify a general principle of law that is 'common to the various legal systems of the world',[351] an empirical assessment of national legal systems is required that is 'wide' and 'representative' comprising 'national laws and decisions of national courts, and other relevant materials'.[352] As State succession is one that by its very nature can concern any State and successions have taken place throughout the world, inquiry into the national legislation and court decisions of States to have engaged with succession and nationality meets the criteria of breadth and diversity in terms of geography, language, and legal tradition.[353]

In seeking to determine whether a 'general' principle exists on a given issue (e.g.—the 'right of option' for natural persons and nationality) the critical issue of interpretation is the meaning of a nationality law in the specific context of the legal system of the State in question. Constitutional provisions on nationality, for example, frequently operate at a high level of generality and do not comprehensively address the complex questions of nationality that arise.[354] Once the meaning of the nationality laws can be determined in the specific context of the internal legal system, the comparative exercise across legal systems is 'not a light one ... [but] relatively clear: one has to compare rules existing in national legal systems and extract the principle that is common to them, or distil the principle underlying those rules'.[355]

### (b)  Transposition to the International Legal System

The rationale for this second criterion is that 'municipal law and international law have unique features and differ in many important aspects, and the principles existing in the former cannot be presumed to be always capable of operating in the former'.[356] While doctrine only describes this part of the methodology only in broad terms,[357] the ILC Special Rapporteur has described transposition as requiring that the principle be compatible with fundamental principles of international law and the conditions exist for its application in the international legal system.[358] A general principle of law must be 'capable of existing within the broader

---

[351] ILC, 'General principles of law: Consolidated text of draft conclusions 1 to 11 provisionally adopted by the Drafting Committee', UN Doc A/CN.4/L.971 (21 July 2022) conclusions 3(a), 4(a), 5. See further: Second Vázquez-Bermúdez Report (n 346).

[352] ILC Conclusions (n 310) conclusion 5.

[353] Second Vázquez-Bermúdez Report (n 346) paras 25–54.

[354] On the merger of North Viet Nam with South Viet Nam in 1976, for example, see Chapter 7.

[355] Second Vázquez-Bermúdez Report (n 346) para 56.

[356] Ibid, para 73.

[357] Ibid, para 74.

[358] Ibid, paras 75–96.

## 58 THE NATURE OF STATE SUCCESSION

framework of international law', which must permit 'the adequate application of the principle'.[359]

As described in Chapter 7, these criteria are applicable because general principles of law on succession and nationality apply in default of a rule of internal law regulating the question of nationality at the date of succession. However, their scope is limited to the determination of 'nationality' for the purposes of international law (e.g.—diplomatic protection). They therefore perform a limited function for the purposes of the international legal system to enable the status of persons to be determined in the absence of a nationality law.[360] There is consequently no doubt that such general principles of law are compatible with international law.

However, there must also be evidence confirming transposition to the international legal system.[361] Whereas the ILC Special Rapporteur has provided the example of 'treaties or other international instruments', this is a limited source of evidence in the field of succession. However, it is suggested that decisions of national and international courts and tribunals and the pleadings of disputing parties can serve as evidence of transposition. In this context, it is argued in Chapter 7 that the general principles of law proposed on the basis of State practice have yet to be transposed to international law.

### 2.5.3 The Persuasive Authority of International Courts and Tribunals

While questions of State succession often came before the Permanent Court of International Justice ('PCIJ') and arbitral tribunals after the First World War, they have arisen rarely in the ICJ and arbitral tribunals in the UN era when compared to the voluminous national court decisions. Though binding in their dispositive part only upon disputing parties,[362] the reasoning part of a judgment or award can carry persuasive authority in its treatment of the general law of succession.[363] The pronouncements of the PCIJ in the area of succession and private property, for example, have influenced the development of the 'doctrine of acquired rights'.[364]

---

[359] Ibid, paras 75, 85.

[360] E.g. – *Civilians Claims: Eritrea's Claims 15, 16, 23 & 27–32* (Partial Award) Eritrea-Ethiopia Claims Commission (17 December 2004) para 51.

[361] Second Vázquez-Bermúdez Report (n 346) paras 97–106.

[362] E.g. – Statute of the International Court of Justice (24 October 1945) 15 UNCIO 355, art 59.

[363] Ibid, art 38(1)(d). For critique of the idea of 'persuasive authority', see, e.g. – Ingo Venzke, 'Between Power and Persuasion: On International Institutions' Authority in Making Law' (2013) 4 Transnational Legal Theory 213.

[364] E.g. – *Certain German Interests in Upper Silesia* (Merits) (Judgment of 25 May 1926) PCIJ Series A (No 7) 6–7, 9–11. See Chapter 8.

On the relatively few occasions when the ICJ has been seized of a succession issue, however, it has rarely provided an incisive answer on a point of principle.[365] While investor-State arbitral tribunals have engaged with succession issues in recent years, their findings have largely been based on the agreement of disputing parties on a general rule as well as factual findings concerning their conduct on the question.[366] The underlying agreement of the disputing parties carries weight to identify the legal positions of States but the persuasive authority of a judgment or award is nevertheless constrained by a general lack of engagement with the general law of succession.

## 2.6 Conclusions

Even as a succession of States necessarily engages with political questions, it is not an intrinsically political phenomenon that is incapable of legal definition in a neutral and objective fashion. Rather, State practice supports the traditional understanding in doctrine of State succession as a territorial transfer from one State to another. Whereas the grand theories seeking to extrapolate predetermined outcomes from the definition of a succession are not supported by State practice, States have consistently considered their territorial rights of jurisdiction and ownership to derive from their predecessors. This definition of the event as a legal phenomenon does not prejudge outcomes on a host of other succession matters, each of which must be determined according to the applicable rules and factual circumstances.

In permitting the politics of decolonization to influence its definition of State succession, the ILC attributed to the law of decolonization an intention to invalidate the territorial titles of metropolitan States that was supported neither by the relevant resolutions of the General Assembly nor the practice of (decolonized) States. This crucial error led to an insufficiently coherent typology entailing not only the misclassification of historical successions but also a failure to distinguish between the respective classes of succession. While the basic distinction between total and partial successions is reflected in the ILC system of classification, State practice supports the intention of Waldock to group 'colonies' with other dependent territories while treating protected States and territories separately due to their limited international legal personality providing for a rule of continuity in certain circumstances.

---

[365] Andreas Zimmermann, 'The International Court of Justice and State Succession to Treaties: Avoiding Principled Answers to Questions of Principle' in Christian Tams and James Sloan (eds) *The Development of International Law by the International Court of Justice* (OUP 2013) 53–70, 60.
[366] See Chapter 1.

## 60 THE NATURE OF STATE SUCCESSION

In light of the irrelevance of the VCSST and VCSSP as treaty law, the interpretation of State practice to identify general rules has principally concerned succession agreements and the jurisprudence of national courts. While specific laws adopted by the parties to a succession and interested third States play an important role, general rules also perform important functions to supplement and construe any specific rules. As secession is the most common class of succession in modern times, the rich practice arising from decolonization is highly significant to identify general rules in every class of succession.[367]

---

[367] Successions taking place during the 'decolonization' era that were not secessions or accessions to independence include the cessions of Newfoundland (1949), French India (1952 and 1963), and Ifni (1969) as well as the mergers of Egypt and Syria (1958), Somalia and Somaliland (1960), and Tanganyika and Zanzibar (1965).

# 3

# Succession to Territorial Rights and Obligations

## 3.1 Introduction

Prior to the codification projects of the International Law Commission ('ILC'), received doctrine on the law of State succession had not identified territorial rights and obligations as a discrete field governed by rules of succession. As O'Connell observed in his *magnum opus* published months prior: 'The traditional law of State succession distinguished between 'personal' and 'dispositive'—or 'real'—treaties, and regarded the latter as transmissible and the former as not.'[1] Despite the traditional doctrine defining State succession as a transfer of territorial sovereignty,[2] the attention of writers focused not on the territorial rights or obligations but rather on the status of the treaty on which they were based.[3]

In reviewing the literature, the Special Rapporteur on succession to treaties, Sir Humphrey Waldock, observed: 'The weight of opinion amongst modern writers ... seems still to support the traditional doctrine that treaties of a territorial character constitute a special category which, in principle, are inherited by a new State.'[4] Noting another doctrinal view held by the International Law Association ('ILA') Committee on State Succession—led by O'Connell—whereby boundaries and other 'real' rights and obligations are independent of 'executed' territorial treaties,[5] Waldock observed: 'The diversity of opinion amongst writers makes it difficult to discern whether and, if so, to what extent and upon what basis, international law today recognizes any special category or categories of treaties of a territorial character which are inherited automatically by a successor State.'[6]

This conceptualization of the doctrinal issue as the status of territorial *treaties* is attributable to the fact that territorial rights and obligations are generally created by treaty. In examining the treatment of territorial rights and obligations separately

---

[1] DP O'Connell, *State Succession in Municipal Law and International Law* vol II (OUP 1968) 231.

[2] See Chapter 1.

[3] Mohammed Bedjaoui, 'First report on succession of States in respect of rights and duties resulting from sources other than treaties' UN Doc. A/CN.4/204 (5 April 1968) 94 ('First Bedjaoui Report') para 118.

[4] Humphrey Waldock, 'Fifth report on succession in respect of treaties' (10 April, 29 May and 8, 16, and 28 June 1972) UN Doc A/CN.4/256 & Add.1-4, 48.

[5] Ibid, 48–49.

[6] Ibid, 49.

---

*The Law of State Succession*. Arman Sarvarian, Oxford University Press. © Arman Sarvarian 2025.
DOI: 10.1093/oso/9780198817956.003.0003

from the treaty, however, State practice is coherent: 'The weight of the evidence of State practice and of legal opinion in favour of the view that in principle a boundary settlement is unaffected by the occurrence of a succession of States is strong and powerfully reinforced by the decision of the United Nations Conference on the Law of Treaties to except from the fundamental change of circumstances rule a treaty which established a boundary.'[7] On this basis, Articles 11 ('Boundary regimes') and 12 ('Other territorial regimes') of the 1978 Vienna Convention on Succession of States in respect of Treaties ('VCSST')[8] provide for succession to boundaries and other territorial rights and obligations independent of the treaty that created them.[9]

While the VCSST has yet to be applied as a treaty due to the low number of participating States,[10] the approach of the ILC in conceiving of succession to territorial rights and obligations as distinct from succession to the underlying treaties accords with prior and subsequent State practice. International boundaries fixed before a succession have been consistently addressed by States separately from the delimitation treaties, as have leases and other 'territorial regimes' created by treaty. Although succession to territorial claims was not examined by the ILC, State practice in that field has shown that territorial rights and obligations are discrete from treaties in the law of succession because such claims do not depend on the existence of a treaty at all.

The significance of this conceptualization goes beyond the doctrinal question of succession to territorial rights and obligations to the definition of State succession itself. As explained in Chapter 2, the practice of successors in asserting territorial claims as 'successor-in-interest' or 'successor-in-title' in dispute settlement without any prior declaration of succession to the claim proves that a succession is a transfer of territorial title rather than a factual replacement of one State by another. This in turn means that the source of the title of a successor, such as its jurisdiction over a continental shelf and ownership of the natural resources therein,[11] derives from the predecessor rather than its own 'sovereignty'. Independent of treaty, the question is whether State practice is sufficiently coherent as to support the existence of

---

[7] Ibid, 49–54.

[8] Vienna Convention on the Succession of States with respect to Treaties, 23 August 1978 (entered into force 6 November 1996) 1946 UNTS 3 ('VCSST').

[9] ILC Draft Articles on Succession of States in respect of Treaties with commentaries (1974) ILC Yearbook vol II 174 ('ILC Articles') 201, 207.

[10] See Chapter 5.

[11] E.g. – ILC, 1221st Meeting (6 June 1973) UN Doc A/CN.4/SR.1221, para 11 (Martínez Moreno); ILC, 1222nd Meeting (7 June 1973) UN Doc A/CN.4/1222, para 19 (Bedjaoui); Manlio Udina, 'La succession des États quant aux obligations internationales autres que les dettes publiques', 4 (1933-II) RdC 665, 704–58; AN Sack, 'La succession aux dettes publiques d'état' (1928-III) 23 RdC 145, 155–227, 262–321.

a given rule of customary international law for the transfer of territorial obligations appurtenant to the transferred title.[12]

## 3.2 Territorial Rights

In an analogy with Roman law, territorial rights concern rights of prescriptive and enforcement jurisdiction (*imperium*) and profits or benefits (*dominium*). Unlike the hierarchical structure of the Roman legal system, however, the essential element of territorial rights in an international legal system founded upon the equality of States is the right to exclude other States from their exercise over the territory in question. The concept of 'territory' embraces not only the land but also the realms of the subsoil, air, and sea that are dependent upon the rights to the land. For coastal States, for example, terrestrial rights generate a right to a territorial sea under customary international law.

To determine the origin of territorial rights acquired by a successor as 'original' or 'derivative',[13] State practice on the exercise of these aforementioned rights is largely indeterminative. This is because successors rarely have occasion to explain in the ordinary course of exercising their territorial rights whether, in their view, they were based upon an original acquisition of title or a derivative transfer from the predecessor. However, the question has arisen in two areas that concern the *limits* of the title of a successor: (1) succession to territorial claims asserted by a predecessor towards a neighbouring State; and (2) succession to boundaries delimited by a predecessor with a neighbouring State. It is in these two fields that the nature of succession to territorial rights as derivative rather than original is revealed in the practice of States.

### 3.2.1 Territorial Claims

The doctrinal distinction drawn by the ILC between succession to territorial rights and obligations established by treaty and succession to the treaty itself is also demonstrated by State practice concerning succession to territorial claims, which was not examined in its codification projects.[14] Unlike boundaries, leases, and other types of territorial rights and obligations, claims to territory are not created by

---

[12] E.g. – ILC Draft Conclusions on Identification of Customary International Law in 'Report of the International Law Commission: Seventieth Session (30 April-1 June and 2 July-10 August 2018)' UN Doc A/73/10, conclusion 11.

[13] See Chapter 2.

[14] First Bedjaoui Report (n 3) paras 117–32. See also: UNGA Sixth Committee, 1327th Meeting (9 October 1972) UNGAOR: Twenty-seventh Session, paras 22–23 (Venezuela).

treaty but rather asserted by a State through its conduct.[15] There is abundant State practice in dispute settlement, including many examples of explicit *opiniones juris* as 'successor-in-title' or 'successor-in-interest', to support a rule of customary international law providing that a predecessor automatically transfers to a successor those claims that are appurtenant to the territorial title.

Successors have asserted succession to territorial claims that had been made by their predecessors in a variety of ways. These have included diplomatic means, such as the successions of Brazil to the claim of Portugal to the island of Trinidade,[16] the United States to the claims of Spain and the United Kingdom to territories in Oregon,[17] and Viet Nam to South Viet Nam in the Gulf of Thailand.[18] There are many examples of the acceptance by other disputing parties of these declarations of succession in settling the dispute, such as: the 1963 China–Pakistan delimitation treaty by which Pakistan relinquished approximately two-thirds of the territorial claim of the United Kingdom;[19] the 1974 settlement between India and Bangladesh of the claims of Pakistan to an area known as 'Beraburi Union No. 12';[20] and the acquiescence of the United States in 1979 to the claim of Kiribati to the Phoenix and Line Island Groups in succession to the United Kingdom.[21]

Succession to claims has also been asserted on numerous occasions in the adjudication and arbitration of territorial disputes. These comprise:

- the American claim to the Island of Palmas in 1928, based on the cession of the Philippines by Spain;[22]

---

[15] E.g. – MG Kohen and Mamadou Hébié, 'Territory, Acquisition' MPEPIL (November 2021) paras 26–31, 40.

[16] Geoffrey Marston, 'The Anglo-Brazilian Dispute over the Island of Trinidade' (1983) 54 BYIL 222.

[17] E.g. – *Harcourt v Gaillard*, Supreme Court of the United States (3 March 1827) 2 AILC 389, 390, 393–94; JB Moore, *A Digest of International Law* vol I (US Government Printing Office 1906) 439, 457–58. They also asserted succession to the claims of Hawai'i to atolls – *United States v Fullard-Leo et al.*, US Ninth Circuit Court of Appeals (23 May 1946) 13 ILR 35, 36.

[18] DM Johnston and MJ Valencia, *Pacific Ocean Boundary Problems: Status and Solutions* (Springer 1991) 134, 138–39.

[19] Agreement on the Boundary between China's Sinkiang and the Contiguous Areas (China–Pakistan) (2 March 1963) III PTS (1961–1966) 230, arts 1–3, 6; International Law Association, *The Effect of Independence on Treaties* (Stevens & Sons 1965) ('ILA Handbook') 363.

[20] Demarcation Agreement (Bangladesh–India) (16 May 1974) India Treaties Database No BG74B2547, art 1; Protocol to the Demarcation Agreement (Bangladesh–India) (6 September 2011) India Treaty Database No BG11B0578, arts 2–3. For background, see, e.g. – *India v Sukumar Sengupta*, Supreme Court of India (3 May 1990) 92 ILR 554, 567–74.

[21] Treaty of Friendship (Kiribati–United States) (adopted 20 September 1979, entered into force 23 September 1983) 1643 UNTS 239, preamble, art 1; 'United Kingdom Materials on International Law 1979' (1979) 50 BYIL 302, 303.

[22] *Island of Palmas (or Miangas)* (Award) Permanent Court of Arbitration (Arbitrator Max Huber) (4 April 1928) 4 ILR 103, 104–07, 113–14. See also: 'Digest of Decisions of National Courts relating to Succession of States and Governments: Study prepared by the Secretariat' (18 April 1963) UN Doc A/CN.4/157 II ILC Yearbook (1963) paras 31–32.

# TERRITORIAL RIGHTS  65

- the Mexican claim to Clipperton Island in 1931 on the basis of discovery by Spain;[23]
- the Pakistani claim in 1968 to the Rann of Kutch in succession to the Indian State of Sind alongside the Indian claim in succession to the Indian States of Kutch, Jodhpur, Wav, Suigam, Tharad, and Santalpur;[24]
- the Libyan claim in 1994 to the Aozou Strip in succession to the claims of Italy and the Ottoman Empire;[25]
- the Eritrean claim in 1998 to disputed Red Sea islands in succession to Ethiopia and Italy;[26]
- the Namibian and Botswanan claims in 1999 to the disputed Kasikili/Sedudu Island in succession to Germany and the United Kingdom;[27]
- the claim of the Philippines to North Borneo in 2001 in succession to the Sultanate of Sulu and the United States;[28] and
- the claims of Malaysia and Indonesia in 2002 to Pulau Ligitan and Pulau Sipadan in succession to the United Kingdom and the Netherlands.[29]

While there is no example of such a claim being successful on the merits, in no case has a disputing party raised an objection to it. Still less did the international court or tribunal hold the claim to be inadmissible; for example, on the ground that the successor could not succeed to it in the absence of an act of succession made prior to the dispute being submitted to adjudication or arbitration.[30] By the general principle of law that a State may not transfer any right greater than it possess (*nemo plus juris ad alium transfere potest quam ipse habet*)[31] a predecessor may not transfer to

[23] *Affaire de l'île de Clipperton (Mexique c. France)* (Award) Sole Arbitrator (28 January 1931) II RIAA 1105, 1109 (French).

[24] *The Indo-Pakistan Western Boundary (Rann of Kutch) Case (India v Pakistan)* (Award) Arbitral Tribunal (19 February 1968) 50 ILR 2, 77–81.

[25] Note 224.

[26] *Territorial Sovereignty (Eritrea v Yemen)* (Award) Permanent Court of Arbitration (9 October 1998) XXII RIAA 211, paras 13–54, 96–100, 441–524.

[27] Note 250.

[28] *Pulau Ligitan and Pulau Sipadan (Indonesia v Malaysia)* (Application by the Philippines to Intervene) [2001] ICJ Rep 575, paras 40–41; Oral Proceedings (25 June 2001) CR 2001/1, Verbatim Record, 19 (para 17); ibid (26 June 2001) CR 2001/2, 20 (para 7), 22 (para 13); ibid (28 June 2001) CR 2001/3, 14 (para 8) 23–24, 26 (paras 13, 15, 21); ibid (29 June 2001) CR 2001/4, 26 (para 2).

[29] *Pulau Ligitan and Pulau Sipadan (Indonesia v Malaysia)* (Merits) (Judgment of 17 December 2002) [2002] ICJ Rep 625, paras 32–33, 93–125, 148–50. On the succession of Belgium to the claim of the Netherlands in Eupén-Malmedy, see: *Kepp and Associates v Belgian State*, Court of Cassation of Belgium (22 May 1925) 3 ILR 120, 121.

[30] In 2019, Belize and Guatemala submitted their pending dispute to the ICJ to determine the terrestrial, insular, and maritime claims of Guatemala against Belize – Special Agreement to submit to the International Court of Justice Guatemala's Territorial, Insular and Maritime Claim (Guatemala–Belize) 3261 UNTS I-55299, art 2. Guatemala claimed the territory of British Honduras from 9 April 1946 in succession to the territorial rights of Spain by denouncing a delimitation treaty with the United Kingdom of 30 April 1859; after Belize was admitted to the UN over Guatemalan protests in 1981, Guatemala recognized Belize in 1991 – *Belize Case*, Constitutional Court of Guatemala (3 November 1992) 100 ILR 305.

[31] E.g. – *Island of Palmas* (n 22).

## 66 SUCCESSION TO TERRITORIAL RIGHTS AND OBLIGATIONS

a successor any claim that it had renounced[32] or omitted to assert[33] at the date of succession.[34]

### 3.2.2 Boundaries

Unlike inchoate claims, territorial rights are perfected and usually based on a delimitation treaty, judgment or arbitral award.[35] In concluding that 'boundary settlements are not affected by the occurrence of a succession of States as such',[36] the ILC proposed the provision that became Article 11 of the VCSST: 'A succession of States does not as such affect: (a) a boundary established by a treaty; or (b) obligations and rights established by a treaty and relating to the regime of a boundary.' Referring to delimitation treaty provisions establishing a boundary[37] as the 'title deeds' for the territory,[38] the ILC formulated Article 11 'not in terms of the treaty itself but of a boundary established by a treaty and of a boundary regime so established'.[39]

A rationale that was considered was the doctrine of separability of treaty provisions,[40] which is expressed in the Vienna Convention on the Law of Treaties ('VCLT') with respect to denunciation, withdrawal, or suspension of a treaty.[41] Separability has appeared rarely in State practice on succession to treaties.[42] It does not expressly underpin Article 11 and has not appeared in *opiniones juris* on succession to boundaries.

The better doctrinal rationale for Article 11 is the 'real' nature of the rights and obligations: a succession of States is a transfer of territorial title from which the successor receives from the predecessor the title as delimited by the agreed boundaries with a third State. A successor need not succeed to the separate provisions of

---

[32] E.g. - *Eritrea v Yemen* (n 26).

[33] E.g. - *Bering Fur Seals (United States v United Kingdom)* (Award) Arbitral Tribunal (15 August 1893) XXVIII RIAA 263, 268, 269. See also: LB Schapiro, 'The Limits of Russian Territorial Waters in the Baltic' (1950) 27 BYIL 439, 440, 445-46; Jamie Trinidad, 'The Disputed Waters around Gibraltar' (2015) 86 BYIL 101, 105-26.

[34] E.g. - *Rights of Passage* (n 163) 39.

[35] *Arbitration between Guyana and Suriname* (Award) PCA Case No 2004-04 (17 September 2007) 30 RIAA 1, 29-39, 69-77, 87-106.

[36] ILC Articles (n 9) 201.

[37] In this book, the term 'boundary' is used interchangeably for both 'boundaries' proper, as one-dimensional lines having only length, and 'frontiers', which are two-dimensional zones having both length and width - Malcolm Shaw, *Title to Territory in Africa* (OUP 1986) 223.

[38] ILC Articles (n 194) 201 (para 20).

[39] Ibid.

[40] E.g. - UNGA Sixth Committee, 1323rd Meeting (5 October 1972) GAOR (Twenty-seventh Session) para 3 (Egypt).

[41] VCLT (n 201) art 44. See also: Martyna Falkowska, Mohamed Bedjaoui, and Tamara Leidgens, 'Article 44 Convention of 1969' in Olivier Corten and Pierre Klein (eds) *The Vienna Convention on the Law of Treaties: A Commentary* vol II (OUP 2011) 1046, 1054-57; Pierre Bodeau-Livinec and Jason Morgan-Foster, 'Article 53 Convention of 1969' in Corten and Klein, ibid, 1224, 1231.

[42] E.g. - *UN Materials on Succession of States* (1967) UN Doc ST/LEG/SER.B/14 223-24.

the treaty dealing with the boundary in question; rather, the relevant provisions evince the limits of its territorial title. In an analogy from the Roman law of property, this rationale is given expression by the maxim *uti possidetis, ita possideatis* ('as you possess, so may you possess').[43] Apart from the preservation of boundaries, this doctrine has also been invoked for the adoption of internal borders (administrative, intra-colonial, etc.) as boundaries.

### (a) The Retention of Existing Boundaries

The scope of Article 11 of the VCSST is confined to the preservation of an international boundary adopted by the predecessor with a third State before the date of succession. In delimiting the territorial title transferred to the successor, it entails reciprocal rights and obligations between the successor and the third State to respect their respective titles.[44] It is thus closely related to the principle of territorial integrity, which is a rule of customary international law expressed in Article 2, paragraph 4, of the UN Charter.[45]

Article 11 was adopted in 1978 at the UN Diplomatic Conference on the Succession of States in respect of Treaties by a vote of 71-1-8.[46] Though a plurality of the UN membership of 151, it comprised a majority of the 100 delegations that participated in the Conference.[47] Based on the cohesive State practice that preceded the UN Conference, it is suggested that the vote as expressions of *opiniones juris* crystallized the principle as a general rule of customary international law. In classical State practice, there was considerable practice featuring the retention of boundaries by successors with third States. Nineteenth-century examples included the retention of the Franco–Portuguese boundary after the secession of Brazil[48] and the Moroccan–Algerian boundary on the subjugation of the Beylik of Algiers by France.[49]

By the early decolonization period, however, the practice had not yet coalesced into a settled rule of customary international law. While Israel implicitly agreed

---

[43] Malcolm Shaw, 'The Heritage of States: The Principle of *Uti possidetis juris* Today' (1996) 67 BYIL75, 98; LI Sánchez Rodríguez, 'L'*uti possidetis* et les effectivités dans les contentieux territoriaux et frontaliers' (1997) 263 RdC 149, 349–69; Edward McWhinney, 'Self-Determination of Peoples and Plural-Ethnic States' (2002) 294 RdC 167, 229–35.

[44] This is also known as the principle of 'stability of boundaries'; e.g. – Shaw (n 43) 81–97; Hugh Thirlway, 'The Law and Procedure of the International Court of Justice: Part Seven' (1995) 66 BYIL 1, 15–31.

[45] Malcolm Shaw, International Law (CUP 2021) 259.

[46] United Nations Conference on Succession of States in respect of Treaties: Official Records vol I (1978) UN Doc A/CONF.80/16/Add.1 (1979) 11 (para 23) 129 (para 9) 232 (para 7).

[47] G Hafner and I Buffard, 'Les principales différences entre les propositions de la Commission du Droit International et le résultat de la Conférence des Nations Unies à Vienne sur la succession d'États en matière des traités' in Giovanni Distefano, Gloria Gaggioli and Aymeric Hêche (eds) *La Convention de Vienne de 1978 sur la succession d'États en matière de traités*, vol 1 (Bruylant 2016) 1494–495.

[48] *Arbitral Award relating to the boundaries between Brazil and French Guiana* (1 December 1900) XXVIII RIAA 349, 374.

[49] Treaty of Lalla-Marnia (n 261) art I.

68   SUCCESSION TO TERRITORIAL RIGHTS AND OBLIGATIONS

with the Lebanon in 1948 to adopt the 1923 Franco–British line as their boundary, for example, it did not reach a comparable agreement with Syria for the same boundary.[50] Saudi Arabia accepted the Saudi–Kuwaiti boundary delimited in 1922 on the accession to independence of Kuwait in 1971 but rejected the 'Blue and Violet lines' in the 1913 Anglo-Turkish treaty on the accession to independence of the United Arab Emirates.[51]

As the secession of former colonies in Africa gathered pace in the 1960s, it was consequently not evident that they would be obliged to accept the boundaries that had been delimited for their territories by their predecessors.[52] In 1964, the Member States of the Organization for African Unity ('OAU') adopted a resolution by which, 'despite their initial feelings of reaction against the maintenance of "colonial" frontiers', they agreed to 'pledge themselves to respect the boundaries existing on their achievement of national independence'.[53] This declaration endorsed the prevailing practice on the retention of boundaries by successors, which was consistently endorsed in subsequent practice. Several delimitation treaties concluded between the 1964 OAU Resolution and the 1978 UN Diplomatic Conference affirmed the boundaries agreed between their predecessors, such the 1966 agreement between Ghana and Burkina Faso ('Upper Volta').[54] In this context, it is arguable that *uti possidetis juris* crystallized into a regional custom between those dates. In parallel, State practice in other regions also coalesced around the maintenance of boundaries; examples include the retention of the Iraqi–Kuwaiti boundary in 1963 on the accession to independence of Kuwait[55] and the preservation of the Anglo-Brazilian boundary on the secession of Guyana in 1966.[56]

By the time the UN Conference on the Succession of States to Treaties was convened in 1977 and 1978, there thus existed a considerable amount of State practice in favour of the presumptive succession to a boundary. Alongside Article 12, Article 11 of the VCSST had nevertheless been one of the most controversial provisions of

[50] General Armistice Agreement (Israel–Syria) (20 July 1949) 42 UNTS 327, art V(1). See further: UNSC 639th Meeting (18 November 1953) SCOR, para 68; UNSC 633rd Meeting (30 October 1953) SCOR, para 165.

[51] Nabil Adamy, 'Boundaries and Boundary Disputes in South Arabia', Gulf Centre for Strategic Studies, Monograph 6 (May 1990) 5–7. See further: HM Albaharna, *The Legal Status of the Arabian Gulf States* (MUP 1968) 196–207.

[52] Shaw (n 43) 101–04. One author considers the rule to have started with the independence of Libya in 1951, crystallizing by December 1961 – DM Ahmed, *Boundaries and Secession in Africa and International Law* (CUP 2015) 68, 85–100.

[53] OAU Doc AHG/Res16(1) in ILC Articles (n 9) 199 (n 187). Negative votes were cast by Somalia and Morocco.

[54] Shaw (n 37) 257.

[55] Agreed Minutes regarding the Restoration of Friendly Relations (Iraq–Kuwait) (4 October 1963) 485 UNTS 321. See further: Maurice Mendelson and SC Hulton, 'The Iraq–Kuwait Boundary' (1993) 64 BYIL 135.

[56] Treaty for the Settlement of the Boundary (Brazil–British Guiana) (adopted 22 April 1926, entered into force 16 April 1929) 123 BFSP 468, Art 1; *Guiana Boundary Case (Brazil v Great Britain)* (Arbitral Award) (6 June 1905) XI RIAA 21.

the draft ILC Articles in the Sixth Committee.[57] As the ILC Chairman observed at the conclusion of the Sixth Committee debate in 1972:

> Articles 29 and 30 had been the subject of the most comments, probably because they touched on the most difficult problems. From the discussion in the Committee it appeared that a majority recognized the need to include in the draft articles rules relating to boundary regimes and other territorial regimes ... It had on the other hand been said that the inheritance of a boundary regime infringed the right to self-determination and the contractual freedom of new States ... It should be stressed that articles 29 and 30 were confined strictly to the right of succession.[58]

Consequently, *uti possidetis juris* had yet to crystallize into a general rule of customary law before the UN Diplomatic Conference in 1978.[59]

However, the affirmative vote of a clear majority of UN Member States at the Diplomatic Conference provided the catalyst whereby *opiniones juris* coalesced in favour of a general rule of customary international law. This is shown by the subsequent State practice and *opiniones juris* that have consistently affirmed the principle.

In agreeing on numerous occasions to resolve their territorial disputes on the basis of the boundaries delimited by their predecessors, disputing parties have expressly endorsed *uti possidetis juris* and Article 11 of the VCSST as customary international law. Examples from Africa include the arbitration between Guinea and Guinea-Bissau in 1985,[60] the arbitration between Senegal and Guinea-Bissau in 1989,[61] the adjudication between Libya and Chad of the Aozou Strip in 1994,[62]

---

[57] UNGA Sixth Committee, 1318th Meeting (2 October 1972) GAOR: Twenty-seventh Session, paras 4–8; 1323rd Meeting (5 October 1972) ibid, para 21; 1326th Meeting (9 October 1972) ibid, para 19; 1490th Meeting (1 November 1974) ibid, para 5; 1492nd Meeting (5 November 1974) ibid, para 62; 1493rd Meeting (6 November 1974) ibid, para 50; 1495th Meeting (8 November 1974) ibid, para 17; 1496th Meeting (11 November 1974) ibid, paras 20–24; 1537th Meeting (13 October 1975) ibid, para 25; Sixth Committee, 1528th Meeting (1 October 1975) GAOR: Thirtieth Session, para 44; 1540th Meeting (15 October 1975) ibid, paras 5–7; 1543rd Meeting (20 October 1975) ibid, paras 3–7; 1545th Meeting (21 October 1975) ibid, para 32; 1547th Meeting (23 October 1975) ibid, para 30; 1548th Meeting (24 October 1975) ibid, paras 11, 26, 52; 1549th Meeting (27 October 1975) ibid, paras 22, 59. For rebuttals, see, e.g. – ibid, 1326th Meeting (9 October 1972) ibid, paras 26–27; UNGA Sixth Committee, 1487th Meeting (29 October 1974) GAOR: Twenty-Ninth Session, para 2; 1489th Meeting (31 October 1974) ibid, para 31; 1496th Meeting (11 November 1974) ibid, paras 14, 26, 32; 1537th Meeting (13 October 1975) ibid, paras 52; 1545th Meeting (21 October 1975) ibid, paras 2, 11.

[58] UNGA Sixth Committee, 1328th Meeting (10 October 1972) GAOR: Twenty-seventh Session, para 18.

[59] UNGA Sixth Committee, 1326th Meeting (9 October 1972) GAOR: Twenty-seventh Session, para 11.

[60] *Guinea – Guinea-Bissau Maritime Delimitation Case* (Award) Court of Arbitration (14 February 1985) 77 ILR 636, 652, 654–57.

[61] *Arbitral Award of 31 July 1989 (Guinea-Bissau v Senegal)* Arbitral Tribunal (31 July 1989) 83 ILR 1, 22, 35–38. See also: JC Gautron, 'Sur quelques aspects de la succession d'Etats au Senegal' (1962) 8 AFDI 838, 846.

[62] *Territorial Dispute (Libya v Chad)* (Judgment of 3 February 1994) [1994] ICJ Rep 6 para 75.

## 70    SUCCESSION TO TERRITORIAL RIGHTS AND OBLIGATIONS

the arbitration between Eritrea and Ethiopia in 2002,[63] the adjudication of the boundary dispute between Cameroon and Nigeria in 2002[64] and and the secession of South Sudan in 2011.[65]

Concerning the pending dispute between Gabon and Equatorial Guinea over the islands of Mbanié/Mbañe, Cocotiers/Cocoteros, and Conga, Gabon declared them a military zone in April 1974 and the President of Equatorial Guinea announced in July 1974 that he accepted the current boundaries.[66] In 2020, the Parties submitted their dispute to the ICJ in which Gabon recognized 'as applicable to the dispute' the 1900 Franco-Spanish delimitation treaty and the 1974 Guinean-Gabonese demarcation treaty while Equatorial Guinea only recognized the former.[67] They reserved the right to invoke other legal titles.[68]

In its pleadings, Equatorial Guinea based its claim to the disputed land territories on its succession to the territorial title of Spain, which it argued was established by Article 4 of the 1900 delimitation treaty between Spain and France.[69] While Gabon accepted that it had succeeded to the titles of France and Equatorial Guinea to the titles of Spain, it argued that the 1900 treaty had not covered the disputed territories in question.[70]

Outside Africa, State practice for other successions has likewise been coherent on the retention of boundaries. Delimitation treaties affirming existing boundaries have been concluded concerning: the accessions to independence of Jordan in 1946 and Israel in 1948;[71] the secession of Bangladesh in 1974;[72] the secession

---

[63] Agreement for the Settlement of Displaced Persons (Ethiopia–Eritrea) (12 December 2000) 2138 UNTS 93, art 4; *Decision regarding Delimitation of the Border (Eritrea v Ethiopia)* PCA Case No 2001-01 Eritrea–Ethiopia Boundary Commission (13 April 2002) paras 3.3, 8.1.

[64] *Land and Maritime Boundary (Cameroon v Nigeria, Equatorial Guinea intervening)* (Judgment of 10 October 2002) [2002] ICJ Rep 303, paras 210–17, 325. See further: Maurice Mendelson, 'The *Cameroon–Nigeria* Case in the International Court of Justice: Some Territorial Sovereignty and Boundary Delimitation Issues' (2004) 75 BYIL 223.

[65] E.g. – RO Collins, 'The Illami Triangle' (2004) 20 Annales d'Éthiopie 5; Philip Winter, 'A Border Too Far: The Ilemi Triangle Yesterday and Today', Durham Middle East Paper No 100 (2019).

[66] Shaw (n 37) 259.

[67] Special Agreement (n 251) art 1.

[68] Ibid.

[69] *Land and Maritime Delimitation and Sovereignty over Islands (Gabon v Equatorial Guinea) (Memorial of Equatorial Guinea of 5 October 2001)* Vol. I, 99–109, 143–44; ibid., Reply of Equatorial Guinea, 13–19; CR 2024/29 (30 September 2024, 10 a.m.) 21 (Smith), 27–35 (d'Argent); CR 2024/30 (30 September 2024, 3 p.m.) 10–11, 17–19 (Akande); CR 2024/33 (3 October 2024, 3 p.m.) 14–17 (d'Argent), 49–55 (Akande).

[70] Ibid., Counter-Memorial of Gabon, Vol. I, 93–94; ibid., Rejoinder of Gabon, 7–12; CR 2024/29 (30 September 2024, 10 a.m.) 59–70 (Reichler); CR 2024/31 (2 October 2024, 10 a.m.) 25–32 (Pellet); CR 2024/33 (3 October 2024, 3 p.m.) 47–48 (Reichler); CR 2024/34 (4 October 2024, 3 p.m.) 33–34 (Miron), 51–59 (Pellet).

[71] Treaty of Peace (Israel-Jordan) (adopted 26 October 1994, entered into force 10 November 1994) 2042 UNTS 351art 3(1), annex I(a). There is no evidence that a maritime boundary had been drawn during the Mandate – Maritime Boundary Agreement (Israel–Jordan) (adopted 18 January 1996, entered into force 7 February 1996) Israel Treaty Database, preamble, art 1.

[72] On the 'Radcliffe Line' between India and East Pakistan see n 20.

of Suriname in 1975;[73] the absorption of East Germany in 1990;[74] the dismemberment of the Socialist Federal Republic of Yugoslavia (SFRY) from 1991 to 1992;[75] the dismemberment of Czecho-Slovakia in 1993;[76] the various secessions from the USSR in 1991;[77] the secession of Eritrea in 1993;[78] the secession of Timor-Leste in 2002 with retroactive effect to 1975;[79] and the secession of Montenegro in 2006.[80] In adjudication, the principle has also been applied to the accessions to

[73] 'Communiqué conjoint franco-surinamien' (15 March 2021) <https://www.diplomatie.gouv.fr/fr/dossiers-pays/suriname/evenements/article/communique-conjoint-franco-surinamien-15-03-21> accessed 1 January 2024; Patrick Blancodini, 'Guyane française – Suriname: le tracé définitif de la frontière officiellement fixé sur 400 km' (March 2021) *Géoconfluences* <http://geoconfluences.ens-lyon.fr/actualites/veille/breves/trace-frontiere-france-suriname> accessed 1 January 2024. See also: *Delimitation Award regarding the Limits of Colonies in Guyana* Arbitral Tribunal (25 May 1891) XXVIII RIAA 249; Delimitation Convention (France–Netherlands) (adopted 30 September 1915, entered into force 16 September 1916) 110 BFSP 872, art I.

[74] Treaty concerning the Common Frontier (Czechia–Germany) (adopted 3 November 1994, entered into force 1 September 1997) 2292 UNTS 379, preamble, art 2(1); Treaty concerning the Established State Frontier (Germany–Poland) (14 November 1990) 1708 UNTS 383, preamble, art 1. See also, e.g. – RW Piotrowicz, 'The Polish–German Frontier in International Law: The Final Solution' (1992) 63 BYIL 367.

[75] On the border with Italy, for example, see: Convention on the State Border (Italy-Slovenia) (7 March 2007) Italy Treaty Database, No BILSVN029 (Italian) preamble, arts 1–2, 16(4); Delimitation Accord (Italy–SFRY) (adopted 8 January 1968, entered into force 21 January 1970) Italy Treaty Database, No BILHRV031 (Italian); *Gulf of Piran Arbitration (Croatia v Slovenia)* (Final Award) Permanent Court of Arbitration Case No 2012-04 (29 June 2017) paras 9, 685. The boundary established by the 1975 Treaty of Osimo does not appear to concern Bosnia, which has but a 20-kilometre coastline.

[76] E.g. – Bilateral Agreements in Force (n 203); Exchange of Notes regarding Austrian-Czechoslovak Treaties (n 203); Agreement on the Common State Border (Slovakia-Poland) (adopted 6 July 1995, entered into force 16 February 1996) UNTS I-55060, arts 1(2) 28; Agreement on Common State Borders (Czechia–Germany) (adopted 3 November 1994, entered into force 1 September 1997) 2292 UNTS 379, arts 2(1)(b), 30. See also: Zimmermann (n 227) 90.

[77] E.g. – Memorandum of Understanding concerning Legal Succession concerning the Agreements of the former USSR (6 July 1992) (1993) 26 RBDI 627, para 3; Agreement on the China–Tajik State Border (China–Tajikstan) (adopted 13 August 1999, entered into force 4 July 2000) China Treaty Database, art 1 (Chinese, Tajik, Russian); Agreement concerning the Polish–Ukrainian State Border (adopted 12 January 1993, entered into force 21 December 1993) UNTS No 57046, art 1(1); Agreement on Friendly Relations (Slovakia–Ukraine) (adopted 29 June 1993, entered into force 16 June 1994) 42 Zakon (1 November 2006) 192, art 1 (Ukrainian).

[78] E.g. – *Maritime Delimitation Arbitration (Eritrea v Yemen)* (Second Stage) XII RIAA 335, paras 10–38, 75–86.

[79] Provisional Agreement on the Land Boundary (Indonesia–Timor-Leste) (adopted 8 April 2005, entered into force 7 May 2005) Indonesia Treaty Database, arts 1–2, 7, annex B. See further: *Boundaries of the Island of Timor (Netherlands v Portugal)* (Award) Permanent Court of Arbitration (25 June 1914) in GG Wilson, *The Hague Arbitration Cases* (Ginn & Co 1915) 380, 445–47 (annexes A & C); Treaty regulating the Archipelago of Timor (Portugal-Netherlands) (adopted 28 April 1859, entered into force 21 August 1860) 50 BFSP 1116, arts I–VII (French); Boundary Convention (Portugal-Netherlands) (adopted 10 June 1893, entered into force 31 January 1894) 85 BFSP 394, arts I–III (French); Convention for the Settlement of the Boundary between their Possessions in the Island of Timor (Netherlands-Portugal) (adopted 1 October 1904, entered into force 29 October 1908) 101 BFSP 497, arts III–V (French).

[80] Agreement on the State Border (Montenegro–Bosnia) (adopted 26 August 2015, entered into force 20 April 2016) I-55488 UNTS, art 2, annex.

72  SUCCESSION TO TERRITORIAL RIGHTS AND OBLIGATIONS

independence of Qatar and Bahrain in 1971[81] and the secession of Singapore in 1965.[82]

Based on this extensive State practice and *opiniones juris* after 1978, it is suggested that the principle of *uti possidetis juris* crystallized into a general rule of customary international law with the adoption of Article 11 by the UN Diplomatic Conference. While the automatic retention of a boundary is the presumptive rule, the States concerned may modify it by agreement. Examples include the delimitation of the Israeli–Egyptian boundary in 1979 'without prejudice to the status of the Gaza Strip'[83] and the delimitation of the Polish–German terrestrial and Oder Bay boundaries in 1990.[84] The customary rule is also subject to the persistent objector exception, which is explained below.

## (b) The Internationalization of Internal Borders

In contrast to international boundaries, Article 11 of the VCSST does not address the transformation of an internal border within a State into an international boundary. This variation of *uti possidetis juris* was first adopted by the former colonies of the Spanish Empire in 1810 for South America and 1821 for Central America.[85] Although it has since been widely applied by those States,[86] it has never been applied by a State in those regions whose territory had not belonged to Spain (e.g.—Brazil[87] and Guyana[88]). The adoption by the successors to Spain of the

---

[81]  *Maritime Delimitation and Territorial Questions (Qatar v Bahrain)* (Merits) [2001] ICJ Rep 40, paras 35–65. See also: Treaty of Jiddah between the United Kingdom and King Ibn Sa'ud of the Hijaz and Najd and its Dependencies (adopted 20 May 1927, entered into force 17 September 1927) 71 LNTS 153, arts 5–6; Richard Schofield and GH Blake (eds) *Arabian Boundaries: Primary Documents 1853–1957* (Archive Editions 1988) vol 10, xx–xii; vol 15, xx; ibid, vol 19, xxii.

[82]  *Pedra Branca/Pulau Batu Puteh, Middle Rocks and South Ledge (Malaysia v Singapore)* (Judgment of 23 May 2008) [2008] ICJ Rep 12, para 186.

[83]  Treaty of Peace (Israel–Egypt) (26 March 1979) (1979) 18 ILM 362, art II.

[84]  Treaty concerning the State Frontier (n 68) art 1. See also: *Germany–Poland Border Treaty Constitutionality Case*, Federal Constitutional Court of Germany (5 June 1992) 108 ILR 657, 659–61, 663; Zimmermann (n 70) 90.

[85]  The exact dating varies according to the doctrine of the critical date, though the principle was not adopted before 1848 – Santiago Torres Bernárdez, 'The "Uti Possidetis Juris Principle" in Historical Perspective' in Konrad Ginther et al. (eds), *Völkerrecht zwischen normativem Anspruch und politischer Realität* (Duncker and Humblot 1994) 419, 425; Ahmed (n 52) 21–32.

[86]  *Boundary Case between Bolivia and Peru* (Award) Arbitral Tribunal (9 July 1909) XI RIAA 133, 145; *Boundary Case between Costa Rica and Panama* (Award) Arbitral Tribunal (12 September 1914) XI RIAA 519, 531, 534; *Boundaries Case (Colombia v Venezuela)* (Award) Arbitral Tribunal (24 March 1922) I RIAA 223, 228–29 (French); *Honduras Borders (Guatemala v Honduras)* (Award) Arbitral Tribunal (16 July 1930) II RIAA 1307, 1322–25; *Beagle Channel Arbitration (Argentina v Chile)* (Award) Arbitral Tribunal (18 February 1977) 52 ILR 93, 124–25 (paras 9–13), 132–33 (para 21); *Land, Island and Maritime Frontier Dispute (El Salvador v Honduras, Nicaragua Intervening)* (Judgment of 11 September 1992) [1992] ICJ Rep 351, paras 28, 34, 40–46, 56–61, 108, 154, 175–77, 236, 307, 332–33, 350; Boundary Treaty (Colombia–Panama) (adopted 20 August 1924, entered into force 31 January 1925) 33 LNTS 168, art I.

[87]  Torres Bernárdez (n 80) 428–31; Ahmed (n 52) 20–21.

[88]  Note 290. On the relevance of *uti possidetis juris* to succession to claims, see: Humphrey Waldock, 'Disputed Sovereignty in the Falkland Islands Dependencies' (1948) 25 BYIL 311, 325–26.

internal Spanish borders as international boundaries created a regional custom for those States.[89]

When the OAU adopted its resolution on the retention of colonial boundaries in 1964,[90] it applied not only to boundaries between colonies of different predecessors but also internal borders between colonies of a single predecesor.[91] Examples of its application in adjudication are the territorial disputes between Burkina Faso and Mali in 1986,[92] Benin and Niger in 2005,[93] and Burkina Faso and Niger in 2013.[94] As discussed below, Morocco and Somalia were persistent objectors to the regional custom of Africa.

Outside Africa, there are examples of States implicitly adopting the principle for territorial delimitation arising from the decolonization era. Examples include:

- the delimitation of the Indian–Pakistani boundary by the 'Radcliffe Award' prior to their secessions from the United Kingdom;[95]
- the adoption of the colonial border between British India and Burma by Pakistan and Myanmar in 1966[96] and by India and Myanmar in 1967;[97]
- the adoption of a modified version of the 1896 colonial border by Australia and Papua New Guinea in 1985;[98] and
- the adoption of the internal Slovak–Czech border in 1992.[99]

There have also been numerous cases in which States have rejected the adoption of an internal border, including in dispute settlement. Examples include the refusal by Viet Nam of a French internal line between Cochin-China and Cambodia,[100]

---

[89] E.g. – *Sovereignty over Certain Frontier Land (Belgium v Netherlands)* (Judgment) [1959] ICJ Rep 209, 217–22.

[90] n 53.

[91] ibid.

[92] E.g. – *Frontier Dispute (Burkina Faso v Republic of Mali)* (Judgment) [1986] ICJ Rep 554, paras 19–20, 24.

[93] *Frontier Dispute (Benin v Niger)* (Judgment) [2005] ICJ Rep 90, paras 23–31, 63–66. See also: Malcolm Shaw, *Title to Territory in Africa* (OUP 1986) 256–57.

[94] *Frontier Dispute (Burkina Faso v Niger)* (Judgment) [2013] ICJ Rep 44, paras 11–20, 61–68.

[95] *Gudder Singh v The State*, High Court of Punjab (12 August 1953) 20 ILR 145, 146–47.

[96] Demarcation Agreement (Pakistan–Burma) (9 May 1966) 1014 UNTS 3, art 10; *Bay of Bengal Case (Bangladesh v Myanmar)* (Judgment of 14 March 2012) [2012] ITLOS Rep 4, para 157.

[97] Boundary Agreement (India–Myanmar) (adopted 10 March 1967, entered into force 30 May 1967) India Treaty Database No MM67B1503, preamble, art I.

[98] Treaty concerning Maritime Boundaries (Australia–Papua New Guinea) (adopted 18 December 1978, entered into force 15 February 1985) 1429 UNTS 207, arts 2–3. See also: KW Ryan and MWD White, 'The Torres Strait Treaty' (1978) 7 AYBIL 87, 94–98.

[99] Agreement on State Borders (Slovakia-Czechia) (adopted 29 October 1992, entered into force 3 May 1993) No 229/1993 Coll Zákony Prolidi, art 1.

[100] Cambodia had protested the transfer by France of Cochin-China to Viet Nam in 1949, following which Viet Nam claimed seven islands in the Gulf of Siam that had belonged to Cochin-China before 1949 – Nhu Dung Hopt-Nguyen, 'Vietnam', Max Planck Encyclopedia of Public International Law (2009) para 48. The two States eventually delimited their boundary in 2005 without reference to the 1887 line – Nguyen Hong Thao, 'Legal aspects of the supplementary treaty to the 1985 treaty on boundary delimitation between Vietnam and Cambodia' (26 January 2006) Vietnam Law & Legal

# 74 SUCCESSION TO TERRITORIAL RIGHTS AND OBLIGATIONS

the denial by Vanuatu of the 1976 transfer of the Mathew and Hunter Islands from the Anglo–French condominium of the New Hebrides to the French colony of New Caledonia,[101] and the aforementioned arbitration between Eritrea and Yemen concerning the Red Sea islands in which the applicability of an internal line of the Ottoman Empire was rejected by Eritrea and the Arbitral Tribunal.[102] Neither Mauritius nor the United Kingdom invoked the principle with respect to the detachment of the Chagos Islands prior to the secession of Mauritius in 1968.[103]

Amid the dismemberment of the SFRY from 1991 to 1992, the Badinter Commission to the Peace Conference for Yugoslavia produced advisory opinions that influenced the recognition practice of the European Community Member States.[104] In its second opinion on whether the Serbian populations of Croatia and Bosnia-Herzegovina had the right to self-determination, the Commission observed: '[W]hatever the circumstances, the right to self-determination must not involve changes to existing frontiers at the time of independence (*uti possidetis juris*) except where the States concerned agree otherwise' and that self-determination entailed a right of every individual 'to belong to whatever ethnic, religious or language community he or she wishes'.[105] In its third opinion, the Commission expressly invoked *uti possidetis juris* in advising that the internal borders within the SFRY 'may not be altered except by agreement freely arrived at' and that they had become 'frontiers protected by international law'.[106]

The subsequent practice of the successors to the SFRY does not support this conclusion of the Badinter Commission that the internal borders had automatically become international boundaries and could only be altered by mutual agreement. To the contrary, it shows that the successors have adopted internal SFRY borders by specific agreement and that they have considered themselves not to be bound by those borders in the absence of such agreement. For example, Croatia and the FRY agreed in 1996 to delimit their boundary by agreement;[107] however, it

---

Forum Magazine <https://vietnamlawmagazine.vn/legal-aspects-of-the-supplementary-treaty-to-the-1985-treaty-on-boundary-delimitation-between-vietnam-and-cambodia-3800.html> accessed 31 December 2023; Resolution No 52/2005/QH11 (29 November 2005) on the Ratification of the Treaty (on file with author) (Vietnamese); Law No 208/2016/QH13 on Treaties (on file with author) art 60.

[101] E.g. – Morsen Mosses, 'Revisiting the Matthew and Hunter Islands Dispute in Light of the Recent Chagos Advisory Opinion and Some Other Relevant Cases' (2019) 66 NILR 475.

[102] *Eritrea v Yemen* (n 26) paras 13–54, 96–100, 441–524.

[103] *Legal Consequences of the Separation of the Chagos Archipelago from Mauritius in 1965* (Advisory Opinion of 25 February 2019) para 160; ibid, Written Statement (Mauritius) para 6.58 (n 699); ibid, Written Statement (United Kingdom) paras 8.29–8.30; ibid, Oral Proceedings, CR 2018/21 (3 September 2018) 42–43 (United Kingdom); ibid, Oral Proceedings, CR 2018/27 (6 September 2018) 28.

[104] E.g. – Matthew Craven, 'The European Community Arbitration Commission on Yugoslavia' (1995) 66 BYIL 335, 336–42.

[105] Conference on Yugoslavia Arbitration Commission, Opinion No 2 (11 January 1992) 92 ILR 167, 168.

[106] Conference on Yugoslavia Arbitration Commission, Opinion No 3 (11 January 1992) 92 ILR 170, 171–72.

[107] Agreement on Normalization of Relations (Croatia–FRY) (1996) 35(5) ILM 1219, art 2.

has yet to be drawn due to a pending dispute concerning two riparian islands and littoral areas alongside the Danube River.[108] In 2001, North Macedonia and the FRY agreed to delimit their boundary: though largely based on the internal SFRY border, the treaty neither cited nor adopted it in its entirety.[109] In the *Gulf of Piran Arbitration*, Croatia and Slovenia agreed to apply *uti possidetis juris* to the determination of their border as it existed at independence but made no reference to a principle of automaticity while contesting how the border at that time was in fact defined.[110] Though adopting the internal SFRY lines, no reference has been made to the principle or automaticity in delimitation agreements.[111]

This approach of adoption of internal lines on the basis of bilateral agreement has also been followed by the 11 successors to the USSR. In a context in which territorial disputes had already arisen,[112] the hortatory Alma Ata Declaration referred to the inviolability of 'existing borders' but did not define those borders as being the inter-republican lines of the Soviet Union.[113] In delimitation agreements concluded thereafter, no reference was made to *uti possidetis juris* or a principle of automaticity.[114]

For example, Kyrgyzstan and Tajikistan have not considered themselves to be bound by the internal border in delimiting 519 kilometres of their 971-kilometre border in 2016[115] in the context of a pending dispute concerning the Batken and

[108] Duško Dimitrijević, 'A Review of the Issue of the Border between Serbia and Croatia on the Danube' (2012) 3 Megatrend Revija 1, 13–15.

[109] Agreement for the Delineation of the Borderline (North Macedonia-FRY) (adopted 23 February 2001, entered into force 16 June 2001) 2174 UNTS 3, art 2, annex 1. Certain adjustments were made with respect to a disputed riverine island and the maritime boundary – Mladen Klemencic, 'The Border Agreement between Croatia and Bosnia-Herzegovina' (Winter 1999–2000) IBRU Boundary and Security Bulletin 96, 98.

[110] *Gulf of Piran Arbitration* (n 69) paras 37, 256–61.

[111] General Framework Agreement for Peace in Bosnia and Herzegovina (Bosnia-Croatia-FRY) (14 December 1995) <https://www.osce.org/files/f/documents/e/0/126173.pdf> accessed 1 January 2024, art X, annex 2 (Art 1); Treaty on the State Border (Bosnia-Croatia) (30 July 1999) <https://www.un.org/depts/los/LEGISLATIONANDTREATIES/PDFFILES/TREATIES/HRV-BIH1999SB.PDF> accessed 1 January 2024, art 2(1); Protocol on the State Border (Croatia-FRY) (23 April 2002) Croatia Treaty List (Serbo-Croatian) (not published).

[112] For an overview, see, e.g. – Romain Yakemtchouk, 'Les conflits de territoire et de frontière dans les États de l'ex-URSS' (1993) 39 AFDI 393.

[113] Agreement establishing the Commonwealth of Independent States (8 December 1991) 31 ILM 143, art 5; Protocol to the Agreement establishing the Commonwealth of Independent States, 21 December 1991, 31 ILM (1992) 147.

[114] Treaty on Inter-State Relations (Ukraine–Belarus) (adopted 29 December 1990, entered into force 31 August 1991) 1669 UNTS 3, art 6; Treaty of Friendship (Ukraine–Belarus) (adopted 17 July 1995, entered into force 6 August 1997) 1993 UNTS 108, art 1; Treaty on State Boundary (Ukraine–Belarus) (adopted 12 May 1997, entered into force 18 June 2013) 3018 UNTS I-52468, preamble, art 1; Treaty on the State Border (Ukraine-Moldova) (18 August 1999) 34 Tratate Internationale No 332, preamble, art 1 (Romanian); Agreement on the State Border (Kazakhstan–Kyrgyzstan) (adopted 15 December 2001, entered into force 5 August 2008) <https://adilet.zan.kz/rus/docs/Z030000459_#z1> accessed 1 January 2024, art 1 (Kazakh); Agreement on the State Border (Turkmenistan–Uzbekistan) (21 September 2000) cited in Agreement on the Joint Point of the State Borders of the Three States (Turkmenistan–Uzbekistan) (10 November 2017) <https://adilet.zan.kz/rus/docs/Z1800000190> accessed 1 January 2024, art 1 (Kazakh).

[115] Agreement on Intergovernmental Relations (Kyrgyzstan-Tajikistan) (adopted 12 July 1996, entered into force 16 October 1997) 2015 UNTS 139, art 1.

76 SUCCESSION TO TERRITORIAL RIGHTS AND OBLIGATIONS

Sughd districts, enclaves in the Ferghana Valley and other border regions.[116] The claim of Russia[117] to the Crimea was not definitively abandoned until 1994.[118] Armenia and Azerbaijan have contested the applicability of the principle to their pending dispute concerning the territory of Nagorno-Karabakh.[119]

It is suggested that the vagueness of the Alma Ata Declaration, coupled with the lack of State practice in 1992, did not result in a regional custom. As in the case of the former SFRY, most of the successors to the USSR have since specifically agreed to internationalize the internal Soviet borders by bilateral agreement.

In no case has an international court or tribunal applied *uti possidetis juris* to an internal border without the joint consent of the disputing parties. Most significantly, the Arbitral Tribunal in the *Eritrea v Yemen* arbitration rejected an argument to apply the principle in the face of an objection by one disputing party.[120] In contrast to its application to international boundaries in existence at the date of succession, there is consequently no presumption of the automatic 'internationalization' of internal borders. Rather, specific consent must be provided by the neighbouring States, whether in the form of a regional custom adopted by the several successors (as in Spanish Central and South America as well as Africa) or by bilateral agreement (as in the former SFRY and USSR). If adopted, the doctrine applies only to the extent that a border was delimited at the critical date with respect to the territory in question.[121]

---

[116] Kemel Toktomushev, 'Understanding Cross-Border Conflict in Post-Soviet Central Asia: The Case of Kyrgzstan and Tajikstan' (2018) 17(1) Connections 21, 27 (n 28).

[117] Constitution of Russia (12 December 1993) in *CIS Legislation Database* <https://cis-legislation.com/> accessed 1 January 2024, art 5(1); Law No 4730-1 (1 April 1993) in *CIS Legislation Database*, ibid, art 2.

[118] Memorandum on Security Assurances (Russia–Ukraine) (5 December 1994) UNTS No I-52241, para 1. See also: UNGA Res 68/262 (1 April 2014); UN Doc A/68/PV.80 (27 March 2014). See also: State Border Treaty (Ukraine–Russia) (adopted 28 January 2003, entered into force 23 April 2004) 3161 UNTS I-54132, preamble, art 2.

[119] Declaration on Independence of Armenia (23 August 1990) in *CIS Legislation Database* (n 112) preamble; Armenia Law No ZR-265 on the Frontier (17 December 2001) in *CIS Legislation Database*, ibid, arts 2, 4–5; Constitution of Armenia (5 July 1995) in *HeinOnline World Constitutions Illustrated Database* <https://home.heinonline.org/content/world-constitutions-illustrated/> accessed 1 January 2024, preamble; Constitution of Azerbaijan (12 November 1995) in *World Constitutions Illustrated Database*, ibid, art 11 (Russian); Law No 13 on the State Border (9 December 1991) in JN Hazard and Vratislav Pechota (eds) *Russia and the Republics: Legal Materials* (1993) binder 1 (arts 2, 7).

[120] n 97. See also: *Dubai–Sharjah Border Arbitration, ad hoc* Court of Arbitration (19 October 1981) 91 ILR 543, 577–80; Derek Bowett, 'The Dubai Sharjah Boundary Arbitration of 1981' (1994) 65 BYIL 103, 104–07, 114–18, 132–33; United Arab Emirates Constitution of 1971, <https://www.constituteproject.org/constitution/United_Arab_Emirates_2004.pdf> accessed 1 January 2024, arts 2–3, 9.

[121] *Delimiting Abyei Area (Sudan v Sudan People's Liberation Movement/Army)* (Final Award) Permanent Court of Arbitration Case No 2008-07 (22 July 2009) paras 113–32, 452–503, 559–672. See also: *Maritime Delimitation and Territorial Questions (Qatar v Bahrain)* (Judgment of 16 March 2001) [2001] ICJ Rep 40, para 148.

## 3.3 Territorial Obligations

An analogy from Roman law,[122] servitudes are obligations appurtenant to the territorial title of the State whereby the territory of a 'servient' State is permitted to be used in a specified way by the territory of a 'dominant' State.[123] Though 'real' rights and duties that 'run with the land',[124] most of the technicalities that characterize servitudes or easements in internal law do not apply in international law. However, there must be a *prædium dominans* ('dominant tenement') as the territory of one State and a *prædium serviens* ('servient tenement') as the territory of another.[125]

During its codification project, the ILC debated '[o]ne of the most widely discussed questions of international law ... that of the existence of *international servitudes* ... usually understood to mean restrictions of a territorial nature which continue even if the sovereignty over the territory changes'.[126] Servitudes could 'be negative or positive, according to whether a restriction is laid upon the authority of a State over a certain part of its territory, or rights in that territory are accorded to some foreign State'.[127] One of the most controversial,[128] the ILC developed the following provision that would become Article 12 of the VCSST:

1. A succession of States does not as such affect:
   (a) Obligations relating to the use of any territory, or to restrictions upon its use, established by a treaty for the benefit of any territory of a foreign State and considered as attaching to the territories in question;
   (b) rights established by a treaty for the benefit of any territory and relating to the use, or to restrictions upon the use, of any territory of a foreign State and considered as attaching to the territories in question.

---

[122] E.g. – WW Buckland, *A Text-Book of Roman Law from Augustus to Justinian* (CUP 1932) 259–73; Hersch Lauterpacht, *Private Law Sources and Analogies of International Law* (Longmans, Green & Co Ltd, 1927) 121.

[123] E.g. – HW Reid, 'Les servitudes internationales' (1933-III) 45 RdC 1, 6–15; Georg Crusen, 'Les servitudes internationales' (1928-II) 22 RdC 1, 19–31; Manlio Udina, 'La succession des États quant aux obligations internationales autres que les dettes publiques' (1933-II) 44 RdC 665, 704–58.

[124] RWG de Muralt, *The Problem of State Succession with regard to Treaties* (van Stockum 1954) 40–59.

[125] E.g. – 'Report of the International Committee of Jurists entrusted by the Council of the League of Nations with the task of giving an advisory opinion upon the legal aspects of the Aaland Islands question', LNOJ: Special Supplement No 3 (October 1920) (*Åland Islands Advisory Opinion*). See also: *North Atlantic Coast Fisheries Case (Great Britain v United States)* (Award) Arbitral Tribunal (7 September 1910) XI RIAA 167, 181–82; *S.S. 'Wimbledon' (United Kingdom et al. v Germany)* (Judgment of 17 August 1923) Permanent Court of International Justice, Series A No 1, 24–25.

[126] Fifth Waldock Report (n 4) 47.

[127] Ibid.

[128] E.g. – UNGA Sixth Committee, 1318th Meeting (2 October 1972) GAOR: Twenty-Seventh Session, para 5 (Afghanistan).

78   SUCCESSION TO TERRITORIAL RIGHTS AND OBLIGATIONS

Corresponding provision was made for obligations and rights for the benefit of 'a group of States or of all States'.[129]

On the conclusion of the debate in the Sixth Committee on the draft articles at first reading, the ILC Chairman observed:

> The rule laid down related essentially to a treaty in which rights and obligations had attached to specific territories situated in two different States, such as agreements governing the use of the waters of an international river. In that connexion, it should be borne in mind that it could not be known in advance whether the successor State would be the inheritor of rights or the inheritor of obligations. It was just as likely in any particular situation that a new State would be harmed rather than helped by a rule which permitted the termination of a territorial regime because a succession had taken place. One might consider, for example, the situation of the new State whose economic prosperity depended on water resources provided in accordance with a pre-existing treaty governing the uses of an international river. It would be inequitable to permit the upstream riparian State that was party to the water utilization agreement concluded with the predecessor State to terminate that agreement merely because there had been a succession.[130]

Due to insufficient mass and consistency of State practice, a *general* rule on servitudes with a coherent typology had not yet crystallized as customary law by the year 1972. In examining each type of servitude, however, it is suggested that State practice and *opiniones juris* are sufficiently coherent to establish leases (other than military bases) as territorial obligations that bind a successor in the absence of persistent objection.

### 3.3.1  Leases

Leases are positive obligations that permit a dominant tenement to administer territory of the servant tenement. Though based on an analogy with domestic laws of property,[131] international leases lack the many of their technical requirements.[132] For example, there are no formality requirements to create a lease, which may also be of indeterminate duration. The hallmark of a lease is that 'ultimate title' remains with the lessor and is divorced from jurisdiction, which is granted to the lessee (normally for a fee). As there is no general international law of leasehold, the rights

---

[129] VCSST, art 12(2).

[130] UNGA Sixth Committee, 1328th Meeting (10 October 1972) GAOR: Twenty-seventh Session, para 18 (ILC Chairman).

[131] See Chapter 2.

[132] On the controversy concerning the lease of Kwantung as a servitude, see: CW Young, *The International Legal Status of the Kwantung Leased Territory* (OUP 1931) 115–24.

of 'jurisdiction' granted to the lessee and the other terms (e.g.—duration and alienability[133]) are governed by each agreement. State practice and *opiniones juris* are consistent both in recognizing a lease granted by a predecessor to a third State as a real obligation independent of treaty and its binding nature for a successor.[134]

In delimiting their boundary between North Borneo and the Philippines in 1930, the United Kingdom and the United States agreed that title to the Turtle and Mangsee Islands belonged to the United States.[135] They further agreed that the United Kingdom (through a charter company) was to be 'left undisturbed in the administration of the islands in question unless or until the United States Government give notice to His Majesty's Government of their desire that the administration of the islands should be transferred to them ... within one year after such notice is given'.[136] Upon their secession from the United States in 1946, the Philippines served notice on the United Kingdom for the termination of the lease.[137] After seceding from the United Kingdom in 1957, Myanmar ('Burma') agreed with China in 1960 to cede an area of 189 square kilometres in exchange for the cession by China of the Namwan Assigned Tract, which had previously been held by the United Kingdom under a perpetual lease.[138]

A significant case was the lease to the Belbase installations granted in 1921 by the United Kingdom to Belgium for a nominal rent and comprising docks and attendant facilities at the port of Dar-es-Salaam.[139] Nine days before independence, the Trust Territory for Tanganyika declared that it intended to treat the lease as void for having been concluded by the United Kingdom without having the

---

[133] E.g. – *Chagos Marine Protected Area Arbitration (Mauritius v United Kingdom)* (Award) Permanent Court of Arbitration (18 March 2015) paras 69–87; Convention for the Construction of a Ship Canal (Panama-United States) (adopted 18 November 1903, entered into force 25 February 1904) 96 BFSP 553, arts II–III; *Government v Diaz*, US District Court for the Canal Zone (31 January 1924) 2 ILR 95, 96.

[134] The cession of a lease ('administrative cession') from one State to another implicitly recognizes the binding nature of a lease on the holder of 'ultimate title'. On the Kwantung lease, see: Treaty of Peace (Japan–Russia) 23 August and 6 September 1905 (entered into force 15 October 1905) 98 BFSP 735, arts V–VI (French); CW Young, *The International Legal Status of the Kwantung Leased Territory* (OUP 1931) 1–37, 50–73, 97–152. The protest of China against the 'cession' of the Shantung lease from Germany to Japan was based on the specific terms of the lease that prohibited alienability without its consent rather than opposition to a general rule prohibiting alienability of leases: Treaty of Versailles, 28 June 1919 (10 January 1920) (1919) 225 CTS 188, art 156; Treaty for the Settlement of Outstanding Questions Relative to Shantung (Japan–China) (4 February 1922) 10 LNTS 310, art 1; Kiaochow Convention (6 March 1898) in WF Mayers, *Treaties between the Empire of China and Foreign Powers* (4th edn, North-China Herald Office 1902) 280–81 (art V).

[135] Boundary Convention (n 247).

[136] Agreement relative to the Sulu Archipelago (20 August 1899) 92 BFSP 1323.

[137] VA Santos and CDT Lennhoff, 'The Taganak Island Lighthouse Dispute' (1951) 45(4) AJIL 680, 682–83; I ILA Handbook (n 19) 354.

[138] Boundary Treaty (China–Burma) (adopted 1 October 1960, entered into force 4 January 1961) 1010 UNTS 111, arts I–II, IX. See further: ILA Handbook (n 19) 97–99, 363.

[139] Convention on facilitating Belgian Traffic through the Territories of East Africa (Belgium-United Kingdom) (15 March 1921) 5 LNTS 319, arts II, V. See further: Léon Darcis, 'Les Belbase: une réalization peu connue de l'expansion belge en Afrique de l'Est' (2007) 53(2) Bulletin des séances 131, 140; Earle Seaton and ST Maiti, *Tanzania Treaty Practice* (OUP 1973) 85–92.

# 80    SUCCESSION TO TERRITORIAL RIGHTS AND OBLIGATIONS

power to bind it 'in perpetuity'.[140] Commenting on draft Article 12 in the Sixth Committee, Tanzania averred:

> On the question of territorial treaties, however, the Commission had been hesitant to draw what was ... the logical conclusion, namely that the Administering Authority of a Trust Territory could not conclude a treaty on behalf of the Trust Territory so as to bind it in perpetuity. In respect of Tanganyika, for example, the United Kingdom as the Administering Authority of the Trust Territory had had no power to grant a lease in perpetuity because the trusteeship had not been in perpetuity. Nevertheless, the process of succession had not generated serious problems and any problems that might exist were being solved without much ado.[141]

Tanzania based this position on the general principle of law that States cannot transfer more rights than they possess.[142] Following the secession of the Democratic Republic of the Congo ('DRC') in 1960 and the accessions to independence of Rwanda and Burundi in 1962, the disputing parties agreed that the rights arising from the lease, including the question of compensation for its revocation, had been transferred from Belgium to Rwanda, Burundi, and the DRC.[143]

State practice and *opiniones juris* are coherent in exempting military base leases from the scope of the territorial obligation. While the ILC had not taken a position on the question of bases,[144] an exception for such bases was added by the Contracting States at the UN Conference: 'The provisions of the present article do not apply to treaty obligations of the predecessor State providing for the establishment of foreign military bases on the territory to which the succession of States relates.'[145] Adopted by a vote of 86-0-1,[146] the weight of State practice supports this exception.

Following the cession of Newfoundland by the United Kingdom to Canada in 1949, Canada considered itself to be bound by leases of military bases to the United States that included a restriction against civilian aircraft.[147] The United States and

---

[140] *UN Materials* (n 42) 187–88.

[141] UNGA Sixth Committee, 1325th Meeting (6 October 1972) GAOR para 28 (Tanzania). Tanzania also stated that services had been continued – UNGA Sixth Committee, 1487th Meeting (n 57) 26.

[142] ILC Articles (n 9) 203 (para 24); ILA Handbook (n 19) 372.

[143] O'Connell (n 1) 242–43; Darcis (n 134) 143.

[144] ILC Articles (n 9) 203 (para 25). Doubts had been expressed by certain States; e.g. – UNGA Sixth Committee, 1322nd Meeting (5 October 1972) GAOR: Twenty-Seventh Session, para 4 (Cuba).

[145] VCSST, art 12(3).

[146] Distefano, 'Article 12' in Distefano (n 47) 399–458, 419–21.

[147] Agreement regarding Leased Naval and Air Bases (United States–United Kingdom) (27 March 1941) 204 LNTS 15, art XI(5). See also: UN Secretariat, 'Succession of States in respect of bilateral treaties: second study – Air transport agreements', UN Doc A/CN.4/253 (24 March 1971) (1971) ILC Yearbook vol II 111 (para 98).

TERRITORIAL OBLIGATIONS 81

Canada agreed to modify the leases to permit civilian aircraft to use the bases.[148] For leases granted by the United Kingdom in the West Indies under the same treaty, however, the United States 'took the view that it could not, without exposing itself to criticism, insist that restrictions imposed upon the territory of the West Indies while it was in a colonial status should continue to bind it after independence'.[149] The leases were consequently not considered to bind the territories of the West Indies Federation, which maintained that 'on its independence it should have the right to form its own alliances generally an to determine for itself what military bases should be allowed on its soil and under whose control such bases should come'.[150]

On acceding to independence in 1956, Morocco insisted upon an exception to its general acceptance of succession to the treaties applied to it by France for the 1950 secret treaty whereby France had granted the use of French military bases in Morocco to the United States.[151] In anticipation of the military withdrawal of France from Morocco in 1961, the United States entered into negotiations with Morocco which resulted in their agreement to withdraw from Morocco on 17 December 1963.[152]

In seceding from France in 1960, Mali rejected succession to military base leases while Senegal agreed with France to succeed to the leases 'without prejudice to any adjustments that may be deemed necessary by mutual agreement'.[153] On seceding from Malaysia in 1965, Singapore did not accept an obligation to succeed to the military base leases concluded by Malaysia with the United Kingdom in 1957.[154] However, it made a new agreement to 'afford to the ... United Kingdom the right to continue to maintain the bases and other facilities and ... [to] permit the ... United Kingdom to make such use of these bases and facilities as that Government may consider necessary for the purposes of assisting in the defence of Singapore and Malaysia and for Commonwealth defence and for the preservation of peace in South-East Asia'.[155]

---

[148] Ibid, para 99; Agreement relating to the Use by Civil Aircraft of certain Air Bases in Newfoundland (Canada-United States) (4 June 1949) 200 UNTS 201; United States Department of State, *Treaties in Force* (2021) 64.

[149] ILC Articles (n 9) 203 (para 25).

[150] Ibid.

[151] Diplomatic Accord (France–Morocco) (28 May 1956) (1957) 51 AJIL 679, art 11, annexed protocol (art II). See also: ILA Handbook (n 19) 368; O'Connell (n 1) 257.

[152] O'Connell (n 1) 258.

[153] Rosalyn Cohen, 'Legal Problems arising from the Dissolution of the Mali Federation' (1960) 36 BYIL 375, 382; UN Secretariat, 'Succession of States in respect of bilateral treaties: second study – Air transport agreements', UN Doc A/CN.4/253 (24 March 1971) (1971) ILC Yearbook vol II 111 (para 176).

[154] Agreement on External Defence (Malaya–Singapore) (12 October 1957) 285 UNTS 59.

[155] Agreement relating to the Separation of Singapore (Singapore–Malaysia) (adopted 7 August 1965, entered into force 9 August 1965) 563 UNTS 89, art 13.

## 3.3.2 Neutralization

Unlike a lease providing for positive rights of use to the dominant tenement, neutralization is a negative form of servitude whereby the servient tenement pledges not to use a territory for military purposes. While there exist a few examples of States supporting the status of neutralization as a real obligation independent of treaty, the practice is too sparse and *opiniones juris* insufficiently precise to support an obligation of automatic transfer without the specific consent of the successor.

Belgium accepted the demilitarization of the Franco-Dutch boundary after the 1815 Congress of Vienna while France endorsed the neutralization of Chablais and Faucigny when Sardinia ceded Nice and Savoy to it in 1860.[156] On the secession of Finland from Russia in 1920, Sweden invoked the neutralization obligation under 1856 Åland Islands Convention[157] and argued that the 1856 Convention had created a 'real servitude' attaching to the Islands.[158]

A Committee of Jurists appointed by the League of Nations reported that 'the existence of international servitudes, in the true technical sense of the term, is not generally admitted' while Sweden was not a dominant tenement because it was not party to the treaty or mentioned in the relevant documents.[159] Rather, the Committee considering Finland to be bound by the duty of demilitarization as one imposed by 'definite international settlement relating to its territory' as a condition of recognition of its independence.[160] Whereas France and Italy had engaged to refrain from occupying Doumeirah Island and its adjacent islets in their 1900 delimitation treaty, Eritrea briefly occupied it in 2008, before withdrawing.[161]

## 3.3.3 Customs Restrictions

A negative obligation, customs restrictions concern the duty of the servient tenement to refrain from applying customs taxes to a territory for the benefit of the dominant tenement. Confined to a single known case, State practice is insufficient to support its automatic transfer to a successor without specific consent.In the *Free Zones of Upper Savoy Case*, the PCIJ held restrictions placed by the 1816

---

[156] ILC Articles (n 9) 204–05 (para 31). See also: *Beagle Channel Arbitration (Argentina v Chile)* (Award) 52 ILR 93, 130.

[157] Convention respecting the Åland Islands (Russia–France–United Kingdom) (adopted 30 March 1856, entered into force 27 April 1856) 46 BFSP 23, art I (French).

[158] *Åland Islands Advisory Opinion* (n 120) 3, 16.

[159] Ibid, 16–17; Aland Islands Convention (n 152) art I.

[160] Ibid, 18. The ILC interpreted the opinion of the Committee as based not on 'the territorial character of the treaty' but rather 'on the theory of the dispositive effect of an international settlement' – ILC Articles (n 9) 198 (para 5).

[161] UNSC 5924th Meeting (24 June 2008) UN Doc S/PV.5924, 4, 7, 8–9, 12, 14. See also: Protocols respecting the Delimitation of the Coast of the Red Sea and the Gulf of Aden (Italy–France) (24 January 1900 and 10 July 1901) 94 BFSP 588, arts I, III.

Swiss–Sardinian delimitation treaty on the imposition of customs dues by Sardinia in the District of Saint-Gingolph to have bound France after its cession in 1860 due to the nature of the rights concerned as attaching to the territory which France had respected before proposing the abolition of the regime to Switzerland in 1919.[162] While the German courts recognized customs rights exercised by Germany connected to the maintenance of railway establishments in Basel insofar as Switzerland had 'ceded' them, the case was not one of succession.[163]

### 3.3.4 Rights of Passage

Rights of passage are positive obligations that permit the dominant tenement to use the territory of the servient tenement for passage. State practice on succession to treaty provisions[164] through the territory of the successor or counterparty is limited.[165] Moreover, it is contradictory on their automatic transfer independent of the underpinning treaty.[166]

The civilian and military rights of free passage stipulated in the 1926 Anglo–French treaty concluded on behalf of Mandatory Palestine, Syria, and the Lebanon were not observed by Israel, Syria, and the Lebanon after independence.[167] In the *Rights of Passage over Indian Territory Case*, the ICJ held the 1779 Treaty of Poona between Portugal and the Maratha Empire to have provided Portugal with a right of passage between its territories in respect of private persons, civil officials, and goods (though not for military purposes) and that a 'constant and uniform practice' between Portugal and British India, as well as India, had allowed such free passage.[168] This finding was ambiguous in that it was not clearly based on a real obligation that automatically bound India on its secession in 1947, as opposed to its subsequent consent.

---

[162] *Free Zones of Upper Savoy and the District of Gex (France v Switzerland)* (Judgment of 7 June 1932) PCIJ Series A/B No 46, 145.

[163] *German Railway Station at Basle Case*, District Court of Karlsruhe (22 June 1928) 4 ILR 136, 138. See also: *Poland v Stanek*, Supreme Court of Poland (17 December 1924) 2 ILR 103.

[164] For an example outside of the succession context, see: *Iron Rhine Arbitration (Belgium v Netherlands)* (Award) Arbitral Tribunal (24 May 2005) 27 RIAA 41, paras 28–61.

[165] For example, the question of the rights of passage through the Suez Canal under the 1888 Constantinople Convention with respect to the merger of Egypt and Syria in 1958, followed by the secession of Syria in 1961, did not practically arise due to the succession of the United Arab Republic to the treaties of Egypt.

[166] On the 'controversial nature' of such rights, see: *S.S. Wimbledon Case (Great Britain, France, Italy and Japan v Germany)* (Judgment of 17 August 1923) PCIJ Series A No 1, 24. See also: Treaty for the Settlement of the Dispute regarding Tacna and Arica (Chile-Peru) (adopted 3 June 1929, entered into force 28 July 1929) 94 LNTS 401, art 2; *Maritime Dispute (Peru v Chile)* (Judgment) [2014] ICJ Rep 3, paras 16–24.

[167] Agreement of Good Neighbourly Relations (France–United Kingdom) (2 February 1926) 56 LNTS 79, arts I–II.

[168] *Rights of Passage over Indian Territory (Portugal v India)* (Merits) [1960] ICJ Rep 6, 33, 40, 46. See also: ILC Articles (n 9) 198–99.

# 84 SUCCESSION TO TERRITORIAL RIGHTS AND OBLIGATIONS

## 3.3.5 Navigation and Water Rights

Navigational rights are positive obligations that permit the dominant tenement to navigate waterways running through the territory of the servient tenement. Water rights can be positive obligations for the dominant tenement to use their waters for specified purposes, such as irrigation, or negative obligations restricting the use of water to maintain water flows and levels for the benefit of the dominant tenement. While there exists considerable State practice on navigational and water rights, it is insufficiently coherent to underpin their automatic transfer independent of the underpinning treaty.

Following the cession of Louisiana by France, Spain accepted the binding character of the rights of navigation on the River Mississippi granted to the United Kingdom in the 1763 Treaty of Paris.[169] However, it had been a counterparty to the treaty that had created the rights.[170] There is no evidence to suggest that its acceptance was based on their real character, as opposed to its treaty obligation to recognize them.

Following the accession to independence of Iraq in 1932, Iran rejected its succession to the 1849 Treaty of Erzerum. The navigational rights of both parties on the Shatt-el-Arab under that treaty as well as that of the United Kingdom under a 1930 treaty were recognized in their 1938 delimitation treaty.[171] In the context of a boundary dispute, there is no evidence that Iran and Iraq had recognized those rights between 1932 and 1938.[172]

Granted by earlier treaties and affirmed in the 1926 Franco–Siamese Treaty, the navigational rights of Thailand on the River Mekong were recognized by Cambodia, Laos, and South Viet Nam upon their secessions from France in 1953.[173] Although this indicates recognition of the real character of the right, information on their practice is insufficiently specific to confirm this interpretation. While Belgium considered itself bound by the navigational rights on the Rivers Congo and Niger provided in the 1885 Berlin Act after absorbing the Independent State of the Congo in 1905, it was a participating State to the Berlin Act.[174] Similarly, recognition of these navigational rights by the riparian States to the River Niger was seemingly based upon treaty participation.[175]

---

[169] ILC Articles (n 9) 203 (para 26).

[170] Definitive Treaty of Peace (France-Spain-United Kingdom) (10 February 1763) 42 CTS 279, art VII.

[171] Boundary Treaty (Iran-Iraq) (4 July 1937) 190 LNTS 256, arts 4–5; protocol (art IV).

[172] Hersch Lauterpacht, 'River Boundaries: Legal Aspects of the Shatt-al-Arab Frontier' (1960) 9(2) ICLQ 208, 226–32.

[173] ILC Articles (n 9) 203 (para 26).

[174] *Oscar Chinn Case (United Kingdom v Belgium)* (Judgment of 12 December 1934) PCIJ Series A/B No 63, 65, 79–81.

[175] Act regarding Navigation between the States of the Niger Basin (adopted 26 October 1963, entered into force 1 February 1966) 587 UNTS 9, art 1. See also: ILC Articles (n 9) 205 (para 32).

The most significant case was the 1929 Nile Waters Agreement providing, *inter alia*, that the United Kingdom would not without the prior agreement of Egypt construct 'irrigation or power works or [take] measures ... on the river Nile and its branches, or on the lakes from which it flows, so far as all these are in the Sudan or in countries under British administration, which would, in such a manner as to entail any prejudice to the interests of Egypt, either reduce the quantity of water arriving in Egypt, or modify the date of its arrival, or lower its level'.[176] While Sudan stated in 1956 that it did not regard itself as party to the 1929 Agreement, Egypt declared itself to be party in 1958.[177] In 1959, Egypt and the Sudan concluded a new treaty for expanded regulation of the Nile on the basis of 'existing rights' under the 1929 Agreement.[178]

The 1929 Agreement also concerned the territories of Tanganyika, Kenya, and Uganda; upon independence, Tanzania declared itself not to be bound, to which the United Arab Republic (as successor to Egypt) countered that it considered the Agreement to apply.[179] Since its secession in 2011, South Sudan has not succeeded to the 1959 Agreement, while the 2010 Cooperative Framework Agreement of the Nile Basin Initiative has been signed by Tanzania and Kenya and ratified by Uganda.[180] Consequently, the positions of the riparian States have centred on their participation in the treaties rather than the real character of the obligation to maintain water levels.

In 1953, Syria invoked rights of irrigation, water supply, navigation, and fishing under the Anglo–French Agreements of 1920,[181] 1923,[182] and 1926[183] in objecting to a hydroelectric project of Israel.[184] Israel denied that it was bound in law by the treaties but expressed its willingness '*ex gratia*, to accept all the rights and obligations which would be incumbent upon it in this respect if the treaty were still valid'.[185] This *opinio juris* indicates that Israel did not consider the invoked rights to have a real character independent of the treaties.[186]

---

[176] Exchange of Notes in regard to the Use of the Waters of the River Nile for Irrigation Purposes (7 May 1929) 93 LNTS 43, para 4(i).

[177] ILA Handbook (n 19) 353–54.

[178] Agreement for the Nile Waters (UAR–Sudan) (adopted 8 November 1959, entered into force 12 December 1959) 453 UNTS 63, preamble, art 1.

[179] ILC Articles (n 9) 203–04 (para 27). See also: UNGA Sixth Committee, 1487th Meeting (n 57) 26.

[180] Cooperative Framework Agreement (14 May 2010) (not in force) <https://www.nilebasin.org/index.php/81-nbi/73-cooperative-framework-agreement> accessed 1 January 2024.

[181] Convention on the Mandates for Syria and the Lebanon, Palestine and Mesopotamia (23 December 1920) 22 LNTS 353 art 8.

[182] Agreement respecting the Boundary Line between Syria and Palestine (France–United Kingdom) (7 March 1923) 22 LNTS 363, 372.

[183] Agreement of Good Neighbourly Relations concluded on behalf of the Territories of Palestine, Syria and Great Lebanon (France–United Kingdom) (2 February 1926) 56 LNTS 80, art III.

[184] UNSC 636th Meeting (10 November 1953) SCOR, paras 11, 37, 87; UNSC 639th Meeting (18 November 1953) SCOR, paras 81–87.

[185] UNSC 639th Meeting, ibid, para 87.

[186] The provisions of the 1994 Israel–Jordan peace treaty on water also omitted reference to the Anglo-French treaties – Treaty of Peace (Israel–Jordan) (adopted 26 October 1994, entered into force 10 November 1994) 2042 UNTS 351 art 6; annex II.

## 86   SUCCESSION TO TERRITORIAL RIGHTS AND OBLIGATIONS

The legal positions of States concerning water rights in other treaties are opaque, including: Afghanistan and Pakistan concerning the water rights prescribed in the 1921 Anglo–Afghan treaty;[187] the DRC and the Sudan regarding the prohibition of works on the Semliki and Isango Rivers to maintain the water level of Lake Albert under the 1906 treaty between the United Kingdom and the Congo Free State;[188] the successors to the Ottoman Empire (Syria, Lebanon, Saudi Arabia, Jordan, Sudan, Libya, Yemen, Iraq, Morocco, and Tunis) concerning navigational rights under the 1888 Suez Canal treaty;[189] and Namibia and Angola on the damming of the Kunene River for irrigation and hydro-electricity production under the 1926 South Africa–Portugal treaty.[190]

### 3.3.6   Fishing and Grazing Rights

Fishing and grazing rights are positive obligations permitting the dominant tenement to use the territory of the servient tenement for agricultural purposes. State practice and *opiniones juris* are insufficiently cohesive on the recognition of such rights as real obligations. Rather, questions of succession to such rights have been addressed with reference to the treaties that created them.

In the 1910 *North Atlantic Fisheries Case*, the United States argued that their rights under the 1818 Treaty of Ghent constituted 'an International servitude in their favour over the territory of Great Britain, thereby involving a derogation from the sovereignty of Great Britain, the servient State, and that therefore Great Britain [was] deprived, by reason of the grant, of its independent right to regulate the fishery'.[191] The Arbitral Tribunal rejected the contention, finding, *inter alia*, that a servitude in international law predicated an express grant of a sovereign right, involving an analogy to a *prædium dominans* and *prædium serviens*, whereas the 1818 Treaty granted not a sovereign right but a 'purely economic right, to the inhabitants of another State'.[192]

---

[187] Treaty for the Establishment of Neighbourly Relations (Afghanistan–United Kingdom) (22 November 1921) XIV LNTS 47, art II.

[188] Agreement modifying the Agreement signed at Brussels, May 12, 1894, relating to the Spheres of Influence in East and Central Africa (Congo Free State–United Kingdom) (9 May 1906) 99 BFSP 173, art III. See also: Treaty of Cession of the Independent State of the Congo (Belgium–Congo Free State) (28 November 1907) 100 BFSP 705, art 1 (French); Law on the Government of the Belgian Congo (18 October 1908) 101 BFSP 733, ss 27–28 (French); O'Connell (n 1) 36; Céléstin Nguya-Ndila, *Indépendance de la République Démocratique du Congo et les engagements internationaux antérieurs* (University of Kinshasa 1971) 82–84.

[189] Convention respecting the Free Navigation of the Suez Maritime Canal (adopted 29 October 1888, entered into force 22 December 1888) 79 BFSP 18, art I (French); *UN Materials* (n 42) 158.

[190] Agreement regulating the use of the Kunene River (Portugal-South Africa) (adopted 1 July 1926, entered into force 14 February 1928) 70 LNTS 315, arts 1–14.

[191] *The North Atlantic Fisheries Case (Great Britain v United States of America)* (Award) Permanent Court of Arbitration (7 September 1910) XI RIAA 167, 181.

[192] Ibid, 181–83.

THE PROCESS OF SUCCESSION    87

While Canada accepted the continuation in force of fishery rights in Newfoundland waters that had been granted the United States in the 1818 Treaty of Ghent,[193] there is no evidence that its acceptance was based on their real character. Similarly, the grazing rights provided for Somali nationals by the Anglo–Ethiopian treaties of 1897[194] and 1954[195] in the Ogaden territorial dispute were stated by Ethiopia to be 'automatically invalid' even as Somalia rejected succession to the treaties.[196] The positions of Zambia and Angola are not known concerning rights established by a 1954 Anglo–Portuguese treaty of camping, fishing, grazing, agricultural, and watering for authorized Zambian villages in Angolan territory and Angolan villages in Zambian territory.[197]

## 3.4  The Process of Succession

As a succession of States is a transfer of territorial title, a successor automatically receives the territorial claims and other rights that are appurtenant to the transferred title. Since this transfer occurs by operation of law, no declaration of succession is necessary by the successor to claim them. A successor may consequently assert a territorial claim or other right from the date of succession without any prior formality.

As the successor receives from the predecessor no more rights than the predecessor possessed, a legal presumption is that the successor is bound by the boundaries of the title delimited by the predecessor with neighbouring States. For the successors to Spain in Central and South America and the Member States of the African Union, a regional custom of transformation of internal borders into boundaries also applies. Except for those pertaining to military bases, a successor is also bound by leases granted by a predecessor to a third State. These general rules of customary international law that apply automatically to a succession can be displaced by a successor in exercise of the persistent objector principle for which a high evidentiary burden applies.

For regions outside Central and South America and Africa, the transformation of internal borders applies not by operation of law but rather the mutual consent of the States concerned. The same rule of consent applies to servitudes other than

---

[193]  ILC Articles (n 9) 202 (para 22); Gonçalves Pereira (n 215) 119.

[194]  Treaty between Great Britain and Ethiopia (14 May 1897) 89 BFSP 31, annex 3.

[195]  Agreement relating to certain matters connected with the Withdrawal of British Military Administration from the Territories designated as the Reserved Area and the Ogaden (Ethiopia–United Kingdom) (29 November 1954) 161 BFSP 93, arts I–II, schedule.

[196]  DJL Brown, 'Recent Developments in the Ethiopia–Somaliland Frontier Dispute' (1961) 10 ICLQ 167, 168–78, 171; ILA Handbook (n 19) 354. See also: Colonial Office, 'Report of the Somaliland Protectorate Constitutional Conference' (May 1960) Cmd 1044, annex VIII ('Draft Somaliland Ordinance') para 14; *UN Materials* (n 42) 185; O'Connell (n 1) 302–04.

[197]  Agreement with regard to certain Angolan and Northern Rhodesian Natives living on the Kwando River (8 November 1954) 161 BFSP 167, arts 1–2.

leases. In such cases, the question is the manifestation of consent, for which a key problem is the interpretation of silence in the legal position of a State.[198] The rules of acquiescence and estoppel in general international law can resolve evidentiary ambiguity.

### 3.4.1 Territorial Treaties

In the course of its codification project on succession to treaties, the ILC considered whether succession is automatically effected by operation of law to territorial (also termed 'real', 'dispositive', or 'localized') treaties from the date of succession.[199] Such treaties had been defined by the ILA as follows: 'Treaties may be 'localized' if they: (a) are in the nature of objective territorial regimes created in the interests of one nation or the community of nations; (b) are applied locally in virtue of territorial application clauses; (c) touch or concern a particular area of land.'[200] Candidates for inclusion in this category were treaties on border delimitation and demarcation, border management (e.g.—traffic, customs), and riparian navigation.[201] The ILC also referred in an open list to 'demilitarization or neutralization of particular localities.'[202]

In their comments on the 1972 draft articles adopted by the ILC at first reading, States were divided in the Sixth Committee on the question of automatic succession to 'so-called "dispositive", "territorial" or "localized" treaties.'[203] The ILC ultimately considered State practice not to support a general rule of automatic succession to territorial treaties.[204] State practice and *opiniones juris* preceding the codification project confirm this rejection of an exception for territorial treaties to the general rule of customary law of succession to bilateral treaties by consent.[205] The reliance of the ILC on the exception for treaties 'establishing a boundary' from the rule on fundamental change of circumstances as grounds for treaty termination or withdrawal[206] is misplaced because State succession is excluded from the scope of the VCLT.[207]

---

[198] E.g. – Danae Azaria, 'State Silence as Acceptance: A Presumption and an Exception' (2024) BYIL 6–19, https://doi.org/10.1093/bybil/brae002.

[199] ILC Articles (n 194) 196–99.

[200] ILA Handbook (n 19) 352.

[201] Ibid, 353.

[202] ILC Articles (n 194) 197 (para 1).

[203] Humphrey Waldock, 'Fourth report on succession in respect of treaties' (24 June 1971) UN Doc A/CN.4/249 (1971) ILC Yearbook vol II 143, para 5. See also: GAOR (Twenty-fifth Session) Annexes Doc A/8147, paras 73–97.

[204] ILC Articles (n 194) paras 17–18.

[205] See Chapter 5.

[206] Vienna Convention on the Law of Treaties, 23 May 1969 (entered into force 27 January 1980) 1155 UNTS 331 ('VCLT') art 62(2)(a); Malcolm Shaw and Caroline Fournet, 'Article 62 Convention of 1969' in Corten and Klein (n 41) 1411, 1421–424.

[207] Ibid, art 73; René Prevost, 'Article 73 Convention of 1969' in Corten and Klein (n 41) 1645, 1646–649.

Territorial treaties were frequently included in succession agreements without distinction from other types of treaty.[208] *Opīniōnes juris* in support of automatic succession were expressed at various times by Tanzania ('Tanganyika'),[209] Uganda,[210] Zambia,[211] the United Kingdom,[212] and Cyprus.[213] While Tanzania and the United Kingdom provided examples of treaties that they considered to be 'territorial', the other States did not.[214]

However, there are many examples of States rejecting automatic succession to treaties of delimitation, border management, and navigation. In 1935, Iran ('Persia') considered the consent of both Iraq and Turkey to be necessary to succeed to the 1849 Treaty of Erzerum delimiting the Ottoman–Iranian border and regulating navigation on the Shatt al-Arab.[215] While the 1888 Constantinople Convention on the Suez Canal lacks a depositary,[216] the successors to the Ottoman Empire (Syria, Saudi Arabia, Jordan, Lebanon, Libya, Yemen, Iraq, Morocco, Tunis, and the Sudan) were not invited to a conference of counterparties in 1956.[217] Afghanistan rejected the succession of Pakistan to the 1919 Anglo–Afghani delimitation treaty.[218]

Whereas Morocco agreed with Spain on 16 March 1967 to transfer responsibility for the Tetuan and Nador aeroports in the former Spanish Zone, it did not consider itself to be obliged to succeed to air transport agreements.[219] Algeria generally declined succession to the bilateral treaties of France,[220] including the 1842 Franco–Moroccan delimitation treaty. Tanganyika rejected succession to the 1929 Anglo–Belgian treaty on the port of Dar-es-Salaam and the 1929 Nile Waters Agreement, as did the Sudan.[221]

In its practice, Thailand did not accept automatic succession to territorial treaties. It expressly agreed with India to provisionally continue the 1937

---

[208] E.g. – ILA Handbook (n 19) 95, 367; 168 BFSP 224 (n 5).

[209] Notes 304, 307. In view of its position on the Nile Waters Agreement, Tanzania excluded river treaties from its definition – Seaton and Maiti (n 134) 28. On Nauru, see: Humphrey Waldock, 'Third report on succession in respect of treaties', UN Doc A/CN.4/224 and Add.1 (22 April and 27 May 1970) (1970) ILC Yearbook vol II, 36–37. On Kenya, see: ILC Articles (n 194) 190.

[210] *UN Materials on Succession of States* (1967) UN Doc ST/LEG/SER.B/14, 179–80.

[211] n 59.

[212] Third Waldock Report (n 204) 36–37.

[213] *UN Materials* (n 42) 182–83; 431 UNTS 294.

[214] Third Waldock Report (n 204) 36–37.

[215] 16(2) LNOJ (1935) 117, 120. See further: Hersch Lauterpacht, 'River Boundaries: Legal Aspects of the Shatt al-Arab Frontier' (1960) 9(2) ICLQ 208; KH Kaikobad, 'The Shatt-al-Arab River Boundary: A Legal Reappraisal' (1985) 56 BYIL 49, 52–69.

[216] Convention respecting the Free Navigation of the Suez Maritime Canal (adopted 29 October 1888, entered into force 22 December 1888) 79 BFSP 18, arts XVI–XVII (French).

[217] *UN Materials* (n 42) 158.

[218] Note 276.

[219] Agreement on Transfer of Responsibility of Tetuan and Nador Airports (Spain-Morocco) (16 March 1967) 1 SPTI 340.

[220] André Gonçalves Pereira, *La succession d'États en matière de traité* (Pedone 1969) 79.

[221] ILA Handbook (n 19) 353–54.

90 SUCCESSION TO TERRITORIAL RIGHTS AND OBLIGATIONS

Anglo–Thai treaty of friendship, commerce, and navigation[222] before replacing it in 1968.[223] It denied the succession of Myanmar ('Burma') to the 1941 Anglo–Thai treaty on border traffic.[224] Though it initially did 'not question the continuity of the Treaty of 1934 relating to the Pak Chan River', it ultimately did not did not accept the succession of Burma to it.[225]

Although disputing parties periodically invoked automatic succession to territorial treaties in dispute settlement, their *opiniones juris* have been inconsistent. In the *Temple of Preah Vihear Case*, Thailand argued that customary international law on State succession did not provide that, following its secession from France, Cambodia automatically succeeded to the boundary provisions of the 1904 Franco–Siamese delimitation treaty but not its dispute settlement provisions.[226] Cambodia claimed succession not only to boundaries but also to the dispute settlement provisions in those treaties.[227] The Court did not pronounce on the question of succession, though it noted it to be 'common ground' between the Parties that the treaty applied to their dispute.[228]

In their territorial dispute concerning the Aozou Strip, Libya opposed the argument of Chad that the 1935 Franco–Italian treaty had delimited their frontier on the ground that it had never entered into force.[229] While the ICJ accepted the argument of Chad that the 1955 treaty had delimited a complete boundary between them in reference to prior treaties, including the contested area,[230] it did not rule that Libya and Chad had automatically succeeded to the 1955 treaty but rather relied on the fact that they had not contested the frontier in the two decades after its conclusion.[231]

---

[222] 'Succession of States in respect of bilateral treaties: third study – Trade agreements' (9 April 1971) UN Doc A/CN.4/253/Add.1, para 28.

[223] Trade Agreement (Thailand–India) (13 December 1968) 656 UNTS 3. The 1941 treaty is omitted from the treaty databases of both India and Thailand.

[224] ILA Handbook (n 19) 192––93.

[225] Ibid. The 1934 border treaty is omitted from the Thailand treaty database and the 1994 Thai–Burmese treaty refers to the 1868 Anglo–Thai border delimitation treaty but not the 1934 treaty – Agreement on the Friendship Bridge (Thailand–Myanmar) (17 October 1994) Thailand Treaty Database, art 11; Exchange of Notes regarding the Boundary (Thailand-United Kingdom) (1 June 1934) Treaty Series No 19 (1934) Cmd 4671.

[226] *Temple of Preah Vihear (Cambodia v Thailand)* (Preliminary Objections) vol I (Pleadings) Preliminary Objections of Thailand (23 May 1960) 145–47 (paras 40–41); vol II (Oral Arguments) 22, 31–40, 106–09.

[227] Ibid, Observations du gouvernement Royal du Cambodge (22 July 1960) 164–66 (paras 30–34); *Oral Pleadings* (n 221) 77–79, 83.

[228] *Temple of Preah Vihear* (n 220) (Judgment of 26 May 1961) [1961] ICJ Rep 17, 38; *Temple of Preah Vihear Case (Thailand v Cambodia)* (Merits) (Judgment of 15 June 1962) [1962] ICJ Rep 6, 16, 32; Counter-Memorial of Thailand (29 September 1961) para 40. See also: Memorial of Cambodia (20 January 1960) para 5; *ICJ Pleadings, Temple of Preah Vihear* vol II, 161, 263–64; ILC Articles (n 194) 198 (para 7).

[229] *Libya v Chad* (n 62) paras 18–21. See also: Shaw (n 88) 253.

[230] Ibid, paras 40–51.

[231] Ibid, paras 66–71.

The conclusion of the ILC that State practice and *opiniones juris* were insufficiently coherent to support a customary rule of automatic succession to territorial treaties has been fortified by State practice arising after the conclusion of the VCSST. While West Germany provisionally continued participation in certain East German bilateral treaties on river management and border crossings,[232] neither its succession to those treaties nor the extension to East Germany of its own treaties on those fields was considered to be automatic.[233] Yemen succeeded neither to the 1934 Saudi–Yemeni delimitation treaty ('Treaty of Taif')[234] nor to a *modus vivendi* treaty between North Yemen and the United Kingdom.[235]

The 1968 Italy–Yugoslavia continental shelf delimitation treaty is listed by Italy as being in force with respect to Croatia from 8 October 1991 by an agreement concluded on 29 July 2005.[236] The provisions of the 1994 Israel–Jordan peace treaty dealing with water[237] omitted reference to the provisions of the 1920 and 1923 Anglo–French boundary treaties concerning the River Jordan and its tributaries.[238] While Austria regarded its succession agreements with the successors to Czecho-Slovakia and the SFRY[239] to be 'confirmatory' of a customary rule of automatic succession to delimitation and border management treaties,[240] the successors considered their succession to have been effected by consent.

*Opīniōnes juris* in favour of automatic succession were seemingly expressed by the successors to the USSR (save Georgia) when they agreed in 1992 that Soviet delimitation agreements with a third State were to remain in force 'according to

---

[232] Andreas Zimmermann, 'State Succession in Respect of Treaties' in Jan Klabbers et al. (eds) *State Practice regarding State Succession and Issues of Recognition* (Kluwer, 1999) 80, 84 (n 179) 87, 92.

[233] Protocol concerning the Reunification of Germany for their Bilateral Treaty Relations (West Germany-Netherlands) (adopted 25 January 1994, entered into force 19 July 1994) 2441 UNTS 135, annex I.

[234] Treaty of Islamic Friendship and Brotherhood (Yemen–Saudi Arabia) (adopted 20 May 1934, entered into force 22 June 1934) 2389 UNTS 231, art 22; International Boundary Treaty (Yemen–Saudi Arabia) (adopted 12 June 2000, entered into force 4 July 2000) 2389 UNTS 203, arts 1–2; Memorandum of Understanding (Yemen–Saudi Arabia) (adopted 26 February 1995, entered into force 15 May 1995) 2389 UNTS 193, arts 1, 10. See further: AH Al-Enazy, '"The International Boundary Treaty" (Treaty of Jeddah) concluded between the Kingdom of Saudi Arabia and the Yemeni Republic on June 12, 2000' (2002) 96(1) AJIL 161 (note 3) 161, 163, 167 (note 48); Richard Schofield, 'Negotiating the Saudi-Yemeni international boundary' (July 2000) <https://al-bab.com/negotiating-saudi-yemeni-international-boundary> accessed 1 January 2024.

[235] Agreement regarding Relations between the United Kingdom and Yemen (20 January 1951) 101 UNTS 39.

[236] Accord on the Delimitation of the Continental Shelf (Italy–SFRY) (adopted 8 January 1968, entered into force 21 January 1970) 7(3) ILM 547.

[237] Treaty of Peace (n 181) art 6, annex II.

[238] Convention on the Mandates for Syria and the Lebanon, Palestine and Mesopotamia (n 176) art 8.

[239] E.g. – Exchange of Notes regarding Austrian-Czechoslovak Treaties (Austria–Slovakia) (14 January 1994) 1046 BGBl (28 December 1994) (German); Bilateral Agreements in Force (Austria–Czechia) 123 BGBl (31 July 1997) (German).

[240] Helmut Tichy, 'Two Recent Cases of State Succession – An Austrian Perspective' (1992) 44 AJPIL 117, 135; *Case No 7Ob573/93* Supreme Court of Austria (6 October 1993) (German).

## 92  SUCCESSION TO TERRITORIAL RIGHTS AND OBLIGATIONS

international law'.[241] While affirming the Soviet boundaries, their subsequent practice has been nevertheless based on succession agreements reached with third States rather than automatic succession. For example, Azerbaijan, Kazakhstan, and Turkmenistan rejected succession to the two Soviet–Iranian treaties on navigation, commerce, and fishing concerning the Caspian Sea[242] and the 2018 Convention on the Legal Status of the Caspian Sea makes no reference to the Soviet–Iranian treaties in addressing questions of delimitation, navigation, fishing, and demilitarization.[243]

In the *Gabčikovo-Nagymaros Project Case* concerning the status of a Hungary–Czechoslovakia bilateral treaty on the construction of a barrage system on the Danube River, Hungary and Slovakia agreed that Slovakia was 'the sole successor State in respect of rights and obligations relating to the ... Project'.[244] However, Hungary argued that the treaty had lapsed by the dismemberment of Czecho-Slovakia on 31 December 1992 because it had rejected a proposal by Slovakia to succeed to the treaty while there was no general rule of automatic succession to bilateral treaties.[245] Slovakia argued the treaty to have continued to apply in virtue of a 'general rule of continuity which applies in the case of dissolution'; alternatively, as a treaty of 'a territorial or localized character' per Article 12 of the VCSST.[246]

The ICJ held the treaty to have become automatically binding upon Slovakia but not Czechia in virtue of customary international law on automatic succession to territorial treaties, as expressed in Article 12 VCSST.[247] Holding the treaty to have been of a territorial character, the Court observed:

> Article 12, in providing only, without reference to the treaty itself, that rights and obligations of a territorial character established by a treaty are unaffected by a succession of States, appears to lend support to the position of Hungary rather than of Slovakia. However the Court concludes that this formulation was devised rather to take account of the fact that, in many cases, treaties which had established boundaries or territorial regimes were no longer in force ... [t]hose that remained in force would nonetheless bind a successor State.[248]

---

[241] CIS Memorandum of Understanding concerning Legal Succession concerning the Agreements of the former USSR (6 July 1992) (1993) 26 RBDI 627, arts 1–3 (French). See also: Agreement establishing the Commonwealth of Independent States (8 December 1991) (1992) 31 ILM 143, art 12.

[242] E.g. – Barbara Janusz-Pawletta, *The Legal Status of the Caspian Sea* (Springer 2015) 20.

[243] Convention on the Caspian Sea (12 August 2018) (not in force) Russia Treaty Database, No 20180068 (Russian).

[244] Special Agreement (Hungary–Slovakia) (2 July 1993) <https://www.icj-cij.org/case/92/institution-proceedings> accessed 31 December 2023, preamble, art 2(b).

[245] *Gabčikovo-Nagymaros Project (Hungary v Slovakia)* (Judgment) [1997] ICJ Rep 7, paras 118–19. Agreement had not been reached by the start of the proceedings – ibid (Memorial of Hungary) paras 10.118–10.120.

[246] Ibid, paras 120–22.

[247] The Court noted that neither of the Parties disputed the customary character of Article 12 – *Gabčikovo-Nagymaros Project* (n 240) para 123.

[248] Ibid.

The negotiating history of Article 12 supports the legal position of Hungary rather than the finding of the Court.[249] The intention of the ILC to distinguish between 'rights and obligations of a territorial character established by a treaty' and the treaty itself, as affirmed by the Contracting States to the VCSST, [250] supports the argument of Hungary that the succession of Slovakia to the Hungary–Czechoslovakia treaty did not occur in the absence of agreement between the successor and the counterparty. Consequently, the interpretation of Article 12 as applying to succession not only to territorial rights and obligations but also to the underlying treaty is wrong.

In this context, State practice supports the application to territorial treaties of the customary rule of succession by agreement to bilateral treaties.[251] This can be done by express agreement, as for the succession of the Philippines to the 1930 Anglo–American delimitation treaty on the cession of the lease to the Turtle and Mangsee Islands by the United Kingdom in 1948.[252] A successor and counterparty can also implicitly[253] agree to a succession by declaring in their delimitation treaty that prior treaties between the predecessor and counterparty are terminated.[254] Agreement can also be manifested in dispute settlement, as when Namibia and Botswana agreed to submit their territorial dispute to the ICJ 'on the basis of the Anglo-German Treaty of 1 July 1890'.[255] Similarly, Equatorial Guinea and Gabon agreed in 2021 to submit a territorial dispute to the ICJ to which they recognized as applicable the 1900 France–Spain delimitation treaty.[256]

---

[249] ILC Articles (n 194) 206 (para 36). See also: PK Menon, *The Succession of States in respect to Treaties, State Property, Archives and Debts* (E. Mellen Press 1991) 9–15.

[250] For support of the description adopted by the ILC, see: UNGA Sixth Committee, 1320th Meeting (4 October 1972) GAOR (Twenty-Seventh Session) para 16 (Poland); ibid, 1321st Meeting (4 October 1972) para 33; ibid, 1325th Meeting (6 October 1972) para 2, 1322nd Meeting (5 October 1972) para 6.

[251] See Chapter 5.

[252] Exchange of Notes regarding the Turtle and Mangsee Islands (Philippines–United Kingdom) (20 April 1948) Treaty Series No 58 (1951) Cmd 8320; Convention regarding the Boundary between the Philippines and North Borneo (United States–United Kingdom) (2 January 1930 and 6 July 1932, entered into force 13 December 1932) Treaty Series No 2 (1933) Cmd 4241.

[253] See Chapter 5.

[254] Boundary Treaty (China–Burma) (adopted 1 October 1960, entered into force 4 January 1961) 1010 UNTS 111, art XII.

[255] *Kasikili/Sedudu Island (Botswana v Namibia)* (Judgment) [1999] ICJ Rep 1045 paras 9, 18, 71–72, 87, 94–95, 99. See also, e.g. – *S v Malumo* (CC 32-2001) High Court of Namibia (7–14 September 2015) [1025] NAHCMD 213, paras 1008–1018.

[256] Special Agreement (Gabon–Equatorial Guinea) (15 November 2016) < https://www.icj-cij.org/case/179> accessed 1 January 2024, arts 1–3; Convention for the Delimitation of the French and Spanish Possessions on the Coast of the Sahara and the Gulf of Guinea (France–Spain) (27 June 1900) 92 BFSP 1014, art IV (French). See also: Shaw (n 37) 258–59.

## 94 SUCCESSION TO TERRITORIAL RIGHTS AND OBLIGATIONS

### 3.4.2 Persistent Objection

A successor may exempt itself from the application of a customary rule by 'persistently objecting' to it within a reasonable period of the succession.[257] If the successor omit to object when the circumstances call for an objection, it is deemed to have acquiesced to it. Whilst the time limit is a question of fact, there is no example of a persistent objector that has asserted a territorial claim more than one year after the date of succession.

The only examples of persistent objections in State practice concerning succession to territorial rights and obligations concern the application of the *uti possidetis juris* rule for the automatic retention of boundaries. As the retention of a boundary concerns mutual rights and obligations of a successor and a third State, the third State may also persistently object to the application of the rule. The best-known persistent objectors are Morocco and Somalia, which were the two States to vote against the 1964 Cairo resolution of the OAU.[258] However, other, non-African States to have persistently objected to the application of the rule have been South Yemen, Afghanistan, and China.

From its accession to independence in 1956, Morocco asserted territorial claims to the Algerian Sahara, Ceuta and Melilla, and the Western Sahara. The Algerian Sahara had not been delimited by a treaty concluded with France in 1845,[259] which had referred to the area in terms of the authority exercised by the counterparties over the nomadic tribes that used it.[260] Morocco had implicitly recognized subsequent encroachments by France in 1901 with rights to establish military and customs posts 'at the extremity of the tribal territories that form part of the Moroccan Empire'.[261]

Following the establishment of the French protectorate over Morocco,[262] the 'Varnier line' was drawn by France with vague and conflicting interpretations.[263] On acceding to independence in 1956, Morocco claimed territories under French control in the Algerian Sahara and maintained its claims after the secession of Algeria in 1962.[264] Though taking the 1845 treaty as the 'starting-point' of its boundary dispute with Algeria, it did not accept that that treaty was in force.[265]

---

[257] See Chapter 2.

[258] n 53. See further: Shaw (n 37) 187–201.

[259] Treaty between the Emperor of France and the Emperor of Morocco (18 March 1845) 34 BFSP 1287, arts IV–VI (French).

[260] ILA Handbook (n 19) 364–65.

[261] Protocol on the 1845 Treaty in South-West Algeria (France–Morocco) (20 July 1901) 101 BFSP 428, arts I–V.

[262] Treaty for the Establishment of a Regular Regime (France–Morocco) (30 March 1912) 106 BFSP 1023 (French).

[263] Shaw (n 37) 239 (note 151) 251.

[264] O'Connell (n 1) 290; Ahmed (n 52) 83.

[265] Shaw (n 37) 239 (notes 153–55) 251 (notes 250–51). Algeria repudiated succession to the treaties of France – Gonçalves Pereira (n 215) 79.

In the wake of the Sand War of October 1963, Morocco and Algeria delimited their entire boundary in 1969–70 whereby they recalled the 1845, 1901, and 1902 Franco–Moroccan treaties but established a new boundary for the areas covered in those treaties.[266] Since independence, Morocco has also maintained its pending claims to the Spanish exclaves of Ceuta and Melilla and the former Spanish territory of the Western Sahara.[267] Morocco has consistently refrained from invoking the *uti possidetis juris* rule in those disputes.[268]

Following the accession to independence of the Trust Territory for Somalia and its immediate merger with Somaliland in 1960,[269] Somalia claimed the Somali-populated Ogaden region of Ethiopia and Northern Frontier District of Kenya.[270] Though asserting that it 'ha[d] no ambitions or claims for territorial aggrandizement', it pressed 'for self-determination for the inhabitants of the Somali areas adjacent to the Somali Republic'.[271] Ethiopia retorted that 'questions of frontiers between Ethiopia and the Somali Republic are regulated by an international treaty'.[272] Having voted against the 1964 OAU Cairo resolution,[273] Somalia rejected the relevant delimitation treaties between Ethiopia, Italy, and the United Kingdom in the Ogaden War of 1977 and 1978.[274] After voting against Article 12 of the VCSST and making detailed statements against it, Somalia abandoned any territorial claims towards its neighbours in 1983.[275]

One day prior to the secession of the colonial protectorate of South Yemen ('South Arabia') in 1967,[276] the United Kingdom retroceded to Oman ('Muscat') the Khuriya Muriya Islands, which it had administered as part of the Aden Colony from 1886 after its cession by Oman in 1854.[277] From 14 December, South Yemen

---

[266] Convention concerning the State Frontier Line (Morocco–Algeria) (adopted 15 June 1972, entered into force 14 May 1989) 2189 UNTS 87, preamble, art 1.

[267] Mohamed Lamouri, *Le contentieux relatif aux frontières terrestres du Maroc* (FeniXX 1979) 24–26, 32–35, 47–50; Rachid Lazrak, *Le Contentieux Territorial entre le Maroc et l'Espagne* (Dar el Kitab 1974) 11–28. The claims also embrace four other Spanish territories on or just off the Moroccan coast – Jamie Trinidad, 'An Evaluation of Morocco's Claims to Spain's Remaining Territories in Africa' (2012) 61 ICLQ 861.

[268] Jamie Trinidad, *Self-Determination in Disputed Colonial Territories* (CUP 2018) 39–56.

[269] Law of Union between Somaliland and Somalia (27 June 1960) 164 BFSP 697, ss 2–3, 11.

[270] ILA Handbook (n 19) 361–62; Brown (n 191) 171; Draft Somaliland Ordinance (n 191) para 14.

[271] 'Speeches & Statements made at the first Organization of African Unity Summit' (May 1963) <https://au.int/en/speeches/19630508/speeches-and-statements-made-first-organization-afri can-unity-oau-summit-1963> accessed 1 January 2024, 108–10.

[272] Ibid, 112.

[273] Saadia Touval, 'The Organization of African Unity and African Borders' (1967) 21(1) International Organization 102, 124–25.

[274] UNGA, 33rd Plenary Meeting (13 October 1977) GAOR: 33rd Session, paras 169–91; UNGA 19th Plenary Meeting (3 October 1979) GAOR: 34th Session, para 161; UNGA 15th Plenary Meeting (29 September 1980) GAOR: 35th Session, paras 138, 141; UNGA 18th Plenary Meeting (29 September 1981) GAOR: 36th Session, para 8; UNGA 18th Plenary Meeting (5 October 1982) GAOR: 37th Session, paras 239, 241–45.

[275] UNGA 13th Plenary Meeting (30 September 1983) GAOR: 38th Session, paras 224, 227.

[276] Memorandum on Independence for South Arabia (29 November 1967) (1967–68) 169 BFSP 136.

[277] Treaty of Cession relating to the Kuria Muria Islands (Oman–United Kingdom) (15 November 1967) Cmd 3505 (January 1968) preamble, arts I–II.

96    SUCCESSION TO TERRITORIAL RIGHTS AND OBLIGATIONS

claimed the Islands.[278] Following the merger of South Yemen with North Yemen in 1990,[279] Yemen recognized the Islands as Omani territory in their delimitation treaty of 1992, in which no reference was made to the 1967 Anglo–Omani treaty of retrocession.[280]

In 1919, Afghanistan and the United Kingdom delimited the 'Durand Line' as the boundary between Afghanistan and British India.[281] After the North West Frontier Province referendum of July 1947 and the secession of Pakistan the next month,[282] Pakistan affirmed the Durand Line and claimed succession to the 1919 Treaty[283] while Afghanistan rejected the succession of Pakistan in 1953, 1956, and 1976.[284] On 21 November 1953, Afghanistan invoked the termination clause of the 1921 Anglo–Afghan delimitation treaty to take effect one year thereafter.[285] While Afghanistan repeatedly criticized Article 11 of the VCSST at the UN Conference, it ultimately abstained in the vote on its final adoption on the basis that it would not apply to its own dispute with Pakistan due to the Durand Line being an invalid boundary.[286] During the 1978 UN Conference, Pakistan declared its intention to settle the dispute on 'an equitable basis'.[287]

In the context of maritime delimitation negotiations in the Gulf of Tonkin between 1974 and 2000, China rejected the invocation by Viet Nam of the boundary agreed between China and France in 1887.[288] Viet Nam implicitly abandoned that position when it agreed to a new boundary with China that made no reference to the 1887 line.[289] Following the secession of India in 1947, China has also rejected since 1958[290] the succession of India to the 'McMahon Line' delimited between the

---

[278] UNGA 1630th Plenary Meeting (14 December 1967) GAOR: 22nd Session, paras 99–100.

[279] Agreement proclaiming the Republic of Yemen (North Yemen–South Yemen) (adopted 22 April 1990, entered into force 22 May 1990) 2373 UNTS 131, arts 1, 8.

[280] International Boundary Agreement (Yemen–Oman) (adopted 1 October 1992, entered into force 25 December 1992) 1709 UNTS 409, arts 1–2; ibid, Joint letter dated 25 December 1992.

[281] Treaty establishing Friendly Relations (Afghanistan–United Kingdom) (adopted 22 November 1921, entered into force 6 February 1922) 114 BFSP 174, art II. See also: Translation of the Final Protocol embodying the Settlement of the North-West Frontier of Afghanistan (10 July 1887) in CU Aitchison, *Collection of Treaties, Engagements and Sanads Relating to India and Neighbouring Countries* (1933) vol 11 351 (arts 1–2); Agreement regarding the Indo-Afghan frontier (Afghanistan–United Kingdom) (12 November 1893) in Aitchison, ibid, 361 (arts 1–3, 6).

[282] Indian Independence Act 1947 c 30, ss 1–2, 7.

[283] *UN Materials* (n 42) 186–87.

[284] Ibid, 2–4. See also: MM Whiteman, *Digest of International Law* vol II (Government Printing Office 1964) 952.

[285] Ibid, 1.

[286] *UN Conference on Succession of States to Treaties* vol I, 10–11 (paras 22–23).

[287] Ibid, 10 (para 17) 232 (para 25).

[288] Convention on the Delimitation of the Frontier between China and Tonkin (France–China) (26 June 1887) 85 BFSP 748, art 2 (French).

[289] Agreement on the Delimitation of the Beibu Gulf (China–Vietnam) (adopted 25 December 2000, entered into force 30 June 2004) in Keyuan Zou, 'The Sino-Vietnamese Agreement on Maritime Boundary Delimitation in the Gulf of Tonkin' (2005) 36(1) ODIL 13, arts 1–2. See also: Johnston and Valencia (n 18) 144–51. China did not comment or vote on Article 11 of the VCSST.

[290] Exchange of Notes on the Tibet–Sikkim and Sino–Indian Border Dispute (India–China) (12 and 16 September 1965) 168 BFSP 220, 224 (n 5).

United Kingdom and Tibet in 1915 with respect to their boundary dispute, which has remained pending since the 1962 Sino–Indian War.[291]

A potential persistent objector appears to be Namibia with respect to its boundary with South Africa. Coinciding with its accession to independence, Namibia asserted a territorial claim on its southern border 'to the middle of the Orange River'.[292] In recognizing the independence of Namibia, South Africa implicitly rejected the claim.[293] Reportedly, it invoked the *uti possidetis juris* principle in 2001 in communicating a denial of the Namibian claim, invoking the boundary defined in the 1890 Anglo–German delimitation treaty as running along the north bank of the Orange River.[294]

Although a State must maintain its objection to the application of the rule to its own succession by rejecting the boundary in question, it is possible for the objection to be couched in imprecise terms; for example, to be conflated with a rejection of the validity of the delimitation treaty, judgment, or award.[295] An example of this distinction appears in the pending dispute between Guyana and Venezuela concerning the Guayana Esequiba territory, which is focused on the validity of an arbitral award of 1899[296] rather than the succession of Guyana to boundary delimited by Venezuela and the United Kingdom.[297]

In proposing Article 11 of the VCSST, the ILC emphasized that grounds for challenging a boundary on the basis of invalidity, self-determination, and other grounds would remain unaffected.[298] This point was emphasized at the UN Diplomatic Conference.[299] In rejecting the boundary, the State implicitly objects

---

[291] China contests the validity of the 1915 treaty on the ground that Tibet had not obtained its approval as suzerain, as China had initialled but refused to sign it – ILA Handbook (n 19) 95, 363; Convention between Great Britain and Thibet (adopted 7 September 1904, entered into force 27 April 1906) 98 BFSP 148, art I; Convention respecting Tibet (China–United Kingdom) (adopted 27 April 1906, entered into force 23 July 1906) 99 BFSP 171, art I, annex; Joint Communique regarding the Sino–Indian Border Dispute (25 April 1960) 164 BFSP 584.

[292] Constitution of Namibia (21 March 1990) UN Doc S/10967/Add.2, art 1(4).

[293] Recognition of the Independence of Namibia Act, 20 March 1990, 297 GG (20 March 1990) para 3.

[294] Agreement respecting Zanzibar, Heligoland, and Spheres of Influence (Germany–United Kingdom) (1 July 1890) 82 BFSP 35, art III(1); Climate Diplomacy, 'Transboundary Water Disagreements between South Africa and Namibia' <https://climate-diplomacy.org/case-studies/transboundary-water-disagreements-between-south-africa-and-namibia#:~:text=Since%20Namibia%20gained%20independence%20and,Highlands%20Water%20Project%20(LHWP)> accessed 1 January 2024.

[295] *Arbitral Award of 3 October 1899 (Guyana v Venezuela)* (Jurisdiction) [2020] ICJ Rep 455, paras 23–60.

[296] *Boundary between the Colony of British Guiana and Venezuela* (Award) Arbitral Tribunal (3 October 1899) XXVIII RIAA 331.

[297] Agreement to Resolve the Frontier between Venezuela and British Guiana (Venezuela-United Kingdom) (17 February 1966) 561 UNTS 322, arts I, VIII.

[298] ILC Articles (n 9) 201–02 (para 20).

[299] Afghanistan and Spain understood Article 11 to be qualified by Article 13 so that invalid colonial treaties did not benefit from it; India understood States to be entitled to challenge existing boundaries through peaceful negotiations, while concerns were also expressed by Thailand, Morocco, and South Yemen – *UN Conference* vol I, 10 (paras 20–24), 113–17 (paras 10–20, 23–37), 120 (paras 15–17), 121 (paras 22–26), 122 (para 33). The second Special Rapporteur (Sir Francis Vallat) as Expert Consultant,

## 98 SUCCESSION TO TERRITORIAL RIGHTS AND OBLIGATIONS

to the reliance of the neighbouring State on the application of the *uti possidetis juris* rule to that boundary. Consequently, the rule does not apply for so long as the objection is maintained, leaving the question of delimitation to be resolved by other means.

### 3.4.3 Acquiescence

Adapted from the Roman law, the doctrine of acquiescence is a general principle of law providing that a State is deemed to implicitly consent to a legal claim when silent in circumstances in which it could and should have voiced its objection (*Qui tacet consentire videtur si loqui debuisset ac potuisset*).[300] This rule can apply when a successor or third State invokes succession to territorial claims, boundaries, or leases. In such cases, the other party concerned must express within a reasonable time its objection to the application of the customary rule or else it is deemed to have tacitly consented to its application. Such consent is interpreted restrictively in favour of the acquiescing State until confirmed by evidence of reliance by the other State.[301]

A potential case of acquiescence is the absence of protest by Egypt to the administration of the Sudan of three disputed border areas (one of which is known as the 'Hala'ib Triangle') between 1902 and 1958.[302] Following a brief occupation by Egypt in 1958, the dispute remained dormant until border clashes on 6 April 1992 and renewed Egyptian occupation from January 1993 to the present day.[303] Following the 2016 Saudi–Egyptian maritime delimitation treaty that ostensibly recognized Egyptian title to the Triangle, Sudan rejected the claim in 2017.[304] Other potential examples of acquiescence include Armenia and Azerbaijan to the Soviet–Iranian boundary.[305]

---

advised that the intention of the ILC was to avoid prejudicing questions on validity in Articles 11 and 12, which was the purpose of Article 13 – ibid, 123 (para 48).

[300] *Temple of Preah Vihear Case (Thailand v Cambodia)* (Merits) [1962] ICJ Rep 6, 16, 23, 32–33; *Pedra Branca Case* (n 77). See also, e.g. – ILA Handbook (n 19) 364–65.

[301] *Rann of Kutch Case* (n 24) 4–7.

[302] Shaw (n 37) 251–53.

[303] EF Kisangani and Jeffrey Pickering, *African Interventions: State Militaries, Foreign Powers, and Rebel Forces* (CUP 2021) 184–85.

[304] 'Declaration by the Republic of the Sudan Ministry of Foreign Affairs, 5 December 2017' (2018) 96 Law of the Sea Bulletin 29.

[305] Agreement concerning Frontier and Financial Questions (Iran-USSR) (adopted 2 December 1954, entered into force 20 May 1955) 451 UNTS 227, arts I–II; Treaty concerning the Soviet–Iranian Frontier (Iran–USSR) (adopted 14 May 1957, entered into force 20 December 1962) 457 UNTS 161; Additional Protocol concerning the Line to be taken by the New Frontier (Iran–USSR) (adopted 7 May 1970, entered into force 11 May 1971) 787 UNTS 356. See also: Azerbaijan Law No 13 on the State Border (9 December 1991) in Hazard and Pechota (n 114) binder 1, *CIS Legislation Database*, arts 2, 7; Constitution of Azerbaijan (12 November 1995) in *World Constitutions Database* art 11(1) (Russian).

### 3.4.4 Estoppel

Inspired by the English common law and linked to the general principle of good faith in the law of treaties,[306] the doctrine of estoppel is a general principle of law whereby a State may not renege on 'a statement or representation made by one party to another and reliance upon it by that other party to his detriment or to the advantage of the party making it'.[307] It can be engaged, for example, by an act of recognition in a treaty or unilateral statement made with the intention of incurring a legal obligation.[308] For succession to territorial rights and obligations, it applies when a successor or third State recognizes the application of a customary rule or acknowledges the rights of the other State concerned.

While Tanganyika considered itself to have automatically succeeded in customary law to an Anglo–Belgian treaty delimiting its boundary with Rwanda and Burundi[309] and an Anglo–German treaty defining its boundary with Kenya,[310] it contested the boundary on the eastern shoreline of Lake Malawi ('Lake Nyasa') prescribed by the same treaty with respect to Malawi ('Nyasaland').[311] Six months after independence, it declared on 11 June 1962 that no part of Lake Malawi was within Tanganyika:

> There is no question of the boundaries of Tanganyika having been altered by any Agreement or Treaty entered into by the British Government after the assumption of the Mandate. The Prime Minister's statement of November 30, 1961, on the subject of treaty succession, has, therefore, no relevance to this issue. Whatever may be the disadvantages to Tanganyika of the present position, the Tanganyika Government could not contemplate entering into negotiations with the Federal Government of Rhodesia and Nyasaland or the British Government for an alteration of the boundaries of Nyasaland. If there are to be negotiations on this question, they must be with the Government of Nyasaland itself and must await the demand by Nyasaland for full independence.[312]

On 18 November 1954, Portugal and the United Kingdom had concluded a delimitation treaty to replace their 1891 treaty to delimit the Mozambique-Nyasaland

---

[306] Arnold McNair, *The Law of Treaties* (OUP 1961) 485–89.

[307] *Land, Island and Maritime Frontier Dispute (El Salvador v Honduras)* (Application to Intervene) [1990] ICJ Rep 92, para 63. See also, e.g. – Humphrey Waldock, 'Second report on succession in respect of treaties' (18 April, 9 June, and 22 July 1960) UN Doc A/CN.4/214 ILC Yearbook (1969) vol II 66.

[308] E.g. – *Nuclear Tests (Australia v France)* [1974] ICJ Rep 253, paras 42–52.

[309] Agreement respecting the Boundary between Tanganyika and Ruanda-Urundi (Belgium-United Kingdom) (5 August 1924) 123 BFSP 462.

[310] Agreement respecting Spheres of Influence (n 289) 35, art I(1).

[311] Ibid, art I(2). See also: Shaw (n 37) 236 (notes 124–25) 253–57; Seaton and Maiti (n 204) 59–63; Aditi Lalbahadur, 'A Stitch in Time: Preventative Diplomacy and the Lake Malawi Dispute' (2016) 32 Policy Insights 1.

[312] ILA Handbook (n 19) 363.

100    SUCCESSION TO TERRITORIAL RIGHTS AND OBLIGATIONS

boundary whereby they agreed that 'the frontier on Lake Nyasa shall run due west from the point where the frontier of Mozambique and Tanganyika meets the shore of the Lake to the median line of the waters of the same lake and shall then follow the median line to its point of intersection with the geographical parallel of Beacon 17 ... which shall constitute the southern frontier.'[313] In demarcating that boundary, a sketch map depicted the Tanganyika–Nyasaland boundary as running through the middle of the Lake.[314]

In 1967, Tanzania notified Malawi that it rejected the eastern shoreline boundary and proposed that the boundary run through the middle of the Lake, which Malawi declined.[315] Although the Tanzanian claim was 'suspended' in 1968,[316] the grant by Malawi of oil exploration licences in 2011 prompted its revival.[317] Since 2012, the dispute has reportedly been under the mediation of the Southern African Development Community.[318]

By its recognition of Ukrainian title to the Crimea in 1994, 1997 and 2003, Russia was estopped from directly claiming title to the territory on the basis of historical title.[319] In the *Pedra Branca Case*, Singapore argued that Malaysia was estopped from claiming title on the basis of a reply from the Indonesian state of Johor in 1953 to an enquiry in which it confirmed that it did not claim ownership over Pedra Branca/Pulau Bau Puteh.[320] As Singapore did not contend that it had relied on the Johor Reply in its subsequent conduct, the Court did not consider the argument of estoppel further.[321]

### 3.5 Conclusions

In codifying rules concerning succession to territorial rights and obligations, the debates of the ILC were dominated by the central problem of their relationship with the treaty that had created them. In proposing that the existence of boundaries and other territorial rights and obligations was independent of treaty, the

---

[313] Agreement with regard to the Nyasaland–Mozambique Frontier (Portugal–United Kingdom) (18 November 1954) Portugal Archives 'Ministério do Ultramar, Delegação Portuguesa de Delimitação de Fronteiras Moçambique-Niassalândia' (1956) arts 1–4.

[314] Exchange of Notes on Demarcation (Portugal–United Kingdom) (27 August 1956) annex A, Portugal Archives 'Ministério do Ultramar, Delegação Portuguesa de Delimitação de Fronteiras Moçambique-Niassalândia' (1956).

[315] Shaw (n 37) 255; Seaton and Maiti (n 204) 55–56.

[316] Ibid, 256.

[317] Christopher Mahony et al., 'Where Politics Borders Law: The Malawi-Tanzania Boundary Dispute', New Zealand Centre for Human Rights Law, Policy and Practice: Working Paper 21 (February 2014), < https://www.legal-tools.org/doc/f78000/pdf/> accessed 1 January 2024.

[318] Gbenga Oduntan, 'Why Malawi and Tanzania should stick to mediation to settle lake boundary dispute', *The Conversation* (3 July 2017).

[319] n 113.

[320] *Pedra Branca Case* (n 77) paras 223, 226–27.

[321] Ibid, para 228.

ILC successfully resolved that doctrinal controversy with the endorsement of the Contracting Parties to the VCSST. It is consequently suggested that Articles 11 and 12 are an accurate statement of customary international law on that matter.

However, the ILC did not adopt a definitive position concerning the doctrinal rationale for the proposition as the separability of the relevant provisions of the treaty or the 'real' character of the rights and obligations concerned. As the issue was framed as a matter concerning treaties, however, the enquiry of the ILC did not consider the question of succession to territorial claims for which no treaty is engaged. A point that had attracted scant consideration in received doctrine, State practice is nonetheless coherent and extensive in favour of automatic succession to such claims. It is suggested that this rule of customary international law resolves the doctrinal question in favour of succession to territorial rights and obligations as a separate category rather than succession to the 'separate' treaty provisions.

More widely, the customary rule concerning automatic succession to territorial claims demonstrates the definition of State succession as a transfer of territorial title. As a factual replacement of one State by another would demand a declaration or other formality by the successor to appropriate the territorial claim, the consistency of State practice in favour of automatic succession shows that a succession is a legal event that intrinsically involves a transfer of territorial rights and obligations. This conclusion provides clarity for the source of the rights of jurisdiction and ownership of successors, such as maritime and airspace entitlements, from the date of succession.

For the transfer of territorial obligations, State practice has varied according to the nature of the obligation in question. Whereas there is a broad base of affirmative practice supporting the customary status of Article 11 of the VCSST for the presumptive retention of boundaries, persistent objection has also enabled a minority of successors or third States to reject its application to their own succession to a particular boundary. Apart from the successors to Spain in Central and South America and the African Union, States have rejected the automatic internationalization of internal borders as derivative title in favour of a rule of bilateral consent as original title. While State practice on servitudes is not sufficiently extensive or consistent to support a general rule of automatic succession for each type of obligation that is doctrinally considered to be a servitude, the practice on leases is coherent to sustain a rule of automatic succession with an exception for military bases.

# 4

# Succession to State Property and Debt

## 4.1 Introduction

When the International Law Commission ('ILC') decided in 1969 to give priority
to the topic of State property and debt, it 'considered that an empirical method
should be adopted for the codification of succession in economic and financial
matters'.[1] While there was broad consensus in doctrine that State property transferred to a successor, its definition was opaque.[2] Controversy also centred on the
transferability of various categories of State debt; in particular, the general debt of
the predecessor versus the local debt of a transferred territory.[3] Overlaying these
questions was the applicability of an overarching principle of equity, expressed by
the maxim 'the burden passes with the benefit' (*res transit cum suo onere*), to regulate the *general* allocation of property and debt through a negotiated settlement or
the application of default rules in dispute settlement.[4]

Following 11 reports produced by the Special Rapporteur, Mr Mohammed
Bedjaoui, the ILC adopted draft articles with commentaries on succession to State
property and debt in 1981.[5] Held between 1 March and 8 April 1983 at Vienna,[6] the
UN Conference on Succession of States in respect of State Property, Archives and
Debts saw delegations attend from 90 of the 157 UN Member States.[7] Amid deep
division, the 1983 Vienna Convention on Succession of States in respect of State
Property, Archives and Debts ('VCSSP')[8] was adopted on 8 April 1983 not by con-
sensus but on a vote of 54-11-11 with socialist and non-aligned States voting largely

---

[1] 'Report of the International Law Commission on the work of its twenty-first session, 2 June – 8
August 1969', UN Doc A/7610/Rev.1, para 61. See further Chapter 8.

[2] E.g. – DP O'Connell, State Succession in Municipal Law and International Law vol I (OUP 1968)
199–204; Mohammed Bedjaoui, 'First report on succession of States in respect of rights and duties
resulting from sources other than treaties' UN Doc A/CN.4/204 (5 April 1968) 94 ('First Bedjaoui
Report') para 78.

[3] Ibid, 369–370, 416–418; First Bedjaoui Report (n 2) paras 95–96.

[4] First Bedjaoui Report (n 2) paras 97–100.

[5] Draft Articles on Succession of States in respect of State Property, Archives and Debts with commentaries 1981, ILC Yearbook (1981) vol II, Part Two, 20 ('ILC Articles').

[6] UNGA Res 36/113 (10 December 1981) paras 2–3; UNGA Res 37/11 (15 November 1982) para 1.

[7] Final Act, UN Doc A/CONF.117/15, *United Nations Conference on Succession of States in respect of
State Property, Archives and Debts: Official Records* UN Doc A/CONF.117/16 vol II, 137.

[8] Vienna Convention on Succession of States in respect of State Property, Archives and Debts 1983
(adopted 8 April 1983, not in force) 22 ILM 306 ('VCSSP').

---

*The Law of State Succession*. Arman Sarvarian, Oxford University Press. © Arman Sarvarian 2025.
DOI: 10.1093/oso/9780198817956.003.0004

in favour and capitalist States voting against or abstaining.[9] No participating State signed the VCSSP at the time and it has yet to enter into force.[10]

Relying frequently on State practice from the eighteenth, nineteenth, and early twentieth centuries,[11] a single empirical study was supplied by the UN Secretariat, in contrast to the 15 provided for the succession to treaties project.[12] Related to this relative lack of information on modern practice was the methodological decision of Bedjaoui to disregard succession agreements concluded between a colony and the metropolitan State.[13] This was to promote the perceived interests of decolonized States by formulating privileged rules for the widetransfer of State property with no transfer of State debt (the 'clean slate') to newly independent States.[14]

In the absence of detailed information on State practice for the elaboration of a default rule, the ILC also relied on two broad concepts: (1) an obligation to negotiate in good faith; and (2) the principle of equity.[15] When the seventh committee of the Institut de droit international ('IDI') drafted guiding principles on State succession to State property and debt in 2001,[16] the VCSSP was described as the 'worst' codification convention while it was acknowledged that some of its provisions were 'acceptable' due to representing 'traditional international law'.[17] In principally focusing upon the problems arising from desovietization,[18] the IDI only occasionally referred to earlier practice.[19] While the IDI progressed from the VCSSP in several respects, such as the typology of successions,[20] the lack of a deep empirical basis for its study meant that it too frequently relied on equity and a duty to negotiate[21] instead of specific rules for the allocation of property and debt, as distilled from State practice.

---

[9] 10th Plenary Meeting (7 April 1983) UN Doc A/CONF.117/SR.10, *Official Records* (n 7) Vol I, para 62

[10] <https://treatiesun.org/Pages/ViewDetailsaspx?src=IND&mtdsg_no=III-12&chapter=3&clang=_en> accessed 16 February 2024.

[11] E.g. – n 302.

[12] See Chapter 1.

[13] First Bedjaoui Report (n 2) para 33.

[14] International Law Association Committee: Aspects of the Law of State Succession, Final Report, Seventy-Third Conference, Rio de Janeiro (2008) 73 ILA Reports 250 ('ILA Report'), 328; ILA Resolution No 3/2008, 'Aspects of the Law on State Succession', (2008) 73 ILA Reports 40, 43 (para 14).

[15] Institut de droit international, 'State Succession in Matters of Property and Debts', Seventh Commission (Rapporteur: M. Georg Ress) (2001) 69 IDI Annuaire 119 ('IDI Report') 166.

[16] Institut de droit international, 'State Succession in Matters of Property and Debts', Seventh Commission, Vancouver, Resolution (2001) 69 IDI Annuaire 711 ('IDI Resolution').

[17] IDI Report (n 15) 121–23, 129–30, 13435, 142, 148, 154, 199, 203. *Contra*: ibid, 175–176, 341, 344, 350.

[18] Ibid, 135, 136, 150–51, 157–61, 164–65, 189–95, 243–49, 332–33. However, the final report of the Rapporteur was completed before the 2001 agreement on the successors to the SFRY – ibid, 337–40.

[19] Ibid, 139, 142–44, 174, 179, 345, 351–52.

[20] Ibid, 218, 250–51, 342, 345.

[21] IDI Resolution (n 16) arts 5(1), 6, 8, 9(2), 10(3), 13(2), 16(2), 19(3), 20(2), 23(2), 26(2), 28(2), 29(5).

104    SUCCESSION TO STATE PROPERTY AND DEBT

## 4.2  The General Principle of Automaticity

Across the classes of succession, State practice has featured two principles for the automatic transfer to a successor of State property and debt in the absence of specific agreement to the contrary: (1) the principle of territoriality; and (2) the principle of equitable apportionment. Both concern the allocation of property and debt without compensation[22] according to different methods: whereas territoriality entails the assignment of an individual asset or debt to a single State, equitable apportionment concerns the distribution of a portion of one or more assets or debts among multiple States according to a 'key' or ratio of shares. As for other rules of succession, the default rules for the automatic transfer of property and debt are displaced by specific agreement of the States concerned.

In drafting Articles 37(2), 40(1), and 41 of the VCSSP, the ILC posited that State debt passes to a successor in cases of cession, secession, and dismemberment in 'equitable proportion, taking into account, in particular, the property, rights and interests which pass to the successor State in relation to that State debt'. This notion of a 'correlation between the proportion of property and debt' under an equitable principle of unjust enrichment was likewise adopted by the IDI, which also posited that the correlated property and debt should pass together under a principle of synchronization.[23] As State practice in favour of such a correlation is rare, these principles of synchronization and unjust enrichment do not reflect customary international law.[24]

Whereas a succession agreement is frequently used to effect a transfer of State property and debt,[25] a specific asset or debt can also transfer by operation of law in the absence of such an agreement.[26] This is particularly significant during an 'intermediate period' in which a succession agreement has not been concluded.[27] When individual assets and debts have been assigned during that period, set-off can be applied to make corresponding adjustments in a subsequent negotiation for a general allocation.

---

[22]  IDI Resolution (n 16) art 7.

[23]  In basing these principles upon the VCSSP and the advisory opinions of the Badinter Commission, the IDI acknowledged their hortatory nature by using the word 'should' – ibid, art 9; IDI Report (n 15) 123, 131, 149, 154, 166, 185, 187, 196, 201, 221, 226–27, 232, 259–60, 267, 282, 286–87, 333–34, 348–49, 356–59, 361, 364.

[24]  For example, the adjustment of the IMF key for diplomatic and consular property was not 'correlated' to the proportions of State debt that North Macedonia and Bosnia-Herzegovnia would receive under the key – Agreement on Succession Issues between the Five Successor States of the former State of Yugoslavia (adopted 29 June 2001, entered into force 2 June 2004) 2262 UNTS 251 ('Agreement on Succession Issues').

[25]  There is no duty for the States concerned to reach an agreement – IDI Resolution (n 16) arts 5(1), 6(1); IDI Report (n 15) 152, 162, 164–66, 170, 182, 212, 224–25, 231, 258, 284, 342, 345, 348, 367.

[26]  While succession agreements are necessarily concluded in diverse contexts, general principles can be distilled from them. See, e.g. – IDI Report (n 15) 152, 170, 345, 352–53, 367.

[27]  On the SFRY, see, e.g. – IDI Resolution (n 16) art 5(1); IDI Report (n 15) 125, 208, 211–213.

State practice has consistently supported the prioritization of territoriality over equitable apportionment, including when applied together in a succession agreement.[28] Even when a collection of assets or debts has been apportioned among multiple States, for example, specific assets and debts have been separately assigned to a State when they have had a specific link to its territory. However, the application of these principles varies according to the class of succession: for example, whereas the extinction of the predecessor means that *all* of its property and debt is allocated to multiple successors in dismemberment (whether by assignment or apportionment) the presence or absence of financial autonomy for a seceding territory is critical to determine whether it succeed to local property and debt versus an equitable share of the property and debt of the predecessor.

## 4.2.1 Territoriality

The principle of territoriality is the assignment of a specific asset or debt to a successor on the basis of a territorial link.[29] Apart from mergers and absorptions, there are always more than one 'States concerned' in a succession with potential claims to the property and debt of the predecessor. These are the multiple successors to an extinct predecessor in a dismemberment, a single predecessor with a single successor in a cession, and a single predecessor with one (or, rarely, multiple) successors in a secession or accession to independence.

To give doctrinal expression to this practice, it is proposed that the legal norm or standard be one of dominant connection to territory.[30] This denotes the exclusivity required to assign a single asset or debt to a single State. While the identity of the owner is often evident (e.g.—ownership of diplomatic estates of the predecessor in secession) the principle is particularly important when assets or debts have factual links to multiple territories.[31]

Due to the diverse nature of State property and debt, its application accordingly varies according to the type of asset or debt. Customary international law recognizes rebuttable presumptions of fact on the basis of the type and location of the asset or debt. For example, the inclusion of credits and debits in the accounts of a local government of the transferred territory generates a presumption of assignment to the successor that can be rebutted by evidence of a dominant connection between a particular credit or debt and the territory of another State.[32]

---

[28] IDI Resolution (n 16) art 16(1); IDI Report (n 15) 139, 267.

[29] IDI Resolution (n 16) art 11(1); IDI Report (n 15) 214–15, 225–26, 229.

[30] Ibid, art 16(1). E.g. – Agreement on Certain Economic Matters (Sudan–South Sudan) (adopted 27 September 2012, entered into force 17 October 2012) <https://www.peaceagreementsorg/view/857/Agreement%20between%20Sudan%20and%20South%20Sudan%20on%20Certain%20Economic%20Matters> accessed 31 December 2023, arts 4.1.1–4.1.2.

[31] E.g. – *Ališić and others v Bosnia and Herzegovina, Croatia, Serbia, Slovenia and Macedonia* No 60642/08, European Court of Human Rights (16 July 2014).

[32] E.g. – Guinea (n 329).

## 4.2.2 Equitable Apportionment

When the primary principle of territoriality cannot be applied to an asset or debt, the secondary principle is its apportionment (whether singly or as part of a group) into equitable shares among the States concerned.[33] This principle is particularly important in cases of dismemberment because the totality of the property and debt (e.g.—extraterritorial property and the external debt) of the predecessor transfers to the successors. It also applies when a seceding territory lacks financial autonomy from the metropolitan State so that the successor receives not the local property and debt of the autonomous territory (e.g.—DRC) but rather a share of the metropolitan property and debt (e.g.—USSR). More rarely, it can also be used to distribute the assets and debt of a territorial sub-unit of the predecessor among multiple seceding territories (e.g.—French Indochina).

To calculate the shares equitably, the basic criterion is the relative economic sizes of the States concerned.[34] However, States have used a variety of methods to measure size:

- mean average revenue contributions to the national treasury;[35]
- mean average contributions to gross domestic product;[36]
- population sizes at the date of succession;[37]
- proportions of note circulation;[38]
- population, foreign currency reserves, and proportionality;[39]
- population sizes, import earnings, export earnings, and gross national product;[40]
- relative levels of physical infrastructure development, human development, and population;[41] and
- the 'IMF key' combining central budget contributions, gross domestic product, export earnings over a five-year period, population shares, and territorial shares.[42]

---

[33] IDI Resolution (n 16) art 16(2).

[34] Ibid, art 11(3); IDI Report (n 15) 124–125, 162–164, 187–188, 233, 257, 271, 287.

[35] On Indonesia, for example, see: Round Table Conference Agreement, Financial and Economic Agreement (n 321) art 1, Round Table Conference Report, ibid, paras 8–9; 'Economic Situation of the Netherlands in June 1951', IMF Doc 623 (17 September 1951) 16. On the secession of Bulgaria in 1878, see: Makarov and Schmitz (n 178) 616–619.

[36] E.g. – Montenegro (n 376).

[37] E.g. – Czecho-Slovakia (n 261). Examples in classical practice includes the cession of Venetia-Lombardy by Austria-Hungary to Sardinia in 1866 and the secession of Panama in 1903.

[38] On British India, see: 3 Partition Proceedings 95, 96.

[39] E.g. – Bangladesh (n 353).

[40] TE Ushakova, 'Pravopreemstvo Respubliki Belarus' v Otnoshenii Gosudarstvennoi Sobstvennosti' (1999) 1 BJILIR, note 4.

[41] E.g. – South Sudan (n 377).

[42] E.g. – Czecho-Slovakia (n 261); SFRY (notes 268–267 above).

THE GENERAL PRINCIPLE OF AUTOMATICITY   107

While State practice and *opiniones juris* have yet to coalesce around a single technique, the IMF key has been a preferred method in the most recent cases of succession.[43]

The validity of a succession agreement is not contingent upon an equitable apportionment of the property and debt that it covers.[44] However, the parties can apply equivalence and set-off to approximate their shares by balancing property and debt.[45] There is no evidence of support in State practice for an equitable principle of unjust enrichment,[46] though the financial resources available to a State can be considered.[47]

Customary international law does not prescribe any particular method for the valuation of property and debt. The sparse data on State practice with respect to valuation methodology[48] indicates that the date of succession applies in default of an agreed alternative.[49] For example, an outstanding debt is to be appraised retrospectively by accounting for interest payments, discounts, and the date of redemption with an interest rate based on an average yield.[50] However, a fluctuation in the value of an asset or debt (e.g.—real estate, pensions, or currency) may be accounted by estimating its market value according to the date of valuation.[51]

### 4.2.3  State Property

Customary international law provides no unitary definition of 'State property' for which a variety of terms (e.g.— 'property', 'land', 'rights', 'interests', and 'assets') has been used in State practice. Amid this diversity,[52] the principal types of property to have featured are:

- immovable property (e.g.—land and structures);[53]
- movable property (e.g.—gold bullion);[54]

---

[43] IDI Resolution (n 16) art 11(3)(d).

[44] On British India, for example, see: Rights, Property and Liabilities Order (n 264) art 9; *Partition of Property Case* (n 119).

[45] E.g. – British India (n 264); SFRY (n 270); Israel (n 387); USSR (n 372).

[46] IDI Resolution (n 16) art 11(1).

[47] E.g. – *Sarah Campbell and W. Ackers Cage*, Anglo-Venezuelan Mixed Claims Commission (1 October 1869) II Recueil des arbitrages internationaux (1923) 552, 556.

[48] E.g. – SFRY (n 276); French India (n 285).

[49] E.g. – SFRY (n 276). See also: *Ottoman Public Debt (Bulgaria, Iraq, Palestine, Transjordan, Greece, Italy and Turkey)* Sole Arbitrator (Borel) 1 RIAA 529, 535, 551–553.

[50] E.g. – British India (n 264).

[51] E.g. – Guinea (n 331); SFRY (note 275).

[52] E.g. – Constitutional Act No 541/1992 Coll. Zákony Prolidi (13 November 1992) arts 1–3, 7 (Czecho-Slovak).

[53] E.g. – Evian Agreements (n 319) ch III; Declaration of Principles concerning Economic and Financial Cooperation, art 19.

[54] E.g. – Viet Nam (n 233).

## 108   SUCCESSION TO STATE PROPERTY AND DEBT

- financial assets (e.g.—loans,[55] shares,[56] tax arrears[57]);
- monetary assets (e.g.—foreign exchange reserves);[58] and
- legal interests (e.g.—claims to enemy property detained in wartime).[59]

While these terms have rarely been defined expressly,[60] they have at times been defined implicitly through an itemized list.[61] A few succession agreements have solely addressed immovable property,[62] though agreements including both forms of property have generally drawn no distinction for the purposes of the substantive rule.[63]

State archives have been treated in practice as a form of State property.[64] In some succession agreements, separate provision has been made for them to deal with special features like the reproduction of documents.[65] Acknowledging this, the ILC drafted a separate Part III in the VCSSP for State archives;[66] though 'unable to define property or archives', it acknowledged that such definitions might emerge in customary international law.[67]

In place of a unitary definition, State practice has defined State property according to the applicable treaty[68] or decision[69] or, in default, the national law in force at the time of its acquisition. As autonomous definitions of State property are rare,[70] referential definitions to national law have been the norm. There exists great

---

[55] E.g. – *Slovenia v Croatia* (n 279) paras 12–16, 31, 73–79; *Polish State Treasury v Paduchowa and Others*, Supreme Court of Poland (20 March 1927) 4 ILR 74, 75.

[56] E.g. – *Polish State Treasury v Deutsche Mittelstandkasse*, Supreme Court of Poland (4 April 1929) 5 ILR 55, 56.

[57] E.g. – *Attorney-General v Levitan*, Supreme Court of Israel (3 May 1954) 18 ILR 64; *Tripura v East Bengal*, Supreme Court of India (4 December 1950) 3 CILC 274, 275; *India v Manmul Jain and Others*, High Court of Calcutta (11 August 1954) [1954] AIR (Cal.) 615, 616; *Sree Rajendra Mills Ltd. v Income-Tax Officer*, High Court of Madras (10 April 1957) 26 ILR 100, 101.

[58] E.g. – 'Namibia – Recent Economic Developments' (22 May 1991) IMF Doc SM/91/105 40–41.

[59] E.g. – *Polish State Treasury v Skibniewska*, Supreme Court of Poland (24 January 1928) 4 ILR 73, 74. On Indonesia, see: Agreement concerning the Transfer of Claims (Indonesia-Netherlands) (11 August 1954) 241 UNTS 134, arts 1–2; *Nederlands Beheers-Instituut v Handels-Vereeniging Amsterdam*, Court of Appeal of The Hague (20 November 1957) 24 ILR 60, 61. On Israel, see: Absentee Property Law, 4 Israel Laws 68, ss 1, 4, 7–8, 11, 19–21, 27–28; *Jabbour v Custodian*, Queen's Bench Division (27 November 1953) 7 BILC 219, 221–232.

[60] Cyprus Independence Treaty (n 316) annex B, part III, s 1.

[61] This technique was frequently used by France and its successors – *UN Materials* (n 287) 127, 152–53, 159–60, 166–67, 185, 225–28, 318–23, 330–33, 340–43, 345–48, 385–86, 420–24, 438. On the SFRY, see: Agreement on Succession Issues (n 24) appendix.

[62] E.g. – Algeria (n 319).

[63] On Singapore, including a share in Malaysian Airways Ltd, see: Independence of Singapore Agreement (n 323) annex B (para 9); 'Succession of States in respect of bilateral treaties: second study – Air transport agreements' (24 March 1971) UN Doc A/CN.4/253, paras 107–08; *Official Records* (n 9) vol I, 53 (para 21) 53 (para 25). See also: *Sudapet v South Sudan* (n 380) paras 416, 443.

[64] E.g. – Czecho-Slovakia (n 261).

[65] E.g. – Libya (n 322).

[66] *Official Records* (n 9) vol I, 45 (para 27), 189 (para 30).

[67] Ibid, 188 (para 13) 189 (para 31).

[68] E.g. – Cyprus (n 316).

[69] E.g. – Libya (n 322).

[70] *Italy v Libya*, UN Tribunal for Libya (27 June 1955) 22 ILR 103, 106, 108.

THE GENERAL PRINCIPLE OF AUTOMATICITY    109

diversity among national legal systems with respect to types of property owned by the State, such as Crown property,[71] federal property,[72] metropolitan property,[73] patrimonial property,[74] shares in State-owned enterprises,[75] central banks,[76] party political assets,[77] and social property.[78] A proprietary right or interest must have been owned by the predecessor at the date of succession.[79]

Article 8 of the VCSSP defines 'State property of the predecessor State' as 'property, rights and interests which, at the date of the succession of States, were, according to the internal law of the predecessor State, owned by that State'. In concluding that customary international law provided no autonomous definition, the ILC decided to refer to the 'internal law of the predecessor State'.[80] Though acknowledging the existence of autonomous definitions provided in treaties, it did not explain whether the expression was intended to cover such treaties.[81]

At the UN Conference, the reference to the internal law of the predecessor received general support.[82] An amendment proposed by the United Kingdom and intended to give effect to local property—a concept omitted from the substantive rules for each class of succession—by distinguishing between property owned by metropolitan and colonial governments was withdrawn in the face of opposition.[83] The issue recurred with respect to Articles 11 and 23.[84]

---

[71] On Hyderabad, see: *Rahimtoola v Nizam of Hyderabad* (n 243) 182–184. On British India, see, e.g. – *Ahmadunnissa Begum v India*, High Court of Anhra Pradesh (29 January 1968) 4 CILC 463, 469–475. On East Germany, see: *Germany v Elicofon (Grand Duchess of Saxony-Weimar intervening)* US Second Circuit Court of Appeals (25 April 1973) 61 ILR 143, 146–147, 149, 153–154; *Kuntstsammlungen zu Weimar v Elicofon*, US Second Circuit Court of Appeals (5 May 1982) 94 ILR 135, 178–181, 192–193.

[72] E.g. – Malaya (n 313).

[73] E.g. – State Property Convention (France–Madagascar) (adopted 4 June 1973, entered into force 19 March 1975) 978 UNTS 368, art 1, annex; Property Agreement (France–Madagascar) (18 October 1961) France Treaty Database, No TRA19610006, arts 1–6 (French).

[74] E.g. – Morocco (notes 391).

[75] E.g. – *Sudapet* (n 380) paras 421–423, 445–541. On the Transvaal Republic, see: *Nederlandsche Zuid Africaansche Spoorweg Maatschappij v Douglas Colliery Ltd. and the Central South African Railways*, Supreme Court of the Transvaal (14, 23 June 1905) 8 CILC 18, 21–23.

[76] E.g. – Bangladesh (n 343).

[77] E.g. – Libya (n 322).

[78] E.g. – *Belgrade v Sidex Intern. Furniture*, US Southern District Court of New York (31 March 1998) 2 F Supp 2d 407 (SDNY 1998).

[79] E.g. – *Tyre Shipping Co. Ltd v Attorney-General*, Admiralty Court of Israel (22 June 1950) 17 ILR 107, 109; *Diamond v Minister of Finance*, Supreme Court of Israel (20 April 1950) 17 ILR 113, 115; *Certain German Interests in Upper Silesia (Poland v Germany)* (Merits) (Judgment of 25 May 1926) PCIJ Series A No 7 41. See also: IDI Resolution (n 280) art 12.

[80] ILC Articles (n 5) 25–26 (paras 8–9); *Official Records* (n 9) vol I, 60 (para 26) 64–65 (para 28). See also: Comments and observations of Governments (n 298) 172 (para 5).

[81] Ibid, 25–26 (paras 2–3, 4–6, 11).

[82] *Official Records* (n 9) vol I, 44 (para 22), 45 (para 28), 45 (para 30), 45 (para 33), 45 (paras 32, 38).

[83] Ibid, 45 (para 29) 46 (paras 47, 50), 60 (para 28), 256–257 (paras 5–10, 12, 14, 23–24) 261 (para 57) 259 (para 30, 40) 260 (paras 43, 45, 48) 261 (para 59) 262 (paras 69–70, 73); vol II, ibid., 116 (para 240).

[84] Ibid, vol I, 51 (paras 51, 1, 4) 52 (paras 5–6, 12, 18–19, 8) 52–53 (paras 21–22, 31), 148–149.

110   SUCCESSION TO STATE PROPERTY AND DEBT

Considerable debate took place concerning the meaning of 'property, rights and interests' in Article 8.[85] At the UN Conference, the Special Rapporteur acknowledged '[t]hat definition was not perfect, but it had been the best solution that the [ILC] had been able to arrive at'.[86] Save insofar as Article 8 does not expressly refer to the possibility of a supervening definition being provided by treaty or international decision, its reliance on the national law of the predecessor reflects State practice.[87] Since its adoption, it has seemingly been applied to Namibia[88] and Czecho-Slovakia[89] and has been recognized as customary international law in dispute settlement on the Socialist Federal Republic of Yugoslavia (SFRY)[90] and South Sudan.[91]

Acknowledging the 'linkage of [State] property to the territory' as the key criterion applicable to all classes of succession, the ILC considered the location of immovable property to be the decisive factor.[92] As a movable asset could be situated 'by chance', it substituted for the test of location the formula 'connected with the activity of the predecessor State in respect of the territory to which the succession of States relates'.[93] At the UN Conference, a proposed amendment of France to substitute the formula 'direct and necessary link' was rejected, with some delegations stating that it was restrictive[94] and others considering it to be an improvement on the 'vague' ILC variation.[95] As each formula for movable property assumes the existence of an *exclusive* link between an asset and a territory, neither acknowledges the possibility of connections between an asset and multiple territories.[96]

While the underlying principle of territoriality accords with State practice,[97] the conclusive nature of the test of location for immovable property does not account for the possibility of rebuttal due to other factors. For example, real estate might be located outside the territory of a successor that is nonetheless claimed as local property.[98] Conversely, it might be situated in the territory of a successor but nevertheless belong to the predecessor due to its 'national' character (e.g.—military

---

[85]   Ibid, 45 (paras 30–31, 38–39), 46 (paras 40–42, 52–53), 61 (para 32), 85 (paras 5–8). See also: ILC Articles (n 5) para 10.

[86]   *Official Records* (n 9) vol I, 60 (para 29).

[87]   IDI Resolution (n 16) art 12; IDI Report (n 15) 136–37, 210–11.

[88]   Note 405.

[89]   Note 406.

[90]   *Croatia et al. v Girocredit Bank A.G. der Sparkassen*, Supreme Court of Austria (17 December 1996) in August Reinisch and Konrad Bühler, 'Introductory Note' (1997) 36 ILM 1520.

[91]   *Sudapet* (n 380) paras 429, 434, 443, 498–499, 512, 525–527.

[92]   ILC Articles (n 5) 29 (paras 6–7); IDI Resolution (n 280) art 19(1); IDI Report (n 17) 136, 262.

[93]   Ibid, 30 (paras 9–11); IDI Resolution (n 280) art 20(1).

[94]   *Official Records* (n 9) vol I, 86 (para 26), 87 (paras 28, 34), 88 (para 51).

[95]   Ibid, 87 (para 36), 88 (paras 46–47).

[96]   E.g. – British India (n 264).

[97]   E.g. – *Sudapet* (n 380) para 431.

[98]   E.g. – British India (n 264).

THE GENERAL PRINCIPLE OF AUTOMATICITY    111

assets[99]). Thus, customary international law provides for a *presumption* of location for immovable property that may be rebutted by other factors.

## (a) Local Property

Local property comprise assets belonging to local governments (provincial, municipal, etc.) in the transferred territory.[100] Local property is automatically transferred without compensation to the successor unless otherwise agreed,[101] including debts owed by the central government of the predecessor.[102] While the power to contract a local debt can correlate to the capacity of a local government to own a separate 'portfolio' of assets,[103] it is also possible for a local government to own property without the power to contract debt.

The customary test of dominant connection is manifested in the ownership of the local government.[104] The 'local' character of a contested asset is determined by applying relevant factors under the applicable law, such as the origin of the order to produce the asset and the State organ in whose name title was held.[105] When the territory of a local government is partitioned, the test of dominant connection applies to assign its property and the principle of equitable apportionment applies in default.

## (b) Localized Property

Localized property comprises assets vested in the central government or other agencies of the predecessor with a dominant connection to the transferred territory.[106] The presence of immovable property in the transferred territory generates a presumption of dominant connection[107] that can be rebutted by other factors, such as its acquisition by the budget of the central government.[108] Title to military

---

[99] E.g. – Military Convention (France–Madagascar) (adopted 4 June 1973, entered into force 19 March 1975) 978 UNTS 354, arts 1–2.

[100] There is no special rule for federal States – IDI Resolution (n 16) arts 16(1), 29(1); IDI Report (n 15) 124, 158–60, 216, 228–29, 236, 269.

[101] E.g. – Independence of Singapore Agreement (Malaysia–Singapore) (7 August 1965) 4 ILM 928, annex B (para 9).

[102] E.g. – Financial Agreement (France–Guinea) (n 331) art III.

[103] E.g. – DRC (n 335).

[104] E.g. – *Germany v Elicofon* (n 71) 146–147, 149, 153–154; *Kuntstsammlungen v Elicofon*, ibid, 178–181, 192–193.

[105] E.g. – 'Allemagne (R.D.A.) et Allemagne (R.F.A.): Problème de la succession aux droits et titres de l'Etat prussien' (1976) 130 RGDIP 213–14.

[106] On the assets of the Portuguese state airline that had been 'produced' by Angola and Mozambique, see: Memorandum between Brazil and Portugal (14 September 1973) Portugal Archives Box 55344 (Portuguese).

[107] On East Germany see, e.g. – *Restitution of Property (Rheinland-Pfalz) Case*, Court of Appeal of Neustadt (7 November 1950) 18 ILR 45, 46.

[108] E.g. – Burma (n 312); DRC (n 335). On the New Panama Canal Company, see: 'Informe del Diputado Arosemena a la Asamblea Nacional de Panamá sobre el Tratado con Colombia' (1909) 1 Tratados de Colombia con los Estados Unidos y con Panama 71. On Mandatory Palestine, see: *Khayat v Attorney-General*, District Court of Haifa (27 April 1954) 22 ILR 123, 125–26.

112    SUCCESSION TO STATE PROPERTY AND DEBT

property located in the transferred territory, for example, has typically remained with the predecessors,[109] or been donated[110] or sold[111] to the successor.

The test of dominant connection also applies to movable assets lacking a physical location, such as financial assets and proprietary claims.[112] Unlike mergers and absorptions, movable and immovable assets located outside the territory of the predecessor in dismemberments are allocated by equitable apportionment unless otherwise agreed.[113] In partial successions, the location of immovable property outside the transferred territory (e.g.—diplomatic and military premises) generates a presumption that title remain with the predecessor.[114]

### (c) State Archives

State archives are original documents owned by the predecessor concerning the governmental administration of the transferred territory.[115] The definition of a 'document' is a broad one in that they may be held in a variety of media (e.g.— printed or electronic) and formats (e.g.—script, graphs, maps, sound). Archives need not be declassified, published, or held by a particular form of institution.

As a form of State property, the principle of territoriality determines title to the original documents.[116] In applying the test of dominant connection, a presumption of origin applies whereby archives *created* in a territory are presumed to relate to that territory – irrespective of their physical location at the date of succession.[117] However, this presumption may be rebutted by reference to their content; for example, records produced by the central government of the predecessor that relate to the transferred territory[118] or generated by the local government of the transferred territory that relate not to its administration but to other matters.[119]

---

[109] E.g. – Evian Agreements (n 319) Declaration of Principles concerning Economic and Financial Cooperation, art 19.

[110] On Mauritius, see, e.g. – Defence Agreement (Mauritius–United Kingdom) (12 March 1968) 648 UNTS 3, art 8; Treasury Minute concerning the Gift of Land and Fixed Assets to Mauritius (5 March 1968) Cmd 3563. On Burma, see: *U Kyaw Myint and U Kyaw Thein v Burma*, High Court of Burma (25 July 1955) [1956] BLR 175, 186.

[111] On the Philippines see, e.g. – Agreement for the Sale of Surplus War Property (Philippines– United States) (11 September 1946) 43 UNTS 232, preamble, arts 1–3.

[112] On Indonesia, see: *Nederlands Beheers-Instituut* (n 59) 61.

[113] E.g. – SFRY (n 275).

[114] On the claims of Pakistan and India to the British Embassy premises in Kabul, see: 'Succession of States in respect of matters other than treaties', UN Doc A/CN.4/338 (4 May–24 July 1981) ILC Yearbook vol I, 109 (para 15); Katherine Himsworth, *A History of the British Mission in Kabul, Afghanistan* (British Embassy 1976) 1, 7.

[115] E.g. – JP Wallot, 'Les grands principes internationales concernant la migration des archives' (1996–97) 28 Archives 3; Ernst Posner, 'Effects of Changes of Sovereignty on Archives' in Ken Munden (ed) *Archives and the Public Interest* (Public Affairs Press 1967) 168–81.

[116] E.g. – Definitive Treaty of Peace (France–Spain–Great Britain) (10 February 1763) 42 CTS 279, art XXII.

[117] E.g. – SFRY (n 273).

[118] E.g. – Portuguese India (n 286).

[119] E.g. – French India (n 285); *Partition of Property of Local Communities (Italy v France)* (Decision No 163) Franco-Italian Conciliation Commission (9 October 1953) XIII RIAA 503, 516–517 (French).

THE GENERAL PRINCIPLE OF AUTOMATICITY 113

The reference to 'all documents of whatever kind' in the definition of State archives in Article 20 of the VCSSP was intended to cover two conditions: first, they must have 'belonged to the predecessor State according to its internal law'; and second, they must have 'been kept by the predecessor as archives' to avoid the exclusion of 'living archives' pending the expiry of a declassification period.[120] The phrase 'documents of whatever kind' was to be understood 'in its widest sense' while excluding their housing and cultural property.[121]

Following extensive debate at the UN Conference,[122] a compromise text was adopted by consensus[123] that was intended to preserve a broad understanding of 'documents' while amending the ILC text to align more closely to archival practice.[124] It is suggested that this broad and flexible definition reflects customary international law.[125] Special provision has sometimes been made in succession agreements to address particular characteristics, such as the records' sensitivity, relevance to multiple territories, vulnerability to damage or destruction, and scope for reproduction.[126]

In proposing Article 24 of the VCSSP on 'the preservation of the integral character of groups of State archives', the ILC intended it to reflect 'the principle of [unity] of archives, irrespective of the specific category of succession of States involved'.[127] At the UN Conference, Pakistan proposed its deletion, but withdrew its amendment in the face of opposition by the Special Rapporteur.[128] While UNESCO observed that the principle of unity of all archives accumulated by an administrative authority was key to archival science[129] and Switzerland proposed an amendment providing that 'the archival concept of joint heritage' would 'guide' predecessors and successors to preclude divisibility,[130] other delegations criticized the proposal as contrary to the division of archives in the majority of cases,[131] and the amendment was rejected by a vote of 32-17-14.[132] In light of the drafting

[120] ILC Articles (n 5) 50 (para 1).

[121] Ibid, 50–52 (paras 3–10). See further: Mohammed Bedjaoui, 'Thirteenth Report on the Succession of States in Respect of Matters Other than Treaties' (6 & 29 May, 6 & 16 June 1981) UN Doc A/CN.4/345, para 227; *Official Records* (n 9) vol I, 123 (para 11) 134 (para 10) 142 (para 36).

[122] *Official Records* (n 9) vol I, 122 (paras 7–8) 123–24 (paras 20, 23–24) 125 (paras 29–30, 35, 38–40) 126 (para 43) 126–27 (paras 1–7, 15) 128 (paras 21, 24, 28) 129 (paras 32, 36–37) 130 (para 45) 131 (para 48) 133 (paras 2, 6) 134 (para 13) 135 (paras 19–21); Vol II, 105 (paras 94–95).

[123] Ibid, 128 (para 17) 130 (paras 41, 46) 131 (para 49) 134–35 (paras 17–18) 136 (para 35) 155 (para 61).

[124] Ibid, 168 (para 67) 169–173.

[125] Jakubowski (n 135) 167, 171.

[126] E.g. – British India (n 264).

[127] ILC Articles (n 5) 53.

[128] *Official Records* (n 9) vol I, 155–156 (paras 62–69) 158 (para 1) 162 (para 48) 162 (para 51).; vol II, 108 (para 135).

[129] Ibid, 157 (paras 78–79).

[130] Ibid, vol I, 156 (para 70); vol II, 108 (para 136).

[131] Ibid, 155 (para 85) 158 (para 7) 159 (paras 8, 15–16) 160 (paras 20, 23, 29) 161 (para 34). On joint ownership in the case of Austria-Hungary, see: ibid, 156 (para 3) 158 (para 5) 159 (paras 10, 13) 160 (para 28).

[132] Ibid, 163 (para 66).

114    SUCCESSION TO STATE PROPERTY AND DEBT

history of Article 24 and State practice, it is suggested that the principle of unity is not a customary rule.[133]

### (d) Cultural Property

Cultural property (e.g.—architectural monuments, artworks, and historical manuscripts) is a form of State property[134] distinct from State archives.[135] It is defined in the 1954 Hague Convention as 'movable or immovable property of great importance to the cultural heritage of every people'.[136] There is no duty for a predecessor to facilitate the acquisition by a successor of cultural property in private ownership, such as museums and libraries.[137]

Information on State practice for the allocation of cultural property is limited, with the majority of known cases settled by *ex gratia* arrangements.[138] Applying the principle of territoriality to a particular asset can be complicated by long, obscure, and multinational histories—including prior successions.[139] As for State archives, a presumption of geographical origin applies rather than a connection to a nation or ethnic group.[140] Whereas 'territorial origin' is presumed to be the place of production,[141] this can be rebutted in favour of another territory of greater significance to the character of the asset.[142]

As for State archives, there is no legal recognition of the curatorial principle of unity of collections, though joint management of a collection may be specially agreed.[143] For movable assets, the lack of a legal presumption of title on the basis of location at the date of succession is particularly significant due to the fact that cultural assets 'originating' from various territories are often collected in a single location, such as a museum.[144] A decisive factor for a dominant territorial connection is the acquisition of title by purchase or donation.[145]

[133] E.g. – Jakubowski (n 134), 202 (Czecho-Slovakia).

[134] E.g. – Kuhr Siehr, 'International Art Trade and Law' (1993) 243 RdC 9.

[135] E.g. – Treaty of Peace with Italy (adopted 10 February 1947, entered into force 15 September 1947) 49 UNTS 3, art 12(1); Treaty of Peace with Hungary (adopted 10 February 1947, entered into force 15 September 1947) 48 UNTS 168, art 11; Jakubowski (n 134) 166, 226–27, 232–33 (SFRY).

[136] Convention for the Protection of Cultural Property in Armed Conflict (adopted 14 May 1955, entered into force 7 August 1956) 249 UNTS 240, art 1. See also: World Heritage Convention (adopted 16 November 1972, entered into force 17 December 1975) 1037 UNTS 151, art 1.

[137] ILC Articles (n 5) 68–69 (Iceland). On Iceland, see: 'Mesures consecutives à la liquidation de l'union réelle dano-islandaise: Restitution d'archives' (1967) 121 RGDIP 401, 402.

[138] Jakubowski (n 134) 121.

[139] Ibid, 201 (Austria-Hungary, Czecho-Slovakia).

[140] Ibid, 126–28 (Indonesia), 157–58 (DRC), 224–26 (Papua New Guinea), 214 (SFRY, USSR), 230–32 (Czecho-Slovakia), 235 (SFRY). See also: IDI Resolution (n 280) art 16(5).

[141] Ibid, 215 (Ukraine). See also: IDI Report (n 17) 340–41, 343, 347, 354, 416–17.

[142] Ibid, 123–24, 201–02, 217–18, 286–88, 295–300, 312–18 (Algeria, Slovakia, Libya, Belarus, Lithuania, Slovenia, Peru).

[143] Ibid, 121–23 (French Indochina), 206–17, 228–29 (Russia, Serbia).

[144] Ibid, 295–300 (Libya).

[145] E.g. – Peace Treaty with Italy (n 135) art 12(1), annex XIV (art 4); Peace Treaty with Hungary (n 135) art 11(2); Agreement on Succession Issues (n 24) annex D (art 9). See also: Jakubowski (n 134) 91–93, 136–38 (Nigeria).

THE GENERAL PRINCIPLE OF AUTOMATICITY    115

The exclusion of cultural property from the definition of State archives in Article 20 of the VCSSP reflects State practice.[146] While a cultural artefact could also be regarded as a 'State archive' in rare cases,[147] subsequent practice suggests that it be treated as a 'historical archive' (i.e.—cultural property) rather than an 'administrative archive' (i.e.—State archive).[148]

### 4.2.4  State Debt

State debt is defined as any financial obligation owed by the predecessor to any person at the date of succession,[149] including the internal debt owed to nationals of the State and the external debt owed to States, international organizations, and foreign nationals.[150] The features of a particular debt (e.g.—fixed sum or contingent liability) are defined by its governing instrument (e.g.—contracts, promissory notes, balance-of-payment support loans), and applicable law (e.g.—internal law).[151] There is no distinction between foreign and domestic creditors[152] but the nationality of the creditor is pertinent to enforcement in that a change of nationality could enable diplomatic protection.[153] Debts owed to private bondholders qualify as 'property' for the international minimum standard of treatment of foreign nationals.[154]

Article 33 of the VCSSP defines 'State debt' as 'any financial obligation of a predecessor State arising in conformity with international law towards another State, an international organization or any other subject of international law'. Explaining the concept of debt to be personal to the debtor and creditor in private law, the ILC acknowledged debt-claims owed by a third State to a predecessor to be a form of State property, while debts of the predecessor owed to a third State may be 'transmitted' to the successor.[155] In defining 'State debts' as contracted by central governments,[156] however, the ILC disregarded abundant State practice concerning

---

[146] E.g. – Comments and observations of Governments (n 298) 176 (para 17).

[147] *Official Records* (n 9) vol I, 212 (paras 67–68).

[148] Jakubowski (n 134) 217–18 (Lithuanian Metrica).

[149] E.g. – Eulálio do Nascimento e Silva, 'Succession of State Debts' in M Rama-Montaldo (ed) *Liber Amicorum Eduardo Jiménez de Aréchaga* vol II (FCU 1994) 947–62, 951–53.

[150] IDI Resolution (n 16) art 22; IDI Report (n 17) 202, 274, 276–78. E.g. – *Belgium v Banque Indosuez Case* C-177/96 Court of Justice of the European Union (16 October 1997) [1997] ECR I-05659, paras 16–25; Opinion of Advocate General Jacobs (3 July 1997), ibid, paras 16–32; IDI Resolution (n 280) art 22.

[151] ILC Articles (n 5) 78 (para 35). For example, the withdrawal of a currency – Spanish Morocco (n 394).

[152] E.g. – *Pamanoekan & Tjiasemlanden v Netherlands*, District Court of The Hague (3 April 1952) 19 ILR 116, 117.

[153] See Chapter 7.

[154] See Chapter 8.

[155] ILC Articles (n 5) 72–74 (paras s-12).

[156] Ibid, 73–75 (paras 10–17).

116  SUCCESSION TO STATE PROPERTY AND DEBT

succession to the local debt of financially autonomous territories.[157] A proposal by the United Kingdom to broaden the definition of 'State debt' in Article 2 to cover local debts for all classes of succession was withdrawn in the face of opposition.[158]

The ILC also excluded from Article 33 the debts of 'public establishments', which it defined as 'entities distinct from the State which have their own personality and usually a degree of financial autonomy'.[159] On a tied vote at second reading, the ILC also rejected a proposal to amend Article 33 to cover 'any other financial obligation chargeable to a State' as debts owed to private creditors but added a 'safeguard clause' in Article 6.[160] In an intense debate that largely replicated those in the ILC,[161] a proposal by Brazil to add this amendment was rejected by a vote of 35-23-5 and Article 33 was adopted on a vote of 40-17-6.[162]

It is suggested that Article 33 does not reflect customary international law because State practice and *opiniones juris* have consistently defined 'State debt' to include debts owed by any organ or agency of the State, as defined by the applicable law.[163] This includes the debts of local governments in the transferred territory and State-owned bodies (e.g.—public corporations).[164] Article 33 also diverges from the customary rule in that the latter does not distinguish between creditors (e.g.—individuals and companies).[165]

### (a) Local Debt

Local debt are monetary loans contracted by local governments of the transferred territory (e.g.—provinces, districts, or municipalities).[166] According to the principle of territoriality, the credits (e.g.—claims for repayment) and debts of local budgets are transferred to a successor.[167] Whereas the local government can 'continue' to service the debt under its applicable law, a succession to the debt nevertheless occurs due to the changed status of the local government (e.g.—its name

---

[157] Ibid, 101 (para 52).

[158] *Official Records* (n 9) vol I, 194 (paras 6–8).

[159] ILC Articles (n 5) 76–77 (paras 29–30). See also: *Official Records* (n 9) vol I, 194 (paras 6–8) 266–71.

[160] Ibid, 24, 79 (para 45). See also: Comments and observations of Governments (n 298) 176–177 (para 6) 194 (para 9).

[161] *Official Records* (n 9) 194 (para 10) 195 (para 23) 198 (para 42) 199 (para 58) 201 (para 4) 202 (para 20) 203 (para 28) 204 (paras 45, 51) 205 (paras 59–60) 207 (para 5); ibid, vol II, 112 (para 181).

[162] *Official Records* (n 9) vol I, 194 (paras 10–12, 14), 195 (paras 15, 20–21), 196 (paras 25, 30, 32), 197 (paras 37–38), 198 (para 42), 199 (paras 50, 51, & 55), 200 (paras 65, 68), 201 (paras 9–11), 202 (para 20), 203 (paras 29–30, 37), 204 (paras 47–48), 205 (para 63), 206 (paras 70, 72), 207 (para 9), 208 (paras 12–14), 209 (para 24), 210 (para 38).

[163] IDI Report (n 17) 235, 237.

[164] E.g. – Algeria (n 318); Bangladesh (n 343); Malaya (n 313); South Yemen (n 314).

[165] IDI Resolution (n 16) art 22(b); IDI Report (n 17) 124, 153, 234.

[166] IDI Resolution (n 16) art 29; IDI Report (n 17) 135, 137, 158–59, 174, 195.

[167] E.g. – *UN Materials* (n 287) 127, 152–53, 159–60, 166–67, 185, 225–28, 318–23, 330-333, 340–43, 345–48, 385–86, 420–24, 438 (Barbados, Côte d'Ivoire, Benin, Central African Republic, Chad, Republic of the Congo, Gabon, Mali, Mauritania, Senegal, Togo, Tonga, and Burkina Faso). See also: IDI Resolution (n 280) art 29(1); IDI Report (n 17) 159, 174; EJS Castrén, 'Aspects récents de la succession d'états' (1951-I) 78 RdC 379, 411–12, 471–78.

and governing statute).[168] The succession is also demonstrated by the possibility that the central government of the successor abolish the autonomy of the local government and assume the debt itself.[169]

Financial autonomy entails a budget separate from that of the central government with the power to borrow.[170] Requirements in internal law to obtain approval from the central government do not affect the separate character of the local budget.[171] To determine whether a debt is a 'local' one, the relevant factors are the identity of the debtor in the debt instrument, the purpose of the contracted debt, and its inclusion in the accounts of the local government.[172] Subject to the rule on odious debt, the local debt includes debts owed by the local government to the central government.[173] Unless localized,[174] the predecessor retains debts contracted by the central government for the transferred territory before financial autonomy[175] and its guarantees issued for debts contracted thereafter (e.g.—development loans).[176]

## (b) Localized Debt

The general debt comprise monetary loans contracted by the central government of the predecessor.[177] When a transferred territory in partial succession lacks financial autonomy, customary international law provides for the transfer of an equitable proportion of the general debt.[178] As for other general rules, the predecessor may waive a claim for apportionment; for example, to provide economic aid.[179]

Localized debt are those monetary loans contracted by the central government of the predecessor to benefit the transferred territory (also known as the 'primary final beneficiary principle') for purposes such as infrastructure projects.[180] In contrast to local debt, the test of dominant connection for such 'project debts' and

---

[168] E.g. – Hong Kong (n 288).

[169] E.g. – Portuguese India (n 286).

[170] IDI Report (n 15) 159, 174. On the lack of financial autonomy for the constituent republics of the USSR, see: LT Orlowski, 'Direct Transfers between the Former Soviet Union Central Budget and the Republics' (November 1992) Kiel Working Paper No 543.

[171] E.g. – Madagascar (n 318).

[172] E.g. – Algeria (n 319). The debt might also be identifiable by its denominated currency; e.g. – DRC (n 334). See also: ILC Articles (n 5) 75–76 (paras 17–26).

[173] E.g. – Burma (n 312); Malaya (n 313); Mauritius (n 315); French India (n 285); Morocco (notes 393–394).

[174] E.g. – Guinea (n 330).

[175] E.g. – Philippines (n 320).

[176] IDI Report (n 17) 137, 227–228; ILC Articles (n 5) 78 (para 38). E.g. – Algeria (n 319); DRC (n 334).

[177] IDI Resolution (n 16) art 27(1); ILC Articles (n 5) 75 (paras 17–18).

[178] E.g. – Bangladesh (n 351); USSR (n 372); South Sudan (n 377). On the lack of autonomy for Bulgaria, see: AN Makarov and Ernst Schmitz (eds) Fontes Juris Gentium: Digest of the Diplomatic Correspondence of the European States (1871–1878) vol I (Carl Heymanns Verlag KG 1937) 613.

[179] E.g. – Libya (n 322).

[180] IDI Resolution (n 16) art 28(1); IDI Report (n 15) 137, 229, 280–81. E.g. – Yemen (n 184).

118  SUCCESSION TO STATE PROPERTY AND DEBT

'programme debts' is met by their primary territorial *benefit*.[181] Localized debts are assigned to a single territory if it primarily benefited that territory[182] but are apportioned if the benefit was equally shared by multiple territories.[183] State practice and *opiniones juris* are abundant in support of this general rule,[184] which may be displaced by specific agreement.[185]

## (c) Secured Debt

Secured ('bonded', 'mortgaged', or 'hypothecated') debt entails a pledge of property (e.g.—tax revenues[186]) as security for repayment of a monetary loan.[187] A secured debt is automatically transferred with the property to which it pertains. Though rare in modern practice,[188] secured debts were more common in classical practice.[189]

While the entry of the maxim *res transit cum suo onere* ('a thing passes with its burden') into the doctrine of the law of succession is obscure,[190] it has been cited in analogy with the Roman law of inheritance whereby debt attached to mortgaged property passed to an heir.[191] Although France withdrew a proposal at the UN Conference to amend Article 8 of the VCSSP to add a reference to the passage of debt attached to State property, it did so on the basis of a 'general understanding that when State property passed, obligations also passed'.[192]

## (d) Administrative Debt

Administrative debts comprise a wide range of sums owed by a State to private persons, States, or international organizations in the ordinary course of governmental business.[193] Examples include tax

---

[181] The physical location of a project is a relevant factor; e.g. – South Sudan (note); Bangladesh (notes 350–349). See also: IDI Resolution (n 280) art 28.

[182] E.g. – Bangladesh (notes 350, 348–349). In *Ališić* (n 31) the head office of the Ljubljana Bank was located in Slovenia and its local office was located in Croatia.

[183] E.g. – Constitutional Charter of Serbia and Montenegro (n 376) art 16; 2008/784/EC 'Council Decision of 2 October 2008 establishing a separate liability of Montenegro', L 269/8 OJEU (10 October 2008) art 1(1).

[184] E.g. – *Yemen v Compagnie d'Enterprises CFE SA*, Supreme Court of Cyprus (28 June 1992) Case No 10717 ORIL paras F1–F4.

[185] E.g. – *Scindia Steam Navigation Co. Ltd. v India*, Supreme Court of India (31 August 1961) 4 CILC 216, 219–56.

[186] E.g. – Austria (n 257).

[187] E.g. – ILC Articles (n 5) 78 (para 37).

[188] E.g. – South Yemen (n 314). On East Germany, see: 114 CCFB (1987) 16; Agreement on the Settlement of Financial Questions (Finland–East Germany) (adopted 3 October 1984, entered into force 26 December 1984) 1392 UNTS 502, arts 1–2.

[189] E.g. – Robert Phillimore, *Commentaries upon International Law* (Butterworths 1854) 18–19, 388–92.

[190] E.g. – ILC Articles (n 5) 105; *Official Records* (n 9) vol I, 220 (para 46) 223 (para 77).

[191] E.g. – Henry Bracton, *Tractatus de legibus et consuetudinibus regni Angliae* (c 1188) Fol. 382, 382b; Justinian, *Corpus iuris civilis* (c 529–34) 50 17 54; Ulpian, *Libri ad edictum* (c 211) Lib LXVI

[192] *Official Records* (n 9) vol I, 61 (paras 35–36) 63 (paras 7, 12), 62 (para 40), 63 (para 4), 64 (paras 19, 25, & 45) 65 (para 39) 66 (para 45) 69 (paras 11 & 16) 203 (para 31).

[193] E.g. – O'Connell (n 254) vol I, 193–200; ILC Articles (n 5) 77 (para 32).

THE GENERAL PRINCIPLE OF AUTOMATICITY    119

deposits,[194] social security pensions,[195] membership dues,[196] rent arrears,[197] and liquidated judgment-debts.[198] The scope of the debt to be transferred to the successor is determined by its governing instrument (e.g.—the internal law of the predecessor) up to the date of succession.[199]

The test of dominant connection under the principle of territoriality is principally determined by reference to the budget to which the administrative debt was charged. Alternative methods for the allocation of administrative debt that have been adopted by special agreement are the permanent residence of the claimant at the date of succession,[200] the nationality of the claimant,[201] and fixed contributions.[202] When nationality is used, the effect of the succession on the claimants' nationality must be determined to identify the debtor.[203]

Debts of mixed location, such as civil service pensions,[204] are assigned with reference to the time-periods pertaining to the transferred territory; for example, the duration of service of a civil servant in proportion to his entire service.[205] In

[194] On British India, see: *Gwalior Rayon Silk Manufacturing v India*, High Court of Madhya Pradesh (30 April 1960) 4 CILC 172, 176–79. This does not apply to tax rates, e.g. – *C. v Commissioner for Taxes* Malawi Court of Special Arbitrator for Income Tax (11 August 1965) 3 ALR 350, 354.

[195] On Equatorial Guinea, see, e.g. – Judgment of the Supreme Court of Spain (23 November 1977) (1981) 33(1) REDI 226 (Spanish). On Algeria, see: *Sadok*, Conseil d'État de France (15 March 1972) 73 ILR 36, 37; *Rekhou*, Conseil d'État de France (29 May 1981) 106 ILR 222, 223–224; *Si Amer v France* Case No 29137/06 European Court of Human Rights (29 October 2009) paras 44–47 (French). On Indonesia, see: *Ter K. v Netherlands, Surinam and Indonesia*, District Court of The Hague (28 May 1951) 18 ILR 223, 225; *Stichting tot Opeising v Netherlands*, Court of Appeal of The Hague, Judgment (30 November 1955) in *UN Materials* (n 287) 113.

[196] On East Germany, see: Konrad Bühler, 'State Succession, Identity/Continuity and Membership in the United Nations' in Eisemann and Koskenniemi (n 372) 187, 237–241. On Austria, see: League of Nations, Board of Liquidation Final Report (31 July 1947) League of Nations Doc C 5.M.5. (1947) 40.

[197] E.g. – *K v Vietnam* (n 236); *West Bengal v Serajuddin Batley*, Supreme Court of India (24 November 1953) [1954] AIR (SC) 406, 407; *Tanganyika Succession Case*, German *Reichsgericht* in Civil Matters (10 October 1922) 1 ILR 61, 62.

[198] On Vanuatu, see: *Russet*, Conseil d'Etat of France (5 October 1984) 89 ILR 15, 16–17; *Société Anonyme Ballande-Vanuatu c République Française* No 49300, Conseil d'État of France, (27 September 1985) (French).

[199] E.g. – Equatorial Guinea (n 324). The terms and conditions of service (e.g. – notice periods and entitlements for termination) may not be retroactively amended by a successor, which may argue for a narrow construction of entitlements according to the law in force at the time; e.g. – *Murphy v Liquidating Agency*, High Court of Malawi (1 July 1966) (1966–68) ALR Mal. 15, 19–22, 28–29, 33–38.

[200] E.g. – *UN Materials* (n 287) 126 (Barbados).

[201] On Mauritius, see: Agreement concerning Public Officers' Pensions (Mauritius–United Kingdom) (adopted 3 July 1975, entered into force 31 July 1975) 1018 UNTS 133, art 1(e). On French Indochina, see, e.g. – Financial Agreement (France–South Viet Nam) (24 March 1960) France Treaty Database, No TRA19600378, art I (French); *Ministre du budget v N'guyen Van Gio*, Conseil d'État of France (27 February 1987) 106 ILR 224, 225. See also: Karl Zemanek, 'State succession after decolonization' (1965-III) 116 RdC 181, 266–69.

[202] E.g. – Equatorial Guinea (n 324).

[203] See Chapter 7.

[204] The term 'civil servant' is defined with reference to the internal law of the predecessor, such as diplomats, soldiers and judges. See, e.g. – Upper Silesia Convention (15 May 1922) XVI MNRG 645, arts 1, 2(3) 6, 25–39, 207–08, 396, 562, 587 (French); Final Protocol, ibid, art IV (French); *Ul Ltd. v Polish State*, Upper Silesian Arbitral Tribunal (21 July 1932) 6 ILR 70, 71; *Grzesik v Polish State*, Upper Silesian Arbitral Tribunal (4 March 1935) 8 ILR 136, 137.

[205] E.g. – Agreement concerning Public Officers' Pensions (n 201) arts 2–4; *U Tha Din v Ministry of Co-Operative and Commodity Distribution*, Supreme Court of Burma (30 October 1959) [1959]

# 120    SUCCESSION TO STATE PROPERTY AND DEBT

a partial succession, a predecessor retains debts contracted with respect to its entire territory (e.g.—military pensions).[206] It may also agree to retain the entirety of pension debts as financial assistance.[207]

## (e) Tortious Debt

Tortious ('delictual') debts are damages owed for breaches committed by the predecessor of its internal law prior to the date of succession, as distinguished from wrongs committed under international law by the predecessor.[208] When a claim is filed before the courts of the predecessor prior to the date of succession, a remedy awarded by the adjudicating court for execution is a 'liquidated' judgment-debt as a form of administrative debt. In contrast, tortious debts are 'unliquidated' legal claims against the predecessor for which judgment had not been rendered before the date of succession.

The customary test of dominant connection under the principle of territoriality is principally determined by reference to the locality of the wrong and the identity of the tortfeasor.[209] Though limitation periods and other rules can apply,[210] there is no requirement in international law that a claim be filed prior to the date of succession. Subject to the odious debt rule, a claim with a dominant connection to the transferred territory passes to the successor.[211] A successor may also retain the debt by special agreement.[212]

---

BLR 94, 105–09; Public Officers Agreement (Malaya–United Kingdom) (27 July 1959) 374 UNTS 22, arts 1–4, 6–7; No 43440/98 *Janković v Croatia*, European Court of Human Rights, Decision (12 October 2000).

[206] E.g. – Guinea (notes 328 & 331).

[207] On the DRC, see, e.g. – *Met den Ancxt v Belgium*, Court of Appeal of Belgium (9 January 1968) (1970) 6(2) RBDI 687–88 (French). On Morocco, see: Exchange of Letters (17 October 1964) in Decree No 69-283 (24 March 1969) 101 JORF (30 March 1969) 3180 (French).

[208] See Chapter 6. Confusion arose during the drafting of the VCSSP: ILC Articles (n 5) 78 (para 36); *Official Records* (n 9) vol I, 198 (paras 47–48), 201 (para 7); IDI Report (n 15) 160, 229–230, 282.

[209] E.g. – SFRY (n 276). On Indonesia, see, e.g. – *Van Os v Netherlands*, Court of Appeal of The Hague (7 April 1954) 21 ILR 77, 78–79. On Bangladesh, see: *Bangladesh (substituted in place of the Province of East Pakistan) v Naziruddin Ahmed*, High Court of Bangladesh (15 December 1972) I DLR (1973) 1, paras 7–8. On German East Africa, see, e.g. – *South-West Africa (Succession) Case*, Reichsgericht of Germany (3 April 1930) 5 ILR 60, 61; FA Mann, 'The Liability for Debts of the Former German Protectorates in Africa Considered in the Light of Decisions of the German Supreme Court' (1934) 16 JCLIL 281. On Malaya, see: *Keyu v Secretary of State for Foreign and Commonwealth Affairs*, Supreme Court of the United Kingdom (25 November 2015) [2015] UKSC 69, paras 64–65, 188–200, 202, 284.

[210] E.g. – *Pales v Ministry of Transport*, Supreme Court of Israel (17 March 1955), 22 ILR 113, 119.

[211] E.g. – *UN Materials* (n 287) 123 (Barbados), 135–36 (Swaziland), 150 (Central African Republic), 157 (Chad), 164 (Congo), 182–83 (Gabon), 253 (Kenya), 290 (Madagascar), 315 (Mali), 388 (Sierra Leone), 402 (Somaliland). On Indonesia, see: *Poldermans v Netherlands*, Supreme Court (15 June 1956) 24 ILR 69, 71–72. *Contra: Pittacos* (n 340) 31–32.

[212] On the Pacific Islands, see: Proclamation 5564 (3 November 1986) 51 Federal Register 40339, title one art VII (s 174).

## (f) Odious Debt

Odious ('war' or 'subjugation') debt are monetary, administrative, and tortious debts contracted by the central or local governments of the predecessor to prevent the succession itself.[213] Such debts include monetary loans contracted to procure military munitions,[214] military pension liabilities for personnel serving in a war of insurrection, and tortious debts for injuries caused to civilians.[215] They exclude, however, debts contracted for civilian purposes (e.g.—agriculture, infrastructure) or military activity against third parties.[216] Though rare, State practice and *opiniones juris* underpinning this general rule are coherent.[217] In claims for damages arising from alleged torture of civilians by agents of the Colony of British Kenya in the Mau Mau rebellion, the High Court of England and Wales found tortious liability to have passed by the independence statutes to Kenya,[218] while the claimants had not discharged their burden of proof for the existence of a sufficiently 'extensive and uniform' rule of customary international law on State succession.[219]

The definition of 'State debt' in Article 33 of the VCSP was stated by the ILC to include odious debts.[220] Whereas Syria withdrew a proposal at the UN Conference to exclude odious debts—defined as debts 'contracted by the predecessor State to the detriment of the successor'—from the scope of succession, delegations opposing the proposal on grounds of vagueness while opining that odious debts were not to pass.[221] It is suggested that this drafting history indicates general agreement among States, consistent with State practice, that odious debts comprise an exception to the general rules of succession to State debt.

---

[213] E.g. – Jeff King, *The Doctrine of Odious Debt in International Law* (CUP 2016) 64–82; HJ Cahn, 'The Responsibility of the Successor State for War Debts' (1950) 44 AJIL 477, 478–79, 485–86. A broader definition of debts connected to the conduct of war or international crimes was not adopted – IDI Resolution (n 16) art 22(1); IDI Report (n 15) 229–30, 283.

[214] E.g. – *Agent Judicaire v Labeunie*, Court of Cassation of France (15 June 1971), 72 ILR 53, 55–56.

[215] E.g. – *Re Société d'Assurances la Nationale*, Conseil d'État (12 April 1967), 48 ILR 61; *Bounouala*, Conseil d'État of France (25 May 1970) 71 ILR 56, 57–58. On the 1871 Treaty of Frankfort, see: Makarov and Schmitz (n 178) 603–605. On the rejection of odious debts for Cuba, see: Moore (n 263) 357–74, 379–85.

[216] E.g. – Indonesia Civil Service Personnel Guarantee Act 1950, 268 *Staatsblad* 1950, Arts 1–4 (Dutch).

[217] E.g. – Algiers Peace Agreement (12 December 2000) 2138 UNTS 85, art 5.

[218] E.g. – *Mutua v Foreign and Commonwealth Office*, High Court of England (21 July 2011 & 5 October 2012) 156 ILR 629, 638–39, 643, 652–55, 666–67, 696–717.

[219] State practice was not argued in detail – ibid, 668–74.

[220] ILC Articles (n 5) 78–79 (paras 41–43).

[221] *Official Records* (n 9) vol I, 193 (paras 82, 4) 196 (paras 26, 31) 197 (para 40) 199 (paras 53, 55, 57, 60) 200 (paras 66, 69, 1) 201 (para 5) 202 (paras 17, 24) 203 (para 34) 204 (para 46) 205 (paras 56, 64) 206 (paras 67, 69, 71, 75); ibid, vol II, 112 (para 181).

## 4.3 Application to the Classes of Succession

In a total succession,[222] the extinction of the predecessor prompts the transfer of the totality of its property and debt by operation of law. State practice concerning mergers and absorptions is relatively simple due to the extinction of the predecessor and the creation of a single successor from which no dispute can arise with the extinct predecessor or among multiple successors. In contrast, the dismemberment of a State offers considerable scope for complexity due to the existence of multiple successors that might contest allocations. The extinction of the predecessor is the key distinction between a total succession and partial succession, such as a dismemberment and a secession.[223]

In cases of partial succession,[224] the continuity of the legal personality of the predecessor[225] means that the transfer of State property and debt is determined by territoriality whereby those assets and debts with a dominant connection to the transferred territory are transferred to the successor and the predecessor retains the remainder. Disputes on State property are generally confined to the predecessor and the successor while disputes on State debt can also involve third-party creditors. In rare cases of multiple successions, disputes might also arise amongst the successors with respect to the allocation of local property and debt of a territorial unit of the predecessor to which they previously belonged (e.g.—a federal province).[226]

The distinctions drawn in the VCSSP between the classes of partial succession in the substantive rules of succession to State property and debt do not reflect customary international law. The most significant divergence from State practice is that State property and debt pass to a seceding territory under specified conditions while newly independent States receive a broader allocation of State property but do not succeed to State debt. Neither this distinction nor the specific tests for the transfer of State property and debt in the respective provisions accord with State practice. Even for the comparatively simpler class of cession, the VCSSP inaccurately provides for broad principles of 'equity' and 'equitable apportionment' while State practice has recognized the primacy of territoriality.

---

[222] See Chapter 2.
[223] IDI Report (n 15) 138, 146, 174, 197, 342, 345.
[224] See Chapter 2.
[225] IDI Resolution (n 16) art 2; IDI Report (n 15) 144, 206–07, 252–54.
[226] On British India, for example, see: Patrick Spens, 'The Arbitral Tribunal in India 1947–48' (1950) 36 Transactions of the Grotius Society 61, 68–69.

APPLICATION TO THE CLASSES OF SUCCESSION    123

## 4.3.1 Merger

When one State merges with another State to create a new State, customary international law provides for the automatic transfer of the entirety of the property and debt of the merging States to the new State. The successor may assign the property and debt of its predecessors to its new central government or to regional governments corresponding to their former territories.[227] State practice underpinning this rule comprises the mergers of:

- Syria with Egypt to form the United Arab Republic in 1958;[228]
- Somaliland with the Trust Territory for Somalia to create Somalia in 1960;[229]
- Tanganyika with Zanzibar to become Tanzania in 1964;[230]
- North Viet Nam with South Viet Nam to create Viet Nam in 1976; and
- North Yemen with South Yemen to form Yemen in 1990.[231]

While *opiniones juris* in favour of automatic succession were implied in the consistent practice of the successors, the basic principle was tested in the case of Viet Nam. After proclaiming their 'union' in 1976,[232] Viet Nam received the gold deposits and foreign exchange reserves owned by South Viet Nam.[233] Initially refusing to assume its external debt, it decided from 1976 to negotiate its settlement on a country-by-country basis.[234]

Third State creditors considered the external debt to have transferred to Viet Nam by succession.[235] In 1981, the Court of Appeal of Berne held Viet Nam to have succeeded to an administrative debt of South Viet Nam with respect to rent arrears for a contractual lease of diplomatic premises because general rules of international law provided for its succession to the rights and corresponding

---

[227] Eugene Cotran, 'Some Legal Aspects of the Formation of the United Arab Republic and the United Arab States' (1959) 8(2) ICLQ 346, 368.

[228] Provisional Constitution of the United Arab Republic (5 March 1958) in Eugene Cotran, 'Some Legal Aspects of the Formation of the United Arab Republic and the United Arab States' (1959) 8(2) ICLQ 346, arts 29, 70.

[229] Somalia Law of Union (27 June 1960) 164 BFSP 697, ss 2–3, 11; Somalia Law No 5 (31 January 1961) 2 Official Bulletin of the Somali Republic (1961) arts 1(1) 3–5, 9–10.

[230] Acts of Union (1 May 1964) 3(4) ILM 763, s 5(1), sch (para 9); Tanganyika (Constitution) Order in Council 1961, sch (para 3(3)).

[231] E.g. – 'People's Democratic Republic of Yemen: Recent Economic Developments' (17 May 1990) IMF Doc SM/90/93, 40–43; 'Republic of Yemen – Recent Economic Developments' (12 March 1992) IMF Doc SM/92/53, 32–33; 4, 20–21, 25–28, 36–37.

[232] E.g. – Resolution of the National Assembly of the Socialist Republic of Vietnam on the Organization and Operation of the State (2 July 1976) s 1 (Vietnamese).

[233] E.g. – 'Viet Nam International Reserves' (January 1975) IMF Archives File Nos 54732 and 96414.

[234] E.g. – 'Note on Viet Nam's foreign debt' (8 March 1982) in 'Viet Nam – Briefing Paper' (26 February 1985) IMF Archives, File 64598, 1 (note), 2.

[235] E.g. – 'Relations with Cambodia and South Vietnam' (30 June 1975) IMF Doc EBS/75/227 3, 11, 12. See also: *Vietnam v Pfizer Inc and Others*, Eighth Circuit Court of Appeals (15 June 1977) 94 ILR 199; *Can and Others v United States*, Second Circuit Court of Appeals (13 January 1994) 107 ILR 255, 258.

124   SUCCESSION TO STATE PROPERTY AND DEBT

obligations of its predecessor.[236] In 1997, Viet Nam settled the largest external debt owed to the United States.[237]

Like the VCSST, the VCSSP does not distinguish between mergers and absorptions[238] but rather provides for a 'uniting of States' in Articles 16, 29, and 39 by which 'the [State property, State archives and State debt] of the predecessor States shall pass to the successor State'. However, the State practice considered by the ILC was composed entirely of mergers.[239] At the UN Conference, these provisions prompted scant debate, with no amendments proposed.[240] In providing for the automatic transfer of the totality of the State property and State debt, they reflect customary international law.[241]

## 4.3.2 Absorption

When one State absorbs another, customary international law provides for the transfer of the entirety of the property and debt of the absorbed State to the absorbing State. As in cases of merger, the central government of the successor may assign the transferred assets and debt to its central or local governments. Modern practice for this rule comprises the absorptions of:

- Austria by Germany in 1938;
- the Free City of Danzig by Poland in 1945;[242]
- Hyderabad by India in 1950;[243] and
- East Germany by West Germany in 1990.[244]

Further support exists in classical practice, such as the absorptions of Texas (1844),[245] the Italian States (1861)[246] and German States (1866 and

---

[236] *K v Vietnam*, Court of Appeal of the Canton of Berne (20 January 1981) 75 ILR 122, 125.

[237] Agreement regarding the Consolidation and Rescheduling of certain Debts (Vietnam–United States) (adopted 7 April 1997, entered into force 23 June 1997) in *Treaties in Force* (US Department of State 2021) 486.

[238] ILC Articles (n 5) 43–44.

[239] Ibid, 66–67, 105–107; *Official Records* (n 9) vol I, 263 (para 11).

[240] *Official Records* (n 9) vol I, 113–14, 186, 234.

[241] ILA Committee Resolution (n 14) para 17.

[242] 91 CCFB (1964) 301–02; 103 CCFB (1976) 12, 19–20, 45–47.

[243] Constitution of India (26 November 1949) 157 BFSP 34, arts 295–296; Rights, Property and Liabilities Order (n 264) art 4(d); *Rahimtoola v Nizam of Hyderabad*, House of Lords (7 November 1957) 24 ILR 175, 182–84.

[244] Treaty on German Unity (West Germany–East Germany) (adopted 30 August 1990, entered into force 3 October 1990) 30 ILM (463, arts 21–24, 24(7) 26–27, 30.

[245] E.g. – *Texas Bond Cases* (Award) British–American Claims Commission (29 November 1854) IV Moore 3591, 3594. See further: EH Feilchenfeld, *Public Debts and State Succession* (Macmillan 1931) 271–286.

[246] Feilchenfeld (n 245) 263. In dozens of cases, the Italian courts held Italy to have succeeded to the various forms of debt of the absorbed Italian States; e.g. – *Antona-Traversi v Ministero delle finanze*, Court of Cassation of Turin (19 February 1881) II Giurisprudenza 1144, 1145–1146 (Italian).

APPLICATION TO THE CLASSES OF SUCCESSION   125

1871),[247] Fiji (1874),[248] the Transvaal Republic (1902),[249] Madagascar (1896),[250] and Hawai'i (1898).[251]

A challenge to the basic rule was made by Germany when, for financial rather than legal motives,[252] it took the initial position in 1938 that it was not obliged to assume the external debt of Austria[253] despite its assumption of its public and private ('patrimonial') property.[254] While refusing to negotiate collectively with creditors with which it exchanged legal argument,[255] Germany secretly accepted succession to the debt owed to Italy[256] before publicly accepting the debt owed to the United Kingdom (the largest creditor) 'without admission of legal liability' at reduced rates of interest.[257]

Omitting a no-admission proviso, Germany then settled the debts owed to France, Sweden, Belgium, and the Netherlands, with which it had favourable exchange rates.[258] In 1939, Germany settled the external debt with private bondholders by agreeing to convert the Austrian bonds to German bonds at reduced interest.[259] Despite the legal position initially adopted for financial reasons, Germany ultimately accepted the principle of succession to the totality of the Austrian debt while renegotiating its terms.

While the customary rule is similar to that of a merger in that the totality of the State property and debt of the predecessor is transferred, the critical difference is that the successor is not a newly created State and so continues to hold the property and debt that it held before the succession. The VCSSP does not distinguish between mergers and absorptions but the absorption of East Germany by West

---

[247] Ibid, 286.

[248] Ibid, 294–95. See also: Charles Rousseau, *Droit international public* (1977) vol III, 437.

[249] Ibid. The United Kingdom assumed its debts but its courts declined jurisdiction to adjudicate claims under the 'act of State' doctrine; e.g. – *Postmaster-General v Taute, Treasurer-General v Van Vuren, Postmaster-General v Parsons, Master of the Supreme Court v Roth*, Supreme Court of the Transvaal (22 August & 22 September 1905) 3 CILC 92, 96–97, 99–100, 103.

[250] Daniel Bardonnet, *La Succession d'États à Madagascar* vol I (Librairie Générale de Droit et de Jurisprudence 1970) 131–206.

[251] Joint Resolution annexing the Hawaiian Islands (7 July 1898) 90 BFSP 1250, s 1. See further: Moore (n 263) vol I, 309, 336–338.

[252] RE Clute, *The International Legal Status of Austria 1938–1955* (Springer 1962) 91, 93–94.

[253] II FRUS (1938) 483, 486. See also: *United States ex rel. d'Esquiva v Uhl, District Director of Immigration*, US Second Circuit Court of Appeals (18 August 1943) 11 ILR 23, 26.

[254] JW Garner, 'Questions of State Succession Raised by the German Annexation of Austria' (1938) 32 AJIL 421, 424–25.

[255] II FRUS (1938) 487, 490–492; Clute (n 252) 95–96; Garner (n 254) 766; 337 Hansard series 5 col 34.

[256] Convention on Payments (Germany–Italy) (28 May 1938) 39 MNRG 302, art 4. See further: HH Brandt, 'Die Regelung der österreichischen Bundesschulden' (1939) 9 HJIL 127, 137–38; Clute (n 252) 93.

[257] Transfer Agreement (Germany–United Kingdom) (1 July 1938) 36 MNRG 370, preamble, art 2 and annex (paras 1–2, 4–5), art 3.

[258] 'Re Austrian Foreign Bonds', FBPC (1938) 664; Brandt (n 256) 140–41. It did not reach agreement with Switzerland and the United States, with which it had poor rates – II FRUS (1938) 483–502; II FRUS (1939) 559–566; 1 Hackworth 544–48.

[259] Clute (n 252) 96.

126   SUCCESSION TO STATE PROPERTY AND DEBT

Germany in 1990 prompted the IDI to acknowledge the existence of a separate category in its guiding principles.[260]

### 4.3.3  Dismemberment

When a State is dismembered to transfer title to multiple parts of its territory to existing States or new States, the entirety of its property and debt is transferred by operation of law to the successors. As there are multiple successors with potential proprietary claims as well as third-party creditors for the State debt, the likelihood of disputes arising is necessarily greater than in cases of merger or absorption. In this context, the key doctrinal issue are the methods to be used to allocate the property and debt among the several successors.

While dismemberments are rare, the basic rule of the complete transfer of State property and debt is consistently supported by State practice. Modern practice underpinning this customary rule comprise the dismemberments of Czecho-Slovakia (1992)[261] and the SFRY (1991–92). Additional examples from classical practice are the Austro-Hungarian Empire (1920)[262] and the Union of Colombia (1830).[263] Though not true dismemberments, the dissolution of the colonial units of British India,[264] French Indochina,[265] and Rhodesia

---

[260]   IDI Resolution (n 16) art 2; IDI Report (n 15) 141.

[261]   E.g. – Czechia Constitutional Act No 542/1992 Zákony Prolidi Coll (25 November 1992) arts 1, 4–5 (Czecho-Slovak); Constitution of Slovakia (1 September 1992) 460/1992 Coll. Pravne Predpisy, art 153 (Czecho-Slovak); Constitutional Act No 624/1992 Coll. Zákony Prolidi (17 December 1992) art 4 (Czecho-Slovak); UN Doc A/47/848 (31 December 1992) annexes I–II; 'Czech Republic and Slovak Republic – Quota Calculations' (16 December 1992) IMF Doc EBS/92/213 7–10. See also: *Succession of States and Individuals Case*, Constitutional Court of the Czech Republic (30 January 2001) 142 ILR 175, 181–85.

[262]   E.g. – Treaty of Saint-Germain-en-Laye, 10 September 1919 (16 July 1920) (1919) 226 CTS 8, preamble, arts 203, 205–06, 208, part IX (annex); Treaty of Trianon, 4 June 1920 (26 July 1921) 3 Malloy 3539, preamble, art 186, 191; *Victor Rubens v Austria* (Decision) Anglo-Austrian Mixed Arbitral Tribunal (2 May 1923) III Recueil des Décisions 38, 39–40 (French); *Municipal Trust Company Limited v Hungary* (Decision) Anglo-Hungarian Mixed Arbitral Tribunal (26 July 1923) III Recueil des Décisions 248, 251 (French); *German Reparations under Article 260 of the Treaty of Versailles (Germany v Reparations Commission)* (Award) Arbitral Tribunal (3 September 1924) I RIAA 429, 440 (French); Commission des réparations, *La répartition de la dette publique d'avant-guerre autrichienne et hongroise* vol VII (1925) 12–13, 18–20, 39 (annexe D) 45–48 (annexe G); *State Succession (Gold Bonds) Case*, Supreme Court in Civil Matters of Austria (5 March 1929) 5 ILR 65, 66. See further: Feilchenfeld (n 245) 435–36, 447–48, 454–56.

[263]   JB Moore, *International Arbitrations to which the United States has been a Party* vol II (1898) 1572. See also: *Consolidated Debt of New Grenada Cases*, US–Colombian Claims Commission (1864) IV Moore 3612.

[264]   E.g. – Indian Independence (Rights, Property and Liabilities) Order 1947, 3 CILC 134, arts 1, 3–4, 6, 8–10; Financial Agreement (India–Pakistan) (14 August 1947) 147 BFSP (1947) 865, arts I–IV. See further, e.g. – Isaac Paenson, *Les conséquences financières de la succession d'États* (Éditions Domat-Montchrestien 1954) 66.

[265]   E.g. – Protocol No 2 on the Liquidation of the former Indochina Treasury (France–Cambodia–Laos–South Viet Nam) Documentation française, *Notes et Études Documentaires*, Doc No 1973 (1955) 17, arts II–XI, tables 1–3 (French); Provisional Financial Convention (Federal Government of Indochina–Cambodia) (27 May 1946) France Treaty Database, Doc TRA19460073, arts 3–5 (French).

APPLICATION TO THE CLASSES OF SUCCESSION 127

and Nyasaland[266] also featured analogous practice in the context of multiple secessions.

The most recent and difficult case of the SFRY has affirmed the basic rule. In the 1990s, each of the successors accepted assignment of project debts localized in their respective territories[267] and apportionment of the general debt according to the 'IMF key' adopted in 1992.[268] After the Federal Republic of Yugoslavia ('FRY') abandoned its claim to the legal personality of the SFRY in 2000,[269] the successors concluded the 2001 Agreement on Succession Issues in which they apportioned assets held at the Bank for International Settlements according to the IMF key.[270]

Movable and immovable property located in the territory of the SFRY passed to the successor on whose territory it was located on its respective date of independence.[271] Each successor was empowered to designate the 'State property' of the SFRY.[272] State archives and social security debts were also assigned on the basis of territoriality.[273] Civil service pension debts were assigned according to a special test of residence or domicile of the creditor.[274]

In contrast, movable and immovable assets situated outside the SFRY were apportioned according to an agreed key[275] with other listed properties and their movable contents to be subsequently allocated by agreement on a similar basis.[276]

---

[266] Federation of Rhodesia and Nyasaland (Dissolution) Order in Council 1963 No 2085, arts 6–7, 10–11, 12, 14, 16–18, 20, 24–25, sch I.

[267] Mrăk (n 346) 160–61, 163–64.

[268] Ibid, 177. See further: Arthur Watts, 'State Succession: Some Recent Practical Legal Problems' in PC Götz, Peter Selmer. and Rüdiger Wolfrum (eds) *Liber amicorum Günther Jaenicke* (Springer 1998) 408; Ana Stanič, 'Financial Aspects of State Succession: The Case of Yugoslavia' (2001) 12 EJIL 751, 761–63.

[269] 'Letter dated 6 May 1992 from the Permanent Mission of Yugoslavia to the United Nations', UN Doc A/46/915 (7 May 1992); Application of the FRY for Admission to Membership in the United Nations, UN Doc A/55/528-S/2000/1043 (30 October 2009).

[270] Agreement on Succession Issues between the Five Successor States of the former State of Yugoslavia (adopted 29 June 2001, entered into force 2 June 2004) 2262 UNTS 251, appendix (para 1).

[271] Ibid, annex A (arts 2(1) 3, 7). This relativistic approach avoided 'making a final and binding determination of the actual date of succession, by relying on an agreed fiction' – Carsten Stahn, 'The Agreement on Succession Issues of the Former Socialist Federal Republic of Yugoslavia' (2002) 96 AJIL 379, 386–87.

[272] Ibid, annex A (art 6). See also: Stanič (n 268) 764–65; Degan, 'Disagreements over the Definition of State Property in the Process of State Succession to the Former Yugoslavia' in Mrăk (n 346) 39–43; *Haakon Korsguard v Croatia* (Award) UNCITRAL *ad hoc* Arbitral Tribunal (7 November 2022) (not published) reported in Vladislav Djanić, 'Croatia claims victory in under-the-radar treaty arbitration' (10 November 2022), <https://www.iareporter.com/articles/croatia-claims-victory-in-under-the-radar-treaty-arbitration/> accessed 26 December 2023.

[273] Ibid, annex D (arts 1(1) 2, 4), annex E (art 1). E.g. – Social Insurance Agreement (Slovenia–Croatia) (28 October 1997) 71 Uradni list (21 November 1997) arts 35–36 (Slovene).

[274] Ibid, annex E (art 2).

[275] Ibid, annex B (arts 1(1) 2). On the sale of the Park Avenue tenement used by the UN Mission, see: Večernji List <https://www.vecernji.hr/vijesti/titov-stan-u-new-yorku-prodan-za-12-milijuna-dol ara-1249483> accessed 2 January 2024 (Serbo-Croatian).

[276] Ibid, annex B (arts 3–4), appendix.

128    SUCCESSION TO STATE PROPERTY AND DEBT

This allocation remains pending[277] while the FRY reached agreements for the assumption of its portion of the external debt on restructuring terms.[278]

Overall, the 2001 Agreement showed that the successors prioritised the principle of territoriality for the assignment of State property and debt, whether movable or immovable, where a link existed between an asset or debt and a particular territory of the SFRY. In contrast, diplomatic and military property and the general debt of the SFRY were equitably apportioned because they lacked a territorial link. Despite the invocation of territoriality by Serbia and Slovenia for the allocation of localized debts owed to foreign currency depositors, the European Court of Human Rights wrongly held in 2014 that equitable apportionment applies in the absence of agreement.[279]

On the critical issue of allocation, State practice on dismemberments thus supports a default rule whereby priority is given to the assignment of a specific asset or debt according to its dominant connection to a transferred territory. This applies both to the property and debt of local governments and to the property or debt that had belonged to the central government but was 'localized' in a particular territory. When an asset or debt has no dominant connection, the secondary principle is that it be equitably apportioned among the successors according to their relative economic sizes.

These customary rules are not reflected in Articles 18 and 41 of the VCSSP.[280] State practice has not followed the absolute rule in Article 18 for the assignment of immovable property located within the territory of the predecessor.[281] Rather, a presumption applies that may be rebutted by evidence of a dominant connection to the territory of another successor. Similarly, assignment according to territoriality can apply to immovable property located outside the territory of the predecessor if it have a dominant connection. The vague test for movable property 'connected with the activity of the predecessor State in respect of the territories to

---

[277] In 2009 and 2015, the Standing Joint Committee advised the Contracting Parties to establish 'without any further delay' a joint committee on succession to movable and immovable property, to disclose outstanding information on State property and to implement pending allocations of military and diplomatic property – Recommendations 1–6 to the Governments of the Successor States of SFRY, Standing Joint Committee (17/18 September 2009) (on file with author); Recommendations 7–11 to the Governments of the Successor States of SFRY, Standing Joint Committee (17 September 2015) (on file with author).

[278] 'Serbia and Montenegro – Staff Report for the 2005 Article IV Consultation', IMF Doc SM/05/216 (14 June 2005) 26–27, 36, 46–47, 49.

[279] *Ališić* (n 31) paras 9–11, 60. This position was also taken by Croatia: *Kovačić and others v Slovenia* Nos 44574/98, 45133/98 & 48316/99, European Court of Human Rights (3 October 2008) paras 27–163, 255–69; *Slovenia v Croatia* No 54155/16, European Court of Human Rights (16 December 2020) paras 12–16, 31, 73–79.

[280] *Official Records* (n 9) vol I, 121–22, 190 (paras 41–53) 236–37 (paras 79–106). See also: IDI Resolution (n 16) art 19(3); ILA Committee Report (n 14) 250–363.

[281] E.g. – *Croatia v Serbia*, High Court of England (2 July 2009) 164 ILR 429, 432–36, 441–48. See also: 'Flat 4 Zetland House, Marloes Road, London, W8 5LB (Leasehold)' Title No NGL216972 (21 August 2022) HM Land Registry.

APPLICATION TO THE CLASSES OF SUCCESSION 129

which the succession of States relates' also does not fully articulate the customary principle of territoriality.

In contrast, the primacy given to the principle of territoriality over equitable apportionment in Article 31 on State archives accurately reflects the default rule for State property even as its formulae for the identification of territorial connection have not been adopted in subsequent practice. In prescribing a single rule of equitable apportionment of State debt, Article 41 does not acknowledge the principle of territoriality for the assignment of specific debts.[282] Omitting any criteria for the evaluation of equitable apportionment, it also stipulates that State debt be apportioned by taking particular account of the State property passing to the successor concerned. This *general* link between State property and debt only applies to those assets and debts that are incapable of being assigned by territoriality.

## 4.3.4 Cession

When one State cedes territory to another, customary international law provides for the automatic transfer of State property and debt with a dominant connection to the ceded territory by operation of law unless otherwise agreed. State practice is consistent in supporting the transfer of local and localized property and debt while all other property and debt remains with the predecessor. Though rare in modern practice, ten cessions in the UN era evince this basic rule.[283] These include the cessions of Newfoundland (1949),[284] French India (1952 and 1963),[285] Portuguese

---

[282] IDI Resolution (n 16) art 11(1).

[283] Classical practice includes: Venetia-Lombardy (1866); Atacama (1904); the First World War peace treaties (1919); and Alexandretta (1939).

[284] British North America Act 1949 (23 March 1949) 153 BFSP 130, ss 1–2; sch ('Terms of Union of Newfoundland with Canada') paras 18(1), 23, 31–39, 50. See also, e.g. – *Charles R. Bell Ltd v Canadian National Railways*, Newfoundland Supreme Court (21 February 1951) 2 DLR 346, 348–49.

[285] Treaty of Cession of Chandernagore (France–India) (adopted 2 February 1951, entered into force 9 June 1952) 158 BFSP (1951) 599, arts V–VIII, protocol (art II); Treaty ceding the French Establishments to India (France–India) (adopted 28 May 1956, entered into force 16 August 1962) 162 BFSP 848, art 1, 14, 19, 26–27; protocol (art 8); Decree No 47-2121 (7 November 1947) 263 JORF (8 November 1947) 11006, arts 21–32 (French). See also, e.g. – 'Changernagore: Mixed Commission and Financial Matters (1 January 1949–31 December 1951)', France Archives, Series E Carton 81 Folder 1C, 180–96, 224–40 (French); 'Chandernagore: Mixed Commission and Financial Questions' (1 January 1949–31 December 1951)', France Archives, Series E Carton 81 Folder 1C, 140–67 (French and English); 'Mixed Commission (1 January 1952–31 December 1955)', France Archives, Series E Carton 81 Folder 5, 31–90 (French & English); *D. Gobalousamy v Pondicherry*, High Court of Madras (6 April 1966) 8 CILC 212, 216–17, 219, 221–23.

130 SUCCESSION TO STATE PROPERTY AND DEBT

India (1961 and 1962),[286] North Borneo, Sarawak and Singapore (1963),[287] Hong Kong (1997),[288] and Macao (1999).[289]

Article 14(2) of the VCSSP provides that immovable State property passes by location and movable State property passes if 'connected with the activity of the predecessor in respect of the territory'. The ILC considered that the 'general principle of equity' demanded that movable State property located in the territory but not linked to it should not pass, while a rebuttable presumption existed that movable property located outside the territory remain with the predecessor.[290] To reflect its succession agreements in the context of decolonization, France proposed amendments to replace the ILC test for movable property with a formula of 'direct and necessary connection with the administration and management of the territory' and to distinguish between 'public' and 'private or patrimonial' State property.[291] After criticism on grounds of vagueness, superfluity, and arrogation by a predecessor of patrimonial property,[292] the amendments were each rejected on votes of 35-19-6, 31-20-7, and 39-10-10, following which Article 14 was adopted on a vote of 40-0-18.[293]

The test of location for immovable property in subparagraph (a) and the test of territorial connection for movable property in subparagraph (b) are consistent with State practice.[294] However, States have departed from them in the face of evidence showing a dominant connection of a particular asset to transferred territory. In formulating the two tests as absolute rules rather than rebuttable presumptions, Article 14(2) therefore does not reflect customary international law.

Article 27(2) provides for the transfer of the part of State archives of the predecessor 'for normal administration of the territory to which the succession of States

---

[286] E.g. – Treaty on Recognition of India's Sovereignty over Goa (Portugal–India) (adopted 31 December 1974, entered into force 3 June 1975) 982 UNTS 153, arts I, III, V; exchange of letters (14 March 1975); Dadra and Nagar Haveli Act No 35 1961 < https://www.indiacode.nic in/bitstream/123456789/1640/2/A1961-35.pdf> accessed 30 December 2023, ss 6–8. See also, e.g. – *Sagoon Jayaidee Dhond v Sociedade Civil e Particular Dos Taris*, Judicial Commissioner's Court of Goa (29 April 1966) 8 CILC 225, 228, 230–31; *Cipriano Negredo v India*, Judicial Commissioner's Court of Goa, Daman and Diu (13 January 1969) 8 CILC 299, 304–06.

[287] Agreement (Malaysia–United Kingdom) Cmd 2094 (July 1963) art VII, annex A (arts 75–76), annex G, annex H (arts 1–3, 5), annex I (arts 1–3, 5); *UN Materials on Succession of States* (1967) UN Doc ST/LEG/SER.B/14, 92–93.

[288] Joint Declaration on the Question of Hong Kong (China–United Kingdom) (19 December 1984) 1399 UNTS 33, arts 1–3, annex I (arts III–VII); 'United Kingdom–Hong Kong: Selected Issues', IMF Doc SM/97/43 (21 May 1997) paras 21–22, 36, 64–76, 78–83.

[289] Joint Declaration on Macao (Portugal–China) (adopted 13 April 1987, entered into force 15 January 1988) 1498 UNTS 228, arts 1–3; annex I (arts I, III–IV, VI, VIII–IX, XI–XII, XIV); 'Portugal–Macao: Recent Economic Developments', IMF Doc SM/99/64 (10 March 1999) paras 18–25.

[290] ILC Articles (n 5) 30–35 (paras 9–13, 20–29).

[291] *Official Records* (n 9) vol I, 84–85 (paras 1–4), 90–91 (paras 5–12) 220 (para 48).

[292] Ibid, 85–86 (paras 12–13), 86 (para 17), 86 (para 22), 86 (para 24), 86 (para 25), 86 (para 26), 87 (para 27), 87 (para 33), 87 (para 34), 87 (para 39), 88 (para 34), 88 (para 49), 88 (para 51), 89 (paras 56–59).

[293] Ibid, 92 (paras 19–20).

[294] IDI Resolution (n 16) arts 19(1), 20(1); IDI Report (n 15) 214–15, 219–21, 268, 273.

APPLICATION TO THE CLASSES OF SUCCESSION    131

relates' and the part 'that relates exclusively or principally to the territory' unless otherwise agreed. In principally surveying classical practice,[295] the ILC described it as 'somewhat suspect'[296] but did not examine detailed practice pertaining to State archives in the modern case of French India. Based on the practices of archivists, the ILC posited an 'archives–territory link' in Article 27(2) with its twin principles of 'territorial origin' and 'territorial or functional connection'.[297] However, Austria remarked that the ILC approach was 'somewhat at variance with the established treaty practice'[298] and proposed an amendment to replace the words 'that relates exclusively or principally' in paragraph 2(b) with the words 'belonging or having belonged' in order to emphasize 'the functional connection between archives'.[299] Criticized by the Special Rapporteur as relating to 'local archives',[300] the Austrian amendment was rejected by a vote of 21-12-35 and Article 25 adopted by a vote of 59-1-9.[301]

Article 27(2)(b) reflects customary international law in providing for the transfer of State archives relating 'exclusively or principally' to the ceded territory, as does the 'functional test' provided in subparagraph (a). Contrary to the assertion of the Special Rapporteur, however, archives held by local governments have been included in the definition of 'State archives' in State practice.

Article 37 of the VCSSP states that State debt passes to the successor in an equitable proportion in relation to the passage of State property. Noting a doctrinal disagreement, the ILC principally analysed classical practice to conclude 'that, while there appears to exist a fairly well-established practice requiring the successor State to assume a localized State debt, no such consensus can be found with regard to general State debts'.[302] Asserting it to be 'useless ... to seek ... an incontestable rule of international law' to avoid a successor receiving State property without State debt, the ILC proposed 'the introduction of the concept of equity as the key to the solution of problems relating to the passing of State debts'.[303]

At the UN Conference, Pakistan tabled an amendment to delete the words 'in an equitable proportion' because it considered it to be 'almost impossible to produce ... a [universal] formula for the simple reason that the words "equitable proportion" emphasized the fact that each case had to be treated on its merits'.[304] The Special Rapporteur opposed the proposal because the formula had 'seemed to

---

[295] ILC Articles (n 5) 54–58 (paras 3–14).

[296] Ibid, 54 (paras 1–2).

[297] Ibid, 58–59 (paras 15–16).

[298] 'Comments and observations of Governments on the draft articles on succession of States in respect of matters other than treaties' UN Doc A/CN.4/338 (1981) ILC Yearbook vol II, part 2, 173 (para 8).

[299] *Official Records* (n 9) vol I, 164 (paras 8, 11); vol II, 109 (para 145).

[300] Ibid, vol I, 165 (para 24) 167 (para 48).

[301] Ibid, 167 (paras 46, 51–52).

[302] ILC Articles (n 5) 84 (para 1) 84–90, 90 (para 36).

[303] *Official Records* (n 9) vol I, 90 (para 37).

[304] Ibid, 220 (para 42).

132  SUCCESSION TO STATE PROPERTY AND DEBT

rectify the rather mechanical correspondence between the property and the debt which passed to the successor State'.[305] The amendment was rejected by a vote of 40-1-18 and Article 37 was adopted on a vote of 57-0-5.[306]

Article 37 does not reflect customary international law, which provides for the transfer of local debt and localized debt according to the primary principle of territoriality. While modern practice has exclusively featured the cession of territories with financial autonomy, classical State practice showed the transfer of an equitable proportion of the general debt of the predecessor to be the secondary principle for territories lacking such autonomy.[307]

### 4.3.5 Secession

When a territory secedes from a State to create a new State, customary international law provides for the automatic transfer to the successor of State property and debt with a dominant connection to the seceding territory unless otherwise agreed. State practice is consistent in supporting the transfer of local and localized property and debt while all other property and debt remains with the predecessor. While these basic rules are the same as for cession, territoriality is particularly important because seceding territories have typically exercised financial autonomy before the date of succession.

The most frequent type of succession in the UN era, secession includes a rich source of practice in the form of the secessions of former colonies from metropolitan States.[308] Representative examples of this extensive and cohesive practice from a variety of legal systems and regions of the world in favour of the basic rule of succession to State property and debt. Classical State practice also supported this principle, though a minority of successors (e.g.—United States, Mexico, Brazil, Panama) denied a duty to succeed while accepting succession.[309]

The secessions of colonial territories of the British Empire generally featured the transfer to the successor of local and localized property and debt.[310] Examples include the secessions of India and Pakistan (1947),[311]

---

[305]  Ibid, 220 (para 45).

[306]  Ibid, 221 (paras 50–51).

[307]  For example, the cession of the Spanish territories of Cuba, Puerto Rico, Guam, and the Philippines in 1899.

[308]  IDI Report (n 17) 131, 144; First Bedjaoui Report (n 2) para 33.

[309]  Feilchenfeld (n 245) 53–54, 147–48, 251–57, 347–51; Rousseau (n 248) 433.

[310]  On Sri Lanka (1948), Ghana (1957), Sierra Leone (1961), Jamaica (1962), Trinidad and Tobago (1962), Uganda (1962), Kenya (1963), Zanzibar (1963), Malta (1964), the Gambia (1965), Barbados (1966), Botswana (1966), Guyana (1966), Lesotho (1966), and Swaziland (1968), see: *UN Materials* (n 287) 123–40, 166–204, 239–66, 278–82, 303–09, 34–337, 386–90, 402–08, 425–37, 452–77.

[311]  Note 264.

APPLICATION TO THE CLASSES OF SUCCESSION    133

Myanmar ('Burma', 1948),[312] Malaya (1957),[313] South Yemen ('South Arabia', 1967),[314] and Mauritius (1968).[315] Although the case of Cyprus (1960) had special complexities, it largely followed the same pattern.[316]

The bureaucratic techniques employed by France differed from those of the United Kingdom (e.g.—in the greater use of itemized lists) but its succession agreements were similar in substance. Examples include the secessions of South Viet Nam, Laos, and Cambodia (1953),[317] the Malagasy Republic ('Madagascar', 1960),[318] and Algeria (1962).[319] Other decolonization examples include the secessions of Philippines from the United States (1946),[320] Indonesia from the

[312] E.g. – Treaty on Burmese Independence (Burma–United Kingdom) (adopted 17 October 1947, entered into force 4 January 1948) 70 UNTS 183, arts 6–7, annex (Defence Agreement) arts 3, 5, annex (para 3), Exchange of Notes (29 August 1947); Burma Independence Act 1947 (10 December 1947) 11 Geo 6 c 3, s 4(2); Constitution of Burma (adopted 24 September 1947, entered into force 4 January 1948) in Maung Maung, *Burma's Constitution* (Springer 1961), 208–09, arts 5, 209, 223–25, 229.

[313] E.g. – Order in Council regarding the Federation of Malaya (26 January 1948) 150 BFSP 30, art 4, sch I, arts 166–167, sch II, arts 111–23, 140–41, 145; Federation of Malaya Independence Act 1957 in *UN Materials* (n 287) 76, s1(1); Agreement on the Independence of Malaya (5 August 1957) 163 BFSP 46, art 3; 'Federation of Malaya – Background Material' (22 September 1958) IMF Doc SM/58/72, 13.

[314] E.g. – Aden, Perim and Kuria Muria Islands Act 1967, 15 & 16 Eliz 2 c 71, s 1; Aden, Parim and Kuria Muria Islands Act 1967 (Appointed Day) Order SI 1967/1761; Memorandum on Independence for South Arabia (National Front for the Liberation of Southern Yemen–United Kingdom) (29 November 1967) 169 BFSP 136, paras 2, 7, 9–10, 12–17; 'Southern Yemen – Recent Economic Developments' (3 June 1970) IMF Doc SM/70/116 28–46, 58–59, 68, 70.

[315] E.g. – Mauritius Independence Act 1968, 16 & 17 Eliz II c 8, s 1(1); Mauritius Independence Order 1968, Government Notice No 54 (6 March 1968) art 3(1); 'The Economy of Mauritius' (10 September 1963) IBRD/IDA Report No EA-139a, paras 1–7; 'Current Economic Position and Prospects of Mauritius' (5 August 1968) IBRD/IDA Report No AF-80, ii, 16, appendix (table 1).

[316] E.g. – Treaty concerning the Republic of Cyprus (Cyprus–Greece–Turkey–United Kingdom) (16 August 1960) 382 UNTS 8, annexe E; 'Cyprus – 1962 Article XIV Consultations', IMF Doc SM/62/55 (27 June 1962) 24–27, 53.

[317] E.g. – Financial Convention (Indochina–Cambodia) (27 May 1946) France Treaty Database No TRA9460073, arts 3–4 (French); Financial Convention (France–Laos), France Treaty Database, No TRA19500158, arts 1, 3 (French); *UN Materials* (n 287) 11–20, 266–271, 441–452; State Property Protocol (France–South Viet Nam) (14 November 1959) France Treaty Database No TRA19590338, arts I–IV, annexes I–IV (French); 'Laos: Economic Situation', IMF Doc SM/62/16 (8 March 1962) 17–19.

[318] E.g. – Agreement on Co-operation in Monetary, Economic and Financial Matters (France–Madagascar) (adopted 27 June 1960, entered into force 18 July 1960) 820 UNTS 248, arts 32–37; ILC Articles (n 5) 95–96 (paras 22–24); 'Malagasy Republic – 1965 Article XIV Consultations' (28 September 1965) IMF Doc SM/65/82, 36. This practice was typical of the secessions in Africa, such as Mauritania and Senegal – Rousseau (n 248) 378–79; Daniel Bardonnet, *La Succession d'États à Madagascar* vol II (Libraire Générale de Droit et de Jurisprudence 1970) 584–628, 648–63.

[319] E.g. – Declarations drawn up in Common Agreement at Evian (France–Algerian National Liberation Front) (18 March 1962) 1(2) ILM 214, Declaration of Principles concerning Economic and Financial Cooperation, arts 15–16, 18–19; *UN Materials* (n 287) 112–113 (French); Agreement on Certain Financial Questions (France–Algeria) (23 December 1966) France Archives No TRA19660023 (on file with author) arts 1–2, 5, annexes I, IV–VI (French). See also: Charles Rousseau, 'Algérie et France: Conséquences financières de l'accession de l'Algérie à l'indépendance. Succession aux dettes publiques', (1967) 38(3) RGDIP 721, 722–23.

[320] E.g. – Act for the Independence of the Philippines Islands (24 March 1934) 137 BFSP 690, ss 2(a) (7) 2(b)(3) 5, 9; Treaty of General Relations (Philippines–United States) (adopted 4 July 1946, entered into force 22 October 1946) 7 UNTS 3, art IV; Constitution of the Philippines (23 March 1935) in AJ Peaslee, *Constitutions of Nations* (Martinus Nijhoff 1950) 789–809, art XVI(I)(3).

134   SUCCESSION TO STATE PROPERTY AND DEBT

Netherlands (1949),[321] Libya from Italy (1951),[322] Singapore from Malaysia (1965),[323] Equatorial Guinea from Spain (1968),[324] and Mozambique from Portugal (1975).[325]

Disputes concerning State property and debt arose for the secessions of French Guinea from France (1958), the Democratic Republic of the Congo from Belgium (1960), and Bangladesh from Pakistan (1971), in which none of the successors contested the basic principle of succession to the local property and debt of a financially autonomous dependent territory, alongside debts of the metropolitan State localized to its territory, or a proportion of the property and general debt of the metropolitan State in the absence of such autonomy. The practice also illustrates the sophistication of the assignment of particular assets and debts according to territoriality, such as funds owned by local government and held in metropolitan accounts and immovable assets located in the transferred territory and owned by the metropolitan government.

In 1958, French Guinea seceded from France as the sole overseas territory to reject the enhanced autonomy in the French Community.[326] Prior to independence, 40 per cent of its ordinary budget had been subsidized by grants from metropolitan France alongside extensive loans.[327] Following a rupture in diplomatic relations and the cessation by France of pension payments to Guinean nationals, Guinea suspended payment on its debts to France while assuming payment of the pensions.[328]

In 1965, Guinea and France reached a first settlement of their outstanding claims whereby France reimbursed Guinea for civil service pension payments

---

[321] E.g. – Round-Table Conference Agreement (2 November 1949) (Indonesia–Netherlands) 69 UNTS 200, Financial and Economic Agreement, arts 25–27; Transitional Agreement (Netherlands–Indonesia) 69 UNTS 266, art 4(1); Economic Agreement (Netherlands–Indonesia) (11 February 1952) 165 UNTS 77, art 1.

[322] UNGA Res 388(V)(A) (15 December 1950) arts I–IV, VI(1) IX(1), X(1)(b). See also: 'Former Italian Colonies, Economic and Financial Provisions Relating to Libya: Report of the Ad Hoc Political Committee' (14 December 1950) UN Doc A/1726, 9.

[323] Independence of Singapore Agreement (Malaysia–Singapore) (7 August 1965) 4 ILM 928, art II, annex B (para 9); Constitution and Malaysia (Singapore Amendment) Act 1965, ibid, 938, ss 3, 6; 'Singapore – Calculation of Quota' (6 October 1965) IMF Doc EB/CM/Singapore/65/1, 2, 5.

[324] E.g. – Decree No 2467 ('Constitution of Equatorial Guinea') (9 October 1968) BOGE (24 July 1968) art 3; Transitional Convention (Spain–Equatorial Guinea) (adopted 12 October 1968, entered into force 14 February 1972) 50 BOE (28 February 1972) 3511, arts III–VI, VIII–XII (Spanish); 'The Economy of Equatorial Guinea' (15 September 1971) IMF Doc SM/71/235, 5–10.

[325] 'High Commission of Mozambique' Portugal Archives Box 40603 (Portuguese). On the financial autonomy of Portuguese Overseas Territories, see: 'Finances – Current Accounts with the Metropole' Portugal Archives Box 55344 Folder J/11–1 Files J/9-a and J/5-aJ3 (Cabinet Division Archive) (Portuguese).

[326] Georges Fischer, 'L'indépendance de la Guinée et les accords franco-guinéens' (1958) 4 AFDI 711, 717–18; ILC Articles (n 5), 95 (para 21).

[327] 'Guinea – 1965 Article XIV Consultations' (30 December 1965) IMF Archives Doc SM/65/105, 6–7, 26–28, 32, 49–50.

[328] Ibid, 6, 38. See also: 'Guinea: Recent Economic Developments', IMF Doc SM/72/163 (27 June 1972) 25–26, 38; Re Marchi, Administrative Court of Paris (22 June 1965) 47 ILR 83, 84.

APPLICATION TO THE CLASSES OF SUCCESSION 135

and settled an outstanding debt owed by the metropolitan treasury to the colonial treasury while Guinea settled 22 debts owed to the metropolitan treasury.[329] Guinea had initially resisted the debts on the ground that they had been contracted by the French colonial administration in which no indigenous Guinean was represented but ultimately accepted them with extended maturities.[330] Having inventoried and revaluated civil service pensions, France and Guinea agreed in 1977 on a lump sum payment by France to discharge its pre-independence debts,[331] the release of frozen funds owned by French Guinea, the transfer of administrative archives pertaining to French Guinea, and compensation to France for the seizure of assets of metropolitan France situated in French Guinea.[332]

Prior to its rapid secession from Belgium in 1960, the DRC concluded a settlement of the debt of the financially autonomous Colony of the Belgian Congo[333] by which it assumed debts denominated in Congolese francs while Belgium assumed debts denominated in foreign currencies that its metropolitan budget had guaranteed.[334] The property portfolio of the Belgian Congo, comprising movable and immovable assets within and without its territory, was transferred to the DRC.[335]

Disputes arose in the Belgian courts concerning the effect of a Belgian law guaranteeing pensions and other charges of the Belgian Congo.[336] The courts held the legislation to have had the special effect of retaining these administrative debts despite the financial autonomy of the Colony in its 1908 charter.[337] This showed the default rule to have been the transfer of these administrative debts but for the adoption of the special law of guarantee.

However, the Belgian courts came to divergent conclusions on contractual and tortious debts. Applying general international law, one line of judgments held such debts to have been automatically transferred to the DRC in the absence of special agreement due to the financial autonomy of the Belgian Congo.[338] In another line,

---

[329] Ibid, 6, 69, 73–74, 100, 103–04.

[330] Ibid, 105.

[331] Financial Agreement (France–Guinea) (26 January 1977) JORF (14 February 1978) 711, art I (French).

[332] Ibid, arts II–III.

[333] Convention for the Settlement of Questions relating to the Public Debt and Portfolio of the Belgian Congo Colony (Belgium–Democratic Republic of the Congo) (adopted 6 February 1965, entered into force 11 May 1965) 540 UNTS 227, art 2, sch 1. See also, e.g. – CRISP, *Congo 1965: Political Documents of a Developing Nation* (1967) 237–42 (French); 'Economic and Financial Developments in the Republic of the Congo', IMF Doc SM/61/38 (24 April 1961).

[334] Ibid, arts 2–4, schs 2–3.

[335] Ibid, arts 15–17, Sch 5.

[336] Law modifying the General Law on Civil Pensions, 79 Moniteur Belge (1 April 1960) 2475, art 1.

[337] *État Belge v Dumont*, Court of Appeal of Brussels (4 December 1963) 48 ILR 8, 9; *Chimique du Congo c Coelho»*, Cour de Cassation (4 June 1964) 2(2) *RBDI* (1966) 546–47 (French); 2(2) *RBDI* (1966) 547–48; 3(2) *RBDI* (1967) 567; 6(2) *RBDI* (1970) 687 (French). See also: *Prosecutor General Dumont*, Civil Court of Brussels (26 December 1961) (1965) 1(1) RBDI 509–511 (French); TM Franck, John Carey and LM Tondel, *Legal Aspects of the United Nations Action in the Congo* (Oceana Publications, 1963) 108 (app E) arts 188–90; 1(1) RBDI (1965) 500, 501–03, 505–09.

[338] E.g. – *Creplet v Belgium*, Civil Court of Brussels (30 January 1962) (1965) 1 RBDI 514, 515 (French); *Soc. Forces de l'Est v Belgium*, Civil Court of Brussels (22 May 1962) (1965) 1 RBDI 515, 516

136    SUCCESSION TO STATE PROPERTY AND DEBT

the courts held international law to admit claims against metropolitan Belgium when contracted 'in its interest', in contrast to local debts contracted in the exclusive interest of the Belgian Congo.[339] The Court of Cassation definitively ruled that Belgium was not liable for tortious debts due to the segregation of the finances of Belgium and the Belgian Congo.[340]

In seceding from Pakistan in 1971,[341] Bangladesh took over the budget of East Pakistan, which had lacked financial autonomy.[342] It also assumed the assets and debts of the State Bank of Pakistan and other public bodies located in its territory[343] as well as the former local government bodies of East Pakistan.[344] It substituted itself for East Pakistan as respondent to pending tortious claims.[345]

From 1972, Bangladesh accepted the principle of succession to the external debt of Pakistan while contesting its apportionment.[346] It succeeded to debts for projects located in its territory[347] and programme debts from which it had benefited.[348] From 1973, it concluded bilateral agreements with creditor countries for projects 'visibly located' in Bangladesh.[349] Accepting the principle of succession to the general debt,[350] in 1974 bilateral negotiations with Pakistan for its apportionment failed, in which Bangladesh reportedly claimed 56 per cent of all common property (e.g.—assets of

(French); *Baugnet-Hock v Belgium*, Court of Appeal of Brussels (4 December 1962) (1965) 1 RBDI 513, 514 (French).

[339] E.g. – *(1) De Keer Maurice v Belgium*, Court of First Instance of Ghent (9 December 1963); *(2) Demol v Belgium*, Court of First Instance of Brussels (23 September 1964) 47 ILR 75, 77–78.

[340] E.g. – *Belgium v Dumont, Pittacos v Belgium*, Court of Cassation of Belgium (26 May 1966) 48 ILR 20, 21–23, 25. See also, e.g. – *Dupont v Belgium*, Court of Cassation of Belgium (8 February 1968) (1970) 6(2) RBDI 684, 685 (French).

[341] Bangladesh Proclamation of Independence (10 April 1971) 24 DLR (1972) 1; Provisional Constitution of Bangladesh Order 1972 (11 January 1972) 24 DLR (1972) 29.

[342] E.g. – Finance (1971–72) Order 1972 BGE (24 May 1972) 921, arts 18–21.

[343] Bangladesh Bank (Temporary) Order, 1971, 24 DLR (1972) arts 2–4; Bangladesh (Demonetization of Bank Notes) Order 1972 (8 June 1972) ibid, 107 (arts 5–6). See also: *Bangladesh Enemy Property Management Board v Md. Abdul Majid*, Supreme Court of Bangladesh (1975) 27 DLR (1975) 52, 54–55, 58; *Benoy Bhusan v Sub-Divisional Officer*, Supreme Court of Bangladesh (29 November 1977) 30 DLR (1978) 139, 145, 147, 151–55, 158.

[344] Bangladesh Local Councils Order 1972 24 DLR (1972) 14, art 5.

[345] E.g. – High Court of Bangladesh Order 1972, 24 DLR (1972) 12 (arts 2–3, 6); Bangladesh (Legal Proceedings) Order 1972, ibid, 28 (art 3).

[346] 'Memorandum: Assumption of Pakistan's External Debt by Bangladesh' (27 June 1975) IMF Archives No 45300. See also, e.g. – TS Cheema, *Pakistan Bangladesh Relations* (Unistar 2013) 75–76; IFI Shihata, 'Matters of State Succession in the World Bank's Practice' in Mojmir Mrăk (ed) *Succession of States* (Kluwer 1999) 75, 89; 'Minutes of Meeting' (29 January 1972) World Bank Archives Folder ID 1771155, para 3.

[347] 'Memorandum' (24 September 1973) World Bank Archives Folder 177115.

[348] 'Memorandum from Mr William Diamond to Mr Robert S McNamara' (8 July 1974) World Bank Archives, Folder ID 1770953.

[349] 'Memorandum' (8 July 1974) World Bank Archives Folder ID 1770953, para 2(c)(i). See also, e.g. – Agreement on the Assumption of Debt Liabilities (Switzerland–Bangladesh) (adopted 4 December 1974, entered into force 10 October 1975) 1127 UNTS 318, art 1, annexe.

[350] 'Memorandum' (2 January 1974) World Bank Archives Folder 1771155, paras 4–5. See also: Mohammed Bedjaoui, 'Eighth report on succession of States in respect of matters other than treaties' (8 April 1976) UN Doc A/CN.4/292, para 59.

Pakistan International Airlines).[351] While a settlement was reportedly reached in 1975 whereby Bangladesh accepted half of the pre-1971 external debt,[352] no treaty is published in the Pakistan Treaty Series or other source.[353]

In drafting the VCSSP between 1978 and 1983, Article 17(1) of the VCSSP provides for the passage of immovable property by location, movable property by connection to activity in the transferred territory, and other movable property by equitable apportionment. At the UN Conference, it was heavily debated with respect to the equities, the clarity of the articulated tests, and their empirical basis in State practice.[354] Amendments proposed by Pakistan to delete equitable apportionment and to substitute a formula of 'direct and necessary connection with the administration and management of the territory' for movable property were rejected on votes of 37-13-12 and 30-18-12, with Article 17 thereafter adopted by a vote of 46-0-17.[355]

The absolute rule in Article 17 for the transfer of immovable property in subparagraph (a) according to its location does not reflect the prior State practice, which recognized a rebuttable presumption.[356] While the formula 'connected with the activity' in subparagraph (b) is vague, its underlying principle of territoriality accords with that practice. However, the most significant weakness is the failure to distinguish between the assignment of local property and debt for financially autonomous territories and the equitable apportionment of the general property and debt of the predecessor for other territories.[357]

In drafting Article 30 on State archives, the ILC relied on classical practice comprising the secessions of Norway (1906) and Iceland (1918).[358] Paragraph 1 provides that the part of State archives of the predecessor passes that: (a) is 'for normal administration of the territory'; or (b) 'relates directly to the territory'. Paragraph 4 affirms that the predecessor and successor shall 'at the request and at the expense of one of them or on an exchange basis' make available 'appropriate reproduction to their State archives connected with the interests of their respective territories'.[359] While paragraph 1 was criticized for vagueness,[360] Article 30 was adopted on a vote of 43-21-1.[361]

---

[351] Rousseau (n 248) vol III 454; 'Chronique des faits internationaux' (1975) 79 RGDIP 165; Provisional Constitution (n 341) sch 4 (para 16(3)).

[352] ILC Yearbook (1981) vol I, para 15.

[353] Other sources indicate that negotiations failed in 1980 and 1992 – Cheema (n 346) 76–81, 95–97; Sanam Noor, 'Outstanding Issues between Pakistan and Bangladesh' (2005) 58(1) Pakistan Horizon 47, 58.

[354] Official Records (n 9) vol I, 114–15 (para 53) 115 (paras 55, 59) 116 (para 64) 115 (para 60) 116 (para 1) 117 (para 6) 119 (paras 23–27, 31, 33) 120–21 (para 45).

[355] Ibid, vol II, 104 (para 80) 120 (para 37), 132 (paras 59–61).

[356] E.g. – British India (n 264).

[357] E.g. – Bangladesh (n 351); USSR (n 372); Eritrea (n 374); South Sudan (n 377).

[358] ILC Articles (n 5) 68 (paras 2–3).

[359] Official Records (n 9) vol I, 186 (para 35) 189 (para 36) 190 (para 40).

[360] Ibid, 187 (paras 44–45) 188 (paras 5–8) 188 (para 18) 189 (para 22).

[361] Ibid, 189 (para 37).

138 SUCCESSION TO STATE PROPERTY AND DEBT

Despite its opacity, the principle of territoriality underlying Article 38(1) reflects the customary rule. While detailed information on the treatment of State archives in cases of secession is scant, the cases of Iceland,[362] French Indochina,[363] and Libya[364] are consistent with the rule. Moreover, the succession agreement for South Sudan[365] appears to have been based on paragraph 1.

Developed as a common rule of equity with Article 41 on 'dissolution',[366] Article 40(1) of the VCSSP provides that State debt passes in an equitable proportion in relation to State property.[367] At the UN Conference, multiple delegations criticized the vagueness of 'equitable proportion' as lacking objective criteria, particularly in relation to different categories of debt.[368] No amendment was proposed and the provision was adopted by a vote of 60-0-2.[369]

This broad principle of equity in relation to State property does not reflect prior State practice and *opiniones juris* that consistently recognized the primary of the principle of territoriality for the transfer of local debt for financially autonomous territories[370] and the principle of equitable apportionment of the general debt for other territories.[371] In distinguishing among different types of debt (e.g.—localized debt) State practice did not feature an overarching correlation of property and debt even in negotiated settlements.

Subsequent secessions have affirmed the principles applied in State practice before the elaboration of the VCSSP in 1983. For the 11 secessions of constituent republics from the USSR in 1991, State property and the general debt was apportioned because the republics had lacked financial autonomy[372] while Russia, as

---

[362] Following the secession of Iceland, an archival exchange agreement was reached in 1927 by a bilateral commission tasked with the claims of Iceland to the originals of archival documents from the Arnamagnæan Institute (e.g. – manuscripts from government offices that an Icelandic scholar had removed to Denmark in the 18th century), the National Archives, the Supreme Court of Denmark and the Royal Library. The agreement resulted in the 'Danish delivery of 1928' of the originals of government documents that partly or solely concerned Iceland while the original documents of equal importance were retained and manuscripts, as cultural property, were not transferred. A second agreement was concluded in 2003 for the reciprocal transfer of original documents of primary concern to the respective States – Njörður Sigurðsson and Bjarni Már Magnússon, 'Did the 1918 Danish–Icelandic Actof Union pave the way for transfers of manuscripts and records to Iceland in 1928?' (on file with author).

[363] Note 317.

[364] Note 322.

[365] Note 377.

[366] ILC Articles (n 5) 108 (para 2), 112 (para 20), 113 (paras 23–24).

[367] *Official Records* (n 9) vol I, 234–35.

[368] Ibid, 234 (paras 53–55).

[369] Ibid, 235 (para 68).

[370] E.g. – Philippines (n 320); Burma (n 312); Malaya (n 313); French Indochina (n 317); Guinea (n 329); Madagascar (n 318); DRC (n 334) Bangladesh (nn 343 & 351). The special rule adopted for Libya (n 322) implicitly proves the general rule.

[371] E.g. – Montenegro (n 376); South Sudan (n 377).

[372] Agreement on the Division of all Property of the former USSR abroad (6 July 1992) 2380 UNTS 69, arts 1–4; Agreement on the Resolution of Succession Issues in respect of the External Public Debt and Assets of the former USSR (Russia–Moldova) (adopted 19 October 1993, entered into force 9 April 1997) Russia Treaty Database No 19930121, arts 3–4 (Russian). See also: NV Dronova, 'The Division

the continuing State, retained responsibility for contractual and administrative debts that were not localized.[373] While Eritrea had also lacked autonomy, it did not succeed to the general debt but rather appropriated State property located in its territory while Ethiopia retained all other property (e.g.—exchange reserves) in set-off.[374]

In seceding from Portugal in 2002 with retroactive effect to 1975, Timor Leste succeeded to the local property of Portuguese Timor and the local property and budget of the UN transitional administration.[375] As Montenegro had lacked financial autonomy before seceding from the FRY in 2006, it succeeded to localized property and debt alongside a general apportionment of property and debt.[376] Since South Sudan had not been autonomous before seceding from the Sudan in 2011, the parties likewise applied territoriality for localized ('domestic') property and debts and equitable apportionment for the external assets and debt.[377]

In the rare cases in which succession disputes have been arbitrated in international courts and tribunals, they have been hampered by a lack of information on State practice. In 2005, the Ethiopia–Eritrea Claims Commission rejected an Eritrean claim for reimbursement of payments made by Eritrea for civil service pension debts.[378] As the argument of Eritrea that the customary international law of State succession obliged Ethiopia to pay the debt was not made in detail, the Commission was not persuaded it 'allocates to the predecessor State primary responsibility for official pensions when unitary States divide.'[379]

---

of State Property in the Case of State Succession in the Former Soviet Union' in Pierre Eisemann and Martti Koskenniemi (eds) *State Succession: Codification Tested against the Facts* (Martinus Nijhoff 2000) 781, 795, 798, 811–15; Tarja Långström, 'The Dissolution of the Soviet Union in the Light of the 1978 Vienna Convention on Succession of States in Respect of Treaties' in Eisemann and Koskenniemi, ibid, 723–779, 730.

[373] E.g. – *Coreck v Sevrybokholodfloti*, Court of Session of Scotland (19 March 1993) 107 ILR 659, 665–66; *The Soviet Embassy Building in Vienna* Case OGH 5 Ob 152/04w; Supreme Court of Austria (9 November 2004) (2004) 9 ARIEL 231, 244; *Manuata v Russian Embassy*, Supreme Court of Argentina (22 December 1994) 113 ILR 429, 430.

[374] 'Eritrea – Recent Economic Developments' (28 November 1994) IMF Doc SM/94/285 34–35, 61–69.

[375] Constitution of Timor-Leste (adopted 22 March 2002, entered into force 25 May 2002) <http://timor-leste.gov.tl/wp-content/uploads/2010/03/Constitution_RDTL_ENG.pdf> accessed 31 December 2023, arts 1(2) 165; Timor-Leste, Law on Real Estate Property No 1/2003 Series I JDR, arts 4(1)(a), 16 (Portuguese & Tetum); 'East Timor: Calculation of Quota' (1 April 2002) IMF Doc EB/CM/East Timor/02/1, paras 32, 53.

[376] 'Constitutional Charter of the State Union of Serbia and Montenegro' (2003) 70(2) Rivista di studi politici internazionali 292, art 24; Agreement on Division of Financial Rights and Liabilities (Serbia-Montenegro) (10 July 2006) 45(6) Crne Gore 17, arts 2, 8–15, 16–21 (Montenegrin).

[377] E.g. – Agreement on Certain Economic Matters (n 30) arts 3.1, 3.2, 4.1.1–4.1.2, 3.1.4–3.3, 4.2–4.3, 6; 'Sudan: Enhanced Heavily-Indebted Poor Countries Initiative – Preliminary Document' (2021) <https://www.elibrary.imf.org/view/journals/002/2021/066/article-A002-en.xml> accessed 3 January 2024; 'Sudan – debt treatment – July 15, 2021' <https://clubdeparisorg/en/traitements/sudan-15-07-2021/en> accessed 3 January 2024.

[378] *Pensions: Eritrea's Claims 15, 19 & 23* (Final Award) Eritrea–Ethiopia Claims Commission (19 December 2005) paras 11–12.

[379] Ibid, paras 41–42.

In an investor-State arbitration concerning a claim brought by the State-owned oil company of the Sudan,[380] South Sudan successfully argued on the basis of the succession agreement that the contested assets 'vested in it by operation of law' upon independence even though the disputing parties were not able to cite comparable precedents.[381] While the primary issue was the character of the contested assets as State property or private property,[382] the Arbitral Tribunal found South Sudan and the Sudan to have deliberately adopted the principle of territoriality for both immovable and movable property by 'drawing upon international law and practice, including where relevant the VCSSP.'[383] Amid disagreement concerning the status of the territorial principle for movable property in Article 17(1)(b),[384] the Arbitral Tribunal held there to be no need to decide the issue because South Sudan and the Sudan had adopted a specific rule of territoriality for movable property.[385]

## 4.3.6 Accession to Independence

When a protected State or Territory ('newly independent State') accedes to independence, a rule of continuity applies whereby it retains the property and debt that was vested in its international legal personality before the date of succession. Alongside this continuity of rights and obligations, the same rules of succession apply to the newly independent State with respect to the property and debt vested in the protecting State. In applying the primary principle of territoriality, the default rule is that protecting State transfers to the newly independent State localized assets and debts unless otherwise agreed.

There is no example in State practice of the application of the principle of equitable apportionment because the limited title of administration held by the protecting State has ensured financial autonomy for the protected State or Territory. While the rule of continuity for newly independent States produces a similar outcome as for the rule of succession to local property and debt, no transfer or allocation of local property and debt (e.g.—as part of a negotiated settlement) is necessary: the rights and obligations continue to be vested in the newly independent State.

State practice with respect to newly independent States is cohesive in favour of these twin rules of continuity and succession. Representative examples of State practice include the accessions to independence of:

---

[380] *Sudapet v South Sudan* (Award) ICSID Case No ARB/12/26 (30 September 2016) paras 1, 319.
[381] Ibid, para 320, 322.
[382] Ibid, paras 445–541.
[383] Ibid, paras 440–43.
[384] Ibid, para 429.
[385] Ibid, paras 440–44, 522–40.

## APPLICATION TO THE CLASSES OF SUCCESSION 141

- the Mandatory Territory for Syria and the Lebanon from France (1943);[386]
- the Mandatory Territory for Palestine from the United Kingdom (1948);[387] and
- the Trust Territory of Western Samoa from New Zealand (1962).[388]

While few disputes have arisen, the accession to independence of Morocco in 1956 was particularly significant because of the extensive scope of the French and Spanish protectorates.[389] France transferred the 'public property' that it had held on behalf of Morocco[390] but sold its own 'patrimonial property' at discounted prices.[391] In contrast, Spain transferred to Morocco title to all property acquired before independence and situated in the zones.[392] Morocco retained responsibility for pre-independence debts owed to France[393] and assumed the local debts of the Spanish Zones, less expenses chargeable to Spain.[394]

Articles 15, 28, and 38 of the VCSSP provide for preferential treatment on the basis of equity[395] for a class of 'newly independent States' that includes former colonies and overseas territories that lacked international legal personality before the succession.[396] This failed to acknowledge the rule of continuity in State practice for the 'special cases' of protected States and Territories. It also overlooked State practice on protected States or Territories in its empirical study, which exclusively concerned colonies.[397]

---

[386] E.g. – Agreement concerning Monetary and Financial Relations (Lebanon–France) (adopted 24 January 1948, entered into force 16 February 1949) 173 UNTS 99 arts 2–3, 8–9; annex I; annex II; Exchange of Letters, ibid, 141; Liquidation Convention of the Bank of Syria and the Lebanon (7 February 1949) in Decree No 50-281 (6 March 1950) 60 JORF (10 March 1950) 2697, art 1 (French).

[387] E.g. – Law and Administration Ordinance 5708-1948, I Laws of the State of Israel 7, ss 7, 11, 15, 17, 19(a), 21; Palestine Act 1948 c 27, ss 1–2; Financial Agreement (Israel–United Kingdom) (30 March 1950) 86 UNTS 231, preamble, arts 2–4, 6–8, 9; State Property Law No 5711-1951 V Israel Laws (1950–51) 45, ss 1–2; *Shimshon Palestine Portland Cement Factory Ltd v Attorney-General*, Supreme Court of Israel (12 April 1950) 17 ILR 72, 75–78; *Richuk v Israel*, Supreme Court of Israel (11 June 1959) 28 ILR 442, 452, 456–57.

[388] *UN Materials* (n 287) 116–19.

[389] On the termination of the International Tangier Zone, see: Final Declaration and Annexed Protocol of the International Conference of Tangier (29 October 1956) (1957) 51(2) AJIL 460, art 2.

[390] E.g. – Agreement on Financial and Monetary Questions (France–Morocco) (2 March 1956) France Archives Doc TRA19560203 (French); '1959 Consultations – Morocco' (15 October 1959) IMF Archives Doc SM/59/57, suppl 1, 2–3.

[391] E.g. – Agreement on Military Real Estate (Morocco–France) (21 June 1958) France Archives Doc TRA19580211 (French).

[392] E.g. – Agreement on the Transfer of Property of the Spanish State in the former Northern Zone (Spain–Morocco) (10 July 1978) 1120 UNTS 383, arts 1–3.

[393] '1959 Consultations – Morocco' (n 390) 24–26.

[394] Agreement on the Withdrawal of the Peseta (Spain–Morocco) (adopted 7 July 1957, entered into force 7 July 1970) 1353 UNTS (1984) 287, art V; Additional Protocol (7 July 1970) ibid, 294, art I.

[395] ILC Articles (n 5) 38 (para 5); *Official Records* (n 9) vol I, 106 (para 5). The customary status of Articles 15, 28 and 38 has been denied; e.g. – *Sudapet* (n 380) para 429.

[396] See Chapter Two.

[397] ILC Articles (n 5) 38–41 (paras 9–23), 94–98 (paras 13–38).

142 SUCCESSION TO STATE PROPERTY AND DEBT

Consequently, the expansive rules in Article 15(1) providing for the passage to a successor of immovable and movable property do not reflect prior State practice with respect to newly independent States. It does not recognize the rule of continuity and draws a firm distinction between immovable and movable property according to location while State property owned by the protecting State on behalf of the protected State or Territory has been transferred in practice, irrespective of its portability or location.

Though scant information is available on prior State practice for State archives, subparagraphs (b) and (c) of Article 28(1) correspond to the known practice concerning the transfer of archives produced during the protectorate.[398] As a protecting State has invariably assumed responsibility for the production and maintenance of archives, the transfer of originals according to the principle of territoriality applies instead of a rule of continuity. There is no data on subparagraph (a) covering 'archives' that existed before the protectorate as opposed to State archives produced during the protectorate.[399]

In proposing Article 38(1) providing that no State debt pass to a newly independent State without its consent, the ILC principally based it on 'the extensive debt problem' and 'the capacity to pay' of decolonized States.[400] At the UN Conference, several delegations opposed Article 38 as being based on policy considerations in drawing no distinction between different categories of State debt and not reflecting State practice, particularly on local debts.[401] An amendment proposed by Italy to insert an exception for State debts relating 'to public works in the process of execution in the territory of the successor State'[402] was withdrawn in the face of opposition from several delegations.[403] Article 38(1) did not reflect the prior State practice whereby a rule of continuity applied to State debt contracted by protected States and Territories (e.g.—before the protectorate) in their own capacity while a rule of succession applied to State debt contracted by the protecting State on behalf of the protected State or Territory (e.g.—as a charge to its accounts) insofar as it related to the protectorate.

Two accessions to independence have taken place since the adoption of the VCSSP in 1983. In the unusual case of South West Africa (1990), the UN had claimed the right to administer after revoking the Mandate in 1967 but South

---

[398] On Western Samoa, see: DL Thomas, 'Western Samoa: Establishment of a National Archive' (11 February 1986) UNESCO Doc RP/1984-1985/VII.2.1, paras 3–28. On Tanganyika, see: Leander Schneider, 'The Tanzania National Archives' (2003) 30 *History in Africa* 447, 447–50. Records concerning the Trust Territory of Papua New Guinea are held by the National Archives of Australia.

[399] ILC Articles (n 5) 62 (paras 5–6); *Official Records* (n 9) vol I, 179 (para 35) 180 (para 41) 183–84 (paras 88–94).

[400] Ibid, 98 (para 40), 98–101 (paras 39–51), 103 (para 62), 104 (para 64).

[401] Ibid, 223 (paras 77–78). See also: *Official Records* (n 9) vol I, 224 (para 14) 225 (paras 19, 21) 232 (para 24) 233 (para 40).

[402] *Official Records* (n 9) vol I, 221 (para 65); vol II, 114–15 (para 213).

[403] Ibid, vol I, 222 (paras 68, 71, 76), 224 (para 16), 228 (paras 57, 60), 228 (paras 57, 62), 229 (paras 70, 83), 230 (paras 88, 95), 232 (paras 16, 24).

CONCLUSIONS    143

Africa effectively administered the Mandatory Territory.[404] On acceding to independence, Namibia elected to regard itself as continuing the legal personality of the UN Council for Namibia and succeeding to South Africa (i.e.—for local property and debt).[405] When Micronesia and the Marshall Islands acceded to independence in 1986 and Palau in 1994, they continued the local property and debt of the Trust Territory for the Pacific Islands with respect to their local 'Districts' and succeeded to the United States for property held for them in the Trust Territory.[406] These cases are consistent with the practice on the accessions to independence of protected States and Territories in applying the rules of continuity and succession.

## 4.4 Conclusions

A traditional problem posed in doctrine has been the equity of the transfer of State property to a successor without a transfer of State debt according to some form of proportional relationship. While this theme threaded the drafting process that led to the adoption of the VCSSP, it produced substantive provisions with a 'heavy reliance throughout on equity' that made it 'too vague for application to specific situations'.[407] Even as the normative bias in favour of newly independent States (as erroneously defined by the ILC) was one reason for the deep splits at the UN Conference, the failure to reflect the nuance to be found in the rich and important source of State practice arising from decolonized States (e.g.—the rule of continuity for protected States and Territories) was even more significant.

In particular, the VCSSP gave insufficient recognition to the suppleness of State practice to apply the principle of territoriality according to the type of asset or debt; for example, the rebuttable tests of location for immovable property and functionality for movable property. Those provisions that have since been accepted as customary international law (e.g.—Article 8 on the definition of State property and

---

[404] UNGA Resn 65(I), 14 December 1946; UNGA Resn 2145 (XXI), 27 October 1966; UNSC Resn 264 (1969), 20 March 1969; *International Status of South-West Africa (Advisory Opinion)*, [1950] ICJ Rep. 128, 131–38, 144; UNSC Resn 435 (1978), 1.

[405] E.g. – UNGA Res 44/243(A) (1990) 4; Constitution of Namibia (21 March 1990) UN Doc S/10967/Add.2, sch 5, para 1, art 140; 'Namibia – Staff Report for the 1991 Article IV Consultation' (2 May 1991) IMF Doc SM/91/83, 6; *Minister of Defence, Namibia v Mwandinghi*, Supreme Court of Namibia (25 October 1991) 91 ILR 341, 346, 353–55, 359, 369–70. See also: HA Strydom, 'Namibian Independence and the Question of the Contractual and Delictual Liability of the Predecessor and Successor Governments' in DH Van Wyk, Marinus Wiechers, and Romaine Hill (eds) *Namibia: Constitutional and International Law Issues* (University of South Africa 1991) 111–21.

[406] E.g. – US Department of Interior Secretarial Order No 3039 (25 April 1979) ss 1–4, 7; Proclamation 6826 (27 September 1994) 108 Stat 5631, s 1; 'Staff Report for the 1992 Article IV Consultation: Marshall Islands' (4 September 1992) IMF Doc SM/92/173 2, 3, 12; 'Memorandum: Micronesia – Recent Economic Developments' (28 April 1994) IMF Doc SM/94/105 iii, 2a, 14, 34; 'Staff Report for the 1999 Article IV Consultation: Palau', IMF Doc SM/99/234 (16 September 1999) 6, 14.

[407] E.g. – Anthony Aust, 'Vienna Convention on the Succession of States in respect of State Property, Archives and Debts', UN Audiovisual Library of International Law (2009).

Article 20 on the definition of State archives) were well grounded in State practice. While the work of the IDI and the ILA has advanced doctrine beyond the VCSSP in recognizing nuances that were disregarded by the ILC, they principally examined the SFRY and other recent cases of desovietization rather than a holistic review of State practice. Classical and modern practice alike show a greater level of coherence and sophistication in the application of the general principles of territoriality and equitable apportionment than has been recognized in doctrine hitherto.

In summary, default rules of customary international law regulate the automatic transfer of State property and debt unless otherwise agreed by the States concerned. As for other fields of the law of succession, the test of dominant connection under the general principle of territoriality for the transfer of individual assets and debt takes priority over the general principle of equitable apportionment. The application of the test varies for the different types of State property and debt according to their particular characteristics. For example, a presumption of geographical origin applies to cultural property and the originals of State archives while the financial autonomy of a transferred territory is a critical factor for the rule on local debt. The following rules of customary international law apply to the various classes of succession as follows:

- for mergers, the entirety of the property and debt of the predecessors is transferred to the successor;
- for absorptions, the entirety of the property and debt of the predecessor is transferred to the successor;
- for dismemberments, individual assets and debts of the predecessor are transferred to the various successors according to the principle of territoriality and the remainder is distributed by equitable apportionment;
- for cessions, individual assets and debts of the predecessor are transferred to the successor according to the principle of territoriality and the remainder is retained by the predecessor;
- for secessions, individual assets and debts of the predecessor are transferred to the successor according to the principle of territoriality while equitable apportionment applies to territories lacking a local debt for want of financial autonomy;
- for accessions to independence, the successor retains the property and debt vested in it before the date of succession and the property and debt of the predecessor with a dominant connection to the territory of the successor are also transferred.

# 5

# Succession to Treaties

## 5.1 Introduction

When the International Law Commission ('ILC') proposed the draft articles with commentaries that would become the 1969 Vienna Convention on the Law of Treaties ('VCLT')[1] it expressly excluded questions of State succession, which had been designated a separate topic by the ILC.[2] Following two sets of draft articles in 1972 and 1974,[3] the Vienna Convention on the Succession of States with respect to Treaties ('VCSST')[4] was concluded in 1978. . While the ILC made considerable use of the 14 empirical studies and memoranda on State practice produced by the Secretariat, it also based its proposals in certain cases on doctrinal considerations of the law of treaties, as for its denial of constitutive effect for devolution agreements.[5] Today, 23 States participate in the VCSST,[6] which has never been applied to a succession since its entry into force in 1996.[7]

Consequently, the primary source of law for the general rules on succession to treaties is customary international law.[8] Like the VCLT, the VCSST acknowledges the possibility of customary international law evolving in a manner that diverges from its provisions as a treaty regime.[9] In its focus on 'testing codification against

---

[1] Vienna Convention on the Law of Treaties (adopted 23 May 1969, entered into force 27 January 1980) 1155 UNTS 331 art 73.

[2] ILC, 'Draft articles on the Law of Treaties with commentaries' (1966) ILC Yearbook vol II 214, 237, 256, 260, 267.

[3] ILC, 'Draft articles on Succession of States in respect of Treaties with commentaries' (1974) ILC Yearbook vol II, part I 174 ('ILC Articles'). See also: Patrick Dumberry, *A Guide to State Succession in International Investment Law* (Elgar 2018) 97–133.

[4] Vienna Convention on the Succession of States with respect to Treaties 1978 (adopted 23 August 1978, entered into force 6 November 1996) 1946 UNTS 3.

[5] Humphrey Waldock, 'Second report on succession in respect of treaties' (18 April, 9 June, & 22 July 1960) UN Doc A/CN.4/214 (1969) ILC Yearbook vol II 55–56.

[6] Vienna Convention on the Succession of States to Treaties (adopted 23 August 1978, entered into force 6 November 1996) Status List (UN Secretariat) < https://treaties.un.org/Pages/ViewDetails.aspx?src=IND&mtdsg_no=XXIII-2&chapter=23&clang=_en> accessed 4 January 2024.

[7] No State accepted the declarations of Czechia and Slovakia under Article 7 – 1946 UNTS 4; 2073 UNTS 240. Montenegro succeeded to the VCSST but made no declaration – Dumberry (n 3) 48–50; 2390 UNTS (2006) 228, A-33356; *Multilateral Treaties Deposited with the Secretary-General*, UN Doc ST/LEG/SER.E/26 (1 April 2009) vol I, xxxii (n 1).

[8] See Chapter 2.

[9] VCSST (n 4) preamble; Daniel Rietiker, 'Préambule' in Giovanni Distefano, Gloria Gaggioli, and Aymeric Hêche (eds) *La Convention de Vienne de 1978 sur la succession d'États en matière de traités*, vol 1 (Bruylant, 2016) 7–60, 33–39, 53–57.

---

*The Law of State Succession*. Arman Sarvarian, Oxford University Press. © Arman Sarvarian 2025.
DOI: 10.1093/oso/9780198817956.003.0005

146 SUCCESSION TO TREATIES

the facts',[10] subsequent doctrine has not sufficiently acknowledged the fact that the ILC had designed the treaty not only as a statement of prior State practice but also as an autonomous regime. In focusing principally upon the evaluation of State practice, doctrinal inquiry should consequently refer to the VCSST not as an authoritative baseline but rather as a point of comparison.

## 5.2 The General Principle of Consent

To formulate a general law of succession to treaties, a classical problem posed in doctrine was the consistency with the law of treaties of a right for a successor to 'pick and choose' to succeed to treaties applied to its territory by the predecessor.[11] While this dynamic ostensibly conflicted with the rights of third parties under the law of treaties, the tension is a false one because there are many examples of the rejection of succession to a treaty by successors and treaty counterparties alike. As in other fields of international law, the true problem has been the identification of consent amid silence from the State concerned.[12] This particularly applies during the interim or 'twilight period' between the date of succession and the definitive expression of a position, which might not come until its invocation in dispute settlement.[13]

The juxtaposition of competing principles of automatic succession and the clean slate is likewise a false paradigm.[14] The metaphor of the 'traditional clean slate view'[15] is inaccurate because it implies that the treaties of the predecessor, as applied to the transferred territory, automatically cease to apply from the date of succession.[16] Rather, State practice has shown the default position to be often opaque at that point in time: whereas there are numerous cases of States specifically rejecting succession, there are also many examples of successors that have successfully claimed succession after a prolonged period of silence. Reasons for delay include the need for time to collate accurate information concerning the treaties that were applied to its territory by the predecessor.[17]

---

[10] E.g. – PM Eisemann, 'Rapport du directeur d'études de la section de langue française du Centre' in Eisemann and Koskenniemi (n 271) 3–64, 10–21; Martii Koskenniemi, 'Report of the Director of Studies of the English-speaking Section of the Centre' in Eisemann and Koskenniemi (n 271) 65–132, 69–81, 125–132.

[11] E.g. – PM Eisemann, 'Rapport du directeur d'études de la section de langue française du Centre' in Eisemann and Koskenniemi (n 271) 3–64, 51.

[12] Danae Azaria, 'State Silence as Acceptance: A Presumption and an Exception' (2024) BYIL, 6–19, https://doi.org/10.1093/bybil/brae002.

[13] CJ Tams, 'State Succession to Investment Treaties: Mapping the Issues' (2016) 31(2) 314, 331.

[14] DP O'Connell, 'Reflections on the State Succession Convention' (1979) 39 ZaöRV 725, 727–729.

[15] E.g. – ILC Articles (n 3) 211 (para 3); UN Conference (n 390) vol I, 1 (para 4), 3 (para 19).

[16] E.g. – International Law Association Committee: Aspects of the Law of State Succession, Final Report, Rio de Janeiro Conference (2008) 17–18, 27; Zidane Mériboute, La codification de la succession d'États aux traités (Presses Universitaires de France 1984) 26–27, 61–66.

[17] E.g. – ILA Handbook (n 379) 116–17.

When a dispute concerning legal identity exists, the question of identity must be resolved to be able to definitively determine whether the State concerned continues the predecessor's participation in treaties or succeeds to them.[18] As depositaries lack the power to evaluate claims of legal identity, there is no default authority to decide disputes even for multilateral treaties.[19] In the well-known claim of the FRY to continue the legal personality of the SFRY,[20] however, the views of counterparties were pivotal for bilateral treaties.[21] When the FRY accepted the status of successor, its agreements on continuity with counterparties were retrospectively treated as succession agreements.[22]

State practice and *opiniones juris* have shown the basic principle of consent to be that a successor may succeed to multilateral treaties by notification and bilateral treaties by agreement with counterparties, subject to eligibility.[23] The distinction drawn in the VCSST between consent-based succession for 'newly independent States'[24] and automatic succession ('*ipso iure* continuity') for the other classes of succession has not been accepted in subsequent practice.[25] Rather than mandate positive outcomes of succession or non-succession, automaticity performs a negative function by determining eligibility to succeed under the law of treaties.

---

[18] See Chapter 2. On Pakistan, for example, see notes 21, 37, 56, 434, & 179; *Yangtze (London) Ltd v Barles Bros (Pakistan) Ltd*, Supreme Court of Pakistan in ILA Handbook (n 379) 6 (n 5).

[19] On Cambodia, see: *Temple of Preah Vihear (Cambodia v Thailand)* (Preliminary Objections) (Observations of Cambodia) (22 July 1960) 164–66 (paras 30–34) (French); vol II (Pleadings) 77–79, 83 (French). On Morocco, see: 'Digest of Decisions of National Courts relating to Succession of States and Governments: Study prepared by the Secretariat', UN Doc A/CN.4/157 (18 April 1963) (1963) ILC Yearbook vol II, para 28; *Rights of Nationals of the United States of America in Morocco (France v United States of America)* (Judgment) [1952] ICJ Rep 176, 188.

[20] nn 294 & 135. See also: Sally Cummins and David Stewart (eds) *Digest of United States Practice in International Law: 2000* (Office of the Legal Adviser 2001) 563; *Soornack Nandanee* (n 248) para 2.4.

[21] E.g. – Agreement with Serbia and Montenegro regarding Treaties (29 May 2003) Norway Treaty Database, No 29-05-2003 Nr 23 Bilateral (Norwegian); Second Bilateral Treaties Study (n 251) paras 13, 16–17; Third Bilateral Treaties Study (n 253) paras 33–36.

[22] E.g. – Extradition Treaty (Serbia (Yugoslavia)–United Kingdom) (adopted 23 November & 6 December 1900, entered into force 13 August 1901) Australia Treaty Database (19 February 2003); *Croatia Genocide* (n 135).

[23] Humphrey Waldock, 'Fourth report on succession in respect of treaties' UN Doc A/CN.4/249 (24 June 1971) (1971) ILC Yearbook vol II 143, 146.

[24] On the erroneous definition of newly independent States, see Chapter 2.

[25] Andreas Zimmermann, 'La Convention de Vienne sur la succession d'États en matière de traités: codification réussie ou échouée?' in Distefano (n 9) 1557; ILC Articles (n 3) 212–14, 263–65; *UN Conference* (n 390) 23 (para 12), 28 (paras 4–5), 29 (para 14), 30 (para 28), 33 (paras 54–55), 43 (para 41). Many Member States called for the principle of consent to apply to all classes of succession; e.g. – UN Sixth Committee, GAOR: 1489th Meeting (31 October 1974) paras 12, 25, 39; 1490th Meeting (1 November 1974) para 22; 1492nd Meeting (5 November 1974) para 86; 1493rd Meeting (6 November 1974) para 15; 1494th Meeting (7 November 1974) paras 18, 34–37; 1495th Meeting (8 November 1974) paras 5, 12; 1496th Meeting (11 November 1974) para 2.

148   SUCCESSION TO TREATIES

### 5.2.1  Eligibility to Succeed to a Treaty

While States have consistently applied a general principle of consent, the doctrinal issue that arises is whether there are any limits to the discretion of the successor to succeed to any treaty action of the predecessor. State practice has answered this question in the affirmative by recognizing three eligibility requirements.

First, a treaty must permit succession on its terms;[26] for example, it can implicitly exclude succession due to restricted territorial scope. Whereas interpretation can account for factual changes such as party names and place names, a treaty can also exclude succession when its object and purpose is rendered obsolete.[27] If the treaty permits separability or the parties otherwise agree,[28] succession to provisions is possible.[29]

Second, the treaty action in question must have been performed by the predecessor before the date of succession. While a successor may succeed to a treaty action done for a treaty not in force or not manifesting consent to be bound, a succession is effective only to the extent of the treaty action concerned. To build upon that action, the applicable formalities of the treaty in question must be followed.

Third, the successor must be eligible to succeed to the treaty action. If it participated in the treaty in its own capacity before the date of succession, then the rule is one of continuity rather than succession. If the treaty action was not applied to the transferred territory before the date of succession, then it is ineligible to succeed.

### (a)  Succession Clauses

When the question of succession is regulated by a treaty, a successor must comply with its terms to succeed to that treaty. There are only four known examples of such succession clauses, all from the decolonization era,[30] which can permit or preclude succession.[31] Article 10(1) of the VCSST articulates this customary rule by providing that a successor may succeed to a treaty by notification if the treaty provide that it 'have the option to consider [itself] a party to the treaty'.[32]

The possibility of implicit exclusion of succession by the terms of the treaty is addressed by the proviso attached to the general rules of succession (e.g.—Article 17(2)) 'unless…the application of the treaty to that territory would be incompatible

---

[26]  Ibid, art 14; ILC Articles (n 3) 207 (paras 44–45) 208; Czapliński, 'Article 14' in Distefano (n 9) 529–39.

[27]  VCLT (n 1) art 62(1); *UN Materials* (n 377) 232–33.

[28]  Ibid, art 44(1); Martyna Falkowska, Mohammed Bedjaoui, and Tamara Leidgens, 'Article 44 Convention of 1969' in Malcolm Shaw and Caroline Fournet, 'Article 62 Convention of 1969' in Olivier Corten and Pierre Klein, *The Vienna Convention on the Law of Treaties: A Commentary* vol I (OUP 2011) 1046–61, 1048–55.

[29]  E.g. – Humphrey Waldock, 'Third report on succession in respect of treaties' (22 April and 27 May 1970) UN Doc A/CN.4/224 (1970) ILC Yearbook, vol II, 52–64.

[30]  E.g. – ILC Articles (n 3) 193–196; Simon Heathcote, 'Article 10' in Distefano (n 9) 339, 344–54.

[31]  E.g. – Second Bilateral Treaties Study (n 251) paras 100–101.

[32]  Heathcote (n 30) 343.

with the object and purpose of the treaty'. However, there is no practice supporting the requirement in Article 10(2) of the Convention of express acceptance in writing for a succession clause that provide for mandatory succession.[33]

## (b) Constitutive Treaties of International Organizations

When a treaty prescribes a procedure for the admission of a new member to an international organization, that treaty rule displaces the general rule permitting a successor to succeed to the treaty by notification.[34] Examples include the following:

- 1944 Convention on International Civil Aviation;[35]
- 1948 Convention on the Inter-Governmental Maritime Consultative Organization;[36]
- 1951 Peace Treaty with Japan creating the International Military Tribunal for the Far East;[37]
- 1965 International Telecommunication Convention;[38] and
- 1950 Convention establishing a Customs Co-Operation Council.[39]

However, successors may succeed by notification to constitutive treaties that lack a specific admission procedure. Examples include the following treaties:

- International Labour Organization Conventions;[40]
- 1899 and 1907 Hague Peace Conventions;[41] and
- 1932 and 1947 International Telecommunication Conventions.[42]

Article 4(a) of the VCSST provides that the VCSST applies to a treaty constituting an international organization 'without prejudice to the rules concerning

---

[33] ILC Articles (n 3) 195–96.

[34] E.g. – Konrad Bühler, *State Succession and Membership in International Organizations* (Martinus Nijhoff 2001) 285–320; AG Mochi Onory, *La succession d'États aux traités* (Giuffrè 1968) 90–119; *UN Materials* (n 377) 224–25, 227–28.

[35] Convention on International Civil Aviation (adopted 7 December 1944, entered into force 4 April 1947) 15 UNTS 295, arts 2, 92.

[36] Ibid, paras 97–98.

[37] *UN Materials* (n 377) 183–84.

[38] Seventh Multilateral Treaties Study (n 270) para 85; International Telecommunication Convention (12 November 1965) <https://search.itu.int/history/HistoryDigitalCollectionDocLibrary/5.9.61.en.100.pdf> accessed 6 January 2024, 91; International Telecommunication Union Notification No 1032 (information received by 10 July 1970) (on file with author).

[39] Convention establishing a Customs Co-operation Council (15 December 1950) Status List (26 November 2018) (South Sudan) Belgium Treaty Database (French).

[40] DP O'Connell, State Succession in Municipal Law and International Law vol II (OUP 1968) 203, 206–07.

[41] 'Succession of States to multilateral treaties: studies prepared by the Secretariat', UN Doc A/CN.4/200 (21 February 1968) para 127.

[42] Seventh Multilateral Treaties Study (n 270) paras 134–62.

150   SUCCESSION TO TREATIES

acquisition of membership'.[43] This provision accurately expresses State practice in that a successor may apply the general rule of succession by notification unless displaced by treaty rules providing for a specific procedure for admission.[44]

## (c) Territorial Application

A successor can only succeed to a treaty that was applied by the predecessor to the transferred territory before the date of succession.[45] According to the territorial application rule of the law of treaties, a treaty is presumed to have been applied by each party 'in respect of its entire territory' unless a different intention appears from the treaty or is otherwise established.[46] A different intention can 'appear' from a territorial application clause that expressly regulates the issue[47] or prescribes a procedure for its extension.[48] It can be 'otherwise established' when a treaty lacks a territorial application clause, yet implicitly requires extension due to its 'object and purpose'.[49] The subsequent practice of the counterparties (e.g.—to interpret territorial references differently from their 'ordinary meaning'[50]) can also establish it.[51]

If a treaty neither precludes nor regulates its application to the transferred territory, it is a question of fact whether the predecessor applied it.[52] For example, the predecessor can expressly agree to apply a treaty but not a supplementary treaty.[53] It can equally decide not to apply a treaty to the entirety of its territory.[54] There is no requirement for treaty rights to have been exercised by the predecessor[55] but a counterparty to a bilateral treaty may cite territorial application to reject a claim to succeed by a successor.[56]

---

[43]  ILC Articles (n 3) 177–180.

[44]  MP Palchetti, 'Article 4' in Distefano (n 9) 141–63, 147–48.

[45]  E.g. – Multilateral Treaties Study (n 41) paras 181–82; *United States v Lui Kin-Hong*, US First Circuit Court of Appeals (20 March 1997) 114 ILR 606, 623, 626, 629–33.

[46]  E.g. – VCLT (n 1) art 29; Syméon Karagiannis, 'Article 29 Convention of 1969' in Corten and Klein (n 28) vol I, 731–758; ILA Handbook (n 379) 23–24, 115, 122–26, 216; Letter from the UN Secretariat to Malaya, Doc LE 352/2 (28 November 1961) UN Archives Folder No 213 MALA (January 1960–23 January 1963); Letter from UN Secretariat to Pakistan, Doc LE 222 (13 July 1967) UN Archives Folder No 222 PAKI (January 1964 – December 1967).

[47]  E.g. – Pierre Lampué, 'L'application des traités dans les territoires et départements d'outre-mer' (1960) 6 AFDI 907, 919; Third Bilateral Treaties Study (n 253) para 53; Exchange of Letters (Malta–United Kingdom) (31 December 1964) 525 UNTS 221.

[48]  E.g. – *Myncke v Van de Weghe et Neerinckx*, Belgium Court of Assizes (2 October 1967) (1970) 6(2) RBDI 718, 719.

[49]  E.g. – Extension of Extradition Treaty to the Belgian Congo and Ruanda-Urundi (Belgium–Pakistan) (9 September 1952 and 28 July 1953) 173 UNTS 408.

[50]  VCLT (n 1) art 31(3). On Russia, see: Danube Navigation Convention (adopted 18 August 1948, entered into force 11 May 1949) 33 UNTS 181, arts 2–5, 44; Additional Protocol (26 March 1998) (1999) 19 BGBl vol II, art 1(2) (German, French, Russian).

[51]  E.g. – Multilateral Treaties Study (n 41) paras 137, 172, 198, 231.

[52]  E.g. – *Davidson's Case*, Court of Appeal of Aix (22 July 1937) 8 ILR 91, 92; *Wan Kuok Koi v Portugal* No 925/2000, UN Human Rights Committee (8 February 2002) UN Doc CCPR/C/73/D/925/2000 paras 1.2–1.4, 4.1–4.2, 6.2.

[53]  E.g. – *UN Materials* (n 377) 188.

[54]  E.g. – Second Bilateral Treaties Study (n 251) paras 155–58, 161–65.

[55]  Ibid, paras 79–82, 130–32, 147.

[56]  E.g. – *UN Materials* (n 377) 7; Third Bilateral Treaties Study (n 253) paras 33–36.

### (d) Moving Treaty Frontiers

The moving treaty frontiers rule stipulates the automatic adjustment of the territorial application of a treaty in consequences of the acquisition or loss of territory.[57] Its 'negative' limb provides that a treaty automatically ceases to apply through the participation of the predecessor from the date of succession. Though State practice is largely invisible,[58] there are several examples of cessions when predecessors notified depositaries of the cessation of application of multilateral treaties to the ceded territories by their participation from the date of succession.[59]

More significant is its 'positive' limb whereby a treaty to which the successor is party at the date of succession extends automatically to the transferred territory. However, this does not apply to all treaties but only to those whose terms require its application to its entire territory. For instance, the 1905 Hague Convention on Civil Procedure stipulates that it 'automatically' (*de plein droit*) applies to the 'European territories' of the Contracting Parties whereas application to other territories requires affirmative acceptance by each counterparty.[60] Though classical practice was inconsistent,[61] there are many examples in modern practice of automatic extension in the absence of such a qualifier.[62]

In 1956, the United Kingdom consolidated the Gold Coast Colony with two colonial protectorates in 1956 as the Dominion of Ghana. When the Dominion seceded in 1957 and simultaneously merged with the Trust Territory of Togoland, different treaties had applied to the four territories previously administered by the United Kingdom.[63] In notifying the UN Secretary-General in 1958, Ghana made no territorial stipulation and the 12 treaties to which it succeeded used the term 'territory' in a unitary sense.[64]

---

[57] E.g. – Second Waldock Report (n 5) 51–52; *Sanum v Laos* (n 86).

[58] Ibid, 52.

[59] Notes 350–356s.

[60] Hague Convention (n 48) art 26 (French).

[61] E.g. – Second Waldock Report (n 5) 53; Arnold McNair, *The Law of Treaties* (OUP 1961) 634–36; JB Moore, *A Digest of International Law* vol I (US Government Printing Office 1906) vol V, 336–38, 351–52; RWG de Muralt, *The Problem of State Succession with regard to Treaties* (van Stockum 1954) 84–86, 118–19; Daniel Bardonnet, *La Succession d'États à Madagascar* vol I (Librairie Générale de Droit et de Jurisprudence 1970) 87–99. On Yugoslavia, see: *Katz and Klump v Yugoslavia*, Germano-Yugoslav Mixed Arbitral Tribunal (30 September 1925) 3 ILR 33, 34; *Ivanovic v Artukovic*, US Ninth Circuit Court of Appeals (19 February 1954) 21 ILR 66, 67.

[62] E.g. – II RGBl (13 January 1939) 7; Seventh Multilateral Treaties Study (n 270) 129–130; Third Bilateral Treaties Study (n 253) paras 132–133, 137; Trade and Navigation Treaty (Poland–United Kingdom) (adopted 26 November 1923, entered into force 1 July 1924) 57 Dziennik Ustaw 835; Air Services Agreement (France–India) (16 July 1947) 27 UNTS 325, arts 1, 3, annex; Agreement (France–Tanganyika) (29 November 1963 and 3 February 1964) France Treaty Database No TRA19630209 (French); Consular Convention (Italy–United Kingdom) 403 UNTS 275, arts 1, 3, 9–10, 12, 15–16, 24, 38.

[63] E.g. – ILA Handbook (n 379) 217–218.

[64] UNSG Depository Practice (n 251) para 40; Narcotic Drugs Convention (adopted 13 July 1931 and 11 December 1946, entered into force 21 November 1947) 139 LNTS 301, art 26.

## 152  SUCCESSION TO TREATIES

When Italy ceded Eritrea to Ethiopia in 1952, Ethiopia declared that each of its treaties in force would thenceforth apply to Eritrea.[65] While a notification requirement was stipulated by the 1947 International Telecommunication Convention for extension to Mandatory or Trust Territories,[66] Ethiopia made no notification of extension for Eritrea when informing the International Telecommunication Union of the application to Eritrea of telegram tariffs from 15 September 1952.[67]

For the merger of North Yemen and South Yemen in 1990, their general declaration of succession to treaties did not address the question of territorial extension.[68] Depositaries revised status lists to replace entries for the predecessors with the successor.[69] Yemen made no subsequent notification of extension for treaties that use 'territory' in a unitary sense.[70]

While *opiniones juris* are generally implicit, the legal division of the Department of External Affairs of Canada stated in 1967 in answer to a parliamentary enquiry on Newfoundland treaty succession:

> The view of the Government on the question of Newfoundland treaty succession has in the past been that Newfoundland became part of Canada by a form of cession and that consequently, in accordance with the appropriate rules of international law, agreements binding upon Newfoundland prior to Union lapsed, except for those obligations arising from agreements locally connected which had established proprietary or quasi-proprietary rights, and Newfoundland became bound by treaty obligations of general application to Canada.[71]

The automatic extension of treaties to territories acquired by the United States has been stated to be the American practice[72] but has not arisen in dispute settlement since the Northern Mariana Islands were ceded in 1978.[73] After Hong Kong was

---

[65] Seventh Multilateral Treaties Study (n 270) paras 1–2-103; UNSG Depositary Practice (n 251) para 140; Leriche (n 352) 263; MM Whiteman, *Digest of International Law* vol II (Government Printing Office 1964) 967, 939–40.

[66] International Telecommunication Convention, Atlantic City, 2 October 1947 (1 January 1949), 193 UNTS 188, art 18(1).

[67] General Secretariat International Telecommunication Union Notification Nos 655 (1 September 1952) 555 (1 February 1953) and 675 (16 June 1953) (on file with author).

[68] Zimmermann (n 272) 285–286.

[69] E.g. – Additional Protocol to the Geneva Conventions (adopted 8 June 1977, entered into force 7 December 1978) Status List (Switzerland) (French); Switzerland Treaty Database Depositary Notification No p.o.411.619.Yém (31 May 1990).

[70] Note 255.

[71] AE Gotlieb, 'Canadian Practice in International Law during 1967' (1968) 6 CYIL 276.

[72] Nash (n 390) book I, 439–440. This point is not discussed in: *Restatement of the Law Fourth: The Foreign Relations Law of the United States* (American Law Institute 2017) 10–11, 75–80 (paras 301, 307); *Restatement of the Law Third: The Foreign Relations Law of the United States* vol I (American Law Institute 1986) para 210; *Restatement of the Law Second: The Foreign Relations Law of the United States* (American Law Institute 1965) para 160.

[73] Covenant to establish a Commonwealth of the Northern Mariana Islands (adopted 15 February 1975, entered into force 24 March 1976) 14 ILM 344, art I (s 101); *Ahmed v Goldberg* Civil Action No 00-0005, Civil Case No 99-0046 (D.N. Mar. I.) US District Court for the Northern Mariana Islands (11 May 2001) 6–7.

THE GENERAL PRINCIPLE OF CONSENT    153

retroceded to China in 1997, China notified the UN Secretary-General of the extension of its unnamed treaties which 'owing to their nature and provisions, must apply to the entire territory of a State'.[74]

While the positive limb of the moving frontiers rule is clear when the treaty requires its application to the entire territory of the successor, a doctrinal problem arises for a treaty that contains no such requirement. In particular, the absence of a clear statement of intention by the successor creates scope for confusion with potential prejudice to its own rights and those of the counterparty.

In this case, State practice has shown the moving frontiers rule not to apply. While classical practice was ambiguous,[75] there are many examples in modern practice of territorial extension by notification or agreement.[76] Following the absorption of East Germany in 1990, for example, multilateral treaties of West Germany were extended to East Germany by general declaration.[77] Bilateral treaties were extended by agreement, as when the Netherlands rejected automatic extension of the Dutch–West German double taxation treaty but agreed to apply it with effect from 1 January 1991 rather than the date of succession (3 October 1990).[78] Similarly, the retrocession of Hong Kong saw one treaty of mainland China extended by notification while bilateral treaties did not extend except by agreement.[79] *Opiniones juris* against automaticity were expressed with respect to Austria,[80] East Germany,[81] Hong Kong,[82] and Macao.[83]

Article 15(a) of the VCSST accurately expresses the negative limb of the moving treaty frontiers rule in stating that the treaties of a predecessor cease to apply from the date of succession to a territory that 'becomes part of the territory of another State'.[84] However, Article 15(b) provides that the treaties of the successor automatically apply to the transferred territory unless appearing from the treaty or

---

[74] Note 355.

[75] E.g. – AN Makarov and Ernst Schmitz (eds) *Fontes Juris Gentium: Digest of the Diplomatic Correspondence of the European States (1871–1878)* vol I (Carl Heymanns Verlag KG 1937) 751–52; Extradition Treaty (United States–Serbia) (adopted 12 and 25 October 1901, entered into force 13 May 1902) 94 BFSP 727, arts I–II, IV–V, VII; *Artukovic v Rison*, US Ninth Circuit Court of Appeals (1 February 1986) 79 ILR 383, 395; *D.C. v Public Prosecutor*, Supreme Court of the Netherlands (31 August 1972) 73 ILR 38, 39.

[76] E.g. – Third Bilateral Treaties Study (n 253) paras 131, 149–166, 168; Agreement on Extension of the Franco–Malaysian Transport Agreement (France–Malaysia) (30 December 1961, entered into force 13 June 1964) France Treaty Database No TRA19640251 (French).

[77] Zimmermann (n 272) 84 (note 183) 85, 241–45.

[78] Protocol concerning the Reunification of Germany for their Bilateral Treaty Relations (West Germany–Netherlands) (adopted 25 January 1994, entered into force 19 July 1994) 2441 UNTS 135.

[79] *Multilateral Treaties* (n 7) vi–viii (n 2); SJ Cummins and DP Stewart (eds) *Digest of United States Practice in International Law: 1991–1999* vol I (2005) 766–67.

[80] Third Bilateral Treaties Study (n 253) para 130.

[81] Zimmermann (n 279) 80, 84 (n 179) ('Algeria').

[82] *Edwards v The Queen*, Federal Court of Appeal of Ontario (14 October 2003) [2003] FCA 378, paras 17–28.

[83] *Sanum Investments Ltd v Laos* (Award on Jurisdiction) PCA Case No 2013-13 (13 December 2013) paras 54, 58.

[84] ILC Articles (n 3) 208–211; Tanzi and Iapichino in Distefano (n 9) 543–555, 546–549.

## 154 SUCCESSION TO TREATIES

otherwise established that it would be incompatible with its object and purpose or radically change the conditions for its operation. While this provision reflects State practice insofar as automaticity applies to a treaty requiring its application to the entire territory of the successor, it conflicts with practice in providing for the automatic extension of a treaty that has no such requirement.[85]

Since extension requires a positive act by the successor, the critical question of interpretation is whether a treaty requires application to the entire territory of the successor or not. The issue arose in the investor-State arbitration of *Sanum v Laos* in which the Claimant, a Macao company, invoked the 1993 China–Laos bilateral investment treaty while Laos argued that the treaty did not apply to Macao.[86] Whereas the disputing Parties agreed that the general rule in Article 15(b) VCSST reflected customary law, the Claimant disputed its two exceptions.[87]

Relying on a statement of the president of the ILC Drafting Committee and two academic opinions, the Arbitral Tribunal held the two exceptions also to reflect custom.[88] No prior or subsequent State practice was examined in the arbitration or set-aside proceedings in the courts of Singapore, which also denied effect to an agreement on non-succession concluded by the counterparties after the arbitral award.[89] There is no recorded practice of automatic extension of other bilateral treaties to Hong Kong[90] or Macao.[91]

### (e) Localization

Since the general principle of consent applies to treaties not requiring application to the entire territory of the successor, a successor may preserve the territorial limits of a treaty when succeeding to it. This principle of localization is applicable in theory to any class of succession but has principally concerned mergers and absorptions in fact. State practice has been coherent on the preservation of treaty limits in the Southern (Egypt) Region and the Northern (Syria) Region of the UAR[92] and the incorporation of the Southern Cameroons by Cameroon.[93]

---

[85] A proposed amendment was defeated: *UN Conference* (n 390) vol III, 108 (para 52); vol I, 101–04.

[86] *Sanum v Laos* (n 83) paras 18–23, 51–56.

[87] Ibid, paras 212, 219, 264–69.

[88] Ibid, paras 219–24.

[89] *Laos v Sanum Investments Ltd*, Singapore High Court (20 January 2015) [2015] SGHC 15, paras 64–78; *Sanum Investments Ltd v Laos*, Singapore Court of Appeal (29 September 2016) [2016] SGCA 57, paras 36–122.

[90] E.g. – *Company X v Tax Chamber*, Supreme Administrative Court of Poland (16 July 2003) ORIL ILDC 277 (PL 2003) paras F1–F5, H1–H3, A1–A2, A5–A6; *Extradition of Cheung*, US Second Circuit Court of Appeals (23 May 2000) 122 ILR 659, 667–68, 672–77.

[91] Macao SAR, 'International Law' <https://www.io.gov.mo/pt/legis/int/> accessed 6 January 2024 (Portuguese). China states in its treaty database that the 1993 bilateral investment treaty with Laos does not apply to Macao and Hong Kong.

[92] E.g. – Second Bilateral Treaties Study (n 251) paras 155–58, 161–65; Third Bilateral Treaties Study (n 253) paras 149–66.

[93] Note 347.

The principle of localization is not accurately expressed in Articles 31 and 32 of the VCSST, which provide for absorptions and mergers that a treaty applied to the transferred territory continues to apply only to that territory unless the successor extend it by notification or agreement, subject to the terms of the treaty.[94] Whereas State practice has recognized a right of successors to preserve territorial limits by notification or agreement, Articles 31 and 32 articulate a rule of automaticity. In addition to the UAR,[95] Tanzania[96] and Somalia[97] expressed *opiniones juris* concerning the permissibility of maintaining territorial limits but ultimately chose not to do so. Had the preservation of territorial limits been automatic, then Tanzania and Somalia would not have had that option.

## 5.2.2 Multilateral Treaties

The terms 'multilateral treaty', 'plurilateral treaty' and 'bilateral treaty' are not defined in the VCLT or VCSST. Doctrine describes a multilateral treaty as permitting three or more States to participate in the same instrument through which they each have a treaty relationship with one another.[98] An open multilateral treaty permits any State to participate while a closed multilateral treaty ('plurilateral treaty') allows participation by meeting eligibility criteria, such as geography.[99] Examples of the latter include the participation of Guyana, Jamaica, and Trinidad and Tobago in the 1925 Canada–West Indies Trade Agreement;[100] the participation of Russia in the 1948 Danube Convention; and the participation of the successors to the USSR in the 1990 Treaty on Conventional Arms Limitations in Europe.[101]

The participation of the various parties thus comprises a web of bilateral rights and obligations (e.g.—on reservations) with respect to the same treaty. For multilateral treaties, the general principle of consent is manifested by the right of a successor to succeed by notification to a multilateral treaty for which it is eligible. Once notification is received,[102] it applies retroactively to the specified date or to the date of succession by default.

---

[94] ILC Articles (n 3) 254–259.

[95] UNSG Depositary Practice (n 251) para 48.

[96] Note 253.

[97] Note 252.

[98] VCLT (n 1) art 15; Jean-François Marchi, 'Article 15 Convention of 1969' in Corten and Klein (n 27) vol I, 308–31, 316–27; Manfred Lachs, 'Le développement et les fonctions des traités multilatéraux' (1957-II) 92 RdC 229, 273–77.

[99] Marchi (n 98) 319–322; Third Bilateral Treaties Study (n 253) para 48; Dronova (n 373) 745–746.

[100] Third Bilateral Treaties Study (n 253) para 48.

[101] Treaty on Conventional Armed Forces in Europe (19 November 1990) 30 ILM 1, art II(B); Dronova (n 373) 745–46.

[102] An omission to notify renders the succession ineffective; e.g. – Javier González Vega, 'Sent. TS (Sala 1.ª) de 20 de septiembre de 1988' (1989) 41 REDI 226–230 (Equatorial Guinea); International Convention on Bills of Lading, 25 August 1924, Status List (Belgium) (28 May 2021) (French).

## 156 SUCCESSION TO TREATIES

While doctrinal debate in the desovietization period considered automatic succession to 'special' treaties concerning human rights and humanitarian law,[103] States rejected the notion in their practice.[104] Proposals by the Netherlands and the USSR at the Vienna Conference to provide for the automatic succession of newly independent States to 'treaties of a universal character' (e.g.—humanitarian law) were withdrawn in the face of opposition.[105]

### (a) Notification

While a successor must notify the depositary of its succession, there is no time limit to do so: notifications have been tendered many years after the date of succession.[106] While notification must be done in writing, there is no particular form of words that must be used. Rather, the question of fact is whether the successor intends that the treaty continue to apply to the transferred territory.[107] A successor may inform the depositary that it declines succession[108] but the default position is that no succession occurs without a notification of one. Articles 22(3) and 23(3) of the VCSST accurately state that notifications to be done in writing and transmitted to the depositary or to the counterparties in the absence of a depositary.[109]

### (b) The Operative Date

As for other treaty actions,[110] the effective date of a notification is distinct from the operative date for the treaty it covers. The practice of depositaries accords with Articles 22(3)(b) and 23(3) of the VCSST in treating the effective date as the date of receipt.[111] The operative date is the date from which the succession covered by the notification begins to run. For instance, a notification taking effect on 1 February 2025 can state that the succession to the treaty concerned becomes operative from 1 January 2024. Consequently, the operative date of a notification of

---

[103] E.g. – Mehdi Belkahla, 'La succession d'États en matière de traités multilatéraux relatifs aux droits de l'homme' in Distefano (n 9) 1661–702, 1701–702.

[104] E.g. – Switzerland, 'Notification, Geneva Conventions of 12 August 1949: Accession of Uzbekistan', Doc. p.o.411.61.Uzb (13 December 1993); Council of Europe Treaty Office, 'Convention for the Protection of Human Rights and Fundamental Freedoms (ETS No. 005): Chart of signatures and ratifications', https://www.coe.int/en/web/conventions/full-list?module=signatures-by-treaty&treatynum=005, Ukraine (11 September 1997).

[105] UN Conference (n 390) vol I, 161–186. See also, e.g. – UNGA Sixth Committee, 1317th Meeting (n 25) paras 18–19; 1320th Meeting paras 9, 25; 1484th Meeting (24 October 1974) paras 25–29; 1537th Meeting (13 October 1975) paras 9, 17, 26–28, 50.

[106] E.g. – Protocol on the Convention for the Pacific Settlement of International Disputes (14 June 1907) Netherlands Treaty Database No 03308 (Ukraine) (29 May 2015).

[107] ILC Articles (n 3) 231 (paras 3–5).

[108] E.g. – UNSG Depositary Practice (n 251) paras 11, 22.

[109] ILC Articles (n 3) 230–33.

[110] Ferhat Horchani and Yousri Ben Hammadi, 'Article 16 Convention of 1969' in Corten and Klein (n 27) 334, 351–56.

[111] E.g. – ILC Articles (n 3) 232–33 (paras 12–13).

THE GENERAL PRINCIPLE OF CONSENT   157

succession is necessarily retroactive to the specified date[112] or by default to the date of succession.[113]

The doctrinal complication of this practice is the status of a treaty during the 'twilight period' between the date of succession and the effective date of the notification.[114] This carries particular importance for the establishment of temporal jurisdiction in the settlement of a dispute arising from the treaty at its 'critical date'.[115] State practice has shown that succession to a treaty is not constituted until the effective date of a notification but that no prejudice is considered to result from the retroactivity of its operative date.[116] As succession to treaties is necessarily a retrospective exercise, the 'compromise position' is that the treaty is ineffective during the indeterminate period but that it become retroactively effective upon notification.

This temporal issue has not been directly addressed by the ICJ. In the *Bosnia Genocide Case*, Bosnia notified the UN Secretary-General on 29 December 1992 of its succession to the 1948 Genocide Convention with effect from 6 March 1992.[117] After initiating proceedings against the FRY pursuant to Article IX of the Convention on 20 March 1993, the ICJ rejected the preliminary objections of the FRY that it lacked jurisdiction for events taking place before 29 December 1992 (the date of receipt of the notification) or 18 March 1993 (the communication of the notification to the counterparties) because the notification lacked retroactive effect.[118] The Court considered it to be unnecessary to rule on the question;[119] noting the absence of any temporal limitation in the Genocide Convention, it found itself to have jurisdiction from the beginning of the conflict in Bosnia 'in accordance with the object and purpose of the Convention as defined by the Court in 1951'.[120]

Article 23(1) of the VCSST provides that a notification renders the treaty effective from the date of succession or the entry into force of the treaty, whichever be the later, unless the treaty provide otherwise or it be otherwise agreed.[121] While

---

[112] E.g. – IAEA, Convention on Nuclear Material, Status List (21 September 2020) note 1 UN Docs C.N.423.1994.TREATIES-7 and C.N.127.1998.TREATIES-1/1/1.

[113] E.g. – *Multilateral Treaties* (n 7) v–x, xiv, xxxii, xlviii–xlix, liii; UNSG Depositary Practice (n 251) paras 14, 16–18, 35–36, 40, 96, 117–18.

[114] Tams (n 13).

[115] Horchani and Ben Hammadi (n 109) 342–46.

[116] E.g. – *European American Investment Bank AG (Austria) v Slovakia* (Award on Jurisdiction) PCA Case No 2010-17 (22 October 2012) paras 77–81. The Parties had not stipulated the operative date – Exchange of Notes (Austria–Slovakia) (adopted 4 August and 25 November 1994, entered into force 1 January 1995) 318 Bgbl (28 December 1994) No 1046 (German).

[117] 1700 UNTS 30.

[118] *Convention on the Prevention and Punishment of the Crime of Genocide (Bosnia and Herzegovina v Yugoslavia)* (Preliminary Objections) [1996] ICJ Rep 595, paras 1, 7, 47.

[119] Ibid, para 23.

[120] Ibid, paras 24, 34. See also: *Jorgic Case, J (A Bosnian Serb)* Constitutional Court of Germany (12 December 2000) 2 BvR 1290/99, ILDC 132 (DE 2000) paras F1–F4, H5, 14; *Croatia Genocide Case* (n 135) para 109.

[121] ILC Articles (n 3) 233–236.

158   SUCCESSION TO TREATIES

this provision accurately reflects State practice,[122] an early proposal to impose a time limit on notifications was discarded due to disagreements on its duration.[123] To deal with the problem of indeterminacy between the date of succession and the date of notification, Article 23(2) of the VCSST states that a treaty 'shall be considered as suspended' during that period unless provisionally applied or otherwise agreed.[124] Though providing an effective solution, this innovative provision has not yet been adopted in State practice.[125] To the contrary, *opiniones juris* suggests that notifications have been clearly intended to have retroactive effect from the specified, operative date.[126]

### (c)  Successive Treaty Actions

A doctrinal problem that arose in decolonization practice was the legal effect of the deposit by a successor of an instrument expressing consent to be bound to a treaty (e.g.—ratification, acceptance, or accession) after it had deposited a notification of succession.[127] The question arose whether such an instrument of accession superseded the succession so that the latter could no longer be invoked for the period between its operative date and the effective date of the accession.[128] While depositaries changed their registers to replace the effective date of the notification of succession with that of the instrument of accession, this did not deal with the question of the *validity* of the former. The underlying doctrinal issue is whether the retroactive abrogation of a notification of succession prejudices the rights of counterparties that had relied on the successor having the status of a counterparty during its operative period.

This problem first arose on the status of Morocco as party to the treaties that had been extended to its territory by France. In conciliation proceedings concerning the detention by France on 22 October 1956 of a civilian aircraft owned by Morocco, Morocco argued that the 1944 Chicago Convention did not apply because its extension by France to its territory in 1947[129] had been inconsistent with its international legal personality.[130] After Morocco deposited an instrument of adherence on 13 November 1956 with effect from 13 December,[131] France countered

---

[122]  Tryfon Korontzis, 'Article 23' in Distefano (n 9) 811–29, 820–21.

[123]  'Observations of Member States on the draft articles on succession of States in respect of treaties adopted by the Commission at its twenty-fourth session' (1974) UN Doc A/CN.4/275 ILC Yearbook vol II, 318 (para 14) 321 (para 1) 324, 325, 327, 329.

[124]  ILC Articles (n 3) 235–36 (paras 11–13).

[125]  Korontzis (n 121) 823–24.

[126]  E.g. – *Azov Shipping Company v Werf-en Vlasnatie NV*, Court of Appeal of Antwerp (19 March 2001) ORIL ILDC 43 (BE 2001) paras F2, H1, A2.

[127]  For example, by administrative oversight – O'Connell (n 40) 141–43.

[128]  E.g. – 354 UNTS 406; *Ghana Treaty Manual* (n 64) 28.

[129]  Convention on International Civil Aviation, 7 December 1944 (4 April 1947) 15 UNTS 295, 364 (art 2).

[130]  *F. OABV Case (Morocco v France)* Conciliation Commission (1958) 4 AFDI 282, 282–95, 285–87.

[131]  324 UNTS 340.

THE GENERAL PRINCIPLE OF CONSENT    159

that Morocco had continuously applied the Convention for more than a decade after its accession to independence on 2 March 1956.[132] While the conciliation was abandoned,[133] a Moroccan court held in 1964 that the 1929 Warsaw Convention had applied to it through the participation of France on behalf of its 'protectorates' which rendered 'not strictly necessary' an instrument of accession deposited on 5 January 1958.[134]

The issue recurred in the *Croatia Genocide Case* concerning the first preliminary objection raised by Serbia that it had not been party to the Genocide Convention until its accession dated 12 March 2001.[135] Dismissing the objection, the ICJ found the declaration of the FRY dated 27 April 1992 to be the continuing State of the SFRY as 'having had the effects of a notification of succession to treaties, notwithstanding that its political premise was different'.[136] The Court did not address the legal effect of the instrument of accession, yet its reliance on the notification of succession implied that the former had not abrogated the latter. Doctrinally, the position would thus appear to be that a subsequent instrument *continues* the consent to be bound expressed by a prior notification of succession.

### (d) Successive Treaty Versions and Amending Protocols
In decolonization practice, the question arose whether a successor electing to succeed to the 1949 Geneva Conventions without mentioning the 1929, 1906, and 1864 versions implicitly succeeded to the earlier versions.[137] Notifications of succession to the Geneva Conventions have mentioned only the most recent versions, which did not abrogate the prior versions but 'replaced' them.[138] The earlier versions would thus continue to apply to the relations between two States that were not both party to the 1949 Conventions.[139] An open question is whether denunciation by a successor of the latest version of a treaty leaves its participation to prior versions intact.[140]

A related issue arose when a predecessor was party to a treaty that was subsequently amended by a protocol.[141] After the United States applied the 1912

---

[132] *F. OABV* (n 129) 285.

[133] Ibid, 295. See also: Mohammed Bedjaoui, *Law and the Algerian Revolution* (International Association of Democratic Lawyers 1961) 161–71.

[134] *Ecoffard (Widow) v Cie Air France*, Court of First Instance of Rabat (29 April 1964) 39 ILR 453, 455.

[135] 1691 UNTS 347.

[136] *Convention for the Prevention and Punishment of the Crime of Genocide (Croatia v Serbia)* (Preliminary Objections) [2008] ICJ Rep 412, para 111.

[137] Multilateral Treaties Study (n 41) paras 225–27.

[138] E.g. – First Geneva Convention (adopted 12 August 1949, entered into force 21 October 1950) 75 UNTS 31, art 59. For the 1952 and 1960 ICRC Commentaries, see: <https://www.icrc.org/en/war-and-law/treaties-customary-law/geneva-conventions> accessed 6 January 2024.

[139] 1952 ICRC Commentary to Article 59 of Geneva I (n 137).

[140] 2016 ICRC Commentary to Article 59 of Geneva I (n 137) paras 3200–201. See also: Anthony Aust, *Modern Treaty Law and Practice* (CUP 2013) 192–204, 232–44.

[141] 'Succession of States in relation to general multilateral treaties' (n 347) paras 13, 153–54.

160 SUCCESSION TO TREATIES

International Opium Convention to the Philippines,[142] the Philippines accepted the 1946 amending Protocol and subsequently notified of succession to the 1912 Convention.[143] The Protocol did not supersede the Convention but rather provided that each party would apply the amendments 'in respect of the instruments to which it is a party'.[144] While the issue was not tested, it appears that the Philippines became party to the 1912 Convention not through its acceptance of the Protocol but rather by its notification of succession.[145]

### (e) The Powers of Depositaries

Most modern treaties designate a depositary to administer them, which could exceed 145 depositaries today.[146] Apart from the UN Secretary-General, examples of depositaries that have handled successions include the Commission internationale de l'État Civil,[147] the ICAO,[148] the Council of Europe,[149] France,[150] Poland,[151] Canada,[152] Belgium,[153] the Netherlands,[154] and the United Kingdom.[155] Rarely, a succession has impacted on the status of a depositary.[156]

Though not empowered to independently decide the status of a successor,[157] depositaries nonetheless play an important role to handle notifications of succession, interpret the communications of a successor, and revise the status list of the treaty.[158] While there is a general coherence in depositary practice, the point of greatest divergence is the interpretation of notifications.[159] There is no required form of words[160] and communications have often employed vague, tentative, or inconsistent language.[161]

---

[142] E.g. – Narcotic Drugs Convention (n 64) art 26.

[143] 54 UNTS 384; International Opium Convention (adopted 23 January 1912, entered into force 28 June 1919) 8 LNTS 187, art 23; ibid, Status List < https://treaties.un.org/Pages/showDetails.aspx?objid=0800000280046862&clang=_en> accessed 5 January 2024.

[144] Amending Protocol to the Narcotic Drugs Conventions (11 December 1946) 12 UNTS 179, art 1.

[145] E.g. – O'Connell (n 40) 223–24, 227.

[146] Horchani and Ben Hammadi (n 109) 341.

[147] ICCS Conventions, Status List (29 June 2020).

[148] E.g. – Convention on Offences On Board Aircraft (adopted 14 September 1963, entered into force 4 December 1969) Status List (ICAO).

[149] E.g. – 'Accession of the Republic of Montenegro to the Council of Europe', Council of Europe Parliamentary Assembly Opinion No 261 (2007) paras 9–12, 19–20.

[150] ILA Handbook (n 17) 187.

[151] Ibid.

[152] Multilateral Treaties Study (n 41) para 182.

[153] Ibid.

[154] E.g. – 1905 Hague Convention (n 46).

[155] E.g. – Agreement on German External Debts (adopted 27 February 1953, entered into force 16 September 1953) Status List (United Kingdom).

[156] Additional Protocol (n 50) eschatocol.

[157] Note 295.

[158] E.g. – VCLT (n 1) art 77(d); AW Rovine, *Digest of United States Practice in International Law 1973* (Office of Legal Adviser 1974) 182; Nash (n 390) 1204–207; 'Selected Legal Opinions of the Secretariat of the United Nations' (1983) UNJY 192–93.

[159] E.g. – UNGA Sixth Committee, 1318th Meeting (n 15) para 12.

[160] E.g. – Multilateral Treaties Study (n 41) paras 175–78.

[161] E.g. – Bardonnet (n 61) 477–547.

THE GENERAL PRINCIPLE OF CONSENT    161

Particularly influential has been the practice of the UN Secretariat,[162] which has been to solicit from successors written notification for each treaty.[163] In consulting the League and UN archives to identify the treaties applied to the transferred territory, they would interpret their territorial application clauses and adopted the principle of automatic application to all dependent territories in the absence of a clause.[164] In many cases, extensive correspondence has been conducted to clarify eligibility and intentions.[165] The Secretariat does not record a successor as party to a treaty without notification; for example, when no reply is received to a solicitation.[166] A successor may decline to succeed to a treaty in spite of a positive assessment of eligibility[167] but may not succeed despite a negative one.[168]

The practice of Switzerland as depositary for 79 treaties[169] has been most influential on the Geneva Conventions, which have been applied by Contracting States to each territory for which they are responsible if no reservation be made.[170] In comparison with the UN Secretariat, it has been more willing to interpret vague communications without protracted correspondence.[171] In so doing, it emphasizes the essence of a notification as a 'declaration of continuity' of application without interruption from the date of succession.[172]

The practice of the United States as depositary for some 200 multilateral treaties[173] has been a mixture of the UN and Swiss approaches in that they have sometimes made enquiries to clarify ambiguous communications and other times interpreted the notification.[174] Though considering the reply of Syria considering itself to be bound by the IAEA Statute to be 'legally sufficient', for example, they informed Syria that it could instead ratify to reduce its financial obligations.[175] Like Switzerland, they consider the distinction between a succession and an accession to be a substantive rather than a formal one.

---

[162] E.g. – Multilateral Treaties Study (n 41) paras 175–78.

[163] UNSG Depositary Practice (n 251) paras 11, 14.

[164] 'Succession to general multilateral treaties' (n 347) paras 15–20, 23, 132–134, 137–138, 141–142. Until 1962, the Secretariat had revised registers on the basis of devolution agreements – UNSG Depositary Practice (n 251) paras 50–52, 55–56, 61–63, 67, 76–77, 81, 83–84, 91, 93, 101, 108–09, 111–12, 114, 117–18, 123–25, 134. The sole deviation in recent practice concerned East Germany to which West Germany acquiesced – Multilateral Treaties (n 7) xxx.

[165] Ibid, paras 21, 43–44.

[166] Ibid, paras 37, 103–106; 470 UNTS 373; 1108 UNTS 419.

[167] E.g. – 'Succession to general multilateral treaties' (n 347) paras 72–74.

[168] E.g. – UNSG Depositary Practice (n 251) paras 14, 27, 97–98.

[169] E.g. – International Convention on Phosphorus in the Match Industry, Berne, 26 September 1906 (1 January 1912) Status List (French) (Montenegro).

[170] E.g. – Multilateral Treaties Study (n 41) paras 137, 198, 231; 278 UNTS 266 (Jamaica).

[171] Ibid, paras 161–67, 172–73, 225; Letter from Cameroon to Switzerland (16 September 1963) and Letter from Switzerland to the UN Secretariat (11 November 1963) in UN Archives, Folder No (213 CAMER) (January 1960–December 1963) (French).

[172] Ibid, paras 219–24.

[173] US Department of State, 'Depositary Information' <https://www.state.gov/depositary-information/> accessed 7 January 2024.

[174] UN Materials (n 377) 226.

[175] Whiteman (n 65) 988–90.

162   SUCCESSION TO TREATIES

Rare cases of multilateral treaties lacking a depositary principally comprise treaties concluded before the League of Nations.[176] Articles 22(3)(a) and 38(3)(a) of the VCSST provide that notifications be transmitted in the absence of a depositary to 'the parties or the contracting States'. While State practice on this point is scant,[177] these provisions accord with practice on the law of treaties.[178] An outstanding doctrinal question is whether an objection by a single contracting State on eligibility would block succession for which the answer is likely to be that a collective decision of the Contracting States is necessary.

### 5.2.3 Bilateral Treaties

A successor may succeed to a bilateral treaty for which it is eligible by agreement with the counterparty: the successor[179] and the counterparty[180] are equally entitled to reject succession.[181] As the treaty relationship between the predecessor and the counterparty is not affected by a succession, a clone of the treaty is created between the successor and the counterparty. No treaty relationship results between the predecessor and the successor in a single instrument: amendment or termination of the one has no effect on the other.[182]

When a succession to each original counterparty occurs,[183] agreement between one successor and one original counterparty does not establish a treaty relationship between that successor and a successor to the counterparty.[184] As accurately expressed in Articles 25 and 26 of the VCSST, an agreement between the successor to one original counterparty and the successor to the other counterparty is required to create a treaty relationship between them.[185] In rare cases when the geographical scope of a treaty is confined to the territory of the successor, the treaty is not duplicated but the successor is substituted for the predecessor as party to the original

---

[176] E.g. – *UN Materials* (n 377) 157–58.

[177] ILC Articles (n 3) 232–33.

[178] VCLT (n 1) art 78(a); Riad Daoudi, 'Article 78 Convention of 1969' in Corten and Klein (n 27) vol II, 1758–768.

[179] E.g. – Bilateral Treaties Study (n 353) paras 84–86, 106–08.

[180] Ibid, paras 84–86; Hackworth (n 269) 370–72.

[181] E.g. – *Lorra and Tonya v Società Industria Armamenti*, Court of Appeal of Genoa (26 June 1971) 71 ILR 48, 49; Fourth Waldock Report (n 23) 148–49; Klabbers (n 272) 321.

[182] E.g. – *Jhirad* (n 229); *Arnbjornsdottir-Mendler* (n 239); Third Bilateral Treaties Study (n 253) paras 39–43; *Preah Vihear* (n 19) vol I (Pleadings) 145–47 (paras 40–41); ibid, vol II (Pleadings) 22, 31–40, 106–09.

[183] E.g. – Bilateral Treaties Study (n 353) paras 36, 111; Bahamas Bilateral Treaty Register (September 2009) <https://mofa.gov.bs/foreign-policies-and-treaties/treaties/bilateral-treaty-register/> accessed 7 January 2024, 15.

[184] E.g. – Extradition Treaty (Serbia–United Kingdom) (adopted 23 November & 6 December 1900, entered into force 13 August 1901) Australia Treaty Database. See also: Cyprus Bilateral Treaty List < https://www.olc.gov.cy/olc/olc.nsf/inttreatiesarch_el/inttreatiesarch_el?openDocument> accessed 7 January 2024, 118; Bahamas Bilateral Treaty Register (n 182) 62 (n 1).

[185] ILC Articles (n 3) 241–44.

THE GENERAL PRINCIPLE OF CONSENT    163

treaty.[186] In rarer cases still, a bilateral treaty has been converted into a plurilateral treaty – joining the predecessor, successor, and counterparty – when the participation of the predecessor has been necessary (e.g.—for mixed commissions).[187]

The key doctrinal problem in modern practice is the identification of an agreement amid ambiguity or silence. A verbal expression of consent can prompt questions of interpretation (particularly for implied consent) while a more intricate practice has been an expression of consent by conduct in tandem with a verbal expression. Even more complex has been the location of an agreement reached by reciprocal conduct. It is suggested that a 'meeting of minds'[188] can occur in each of these forms of consent for which evidentiary considerations are critical.[189]

Article 24(1) of the VCSST states that succession to a bilateral treaty may be done when the newly independent State and a counterparty 'expressly so agree' or 'by reason of their conduct they are to be considered as having so agreed'.[190] The latter was described by the ILC as 'tacit' agreement,[191] a term since considered to be 'not entirely helpful'.[192] This provision reflects State practice[193] save insofar as it does not distinguish between an implied, verbal agreement and an agreement by conduct as actions and omissions.

## (a) Notification

Unlike for multilateral treaties, a notification by a successor does not itself constitute a succession to a bilateral treaty but rather comprises one-half of the requisite agreement.[194] It can accordingly be combined with an affirmative response to create a verbal agreement[195] or affirmative conduct. By the general principle of acquiescence, implied consent is also expressed by silence or a vague reply.[196]

---

[186] E.g. – Second Bilateral Treaties Study (n 251) paras 130–32, 147, 151; Third Bilateral Treaties Study (n 253) paras 21, 84, 95–104; Bilateral Treaties Study (n 353) paras 138–43, 192.

[187] E.g. – Third Bilateral Treaties Study (n 253) para 21; Protocol to the Soviet≠American Treaty on Strategic Offensive Arms (adopted 23 May 1992, entered into force 5 December 1994) (1992) 96 RGDIP 1030, 1031 (French).

[188] *Gold Pool* (n 224) para 71.

[189] E.g. – *United States v Bowe*, Judicial Committee of the Privy Council (4 August 1989) 85 ILR 128, 137–38, 143–44 ('Bahamas').

[190] ILC Articles (n 3) 236–41.

[191] Ibid, 239–40.

[192] *Gold Pool* (n 224) para 3.

[193] *M v Federal Department of Justice and Police*, Federal Tribunal of Switzerland (21 September 1979) 75 ILR 107, 110–12 ('South Africa'); *R v DPP, ex parte Schwartz*, Supreme Court of Jamaica (1 December 1976) (1976) 24 WIR 491, 73 ILR 44, 46–48, 53–54 ('Jamaica'); *R v Commissioner of Correctional Services, ex parte Fitz Henry*, Supreme Court of Jamaica (1 October 1976) 72 ILR 63, 66–74 ('Jamaica').

[194] E.g. – O'Connell (n 40) 135.

[195] E.g. – *UN Materials* (n 377) 229–30; *Treaties in Force* (n 254) 281–83 ('Malaysia').

[196] E.g. – ILC Articles (n 3) 239 (n 405); Bilateral Treaties Study (n 353) paras 50, 81–82; Extradition Convention (Italy–United Kingdom) (adopted 4 January 1873, entered into force 18 March 1873) Italian Treaty Database No BILMT011 (Italian); 'Extradition treaties with Italy', Malta Treaty Database (25 May 2001) art XVIII.

## 164  SUCCESSION TO TREATIES

As for multilateral treaties, there is no required form of words: the substance must express the will to continue the application of the treaty from the operative date. A notification can pertain to one, some, or all of the bilateral treaties concluded between the predecessor (e.g.—a list of treaties).[197] Either State concerned may reject the succession[198] and it is a question of fact whether a communication expresses an intention to agree to the succession.[199] Whereas Article 2(g) of the VCSST defines a 'notification' exclusively in relation to multilateral treaties, Article 24(a) does not address the definition of a notification for bilateral treaties.

### (b)  Operative Date

When a successor and a counterparty agree on succession, they usually select the date of succession,[200] but may opt for a different date.[201] When a different date is selected,[202] a 'novation'[203] occurs whereby the treaty in question is reconstituted but was not in force between the date of succession and the operative date.[204] The difference is shown by the notification of Tanganyika to counterparties of its desire to 'revive' extradition and judicial assistance treaties, which resulted in a succession rather than a novation because there was temporal continuity with the expiry of its general declaration of provisional application.[205]

When a succession agreement is silent or vague,[206] the operative date intended by the parties is a question of fact. For example, the Franco–Israeli agreement for the 'provisional reinstatement, pending the conclusion of a new extradition treaty' of the 1876 Anglo-French extradition treaty can be interpreted in light of the counterparties' subsequent conduct.[207] While the status of the treaty during the 'twilight period' between the date of succession and the date of agreement is unlikely to be important when the successor and counterparty reach agreement in a short period of time,[208] the scope for dispute expands over time.

---

[197]  E.g. – Whiteman (n 65) 983–84.

[198]  E.g. – AP Lester, 'State Succession to Treaties in the Commonwealth' (1963) 12 ICLQ 475, 500–01.

[199]  E.g. – *Deripaska* (n 549).

[200]  E.g. – Dronova (n 373) 772 (note 304); Agreement on the Application of Certain Treaties (Finland–Montenegro) (18 April 2007) 45 Sähköinen sopimussarja (2007) 456 (Finnish).

[201]  E.g. – Succession Agreement (Norway–Bosnia) (20 August 2008) Norway Treaty Database No 20-08-2008 Nr 20 Bilateral (Norwegian).

[202]  E.g. – Exchange of Notes (United Kingdom–Bosnia) (1 October 1997 and 4 May 1998) Cmd 5028, 1.

[203]  Fourth Waldock Report (n 23) 154.

[204]  E.g. – Air Transport Agreement (Egypt–Syria) (adopted 3 July 1955, entered into force 11 March 1956) 393 UNTS 5652.

[205]  E.g. – *UN Materials* (n 377) 178–179; Bilateral Treaties Study (n 353) paras 60–63; Exchange of Notes (Switzerland–Tanzania) (2 August and 28 September 1967) Switzerland Treaty Database, No 19670196 (French).

[206]  E.g. – Third Bilateral Treaties Study (n 253) paras 27, 30–32, 45; Agreement on the 1985 Franco–Soviet Finance Treaty (France–Turkmenistan) (28 April 1994) France Treaty Database No TRA1994069 (French).

[207]  Bilateral Treaties Study (n 353) paras 40–44; Extradition Convention (Israel–France) (adopted 12 November 1958, entered into force 14 November 1971) 805 UNTS 251, art 23.

[208]  E.g. – Bardonnet (n 61) 444–70; Third Bilateral Treaties Study (n 253) para 28; Trade Agreement (Thailand–India) (13 December 1968) 656 UNTS 3.

THE GENERAL PRINCIPLE OF CONSENT    165

In the *EURAM* arbitration, the disputing parties agreed that Slovakia had succeeded to the 1990 Austria–Czechoslovakia bilateral investment treaty.[209] However, Slovakia argued that the VCLT did not apply to the dispute because it had not succeeded to it by notification until 1 January 1993—after the ratification by Czecho-Slovakia of the bilateral investment treaty but before the entry into force of the Austro-Slovak succession agreement on 1 January 1995.[210] Rejecting this argument, the Arbitral Tribunal held that Slovakia could not have succeeded to the bilateral investment treaty without taking the necessary steps, which it had not done until after it had succeeded to the VCLT, as confirmed by information provided by Austria.[211] As the treaty had to have been operative 'at the earliest' from the date of the exchange of notes (25 November 1994) this implied that the treaty was novated from the date of succession of Slovakia (1 January 1993).

(c) Verbal Agreement

A verbal agreement can be concluded between a successor and a counterparty dealing with one[212] or more[213] treaties. Since the desovietization period, succession agreements have frequently included one list of treaties to which succession applies and another to which it does not.[214] While the possibility of succession to a succession agreement exists, there is still no practice on the point because States have instead replaced succession agreements with new ones that deal with the listed treaties.[215] Due to the general principle of *res judicata*, an agreement not to succeed to a treaty[216] concluded after a decided dispute does not impact on that dispute.[217]

A successor and counterparty can also agree to a succession without naming the treaty. The treaty might be implied in a general agreement to succeed to each of the applicable treaties of the predecessor and counterparty without listing them.[218] A counterparty can also acquiesce to a notification of succession to all applicable treaties.[219] The parties could agree to implement a particular treaty without

[209] *European American* (n 115) para 40.

[210] Ibid, paras 77–78. They had not stipulated the operative date – Exchange of Notes (Austria–Slovakia) (adopted 4 August and 25 November 1994, entered into force 1 January 1995) 318 BGBl (28 December 1994) No 1046 (German).

[211] Ibid, paras 79–81.

[212] E.g. – Bilateral Treaties Study (n 353) paras 23, 33, 46, 89; Third Bilateral Treaties Study (n 253) para 105; *Then v Melendez*, US Ninth Circuit Court of Appeals (7 August 1996) 92 F 3d 851 ('Singapore'); *Extradition of Tuttle*, US Ninth Circuit Court of Appeals (12 June 1992) 96 ILR 110, 111 ('Bahamas').

[213] E.g. – Succession Agreement (Denmark–Croatia) (27 April and 4 May 1998) 2076 UNTS 3.

[214] E.g. – Protocol (Germany–Azerbaijan) (2 July 1996) 2420 UNTS 114.

[215] E.g. – Succession Agreement (France–Montenegro) (30 September 2010 and 13 June 2011) 105 JORF (4 May 2012) 7895 (French).

[216] E.g. – ILA Handbook (n 379) 115.

[217] E.g. – *Sanum* (n 89).

[218] E.g. – Agreement on Treaties (Germany–Georgia) (19 May and 9 September 1992) BGBl vol II (1992) 1128 (German).

[219] E.g. – Agreement relating to Certain Treaties (Congo (Brazzaville)–United States) (12 May and 5 August 1961) 603 UNTS 19; Bilateral Treaties Study (n 353) para 104; *Treaties in Force* (n 254) 94.

166    SUCCESSION TO TREATIES

expressing their positions on its status;[220] they might also annex an incomplete list of treaties to their succession agreement.[221]

A recent example of an implied agreement was the succession of Kazakhstan to the 1989 Soviet–Canadian bilateral investment agreement.[222] While an investor-State arbitral tribunal concluded in the *World Wide Minerals* arbitration in 2015 that Kazakhstan had succeeded by 'tacit agreement' with Canada,[223] another tribunal found in the *Gold Pool* arbitration in 2020 that it had not.[224] In its judgment setting aside the *Gold Pool* award on jurisdiction, the High Court of England and Wales found Canada and Kazakhstan to have implicitly agreed to the succession of Kazakhstan to the treaty in a declaration of economic cooperation of 10 July 1992, as reaffirmed in an exchange of notes of 13 April 1994 and a citation in a trade agreement of 29 March 1995.[225]

## (d) Agreement by Conduct

The most complex form of succession agreement is when a successor or counterparty expresses consent by their conduct. This can either comprise reciprocal conduct or the conduct of one State in combination with a verbal expression of consent by the other.[226] The executive authorities of the States concerned have expressed consent by continuing to implement treaties on matters such as air transport,[227] trade,[228] and border management.[229] For example, they have expressed consent to extradition treaties by making or granting an extradition request.[230]

---

[220] E.g. – Whiteman (n 65) 987; Third Bilateral Treaties Study (n 253) paras 72–83.

[221] Exchange of Notes (Switzerland–Ukraine) (4 August 1997) Switzerland Treaty Database No 99991057; *X and Y* (n 430) paras H7–H10, A2–A8.

[222] Dumberry (n 3) 56–62.

[223] *World Wide Minerals v Kazakhstan (2)* (Award on Jurisdiction) UNCITRAL *ad hoc* Arbitral Tribunal (15 October 2015) (unpublished) in Dumberry (n 3) 92.

[224] *Gold Pool v Kazakhstan* (Award) PCA Case No 2016-23 (30 July 2020) (UNCITRAL) (unpublished) in Vladislav Djanić, 'Kazakhstan fends off claims by Canadian gold miner, as tribunal finds it is not a successor to USSR BIT', IAReporter (4 August 2020).

[225] *Gold Pool JV Limited v Kazakhstan*, High Court of Justice (15 December 2021) [2021] EWHC 3422 (Comm) paras 33–42, 47–50, 55–60, 69–81, 84–96.

[226] Bilateral Treaties Study (n 353) paras 75–80, 132–33.

[227] E.g. – Second Bilateral Treaties Study (n 251) paras 26, 29–58, 83, 111–12, 126–28, 133–37, 144–46, 148–49, 155, 159–75; Third Bilateral Treaties Study (n 253) paras 1–10, 65–70, 169–92; *Nigeria's Treaties in Force* (Federal Ministry of Information 1971) vol I, 7–11; *Nigeria's Treaties in Force* (Federal Ministry of Justice 1990) vol I, v. The Anglo-Dutch air transport treaty remained in effect after the secession of Jamaica through new licences issued by Jamaica to Dutch carriers – Netherlands Treaty Database No 005441, Parliament Paper No 0000001904 (Dutch); Netherlands Treaty Database No 003552, Parliamentary Paper No 0000239810 (Dutch).

[228] E.g. – Third Bilateral Treaties Study (n 253) paras 66–71, 149–66.

[229] E.g. – Second Bilateral Treaties Study (n 251) para 64, 71–78.

[230] E.g. – *Elijah Ephraim Jhirad v Thomas E. Ferrandina*, US Southern District Court of New York (23 January 1973) 22 AILC 261, 263–264 ('India'); *Saroop v Maharaj and Others*, Court of Appeal of Trinidad and Tobago (16 May, 26 July 1995) 3 LRC [1996] 1, 8–10 ('Trinidad and Tobago'); *Extradition of Sacirbegovic*, US Southern District Court for New York (18 January 2005) No 03 Crim Misc 01 Page 19 (SDNY 18 Jan 2005) 21–25 ('Bosnia'); *Extradition of Platko*, US Southern District Court for California (26 July 2002) 213 F Supp 2d 1229 (2002) 1232–1233 (n 3) ('Czechia'); *Sabatier v Dabrowski*, US First Circuit Court of Appeals (15 November 1978) 586 F 2d 866 (1978) 868 ('Canada'); *M v Federal Department of Justice and Police*, (n 193).

THE GENERAL PRINCIPLE OF CONSENT    167

An interruption of treaty performance might[231] or might not[232] indicate a position against succession.

Unlike verbal agreements negotiated by the executive authorities of a State, consent by conduct to a succession can also be expressed by its legislative and judicial organs. For example, the legislatures of the States concerned can adopt corresponding legislation to implement the treaty.[233] When national courts hold a treaty (e.g.—on extradition) to remain in force without any prior action by the executive, the doctrinal question concerning the validity of such an expression of consent is answered by the irrelevance of internal law concerning treaty-making competence under the law of treaties.[234]

Rather, the true question is whether a judgment of a national court expressing the consent of its State to be bound is effective *in itself* to constitute succession. It is suggested that State practice shows the judgment not to constitute a succession on its own but rather requires reciprocal conduct by the other State, whether before or after the judgment, for a 'meeting of minds' to occur. A court can express the consent of a State in response to an expression of consent by the other State concerned but its decision in the absence of such prior conduct needs an affirmative response by the other State to effect an agreement.[235]

An example is the succession of Malawi to the 1962 extradition treaty between South Africa and the Federation of Rhodesia and Nyasaland.[236] The South African courts relied upon the legislative actions of Malawi preserving the implementation of the treaty in its internal law and the request for extradition by South Africa, accepting the official certificate of the Ministry of Justice as persuasive evidence.[237] This agreement by conduct was retrospectively proven by the inclusion of a clause terminating the extradition treaty in its replacement.[238] Other examples include the successions of Zambia[239] and Trinidad and Tobago[240] to the 1931 Anglo-American extradition treaty and Croatia to the 1922 Italo–Yugoslav extradition treaty.[241]

---

[231] E.g. – Second Bilateral Treaties Study (n 251) paras 21–24.

[232] Ibid, paras 71–78, 116–25.

[233] E.g. – Bilateral Treaties Study (n 353) para 58; Third Bilateral Treaties Study (n 253) para 56.

[234] VCLT (n 1) art 46(1).

[235] E.g. – *Schwartz & Fitz Henry* (n 192).

[236] E.g. – John Dugard, 'Succession to Federal Treaties on the Dissolution of a Federation' (1967) 84(3) SALJ 250–54.

[237] *S v Bull*, Transvaal Provincial Division (11 November 1966) 52 ILR 84, 85–86, 88. See also: *S v Eliasov*, Appellate Division (28 September 1967) 52 ILR 408, 411; *S v Devoy*, Natal Provincial Division (3 and 19 November 1970) 55 ILR 89, 91–93.

[238] Extradition Agreement (Malawi–South Africa) (25 February 1972) 81 SAGG (24 March 1972) 3424, art 25.

[239] *Jère* (n 534).

[240] *USA. ex rel Saroop v Garcia*, Third Circuit Court of Appeals (21 March 1997) 109 F 3d 165 (3d Cir 1997) 170–173. See also: *Arnbjornsdottir-Mendler v United States*, Ninth Circuit Court of Appeals (8 December 1983) 96 ILR 105, 107–08 ('Iceland').

[241] *Jadranko*, Court of Cassation of Italy (6 July 1995) in *Mauritius v Nandanee* (n 248) 'Considerato in diritto', para 2.3 (Italian).

168    SUCCESSION TO TREATIES

Equally, however, the courts of a State have rejected succession; for example, when the other State concerned had not expressed its consent to be bound beforehand[242] or an extradition request omitted reference to the treaty concerned.[243] This has applied even when written notification was belatedly provided during extradition proceedings.[244]

Confusion concerning the application of the relevant rules of succession has arisen in judgments of national courts concerning the succession of Mauritius to extradition treaties. In 1976, the Supreme Court of Mauritius relied upon the extradition request of France and the preservation of implementing law by Mauritius as constituting the succession of Mauritius to the 1876 Anglo–French extradition treaty.[245] However, the same court rejected another request under the same treaty in 1992 by holding France not to have considered the treaty to be in force and a declaration of provisional application of bilateral treaties by Mauritius to have lapsed.[246]

Yet, France had made two extradition requests pursuant to the treaty, while Mauritius' declaration of provisional application dated 12 March 1968 exclusively concerned multilateral treaties.[247] Whereas Mauritius had declared its intention in its declaration on multilateral treaties to make a subsequent declaration on bilateral treaties, there is no record of one being made.[248] In 2017, the Court of Cassation of Italy held Mauritius not to have succeeded to the 1873 Anglo–Italian extradition treaty in the absence of affirmative conduct by Mauritius and reciprocal conduct by the executive authorities of Italy, such as listing.[249]

## 5.3 Application to the Classes of Succession

The general principle of consent applies to each of the classes of succession but its manifestation varies according to the particular dynamics of each class. In a total succession, the termination of the international legal personality of the predecessor[250] does not preclude succession to its treaties. In mergers and absorptions,

---

[242] *Re Bottali*, Court of Appeal of Rome (17 October 1980) 78 ILR 105, 108–111 ('India').

[243] E.g. – JN Saxena, 'Extradition of a Soviet Sailor' (1963) 57 AJIL 883, 886.

[244] *Re Westerling*, High Court of the Colony of Singapore (15 August 1950) 17 ILR 82, 83, 88. Indonesia accepted the judgment and concluded a new treaty – 'Letter from R.C. Barnes, British Embassy, Djakarta, to F.A. Warner, Foreign Office' (21 October 1960) UK National Archives Record No FO 372/7568 Doc 1591/60.

[245] *Ex parte Deprez and Fontaine*, Supreme Court of Mauritius (29 January 1976) 87 ILR 311, 314, 316.

[246] *France v Heeralall and Attorney-General*, Supreme Court of Mauritius (30 March 1992) 107 ILR 168, 173.

[247] ILC Articles (n 3) 190.

[248] Ian Brownlie, *Principles of Public International Law* (OUP 1990) 671.

[249] *Mauritius v Soornack Nandanee*, Court of Cassation of Italy (3 February 2017) 'Ritenuto in fatto', para 2.1; 'Considerato in diritto', paras 2–2.2, 2.3–2.5 (Italian) (on file with author).

[250] See Chapter 2.

the key issue is the extension of the territorial application of a treaty of one predecessor to the other territories of the successor. In dismemberment, it has been succession to the 'localized' treaties applied exclusively to the territory transferred.

In a partial succession,[251] the treaties of the predecessor continue in force in its remaining territory under the moving treaty frontiers rule. An important issue is whether the successor may succeed to treaties of the predecessor that were applied to the transferred territory. For cession, an additional question is whether the existing treaties of the successor extend to the ceded territory. When a protected State or Territory accedes to independence, an additional issue is the continued participation of the successor in treaties concluded by the successor or the predecessor on its behalf.

### 5.3.1 Merger

When multiple States merge to form a single State, the successor may succeed to any treaty of the predecessor by notification or agreement. State practice evincing this rule comprises the mergers of:

- Egypt and Syria to create the United Arab Republic ('UAR', 1958);[252]
- the Trust Territory of Somalia with Somaliland to form Somalia (1960);[253]
- Tanganyika with Zanzibar to create Tanzania (1964);[254]
- the Democratic Republic of Viet Nam ('North Viet Nam') with the Republic of Viet Nam ('South Viet Nam') to create the Socialist Republic of Viet Nam ('Viet Nam', 1976);[255] and
- the Yemeni Arab Republic ('North Yemen') with the People's Democratic Republic of Yemen ('South Yemen') to establish the Republic of Yemen ('Yemen', 1990).[256]

---

[251] Ibid.

[252] E.g. – ILC Articles (n 3) 255 (n 15); 'Summary of the Practice of the Secretary-General as Depositary of Multilateral Agreements', UN Doc ST/LEG/7 (7 August 1959) para 48; UN Secretariat, 'Succession of States in respect of bilateral treaties: second study – Air transport agreements', UN Doc A/CN.4/253 (24 March 1971) (1971) ILC Yearbook vol II 111, para 190.

[253] Law No 5 (31 January 1961) 2 Official Bulletin of the Somali Republic (1961) arts 3(1) 3(5) 4–5, 9. See also: O'Connell (n 40) 74.

[254] ILC Articles (n 3) 256–58 (paras 20–23); Multilateral Treaties (n 7) lii; 'Succession of States in respect of bilateral treaties: third study – Trade agreements' (9 April 1971) UN Doc A/CN.4/253/Add.1, para 168. Unlike the treaties of Tanganyika, Tanzania chose not to succeed to those of Zanzibar: EE Seaton and ST Maiti, Tanzania Treaty Practice (OUP 1973) 28, 51–53, 63–75.

[255] Multilateral Treaties (n 7) vol I, lii, 100, 115 (n 14) 124, 130 (n 15) 133 (n 2) 135 (n 2) 146, 154 (n 16), 515 (n 19), 517 (n 2), 520 (n 2), 528 (n 2), 536 (n 2), 546 (n 2), 550 (n 2), 556 (n 5), 572 (n 20); vol II, 19, 20 (n 12), 26 (n 26), 65, 68 (n 9), 127 (n 7), 137 (n 5), 175 (n 3); vol III, 29 (n 2) 116, 117 (n 8), 124 (n 2), 324 (n 2), 796 (n 9), 799 (n 9), 801 (n 4); US Department of State, Treaties in Force (2021) 348.

[256] Ibid, l, lii–liii. See also notes 68, 403, & 521.

## 170 SUCCESSION TO TREATIES

Express *opiniones juris* include the general declarations of succession to the UN Member States of the UAR on 1 March 1958,[257] Tanzania on 6 May 1964,[258] and Yemen on 19 May 1990.[259]

Combining mergers and absorptions as a 'uniting of States',[260] Article 31(1) of the VCSST prescribes a rule of automatic succession unless incompatible with a treaty or otherwise agreed.[261] In contrast, Articles 17, 24, and 30(1) stipulate that 'newly independent States formed from two or more territories' may succeed by notification to multilateral treaties or agreement to bilateral treaties.[262] The latter provision was intended to apply solely to multiple territories combining to form a new State[263] but has yet to be applied in practice.[264]

An important aspect is the application of the moving treaty frontiers rule to determine whether succession to a treaty of one predecessor entails its automatic extension to the territory of the other. In an example of progressive development,[265] Articles 31 and 32 of the VCSST prescribe a rule of automatic non-extension unless a successor make a notification for multilateral treaties (if compatible with the treaty) or agree with the counterparties.[266] For 'newly independent States formed from two or more territories', in contrast, Article 30 provides that a treaty automatically extends to the entire territory of the successor unless incompatible with the treaty or otherwise agreed.[267] These provisions have yet to be applied in subsequent practice[268] and do not match the prior practice, which rather points to the nature of the treaty in question as requiring application throughout the territory of the successor or not.

### 5.3.2 Absorption

When one State absorbs another, bilateral treaties between the predecessor and successor automatically terminate due to the extinction of the predecessor. Subject to eligibility, the successor may succeed by notification or agreement only to localized treaties to be applied exclusively to the absorbed territory. The moving treaty

---

[257] Note 251.

[258] Note 253.

[259] Note 255.

[260] ILC Articles (n 3) 258–59 (para 28); Graf-Brugère (n 263) 1075–79.

[261] Ibid, 259.

[262] Ibid.

[263] Ibid, 248–51.

[264] Lucius Caflisch and Denis, 'Article 30' in Distefano (n 9) 1033, 1040–1047; Graf-Brugère, 'Article 31' in Distefano (n 9) 1069, 1094–100.

[265] Graf-Brugère (n 263) 1099 (notes 104–05).

[266] ILC Articles (n 3) 259.

[267] Ibid.

[268] Caflisch and Denis (n 263) 1047–66; Graf-Brugère (n 263) 1092–1100.

APPLICATION TO THE CLASSES OF SUCCESSION    171

frontiers rule automatically extends the treaties of the successor to the absorbed territory when they so require.

State practice proving the rule of succession by notification or agreement to localized treaties comprises the absorptions of:

- the Memel Territory by Lithuania (1924);[269]
- Austria by Germany (1938);[270]
- the Saar Territory by West Germany (1956);[271] and
- the German Democratic Republic ('East Germany') by the Federal Republic of Germany ('West Germany', 1990).[272]

In the most recent case of absorption, a minority of the East German bilateral treaties were provisionally continued in force or terminated by a superseding agreement.[273] While West Germany denied an obligation to succeed to multilateral treaties[274] and generally declined succession to them,[275] it considered itself to be entitled to succeed.[276]

As for mergers, the VCSST provides for a presumptive rule of automatic succession in absorptions[277] that does not reflect the prior practice and has not been applied subsequently.[278] The general policy of West Germany was one of moving

---

[269] Convention concerning the Territory of Memel (adopted 8 May 1924, entered into force 27 September 1924) 29 LNTS 86, art 4.

[270] II FRUS (1938) 502–505; GH Hackworth, *Digest of International Law* vol V (Government Printing Office 1943) 370–72; Extension of the 1905 Hague Convention to Austria (Germany(n Romania) (11 January 1939) II RGBl (13 January 1939) 7 (German); Günther Jaenicke, Karl Doehring and Erich Zimmermann (eds) *Fontes Iuris Gentium: Decisions of the German Supreme Court relating to Public International Law* (Carl Heymanns Verlag KG 1960) 107.

[271] E.g. – Treaty for the Settlement of the Saar (France(n West Germany) (adopted 27 October 1956, entered into force 1 January 1957) 1053 UNTS 3, arts 34, 51–54, 95; annex 9 (arts 5, 30); annex 12 (art 39); annex 16 (art 2(1)); annex 17 (arts 2–6); ibid, Exchange of Notes (27 October 1956); 'Succession of States to multilateral treaties; seventh study prepared by the Secretariat', UN Doc A/CN.4/225 (24 April 1970) (1970) ILC Yearbook vol II, paras 129–30; *Mrs W v T.S.*, Court of First Instance of Amsterdam (8 April 1954) in *UN Materials* (n 377) 112–13.

[272] Treaty on the Establishment of German Unity (West Germany–East Germany) (adopted 30 August 1990, entered into force 3 October 1990) 30 ILM 463, art 12. See also: Konrad Bühler, 'State Succession, Identity/Continuity and Membership in the United Nations' in Pierre Eisemann and Martti Koskenniemi (eds) *State Succession: Codification Tested against the Facts* (Martinus Nijhoff 2000) 187, 239, 245–47.

[273] Andreas Zimmermann, *Staatennachfolge in völkerrechtliche Verträge* (Springer 2000) 87; Zimmermann (n 189) 63–274.

[274] *Former Syrian Ambassador to the German Democratic Republic*, Federal Constitutional Court of Germany (10 June 1997) 115 ILR 596, 614–617.

[275] E.g. – Agreement on the termination of 'Petrobaltik' (USSR–Poland–East Germany) (12 July 1990) Russia Treaty Database No 19900084, arts 2, 4 (Russian). See also: Zimmermann (n 272) 274, 276; Papenfuß, 'The Fate of the International Treaties of the GDR within the Framework of German Unification' (1998) 92 AJIL 469, 479–80.

[276] Unification Treaty (n 271) art 12(3). The sole, possible exception is: Agreement on 'Intersputnik' (adopted 15 November 1971, entered into force 12 July 1972) 862 UNTS 4, arts 20, 22–23.

[277] VCSST (n 4) art 31.

[278] Graf-Brugère (n 263).

172   SUCCESSION TO TREATIES

treaty frontiers, which contradicted the decision of the ILC to transfer absorptions from Article 14 on moving treaty frontiers in its first draft to Article 31 on 'a uniting of States' in its second draft.[279] Had West Germany applied Article 31, the treaties of East Germany would have automatically remained in force within their territorial limits.[280]

### 5.3.3  Dismemberment

When a State is dismembered to transfer title to its territories to existing States or new States, the successor may succeed by notification or agreement to eligible treaties applied to the transferred territory. State practice underpinning this rule comprise the dismemberments of:

- the Federation of Mali (20 August 1960);[281]
- the Socialist Federal Republic of Yugoslavia ('SFRY', 25 June 1991–27 April 1992); and
- Czecho-Slovakia (1 January 1993).

Affirmative opiniones juris on the right of a new State to succeed were expressed by Senegal and France,[282] the FRY,[283] Slovenia,[284] Croatia,[285] Bosnia,[286] North Macedonia,[287] Czechia,[288] Slovakia,[289] and Austria.[290]

On 1 July 1992, Slovenia notified the UN Secretary-General of its succession to 55 multilateral treaties from its declaration of independence (25 June 1991).[291] Similar notifications were tendered by Croatia,[292] Bosnia,[293] and North Macedonia.[294] Following the change in the policy of the Federal Republic

[279] ILC Articles (n 3) 259 (para 28).

[280] Andreas Zimmermann, 'State Succession in Respect of Treaties' in Jan Klabbers et al (eds) *State Practice regarding State Succession and Issues of Recognition* (Kluwer 1999) 86.

[281] E.g. – Second Bilateral Treaties Study (n 251) para 176; 'Republic of Mali: Multilateral Agreements', UN Archives Folder No 213 MALI; Letter from Mali to the UN Secretariat (11 December 1962) ibid (French). See also: Rosalyn Cohen, 'Legal Problems Arising from the Dissolution of the Mali Federation' (1960) 36 BYIL 375, 382.

[282] Note 280.

[283] Note 294.

[284] Ortega Terol, 'The Bursting of Yugoslavia' in Eisemann and Koskenniemi (n 271) 903–904.

[285] Ibid, 906.

[286] Ibid, 906–907.

[287] Constitutional law on the entry into force of the Constitution of Macedonia (25 November 1991) in Foreign Broadcast Information Service, *JPRS Report: East Europe Recent Legislation* (US Department of Commerce, 10 February 1992) arts 3–4.

[288] UN Doc A/47/848 (31 December 1992) annex I.

[289] Ibid, annex II.

[290] E.g. – Case No 7Ob573/93 (n 510).

[291] *Multilateral Treaties* (n 7) xlix.

[292] Ibid, xiv.

[293] Ibid, v, xlix.

[294] E.g. – UN Doc C/N/1351/2005.TREATIES-3 (5 September 2007).

APPLICATION TO THE CLASSES OF SUCCESSION   173

of Yugoslavia ('FRY') on 8 March 2001 to consider itself a successor with effect from 27 April 1992,[295] Serbia issued three notifications of succession in 2016 and 2019.[296] This also applied to treaties administered by Switzerland,[297] Belgium,[298] the IAEA,[299] the ICAO,[300] the Commission internationale de l'État Civil,[301] the Netherlands,[302] the United Kingdom,[303] and the United States.[304]

The successors have expressly succeeded to numerous bilateral treaties by concluding succession agreements with counterparties, such as Austria,[305] the Netherlands,[306] Italy,[307] France,[308] Switzerland,[309] China,[310] Norway,[311] Romania,[312] Russia,[313] Mexico,[314] Denmark,[315] Spain,[316] Portugal,[317]Australia,[318]

---

[295] *Multilateral Treaties* (n 7) liii–liv.

[296] E.g. – UN Doc C.N.241.2019.TREATIES-XIV.7 (11 June 2019).

[297] E.g. – Convention on the Treatment of Prisoners of War (adopted 12 August 1949, entered into force 21 October 1950) Status List (Switzerland) (French). See also: *Serbia v Ganić*, City of Westminster Magistrates' Court (27 July 2010) (2010) 81 BYIL 395, 397–98.

[298] E.g. – Convention for the Unification of Certain Rules (23 September 1910) Status List (Belgium) (January 2005) (French).

[299] E.g. – Convention on Assistance in Case of a Nuclear Accident (26 September 1986) Registration No 1534, Status List (IAEA) (21 September 2020).

[300] E.g. – Convention on Offences committed on board Aircraft (14 September 1963) Status List (ICAO) (4 December 1969).

[301] E.g. – 'Conventions: Status List' (ICCS) (29 June 2020) (French).

[302] E.g. – Agreement relating to Refugee Seamen (adopted 23 November 1957, entered into force 27 December 1961) Status List Netherlands Treaty Database No 006829.

[303] E.g. – Convention on the Prevention of Marine Pollution by Dumping of Wastes (adopted 29 December 1972, entered into force 30 August 1975) Status List United Kingdom Treaty Database.

[304] E.g. –Treaty on the Non-Proliferation of Nuclear Weapons (adopted 1 July 1968, entered into force 5 March 1970) Status List (United States) (6 October 2010).

[305] E.g. – Agreement on certain Yugoslav–Austrian treaties (Slovenia–Austria) (adopted 16 October 1992, entered into force 24 September 1993) 714/1993 BGBl (German).

[306] E.g. – Joint Declaration (Netherlands–Slovenia) (18 March and 21 April 1992) 98 Tractatenblad (19 April 1995) Netherlands Treaty Database No 011806 (Dutch).

[307] E.g. – Exchange of notes (Italy–Slovenia) (31 July & 8 September 1992) Italy Treaty Database No BILSVN049 (French).

[308] E.g. – Agreement on Succession to Bilateral Treaties (France–FRY) (26 March 2003) 2239 UNTS 325, art 1, annex.

[309] E.g. – Exchange of Notes (Switzerland–North Macedonia) (21 May 1997) Switzerland Treaty Database, No 99990739 (German).

[310] E.g. – Exchange of Letters (China–Croatia) (27 August 1996) China Treaty Database (Chinese).

[311] E.g. – Succession Agreement (Norway–Bosnia) (20 August 2008) Norway Treaty Database No 20-08-2008 Nr 20 Bilateral (Norwegian).

[312] E.g. – Protocol on Succession (Romania–Croatia) (adopted 5 March 2004, entered into force 20 August 2004) Romania Treaty Database.

[313] E.g. – Protocol on Bilateral Agreements (Russia–Croatia) (adopted 12 January 1998, entered into force 9 July 2001) Russia Treaty Database No 19980242 (Russian).

[314] Trade Agreement (Mexico–SFRY) (adopted 17 March 1950, entered into force 25 September 1953) Mexico Treaty Database (Spanish).

[315] E.g. – Agreement concerning Succession (Denmark–Croatia) (27 April and 4 May 1998) 2076 UNTS 3.

[316] E.g. – Exchange of Notes (Spain–Slovenia) (5 February and 9 September 1996) 32 BOE (6 February 1997) 3750 (Spanish); *Guía de tratados bilaterales con Estados* (Ministerio de Asuntos Exteriores de España 14 June 2021) 91, 132 (Spanish).

[317] Agreement on Succession (Portugal–FRY) (3 November 2003) 101 Diário da República I-A (29 April 2004) (Portuguese).

[318] E.g. – Agreement on Yugoslav Citizens in Australia (Australia–SFRY) (adopted 12 February 1970, entered into force 20 May 1970) Australia Treaty Database.

174    SUCCESSION TO TREATIES

Poland,[319] Canada,[320] New Zealand,[321] Czechia,[322] Japan,[323] Egypt,[324] and the United Kingdom.[325] Other treaties are listed by successors or counterparties as remaining in force without providing information on the succession.

For the dismemberment of Czecho-Slovakia, the Czech Republic ('Czechia') notified the UN Secretary-General of its succession to a list of multilateral treaties with effect from 1 January 1993.[326] Slovakia made a similar notification on 19 May.[327] The Secretary-General replaced the entries in status lists for Czecho-Slovakia with their names and the corresponding dates of notification of succession.[328] The successors adopted similar approaches in succeeding to various treaties administered by 14 other depositaries.[329]

The successors also succeeded to numerous bilateral treaties by agreement with France,[330] Austria,[331] Argentina,[332] Colombia,[333] the Netherlands,[334] Norway,[335] Spain,[336] Switzerland,[337] China,[338] Romania,[339] the United Kingdom,[340] Russia,[341]

---

[319] Succession Agreement (Slovenia–Poland) (adopted 1 March 1995, entered into force 9 October 1995) Poland Treaty Database (Polish, Slovenian).

[320] Succession Agreement (Slovenia–Canada) (23 June 1997) 34/1997 Uradni list (Slovenian).

[321] Slovenia–New Zealand, Succession Agreement, 13 March 2003, 13/04 Uradni list (2004) (Slovenian).

[322] Slovenia–Czechia, Succession Agreement, 35/1994 Uradni list (Slovenian).

[323] Slovenia–Japan, Succession Agreement, 8/1994 Uradni list (Slovenian).

[324] Agreement between Egypt and the FRY (23 November 2005) 12 Службени гласник (May 2006) 32, arts 1–2.

[325] E.g. – Exchange of Letters (Slovenia–United Kingdom) (28 May and 3 June 1998) Treaty Series No 39 (1998) Cmd 4046, 35.

[326] Multilateral Treaties (n 7) xiv. See further: Václav Mikulka, 'The Dissolution of Czechoslovakia and Succession in Respect of Treaties' in Mojmir Mrăk (ed) Succession of States (Kluwer 1999) 109, 111 (n 4).

[327] Ibid, xlviii.

[328] Ibid, xiv, xlviii.

[329] Mikulka (n 325) 111–18.

[330] E.g. – Agreement on the Succession to Treaties (Czechia–France) (19 June 1995) France Treaty Database, No TRA19950270 (French).

[331] E.g. – Exchange of Notes regarding Austrian–Czechoslovak Treaties (Austria–Slovakia) (14 January 1994) 1046 BGBl (28 December 1994) (German).

[332] E.g. – Note on Treaties (Argentina–Slovakia) (13 July 1995) Argentina Treaty Database No 5671 (Spanish).

[333] Agreement on Succession to Bilateral Treaties (Czechia–Colombia) (17 and 24 February 1997) Colombia Treaty Database No 043/97 (Spanish, Czecho-Slovak).

[334] E.g. – Exchange of Letters (Netherlands–Slovakia) (8 and 9 December 1994) 27 Tractatenblad (1995) (Dutch).

[335] E.g. – Protocol concerning Bilateral Treaties (Norway–Slovakia) (16 September 1994) Norway Treaty Database No 16-09-1994 No 1 Bilateral (Norwegian).

[336] E.g. – Exchange of Notes (Spain–Czechia) (21 March 1994 and 2 February 1995) 142 BOE (15 June 1995) 17846 (Spanish).

[337] E.g. – Exchange of Notes (Switzerland–Slovakia) (25 November 1994) Switzerland Treaty Database No 99990915 (German).

[338] Exchange of Notes (China–Czechia) (10 August 1994) China Treaty Database (Chinese).

[339] E.g. – Protocol (Romania–Czechia) (adopted 26 May 1995, entered into force 3 March 1997) 339 Monitorul Oficial (11 November 1996) art 1, annex I (Romanian).

[340] Exchange of Notes (United Kingdom–Czechia) (29 August & 16 September 1996) Treaty Series No 96 (1996) Cmd 3528 (January 1997) 8.

[341] E.g. – Protocol (Russia–Slovakia) (adopted 31 October 1995, entered into force 3 July 1996) Russia Treaty Database No 1995082, art 1, annex I (Russian).

Mexico,[342] and Australia.[343] The treaty database of Czechia lists many other Czechoslovak treaties in force with counterparties without including annotations on succession.

In its 1972 draft, the ILC had developed separate provisions dealing with dismemberment and secession.[344] In response to the comments of some Member States, the Commission decided that there was insufficient difference between the two situations to warrant the distinction.[345] The rule of presumptive automaticity in Article 34(1) of the VCSST for both classes has yet to find application in subsequent practice.[346]

This decision overlooks the possibility of incorporation by an existing State of a part of the territory of the predecessor in a dismemberment. Per the moving treaty frontiers rule, treaties of the predecessor cease to apply unless the successor succeed to a localized treaty. State practice for this rule comprises the dismemberment of the Trust Territory of Cameroon ('British Cameroons') in which the Northern Cameroons were incorporated by Nigeria on 1 June 1961[347] and the Southern Cameroons by Cameroon on 1 October 1961,[348] as well as the cession of the Northern Mariana Islands by the United States from the Trust Territory of the Pacific Islands on 9 January 1978.[349]

## 5.3.4 Cession

When one State cedes territory to another, the negative limb of the moving treaty frontiers rule provides that treaties applied to the ceded territory automatically cease to apply to it from the date of succession.[350] State practice evincing this rule includes:

---

[342] E.g. – Aerial Transport Convention (Mexico–Czechoslovakia) (adopted 14 August 1990, entered into force 4 February 1991) Mexico Treaty Database, Note 2 (Spanish).

[343] E.g. – Legal Proceedings Convention (Czechoslovakia–United Kingdom) (adopted 11 November 1924, entered into force 9 November 1933) [1933] ATS 2, Australia Treaty Database.

[344] ILC Articles (n 3) 264–65 (paras 19–20).

[345] Ibid, 265–66 (paras 21–33).

[346] Václav Mikulka, 'Article 34' in Distefano (n 9) 1153–207, 1191–207. The ICJ did not address its status in the *Gabčikovo-Nagymaros Project Case*, the *Bosnia Genocide Case*, or the *Croatia Genocide Case* – Andreas Zimmermann, 'The International Court of Justice and State Succession to Treaties: Avoiding Principled Answers to Questions of Principle' in Christian Tams and James Sloan (eds) *The Development of International Law by the International Court of Justice* (OUP 2013) 53–70, 60.

[347] The notifications of Cameroon and Nigeria make no mention of territorial limitation; e.g. – UN Doc C.N.78.1961.TREATIES-1 (24 July 1961) UN Archives Folder No 213 NIGE (January 1960–December 1963).

[348] E.g. – 'Succession of States in relation to general multilateral treaties of which the Secretary-General is depositary', UN Doc A/CN.4/150 (10 December 1962) para 58; 'Letters from Cameroon to the UN Secretariat dated 21 December 1961, 9 January 1962, 12 February 1962 & 1 March 1962' (French) UN Archives Folder No 213 CAMER.

[349] Note 73.

[350] Note 57.

176   SUCCESSION TO TREATIES

- the Sudetenland by Czecho-Slovakia to Germany (1938);[351]
- Newfoundland by the United Kingdom to Canada (1949);[352]
- Eritrea by Italy to Ethiopia (1952);[353]
- North Borneo, Sarawak, and Singapore by the United Kingdom to Malaysia (1963);[354]
- Ifni by Spain to Morocco (1969);[355]
- Hong Kong by the United Kingdom to China (1997);[356] and
- Macao by Portugal to China (1999).[357]

While a treaty thus ceases to apply to a ceded territory through the consent of the predecessor, a successor may succeed by notification or agreement to treaties that were localized to the ceded territory. Examples include the cessions of North Borneo, Sarawak and Singapore,[358] and Ifni.[359] *Opīniōnes juris* were expressed by on Ifni,[360] Newfoundland,[361] and Singapore.[362]

A special feature of a cession is its effect on bilateral treaties between the ceding State and the cessionaire. As the change to such treaties is typically semantic rather than substantive, they have been treated in practice as continuing in force. Following the cession of Singapore, for example, the British and Malaysian carriers continued to operate the routes through Singapore and Kuala Lumpur under the 1957 Anglo–Malayan aviation agreement.[363]

## 5.3.5 Secession

When a territory secedes from an existing State to become a new State, the successor may succeed by notification or agreement to eligible treaties of the

---

[351] Hackworth (n 269) 372–73.

[352] E.g. – Second Bilateral Treaties Study (n 251) paras 86–90, 93, 96, 100–101. See also: Hans Aufricht, 'State Succession under the Law and Practice of the International Monetary Fund' (1962) 11 ICLQ 154, 161–62.

[353] Antony Leriche, 'De l'application à l'Erythrée des obligations résultant des traités conclus par l'Ethiopie antérieurement à la Fédération' (1953) 57 RGDIP 262, 267.

[354] E.g. – 'Succession of States in respect of bilateral treaties: study prepared by the Secretariat' (28 May 1970) UN Doc A/CN.4/229 paras 116–25. See also: 'Selected Legal Opinions of the Secretariat of the United Nations' (1963) UNJY 178–79.

[355] Treaty on the Retrocession of Ifni (Spain–Morocco) (adopted 4 January 1969, entered into force 9 January 1971) BOE (5 June 1969) 8805, art 1 (Spanish).

[356] E.g. – *Multilateral Treaties* (n 7) vi–viii (n 2); Roda Mushkat, 'Hong Kong and Succession of Treaties' (1997) 46 ICLQ 181, 197.

[357] Ibid, viii–x (n 3).

[358] E.g. – *Treaties in Force* (n 254) 281.

[359] Agreement on Transfer of Responsibility for Tetuan and Nador Airports (Spain–Morocco) (16 March 1967) 1 SPTI 340 (Spanish).

[360] Treaty on the Retrocession of Ifni (n 354) art 1.

[361] AE Gotlieb, 'Canadian Practice in International Law during 1967' (1968) 6 CYIL 276.

[362] Second Bilateral Treaties Study (n 251) paras 122–23.

[363] Bilateral Treaties Study (n 353) para 110.

APPLICATION TO THE CLASSES OF SUCCESSION    177

predecessor. Extensive practice in support of this rule include the secessions of 35 colonial territories from the United Kingdom[364] and 20 colonial territories from France.[365] Other examples are the secessions of:

- Indonesia (1949);[366]
- the Democratic Republic of the Congo ('DRC', 1960);[367]
- Syria (1961);[368]
- Singapore (1965);[369]
- Bangladesh (1971);[370]
- Guinea-Bissau (1973);[371]
- Suriname (1975);[372]
- Mozambique (1975);[373]
- the 11 successors to the Soviet Union (1991);[374]
- Montenegro (2006);[375] and
- South Sudan (2011).[376]

While Equatorial Guinea, South Yemen ('South Arabia'), and Eritrea declined to succeed to any treaty, they expressed no *opinio juris* that they lacked the right to succeed. Affirmative *opiniones juris* have been expressed by Ireland,[377] the Central African

[364] E.g. – Bilateral Treaties Study (n 353) paras 84–86; Third Bilateral Treaties Study (n 253) paras 5–18, 138–48.

[365] E.g. – Second Bilateral Treaties Study (n 251) para 191; UN Doc C.N.45.1963.TREATIES-2 (22 March 1963); Charles Rousseau, 'Algérie et Suisse: Succession de l'Algérie aux conventions internationales sur les télécommunications' (1967) 38(3) RGDIP 724.

[366] E.g. – HF van Panhuys, 'La Succession de l'Indonesie aux Accords Internationaux conclus par les Pays-Bas avant l'Independence de l'Indonesie' (1959) 2 NTVIR 55.

[367] UNGA Sixth Committee, 1535th Meeting (n 25) paras 30–33; Célestin Nguya-Ndila, *Indépendance de la République Démocratique du Congo et les engagements internationaux antérieurs* (Université de Kinshasa 1971) 190–92.

[368] Richard Young, 'State of Syria: Old or New?' (1962) 56(2) AJIL 482, 486–87.

[369] E.g. – Second Bilateral Treaties Study (n 251) para 191.

[370] E.g. – UN Docs C.N.19.1978.TREATIES-1 (7 March 1978) C.N.20.1978.TREATIES-2 (7 March 1978).

[371] *Arbitral Award of 31 July 1989 (Guinea-Bissau v Senegal)* (Award) Arbitration Tribunal (31 July 1989) 83 ILR 1, 35–38; *Guinea – Guinea-Bissau Maritime Delimitation Case* (Award) Court of Arbitration (14 February 1985) 77 ILR 636, 657.

[372] E.g. – *Arbitration between Guyana and Suriname* (Award) PCA Case No 2004-04 (17 September 2007) 30 RIAA 1, paras 176–77, 312.

[373] E.g. – 'Relações com a África do Sul' Portugal Archives File 1928/74 Box 55350 (Portuguese). The South Africa treaty database lists four Portuguese bilateral treaties in force for Mozambique.

[374] E.g. – Hélène Hamant, *Démembrement de l'URSS et problèmes de succession d'États* (Bruylant 2007) 217–47, 390, 435–532; Zimmermann (n 272) 390–421; NV Dronova, 'The Dissolution of the Soviet Union in the light of the 1978 Vienna Convention on Succession of States in respect of Treaties' in Eisemann and Koskenniemi (n 271) 723–780; International Law Association, 'Preliminary Report on Succession of States to Treaties, Helsinki Conference (1996) 655–96.

[375] E.g. – 'Legal Obligations of Montenegro' (2007) 78 BYIL 673, 685.

[376] Convention on the Prohibition of Anti-Personnel Mines (adopted 18 September 1997, entered into force 1 March 1999) ('Succession: South Sudan') 2794 UNTS 210.

[377] JM Jones, 'State Succession in the Matter of Treaties' (1947) 14 BYIL 360, 367.

178  SUCCESSION TO TREATIES

Republic,[378] Italy,[379] and the Republic of Congo.[380]

Applying its broad definition of newly independent States as including colonial territories,[381] Articles 18, 24, and 34(1) of the VCSST provide for automatic succession for seceding territories in contrast to a rule of consent for newly independent States. The rule of automatic succession has not been applied in any subsequent case of succession, all of which have consistently applied the principle of consent in Articles 17 and 24 for newly independent States. While those provisions accurately reflect prior and subsequent practice, the misclassification of colonial territories as newly independent States resulted in a failure to distinguish between the secessions of colonies and the accessions to independence of protected States and Territories.

### 5.3.6  Accession to Independence

When a protected State or Territory accedes to independence, the successor may succeed by notification or agreement to treaties applied to the transferred territory by the protecting State.[382] When exercising their powers to apply treaties to protected States and Territories, protecting States have employed the formulæ 'on behalf of' for multilateral treaties and 'in the name of' for bilateral treaties.[383] While a protected State or Territory may succeed to these treaties by notification or agreement,[384] a rule of continuity applies to treaties that it concluded itself in exercise of powers delegated by the protecting State.[385] State practice on these rules of succession and continuity includes the accessions to independence of:

- Jordan;[386]
- Iceland;[387]

---

[378] *UN Materials on Succession of States* (1967) UN Doc ST/LEG/SER.B/14, 145.

[379] *Re Bottali* (n 241).

[380] *UN Materials* (n 377) 218; Bilateral Treaties Study (n 353) para 104; International Law Association, *The Effect of Independence on Treaties* (1965) 195.

[381] See Chapter 2.

[382] E.g. – ILA Handbook (n 379) 1, 370 (notes 9–10); Diplomatic Convention (Spain–Morocco) (11 February 1957) 63 BOE (4 March 1957) 1387 (Spanish); *Biria v Kiardo*, Supreme Court of Morocco (5 July 1967) 45 ILR 53, 55; International Opium Convention (adopted 23 January 1912, entered into force 28 June 1919) 8 LNTS 187, art 23, Status List < https://treaties.un.org/Pages/showDetails. aspx?objid=0800000280046862&clang=_en> accessed 5 January 2024 (Syria, Lebanon).

[383] E.g. – Charles Rousseau, *Principes généraux du droit international public* vol I (Pedone 1944) 331; Henri Rolin, 'La pratique des mandats internationaux' (1927) 4 RdC 497, 575–83.

[384] E.g. – 191 UNTS 409.

[385] E.g. – ILA Handbook (n 379) 374–75; Agreement on the Exchange of Planting Material (Malaya–Papua New Guinea) (26 November 1962) 453 UNTS 161; Manfred Lachs, 'Le développement et les fonctions des traités multilatéraux' (1957–II) 92 RdC 229, 259–60.

[386] Third Bilateral Treaties Study (n 253) para 22.

[387] ILC Articles (n 3) 261–62; André Gonçalves Pereira, *La succession d'États en matière de traité* (Pedone 1969) 68–69.

- Syria and the Lebanon;[388]
- Tunisia;[389]
- Morocco;[390] and
- Namibia.[391]

The sole example of a newly independent State that rejected both succession and continuity is Israel.[392] However, it expressed an *opinio juris* whereby its policy of accession to treaties was based not on a rejection of the legal rules but rather of its identity as the continuation of Mandatory Palestine.[393]

Whereas the definition of 'newly independent State' in the VCSST does not reflect customary international law,[394] the ILC had failed to identify the rule of continuity for protected States and Territories. An abortive draft Article 18 developed by the Special Rapporteur accurately expressed the rules of succession and continuity for these 'special cases'.[395] While Articles 17 and 24 of the VCSST articulate the consensual rule of succession for newly independent States, they omit the special rule of continuity for treaties concluded by the protected Territory.

## 5.4 The Process of Succession

Whereas the application of the basic principle of consent varies according to the particular dynamics of each class of succession, the rules concerning the process by which a succession is constituted are the same for each. There are no formalities with which a successor must comply to succeed to multilateral or bilateral treaties.

---

[388] E.g. – Whiteman (n 65); *Shehadeh et al v Commissioner of Prisons, Jerusalem*, Supreme Court of Palestine, 14 ILR 42, 42–43; *Cie d'assurances «La Baloise» v Cie Air France, Cie Air Liban*, Civil Court of Beirut (3 October 1958) (1960) 14 RFDA 92, 93–95.

[389] E.g. – Third Bilateral Treaties Study (n 253) paras 65–71; UN Doc C.N.152.1957.TREATIES-4 (18 November 1957); 'Letter from the UN Secretariat to Dr D.P. O'Connell' (11 December 1957) UN Archives Folder LE 213 (November 1957–December 1959).

[390] E.g. – *Treaties in Force* (n 254) 309–11; Third Bilateral Treaties Study (n 253) paras 62–64; *Guía de tratados* (n 315) 216.

[391] E.g. – Julio Fáundez, *Independent Namibia: Succession to Treaty Rights and Obligations* (UN Institute for Namibia 1989) 57–143; Marian Nash (ed) *Cumulative Digest of United States Practice in International Law: 1981–1988* book I (Office of the Legal Adviser 1993) 1203–207; PC Szasz, 'Succession to Treaties under the Namibian Constitution' in DW van Wyck, Marinus Wiechers, and Romaine Hill (eds) *Namibia: Constitutional and International Law Issues* (University of South Africa 1991) 65–80, 72–73. On twelve other Mandatory and Trust Territories, see: 'Succession of States to multilateral treaties: studies prepared by the Secretariat', UN Doc A/CN.4/200 (21 February 1968) para 171; O'Connell (n 40) 161, 227.

[392] E.g. – UNSG Depositary Practice (n 251) para 30.

[393] E.g. – 'Replies from Governments to Questionnaires of the International Law Commission', UN Doc A/CN.4/19 (23 March 1950) para 23; MC Bassiouni, *International Extradition: United States Law and Practice* (2014) 155–56.

[394] See Chapter 2.

[395] Humphrey Waldock, 'Fifth Report on succession in respect of treaties' UN Doc A/CN.4/256 (10 April 1972) 3.

180   SUCCESSION TO TREATIES

Controversial during the decolonization era, the doctrinal questions of the constitutive effect of a 'devolution agreement' between a predecessor and successor and a general declaration on succession have since been resolved. As the key issue in modern practice is the interpretation of ambiguity or silence, the role of general principles of law is suggested to be critical in the absence of clear proof of intention.

### 5.4.1 Formalities

While a successor must notify the depositary to a multilateral treaty of their succession in writing, there is no formality requirement for bilateral treaties. Succession agreements for bilateral treaties have usually been done in writing but oral agreements have also been concluded in rare cases.[396] Registration of succession agreements with the UN Secretariat is a requirement for the parties to invoke them before UN organs,[397] yet an omission to register does not invalidate them.[398]

It is a question of fact whether a successor or counterparty that notifies the other of the 'termination' of a bilateral treaty invokes a termination clause of the treaty or expresses a position that the treaty was never in force between them.[399] If the former, the termination enters into force in accordance with the notice period prescribed by the treaty;[400] if the latter, it is effective from the date of succession.[401] Whether the treaty was in force between the date of succession and the effective date of termination affects potential disputes in the interim.

### (a) Provisional Treaty Actions

A successor may succeed to a provisional treaty action completed by the predecessor (e.g.—initialling, signature, or exchange of instruments) which was not a definitive expression of consent to be bound but rather was conditional upon the completion of a subsequent action (e.g.—ratification, acceptance, or approval).[402] A paucity of State practice on this point in the early years of decolonization[403] has been filled by subsequent practice.[404]

---

[396] *UN Materials* (n 377) 211–13; Agreement on Treaties (Ghana–United States) (4 September and 21 December 1957) (adopted 12 February 1958, entered into force 12 September 1958) 442 UNTS 175.

[397] Charter of the United Nations, 26 June 1945 (entered into force 24 October 1945) 892 UNTS 119, art 102(2).

[398] VCLT (n 1) arts 2(1)(a), 80.

[399] E.g. – ILA Handbook (n 379) paras 25, 32, 38.

[400] Note 489.

[401] E.g. – Third Bilateral Treaties Study (n 253) paras 26, 54.

[402] VCLT (n 1) arts 12, 18(a); Cedric van Assche, 'Article 12 Convention of 1969' in Corten and Klein (n 27) vol I, 209–42.

[403] UNSG Depositary Practice (n 251) para 151.

[404] E.g. – *Multilateral Treaties* (n 7) xiv, xlviii, xxxii (n 1); Mikulka (n 325) 111 (n 4); *Treaties in Force* (n 254) 85–86; 1946 UNTS 156.

The succession applies only to the extent of the provisional action: it does not constitute definitive participation in the treaty. As for treaties not in force, a successor would succeed to the obligation not to defeat the object and purpose of the treaty prior to its entry into force.[405] The substantive rule expressed in the VCSST accurately expresses the customary rule.[406]

## (b) Reservations

A successor may succeed by notification to a reservation made by the predecessor. State practice was sparse at the time of the conclusion of the VCSST[407] but has since gestated.[408] Affirmative *opiniones juris* were expressed by Tanganyika, Uganda, Zambia, and many others.[409] The doctrinal issue that has arisen is the interpretation of silence by the successor concerning a reservation.[410]

While State practice in the early decolonization period was vague,[411] four approaches to a predecessor's reservation were taken in subsequent practice:

1. successors reproduced the reservation in their notifications of succession, sometimes in modified form;[412]
2. successors claimed succession to the reservation to which they added new reservations;[413]
3. successors omitted the reservation from their notifications but subsequently informed the depositary that they would not succeed to it;[414] and
4. successors formulated new reservations without mentioning the reservation and so the depositary did not list the reservation.[415]

This practice shows that a successor, if omitting a predecessor's reservation when making its notification of succession, is nevertheless to be understood by the depositary as implicitly claiming succession to the reservation unless otherwise notified.[416] When a successor formulates a new reservation without mentioning the reservation, however, the depositary is to construe this as implicitly disclaiming succession.

---

[405] VCLT (n 1) art 18.

[406] VCSST (n 4) arts 19(1) 19(3) 33(1) 33(2) 37(1) 37(2).

[407] E.g. – Multilateral Treaties Study (n 41) paras 138, 228–29.

[408] 'Reservations to treaties in the context of succession of States: memorandum by the Secretariat' (6 May 2009) UN Doc A/CN.4/616, paras 53–69.

[409] Second Waldock Report (n 5) 65.

[410] ILC Articles (n 3) 225 (paras 11–12).

[411] Multilateral Treaties Study (n 41) paras 86–92.

[412] *Multilateral Treaties* (n 7) 84, 136, 149, 166, 376, 379, 389, 390, 631; Secretariat Reservations Memorandum (n 407) paras 57–60, 67–69.

[413] Ibid, 398.

[414] Third Waldock Report (n 29) 48–50.

[415] E.g. – *Multilateral Treaties* (n 7) 396, 398; 683 UNTS 315; UN Doc C.N.112.1978.TREATIES-7 (22 May 1978).

[416] Third Waldock Report (n 29) 48–49.

182    SUCCESSION TO TREATIES

While State practice on succession to an objection by the predecessor to a reservation was also 'sparse',[417] subsequent practice has been affirmative.[418] *Opiniones juris* have been expressed by Slovakia, the FRY, and Montenegro.[419] Though likewise rare, practice has also recognized the right of counterparties to object to a reservation to which a successor succeeds.[420] This is consistent with the 'flexible system' of the VCLT and the customary law of treaties,[421] whereby an objection may be made to reservations in other contexts.[422]

In providing for a default rule of succession to a reservation amid silence, the right to formulate a new reservation, and the right of objection by counterparties, Article 20 of the VCSST provisions accurately reflects State practice.[423] Its restriction of the presumption of succession to reservations to the category of 'newly independent States', however, is inconsistent with the practice, which does not distinguish among classes of succession.[424] While the VCSST omits succession to objections, leaving the matter to be regulated by the law of treaties,[425] the practice shows it to be permitted.

### (c) Treaties not in Force

A successor may succeed to a treaty action of the predecessor with respect to a treaty that was not yet in force at the date of succession. In such cases, the succession applies to the extent of the action completed by the predecessor: for example, a successor may succeed to a ratification that was applied to the transferred territory.[426] The successor is bound by the duty not to defeat the object and purpose of the treaty.[427]

However, a successor may not succeed as *party* to a treaty for which the predecessor had not expressed its consent to be bound.[428] Though not obliged to do so,[429] it may succeed to a treaty action expressing consent to be bound

---

[417] E.g. – ILC Articles (n 3) 225–26 (para 13); Buzzini, 'Article 20' in Distefano (n 9) 765–66, 772–77.

[418] *Multilateral Treaties* (n 7) 95, 97, 112, 116, 257.

[419] Ibid, xxxii, xlviii, liii.

[420] Ibid, 111–12, 129, 152, 167–71.

[421] VCLT (n 1) arts 20(4)(b) 21(3); Daniel Müller, 'Article 20 Convention of 1969' in Corten and Klein (n 27) vol I, 489–534, 495–98, 525–34.

[422] Buzzini (n 416) 761–67.

[423] Ibid, 735–77, 740–42, 770–77; Alain Pellet, 'Sixteenth Report on Reservations to Treaties', UN Doc A/CN.4/626 (19 March 2010) paras 11–28.

[424] ILC, Guide to Practice on Reservations to Treaties 2011 (2011) ILC Yearbook vol II, Part Two, guidelines 5.1.1(1)–(2) 5.1.2(1) 5.1.6; Pellet (n 422) paras 38–40.

[425] ILC Articles (n 3) 225–226; Secretariat Reservations Memorandum (n 407) paras 26–40.

[426] E.g. – 'Succession to general multilateral treaties' (n 347) para 143; Second Bilateral Treaties Study (n 251) 148.

[427] VCLT (n 1) art 18.

[428] E.g. – Multilateral Treaties Study (n 41) paras 181, 183, 185.

[429] E.g. – *UN Materials* (n 377) 193–194; *Medusa Oil and Gas Limited v Montenegro* (Award on Jurisdiction) PCA Case No 2015-39 (UNCITRAL) (17 July 2019) (unpublished) in LE Peterson, 'Veeder-chaired tribunal declines jurisdiction over unusual claim where investor sought to use MFN, domestic law, and unilateral declarations of state to circumvent unratified BIT' IA Reporter (1 August 2019).

(e.g.—ratification).[430] It may not succeed to treaties that were terminated prior to the succession, such as a treaty that was suspended and not revived[431] or a treaty that had been applied to the transferred territory but was superseded by another treaty.[432] Save insofar as they omit bilateral treaties,[433] Articles 18, 32, and 36 of the VCSST reflect State practice in providing that a newly independent State, seceding State, absorbing State, or merging State may succeed by notification to a multilateral treaty not in force unless it would be incompatible with that treaty.

## 5.4.2 General Agreements on Succession

A doctrinal issue arising from decolonization practice was the legal effect of general agreements concerning succession to treaties concluded by a successor with a predecessor or a third State. On the one hand, it was questionable whether a general agreement concluded without the participation of a treaty counterparty could bind that State. On the other hand, it was doubtful whether a general agreement was sufficiently precise to identify the treaties that it purported to cover. These considerations applied with particular force when a general agreement on succession was concluded without accurate information being available to the successor concerning the treaties applied to the transferred territory.

### (a) Devolution Agreements

A succession agreement on treaties between a predecessor and a successor ('devolution agreement') envisages a transfer of treaty rights and obligations applied to the transferred territory.[434] It may be enacted by the predecessor through internal legislation[435] or an agreement concluded between the predecessor and representatives of the transferred territory[436] from the date of succession.[437] The devolution agreement can be a discrete instrument or a part of a broader succession agreement.[438]

---

[430] E.g. – Second Bilateral Treaties Study (n 251) paras 138–43, 192; *MacKinnon v Air-France*, Court of First Instance of the Seine (10 April 1964) (1965) 11 AFDI 949 (French).

[431] E.g. – *X and Y v Government of the Canton of Zurich*, Federal Supreme Court of Switzerland (22 November 2005) ORIL ILDC 340 (CH 2005) paras H7–H10, A2–A8.

[432] E.g. – UNSG Depositary Practice (n 251) para 150; Bardonnet (n 61) 444–70.

[433] ILC Articles (n 3) 218–20, 259–60, 267.

[434] Second Waldock Report (n 5) 54.

[435] E.g. – Indian Independence (International Arrangements) Order 1947, 3 CILC 144; UNGA Res 392(V) (15 December 1950) 1–2.

[436] E.g. – Treaty on Burmese Independence (Burma–United Kingdom) (adopted 17 October 1947, entered into force 4 January 1948) 70 UNTS 183, art 2.

[437] Treaties concluded after the date of succession are invariably done with retroactive effect, e.g. – Ceylon, Morocco, Ghana, Somalia, Nigeria, Sierra Leone, Trinidad and Tobago, Western Samoa, Jamaica, Malta, the Gambia, and the Seychelles.

[438] For example, those for the DRC, Equatorial Guinea, and South Sudan.

184 SUCCESSION TO TREATIES

Early examples of devolution agreements were the accessions to independence of Iraq in 1935 and Jordan in 1948.[439] While different formulae and instruments were employed, the standard British template came to be the exchange of notes with Malaya providing for a transfer of treaty 'rights, benefits, obligations and responsibilities'.[440] Other examples of devolution agreements concerned Indonesia,[441] Laos,[442] Morocco,[443] Côte d'Ivoire,[444] Somalia,[445] Singapore,[446] and Ifni.[447] Obligations of successors varied considerably, such as:

- to provisionally continue the implementation of treaties in force;[448]
- to assume 'all international obligations and responsibilities' applied to it;[449]
- to make a declaration on succession to treaties;[450] or
- to preserve in force specified treaties (e.g.—delimitation treaties).[451]

However, a duty for the successor to succeed to treaties might be qualified by a stipulation that it would 'formally associate or disassociate' itself from those commitments 'as soon as possible thereafter'.[452] A duty may be prescribed for the predecessor is to facilitate accession to treaties or international organizations.[453]

A problem of interpretation is the availability of verified lists of treaties applied to the transferred territory. For example, the United Kingdom sought to provide successors with a collated list of treaties that was not annexed to devolution agreements but furnished separately. Due to administrative mistakes made over decades and centuries, the United Kingdom often cautioned the successor against relying upon the completeness of the lists—though they were generally accurate insofar as the included treaties were concerned.[454] Successors have not always had the resources to undertake an exhaustive study.[455]

---

[439] O'Connell (n 40) 359.

[440] Succession Agreement (United Kingdom–Malaya) (12 September 1957) 279 UNTS 288.

[441] Round-Table Conference Agreements (Netherlands–Indonesia) (2 November 1949) 69 UNTS (1950) 200.

[442] Treaty of Friendship (France–Laos) (22 October 1953) 155 BFSP 658, arts 1, 7 (French).

[443] Diplomatic Accord (France–Morocco) (28 May 1956) (1957) 51 AJIL 679, art 11.

[444] Whiteman (n 65) 983.

[445] Agreement (Italy–Somalia) (1 July 1960) in Law No 367 (1 February 1962) 148 Gazzetta Ufficiale (13 June 1962).

[446] Independence of Singapore Agreement (Malaysia–Singapore) (7 August 1965) 4 ILM 928, art 13.

[447] Note 354.

[448] E.g. – Treaty of Alliance (United Kingdom–Transjordan) (adopted 22 March 1946, entered into force 25 May 1946) 6 UNTS 144, art 8(2).

[449] E.g. – Treaty on the Independence of Cyprus (16 August 1960) 382 UNTS 8, art 8.

[450] Memorandum on Independence for South Arabia (National Front for the Liberation of Southern Yemen–United Kingdom) (29 November 1967) 169 BFSP 136, para 8.

[451] E.g. – Memorandum on Legal Succession concerning the former USSR (6 July 1992) (1993) 26 RBDI 627, arts 1–3 (French).

[452] Note 443.

[453] E.g. – Third Bilateral Treaties Study (n 253) para 60.

[454] E.g. – Replies from Governments to Questionnaires (n 392) paras 19–22.

[455] E.g. – Maung Maung, *Burma's Constitution* (Springer 1961) 208.

In this context, the key doctrinal problem was whether devolution agreements constitute succession in themselves. While the early practice of the UN Secretariat was to revise status lists according to registered devolution agreements, the failure of agreements to list the relevant treaties and the subsequent denial of succession to particular treaties by certain successors prompted the Secretariat to solicit notification for each treaty.[456] A devolution agreement can be treated by the Secretariat as equating to notification 'if the treaties concerned were clearly and specifically identified'.[457]

For bilateral treaties, State practice has shown devolution agreements to have no constitutive effect. There are many examples of successors with devolution agreements that nevertheless considered it to be necessary to conclude succession agreements with the respective counterparties[458] or that have denied constitutive effect in their subsequent practice.[459] Affirmative *opiniones juris* asserting devolution agreements as lacking constitutive effect were expressed by the United Kingdom,[460] Indonesia,[461] Côte d'Ivoire,[462] Argentina,[463] Nigeria,[464] and Thailand.[465] While Laos and Myanmar[466] considered their devolution agreements to be constitutive for bilateral treaties, they accepted the negative views of counterparties.

Article 8(1) of the VCSST accurately articulates the lack of constitutive effect for devolution agreements.[467] While the ILC cited the third-party rule of the law of treaties,[468] State practice has shown successors to consider themselves to be free to formulate policy on a treaty-by-treaty basis. An open question is whether the general principle of estoppel can effect a succession if a third State can demonstrate its reliance on the devolution agreement to its detriment.[469]

There are examples of States including treaties in their published lists and citing the devolution agreements[470] but no case of the devolution agreement being successfully invoked by a counterparty in the face of opposition by the successor.[471] A rare, though abortive, example of enforcement took place in the *F. OABV* conciliation in which France argued that Morocco had been party to the 1944

---

[456] UNSG Depositary Practice (n 251) paras 14, 28–29.
[457] Ibid, para 310.
[458] *UN Materials* (n 377) 211–13, 220–24.
[459] Ibid, 189, 192.
[460] Ibid, 188–89.
[461] Ibid, 37–38, 186.
[462] Bilateral Treaties Study (n 353) para 103.
[463] *UN Materials* (n 377) 6–7.
[464] Ibid, 181.
[465] *Temple of Preah Vihear* (n 181) vol II (Pleadings) 33.
[466] *UN Materials* (n 377) 180–81, 188–89.
[467] ILC Articles (n 3) 182–87.
[468] Ibid, 184–87 (paras 8–19); Assier Garrido-Muñoz, 'Article 8' in Distefano (n 9) 261, 270–73.
[469] VCLT (n 1) art 36; Pierre d'Argent, 'Article 36 Vienna Convention' in Corten and Klein (n 27) vol I, 929–40.
[470] ILA Handbook (n 379) 99–100, 386; *Treaties in Force* (n 254) 202–06.
[471] Second Bilateral Treaties Study (n 251) paras 138–43; *Sanum v Laos* (n 86) paras 254–68.

# 186    SUCCESSION TO TREATIES

Chicago Convention through their devolution agreement.[472] The denunciation by Indonesia of its succession agreement with the Netherlands in 1956[473] had no effect on its own policy concerning treaty succession.[474]

## (b)  Agreements of Provisional Application

A successor may continue to apply a treaty to its territory for a limited time without definitively succeeding to it.[475] This has been done for a variety of reasons, including:

- 'standstill agreements' pending the absorption of the successor;[476]
- to decline succession as general policy, yet temporarily apply specific treaties;[477]
- to prevent services from being suddenly withdrawn;[478]
- to enable treaties to expire upon completion of performance;[479]
- to preserve continuity pending the completion of formalities for new agreements;[480] or
- to maintain the existing situation pending a review of the treaties in force[481] or negotiations with counterparties.[482]

While provisional application agreements are more frequently applied to bilateral treaties, they can also be done on a bilateral basis between a successor and a party to a multilateral treaty.[483] Such agreements are revocable at will or terminate on the expiry of a time limit, whether expressed as a fixed period or implied by reference to an event (e.g.—the conclusion of negotiations on succession).[484] Time limits may be subsequently extended or the treaty allowed to lapse with its expiry.[485]

The parties can intend definitive succession even when using qualified language.[486] Their intention can also change over time: for example, they might

---

[472] *L'affaire du F. OABV* (n 129) 285.

[473] E.g. - ILA Handbook (n 379) 193–94.

[474] E.g. - O'Connell (n 40) 138–139, 203, 207, 208, 225.

[475] E.g. - Case No 7Ob573/93 (n 510).

[476] E.g. - *Babu Ram Saksena v The State* (1950) SCR 573; (1950) ILR 11.

[477] E.g. - *UN Materials* (n 377) 42 (n 1) 229.

[478] E.g. - ILA Handbook (n 379) 382–86.

[479] E.g. - *UN Materials* (n 377) 223–24, 231.

[480] E.g. - FRY (n 323).

[481] E.g. - Montenegro (n 374).

[482] E.g. - Zimmermann (n 279) 87, 92; Helmut Tichy, 'Two Recent Cases of State Succession – An Austrian Perspective' (1992) 44 AJPIL 117, 125; Third Bilateral Treaties Study (n 39) para 47.

[483] E.g. - Bilateral Treaties Study (n 353) paras 75–80; Agreement regarding certain Treaties (United States–Malawi) (17 December 1966, 6 January 1967 & 4 April 1967) 692 UNTS 191.

[484] E.g. - Second Bilateral Treaties Study (n 251) paras 71–78; *VJ v Czech Social Security Administration*, Supreme Administrative Court of Czechia (28 November 2008) ORIL ILDC 1406 (CZ 2008), paras F1–F2, H1–H2, A1–A4 ('Armenia').

[485] E.g. - Bilateral Treaties Study (n 353) paras 90–91; Second Bilateral Treaties Study (n 251) paras 62–63.

[486] E.g. - Third Bilateral Treaties Study (n 253) para 37.

intend at the point of agreement for it to be provisional and subsequently agree to extend the period to facilitate negotiation[487] or to prolong it indefinitely.[488] In cases when the counterparties decide to continue a treaty pending the conclusion of a replacement, it is a question of fact whether their agreement was implicitly conditional upon the completion of planned negotiations.[489] This is important to determine whether any requirement of notice under the treaty applies.[490]

The key doctrinal issue is the distinction between an agreement of 'provisional' continuity versus definitive succession. This is illustrated by the initial agreements between the United States and Trinidad and Tobago in 1961 to provisionally continue the Anglo-American aviation agreement for 11 months, whereupon they further agreed to indefinitely extend their agreement 'until [it is] superseded by other mutually agreed arrangements'.[491] As the second agreement was indefinite, it was an agreement of succession rather than an extension of the time limit for provisional application.[492]

When a time limit is applied but continuity is stated to be provisional upon the conclusion of a new treaty without reference to planned negotiations, the case is one of succession because the continuity is indefinite and unconditional. For example, the agreement of Thailand and Malaya in 1959 to continue the 1911 Anglo–Thai extradition treaty 'pending the conclusion of an Extradition Treaty between ... Malaya and ... Thailand' remains in force to the present day.[493] As for a case of definitive succession,[494] amendments can be made to adjust the treaty to new conditions (e.g.—carriers and routes in air transport agreements).

Article 28 of the VCSST provides that a newly independent State may agree with a counterparty to provisionally apply a bilateral treaty in force by express agreement or conduct.[495] Save insofar as it overlooks the possibility of implied agreement and bilateral agreements for multilateral treaties, Article 28 accurately articulates State practice. However, the requirement in Article 29 of 'reasonable notice'—defined as 12 months from the date of receipt—unless otherwise provided by the treaty or special agreement has not been evinced by prior or subsequent practice.[496]

---

[487] E.g. – Succession Agreement (Norway–Montenegro) (31 October 2011) Norway Treaty Database 31-10-2011 No 43 Bilateral (Norwegian).

[488] ILA Handbook (n 379) 193, 369; Exchange of Notes (Thailand–Malaya) (27 October 1959) Thailand Treaty Database; France–Slovenia (n 307) annexe II; Investment Agreement (France–Slovenia) (11 February 1998) France Treaty Database No TRA19980010, art 12 (French, Slovenian).

[489] Ibid,– 192–93.

[490] E.g.– Second Bilateral Treaties Study (n 251) paras 122–23.

[491] E.g. – UN Materials (n 377) 220–21; Air Transport Agreement (United States–Trinidad and Tobago) (23 May 1990) 2207 UNTS 229, preamble.

[492] E.g. – Exchange of Notes (Switzerland–Malawi) (6 January 1967 and 16 December 1967) Switzerland Treaty Database, No 0.353.953.2 (French, German, Italian).

[493] Exchange of Notes (Thailand–Malaysia) (27 October 1959) Thailand Treaty Database.

[494] E.g. – ILA Handbook (n 379) 209–10, 379–80; Continued Application of certain Agreements (Jamaica–United States) (25 October and 29 November 1962) TIAS 5244.

[495] Elodie Tranchez, 'Article 28' in Distefano (n 99) 989–1011.

[496] ILC Articles (n 3) 246–48; Sandra Krähenmann, 'Article 29' in Distefano (n 9) 1011–29.

188    SUCCESSION TO TREATIES

### 5.4.3  General Declarations on Succession

Starting from the famous 'Nyerere Doctrine' espoused by Tanganyika in 1961,[497] a doctrinal issue was the legal effect of a general declaration on succession to treaties. Such declarations were invariably made by means of a letter addressed to the UN Secretary-General with a request for dissemination to the Member States in his role as chief administrative officer.[498] The purpose of such declarations was typically to enable a successor to collate and review the treaties applied to its territory,[499] potentially with the assistance of a third State.[500]

The difficulty lay in the apparent power of a successor to unilaterally determine the fate of treaties applied to the transferred territory, regardless of third States' views.[501] While this concern prompted the ILC to deny legal effect, this overlooked a significant difference between declarations of provisional application—a time-limited period of review—and declarations of definitive succession. Declarations of provisional application were not treated by depositaries as having constitutive effect[502] but rather, on their own terms,[503] as an offer by a successor to apply a multilateral treaty on a bilateral basis unless a counterparty object.[504] In contrast, declarations of succession have been treated by depositaries as notifications to multilateral treaties while they have no constitutive effect for bilateral treaties in themselves.

A declaration of succession could appear in the internal law of a successor, such as declarations of independence,[505] constitutions,[506] statutory laws,[507] and parliamentary resolutions.[508] State practice has shown these instruments not to constitute succession because 'notification' to counterparties is not achieved[509] unless

---

[497]  Seaton and Maiti (n 253) 76–85.

[498]  Second Waldock Report (n 5) 66; *Croatia Genocide* (n 135).

[499]  E.g. – Letters from Rwanda (18 February 1963) and Burundi (1 February 1963) in UN Archives, 'State Succession to Treaty Rights and Obligations: Kingdom of Burundi', Folder No 213 BURU (January 1960–December 1963).

[500]  E.g. – UNGA Sixth Committee, 1545th Meeting (n 104) para 17.

[501]  E.g. – Second Waldock Report (n 5) 63.

[502]  E.g. – UN Archives, 'State Succession to Treaty Rights and Obligations: Mauritius', File No 18016, 222 MAURS (March 1968–October 1970); UNSG Depositary Practice (n 251) paras 303–07; *UN Materials* (n 377) 181–82.

[503]  *UN Materials* (n 377) paras 177–78; *UN Materials on Succession of States: Supplement*, UN Doc A/CN.4/263 (29 May 1972) 27–28, 45–46, 50–51, 53–54.

[504]  E.g. – JA Boyd, *Digest of United States Practice in International Law 1977* (Office of the Legal Adviser 1979) 394–95; Martin Leich (ed) *Digest of United States Practice in International Law 1980* (Office of the Legal Adviser 1986) 35; Nash (n 390) 254–62.

[505]  E.g. – Tuerk (n 559) para 22; Ortega Terol (n 283) 903–907.

[506]  E.g. – *Arnbjornsdottir-Mendler* (n 239); Maung (n 454) art 227; *UN Materials* (n 377) 145–46.

[507]  E.g. – Bilateral Treaties Study (n 353) paras 90–91; Third Bilateral Treaties Study (n 253) para 56; Whiteman (n 65) 987.

[508]  E.g. – *X and Y* (n 430) para A6.

[509]  For example, the declaration of Slovakia was omitted from its letter to the UN Member States – Constitution of Slovakia (1 September 1992) 460/1992 Coll Pravne Predpisy, art 153 (Czecho-Slovak); Letter from Czechoslovakia (n 527) annexe II.

communicated.[510] For example, the Supreme Court of Austria relied on the general declaration of succession to treaties by Croatia in its declaration of independence to find the 1954 Austro–Yugoslav legal assistance treaty to remain in effect[511] but Croatia omitted the treaty from a 1997 law publishing a list of 17 bilateral treaties with Austria to which it considered itself to have succeeded.[512]

## (a) Provisional Application

General declarations of provisional application can be made by successors to which counterparties acquiesce in the absence of objection. There are three variants of this practice:

- termination on expiry of a stipulated time limit unless succession be done by notification or agreement;[513]
- presumed succession to treaties in the absence of notification of termination;[514] or
- provisional application pending notification of succession or termination.[515]

Counterparties may reciprocally rely on these declarations during their period of application by estoppel. Although there is extensive practice of successors subsequently succeeding to treaties covered by such declarations,[516] either party can terminate provisional application by notification.

Article 27 of the VCSST provides that notification of provisional application of a multilateral treaty may be given by a newly independent State, which is effective for any counterparty agreeing expressly or by conduct unless incompatible with the treaty.[517] Save insofar as it is restricted to newly independent States, this provision accurately expresses State practice. On the critical issue of the application of the doctrine of acquiescence to interpret the silence of a counterparty, paragraphs 1

---

[510] E.g. – Bilateral Treaties Study (n 353) para 45; UNSG Depositary Practice (n 251) para 43; Gamarra (n 528) 408.

[511] Case No 2Ob69/92, Supreme Court of Austria (16 December 1992) (German). The Court found the same treaty not to be in force for North Macedonia, which had made no declaration: Case No 7Ob573/93, Supreme Court of Austria (6 October 1993) (German).

[512] Narodne Novine 1997/1/5 (Serbo-Croatian).

[513] The Tanganyika template was applied by Uganda (1962), Burundi (1964), Malawi (1964), Botswana (1966), Lesotho (1967), Nauru (1968), Kenya (1971), Zimbabwe (1981), Brunei (1984), and Micronesia (1992) – ILC Articles (n 3) 188–91.

[514] The 1965 declaration of Zambia became the model rather than those of Rwanda and Madagascar – ibid, 190, 191; *UN Materials* (n 377) 233. It was applied by Guyana (1966), Barbados (1967), Mauritius (1968), Fiji (1970), Tonga (1970), the Bahamas (1973), Grenada (1974), Suriname (1975), Solomon Islands (1978), Tuvalu (1978), Kiribati (1979), Saint Lucia (1979), Saint Vincent and the Grenadines (1979), Antigua and Barbuda (1981), Belize (1982), Dominica (1982), and Saint Kitts and Nevis (1983).

[515] Originated by Eswatini ('Swaziland') in 1968, this was applied by Papua New Guinea (1975) and Palau (1994) – ibid, 191; *Treaties in Force* (n 254) 354; *Multilateral Treaties* (n 7) xxxiv.

[516] E.g. – ILA Handbook (n 379) 374–75, 386–89; Bilateral Treaties Study (n 353) paras 67–69.

[517] ILC Articles (n 3) 245–246.

190    SUCCESSION TO TREATIES

and 3 correctly express this position through the words use of the words 'by reason of its conduct is to be considered as having so agreed'.[518]

## (b) Succession

A successor may make a general declaration to all counterparties of succession to the relevant treaties applied to the transferred territory. Such declarations were made for the mergers forming the UAR,[519] Tanzania,[520] and Yemen.[521] Unlike general declarations of provisional application, these declarations contained no qualifier and so were treated as definitive notifications of succession by the UN Secretary-General in his depositary functions.[522] An exception was the declaration of Czechia, which was couched in terms of definitive succession, yet was soon followed by notifications for specific treaties.[523]

There is no recorded example of a counterparty to bilateral treaties objecting to these declarations of succession.[524] While Article 9(1) of the VCSST denies succession to treaties 'by reason only of the fact that the successor State has made a unilateral declaration', the cited practice[525] comprised declarations of provisional application but overlooked the general declarations of the UAR and Tanzania.[526] As the declaration of succession by Yemen was generally recognized, Article 9(1) does not accurately reflect State practice.[527]

## (c) Time Limit

The key difference between general declarations of provisional application and definitive succession is the stipulation by a successor of a time limit for the former but not the latter. In the absence of a specified time period, however, a declaration must be interpreted in light of subsequent conduct to determine whether it was intended to be one of provisional application or definitive succession. The general declaration of Czechia,[528] for example, was one of provisional application because it subsequently considered itself not to have succeeded to each treaty of Czecho-Slovakia but rather issued specific notifications of succession to depositaries without succeeding to each treaty action.[529]

---

[518] Marco Pertile, 'Article 27' in Distefano (n 9) 963–87, 986–87.

[519] Note 251.

[520] Note 253.

[521] Note 255.

[522] UNSG Depositary Practice (n 251) para 48; Zimmermann (n 272) 284.

[523] *Multilateral Treaties* (n 7) xiv, xlviii; Mikulka (n 325) 111 (n 4).

[524] Zimmermann (n 272) 285 (Yemen). Treaty lists published by Argentina, Czechia, Russia, Switzerland, the United Kingdom, the Netherlands, and the United States include treaties concluded with its predecessors.

[525] ILC Articles (n 3) 187–93.

[526] Ibid, 255–57.

[527] *Soornack Nandanee* (n 248).

[528] UN Doc A/47/848 (31 December 1992) annexe I.

[529] Yolanda Gamarra, 'Current Questions of State Succession Relating to Multilateral Treaties' in Eisemann and Koskenniemi (n 271) 387–436, 408; Mikulka (n 325) 111–18.

The Tanganyika and Eswatini variations of provisional application[530] specify a precise time period for expiry, which can be extended.[531] However, a failure to convey a decision within the time limit results in the succession or termination of the treaty according to the terms of the declaration, as occurred for Uganda[532] and Lesotho.[533] Although the Zambia variation[534] specifies no time period, the time limit has been regarded in practice (e.g.—Zambia,[535] Suriname,[536] Tuvalu,[537] Belize,[538] and the Bahamas[539]) as being the completion of the period of internal review whereupon succession is constituted in the absence of objection by either party.

Article 29 of the VCSST states that provisional application of a multilateral treaty expires by reasonable notice of 12 months or notice given of the intention of the successor not to succeed to the treaty unless otherwise agreed or provided by the treaty.[540] It is not known whether the default period of 12 months specified in paragraph 3 has been followed in in subsequent practice.[541]

## 5.4.4 The Interpretation of Silence

When a successor notifies a counterparty of its intention to provisionally apply or definitively succeed to a treaty, the legal effect of silence by the counterparty is engaged. Conversely, the question arises whether a counterparty might invoke a treaty when a successor fail to take further action after provisionally applying it. In these situations, it is suggested that the general principles of acquiescence and estoppel apply, which 'follow from the fundamental principles of good faith and

---

[530] nn 512 and 514. See also: Note on the Treaties of Nauru (4 April 1973) Argentina Treaty Database No 7353 (Spanish).

[531] 'Succession to Treaty Rights and Obligations: Nauru' UN Archives Folder 18018 (1 January 1968–31 December 1971).

[532] *Treaties in Force* (n 254) 452–53.

[533] Bilateral Treaties Study (n 353) paras 92–93.

[534] Note 513.

[535] Note 398. The 1931 Anglo-American extradition treaty was held to apply to Zambia, relying on an affirmative opinion of the State Department and the declaration of Zambia in September 1965 – *Extradition of Zwagendaba Jère*, District Court for the District of Columbia (29 March 1966) in O'Connell (n 40) 115 (n 1). The treaty is still listed – *Treaties in Force* (n 254) 494.

[536] *In re R*, Court of Appeal of The Hague (6 July 1976) 74 ILR 115, 116.

[537] Leich (n 503) 35; *Multilateral Treaties* (n 7) 130 (n 12).

[538] *Treaties in Force* (n 254) 36.

[539] *Bowe* (n 188).

[540] ILC Articles (n 3) 248–52.

[541] *Treaties in Force* (n 254) 50, 303, 482, 491. The United States lists provisionally applied treaties as 'under review' – ibid, 458–61, 486–87; *Platko* (n 227); ED Williamson and JE Osborn, 'A US Perspective on Treaty Succession and Related Issues in the Wake of the Break-up of the USSR and Yugoslavia' (1992) 33 VJIL 261, 264–67. On South Viet Nam, see: JA Boyd (ed) *Digest of United States Practice in International Law 1976* (Office of the Legal Adviser 1977) 220–21; *Kasterova v United States*, US Eleventh Circuit Court of Appeals (2004) 365 F 3d 980, 982–84.

192  SUCCESSION TO TREATIES

equity'.[542] Though written for the VCLT with respect to the validity and termination of treaties,[543] they can also extend to the operability of treaties by succession because they engage the same doctrinal issue of the interpretation of the conduct of one State in order to evaluate the status of a treaty with respect to another State.[544]

## (a) Acquiescence

A State that omits to object within a reasonable period of time to a claim asserted by another State is deemed to have implicitly consented to it.[545] The rule has been applied in practice to treaty succession for omissions:

- by a counterparty to object to a notification of succession to bilateral treaties;[546]
- by a successor to object to a notification by a counterparty that the successor has succeeded[547] or not succeeded;[548] and
- by a counterparty to object to an extension of territorial application of the existing treaties of a successor.[549]

After Montenegro sent two *notes verbales* to Russia on succession to the 1995 Russian–Yugoslav bilateral investment treaty, the Arbitral Tribunal in the *Deripaska v Montenegro* arbitration found there to have been no succession agreement because the Montenegrin notes were vague and the Russian reply to the second note ambivalent.[550]

## (b) Estoppel

A State may not renege on 'a statement or representation made by one party to another and reliance upon it by that other party to its detriment or to the advantage of the party making it'.[551] Examples of States arguing that a notification by a successor or counterparty bound the notifying State include the invocation by the United

---

[542] *Delimitation of the Gulf of Maine Area (Canada v United States of America)* [1984] ICJ Rep 305, para 130.

[543] VCLT (n 1) art 45(b).

[544] ILC Articles (n 3) 240 (paras 17–18); *UN Conference* (n 390) vol III, 134, 174; Rietiker (n 9) 53–56.

[545] E.g. – *Temple of Preah Vihear (Cambodia v Thailand)* (Merits) [1962] ICJ Rep 6, 21 31; *Gulf of Maine Area* (n 541) para 130; *Pedra Branca/Pulau Batu Puteh, Middle Rocks and South Ledge (Singapore v Malaysia)* [2008] ICJ Rep 12, para 121.

[546] Note 218.

[547] E.g. – Second Bilateral Treaties Study (n 251) para 64.

[548] *VJ* (n 483).

[549] E.g. – East Germany (n 81).

[550] *Oleg Deripaska v Montenegro* (Award) PCA Case No 2017-07 (25 October 2019) in Vladislav Djanić, 'Revealed: reasons surface for tribunal's decision that Montenegro was not bound by the Russia–Yugoslavia BIT' IA Reporter (3 July 2020).

[551] *Land, Island and Maritime Frontier Dispute (El Salvador v Honduras)* (Application to Intervene) [1990] ICJ Rep 92, para 63; *Nuclear Tests (Australia v France)* (Judgment) [1974] ICJ Rep 253, paras 42–52; McNair (n 61) 485–89.

States of a 1962 notification by Madagascar for the 1909 Franco–American extradition treaty[552] and that by Ghana, supported by the United Kingdom, to France for the 1946 Franco–British air transport treaty.[553]

A doctrinal issue is whether a declaration of provisional application or succession made in internal law but not communicated to third States can engage estoppel if relied upon by counterparties. Whereas succession agreements can be concluded by reciprocal conduct, including a verbal communication of one State to which the other State consents by its actions,[554] the expression of a public position concerning succession to treaties in internal law, treaty lists, or databases has tended to result in ambiguity. It is neither clear whether the declaration or listing expresses definitive consent on a specific treaty nor that the counterparty to that treaty is aware of the position of the State concerned.

State practice has yet to coalesce: while there are examples of the listing of treaties by one State being relied upon by another State to conclude a succession agreement, these eventually involved verbal communication.[555] In the absence of such communication, declarations made in internal law have not been successfully invoked by counterparties.[556]

For example, a statute and 'open letter' on succession were adopted by the parliament of Ukraine in 1991.[557] The Swiss Directorate of Public International Law advised in 1992 that these declarations be treated 'in the absence of recognized principles on state succession to treaties' as effective for provisional application until each treaty could be individually assessed. In extradition proceedings, the Federal Supreme Court of Switzerland found the declarations to be ineffective for the 1873 Swiss–Russian extradition treaty because they had not referred to it.[558] In 2005, the Court left the question open whether the declarations constituted a unilateral obligation applicable to the 1872 Russian–Swiss treaty of commerce.[559]

When Montenegro argued against jurisdiction in *Deripaska v Montenegro* on the basis that it had not succeeded to the Russian–Yugoslav bilateral investment treaty, the Claimant seemingly did not argue that Montenegro was estopped by its general declaration of succession to the treaties of the FRY in its declaration of independence[560] or its two notes communicated to Russia concerning the treaty.[561]

---

[552] E.g. – *UN Materials* (n 377) 233; Bilateral Treaties Study (n 353) paras 101–102; *Treaties in Force* (n 254) 278–80.

[553] Ibid, 191–92; Second Bilateral Treaties Study (n 251) para 25.

[554] Note 225.

[555] E.g. – Agreement (United States–Swaziland) (13 May and 28 July 1970) 756 UNTS 103.

[556] E.g. – Bilateral Treaties Study (n 353) para 88.

[557] Note 506; *X and Y* (n 430) para A6.

[558] *Dvoriantschikov et autres c. Office federal de la police (extradition à l'Ukraine)* Case No 1A/249/1995, Federal Supreme Court of Switzerland (16 January 1996) (French) (on file with author) para C.

[559] *X and Y* (n 430) para A6.

[560] Helmut Tuerk, 'Montenegro', Max Planck Encyclopaedia of Public International Law (2015) para 19; Jure Vidmar, 'Montenegro's Path to Independence: A Study of Self-Determination, Statehood and Recognition' (2007) 3(1) HLR 73, 99.

[561] *Deripaska* (n 549).

The current position appears to be that a general declaration of succession to treaties made in internal law or treaty lists is insufficient to engage estoppel unless specifying the treaty in question.

## 5.5 Conclusions

Despite the fact that the VCSST has not been applied as a treaty regime as it had been intended to function, a significant proportion of its substantive provisions accurately reflect the prior practice from decolonization and beyond. In particular, the rules prescribed for newly independent States manifest the general principle of consent that has become the settled foundation of succession to treaties. The most significant divergence of the VCSST from State practice has been the distinction drawn between the principle of consent for newly independent States and the principle of automaticity for the other classes of succession.

Whilst the law of succession interfaces with the law of treaties at several points (e.g.—the role of depositaries to handle notifications) the preoccupation of Waldock and the ILC with the law of treaties not only overlooked the savings clause in the VCLT but also produced discrepancies with settled practice (e.g.—on general declarations of succession). The perceived dilemma of a successor being able to 'pick and choose' the treaties to which it would succeed, as being inconsistent with the law of treaties, has been shown to be a false one because successors have not been able to impose their will by succeeding to multilateral treaties for which they are ineligible or bilateral treaties without the consent of the counterparty.

The application of the general principle of consent as succession to multilateral treaties by notification and bilateral treaties by agreement applies across the classes of succession. Unlike other field of succession, automaticity applies not to produce a positive outcome of succession or non-succession but rather in a negative way to determine the eligibility of a successor to succeed to a particular treaty. As the dynamics of each class of succession vary, the rules of customary international law may be summarized as follows:

- for mergers, the successor may succeed to any treaty of the predecessor by notification or agreement;
- for absorptions, the treaties of the successor automatically extend to the transferred territory by the moving treaty frontiers rule and the successor may succeed by notification or agreement to localized treaties of the predecessor, which apply only to the transferred territory;
- for dismemberments, the successors may succeed by notification or agreement to any eligible treaties applied to their transferred territories;
- for cessions, treaties of the predecessor cease to apply to the transferred territory in application of the moving treaty frontiers rule but the successor may

succeed by notification or agreement to those localized treaties that were applied exclusively to the transferred territory;
- for secessions, the successor may succeed by notification or agreement to any treaty of the predecessor applied to the transferred territory;
- for accessions to independence, the successor continues to participate in the treaties in which it had participated on its own behalf before the succession and may succeed to any other treaty applied by the predecessor to its territory.

The coherence of the basic principle of consent notwithstanding, two issues in recent practice concerning succession to multilateral treaties and bilateral treaties are inter-related and complex. The first is the interpretation of silence, vague language, or conduct to identify an expression of consent for succession to a bilateral treaty or the bilateral application of a multilateral treaty in response to a general declaration of provisional application. As the guidance provided in Articles 24(1), 27(1), and 28 on the identification of agreement is rudimentary, State practice and the jurisprudence of national and international courts and tribunals has developed techniques to deal with the interpretative problems resulting from vagueness.

While the possibility of a verbal agreement by implication was persuasively reasoned through forensic scrutiny by the High Court of England and Wales in the *Gold Pool v Kazakhstan* case, national courts in dozens of cases (particularly in the United States) have also identified agreements by conduct. Though a complex exercise due to the interpretation of various forms of action (e.g.—extradition requests, implementing legislation, treaty listing), the possibility of succession through a combination of techniques (e.g.—affirmative judgment of a national court granting an extradition request) has enabled agreement to be flexibly reached in the absence of action by executive authorities. The ongoing challenge is to refine these forensic and interpretative techniques to deal with the frequent scenario of treaties that have not been addressed during the twilight period (e.g.—long periods of 'provisional application').

The second problem is the temporal application of a succession to the 'twilight period' between the date of succession and the effective date of a notification or agreement. States have not followed the rule of suspension prescribed in Article 23(2) of the VCSST but the potential for prejudice to the rights of third States from the retroactive effect of a succession has yet to be directly addressed in dispute settlement. It is suggested that the solution to the doctrinal problem lies in the correct application of the operative date. Contrary to the reasoning of the ICJ in the *Bosnia Genocide Case*, the basis of retroactive application is not the object and purpose of a particular treaty but rather a rule of succession whereby the retroactive effect of a notification of succession does not begin until its effective date.

In this respect, a distinction should be drawn between the prejudice to the rights of treaty counterparties and the rights of other entities under the treaty. In the *Sanum v Laos* arbitration, for example, the prejudice to the investor was that the Chinese–Laotian agreement on the inapplicability of their bilateral investment treaty to Macao was struck *after* the conclusion of the arbitration. While there was no prejudice to the rights of China by the retroactive effect of that agreement, the rights of the investor would have been infringed had the courts of Singapore applied the agreement. It is suggested that this same consideration applies to a succession by conduct in which the affirmative action is the judgment of a national court (e.g.—extradition proceedings) in that a verbal agreement on succession or non-succession reached during the proceedings would bind the court, unlike an agreement reached after their conclusion.

# 6

# Succession to International Claims and Responsibility

## 6.1 Introduction

Succession to international claims is the transfer from a predecessor to a successor of rights arising from an internationally wrongful act[1] committed against the predecessor before the date of succession. Succession to international responsibility[2] is the transfer of obligations arising from an internationally wrongful act committed by the predecessor before the date of succession.[3] Mutually complementary, they are 'secondary' rights and obligations under the law of international responsibility: the general rules governing the constitutive elements of the 'primary' rule of international law breached are discrete from the consequences of the breach.[4]

Relative to the other sub-fields of the law of succession, succession to international claims and responsibility is marked by a paucity of State practice.[5] Though it is likely that confidentiality covers unknown practice,[6] it is also probable that claims are rarely pursued.[7] Whether in the context of settlement negotiations,[8] claims commissions, or inter-State arbitration and adjudication, there nevertheless

---

[1] ILC, 'Draft articles on Responsibility of States for Internationally Wrongful Acts, with commentaries' (2001) ILC Yearbook vol II Part 2 31 ('ARSIWA') art 2.

[2] The term 'international responsibility' acknowledges the hypothetical involvement of an international organization – ILC, Draft articles on the Responsibility of International Organizations (2011) ILC Yearbook vol II Part 2.

[3] This excludes injuries resulting from a lawful act: Alan Boyle, 'Liability for Injurious Consequences of Acts Not Prohibited by International Law' in: James Crawford, Alain Pellet, and Simon Olleson (eds) *The Law of International Responsibility* (OUP 2010) 95–104.

[4] On the 'Ago revolution' see: Alain Pellet, 'The ILC's Articles on State Responsibility' in Crawford et al (n 3) 75–94, 76–78.

[5] JP Monnier, 'La succession d'Etats en matière de responsabilité internationale' (1962) 8 AFDI 65, 72, 86; Brigitte Stern, 'Responsabilité internationale et succession d'Etats' in Laurence Boisson de Chazournes and Vera Gowlland-Debbas (eds) *The International Legal System in Quest of Equity and Universality, Liber Amicorum Georges Abi-Saab* (Martinus Nijhoff 2001) 335; Wladyslaw Czaplinski, 'State Succession and State Responsibility' (1990) 28 CYIL 339; MJ Volkovitsch, 'Towards a New Theory of State Succession to Responsibility for International Delicts' (1992) 92 Col LR 2162, 2178–82; Václav Mikulka, 'State Succession and Responsibility' in Crawford et al (n 3) 291–96, 292.

[6] Patrick Dumberry, *State Succession to International Responsibility* (Martinus Nijhoff 2007) 61.

[7] Grega Pajnkihar, *State Succession to Responsibility for Internationally Wrongful Acts* (Brill Nijhoff 2023) 304.

[8] States have taken different views concerning reliance on settlements to identify a general rule. See, e.g. – Sixth Committee, 30th Meeting (n 139) para 11; 33rd Meeting (n 213) para 4; 25th Meeting (n 29) para 47.

---

*The Law of State Succession.* Arman Sarvarian, Oxford University Press. © Arman Sarvarian 2025.
DOI: 10.1093/oso/9780198817956.003.0006

198    SUCCESSION TO INTERNATIONAL CLAIMS AND RESPONSIBILITY

exists a demand for normativity with significant implications for the settlement of disputes. While the dearth of modern practice makes the law in the area subject to rapid change,[9] examples of classical practice are also pertinent.[10]

Due to a divergence of views, the ILC decided to omit 'succession in respect of responsibility for torts' from its programme of work.[11] In his first report on the topic of State responsibility for internationally wrongful acts, the fourth Special Rapporteur, Professor James Crawford SC, cited DP O'Connell in writing that there was 'a widely accepted opinion that a new State generally does not succeed to any State responsibility of the predecessor'.[12] The ILC reserved its collective view in commenting that the question was 'unclear'.[13] While the 2001 ILC Articles on the Responsibility of States for Internationally Wrongful Acts ('ARSIWA') omit a savings clause, the ILC had intended to exclude State succession from their scope.[14]

In 2015, the Institut de droit international ('IDI') adopted its Resolution on State Succession and State Responsibility ('IDI Resolution'), which examines the question of succession to the consequences of an internationally wrongful act.[15] Alongside empirical analysis, considerations of justice and equity were invoked 'where State practice is scarce or … contradictory' for proposed rules 'to discard the application of a general strict non-succession "clean slate" solution'.[16]

When the ILC added the topic 'Succession of States in respect of State responsibility' to its long-term programme of work in 2016,[17] 'some delegations [in the Sixth Committee] supported [its] inclusion … [while] other delegations questioned its contemporary relevance'.[18] The following year, the ILC decided without debate 'in light of the consensus that had emerged from consultations' to move the topic to the main programme of work and to appoint Professor Pavel Šturma as

[9] See Chapter Two. Institut de droit international, 'State Succession in Matters of Property and Debts', Seventh Commission, Report and Resolution (2001) 69 IDI Annuaire 119 (French)

[10] On 'annexation' for example, see: Marcelo Kohen and Patrick Dumberry, *The Institute of International Law's Resolution on State Succession and State Responsibility: Introduction, Text and Commentaries* (CUP 2019) 117.

[11] Report of the Sub-Committee on Succession of States and Governments, UN Doc A/5509 (Annex II) II *Yearbook of the International Law Commission* (1963) 260, 299.

[12] James Crawford, 'First Report on State responsibility' UN Doc A/CN.4/490 (24 April 1998) para 279.

[13] Note 327.

[14] James Crawford, *State Responsibility: The General Part* (2013) 436–37.

[15] Kohen and Dumberry (n 10) 141. See also: International Law Association, 'Final Report on Aspects of the Law of State Succession' Report of the Seventy-Third Conference (Rio de Janeiro 2008) 250–363.

[16] Ibid, 9–11. See also, e.g. – ILC, 3377th Meeting (n 22) 11.

[17] 'Report of the International Law Commission: Sixty-eighth session (2 May–10 June and 4 July–12 August 2016)' UN Doc A/71/10, paras 308–09, annexe B.

[18] 'Report of the International Law Commission on the work of its sixty-eighth session (2016): Topical summary of the discussion held in the Sixth Committee of the General Assembly during its seventy-first session' UN Doc A/CN.4/703 (22 February 2017) para 74. See also: Sixth Committee, 'Summary record of the 21st meeting' (25 October 2016) UN Doc A/C.6/71/SR.21 (16 November 2016) paras 11, 22, 68, 80, 143; Sixth Committee: 'Summary record of the 23rd meeting' (26 October 2016) UN Doc A/C.6/71/SR.23 (14 November 2016) paras 20, 27, 36; Sixth Committee, 'Summary record of the 29th meeting' (2 November 2016) UN Doc A/C.6/71/SR.29 (2 December 2016) para 98.

Special Rapporteur.[19] Twenty-two days later, the Special Rapporteur submitted his first report together with four draft articles in proposing that the ILC adopt 'draft articles with commentaries' as 'both codification and progressive development of international law'.[20]

Introducing his report in the same session, the Special Rapporteur remarked: 'The dearth of examples of State succession made it difficult to identify customary rules on succession of States in respect of State responsibility.'[21] While some Members considered there to be a need to clearly articulate a general rule on succession or non-succession and to provide a stronger foundation in State practice rather than doctrine,[22] others doubted its suitability for codification due to 'the prevailing view that there was no succession to international responsibility ... it appeared that the Commission's project should be purely one of progressive development, guided by the position of the Institute of International Law that responsibility had to remain with at least some successor State'.[23] The ILC referred the four draft articles to the Drafting Committee on the understanding that the Special Rapporteur would take into account the views expressed in the plenary debate for his second report whereupon 'members of the Commission would have a clearer picture of residual rules on non-succession and succession to be proposed'.[24]

In 2018,[25] 2019,[26] and 2020,[27] the Special Rapporteur proposed 16 draft articles that were referred to the Drafting Committee. Though continuing its work on the project, the ILC remained divided on a general rule of succession versus non-succession:

---

[19] ILC, 'Provisional summary record of the 3354th meeting' (9 May 2017) UN Doc A/CN.4/SR.3354 (2 June 2017) 10.

[20] Šturma, First Report (n 44) paras 27–28.

[21] 'International Law Commission: Provisional summary record of the 3374th meeting' (13 July 2017) UN Doc A/CN.4/SR.3374 (14 August 2017) 10.

[22] Ibid, 12–14; ILC, 'Provisional summary record of the 3375th meeting' (14 July 2017) UN Doc A/CN.4/SR.3375 (7 August 2017) 3–6; ILC, 'Provisional summary record of the 3376th meeting' (18 July 2017) UN Doc A/CN.4/SR.3376 (17 August 2017) 1–4, 5–7, 7–8; ILC, 'Provisional summary record of the 3377th meeting' (19 July 2017) UN Doc A/CN.4/SR.3377 (18 August 2017) 6–10; ILC, 'Provisional summary record of the 3378th meeting' (20 July 2017) UN Doc A/CN.4/SR.3378 (18 August 2017) 18; ILC, 'Provisional summary record of the 3379th meeting' (21 July 2017) UN Doc A/CN.4/SR.3378 (16 August 2017) 9–10; ILC, 'Provisional summary record of the 3380th meeting' (25 July 2017) UN Doc A/CN.4/SR.3380 (24 August 2017) 5–6; ILC, 'Provisional summary record of the 3381st meeting' (25 July 2017) UN Doc A/CN.4/SR.3381 (17 August 2017) 3–5.

[23] ILC, 3374th Meeting (n 21) 14–16; ILC, 3376th Meeting (n 21) 8–9; ILC, 3377th Meeting (n 21) 10–14; ILC, 3378th Meeting (n 21) 16–18; ILC, 3379th Meeting (n 21) 3–9; ILC, 3380th Meeting (n 21) 3–5.

[24] ILC, 3381st Meeting (n 21) 9.

[25] Václav Šturma, 'Second Report on Succession of States in respect of State Responsibility' UN Doc A/CN.4/719 (6 April 2018) paras 41, 75, 123, 137, 146, 165, 190.

[26] Václav Šturma, 'Third Report on Succession of States in respect of State Responsibility' UN Doc A/CN.4/731 (2 May 2019) para 138.

[27] Václav Šturma, 'Fourth Report on Succession of States in respect of State responsibility' UN Doc A/CN.4/743 (27 March 2020) paras 47, 65, 97, 121, 136.

200 SUCCESSION TO INTERNATIONAL CLAIMS AND RESPONSIBILITY

While the view was expressed that the proposed draft articles appeared to go in the direction of automatic succession, other members did not share that view. The point was made that the fourth report, while stating that the 'transfer of responsibility' of States is different from the 'transfer of rights and obligations arising from responsibility' of States, did not sufficiently explain such difference. Some members questioned the methodology of the report and the extent to which analysis contained therein was made by drawing parallels with succession of States in respect of debts and inspired by the 1983 Vienna Convention on Succession of States in respect of State Property, Archives and Debts.[28]

In 2021, 12 States concurred with the Special Rapporteur 'that neither the clean-slate principle nor the principle of automatic succession were acceptable as general rules'.[29] Others doubted 'the premise underlying the fourth report that there might be situations where the responsibility or the rights and obligations arising from responsibility might be transferred from a predecessor State to a successor State as *lex lata*'[30] and still others considered the default rule to be 'non-succession with exceptions'[31] or 'succession'.[32] States were also divided in supporting an exercise of progressive development[33] or questioning whether sufficient State practice existed for codification.[34]

In 2022, the ILC decided on the basis of the recommendation of the Special Rapporteur to change the format from 'draft articles with commentaries' to 'draft guidelines' to reflect the views of the majority of Members and commenting States.[35] The principal effect was to provide for a duty of the States concerned to endeavour to agree on issues arising from succession to responsibility, which was later changed to a hortatory guideline alongside a right of successors to succeed to international claims. At its seventy-fifth session in 2024, a working group under the chairmanship of Professor August Reinisch[36] recommended that the ILC

---

[28] 'Report of the International Law Commission: Seventy-second session (26 April–4 June and 5 July–6 August 2021) UN Doc A/76/10, para 135.

[29] Sixth Committee, 'Summary record of the 17th meeting' (26 October 2021) UN Doc A/C.6/76/SR.17 (10 December 2021) para 62; Sixth Committee, 'Summary record of the 23rd meeting' (2 November 2021) UN Doc A/C.6/76/SR.23 (10 December 2021) paras 33, 60; Sixth Committee, 'Summary record of the 24th meeting' (3 November 2021) UN Doc A/C.6/76/SR.24 (9 December 2021) paras 17, 33, 42, 67, 145, 151. Sixth Committee, 'Summary record of the 25th meeting' (3 November 2021) UN Doc A/C.6/76/SR.24 (12 April 2022) paras 14, 39.

[30] Sixth Committee, 23rd meeting (n 29) paras 134, 138. See also: Sixth Committee, 24th Meeting (n 29) paras 2, 48–49.

[31] Sixth Committee, 24th meeting (n 29) para 53.

[32] Ibid, para 110.

[33] Sixth Committee, 23rd meeting (n 29) para 126, 146.

[34] Ibid, paras 44, 53, 72, 82, 86–87, 108–09, 122; Sixth Committee, 24th Meeting (n 29) paras 29, 144; 25th meeting (n 29) paras 13, 21, 24, 58–59.

[35] ILC, 'Provisional summary record of the 3583rd meeting' (17 May 2022) UN Doc A/CN.4/3583 (16 June 2022) 3–8.

[36] ILC, 'Report on the work of the seventy-fourth session (2023)' UN Doc A/78/10 (September 2023) paras 235–46.

INTRODUCTION    201

establish a working group 'for the purpose of drafting a concluding report in its seventy-sixth session in 2025 that would contain a summary of the difficulties that the Commission would face if it were to continue its work on the topic and explain the reasons for the discontinuance of such work'.[37] Such difficulties included the sufficiency of State practice to enable identification of customary international law, a distinction between a transfer of rights versus obligations arising from international responsibility, the applicability of a potential parallel with rules governing State debt, and identification of underlying policy justifications as progressive development.[38]

To accurately categorize and evaluate State practice,[39] a sharp distinction exists between succession to international claims and responsibility concerning breaches of international law and succession to tortious debts ('municipal torts') as breaches of internal law.[40] As O'Connell wrote in 1967:

> It has been taken for granted that a successor State is not liable for the delicts of its predecessor, but what remains unclear is whether the reference is to international delicts giving rise to State responsibility, or to torts in municipal law. Although a tort in municipal law may constitute an international delict, this is not necessarily the case; conversely, an international delict may not amount to municipal law tort. The failure to characterize the event properly has produced a defective jurisprudence on the part of international and municipal tribunals which have pronounced upon the effect of State succession upon international responsibility.[41]

As State practice on tortious debts concerns breaches of internal law,[42] it is irrelevant to the identification of rules on succession to international claims and responsibility unless also comprising a breach of international law, such as the foreign nationality of the injured person in cases of 'indirect injury' to the home State.[43]

As for other areas of the law of succession, general rules provide a template for negotiation of succession agreements and apply in default of agreement being reached for the purposes of dispute settlement.[44] Like most other sub-fields of the

---

[37] ILC, 'Succession of States in respect of State responsibility' UN Doc A/CN.4/L.1003 (12 July 2024) para 23.

[38] Ibid, paras 4–7.

[39] See Chapter 2.

[40] Institut de droit international, 'State Succession in Matters of State Responsibility', Fourteenth Commission, Final Report & Resolution (2015) 76 IDI Annuaire 511, art 2(1). 141. See also: International Law Association, 'Final Report on Aspects of the Law of State Succession' Report of the Seventy-Third Conference (Rio de Janeiro 2008) 250–363. On tortious debts, see: Chapter 4.

[41] DP O'Connell, *State Succession in Municipal Law and International Law* vol I (OUP 1968) 482.

[42] See Chapter 4.

[43] Patrick Dumberry, *State Succession to International Responsibility* (Brill 2024) 30–31. See Chapter 8.

[44] IDI Resolution (n 40) art 4; Kohen and Dumberry (n 10) 29; Šturma, 'First report on succession of States in respect of State responsibility' UN Doc A/CN.4/708 (31 May 2017) para 86.

law of succession, there is no single rule of customary international law applicable to all classes of succession.[45] Rather, the substantive rule of succession for each class must be identified by interpreting the State practice and *opiniones juris* in its own context. The conceptual reason is the fundamental distinction for the purposes of succession to international claims and responsibility between the extinction of the international legal personality of a State in total succession and its continuation in partial succession, which creates different dynamics according to the varying participation of predecessors and successors in each class of succession.[46]

## 6.2 The General Principle of Automaticity

The question of transferability of claims and responsibility is discrete from the existence of an internationally wrongful act,[47] the applicability of a 'circumstance precluding wrongfulness',[48] and other matters under the law of international responsibility. Rather, the law of succession is concerned with the identification of a disputing party in an international dispute.[49] If international claims and responsibility be transferred to a successor, the successor is entitled as a disputing party to assert or deny the existence of an internationally wrongful act or circumstance precluding wrongfulness. As a respondent, for example, it may argue that an impugned act or omission is not attributable to the predecessor[50] or did not constitute a breach of an international obligation owed by it.[51]

While the ARSIWA implicitly excludes State succession from its scope,[52] Article 10(2) states: 'The conduct of a movement, insurrectional or other, which succeeds in establishing a new State in part of the territory of a pre-existing State or in a territory under its administration shall be considered an act of the new State under international law.'[53] Though not stated by the ILC to be designed for dismemberments and secessions, its terms are unlikely to apply in other situations:

[45] Dumberry (n 43) 9–10, 479–80.

[46] See Chapter 2.

[47] ILC, 'Succession of States in respect of State Responsibility: Statement of the Chairperson of the Drafting Committee' (3 August 2018) 4–7 (draft article 6) <https://legal.un.org/ilc/guide/3_5.shtml#dcommrep> accessed 16 February 2024.

[48] ARSIWA (n 1) 71–72.

[49] On the limited jurisprudence with respect to substitution by succession in a pending investor-State arbitration, see: Patrick Dumberry, '*Terra Incognita*: What Happens When a Problem of State Succession Occurs during Arbitration Proceedings?', (2018) 17 LPICT 350, 352–60.

[50] For example, it might argue that the conduct of a non-State actor, such as an armed group, was not attributable to the predecessor under Article 8 of the ARSIWA – IDI Resolution (n 40) art 2(1); Kohen and Dumberry (n 10) 23–25.

[51] For example, Slovakia succeeded by agreement to the international claims and responsibility of Czecho-Slovakia with respect to the dispute in which it contested the 'state of ecological necessity' argued by Hungary as a circumstance precluding wrongfulness and refuted the claims of Hungary on breach of the 1977 Treaty by Czecho-Slovakia – *Gabčikovo-Nagymaros Project Case* (n 197) paras 39–45. See also, e.g. – Burma (n 148), Madagascar (n 152).

[52] Note 14.

[53] ARSIWA (n 1) art 10(2).

This terminology reflects the existence of a greater variety of movements whose actions may result in the formation of a new State. The words do not, however, extend to encompass the actions of a group of citizens advocating separation or revolution where these are carried out within the framework of the predecessor State. Nor does it cover the situation where an insurrectional movement within a territory succeeds in its agitation for union with another State. This is essentially a case of succession, and outside the scope of the articles, whereas article 10 focuses on the continuity of the movement concerned and the eventual new Government or State, as the case may be.[54]

Despite considerable support in State practice for rule of attribution of the conduct of 'an insurrectional movement which becomes the new Government of a State' in Article 10(1),[55] there is scant practice to support Article 10(2).[56] As the provision was intended by the ILC to be a rule of attribution[57] and there is a dearth of State practice, there is no doctrinal or empirical basis for the replication of Article 10(2) in Articles 12(6) and 16(3) of the IDI Resolution as a rule of succession for secessions and accessions to independence.[58]

While violations of international obligations have occurred for direct injuries to predecessors,[59] the more typical example in practice has been indirect injury sustained by a State through personal or proprietary damages caused to its nationals in breach of the international minimum standard of treatment.[60] To constitute a breach of an international obligation owed by the predecessor,[61] a critical issue in the context of a succession is whether the international obligation applied to the impugned conduct of the predecessor or third State. If so, then a rule of succession or non-succession applies to the period from which a breach was committed by the predecessor up to the date of succession.

In contrast, a continuing breach from the date of succession of an obligation owed by the successor is regulated not by the law of succession but by the law of responsibility.[62] If the impugned conduct continue and become *attributable* to the successor from the date of succession, then the law of responsibility applies. When

---

[54] Ibid, 51 (para 10).

[55] Crawford (n 14) 170–80.

[56] E.g. – Michael Akehurst, 'State Responsibility for the Wrongful Acts of Rebels – An Aspect of the Southern Rhodesian Problem' 43 BYIL 49, 55, 61–70. Whereas Croatia invoked it in the *Croatia Genocide Case*, Serbia considered it to be 'progressive development' and the ICJ did not pronounce upon its status – *Croatia Genocide Case* (n 268) paras 104–05.

[57] Ibid.

[58] The sole practice cited by the IDI concerned municipal torts in Algeria – Kohen and Dumberry (n 10) 106–11, 138–39.

[59] E.g. – Viet Nam (n 133); Indonesia (n 252).

[60] Mikulka (n 5) 295. E.g. – UAR (notes 128–129, 130); Viet Nam (n 133); Burma (n 147); East Germany (notes 168–169); Tarapacá (n 224); Estonia and Lithuania (n 344).

[61] ARSIWA (n 1) art 13.

[62] Ibid, art 14(2).

204   SUCCESSION TO INTERNATIONAL CLAIMS AND RESPONSIBILITY

responsibility for the impugned conduct before the date of succession remains with the predecessor due to non-succession while the continuing act becomes attributable to the successor after the date of succession, the injured State may invoke the responsibility of each State in relation to the continuing act.[63]

However, this scenario of a continuing breach shared by a predecessor and successor is highly unlikely to occur in practice. This is because conduct continuing to occur after the date of succession would continue to be attributable to the predecessor or responsibility for the internationally wrongful act taking place before the date of succession would transfer to the successor by the principle of territoriality. There is no example in practice of the problem of a continuing breach in a case of succession.

For these reasons, the replication, *mutatis mutandis*, of Article 14(2) of the ARSIWA in Article 9(1) of the IDI Resolution is misconceived.[64] The sole instance of State practice cited in support of this provision is the *Gabčikovo-Nagymaros Project Case* in which the argument of Hungary on the assumption by Slovakia of responsibility for the alleged internationally wrongful acts of Czecho-Slovakia was interpreted by the IDI to mean that 'Slovakia was not only responsible for the damage resulting from its own illicit act committed upon its creation in January 1993, but also for the consequences arising from the act committed by the predecessor State.'[65] However, the problem of continuing breach did not arise because Slovakia agreed with Hungary (albeit on differing reasoning) on its succession to the responsibility of Czecho-Slovakia for any breaches occurring before the date of succession.[66]

Draft article 7 developed by the ILC Drafting Committee departed from Article 9(1) of the IDI Resolution in stating that the international responsibility of a successor for an internationally wrongful act of a continuing character 'extends only to the consequences of its own act after the date of the succession of States.'[67] This provision was criticized by Czechia in the Sixth Committee as conflating 'two independent acts committed by two different States'[68] and by Thailand in questioning its 'added value' due to its pertaining to a rule of international responsibility rather than succession.[69]

There is also no example of the situation of a successor completing a series of actions or omissions initiated by a predecessor and defined in aggregate as a

---

[63] ARSIWA (n 1) art 47.

[64] Kohen and Dumberry (n 10) 58.

[65] Ibid, 63.

[66] Note 197. While Estonia argued in the *Panavezys-Saldutiskis Railway Case* that the breach by Lithuania was of a continuing character without claiming that Lithuania had succeeded to the alleged breaches by Russia before the date of succession, the case was decided on other grounds – note 341.

[67] 'Text of draft articles 7, 8 and 9 provisionally adopted by the Drafting Committee' (n 119); 'Statement of the Chair of the Drafting Committee' ibid, 3–4.

[68] Sixth Committee, 32nd Meeting (n 116) para 98; Sixth Committee, 24th Meeting (n 29) paras 16–21.

[69] Sixth Committee, 24th Meeting (n 29) para 95.

composite breach of an international obligation.[70] For this hypothetical situation, Article 9(2) of the IDI Resolution provides for the international responsibility of a successor over the entire period of a series of actions or omissions initiated by its predecessor and completed by it.[71]

In contrast, draft article 7*bis* developed by the ILC Drafting Committee stated that the predecessor and successor would be 'responsible only for the consequences of its own act' unless the internationally wrongful act occurred only after the last action or omission of the successor, in which case the successor is responsible for the entire period.[72] While ten delegations expressed interest in draft article 7*bis* in the Sixth Committee, they considered there to be a need for refinement and underpinning in State practice.[73]

## 6.2.1 International Claims and Responsibility

An important doctrinal question has been whether a distinction exists between succession to responsibility for an internationally wrongful act as opposed to succession to its legal consequences, as a duty to repair.[74] Article 1(h) of the IDI Resolution defines 'international responsibility' as 'the legal consequences of an internationally wrongful act' and Article 2(1) states that the Resolution 'applies to the effects of a succession of States in respect of the rights and obligations arising out of an internationally wrongful act that the predecessor State committed against another State or another subject of international law prior to the date of succession, or that a State or another subject of international law committed against the predecessor State prior to the date of succession'.

The phrase 'rights and obligations arising out of an internationally wrongful act' was used throughout the work of the IDI to emphasize that '[t]he question ... is *not* whether the successor State(s) should be "*responsible*" for internationally wrongful acts committed by the predecessor ... [a]s a matter of principle, the successor State(s) cannot be *liable for* internationally wrongful acts committed by *another State*'.[75] It was said that the issue 'is not one of transfer of *responsibility* for internationally wrongful acts, but rather that of the succession to the *consequences* of

---

[70] ARSIWA (n 1) art 15(1).
[71] Kohen and Dumberry (n 10) 63–64.
[72] Šturma, Fourth Report (n 27) paras 109–21.
[73] 'Report of the International Law Commission on the work of its seventy-second session (2021): Topical summary of the discussion held in the Sixth Committee during it seventy-sixth session' UN Doc A/CN.4/746 (28 February 2022) para 52. See further: Sixth Committee, 24th meeting (n 29) para 27; Sixth Committee, 25th meeting (n 29) para 45; Sixth Committee, 23rd meeting (n 29) paras 34, 54, 88, 118.
[74] ARSIWA (n 1) arts 28, 42. See also: IDI Resolution (n 40) arts 1(h) 2(1) 4.
[75] Kohen and Dumberry (n 10) 22.

international responsibility *arising from* the commission of such acts'.[76] This approach was followed by the ILC Special Rapporteur.

Doctrine[77] and modern practice[78] have generally referred to 'succession to responsibility'. Examples include the arguments of Bosnia in the *Bosnia Genocide Case*[79] and of Serbia and Croatia in the *Croatia Genocide Case*,[80] as well as the judgment of the ECtHR in the *Bijelić* case.[81] In the *Gabčikovo-Nagymaros Project Case*, the arguments of Hungary and Slovakia referred to the 'obligation to repair' and the 'rights and obligations arising out of an internationally wrongful act' as well as to 'succession to responsibility'.[82] The clearest articulations of the distinction adopted by the IDI appear in the judgment of the German Federal Administrative Court concerning East Germany[83] and the separate opinion of Judge Kreća in the *Croatia Genocide Case*.[84]

The rationale for the conceptual distinction is that the injured State or the State responsible for the internationally wrongful act in question, as the case may be, is the predecessor rather than the successor.[85] This is technically correct because it is the predecessor that commits the internationally wrongful act before the date of succession. In a subsequent settlement agreement or dispute settlement process, it is plain that the successor was not originally the injured State or the State responsible for the internationally wrongful act in question.

However, the distinction does not lead to any substantive or procedural difference because the principal effect of a succession is the substitution of the successor for the predecessor as party to a dispute. This is described by Bosnia and the ICJ on the status of Montenegro in the *Bosnia Genocide Case*,[86] Croatia and the ICJ in the *Croatia Genocide Case*,[87] the Arbitral Tribunal in the *Mytileanos* arbitration,[88] the ECtHR in the *Matijašević* and *Bijelić* cases, and the Arbitral Tribunal in the *ImageSat* arbitration.[89] As disputing party, a successor is entitled to exercise the procedural rights of a claimant or respondent in the stead of the predecessor with respect to the internationally wrongful act, such as the right to contest the existence of an internationally wrongful act, to counterclaim or to invoke a circumstance precluding wrongfulness.

---

[76] Ibid.

[77] Dumberry (n 43) 3–7, 484–88.

[78] As settlement agreements deal with questions of reparation to settle claims with or without admissions of responsibility, they are not helpful on this point.

[79] Note 264.

[80] Notes 203 & 205.

[81] Note 273.

[82] Notes 192–196.

[83] Note 169.

[84] *Croatia Genocide Case* (n 268) Separate Opinion of Judge Kreća, para 65.4.

[85] E.g. – Kohen and Dumberry (n 10) 19, 22–23.

[86] Notes 264, 267.

[87] Notes 268 & 269.

[88] Notes 271& 275.

[89] Note 278.

A related doctrinal issue has been whether a difference exists in the legal tests on default rules to succeed to international claims as opposed to international responsibility. While the substantive provisions of the IDI Resolution on total succession do not distinguish between the two, those on partial succession (i.e.—Articles 11, 12, and 16) propose different tests for the transfer of claims versus responsibility. The draft articles proposed by the ILC Special Rapporteur did not advance sufficiently to develop provisions on succession to claims for partial successions[90] and the guidelines elaborated by the Drafting Committee made a general distinction between a right to succeed to claims and a duty to negotiate with third States on succession to responsibility even in cases of total succession.[91]

There is no basis in State practice for a distinction between international claims and responsibility in any class of succession. To the contrary, the practice is coherent in showing that a successor that is substituted for a predecessor as disputing party succeeds equally to its claims and responsibility. This is shown by a wide variety of settlement agreements[92] and the equal presentation of claims and defences by Slovakia in the *Gabčikovo-Nagymaros Project Case*.[93] Infrequently, practice has featured succession to responsibility alone because a human rights jurisdiction did not include scope to counterclaim[94] or the successor had no counterclaims to present.[95]

## 6.2.2 Territoriality

Whereas the successor receives the entire territory of the predecessor in cases of merger and absorption, it receives title to only a part of its territory in dismemberment, cession, and secession.[96] State practice supports the principle of territoriality to assign international claims and responsibility to a particular successor, for which a test of dominant connection to territory is proposed as a choice between multiple successors in dismemberments or a predecessor and successor in cessions and secessions. No example has yet arisen in practice of a dispute with an equally strong connection to the territories of multiple States concerned (e.g.—two successors of three or more in a case of dismemberment).

While the principle of territoriality is recognized (albeit for claims only) in Articles 11(2), 12(2), and 15(2) of the IDI Resolution,[97] the test of 'direct link' does

---

[90] For mergers and dismemberments, draft articles 13 and 14 on succession to claims did not differ from draft articles 10 and 11 on succession to responsibility – Second Šturma Report (n 25) annex I; Third Šturma Report (n 26) annex I.

[91] ILC 'Text of draft guidelines' (n 143) draft guidelines 10, 10*bis*, 11, 13, 13*bis*, 14.

[92] UAR (n 131), Viet Nam (n 133), Malaysia (n 251), Malaysia (n 253), Singapore (n 254).

[93] Note 197.

[94] *Bijelić* (n 273).

[95] Union of Colombia (notes 185–187).

[96] See Chapter 2.

[97] Kohen and Dumberry (n 10) 82–86, 98–102, 123–126.

208 SUCCESSION TO INTERNATIONAL CLAIMS AND RESPONSIBILITY

not acknowledge the need to choose among multiple territories in these classes of succession. Czechia had tendered a *note verbale* in 1993 disclaiming succession to the treaty on the Gabčikovo-Nagymaros Project,[98] yet the status of the treaty was a key issue in the *Gabčikovo-Nagymaros Project Case* between Slovakia and Hungary even as the dominant territorial connection between the project and Slovakia was not.[99]

Settlement agreements and other practice arising from cessions[100] and secessions[101] support this principle. While the location of the commission of the impugned conduct in the transferred territory generates a presumption of transfer to the successor, [102] the presumption can be rebutted by other factors (e.g.—the identity of the organ or the purpose of the conduct) that indicate a dominant connection to another territory.

## 6.2.3 Equitable Apportionment

When an internationally wrongful act concerns not one particular territory but rather the entire territory of the predecessor in cases of dismemberment, or the States concerned otherwise agree to share the status of disputing party in any class of succession, the principle of equitable apportionment applies to the distribution of the international claims and responsibility among the States concerned. The two doctrinal issues that arise from this possibility are the capacity of any one of the States concerned to settle the dispute without the consent of the others and the criteria for the calculation of the damages to be awarded to them. In this situation, it is suggested that Articles 46 and 47 of the ARSIWA apply to enable each State to separately claim or respond for the internationally wrongful act in question.[103]

While the ICJ held Serbia to be the sole respondent in the *Bosnia Genocide Case* and *Croatia Genocide Case* due to the absence of consent to the status of respondent by Montenegro, Bosnia had expressly claimed 'joint and several' responsibility of Serbia and Montenegro[104] and Croatia implicitly did likewise.[105]

---

[98] *Gabčikovo-Nagymaros Project Case* (n 197) Memorial of Hungary, para 2.07.

[99] Ibid, Judgment, paras 117–124. On the erroneous interpretation by the Court of Article 12 of the VCSST as expressing a rule of succession to 'territorial treaties', see Chapter 3.

[100] Notes 216 (French India), 217 (Portuguese India), 222 (Tarapacá).

[101] Notes 242 (Mozambique), 250–252 (Indonesia), 253 (Malaysia), 254 (Singapore), 262 (Syria), & 273 (Montenegro).

[102] In the *Bijelić* case, for example, Serbia denied the status of respondent on the ground that the impugned conduct had taken place in Montenegro – n 273.

[103] As the ILC observed, '[i]t is important not to assume that internal law concepts and rules in this field can be applied directly ... [t]erms such as "joint", "joint and several" and "solidary" responsibility derive from different legal traditions and analogies must be applied with care' – ARSIWA (n 1) 124.

[104] Note 264.

[105] Note 268. The joint and several principle was also applied by the successors in the classical case of the Union of Colombia – notes 182, 186–88.

In common law traditions, the concept of joint and several liability requires the participation of each disputing party to settle a dispute.[106] While Serbia expressed no *opinio juris* and Montenegro rejected succession to responsibility, the Court did not rule on the issue.[107] This practice is insufficient to constitute the joint and several principle as a rule of succession but it could give rise to a jurisdictional objection to the settlement of the dispute by one of the States concerned on the basis of the third-party principle.[108]

Although State practice on equitable apportionment is sparse, the cases of the Union of Colombia[109] and British India[110] suggest that the basis of calculation of shares follows the same methodology adopted by the successors for the allocation of State debt.[111] On this open question, Article 7 of the IDI Resolution elaborates objective criteria for apportionment that are inspired by State practice concerning State property and debt.[112] The IDI also cited the equitable principle of unjust enrichment as being 'central to the whole question of succession'[113] but there is no State practice supporting its application.[114]

## 6.3 Application to the Classes of Succession

In total successions, the extinction of the predecessor[115] means that its international claims and responsibility either lapse or transfer to a successor at the date of succession.[116] While it is argued that a default rule of succession applies to mergers in contrast to a rule of non-succession for absorptions and dismemberments, this conclusion is based solely on the sufficiency of State practice. However, the same doctrinal issue of the extinction of the predecessor and the existence of a single successor arises for both classes of succession. In contrast, the existence of multiple successors in dismemberments prompts not only the question of the transferability of claims and responsibility to any of the successors but also that of their allocation to one or more of them.

---

[106] Joint liability enables any party to claim or respond to the full extent of the dispute while several liability allows each party to claim or respond to the extent of its individual share.

[107] Notes 265–66.

[108] However, the ICJ dismissed this argument in the *Certain Phosphate Lands in Nauru Case –* ARSIWA (n 1) 124.

[109] Note 188.

[110] Note 247.

[111] See Chapter 3.

[112] Kohen and Dumberry (n 10) 53–57.

[113] Ibid, 56–57.

[114] See Chapter 3.

[115] See Chapter 2.

[116] Sixth Committee, 'Summary record of the 32nd meeting' (6 November 2019) UN Doc A/C.6/74/SR.32 (27 November 2019) paras 25, 57; Sixth Committee, 'Summary record of the 31st meeting' (5 November 2019) UN Doc A/C.6/74/SR.31 (5 December 2019) para 83.

The continued existence of the predecessor in a partial succession enables the continued exercise of international claims and responsibility. Consequently, the doctrinal question is not the transfer or disappearance of claims and responsibility with potential prejudice to the rights of third States but rather the criteria for the identification of the predecessor or successor as disputing party. While Articles 4 and 5 of the IDI Resolution recognize a basic rule of continuity for the international claims and responsibility of a predecessor, they also state that international responsibility may be transferred in part or whole while a successor may succeed to a claim for an internationally wrongful act that 'affected the territory or persons which ... are under [its] jurisdiction.'[117]

Following the recommendation of the ILC Special Rapporteur to combine draft articles 7, 8, and 9 into a single provision due to comments made in the ILC on their substantive similarity,[118] the Drafting Committee produced a new draft article 9 ('Cases of succession of States when the predecessor State continues to exist') in 2019. This stated that 'an injured State continues to be entitled to invoke the responsibility of the predecessor State even after the date of succession' when the predecessor continues to exist in cessions, secessions, and accessions to independence.[119] This did not receive substantive comment in the Sixth Committee[120] and the Drafting Committee converted it into a hortatory guideline in 2022. It also added draft guideline 12 stating the corresponding right of a predecessor to invoke the responsibility of a wrongful State for internationally wrongful acts committed against it.

Articles 4 and 5 of the IDI Resolution and draft article 9 developed by the ILC Drafting Committee correctly identify the critical characteristic of a partial succession, namely, the continuity of the international legal personality of the predecessor. By including newly independent States in their scope, however, they do not reflect the rule of continuity in the practice on that class of succession.

### 6.3.1 Merger

When one State merges with another State to create a new State, the default rule of customary international law is that the international claims and responsibility of

---

[117] Kohen and Dumberry (n 10) 32–36.

[118] Second Šturma Report (n 25) paras 77–146; Third Šturma Report (n 26) para 65.

[119] ILC, 'Succession of States in respect of State responsibility: Text of draft articles 7, 8 and 9 provisionally adopted by the Drafting Committee at the seventy-first session' UN Doc A/CN.4/L.939/Add.1 (24 July 2019); ILC, 'Succession of States in respect of State responsibility: Statement of the Chair of the Drafting Committee' (31 July 2019) <https://legal.un.org/ilc/guide/3_5.shtml#dcommrep> accessed 7 January 2024, 6–9.

[120] Three delegations welcomed it in general terms while a fourth challenged it as based on an 'erroneous assumption of a transfer of responsibility' – Sixth Committee, 32nd Meeting (n 116) para 99; Sixth Committee, 23rd meeting (n 29) paras 59, 141.

## APPLICATION TO THE CLASSES OF SUCCESSION    211

the merged States automatically transfer to the successor.[121] There is no example of predecessors agreeing to preclude their transfer in the four modern cases featuring relevant practice:

- Egypt and Syria, to form the United Arab Republic ('UAR') in 1958;
- Somaliland and the Trust Territory for Somalia, to create the Republic of Somalia ('Somalia') in 1960;[122]
- Tanganyika and Zanzibar, to establish the Republic of Tanzania (1964);[123] and
- the Democratic Republic of Viet Nam ('North Viet Nam') with the Republic of Viet Nam ('South Viet Nam'), to form the Socialist Republic of Viet Nam ('Viet Nam') in 1976.[124]

There are no direct examples arising from the creation of Yemen in 1990.[125] Except for the declaration of Somalia, *opiniones juris* have been implicit in the positions taken by the States concerned in dispute settlement.

In 1958 and 1959, the UAR concluded settlement agreements with the *Société Financière de Suez*,[126] France,[127] and the United Kingdom[128] whereby it undertook duties of reparation in full and final settlement of claims for direct and indirect injuries caused by the sequestration and nationalization measures of Egypt in 1956 and waived the claims of Egypt arising from injuries inflicted by France and the United Kingdom during the Suez Canal crisis.[129] Neither the UAR nor the counterparties questioned its succession to the claims and responsibility of Egypt.[130]

Following the merger of North Viet Nam and South Viet Nam in 1976, the United States of America and Viet Nam concluded a treaty in 1995 in full and final settlement of their mutual claims and those of their nationals.[131] The claims concerned the expropriation by South Viet Nam of the assets of American nationals and the

---

[121] IDI Resolution (n 40) art 13; Kohen and Dumberry (n 10) 111.

[122] Law No 5 (31 January 1961) 2 Official Bulletin of the Somali Republic No 2 (1961) art 4(1). The impugned action was done by Somalia in 1962, though the Arbitral Tribunal took the 'historic costs' of the concession awarded by the Trust Territory for Somalia in 1950 into consideration – *The Ditta Luigi Gallotti v The Somali Government* (Award) Arbitral Tribunal (5 December 1964) 40 ILR 158, 160, 163.

[123] Tanzania succeeded Tanganyika as party to the dispute that had arisen in 1962 with Rwanda, Burundi, and the Democratic Republic of the Congo concerning the Belbases port installations concession – O'Connell (n 41) vol II, 242. See further Chapters 5 and 8.

[124] Dumberry (n 43) 115; Kohen and Dumberry (n 10) 111–14; Second Šturma Report (n 25) paras 149–54; Third Šturma Report (n 26) paras 68–73, 82.

[125] While Yemen was found to have succeeded South Yemen in the *Yemen v Compagnie d'Enterprises* dispute, its substitution was based on its status as party to the contract. See Chapter 8.

[126] Eugene Cotran, 'Some Legal Aspects of the Formation of the United Arab Republic and the United Arab States' (1959) 8(2) ICLQ 346, 366.

[127] General Accord (22 August 1958) (1958) 62(4) RGDIP 738, arts 3, 5, 7, protocol II (French).

[128] Agreement Concerning Financial and Commercial Relations and British Property in Egypt (1959) 343 UNTS 159 (1960) 54(2) AJIL 511, preamble, arts III, IV.

[129] Ibid, art IV(5), Exchange of Notes (28 February 1959).

[130] Dumberry (n 43) 116–18.

[131] Agreement concerning the Settlement of Certain Property Claims (Vietnam–United States) (28 January 1995) 34 ILM 685, arts 1, 2(1) 3(1).

## 212    SUCCESSION TO INTERNATIONAL CLAIMS AND RESPONSIBILITY

sequestration by the United States of State property owned by South Viet Nam.[132] Neither State questioned the status of Viet Nam as successor to the claims and responsibility of South Viet Nam. Although the treaty did not expressly describe the expropriations as internationally wrongful acts,[133] it omitted any 'without prejudice' clause in contrast to other State practice concerning expropriations.[134]

Article 13 of the IDI Resolution on a 'merger of States' provides for the passage of the rights and obligations to the successor when 'two or more States unite and form a new successor State'.[135] In 2018, the ILC Special Rapporteur proposed draft article 10(1) that replicated Article 13, with the difference that it dealt only with the transfer of obligations.[136] Malaysia was the only State to comment in the Sixth Committee by indicating general support for draft article 10, subject to the inclusion of more examples of State practice.[137]

In 2021, the Drafting Committee amended draft Article 10 to articulate an obligation for the injured State and the successor to 'agree on how to address the injury':[138]

> Several members noted that there was no rule of 'automatic succession' in [a merger of States] and expressed a preference for a text which clearly stipulated it. Other members were concerned that such position, which effectively amounted to the 'clean slate' approach, would risk leaving the injured State without remedy. The Drafting Committee sought to find a middle way between those positions. It did so initially on the basis of a revised proposal submitted by the Special Rapporteur, which sought to establish an obligation ('shall') between the successor State and injured State to 'endeavour to reach an agreement'.[139]

While sceptics of automatic succession had opined that the IDI Resolution was based not on sufficient practice but a policy decision 'to avoid leaving the

---

[132] See Chapter 7.

[133] ILC, 'Provisional summary record of the 3431st meeting' (17 July 2018) UN Doc A/CN.4/SR.3431 (9 August 2018) 17–18; Sixth Committee, 30th Meeting (n 139) para 45.

[134] E.g. – Burma (n 148), Madagascar (n 150).

[135] Kohen and Dumberry (n 10) 111–14.

[136] Second Šturma Report (n 25) para 165.

[137] Sixth Committee, 'Summary record of the 30th meeting' (31 October 2018) UN Doc A/C.6/73/SR.30 (6 December 2018) para 78; 'Statement by Afzan Abd Kahar, Delegate of Malaysia to the UNGA 73rd Session, Agenda Item 82: Report of the International Law Commission on the Work of its Seventieth Session' (31 October 2018) para 37.

[138] Describing modern practice as 'not always consistent' without explanation, he did not locate practice on either Tanzania or Yemen and made no mention of Somalia – Second Šturma Report (n 25) paras 152–56.

[139] ILC, 'Succession of States in respect of State responsibility: Text of draft articles 10, 10 *bis* and 11 provisionally adopted by the Drafting Committee at the seventy-second session' UN Doc A/CN.4/L.954 (19 July 2021); ILC, 'Succession of States in respect of State Responsibility: Statement of the Chair of the Drafting Committee' (28 July 2021) 3–4, <https://legal.un.org/ilc/guide/3_5.shtml#dcommrep> accessed 7 January 2024.

APPLICATION TO THE CLASSES OF SUCCESSION    213

internationally wrongful act unrepaired',[140] no explanation was provided for the
inadequacy of the cited practice on the UAR and Viet Nam. In converting draft
article 10 into draft guideline 10 in 2022, the Drafting Committee also did not cite
State practice for the distinction drawn between a hortatory guideline to negotiate
on responsibility and a right of the successor in draft guideline 13 to succeed to
claims.[141]

Taking into account that only five mergers have taken place in the modern
era,[142] it is suggested that the aforementioned practice concerning the UAR,
Somalia, Tanzania and Viet Nam is sufficiently coherent to support a rule of customary international law. That practice consistently shows none of the disputing
parties to have objected to the status of the successors as disputing parties for the
internationally wrongful acts of their predecessors. Consequently, it is suggested
that Article 13 of the IDI Resolution accurately reflects that practice.

## 6.3.2 Absorption

When one State absorbs another State, the default rule of customary international
law is that the international claims and responsibility of the absorbed State do not
automatically transfer to the absorbing State unless the successor assume them by
agreement with the predecessor or unilateral adoption. While the sole example
of modern practice is the absorption of the German Democratic Republic ('East
Germany') by the Federal Republic of Germany ('West Germany') in 1990,[143]
classical practice also exists on the following cases:

- Burma by the United Kingdom (1886);
- Madagascar by France (1896);
- Hawai'i by the United States (1898); and
- the South African Republic by the United Kingdom (1902).[144]

---

[140] ILC, 'Provisional summary record of the 3552nd meeting' (28 July 2021) UN Doc A/CN.4/
SR.3552 (14 September 2021) 3–4; ILC, 'Provisional summary record of the 3434th meeting' (20 July
2018) UN Doc A/CN.4/SR.3434 (21 September 2018) 6, 10–11, 13–14.

[141] ILC, 'Succession of States in respect of State responsibility: Text of draft guidelines 6, 7 *bis*, 10,
10 *bis*, 11, 12, 13, 13 *bis*, 14, 15 and 15*bis* as provisionally adopted by the Drafting Committee at the
seventy-third session' UN Doc A/CN.4/L.970 (12 July 2022).

[142] Mergers were also rare in classical practice. The Kingdom of the Two Sicilies accepted responsibility for damages to merchant vessels and cargoes of the United States inflicted by Naples between
1809 and 1812 prior to its merger with Sicily by decision of the 1815 Congress of Vienna – Claims
Convention, 14 October 1832 (27 August 1833) II Malloy 1804, art I.

[143] Treaty on the Establishment of German Unity (West Germany–East Germany) (adopted 30
August 1990, entered into force 3 October 1990) 30 ILM 463, arts 1, 3–4. There is no known practice
arising from the absorptions of Austria (1938), Danzig (1945), or Hyderabad (1950). See further: Cecil
Hurst, 'State Succession in Matters of Tort' (1924) 5 BYIL 163, 167–70.

[144] Unlike municipal torts, there is no known practice on international claims and responsibility concerning Texas (1845), Emilia and the other Italian States (1860–61), Hanover and the other German

214 SUCCESSION TO INTERNATIONAL CLAIMS AND RESPONSIBILITY

After the subjugation of Burma by the United Kingdom on 1 January 1886, numerous claims for indirect injury to third States were investigated.[145] A claim for proprietary damages of an Italian national brought by Italy was settled by an *ex gratia* payment without admission of responsibility while three sets of claims for personal and proprietary injuries by French and American nationals were rejected with the acquiescence of the claimant States.[146]

Following the subjugation of the French-protected State of Madagascar by France in 1896,[147] several claims were addressed to France by third States for injuries between 1894 and 1895. While France settled the claims by making *ex gratia* payments without admission of responsibility,[148] it did not reject responsibility on the basis of non-succession.[149] In a settlement reached in 1906 for proprietary damages to a British national, France reserved the question of succession but contested attribution of the impugned conduct to Madagascar.[150]

After its subjugation of the South African Republic in 1902,[151] the United Kingdom addressed unliquidated claims brought by nationals of third States against the Republic.[152] In the *Robert E. Brown Arbitration*,[153] the United States claimed for proprietary injuries to its national for which the United Kingdom denied a basis in State practice or principle for the assumption of 'unliquidated damages' by a 'conquering State [to take over] liabilities for wrongs which have been committed by the Government of the conquered country'.[154]

While the United States initially asserted a principle of succession to 'the legal obligations of [the] defunct Republic',[155] it abandoned the argument and the United Kingdom rebutted it with reference to precedent and principle.[156] Noting the disclaimer of the United States, the Arbitral Tribunal decided in 1923 that it could not find practice to support the doctrine 'that a succeeding State acquiring a

States (1866–67), or the Transvaal Republic (1877). See, e.g. – 'British Proclamation annexing the Transvaal Republic – Pretoria, April 12, 1877' 68 BFSP 140, 144.

[145] Hurst (n 143) 170–72.

[146] Dumberry (n 43) 81–83.

[147] Treaty respecting the Relations between Madagascar and France (18 January 1896) 88 BFSP 1223, arts I–IV.

[148] Daniel Bardonnet, *La Succession d'États à Madagascar* vol I (Libraire Générale de Droit et de Jurisprudence 1970) 307.

[149] Ibid, 304–07.

[150] Ibid, 312. See also: ARSIWA (n 1) 42 (para 13).

[151] For an overview, see: *Madzimbamuto v Lardner-Burke*, Judicial Committee of the Privy Council (23 July 1968) 39 ILR 61, 102–03.

[152] Claims by British nationals were inadmissible due to the 'act of State doctrine' in internal law; e.g. – *West Rand Central Gold Mining Company Limited v The King* Divisional Court of England and Wales (1905) 2 BILC 238, 287–94, 399–402, 411.

[153] *Robert E. Brown Claim (United States v Great Britain)* British-American Arbitral Tribunal (23 November 1923) 2 ILR 66.

[154] Ibid, 128.

[155] Hurst (n 143) 164.

[156] Ibid, 165; Dumberry (n 43) 88–91.

APPLICATION TO THE CLASSES OF SUCCESSION 215

territory by conquest without any undertaking to assume such liabilities is bound to take affirmative steps to right the wrongs done by the former State'.[157]

In the wake of its absorption of Hawai'i in 1898,[158] the United States initially decided claims by Portugal, Denmark, and the United Kingdom for personal injuries to their nationals arising from a revolt in 1895 to be admissible but unfounded on their merits.[159] Two years after the conclusion of the *Robert E. Brown Arbitration*, however, it contested its succession to Hawai'i for responsibility arising out of personal injury to British nationals on the ground that no basis existed in State practice.[160] The United Kingdom contended that the succession of the United States was grounded not in State practice but rather 'natural justice' in distinguishing Hawai'i from the South African Republic as a case of voluntary absorption rather than annexation by force.[161] Rejecting this argument, the Arbitral Tribunal held:

> In the first place, it assumes a general principle of succession to liability for delicts, to which the case of succession of one State to another through conquest would be an exception. We think there is no such principle. It was denied in the Brown case and has never been contended for to any such extent ... nor do we see any valid reason for distinguishing termination of a legal unit of international law through conquest from termination by any other mode of merging in, or swallowing up by, some other legal unit. In either case the legal unit which did the wrong no longer exists, and legal liability for the wrong has been extinguished with it.[162]

While it has been argued that the 'political domination' of the United States over the 'puppet government' of the Republic of Hawai'i should have resulted in the attribution of the conduct of the latter to the former under the law of State responsibility,[163] the arbitration remains significant due to the agreement of the disputing parties and the Arbitral Tribunal on the lack of State practice to underpin a rule of succession.

Effective on the date of succession, West Germany and East Germany agreed on 'settlement of claims and liabilities vis-à-vis foreign countries and [West] Germany'.[164] West Germany undertook the responsibility to repair for the expropriations of private property done by East Germany but not those done by the

---

[157] *Robert E. Brown Claim* (n 153) 129–30.

[158] JB Moore, *International Arbitrations to which the United States has been a Party* vol II (1898) 509–10.

[159] Ibid, vol I, 337, 519.

[160] Ibid, 79 (notes 104–07).

[161] Dumberry (n 6) 78–79 (notes 100–03); Hurst (n 145) 164–65.

[162] *F.H. Redward and others (Great Britain) v United States* (Award) (10 November 1925) 6 RIAA 157, 158.

[163] Dumberry (n 6) 97–98.

[164] Treaty on German Unity (n 145) art 24(1). On claims with respect to cultural property in the possession of Russia, see: Jakubowski, *State Succession in Cultural Property* (OUP 2015) 194–96.

Soviet Union.[165] West Germany compensated nationals of the United States for proprietary damages inflicted by East Germany between 1946 and 1976[166] while the Federal Administrative Court 'rejected, as a matter of principle, the responsibility of [West] Germany' for such injuries against a Dutch national in finding that the obligation to pay compensation had passed to West Germany.[167]

Article 14 of the IDI Resolution provides for a default rule of transfer of 'rights or obligations arising from an internationally wrongful act' in an absorption,[168] which the ILC Special Rapporteur followed in proposing draft article 10(2) in solely examining the case of East Germany.[169] The only State to comment specifically on the question of incorporation of a State in the Sixth Committee, Austria considered a rule of automaticity not to be 'warranted by State practice'.[170] In converting the draft articles into draft guidelines in 2022,[171] the Drafting Committee proposed draft guideline 13*bis* prescribing a right of the absorbing State to invoke responsibility towards a third State for an internationally wrongful act against the absorbed State.[172] As for mergers, the Drafting Committee did not explain the basis in State practice for the divergence between a guideline to endeavour to agree on succession to responsibility and a right to succeed to claims.

It is suggested that classical State practice on the absorptions of Madagascar, Burma, Hawai'i, and the South African Republic is consistent in evincing a default rule of non-succession.[173] While modern practice on the absorption of East Germany supports a trend towards a default rule of succession,[174] it remains *lex ferenda* due to being the only example to date. Consequently, the rule of default succession to international claims and responsibility in Article 14 of the IDI Resolution does not yet reflect customary international law.

---

[165] Ibid, art 41, annex III. See also: *Unification Treaty Constitutionality Case (Merits)* Federal Constitutional Court (23 April 1991) 94 ILR 42, 48–53, 59–66; *von Maltzan and Others, von Zitzewitz and Others, and Ferrostaal and Stiftung v Germany*, App Nos 71916/01, 71917/01, and 10260/02 European Court of Human Rights (Grand Chamber) Decision (2 March 2005) paras 74–114.

[166] Agreement between the Government of the Federal Republic of Germany and the Government of the United States of America concerning the Settlement of Certain Property Claims (adopted 13 May 1992, entered into force 28 December 1992) 1911 UNTS 27, arts 1–2. See further: Dumberry (n 43) 108–10; Crawford (n 14) 449–50; Second Šturma Report (n 25) para 161.

[167] German Federal Administrative Court (Decision) (1 July 1999) (1999) 52 NJW 3354 in Dumberry (n 43) 107. See also: Crawford (n 14) 450; Second Šturma Report (n 25) para 160.

[168] Kohen and Dumberry (n 10) 114.

[169] Though correctly noting that Singapore was 'the territory of the United Kingdom', he nevertheless erroneously categorized its cession to Malaysia as a case of absorption –Second Šturma Report (n 25) paras 157–64.

[170] Sixth Committee, 'Summary record of the 28th meeting' (30 October 2018) UN Doc A/C.6/73/SR.28 (10 December 2018) para 64.

[171] ILC, 'Text of draft articles 10, 10 *bis* and 11' (n 140); ILC, 'Statement of the Chair of the Drafting Committee' (n 141) 6–9.

[172] Ibid, 12–13.

[173] Dumberry (n 43) 75–100; Kohen and Dumberry (n 10) 116–19.

[174] Ibid, 83–93.

### 6.3.3 Dismemberment

When a State is dismembered so that parts of its territory are transferred to existing States or new States, the default rule of customary international law is that international claims and responsibility do not automatically transfer to the successors unless a successor assume them by agreement with the other successors or unilateral adoption.[175] The two cases of modern practice are the dismemberments of the Socialist Federal Republic of Yugoslavia (1991–92) and Czecho-Slovakia (1993). While the classical cases of the Union of Colombia (1829–31) and the Peru-Bolivian Confederation (1839)[176] provide additional information on this rare class, the Allied Powers applied a special rule to the dismemberment of Austria-Hungary (1920)[177] by assigning responsibility for war damages to Austria and Hungary but not the other successors.[178]

After the dismemberment of the Union of Colombia (*Gran Colombia*) in 1830,[179] the United States addressed claims to Venezuela, New Grenada ('Colombia'), and Ecuador for 'joint and several' liability in 1839.[180] In 1852, Venezuela undertook to indemnify in fixed sums for proprietary injuries by the Union of Colombia to American nationals in the years 1818, 1819, and 1827.[181] In 1865, an American–Ecuadorian claims commission[182] decided that claims brought by American

---

[175] Ibid, 103–05; Crawford (n 14) 452; First Šturma Report (n 44) paras 54, 109; Second Šturma Report (n 25) paras 167, 178.

[176] Peru accepted responsibility to 'make full satisfaction' for various claims of American nationals for proprietary damages during the War of the Confederation – Claims Convention (adopted 17 March 1841, entered into force 8 January 1847) II Malloy 1386, art I.

[177] The ILC Special Rapporteur wrongly stated that 'the Allied Powers considered this situation as secession, and they saw Austria and Hungary as continuing legal personality of the Austrian-Hungarian Empire' – Second Šturma Report (n 25) para 82. Two States cannot both continue a single legal personality and the Allied Powers treated Austria as a continuation of the Austrian Empire (*Cisleithania*) and Hungary as a continuation of the Kingdom of Hungary (*Translitheinia*) but not the Dual Monarchy ('Austria-Hungary') for the apportionment of the decentralized State debt: see Chapters 2 and 4.

[178] The description of the event ('whereas the former Austro-Hungarian Monarchy has now ceased to exist, and has been replaced in Austria by a republican government') was vague – Treaty of Saint-Germain-en-Laye, 10 September 1919 (16 July 1920) (1919) 226 CTS 8, preamble, arts 177–90 and Annexes; Treaty of Trianon, 4 June 1920 (26 July 1921) 3 Malloy 3539, preamble, arts 161–74 and annexes. See also: EM Borchard, 'Sequestrated Private Property and American Claims – the Treaties of Versailles and Berlin' (1925) 19(2) AJIL 355–59, 358; *Rothschild v Administrator of Austrian Property*, High Court of Justice of England (31 July 1923) 2 ILR 237, 239; *Groedel v Administrator of Hungarian Property*, High Court of Justice of England (10 November 1927) 4 ILR 304, 306. The jurisprudence of the Austrian courts concerned municipal torts – Dumberry (n 6) 98–123.

[179] O'Connell (n 41) vol I, 43–44; Armas Pfirter and González Napolitano, 'Secession and international law: Latin American practice' in Kohen (ed) *Secession: International Law Perspectives* (2006) 374–415, 382–87.

[180] Dumberry (n 6) 106 (n 219). See also: 'Mr Adams, Secretary of State, to Mr Anderson, min. to Colombia, May 27, 1823' 13 BFSP 459, 480–81; Claims Convention (United States–New Grenada) (adopted 10 September 1857, entered into force 19 August 1865) in Malloy, ibid, vol I, 319 (art V).

[181] Protocol (Venezuela–United States of America) (1 May 1852) in II Malloy 1842, preamble, arts 1, 3. The United States had recognized Gran Colombia as a State in 1822 during its war of secession from Spain, though Spain did not recognize the independence of Ecuador until 1841, Venezuela in 1846 and Colombia in 1881 – Armas Pfirter and González Napolitano (n 179) 375, 382.

[182] Claims Convention (Ecuador–United States–Ecuador) (adopted 25 November 1862, entered into force 8 September 1864) in Malloy, ibid, vol I 432 (arts I, V).

218 SUCCESSION TO INTERNATIONAL CLAIMS AND RESPONSIBILITY

nationals in respect of the seizure of two vessels in 1827 were inadmissible because those vessels had violated forfeited neutral status.[183] On the question of succession, however, it concluded: 'In the dissolution of the original republic, New Grenada, Venezuela, and Ecuador each assumed a proportionate part of the burdens of the parent state, and to that extent became answerable for claims against it.'[184] This finding were followed by the American–Colombian and American–Venezuelan claims commissions.[185]

In another award concerning the seizure and condemnation of the cargo of an American vessel (*The Mechanic*) in breach of a 1795 Spanish–American treaty, the claimants had claimed 'for an award of 21 ½ per cent of the original amount as the proportion of the old Colombian debt, for which Ecuador made herself liable on the disintegration of the Republic of Colombia'.[186] The claims commission decided the claim on the basis that Ecuador had been bound by the 1795 treaty in succession to the Union of Colombia and Spain.[187] Overall, the practice on the American claims shows that the successors to the Union of Colombia each unilaterally adopted responsibility for its internationally wrongful acts in proportion to their shares of its State debt.

In modern practice, the question of succession to the international claims and responsibility of Czecho-Slovakia arose in the *Gabčikovo-Nagymaros Project Case*. In their treaty submitting the dispute, Hungary and Slovakia agreed that Slovakia was 'the sole successor State in respect of rights and obligations relating to the ...Project', including the impugned decision of Czecho-Slovakia to proceed to the 'Variant C solution'.[188] Five weeks beforehand, Czechia had tendered a *note verbale* to the European Commission stating that it 'would not become a succession state [*sic.*] to the Treaty ... on the construction and operation of the Gacikovo-Nagymaros Barrage System of Locks'.[189] In its pleadings, Hungary asserted:

> The first legal consequence is that Slovakia cannot be deemed responsible for breaches of treaty obligations attributable only to Czechoslovakia, which no longer exists. Nevertheless, Czechoslovakia's breaches of ... international law created a series of secondary obligations; namely, the obligation to repair the damage caused by the wrongful acts. These secondary obligations were neither

---

[183] Moore (n 152) 1572–73.

[184] Ibid, 1572.

[185] Ibid, 1573–74.

[186] *Atlantic and Hope Insurance Companies v Ecuador (The Mechanic)* (Opinion) Commissioner Hassaurek (8 January 1865) 29 RIAA 108, 109. See also: *Consolidated Debt of New Grenada Cases*, US–Colombian Claims Commission (1864) IV Moore 3612.

[187] Ibid, 111–14. See also: O'Connell (n 41) vol II, 92.

[188] Special Agreement for submission to the International Court of Justice of the differences between Hungary and Slovakia concerning the Gabčikovo-Nagymaros Project (adopted 7 April 1993, entered into force 26 June 1993) 1725 UNTS 225, preamble, art 2(b).

[189] *Gabčikovo-Nagymaros Project (Hungary v Slovakia)* (Memorial of Hungary) vol 1 (2 May 1994) para 2.07.

APPLICATION TO THE CLASSES OF SUCCESSION 219

extinguished by the termination of the 1977 Treaty nor by the disappearance of Czechoslovakia.[190]

Hungary argued that Slovakia had 'effectively endorsed its international responsibility for Variant C' and by the Special Agreement 'assumed the obligations, as operator of Variant C, to repair damage caused by present and prior breaches of international law'.[191]

Slovakia averred that there 'exists in law no customary rule or general principle supposing the automatic transfer to the State successor of the obligations resulting from the international responsibility of a predecessor State'.[192] While it did not deny responsibility for Variant C, it considered it to be based not upon its adoption of responsibility but rather its own conduct 'as a party to the 1977 Treaty'.[193] Recalling 'the well-established principle that there is in general no succession to international responsibility', Hungary replied that Slovakia had assumed 'the breaches of the law committed by its predecessor' by its own conduct as an exception to that general rule.[194]

The Court did not pronounce on the question of principle in observing 'that Slovakia [was] the sole successor State of Czechoslovakia in respect of rights and obligations relating to the ... Project' and the Parties considered that Slovakia might 'be liable to pay compensation not only for its own wrongful conduct but also for that of Czechoslovakia, and it [was] entitled to be compensated for the damage sustained by Czechoslovakia as well as by itself as a result of the wrongful conduct of Hungary'.[195] While the case 'is an example of succession to [claims and] responsibility by agreement',[196] the *opiniones juris* of Hungary and Slovakia expressly rejected a general rule of automatic succession.

Following the completion of the dismemberment of the SFRY on 27 April 1992, the successors agreed in their 2001 Agreement on Succession Issues that '[a]ll claims against the SFRY ... shall be considered by the Standing Joint Committee established under Article 4 of this Agreement'.[197] This left open the question whether the Standing Joint Committee 'might decide that [any given claim against the SFRY] was now a matter solely for one or other of the successor States, or that it was a matter for two or more of them jointly, or that it [has] nothing to do with any of them—i.e.—in the last case their position would be that the claim died with

---

[190] Ibid, para 8.03.
[191] Ibid, paras 8.04–8.05.
[192] Ibid, Counter-Memorial of Slovakia vol I (5 December 1994) para 3.60.
[193] Ibid, para 12.19.
[194] Ibid, Reply of Hungary vol 1 (20 June 1995) para 3.163.
[195] *Gabčikovo-Nagymaros Project (Hungary v Slovakia)* (Judgment) [1997] ICJ Rep 7, para 151. See further: Dumberry (n 43) 138–144; Crawford (n 14) 446; Second Šturma Report (n 25) para 172.
[196] Crawford (n 14) 447.
[197] Agreement on Succession Issues between the Five Successor States of the former State of Yugoslavia (adopted 29 June 2001, entered into force 2 June 2004) 2262 UNTS 251, annex F, art 2.

220 SUCCESSION TO INTERNATIONAL CLAIMS AND RESPONSIBILITY

the SFRY.[198] While Australia had notified the International Conference on the Former Yugoslavia in 1992 of a claim against the SFRY for personal injuries to an Australian national[199] and the FRY had declared itself to continue the international legal personality of the SFRY while remaining in possession of the consulate from where the impugned conduct was committed,[200] the Standing Joint Committee has confirmed in correspondence with the present author that it has not considered the claim.

In the *Croatia Genocide Case*, the question arose of succession to the international responsibility of the SFRY prior to the date of succession of the FRY (27 April 1992). Croatia argued that the succession 'came about as a result of the application of the principles of general international law regarding State succession' whereby the fact that the FRY 'largely controlled the armed forces of the SFRY during the last year of the latter's formal existence ... justif[ied] the succession of the FRY to the responsibility incurred by the SFRY for acts of armed forces that subsequently became organs of the FRY.[201] It also asserted that 'the FRY, by the declaration of 27 April 1992 ... indicated not only that it was succeeding to the treaty obligations of the SFRY, but also that it succeeded to the responsibility incurred by the SFRY for the violation of those treaty obligations.[202]

Serbia retorted that there was no principle of succession to responsibility in general international law, the declaration of 27 April 1992 being concerned only with succession to treaties so that 'all issues of succession to the rights and obligations of the SFRY are governed by the Agreement on Succession Issues, 2001 ... which lays down a procedure for considering outstanding claims against the SFRY.[203] As the ICJ concluded that acts occurring prior to 27 April 1992 were admissible, it was 'not necessary to decide whether the FRY, and therefore Serbia, actually succeeded to any responsibility that might have been incurred by the SFRY.[204]

---

[198] 'Letter dated 13 November 2002 by Sir Arthur Watts to Patrick Dumberry' in Dumberry (n 43) 150 (note 427).

[199] *J. Tokic v Government of Yugoslavia* Case No S14790/91 Supreme Court of New South Wales (12 December 1991) 9–10 (on file with author). There is no record of the debt being settled – Dumberry (n 43) 152 (note 433). Pursuant to the Foreign State Immunities Act 1985, service of the default judgment on the SFRY was done on 18 March 1992; as the consulate premises were immune from enforcement, the Court ordered the Consul-General on 22 September to give evidence of the commercial assets owned by the SFRY in its jurisdiction, following which no record of further action is in the case file (on file with author).

[200] 'Letter dated 6 May 1992 from the Permanent Mission of Yugoslavia to the United Nations', UN Doc A/46/915 (7 May 1992).

[201] *Convention on the Prevention and Punishment of the Crime of Genocide (Croatia v Serbia)* (Merits) [2015] ICJ Rep 3, para 107.

[202] Ibid; Verbatim Record (21 March 2014) CR 2014/21, paras 39–42.

[203] Ibid, para 108; Verbatim Record, CR 2014/22, 27 March 2014, paras 46–54.

[204] Ibid, paras 114, 117. In voting against the operative paragraph of the Judgment regarding the admissibility of the claim of Croatia for acts prior to 27 April 1992, Judge Xue observed that 'little can be found about State succession to responsibility in the field of general international law' and '[r]ules of State responsibility in the event of succession remain to be developed' – Declaration of Judge Xue, para 23. See also: Separate Opinion of Judge Skoltnikov, paras 2–9; Separate Opinion of Judge ad hoc Kreća, paras 60–65.4; Kohen and Dumberry (n 10) 12 (n 18).

Article 15(1) of the IDI Resolution provides for a default rule of succession to 'one, several or all the successor States' according to different tests for the allocation of international claims and responsibility.[205] This was justified both in reference to the 2001 Agreement on Succesion Issues and the *Gabčikovo-Nagymaros Project Case* as well as the normative argument that 'strict and automatic non-succession is in complete contradiction with the very idea of justice'.[206]

In proposing draft article 11(1) that resembled Article 15(1) save insofar the passage of international responsibility was stated to be 'subject to an agreement' between the successors,[207] the ILC Special Rapporteur noted the Union of Colombia as supporting a general principle of succession.[208] Considering the arguments of the disputing parties in the *Gabčikovo-Nagymaros Project Case* to have been 'contradictory',[209] he described the *Croatia Genocide Case* as 'the most recent pronouncement in favour of [succession to responsibility]' even though 'the Court did not need to decide on the question of succession', while the argument of Serbia supported 'the view that the 2001 Agreement and annex F thereto are indeed relevant to the issues of succession in respect of State responsibility.[210]

Whereas Malaysia and Croatia endorsed a 'general rule of non-succession with some exceptions',[211] the Netherlands supported a rule of automatic transfer in the absence of agreement.[212] The Drafting Committee converted draft article 11 into a guideline exhorting the injured State and 'the relevant successor State or States' to agree on how to address the injury arising from the internationally wrongful act and added draft guideline 14 providing for a right to succeed to international claims 'in particular circumstances', with the wrongdoing State and the 'relevant successor State or States' exhorted to reach agreement.[213]

---

[205] Kohen and Dumberry (n 10) 118–28.

[206] Ibid, 103–04.

[207] Second Šturma Report (n 25) para 190.

[208] Ibid, paras 167–69. He erroneously cited the secession of Syria from the UAR in 1961 as a dismemberment – ibid, para 170. While Egypt continued the name and legal personality of the UAR and the Sixth Committee reported that Syria should be admitted to UN membership, the General Assembly decided in the absence of objection to accredit Syria under its old membership before its merger with Egypt – Richard Young, 'State of Syria: Old or New?' (1962) 56(2) AJIL 482, 482–83, 486–87; MM Whiteman, *Digest of International Law* vol III (Government Printing Office 1964) 987–90.

[209] Ibid, para. 175.

[210] Ibid, paras 182–84. One cited case of the ECtHR is immaterial because a Liechtenstein claimant against Slovenia for proprietary losses sustained by acts of the SFRY failed to exhaust local remedies – *Glas-Metall Trust Reg. v Slovenia* App No. 47523/10 European Court of Human Rights (12 June 2018). Another cited case is irrelevant because it concerned a municipal tort for proprietary injuries inflicted by the SFRY on one of its nationals – *Zaklan v Croatia* App No. 57239/13 European Court of Human Rights (16 December 2021) paras 2, 5–11, 48–50, 55–56.

[211] Sixth Committee, 'Summary record of the 33rd meeting' (6 November 2019) UN Doc A/C.6/74/SR.33 (3 February 2020) para 4; Sixth Committee, 17th Meeting (n 29) para 62. See also: 'Statement by Croatia at the 74th Session of the General Assembly Sixth Committee, Agenda Item 79, Report of the International Law Commission on the work of its seventieth session, Cluster I' (29 October 2019).

[212] Sixth Committee, 24th Meeting (n 29) para 110.

[213] ILC, 'Text of draft articles 10, 10 *bis* and 11' (n 140); ILC, 'Statement of the Chair of the Drafting Committee' (n 141) 9–11.

222 SUCCESSION TO INTERNATIONAL CLAIMS AND RESPONSIBILITY

The classical cases of the Union of Colombia and the Peru-Bolivian Confederation provide limited support for a default rule of succession, yet the *opiniones juris* of Hungary and Slovakia in the *Gabčikovo-Nagymaros Project* agreed upon a rule of non-succession with exceptions for agreement and unilateral adoption. While the ICJ gave no answer to the question of succession to responsibility in the *Croatia Genocide Case*, Croatia expressed an *opinio juris* in favour of a general rule of succession that Serbia opposed on the ground that the successors have adopted a special rule in the 2001 Agreement on Succession Issues. In this context, it is suggested that the default rule of non-succession to international claims and responsibility save by agreement amongst the successors or unilateral adoption was expressed by the disputing parties in the *Gabčikovo-Nagymaros Project Case*. While there are normative arguments in favour of a default rule of succession, Article 15(1) remains potential *lex ferenda*.

### 6.3.4 Cession

When one State cedes a part of its territory to another State, the default rule of customary international law is that international claims and responsibility of the predecessor do not transfer to the successor save by agreement with the predecessor or unilateral adoption. State practice shows the consent of the third State not to be required. While the theoretical possibility exists of a dispute between the predecessor and successor with respect to succession by adoption to international claims, this has yet to occur in practice.

Modern practice comprises the succession agreements that implied succession to international claims and responsibility by asserting that the cessionaire would assume 'all' rights and obligations of the ceding State with respect to the ceded territory. These are the cessions of:

- French India by France to India (1952 and 1954);[214]
- Portuguese India by Portugal to India (1961 and 1962);[215] and
- North Borneo, Sarawak, and Singapore by the United Kingdom to Malaysia (1963).[216]

---

[214] Treaty of Cession of the Free Town of Chandernagore (India–France) (adopted 2 February 1951, entered into force 9 June 1952) 158 BFSP 599, art I; Agreement concerning the future of the French Establishments in India (France–India) (21 October 1954) 161 BFSP 533, art 1.

[215] Dadra and Nagar Haveli Act No 35 1961 < https://www.indiacode.nic.in/bitstream/123456 789/1640/2/A1961-35.pdf> accessed 30 December 2023, s 7; Goa, Daman and Diu (Administration) Act 1962 <https://www.indiacode.nic.in/bitstream/123456789/1369/2/A1962-01.pdf> accessed 30 December 2023, ss 4–5; Treaty on Recognition of India's Sovereignty over Goa, Daman, Diu, Dadra and Nagar Haveli (adopted 31 December 1974, entered into force 3 June 1975) 982 UNTS 153, art I.

[216] Agreement concluded between the United Kingdom and the Federation of Malaya, Cmd 2094 (July 1963) annex A, art 76.

APPLICATION TO THE CLASSES OF SUCCESSION    223

Save with respect to Malaysia,[217] however, there is no subsequent practice concerning international claims and responsibility to confirm this interpretation. To these instances of modern practice may be added the classical cases of Tarapacá (1883), Crete (1913), and Samos (1914).[218] There are no examples of practice from the cessions of North Borneo, Sarawak and Singapore (1963), Ifni (1971), Walvis Bay (1994), Hong Kong (1997), or Macao (1999).[219]

Prior to the cession of the Tarapacá region by Peru to Chile in 1883,[220] Italy addressed a claim to Chile with respect to the expropriation without compensation by Peru of property belonging to its nationals in 1875.[221] After initially denying an obligation to repair, Chile settled the claim with Italy in 1886.[222]

After the cessions by the Ottoman Empire to Greece of Crete in 1913 and Samos in 1914,[223] France brought four sets of claims against Greece on behalf of its national in the *Lighthouses Arbitration* for breaches of concessionary contracts concerning the maintenance of lighthouses in the ceded territories.[224] The Arbitral Tribunal arranged them by chronology:

1. acts preceding 1924 attributable to the Ottoman Empire (Claim No. 12a); and
2. acts attributable to the 'Autonomous State of Crete' preceding 1913 (Claim Nos 4 and 11).[225]

---

[217] Note 253.

[218] The jurisprudence of the Franco–German Arbitral Tribunal on claims brought by French nationals on was based on the special meaning of the term 'national of an Allied or Associated State' as including persons who had been German nationals before being collectively nationalized in consequence of the retrocession of Alsace-Lorraine – Peace Treaty of Versailles (adopted 28 June 1919, entered into force 10 January 1920) 225 CTS 188, arts 51, 79, & annex 1, 302, 304; Dumberry (n 43) 428–30. For the cession of the Dodecanese Islands by Italy to Greece in 1953, no general rule on international claims or responsibility was prescribed – Treaty of Peace with Italy (adopted 10 February 1947, entered into force 30 September 1953) 49 UNTS 3, art 14. While Italy was obliged to retain responsibility for war damages sustained by nationals of third States in the ceded territory, the negotiating history suggests that this was a special treaty rule – ibid, art 78(7); GG Fitzmaurice, 'The Juridical Clauses of the Peace Treaties' (1948) 73 RdC 260, 340. A Greek court held Greece to be responsible in 1952 for violations by Italy in 1933 of the Treaty of Lausanne and the 1907 Hague Convention; however, the case was not one of diplomatic protection because the claimants held Greek nationality – *Nissyros Mines Case*, Greece Council of State (1952) 19 ILR 135, 137; Philippe Drakidis, 'Succession d'Etats et enrichissements sans cause des biens public du Dodécanese' (1971) 24 RHDI 109, 110.

[219] Jurisprudence on the cessions of Bessarabia (1918), Alsace-Lorraine (1919), and Transylvania (1920) entirely concerns municipal torts – Dumberry (n 43) 168–72. E.g. – *Personal Injuries (Upper Silesia) Case*, Court of Appeal of Cologne (10 December 1951) 18 ILR 67.

[220] Treaty of Peace and Friendship (Peru–Chile) (20 October 1883) *Colección de Actos Internacionales Celebrados por la Républica del Peru* (Ministerio de Relaciones Exteriores 1915) 1, art II.

[221] *UN Materials on Succession of States in respect of Matters other than Treaties*, UN Doc ST/LEG/SER.B/17 (1978) 11–16.

[222] Ibid, 16–17.

[223] Treaty of Lausanne, 24 July 1923 (6 August 1924) 28 LNTS 11, arts 12, 15.

[224] *Lighthouse Concession of the Ottoman Empire (France v Greece)* (Award) Permanent Court of Arbitration (24–27 July 1956) XII RIAA 165, 178–86.

[225] Ibid, 167.

224  SUCCESSION TO INTERNATIONAL CLAIMS AND RESPONSIBILITY

For the former set of claims, the Arbitral Tribunal found Greece not to have been subrogated to a duty to compensate for alleged concession violations by the Ottoman naval authorities in 1911 and 1912 because the acts preceded the critical date of succession and were not wrongful.[226] It rejected a general doctrine on State succession to abrogate the legal effects of the attribution of responsibility according to time.[227]

For the latter set, the Tribunal found Greece to be responsible for the 'tortious debts' (*dettes délictuelles*) arising from the specific case of the 'union' of Crete and Greece due to the adoption by Greece of the conduct of the Autonomous State of Crete.[228] Rejecting Claim No. 11 on the merits,[229] it ruled Claim No. 4 admissible in dismissing the doctrinal argument in Germanophone scholarship of a general and absolute rule of non-succession due to the 'personal in the highest degree' (*h öchstpersönlich*) character of responsibility because civil law provided that tortious debts of private persons of the same 'personal character' pass to their heirs.[230] As Greece was ordered to pay damages for the period 1909 to 1914 while the date of succession was 30 May 1913,[231] the example is one of succession to the responsibility of the Ottoman Empire rather than a continuing internationally wrongful act by Greece.[232]

Based on the succession agreements concluded for the cessions of Tarapacá, French India, and Portuguese India and the reasoning of the Arbitral Tribunal in the *Lighthouses Arbitration*, it is suggested that the weight of practice supports a default rule of succession to international claims and responsibility articulated in Article 11(2) of the IDI Resolution on the basis of a 'direct link between the consequences of [an internationally wrongful act committed by the predecessor] and the territory transferred.'[233] However, there is no basis in practice for the alternative test of a direct link with the population of the transferred territory.[234]

State practice also does not support the distinction drawn in Article 11 between international claims, to which paragraph 2 applies, and international

---

[226] Ibid, 188–89.

[227] Ibid, 189–90.

[228] Ibid, 198. In an older judgment concerning the cession of Samos, a Greek court held Greece to have succeeded to a municipal tort by Ottoman customs officials through its substitution for the autonomous Principality of Samos – *Samos (Liability for Torts) Case*, Court of the Aegean Islands (1924) 2 ILR 70.

[229] Ibid, 190–91, 195–96.

[230] Ibid, 199.

[231] Ibid, 254.

[232] *Contra*: Kohen and Dumberry (n 10) 138–41.

[233] Kohen and Dumberry (n 10) 80–82. Save in being confined to the 'obligations arising from an internationally wrongful act', draft article 9 proposed by the ILC Special Rapporteur corresponded to Article 11 – Second Šturma Report (n 25) paras 138–46; ILC Report, Seventieth Session (n 139) 334. The draft provision prompted scant debate in the plenary meetings of the ILC and no specific comments by States in the Sixth Committee – ILC, 'Provisional summary record of the 3433rd Meeting' (19 July 2018) UN Doc A/CN.4/SR.3433 (9 August 2018) 11; ILC, 3434th Meeting (n 141) 8.

[234] Ibid, 85.

responsibility, for which paragraph 3 provides for a test of succession 'when the author of [an internationally wrongful act] was an organ of the territorial unit of the predecessor State that has later become an organ of the successor State'. Cited practice concerning Samos concerned a municipal tort,[235] leaving the reasoning of the Arbitral Tribunal concerning Claim No. 4 in the *Lighthouses Arbitration* as its sole basis.[236] It is suggested that that reasoning is flawed because a ceded territory can lack autonomy,[237] which can also be modified or abolished by the successor.[238]

## 6.3.5 Secession

When a part of the territory of one State secedes to create a new State,[239] the default rule of customary international law is that the new State succeeds to the international claims and responsibility with a dominant connection to the transferred territory and all other claims and responsibility remain with the parent State unless transferred by agreement with the predecessor or unilateral adoption. In rare cases of concurrent secessions by territories that previously formed a single unit (e,g. —British India), claims and responsibility concerning the entire territory of that unit are equitably apportioned on a joint and several basis. These default rules may be displaced by agreement between the predecessor and successor or decision of an international court or tribunal for which the consent of a third State is not required.

Relative to the dozens of instances of secession to have taken place in the modern era, the known State practice on succession to international claims and responsibility is limited:

- India and Pakistan from the United Kingdom (1947);
- Indonesia from the Netherlands (1949);
- Ghana from the United Kingdom (1957);
- Syria from the UAR (1961);
- Singapore from Malaysia (1967);
- Mozambique from Portugal (1975);[240] and

---

[235] *Samos (Liability for Torts) Case* (n 228).
[236] Kohen and Dumberry (n 10) 88–89.
[237] E.g. - JB Moore, *A Digest of International Law* vol I (US Government Printing Office 1906) vol I, 357–74, 379–85 (Cuba, Puerto Rico and the Philippines).
[238] On the abolition of the autonomy of Eritrea by Ethiopia in 1962 after its cession by Italy in 1952, for example, see: Raymond Goy, 'L'indépendance de l'Érythrée' (1993) 39 AFDI 337, 341; UNGA Res 390(V), 2 December 1950, 1.
[239] See Chapter 1.
[240] On 9 April 1975, Switzerland addressed a claim to the Transitional Government of Mozambique for injuries to one of its nationals by an armed patrol in Mozambique on 4 April before Mozambique seceded on 25 June – Letter from Consul-General of Switzerland to Prime Minister of the Transitional Government of Mozambique (9 April 1975) in 'Alto Comissão Moçambique' Portugal Archives Box 40603 (Portuguese).

226    SUCCESSION TO INTERNATIONAL CLAIMS AND RESPONSIBILITY

- Montenegro from the State Union of Serbia and Montenegro ('FRY') in 2006.[241]

The 'complex' example of East Germany is confused[242] and there are no pertinent examples from classical practice.[243]

Following their concurrent secessions from the United Kingdom on 11 August 1947,[244] India and Pakistan agreed in 1948 on the apportionment of the share of compensation for war reparations allocated to British India under a 1946 treaty with Germany.[245] The other Parties neither objected nor ratified the agreement but simply 'took note' of it.[246]

During a transitional period before its secession on 27 December 1949,[247] the Netherlands, 'acting on behalf of the Government of Indonesia formerly the Government of the Netherlands Indies', concluded a treaty with Australia on 12 August 1949 for the settlement of claims and counterclaims concerning the Second World War.[248] Indonesia paid Australia a lump sum to which was applied a set-off for claims of Indonesia.[249] After its secession, Indonesia concluded a similar agreement with Japan in 1958 featuring mutual waivers of claims with respect to

---

[241] Practice concerning the secessions of the Democratic Republic of the Congo (1960), Kenya (1963), Algeria (1963), and Vanuatu (1980) concerns municipal torts because the injuries were caused to nationals of the predecessors under internal law rather than foreign nationals under international law – Dumberry (n 6) 146–48, 173–82, 329–30; Kohen and Dumberry (n 10) 93, 132–33. See also: *Mutua and Others v Foreign and Commonwealth Office*, High Court of Justice (Queen's Bench Division) Judgment (21 July 2011) [2011] EWHC 1913 (QB) paras 80–96.

[242] Dumberry (n 6) 148–49. See also, e.g. –Agreement on the Settlement of Questions relating to Property Rights (Sweden–East Germany) (adopted 24 October 1986, entered into force 19 December 1986) in BW Weston, RB Lillich, and DJ Bederman (eds) *International Claims: Their Settlement by Lump Sum Agreements, 1975–1995* (CUP 1999) 305, arts 1–3, 6–7.

[243] The claims brought against the Netherlands after the secession of Belgium in 1830 concerned actions that it had taken before its annexation by France while the claims brought against Panama after its secession from Colombia in 1903 did not produce a clear outcome – Dumberry (n 43) 215–20.

[244] Prior to independence, India was not a Dominion but rather an autonomous territory of the United Kingdom: see Chapter 2. Their succession agreement on State property and debt included a provision for the assignment of 'liability in respect of an actionable wrong other than breach of contract' according to the territory in which the 'cause of action arose' – Indian Independence (Rights, Property and Liabilities) Order 1947, 3 CILC 134, art 10. Though applied extensively in the Indian and Pakistani courts for the assignment of municipal torts, there is no evidence of its application to international claims or responsibility: see Chapter 4.

[245] Agreement on Reparation from Germany (adopted 14 January 1946, entered into force 15 September 1947) 555 UNTS 69, arts 1–2. The shares of 82.5 per cent to India and 17.5 per cent to Pakistan corresponded to the key that they had agreed for the apportionment of the property of British India: see Chapter 4.

[246] Protocol attached to the Paris Agreement of 14 January 1946 on Reparation (15 March 1948) 555 UNTS 105.

[247] Indonesia agreed with the Netherlands that 'all rights and obligations of Indonesia [*sic*.], under private and public law, are ipso jure transferred to the Republic of the United States of Indonesia, unless otherwise provided for in the special agreements included in the Union Statute' – Agreement on Transitional Measures (Indonesia–Netherlands) (27 December 1949) 69 UNTS 266, art 4(1). The Dutch courts applied this provision to municipal torts – Dumberry (n 43) 249–51. See Chapter 4.

[248] Agreement concerning the Final Settlement of Claims (Indonesia–Netherlands) (12 August 1949) 34 UNTS 213.

[249] Ibid, paras 1–3.

APPLICATION TO THE CLASSES OF SUCCESSION    227

war reparations concerning the Netherlands East Indies.[250] Japan also concluded settlement agreements in 1967 with Malaysia[251] and Singapore.[252]

Following the secession of Ghana on 6 March 1957,[253] the United Kingdom paid compensation in August 1957 to Switzerland pursuant to an agreement reached before the date of succession for proprietary damages sustained by a Swiss national during riots in the Gold Coast.[254] Although one interpretation is that 'the United Kingdom made payment *after* the independence of Ghana simply based on good faith and the fact that it had already agreed to it before the date of succession', the example can also be construed as supporting 'the view that the continuing State (United Kingdom) should remain responsible for internationally wrongful acts committed before the creation of the new State'.[255] While the case is ambiguous, it is suggested that the conclusion of the reparation agreement prior to the date of succession was the manifestation of a distinction between 'liquidated' and 'unliquidated' responsibility.

For the secession of Syria from the UAR on 29 September 1961, no succession agreement on claims and responsibility was concluded. However, the UAR (renamed the 'Arab Republic of Egypt' in September 1971) retained responsibility for the reparation settlements concluded with the United Kingdom and France. After the secession, the UAR concluded additional settlements to compensate Italy,[256] the United Kingdom,[257] Sweden,[258] and the United States[259] for claims of their nationals to damages for proprietary injuries between 1958 and 1961. As the impugned measures took place entirely within the Egypt Region of the UAR, the practice supports the principle of territoriality on the transferability of international claims and responsibility to a seceding State.[260]

For the secession of Montenegro from the State Union of Serbia-Montenegro ('FRY') on 3 June 2006, no succession agreement covering international claims and responsibility was concluded. In two proceedings pending before the ICJ at

---

[250] Treaty of Peace (adopted 20 January 1958, entered into force 15 April 1958) 324 UNTS 227, arts 4(2), 5.

[251] Agreement between Japan and Malaysia (21 September 1967) in RB Lillich and BH Weston, *International Claims: their Settlement by Lump Sum Agreements* (University Press of Virginia 1975) 350, art 2.

[252] Agreement between Japan and Singapore (21 September 1967) in Lillich and Weston (n 251) 350, art 2. See also: Independence of Singapore Agreement (Malaysia–Singapore) (7 August 1965) 4 ILM (1965) 928, Annex B (para 9).

[253] Ghana Independence Act 1957 5 & 6 Eliz c 6, s 1.

[254] Dumberry (n 43) 241.

[255] Ibid.

[256] Agreement relative to the Indemnification of Italian interests in Egypt (Italy–UAR) (adopted 23 March 1965, entered into force 5 September 1966) in Weston et al (n 241) 139, Art 2.

[257] Agreement concerning Financial and Commercial Relations (UAR–United Kingdom) (28 February 1959) (1960) 54(2) AJIL 511, arts 1(3) 2.

[258] Agreement concerning the Compensation of Swedish Interests (UAR–Sweden) (adopted 10 November 1971, entered into force 7 August 1972) 969 UNTS 317, arts 2, 9–10.

[259] Agreement concerning Claims of United States Nationals (UAR–United States) (adopted 1 May 1976, entered into force 27 October 1976) [1976] 4 UST 4214, arts 1–2, 5.

[260] Dumberry (n 43) 135–38. Additional agreements were reached with other States to the same effect – Second Šturma Report (n 25) para 170.

228    SUCCESSION TO INTERNATIONAL CLAIMS AND RESPONSIBILITY

the date of succession, Serbia took the position that it continued the legal personality of the FRY.[261] In the *Bosnia Genocide Case*, the Applicant asserted that the acceptance by Montenegro and the international community of the claim of Serbia to continue the personality of the FRY 'cannot have ... any effect on the applicable rules of state responsibility ... both Serbia and Montenegro, jointly and severally, are responsible for the unlawful conduct that constitute the cause of action in this case'.[262] Montenegro retorted that it was not a respondent because international responsibility remained vested in Serbia according to the Article 60 of the Constitutional Charter of the FRY.[263] Serbia took no clear position on the issue.[264]

The Court decided that Serbia remained the sole respondent in the case because Montenegro did 'not continue the legal personality of [the FRY]; it cannot therefore have acquired, on that basis, the status of Respondent in the present case ... the Applicant did not ... assert that Montenegro is still a party to the present case; it merely emphasized its views as to the joint and several liability of Serbia and of Montenegro'.[265] In the *Croatia Genocide Case*, Croatia took the position that its proceedings were 'maintained against ... Serbia as Respondent' but that this position was 'without prejudice to the potential responsibility of ... Montenegro and the possibility of instituting separate proceedings against it'.[266] The Court reached the same conclusion as in the *Bosnia Genocide Case*.[267]

In an investor-State arbitration pending against the FRY and Serbia at the date of succession, the Claimant did not seek to add Montenegro as a respondent after its secession and the Arbitral Tribunal noted 'that it appears uncontroversial that the Republic of Serbia will continue the legal identity of the [FRY] on the international level'.[268] In the first case pending against the FRY before the European Court of Human Rights to be decided after the date of succession, the respondent was renamed 'Serbia', with the Court noting that the FRY had 'ceased to exist' after the declaration of independence while Serbia had continued its participation in the 1950 European Convention on Human Rights and other Council of Europe treaties.[269] The Court applied this finding to three other cases.[270]

---

[261] *Convention on the Prevention and Punishment of the Crime of Genocide (Bosnia and Herzegovina v Yugoslavia)* (Preliminary Objections) [1996] ICJ Rep 595, paras 68–70.

[262] Ibid, para 71.

[263] Ibid, para 72.

[264] Ibid, para 73.

[265] Ibid, para 76. On the third-party principle of jurisdiction, see, e.g. – Christian Tomuschat, 'Article 36' in Andreas Zimmermann and CJ Tams (eds) *The Statute of the International Court of Justice: A Commentary* (2019) 729–34.

[266] *Convention for the Prevention and Punishment of the Crime of Genocide (Croatia v Serbia)* (Preliminary Objections) [2008] ICJ Rep 412, para 30.

[267] Ibid, para 33.

[268] *Mytilineos Holdings SA v State Union of Serbia & Montenegro and Republic of Serbia* (Partial Award on Jurisdiction) Arbitral Tribunal (UNCITRAL) (8 September 2006) <https://www.italaw.com/cases/documents/726> accessed 10 September 2019, paras 7, 158.

[269] *Matijašević v Serbia* App No 23037/04 European Court of Human Rights (19 December 2006) 48 EHRR (2009) 876, 882, paras 22–25.

[270] *Tomić v Serbia* App No 25959/06 European Court of Human Rights (26 June 2007) paras 1–2, 72; *Jevremović v Serbia* App No 3150/05 European Court of Human Rights (17 July 2007) paras 63, 74; *Ilić v Serbia* App No 30132/04 European Court of Human Rights (9 January 2008) paras 49, 66.

APPLICATION TO THE CLASSES OF SUCCESSION    229

In each of the four cases, the impugned conduct was of entities of the constituent republic of Serbia in the FRY. In a case decided in 2009 concerning impugned conduct of organs of the constituent republic of Montenegro, however, Serbia took the following position:

> [F]irstly ... each constituent republic of the [FRY] had the obligation to protect human rights in its own territory ... [s]econdly, the impugned enforcement proceedings were themselves solely conducted by the competent Montenegrin authorities. Thirdly ... Serbia cannot be deemed responsible for any violations of the Convention which might have occurred in Montenegro prior to its declaration of independence.[271]

While Montenegro supported the position of Serbia, the applicants averred that 'both Montenegro and Serbia should be held responsible for the non-enforcement of the judgement in question'.[272] The Court held that Montenegro was the sole respondent to the claims because 'the impugned proceedings have been solely within the competence of the Montenegrin authorities'.[273] This judgment was followed in subsequent proceedings concerning impugned conduct of organs of the constituent republic of Montenegro.[274]

On 24 May 2006, a claimant requested arbitration under the International Chamber of Commerce ('ICC') pursuant to its contract with the FRY and communicated its request (five days after the secession of Montenegro) on 8 June 2006.[275] In its reply, Serbia informed the ICC that the FRY had 'ceased to exist' and that 'Serbia will act as the Respondent in this phase of the procedure'.[276] In set-aside proceedings, the High Court of England and Wales construed the term 'successor state' in Article 60 of the Constitutional Charter to mean 'continuing State', which conclusion was consistent with the position taken by Serbia before the ICJ and the ECtHR.[277] At no point in the proceedings was the succession of Montenegro to the responsibility of the FRY for the alleged violations of the contract at issue.

---

[271] *Bijelić v Montenegro and Serbia* App No 11890/05, European Court of Human Rights (28 April 2009) 142 ILR 146, para 62. See further: Patrick Dumberry, 'La succession d'États en matière de responsabilité internationale et ses liens avec la responsabilité des États en matière de traités' in Giovanni Distefano, Gloria Gaggioli, and Aymeric Hêche (eds) *La Convention de Vienne de 1978 sur la succession d'États en matière de traités*, vol 1 (Bruylant 2016) 1581, 1600–05.

[272] Ibid, paras 1, 63–64.

[273] Ibid, paras 69–70. On the succession of Montenegro to the Convention, see Chapter 4.

[274] *Mandić v Montenegro, Serbia and Bosnia and Herzegovina* App No 32557/05 European Court of Human Rights (12 June 2012) para 23; *Lakićević and Others v Montenegro and Serbia*, App Nos 27458/06, 37205/06, 37207/06, and 33604/07 European Court of Human Rights (13 December 2011) paras 40–51; *Milić v Montenegro and Serbia* App No 28359/05 European Court of Human Rights (11 December 2012) paras 37–40.

[275] *Serbia v ImageSat International NV*, High Court of England (16 November 2009) 142 ILR 644, paras 1, 38.

[276] Ibid, paras 40, 47, 54.

[277] Ibid, paras 106, 137.

230 SUCCESSION TO INTERNATIONAL CLAIMS AND RESPONSIBILITY

Like Article 11(1) on cession, Article 12(1) of the IDI Resolution states a default rule of retention by the predecessor of international claims and responsibility.[278] While the principle of territoriality for the exceptional transfer of international claims in paragraph 2 accurately reflects State practice, the alternative test of a 'direct link' with the population of the successor does not.[279] The test for the assignment of responsibility on the basis of the identity of 'an organ of a territorial unit' in paragraph 3 is supported by the reasoning of the ECtHR in the *Bijelić v Montenegro* case, which has been argued to contradict earlier practice and to be doctrinally flawed. The assumption of responsibility by a predecessor or successor in paragraph 4 is supported by the example of Ghana, though supporting practice for the principle of equitable apportionment between predecessors and successors in paragraph 5 is scant.[280]

It is suggested that the modern State practice and *opiniones juris* support the default rule of automatic retention by the predecessor of international claims and responsibility articulated in Article 12(1) unless there be a dominant connection with the territory transferred to the successor. The general principle of retention of claims and responsibility is demonstrated by the retention of responsibility by the UAR in its settlement agreements with numerous injured States for internationally wrongful acts that had been committed in the Egypt Region. It is also shown by the assignment to Serbia of the status of respondent in the *Bosnia Genocide Case*, *Croatia Genocide Case*, *Mytilineos Holdings* arbitration, and *ImageSat International* arbitration in which the impugned conduct concerned the entire territory of the FRY.

The exceptional transferability of claims and responsibility on the basis of the principle of territoriality is demonstrated by the succession of India and Pakistan to the claim of British India for war reparations as well as Indonesia to the claims and responsibility of the Netherlands East Indies for war reparations. It is also shown by the claim addressed to Mozambique by Switzerland for an internationally wrongful act committed in the Overseas Territory of Mozambique. While the same principle should arguably have applied to the claim of Switzerland concerning impugned conduct in the territory of the Gold Coast Colony, the retention of responsibility by the United Kingdom should be viewed as a case of unilateral adoption due to the agreement on reparation having been made before the date of succession.

---

[278] Kohen and Dumberry (n 10) 90, 93–98. In 2018, the ILC Special Rapporteur proposed draft article 7 that largely replicated Article 12 except for the omission of a 'direct link to population' for the transfer of international claims and the replication of Article 9 of the ARSIWA on the attribution of conduct of an insurrectional or other movement – Second Šturma Report (n 25) paras 78–123. The substance of draft article 7 did not prompt specific comment from States in the Sixth Committee.

[279] The IDI cited the examples of British India and East Germany, though it did not discuss those of Indonesia, Ghana, and Montenegro – ibid, 100.

[280] Ibid, 105.

While the ECtHR based its reasoning for the assignment of the status of respondent to Montenegro in the *Bijelić v Montenegro* case on the conduct of State *organs* of the constituent republic of Montenegro, this reasoning has two flaws. The first is that it is inconsistent with earlier State practice (e.g.—British India, Mozambique) in which claims and responsibility were assigned not on the basis of identity but rather territorial location. Second, there is no guarantee that the organs of a seceding territorial unit will remain intact after the date of succession. For example, the Provinces of Punjab and Assam were partitioned upon the secessions of British India; the colonial federations of French Indochina and Rhodesia and Nyasaland were dissolved when their constituent members seceded; and the organs of Eritrea, Indonesia, North Viet Nam, and other seceding States bore little resemblance to the local governments that preceded them because 'revolutionary' or 'underground' governments had been created in wars of independence.

## 6.3.6 Accession to Independence

When a protected State or Territory accedes to independence,[281] customary international law provides that the international claims and responsibility of the protecting State do not transfer to the protected State or Territory. Due to the limited international legal personality of the protected State or Territory prior to the date of succession, the claims and responsibility of the protecting State are separate from those of the protected State even when it exercises powers on behalf of the latter.[282] Consequently, the newly independent State retains its own international claims and responsibility after the date of succession but does not succeed to the claims and responsibility of the predecessor.

The two cases of accessions to independence in modern practice on international claims and responsibility are the Trust Territory of Nauru (1968) and the Mandatory Territory for South-West Africa (1990).[283] After the Trust Territory of Nauru acceded to independence in 1968,[284] Nauru initiated proceedings against Australia before the ICJ in 1989 for breaches of the 1947 Trusteeship Agreement for Nauru and general international law for 'its failure to make any provision or any adequate provision for the rehabilitation of the phosphate lands worked out under Australian administration in the period before 1 July 1967 and ... acts of

---

[281] See Chapter 2.

[282] For an example of a protecting State instituting proceedings on its own behalf and on behalf of the protected State, see: *Rights of Nationals of the United States of America in Morocco (France v United States of America)* (Pleadings) vol I 235, vol II 431–34; ibid (Judgment) [1952] ICJ Rep 176, 179, 185.

[283] Whereas practice concerning Morocco clearly defines the principle of separation of the claims and responsibility of the protecting State and protected State *during* the protectorate, the question of succession was not tested after its termination.

[284] UNGA Res 2347 (XII) (19 December 1967) paras 1, 3.

## 232  SUCCESSION TO INTERNATIONAL CLAIMS AND RESPONSIBILITY

maladministration wrongful under international law'.[285] The claim was based on alleged breaches of the 1947 Trusteeship Agreement for Nauru and general international law.[286] Nauru argued:

> The 'transfer' of the Island of Nauru to the Applicant State on independence is not to be regarded as a case of State succession operating against an assumption of a clean slate. The independence of a trust territory is not a case of transfer of territory, since, first, the Administering Authority has no sovereignty over the territory, and, secondly, the people of a trust territory are an already existing international entity to whom duties are owed by the Administering Authority, both under the Trusteeship Agreement or otherwise under general international law. The emergence of a new State from the status of a trust territory in accordance with the principle of self-determination embodied in the trusteeship arrangements is not the emergence *ab initio* of an entirely new legal entity, but the emergence from a state of dependence of a people whose rights and status are already distinctly recognized, and to which the predecessor State is in principle accountable.[287]

In raising preliminary objections, Australia asserted, *inter alia*, that 'any dispute of that type should be regarded as having been settled by the very fact of the termination of the Trusteeship, provided that that termination was unconditional'.[288] It further contended that 'the Nauruan authorities, even before acceding to independence, waived all claims relating to rehabilitation of the phosphate lands'.[289]

Rejecting these objections, the Court held that neither the termination of the Trusteeship nor the alleged waiver had precluded its jurisdiction over the dispute.[290] The case was settled before being heard on the merits.[291] While challenging the jurisdiction of the Court, Australia not only did not question the standing of Nauru to claim for reparation in respect of alleged internationally wrongful acts against the Trust Territory but also invoked the conduct of the local government of the Trust Territory as waiving such claims.

Prior to the accession to independence of the Mandatory Territory for South-West Africa from the United Nations on 21 March 1990, the United Nations Council for Namibia ('UNCN') had initiated a test case against the Netherlands before the District Court of The Hague for unlawful exploitation of its natural resources as

---

[285]  *Certain Phosphate Lands in Nauru (Nauru v Australia)* (Application) (19 May 1989) para 47.

[286]  *Certain Phosphate Lands in Nauru (Nauru v Australia)* (Preliminary Objections) [1992] ICJ Rep 240, para 5.

[287]  Ibid (Memorial of Nauru) vol 1 (April 1990).

[288]  Ibid (Judgment) para 9.

[289]  Ibid, paras 10–12.

[290]  Ibid, paras 8–30, 72.

[291]  Ibid (Order of 13 September 1993) [1993] ICJ Rep 322.

State property.[292] After acceding to independence, Namibia was substituted for the UNCN in the proceedings whereupon it chose to discontinue them.[293] A joint declaration by Namibia and Germany in 2021 concerning 'a moral, historical and political obligation [of Germany] to tender an apology for ... genocide [between 1904 and 1908] and subsequently provide the necessary means for reconciliation and reconstruction' was not made without any legal claim or responsibility being asserted.[294]

In formulating Article 16 of the IDI Resolution, the IDI based its definition of a 'newly independent State' upon the ILC definition.[295] However, the IDI confined its definition to Mandatory Territories, Trust Territories and Non-Self-Governing Territories.[296] Incorrectly including the category of 'non-self-governing territories', the IDI interpretation also omits international protectorates and protected States.[297] In providing for a default rule of non-succession to international responsibility and a limited rule of succession to international claims with 'a direct link with the territory or the population of a newly independent State',[298] paragraphs 1 and 2 of Article 16 neither articulate the rule of continuity for protected States and Territories nor recognize that there is no practice concerning a rule of succession for newly independent States to international claims.[299]

In 2018, the ILC Special Rapporteur proposed draft article 8, which differed from Article 16 in stating that international responsibility may only transfer if the newly independent State agree.[300] He considered that protected States (e.g.— Morocco) were included in the category of 'newly independent State' but 'such cases may be taken into account when it comes to possible exceptions to the rule of non-succession'.[301] In the Sixth Committee, only Austria made specific comment on this draft article whereby it 'doubted whether there was a need for a separate reference to that category of States'.[302]

---

[292] UNGA Res 42/14 A, 75; UNCN, 'Implementation of Decree No 1 for the Protection of the Natural Resources of Namibia: Study on the possibility of instituting legal proceedings in the domestic courts of States' UN Doc A/AC.131.194 (23 October 1985); UNCN Report (1991) GAOR Fifty-third Session, Supplement No 24 (A/43/24) 228, 278, 481–82.

[293] Nele Matz-Lück, 'Namibia' *MPEPIL* (April 2009). This example was also cited by Nauru – *Certain Phosphate Lands* (Memorial of Nauru) (n 287) para 467. The judgment of the Supreme Court of Namibia in *Mwadinghi v Minister of Defence* concerned a municipal tort: Dumberry (n 43) 259–67.

[294] Joint Declaration by Germany and Namibia (28 May 2021) <https://www.parliament.na/wp-content/uploads/2021/09/Joint-Declaration-Document-Genocide-rt.pdf> accessed 8 January 2024, paras III((1) 20.

[295] Kohen and Dumberry (n 10) 129–30.

[296] Ibid, 130.

[297] See Chapter 2.

[298] Kohen and Dumberry (n 10) 128–40.

[299] Cited practice concerned municipal torts (Algeria, the DRC, Kenya, Namibia): Kohen and Dumberry (n 10) 131–40.

[300] Second Šturma Report (n 25) paras 124–37.

[301] Though describing them as 'international protectorates' the Special Rapporteur referred to protected States rather than the rare cases of international protectorates, such as the Free City of Danzig – Second Šturma Report (n 25) paras 127–28. See further Chapter 1.

[302] Sixth Committee, 28th Meeting (n 170) para 64.

In bringing and discontinuing claims against the Trustee and third States with respect to alleged internationally wrongful acts taking place before the date of succession, the two cases of Nauru and Namibia are coherent in favour of a rule of continuity applicable to the accession to independence of a protected State or Territory. The separation of the international claims and responsibility of the protecting State from the protected State as the doctrinal basis for this rule is also supported by State practice with respect to Morocco.

## 6.4 The Process of Succession

The transfer of international claims and responsibility by succession encompasses two types of injury arising before the date of succession:

- direct injuries to territorial, proprietary, treaty, and other rights; and
- indirect injuries sustained by the property and persons of nationals.

Succession to international claims and responsibility arising from these injuries is determined according to the customary rule applicable to each class of succession. When a default rule of succession applies in a case of merger or secession, then the claims and responsibility automatically transfer to the successor. In the other classes of succession in which a default rule of non-succession applies, they can transfer by an agreement on succession between the States concerned or unilateral adoption by the successor.

Whereas the question for the transfer of claims and responsibility by operation of law is the coherence of underpinning State practice and *opiniones juris* for the existence of the rule, the doctrinal issue arising from succession agreements and unilateral adoption is whether they create an obligation for the third State without its consent. It is contended that succession to claims and responsibility by agreement or adoption is compatible with other rules of general international law, such as the third-party principle of the law of treaties or the law of jurisdiction, because those acts do not create a duty for the third State but rather identify the disputing party for the purposes of its dispute.

Concerning indirect injuries, the nationality-of-claims rule of the law of diplomatic protection applies to international claims and responsibility. As discussed in Chapter 7, the effect of the succession on the nationality of the person to which diplomatic protection is to be provided to settle a dispute must be identified in order to determine the admissibility of the claim. However, State practice is coherent in showing that the rule of continuous nationality of the law of diplomatic protection does not apply to a succession of States.

### 6.4.1 Succession Agreements

A succession agreement denotes a treaty concluded between on the transfer or non-transfer of international claims and responsibility. Such agreements can be concluded between:

- a predecessor and successor in cases of absorption,[303] cession[304] and secession;[305] or
- multiple successors in cases of dismemberment[306] and secession.[307]

Apart from the general question of the validity of succession agreements,[308] the key doctrinal issue concerning succession agreements has been whether 'the decision taken by ... parties in such agreements [is] opposable to the other actors involved in the responsibility relationship (either the author or the injured State)'.[309]

In denying constitutive effect to a succession agreement in Article 6(2) of the IDI Resolution, the IDI considered there to be a 'basic need to protect the interests of the injured State or subject who is the *victim* ... if the injured State or subject is a third party to a devolution agreement, it ... needs to consent to the transfer of the obligation to repair from the predecessor State to the successor State.'[310] The situation was said to be 'obviously quite different ... where the third State or subject is ... the *author* of the internationally wrongful act': as the third State or subject has the obligation to repair, the 'only impact of any such agreement would be to change the identification of the State to whom the third State should provide proper reparation'.[311] Draft article 3 proposed by the ILC Special Rapporteur also denied legal effect to devolution agreements between predecessors and successors before the date of succession while recognizing other forms of succession agreement.[312]

State practice and *opiniones juris* are consistent in omitting any requirement for the consent of a third State for succession agreements to have constitutive effect. In the context of settlement agreements, this includes not only agreements between successors concerning succession to claims of which the other States concerned merely 'took note'[313] but also agreements between a predecessor and successor on

---

[303] E.g. – East Germany (notes 166–167).
[304] E.g. – North Borneo, Sarawak, & Singapore (n 216).
[305] E.g. – Indonesia (n 248).
[306] E.g. – SFRY (notes 197 & 203).
[307] E.g. – British India (n 246).
[308] See Chapter 2.
[309] Kohen and Dumberry (n 10) 38.
[310] Ibid, 42.
[311] Ibid, 43.
[312] First Šturma Report (n 44) paras 95–111. Referred to the Drafting Committee, no action was subsequently taken on it – ILC, 3381st Meeting (n 23) 9; ILC, 'Succession of States in respect of State Responsibility: Statement of the Chairman of the Drafting Committee' (31 July 2017) 1, 9.
[313] British India (n 246).

succession to responsibility and claims to which the third State acquiesced.[314] The consent of third parties (e.g.—the United States) was also not considered to be necessary for the succession agreement between West Germany and East Germany to have constitutive effect for the identification of West Germany as the disputing party for the settlement of claims concerning East Germany.[315]

The conclusion of the Special Agreement submitting the *Gabčikovo-Nagymaros Project Case* to the ICJ by Slovakia can be interpreted as an example of unilateral adoption of claims and responsibility.[316] However, the better interpretation is an implied agreement with Czechia[317] because Czechia had disclaimed succession to the bilateral treaty with Hungary five weeks before the Special Agreement was concluded and after Hungary had filed an application against Czecho-Slovakia concerning the dispute on 23 October 1992.[318] As Hungary itself argued, the second preambular paragraph of the Special Agreement referring to Slovakia as the 'sole successor State in respect of rights and obligations relating to the Gabcikovo-Nagymaros Project' was 'a reference to the fact that, *as between the Czech Republic and the Slovak Republic as the successor States* ... it was understood that the Slovak Republic would be solely concerned ... and that this matter would be of no concern to the Czech Republic'.[319]

Doctrinally, the concern of prejudice to the rights of third parties underpinning Article 6(2) of the IDI Resolution is misplaced because no obligation is created by a succession agreement for that third State under the law of treaties[320] and no jurisdiction to settle the dispute is established.[321] For claims and responsibility alike, the principal effect of the succession agreement is rather to identify the party to the dispute. Though open to the third State to address its claims to both of the parties to the succession agreement for tactical reasons,[322] the third State has no legal *right* to choose the disputing party to be prejudiced by a succession agreement.

---

[314] Indonesia (n 248); Malaysia (nn 216 and 251); French India (n 214); Portuguese India (n 215).

[315] Note 166.

[316] Kohen and Dumberry (n 10) 48.

[317] Note 196.

[318] Note 189; *Gabčikovo-Nagymaros Project Case* (n 195) Judgment, para 24.

[319] *Gabčikovo-Nagymaros Project Case* (n 195) Memorial of Hungary, para 2.06.

[320] Vienna Convention on the Law of Treaties (adopted 23 May 1969, entered into force 27 January 1980) 1155 UNTS 331 art 35. See further Chapter 5.

[321] On the *Monetary Gold* or third-party principle, see, e.g. – Christian Tomuschat, 'Article 36' in Andreas Zimmermann et al. (eds) *The Statute of the International Court of Justice: A Commentary* (OUP 2019).

[322] On Montenegro, see: *Bosnia Genocide Case* (n 262); *Croatia Genocide Case* (n 267); *Bijelić* (n 272).

## 6.4.2 Adoption

The adoption of international claims and responsibility refers to a unilateral declaration or other act of a successor to assume the status of party in the place of its predecessor for a particular dispute. Article 6(3) of the IDI Resolution denies legal effect to such unilateral acts of acceptance for the same reason as succession agreements, namely, that the 'injured party must be given the possibility to accept or reject the solution unilaterally adopted by the successor ... to protect the right of the injured State (or subject) to receive proper reparation'.[323] The position of Croatia in the *Croatia Genocide Case* indicates support for the principle.[324]

While the lack of practice leaves the question open, the ILC commented on Article 11 of the ARSIWA:

> In the context of State succession, it is unclear whether a new State succeeds to any State responsibility of the predecessor State with respect to its territory. However, if the successor State, faced with a continuing wrongful act on its territory, endorses and continues that situation, the inference may readily be drawn that it assumed responsibility for it.[325]

The doctrinal implications of a right for a successor to adopt international claims and responsibility are the same as for succession agreements with the difference that a dispute could arise concerning the status of disputing party between multiple successors or a predecessor and successor. This hypothetical possibility does not arise for absorptions due to the extinction of the predecessor and the existence of a single successor[326] and has yet to occur in other classes of succession, most likely because the practice has entirely concerned succession to responsibility.[327] If such a dispute were to arise, then it is suggested that the general principles of territoriality or equitable apportionment would apply according to the connection of the dispute with the territories of the States concerned.

---

[323] Kohen and Dumberry (n 10) 50.
[324] Note 202.
[325] ARSIWA (n 1) 52.
[326] nn 146 (Burma), 149–151 (Madagascar).
[327] Notes 181, 184–185 (Union of Colombia), 222 (Tarapacá), 256–259 (UAR). If the succession agreements concluded by Indonesia, Malaysia, and Singapore are immaterial for their subsequent war reparations settlements with Japan, then that practice could be classified as adoption alongside the Special Agreement between Slovakia and Hungary without the participation of Czechia for the *Gabčikovo-Nagymaros Project Case.*

# 238  SUCCESSION TO INTERNATIONAL CLAIMS AND RESPONSIBILITY

## 6.4.3  Diplomatic Protection

For claims of indirect injury to a State the nationality-of-claims rule under the law of diplomatic protection requires that the injured person be a national of the claimant and not a national of the respondent at the date of claim.[328] While the effective nationality rule[329] could render ineffective a retention or grant of nationality in consequence of a succession, there is no example in practice.[330] However, the rule of 'continuous nationality' between the date of injury and the date of claim does not apply to the law of succession[331] because the rationale of that rule to prevent voluntary changes of nationality for the purposes of prosecuting an international claim does not apply to changes of nationality resulting from State succession.[332]

While standing to claim for injuries to a national is transferred to the successor in consequence of collective nationalization, it is transferred back to the predecessor or to another successor when a right of option is exercised by an injured person.[333] There are few examples of this rule being applied to an international claim in exercise of diplomatic protection that was pending at the date of succession.[334] Until the date of succession, standing to claim for alleged injuries by third States remains vested in the predecessor.[335] In contrast, claims by the predecessor to its own nationals are municipal torts.[336]

---

[328] For an overview, see, e.g. – ILC, 'Draft Articles on Diplomatic Protection with commentaries' (2006) ILC Yearbook vol II Part 2 23, 29–30; CF Amerasinghe, *Diplomatic Protection* (OUP 2008) 91–96, 106–113. This general rule can be displaced by special agreement; e.g. – Agreement for the Settlement of Displaced Persons (Eritrea–Ethiopia) (12 December 2000) 2138 UNTS 93, art 5(9).

[329] *Nottebohm Case (Liechtenstein v Guatemala)* (Second Phase) [1955] ICJ Rep 4, 23. See also: *Flegenheimer Case* (Decision No 182) Italian–United States Conciliation Commission (20 September 1958) XIV RIAA 327, para 62.

[330] See Chapter 7.

[331] IDI Resolution (n 40) art 10(1); Kohen and Dumberry (n 8) 74–75. See further: *Pablo Nájera (France) v Mexico*, France–Mexico Claims Commission (19 October 1928) V RIAA 466, 473–88 (French); *Administrative Decision No V*, US–German Mixed Claims Commission (31 October 1924) 7 RIAA 1, 141–43; *Barcelona Traction, Light and Power Company, Limited (Second Phase) (Belgium v Spain)* [1970] ICJ Rep 3 (Separate Opinion Judge Fitzmaurice) para 62; ibid, (Separate Opinion Judge Jessup) para 73. See also: Dumberry (n 43) 393–465; First Šturma Report (n 44) paras 64, 77–84; Second Šturma Report (n 25) 173–76.

[332] ILC, Draft Articles on Diplomatic Protection (n 328) 32 (art 5(2)). See further, e.g. – John Dugard, 'Addendum to First Report on Diplomatic Protection' UN Doc A/CN.4/506/Add.1 (20 April 2000) para 1; John Dugard, 'Seventh Report on Diplomatic Protection' UN Doc A/CN.4/567 (7 March 2006) para 35; Amerasinghe (n 328) 92–96; Dumberry (n 43) 393–465.

[333] Kohen and Dumberry (n 10) 67. On Alsace-Lorraine, see: *Henriette Levy Case* (Award) French-American Claims Commission (5 June 1881) in Moore (n 158) vol III, 2514–18, 2517.

[334] On the jurisprudence of the UN Claims Commission with respect to Czecho-Slovakia, the SFRY, and the Soviet Union, see: Dumberry (n 43) 371–72, 431–34.

[335] E.g. – *Claim of Finnish Shipowners against Great Britain in respect of the Use of Certain Finnish Vessels During the War (Finland v United Kingdom)* (Award) Sole Arbitrator (Dr Bagge) (9 May 1934) 3 RIAA 1479, 1481. On the jurisprudence of the Mixed Arbitral Tribunals created after the First World War, see: Dumberry (n 6) 370–79.

[336] On Alsace-Lorraine, see: Dumberry (n 43) 170–71, 428–30. See also: Agreement (Mauritius–United Kingdom) (adopted 7 July 1982, entered into force 28 October 1982) Cmd 8785, arts 1–2. Other

In the *Panevezys-Saldutiskis Railway Case* before the Permanent Court of International Justice ('PCIJ'), Estonia claimed for proprietary injuries inflicted by Russia on its national in 1919 before the secession of the Baltic States in 1923.[337] Lithuania raised preliminary objections that no legal relationship existed at the time of the expropriations between Estonia and the nationalized company, noting 'the rule of international law that a claim must be national not only at the time of its presentation but also at the time of the injury'.[338]

Estonia argued, *inter alia*, that the company had acquired *de facto* Estonian nationality by the declaration of independence of Estonia in 1918 and even if it had acquired Estonian nationality by the entry into force in 1923 of the 1920 Treaty of Tartu with Russia, the impugned conduct was of a continuing character.[339] The PCIJ did not uphold the objection on the ground that it would necessitate a decision on the nationality of the company on the merits,[340] it affirmed that the nationality-of-claims rule applied.[341] The question of the succession of Lithuania to the responsibility of Russia was reserved to the merits but was never heard.[342]

## 6.5 Conclusions

As the field of succession with the least amount of State practice, succession to international claims and responsibility rests on doctrinal foundations that remain in construction. As analogies to municipal torts are misplaced due to the significant differences in the practice and procedure concerning breaches of the internal law of a predecessor versus international law, classical practice assumes a greater degree of relative importance. This in turn underscores the importance of accurate classification of individual cases[343] to identify the salient features of the limited practice. In particular, the rule of continuity for newly independent States was not identified by the IDI or ILC due to the perpetuation of the erroneous definition of the class in earlier codification projects.[344]

---

claims were not made on the basis of nationality – Agreement (Israel–West Germany) (adopted 10 September 1952, entered into force 27 March 1953) 162 UNTS 205, preamble; Dumberry (n 6) 386.

[337] *Panevezys-Saldutiskis Railway Case (Estonia v Lithuania)* (Preliminary Objections) PCIJ Series A/B No 76, 5. See also: Dissenting Opinion of Judge van Eysinga, ibid, 31–35.

[338] Ibid, 16.

[339] Dumberry (n 43) 443–56.

[340] Ibid, 17–18.

[341] Ibid, 16–17. See further: ibid (Dissenting Opinion of Judge van Eysinga) 35.

[342] Ibid, 17.

[343] For example, the cession of Singapore to Malaysia rather than its absorption, the secession of Syria rather than the dismemberment of the UAR, and the secessions of India and Pakistan rather than a dismemberment of British India.

[344] See Chapter 2.

In this respect, it is unsurprising that State practice has been most coherent to support a default rule of succession for mergers as the simplest class of succession. While the extinction of the predecessor to leave a single successor in absorptions give rise to no difference in principle, the modern case of East Germany is not yet sufficient to displace the considerable classical practice against a default rule of succession. The practice of Czechia and Slovakia concerning the *Gabčikovo-Nagymaros Project Case* and the 2001 Agreement on Succession Issues supports an exception of succession by agreement of the successors or unilateral adoption.

Whereas the IDI Resolution was underpinned by a willingness to justify departures from a default and general rule of non-succession for all classes of succession on the basis of normative considerations, the lack of State practice to justify the approach proposed by the ILC Special Rapporteur and largely similar to that of the IDI was a key concern. In this respect, the focus of the ILC on the existence of a grand rule of succession or non-succession applicable across different classes of succession was misplaced.[345] This is not only due to the conceptual distinction for the purposes of international responsibility between the continued existence of the predecessor in partial successions and its extinction in total successions but also because State practice has seen different solutions adopted for these different scenarios.

As the ILC codification project will not feature any complete product with proposals for the codification or progressive development of the field, the IDI Resolution and Report remain the principal point of reference in the form of a text. However, it is suggested that its reliance upon analogies with municipal torts and policy considerations means that it does not accurately reflect the limited State practice on certain points. Despite the discomfort expressed by the IDI about devolution agreements concluded between predecessors and successors before the date of succession, they do not feature in the treatment of such agreements by the States concerned. To the contrary, successors and third States alike have consistently treated succession agreements of all kinds, including between successors or a predecessor and successor, as having dispositive effect on the question of succession.

The work of the IDI and ILC Special Rapporteur and Drafting Committee emphasized the importance of a conceptual distinction between succession to the rights and consequences arising from an internationally wrongful act.[346] This has only been articulated by disputing parties (and then inconsistently) in only two cases. Even though the internationally wrongful act is committed by the predecessor at the date of injury, disputing parties have generally referred simply to 'succession to responsibility'. Ultimately, the terms may be used interchangeably (as the disputing parties did in the *Gabčikovo-Nagymaros Project Case*), because the

---

[345] Dumberry (n 43) 469–70.
[346] Ibid, 202–06, 299–303.

CONCLUSIONS 241

salient issue is the status of the successor as party to the dispute in question with the accompanying procedural rights. At least in this regard, a conceptual analogy to 'unliquidated damages' for municipal torts appears to hold.[347]

A related point is that the practice also recognizes, unlike the IDI Resolution, no difference between the substantive tests for international claims and responsibility. This is shown not only in the numerous settlement agreements dealing with both matters equally but also the consistency in the approaches taken in practice concerning succession to claims or succession to responsibility alone. With the exceptions of the *Lighthouses Arbitration* and the *Bijelić* case, the practice is coherent in supporting a principle of territoriality for the assignment of claims and responsibility to one of multiple successors or to a successor rather than a test of identity for the organs of the State that performed the impugned conduct.

The highly limited practice on equitable apportionment in default of assignment supports the application of the same rule used by the successors for State debt rather than the elaboration of separate criteria. In spite of the rare references to joint and several liability by claimants, it is suggested that the principle of separate responsibility in Articles 46 and 47 of the ARSIWA is applicable to the question of invocation of responsibility. In spite of the considerable effort expended by the IDI and ILC Special Rapporteur on the questions of a continuing breach and a composite act, there are no clear examples of such situations arises in State succession. Although these are limited intersections with the ARSIWA, they serve more to illustrate the boundary between the law of succession and the law of responsibility. As for the law of treaties,[348] the implicit exclusion of State succession from the ARSIWA is critical to recall in approaching the practice of succession on its own terms rather than searching for a doctrinal solution by extending a text that was not designed to deal with it.

As most of the limited practice has featured indirect injury to nationals, the nationality-of-claims rule of diplomatic protection can assume considerable importance. Although the continuous nationality rule does not apply to State succession due to its rationale serving no purpose, there are scant examples of its invocation in recent practice. When the nationality of the injured national changes in consequence of a succession, however, the question of its nationality must be answered to determine compliance with the rule.

---

[347] E.g. – *Robert E. Brown Arbitration* (n 154); Tarapacá (n 222); Ghana (n 254).
[348] See Chapter 5.

# 7

# Succession and Nationality

## 7.1 Introduction

Unlike the matters considered in the preceding chapters, State succession with respect to nationality does not entail a primary transfer of rights and obligations from predecessors to successors but rather its secondary consequences for the nationals of the predecessor.[1] The heart of this issue is the identification of those nationals of the predecessor (the 'affected body of nationals') whose nationality is converted into that of the successor by a succession agreement, nationality law, or default rule of the law of succession. The term 'collective nationalization' is used in this chapter to distinguish the collective deprivation of the nationality of the predecessor and the acquisition of the nationality of the successor by operation of law from the acquisition of nationality by individual application ('naturalization').[2]

In international law, 'nationality'[3] is the bond between the natural and legal persons who owe a duty of loyalty to a State and whom that State may protect in its relations with other States.[4] This broad concept differs from the specific types of nationality (e.g.—'citizens',[5] 'subjects',[6] and 'protected persons'[7]) to be found in internal law providing rights of entry, residence, voting, and so on.[8] For most practical purposes, the rights and obligations of nationality flow from internal law such as ownership of private property,[9] civil service employment,[10] military service obligations,[11] or compensation for war

---

[1] E.g. – First Mikulka Report (n 8) para 16.

[2] Ibid, paras 54, 76.

[3] E.g. – AN Makarov, 'Règles générales du droit de la nationalité' (1949-I) 74 RdC 269, 277–94; Karl Zemanek, 'State Succession after Decolonization' (1965-III) 116 RdC 272; DP O'Connell, *State Succession in Municipal Law and International Law* vol I (OUP 1968) 497–542; Jacques de Burlet, *Nationalité des personnes physiques et décolonisation* (Bruylant 1975) 144–80.

[4] E.g. – Jones (n 296) 122.

[5] E.g. – Philippines (n 285).

[6] E.g. – French India (n 255) Burma (n 309) Indonesia (n 329).

[7] E.g. – Morocco (n 465).

[8] The International Law Commission ('ILC') discarded a draft definition – Václav Mikulka, 'First report on State succession and its impact on the nationality of natural and legal persons' (17 April 1995) UN Doc A/CN.4/467, para 37; Václav Mikulka, 'Third report on nationality in relation to the succession of States', UN Doc A/CN.4/280 (27–28 February 1997) 17–18; ILC, 2479th Meeting (20 May 1997) UN Doc A/CN.4/2479, paras 4–5, 12, 60. See also, e.g. – Federico de Castro, 'La nationalité, la double nationalité et la supranationalité' (1961-I) 102 RdC 515, 523–87; JF Rezek, 'Le droit international de la nationalité' (1986-III) 198 RdC 333, 341–50.

[9] See Chapter 7.

[10] See Chapter 4.

[11] E.g. – Bosnia (n 233).

---

*The Law of State Succession.* Arman Sarvarian, Oxford University Press. © Arman Sarvarian 2025.
DOI: 10.1093/oso/9780198817956.003.0007

INTRODUCTION    243

damages.[12] For international law, nationality pertains to limited functions such as the exercise of diplomatic protection,[13] the 'foreign' status of an investor in international investment law,[14] extradition,[15] war reparations,[16] freedom of establishment by treaty,[17] and refugee status.[18]

Conceptually, this 'intractable dualism'[19] restricts the authority of international law to the determination of nationality for its limited purposes. Though necessary to enable third States to identify the nationality of a person (a *de cuius*),[20] this function does not oblige the State concerned to grant a particular form of nationality (e.g.—citizenship) to the national.[21] Consequently, it is possible for international law to designate a *de cuius* as a national in consequence of State succession while the State concerned denies recognition in its internal law.

Although this problem can be avoided by the conclusion of a succession agreement or the coordination of nationality laws between the States concerned, it is likelier to arise when they legislate separately. It is also certain to arise when a State concerned does not adopt a nationality law by the date of succession or overlooks a particular category of national. The key doctrinal issue is consequently the identification of default rules for the loss and acquisition of nationality in consequence of State succession for the affected body of nationals when the States concerned do not determine their status at the date of succession.

Unlike other fields regulated by the law of succession, it is argued that the default rules do not derive from customary international law,[22] as the consequences of State succession on nationality are principally regulated in the practice of predecessors and successors at the national level through internal law and decisions of national courts.[23] Though relevant forms of 'State practice' for the identification of customary international law, the 'psychological' or 'subjective' element of 'acceptance as international law' (*opinio juris*) is not met due to the resolution of

---

[12] E.g. – *In re Nguyen Kim Hai*, Conseil d'État of France (8 July 1966) 47 ILR 97, 98–99.

[13] E.g. – *Mavrommatis Palestine Concessions (Greece v Great Britain)* (Preliminary Objections) PCIJ Rep Series A No 2, 28–32. See further Chapters 6 and 8.

[14] E.g. – *Khudyan* (n 419); Patrick Dumberry, '*Terra Incognita*: What Happens When a Problem of State Succession Occurs during Arbitration Proceedings?' (2018) 17 LPICT 350, 360–64.

[15] See Chapter 5.

[16] E.g. – Hans Ballreich et al (eds) *Fontes Iuris Gentium: Decisions of German Superior Courts relating to International Law* (Heymann 1956) 120.

[17] E.g. – *Micheletti v Delegación del Gobierno en Cantabria* Case C-369/90 Court of Justice of the European Union (7 July 1992) paras 9–12.

[18] E.g. – Timor-Leste (n 392).

[19] ILC, Summary Record of the 2413th Meeting (7 July 1995) UN Doc A/CN.4/SR.2413, para 22 (Crawford).

[20] E.g. – *Aslam Khan* (n 304).

[21] ILC Articles (n 29) 29–30. E.g. – *Nationality Decrees issued in Tunis and Morocco*, PCIJ Series B No 4 (1923) 24; *Acquisition of Polish Nationality*, PCIJ Series B No 7 (1923) 16; *Nottebohm Case (Liechtenstein v Guatemala) (Second Phase)* [1955] ICJ Rep 4, 23.

[22] Third Mikulka Report (n 8) 20 (para 6); 2479th Meeting (n 8) para 2; ILC, 2489th meeting (6 June 1997) UN Doc A/CN.4/2489, para 4.

[23] ILC Articles (n 29) preamble, 24.

244 SUCCESSION AND NATIONALITY

nationality issues through internal law.[24] This is shown by the rarity of *opiniones juris* concerning the existence and content of general rules on succession and nationality.[25]

Based on a hypothesis first proposed by Ian Brownlie,[26] however, it is suggested that the abundant practice at the national level is sufficiently coherent to comprise general principles of law applicable as default rules for the purposes of international law.[27] To identify these general principles of law, the principal sources of practice are succession agreements, nationality laws of predecessors and successors (i.e.—constitutions, statutes, and executive decrees), and decisions of national courts.[28]

From 1993 to 1999, the ILC developed the Articles on Nationality of Natural Persons in relation to the Succession of States ('ILC Articles')[29] in reaction to the successions resulting from desovietization 'which raised concerns among the international community over the impact of this development on the condition of the populations in this region and, in particular, over the risk of the occurrence of statelessness'.[30] In its work, the ILC 'built upon its previous work in both areas by maintaining consistency in a conceptual approach to the phenomenon of succession of States and by putting accent on avoidance of statelessness and human rights dimension of nationality'.[31] A significant constraint was a dearth of information on State practice, for few States submitted information while 'a great many cases of State succession were covered neither by recent documents [provided by the Secretariat] nor by older ones'.[32]

Following the second[33] and fourth[34] reports of the Special Rapporteur, Professor Václav Mikulka, the ILC 'relinquished the question of legal persons in view of the absence of comments from States, which it understood as their lack of interest in this matter'.[35] It completed the first reading of a complete set of draft

---

[24] See Chapter Two.

[25] E.g. – *In re Hehanussa* (n 335).

[26] Ian Brownlie, 'The Relations of Nationality in Public International Law' (1963) 39 BYIL 284, 314–326; Second Mikulka Report (n 33) paras 163–66.

[27] See Chapter 2.

[28] E.g. – ILC, 2390th Meeting (26 May 1995) UN Doc A/CN.4/SR.2390, para 9.

[29] ILC, Draft Articles on Nationality of Natural Persons in relation to the Succession of States with commentaries, (1999) ILC Yearbook vol II Part Two, 42.

[30] Václav Mikulka, 'Introductory Note: Articles on Nationality of Natural Persons in relation to the Succession of States', UN Audiovisual Library of International Law <https://legal.un.org/avl/ha/annp rss/annprss html> accessed 9 January 2024.

[31] ILC Articles (n 29) preamble; Third Mikulka Report (n 8) 20–22, 42–43.

[32] E.g. – ILC, 2488th meeting (5 June 1997) UN Doc A/CN.4/2488, paras 23, 33–34, 36, 40–41, 43, 49.

[33] Václav Mikulka, 'Second report on State Succession and its impact on the nationality of natural and legal persons', UN Doc A/CN.4/474 (17 April 1996) paras 140–72.

[34] Václav Mikulka, 'Fourth report on nationality in relation to the succession of States' (23 April 1998) UN Doc A/CN.4/489 paras 29, 50–52.

[35] Mikulka (n 30).

articles with commentaries in 1997[36] and adopted them in 1999.[37] Following 'increasingly agonizing debates' on the final form to be given to the ILC Articles, the Sixth Committee did not adopt the text.[38] Rather, it recommended to the General Assembly to 'take note of the Articles' and to annex the text to its resolution.[39]

While the General Assembly took no further action on the item,[40] the Council of Europe adopted the 2006 Convention on the Avoidance of Statelessness in relation to State Succession. The Special Rapporteur observed in 2020 that 'the phenomenon of succession of States ... will reoccur even in the future, and the problems accompanying collective naturalizations, including the risk of large scale statelessness, will also reappear'.[41] There is scant evidence of the subsequent application of the ILC Articles,[42] even in international jurisprudence.[43] Overall, they are 'an intricate web of rules that, in many cases, are clear examples of progressive development, rather than mere codification'.[44]

## 7.2 The General Principle of Automaticity

When a succession of States occurs, collective nationalization is the default rule that regulates the loss of the nationality of the predecessor and the acquisition of the nationality of the successor. As secondary rules from which predecessors and successor may derogate, general principles of law apply to the extent that a particular issue (e.g.—the right of option) is not regulated by a succession agreement[45] or nationality law.[46] Recognition by international law of a natural or legal person as

[36] 'Report of the International Law Commission on the work of its forty-ninth session (12 May–18 July 1997)', UN Doc A/52/10, paras 36–43.

[37] Comments and observations received from Governments UN Doc A/CN.4/493 (4 December 1998). For the changes made in the Drafting Committee, see the 2497th, 2498th, 2499th, 2504th, 2505th, 2507th, 2508th, and 2509th meeting records.

[38] Mikulka, 'Introductory Note' (n 30).

[39] UNGA Res 55/153 (12 December 2000).

[40] UNGA Res 59/34 (2 December 2004); UNGA Res 63/118 (11 December 2008); UNGA Res 66/92 (9 December 2011).

[41] Mikulka, Introductory Note' (n 30).

[42] E.g. – Montenegro (n 433) South Sudan (notes 437–42).

[43] E.g. – *Khudyan* (n 419) Eritrea (n 428). The International Criminal Tribunal for the Former Yugoslavia rejected the expert evidence of a Member of the ILC who participated in the drafting of the ILC Articles 'probably cannot be said to reflect binding customary international law, on the basis of State practice and *opinio juris*' – Case No. IT-96-21-T *Prosecutor v Zejnil Delalić*, ICTY Trial Chamber (16 November 1998) *Judicial Reports* (1997) 1031, paras 255–56.

[44] Francesco Costamagna, 'Statelessness in the context of state succession: an appraisal under international law' in Annoni and Forlati (n 13) 37–53, 44.

[45] E.g. – Indonesia (n 331) South Viet Nam (n 355); Algeria (n 369).

[46] E.g. – South Yemen (n 328) Burma (n 309) Hong Kong (n 276); Malaya (n 323); Indonesia (n 332); South Sudan (notes 440–41). See also: *UN Materials* (n 321) 129 (Botswana) 179 (Fiji) 189 (Gambia) 239 (Jamaica) 248 (Kenya) 386 (Sierra Leone), 404 (Swaziland).

246  SUCCESSION AND NATIONALITY

a 'national' of a predecessor or successor does not oblige that State to grant persons a specific type of nationality (e.g.—citizenship) under its internal law.[47]

The stipulations for predecessors and successors to 'withdraw' and 'attribute' their nationality in the ILC Articles[48] was based on the notion of the 'negative' function of international law as being 'at the most to delimit the competence of the predecessor State to retain certain persons as its nationals and of the successor State to claim them ... [i]nternational law cannot prescribe that such persons change their nationality, either automatically or by submission'.[49] However, it is argued that State practice supports a general principle of collective nationalization whereby default rules of international law perform a 'positive function' to automatically attribute nationality for its limited purposes.[50]

Collective nationalization is effective on the date of succession[51] unless displaced by a nationality law or succession agreement.[52] While a successor may adopt or extend a new nationality law,[53] it can also retain the nationality law of the predecessor.[54] Subject to treaty law on statelessness, a predecessor may deprive and a successor may deny its nationality with prospective effect.

In the vast majority of cases, predecessors and successors have retrospectively affirmed collective nationalization from the date of succession.[55] In the rare cases in which a retroactive deprivation,[56] denial,[57] or grant[58] of nationality has been done, this is suggested to be ineffective for the purposes of international law between the date of succession and the date of decision.[59] This does not affect their validity in internal law by means of a succession agreement[60] or nationality law.[61]

---

[47] Notes 3, 13. See also, e.g. – ILC, Summary record of the 2476th meeting (14 May 1997) UN Doc A/CN.4/SR.2476, paras 19–62; ILC, Summary record of the 2478th Meeting (16 May 1997) UN Doc A/CN.4/SR.2478, paras 26–28, 41–42, 44, 55–56.

[48] Second Mikulka Report (n 33) para 85.

[49] First Mikulka Report (n 8) paras 61, 99, 104.

[50] 2476th meeting (n 47) paras 59; ILC, 2477th meeting (15 May 1997) UN Doc A/CN.4/SR.2477, paras 43–45; 2478th meeting (n 47) paras 4, 45, 62.

[51] E.g. – UAR (n 201); French India (n 255); Ifni (n 262); Walvis Bay (n 266); Libya (n 340).

[52] E.g. – North Borneo, Sarawak, & Singapore (n 260); Burma (notes 309–10). The effective date can be moved by special agreement; e.g. – Treaty of Versailles (n 474) Arts 36(2) 91(3) 112(2); Treaty of Peace with Italy (n 47) Annex XIV, para 11.

[53] E.g. – Austria (n 219); Slovenia (n 229); Croatia (n 230); North Macedonia (n 231); Newfoundland (n 246); Burma (nn 314 and 309); Azerbaijan (n 403); Moldova (n 404); Ukraine (n 410); Belarus (n 412); Kazakhstan (n 407); South Sudan (n 439).

[54] E.g. – Yemen (n 211); Philippines (n 285); Laos (n 352); Montenegro (nn 432 and 434); Israel (n 455).

[55] E.g. – FRY (notes 238–39); French India (n 255); Portuguese India (nn 256–57); Burma (n 315); Indonesia (n 331); Libya (n 340); Armenia (n 420); Turkmenistan (n 409); Uzbekistan (n 408); Georgia (notes 414–15); Kyrgzstan (n 406); Montenegro (n 434); Morocco (n 467); Mandatory Palestine (n 454).

[56] E.g. – Eritrea (n 428).

[57] E.g. – DRC (n 373); Israel (n 458).

[58] E.g. – Bosnia (n 233); Libya (nn 341–43); Guinea (nn 357–60); South Sudan (n 440)

[59] E.g. – Burma (n 319); South Sudan (n 442).

[60] E.g. – Czechoslovak–German Treaty on Nationality and Option Questions (n 251) art 1.

[61] E.g. – UAR (n 201); Somalia (n 205); Tanzania (n 207); Viet Nam (nn 208–09, 210); Bosnia (n 233); DRC (notes 374–79).

A nationality law may also be rendered prospective by fixing the date of succession to synchronize with it.[62]

As there is no general right to a nationality, States are not obliged to grant it.[63] When a predecessor deprives a person of nationality to whom the successor declines to grant its nationality, the person concerned becomes stateless.[64] This general position is altered if a State concerned participates in the Statelessness Convention;[65] only Kiribati has succeeded to the Statelessness Convention to date, which was also automatically extended to the territory of East Germany on its absorption. In acceding to the Convention on 29 March 1966, the United Kingdom applied it to 29 territories,[66] of which 13 have seceded and made retroactive declarations of provisional continuity for multilateral treaties.[67]

The 1997 European Convention on Nationality contains duties to avoid statelessness in cases of succession and to regulate nationality by agreement.[68] In deciding to grant nationality due to a succession, Contracing Parties are particularly obliged to take into account specified criteria.[69] Twenty-one members of the Council of Europe are party to the Convention,[70] which has yet to be applied to a succession.

Enacted in response to the call of the UN General Assembly,[71] the Council of Europe Convention requires a successor to grant its nationality to nationals of the predecessor 'who have or would become stateless as a result of the State succession if at that time' if 'habitually resident' in the transferred territory or having 'an appropriate connection with the successor'.[72] A predecessor must refrain from withdrawing its nationality from those who would otherwise become stateless.[73] A successor must not refuse to grant its nationality 'where such nationality reflects the expressed will of the person concerned' even if that person can acquire the nationality of another successor.[74] Seven States are party to the Council of Europe

---

[62] E.g. – Portuguese India (n 258); Bangladesh (n 386); Timor-Leste (n 394).

[63] Costamagna (n 44) 39–40, 42.

[64] Convention relating to the Status of Stateless Persons (adopted 28 September 1954, entered into force 6 June 1960) 360 UNTS 117, art 1. *Contra*: ILC Articles (n 29) art 10.

[65] Convention on the Reduction of Statelessness (adopted 30 August 1961, entered into force 13 December 1975) 989 UNTS 175.

[66] Ibid.

[67] See Chapter 5.

[68] European Convention on Nationality (6 November 1997) CETS 166, arts 18(1), 19.

[69] Ibid, art 18(2).

[70] 'States Parties to Conventions relating to Statelessness and Nationality' (31 August 2021) <https://rm.coe.int/overview-conventions-en/1680a3e690> accessed 10 January 2024.

[71] UNGA Res 59/34 (2 December 2004) para 2.

[72] Convention on the Avoidance of Statelessness in relation to State Succession (adopted 19 May 2006, entered into force 1 May 2009) CETS No 200, art 5. See also: 'Explanatory Report to the Council of Europe Convention on the avoidance of statelessness in relation to State succession' (19 May 2006) <https://rm.coe.int/16800d3815> accessed 10 January 2024, paras 9–10, 18–31.

[73] Ibid, art 6.

[74] Ibid, art 7.

Convention,[75] which was not retroactively applied by Montenegro to its own succession after ratifying it in 2010.[76]

Overall, the impact of the treaties providing for obligations on statelessness resulting from a succession has been 'limited'.[77] Although it is possible for a person to choose to become stateless by renouncing any nationality in consequence of a succession,[78] this results not by operation of international law but rather by the act by the person concerned. As for the exercise of an option, the person holds the nationality resulting from the succession until the effective date of renunciation.

Unless otherwise provided,[79] there is no general right to dual nationality.[80] However, an affected national may hold dual nationality in consequence of a succession if permitted by succession agreements or nationality laws enacted by the date of succession.[81] If multiple predecessors or successors designate persons as their nationals without a right of renunciation, then the conflict of nationality laws must be resolved by agreement.[82]

### 7.2.1  The Affected Body of Nationals

Unless otherwise provided by a succession agreement or nationality law,[83] the affected body of nationals comprises those nationals of the predecessor whose nationality changes in consequence of a succession.[84] It is composed of all persons holding the nationality of the predecessor in total successions under its applicable laws[85] but only those nationals who are connected to the transferred territory in partial successions. If the nationality laws of the predecessor be retained by the successor,[86] they also define the nationality of persons acquiring nationality after the

---

[75]  Note 70.

[76]  Council of Europe Convention, note 72, art 15(1); 2685 UNTS 360; 'Foreign Nationals Law', No 12/2018 Crne Gore, 23 February 2018 (3 March 2018) <https://www.refworld.org/docid/5552f8384.html> accessed 10 January 2024, arts 219–20.

[77]  Costamagna (n 44) 47.

[78]  E.g. – *Schwarzkopf* (n 221) 194; *Compulsory Acquisition of Nationality Case*, Court of Appeal of Cologne (16 May 1960) 32 ILR 166, 167.

[79]  E.g. – Walvis Bay (n 269); Eritrea (n 428).

[80]  E.g. – Montenegro (n 435).

[81]  E.g. – Eritrea (n 428); Montenegro (n 435).

[82]  E.g. – AM Boll, *Multiple Nationality and International Law* (Martinus Nijhoff 2007) 106, 249–60.

[83]  E.g. – Treaty of Peace with Italy (n 47) art 19; *Rimpelt v Clarkson*, Transvaal Provincial Division (1947) 14 ILR (1947) 32, 33 ('South West Africa'); *Westphal et uxor v Conducting Officer of Southern Rhodesia*, Cape Provincial Division of the Union of South Africa (24 January 1948) 15 ILR 211, 212 ('South West Africa').

[84]  ILC Articles (n 29) 26.

[85]  On Hawai'i and Florida, see: *United States et al. v Rodiek*, US Circuit Court of Appeals (17 February 1941) 10 ILR 279, 281; *Canter v The American Insurance Co. and The Ocean Insurance Company v Canter*, Supreme Court of the United States (1 January 1828) 1 Peters 511, 525–42.

[86]  E.g. – FRY (notes 234–236); Viet Nam (n 209); Montenegro (nn 432 and 434); Indonesia (n 331); Eritrea (n 421); South Sudan (n 439); Syria and the Lebanon (n 451). See also: *Khudyan* (n 419); Botswana Independence Order (30 September 1966) SI 1966 part III 2842, s 1.

THE GENERAL PRINCIPLE OF AUTOMATICITY    249

date of succession.[87] In State practice, special categories of persons have been wives and widows who acquired the nationality of the predecessor by marriage as well as minors and wards who are legally incapable of exercising a right of option.

### (a) Wives and Widows

Unless otherwise provided by a succession agreement or nationality law,[88] the wife of an affected national who is herself an affected national (as opposed to a foreign national[89]) is independent of his status. In classical practice, it was commonplace for the nationality of a wife or widow to follow that of her living or deceased husband:[90] his status automatically extended to her unless her prior nationality was preserved after her marriage.[91] A married woman thus automatically acquired nationality by marriage (*ius matrimonii*), which did not apply to maidens or divorced women.[92]

Since the Second World War, succession practice has gradually coalesced around the independent status of a wife,[93] though the right to acquire the same nationality as her husband upon application has also been permitted. If her husband be included in the affected body of nationals, the general principle of law stipulates that his wife must separately qualify for its nationality. However, this can cause the separation of a family unit, for which a duty to 'take all appropriate measures to allow that family to remain together or to be reunited' in Article 12 of the ILC Articles is *lex ferenda*.[94]

### (b) Minors and Wards

Unless otherwise provided by a succession agreement[95] or nationality law,[96] the nationality of a ward under the legal authority of another person follows that of his guardian according to the national law of the successor applicable at the date of succession. The bulk of succession practice has addressed the status of minors, as

---

[87] ILC Articles (n 29) 25.

[88] E.g. – Zanzibar (n 298). See also: *UN Materials* (n 321) 203 (Guyana); 389–90 (Sierra Leone); 429 (Trinidad & Tobago).

[89] E.g. – Indonesia (n 330).

[90] E.g. – Tanganyika (n 471).

[91] E.g. – Treaty of Versailles (n 474) arts 37, 79, 106, 113; Treaty of Saint-Germain (adopted 10 September 1919, entered into force 16 July 1920) 226 CTS 8, art 82; Treaty of Neuilly-sur-Seine (adopted 27 November 1919, entered into force 9 August 1920) 226 CTS 332, arts 40, 45; Treaty of Lausanne (n 451) art 36. See also, e.g. – AN Makarov, 'La nationalité de la femme mariée' (1937-II) 60 RdC 111, 117–70.

[92] E.g. – Indonesia (n 330).

[93] E.g. – Treaty of Peace with Italy (n 47) art 19(1); French India (n 255); Convention on the Nationality of Married Women (adopted 20 February 1957, entered into force 11 August 1958) 309 UNTS 65, arts 1–2. See further: JL Kunz, 'Nationality and Option Clauses in the Italian Peace Treaty of 1947' (1947) 41(3) AJIL 622, 628.

[94] ILC, 2483rd meeting (27 May 1997) UN Doc A/CN.4/2483 paras 41–43, 46, 47, 48, 49; ILC, 2484th meeting (29 May 1997) UN Doc A/CN.4/2484, paras 2–3, 14, 15, 9, 26, 35, 36, 38, 39, 42, 47.

[95] E.g. – Treaty of Peace with Italy (n 47) art 19(1), annexe XIV (para 9).

[96] E.g. – Czechia (n 241); Indonesia (n 332); Timor-Leste (n 393).

250 SUCCESSION AND NATIONALITY

defined by internal law.[97] The usual practice has been to define a minor as below the age of 18 years;[98] persons born in the transferred territory on the date of succession are included in the affected body of nationals but those born afterwards are not.[99]

Unless otherwise provided,[100] in case of 'mixed' parentage in that one parent is a national of the predecessor and the other a national of the successor with dual nationality prohibited, the nationality of a minor is determined by the nationality law on descent (*ius sanguinis*) of the predecessor.[101] Succession agreements and nationality laws of successors have rarely addressed other categories of wards, such as adopted, incarcerated, or insane persons.[102] As for minors, guardianship is determined according to the internal law applicable at the date of succession.

If a succession agreement or nationality law omit a particular category of birth or the identity of a parent cannot be determined (e.g.—an unknown father[103] or a foundling[104]) then the general principle of law is that birth in the transferred territory suffices. The distinction in classical practice drawn between legitimate and natural children to determine whether nationality be derived from the father or the mother[105] is rare in modern practice.[106]

### 7.2.2 The Principle of Territoriality

In default of a succession agreement[107] or nationality law,[108] the general principle of law is that the affected body of nationals automatically lose the nationality of the predecessor and acquire the nationality of the successor according to a principle of territoriality.[109] It is important for the assignment of the nationality of one of multiple successors in dismemberments and (more rarely) one of multiple successors in rare cases of concurrent secessions and accessions to independence. [110] It also

---

[97] E.g. – UAR (n 201).
[98] E.g. – Treaty of Versailles (n 474) arts 37, 106, 113; Treaty of Peace with Italy (n 47) art 19; annexe XIV, s 9; Indonesia (n 332) art 1; Burma (n 312); Pacific Islands (notes 484–486).
[99] For an exception, see: Treaty of Peace with Italy (n 47) art 19.
[100] E.g. – Tanganyika (n 471).
[101] E.g. – Indonesia (n 332).
[102] E.g. – Indonesia (n 332); Malaya (notes 320–23).
[103] E.g. – UAR (n 202).
[104] E.g. – UAR (n 202); Yemen (n 214); North Borneo, Sarawak, & Singapore (n 261); Eritrea (n 421). See, further: Mai Kaneko-Iwase, *Nationality of Foundlings* (Springer 2021) 31–176.
[105] E.g. – Somaliland Nationality and Citizenship Ordinance 1960, XX (30) Somaliland Protectorate Gazette, Supplement No 2 (26 June 1960) s 4.
[106] E.g. – Malaya (notes 320–23); South Yemen (n 327); Madagascar (n 363).
[107] E.g. – Ifni (n 262).
[108] E.g. – *UN Materials* (n 321) 124, 246, 254–255, 282, 472.
[109] E.g. – Libya (n 339); Equatorial Guinea (notes 383–84); Montenegro (n 433). Article 8 is *lex ferenda* – ILC Articles (n 29) 31; *Khudyan* (n 419).
[110] E.g. – British India (n 300); Pacific Islands (notes 481–86).

applies to determine who retains the nationality of the predecessor or assumes that of the successor in cessions and secessions.

To reflect this dynamic of selection from multiple States, it is proposed that the test of territoriality be expressed as one of dominant connection to a particular territory. To apply this test, State practice has featured the following criteria:

- local citizenship;
- indigeneity;
- permanent residence;
- birth; and
- descent.

While the criteria of local citizenship and indigeneity have been prescribed in succession agreements and nationality laws, they are subjective concepts that lack a common definition to apply as general principles.

As the most commonplace criteria across all classes of succession, it is recommended that the objective concepts of permanent residence, birthplace, and descent apply in default of a succession agreement or nationality law. The ILC distinguished among three groups of nationals: (1) those born in the transferred territory and resident therein; (2) those born elsewhere but temporarily or permanently resident therein; and (3) those born in the transferred territory but temporarily or permanently resident in the remaining territory of the predecessor or a third State.[111] Though acknowledging State practice on birthplace and local citizenship,[112] the ILC prioritized permanent residence in Article 8 of the ILC Articles and excluded indigeneity.[113]

### (a) Local Citizenship

Unless otherwise provided in a succession agreement or nationality law,[114] a 'secondary nationality' or local citizenship[115] designates the affected body of nationals pursuant to a nationality law of the central government[116] or a local government[117] of the predecessor, a provision of a succession agreement,[118] or a nationality law of a successor.[119] Unless otherwise provided,[120] the dominant connection of a

---

[111] First Mikulka Report (n 8) para 99.

[112] ILC Articles (n 29) 41 (para 2).

[113] Second Mikulka Report (n 33) paras 125–34; Third Mikulka Report (n 8) 50–51; 2492nd Meeting (n 8) paras 1–34.

[114] E.g. – Equatorial Guinea (notes 380–82); Belarus (n 412).

[115] E.g. – SFRY (notes 229–30, 232, 236–37); Czecho-Slovakia (notes 242–242); Alexandretta (n 252); Laos (n 352); Cambodia (n 353); Montenegro (notes 430, 434).

[116] E.g. – Libya (n 339).

[117] E.g. – Laos (n 349); Philippines (n 285); Montenegro (n 429); Pacific Islands (notes 481, 483, 485, & 486).

[118] E.g. – North Borneo & Sarawak (n 261).

[119] E.g. – Indonesia (n 331); Bangladesh (n 386).

[120] E.g. – Czecho-Slovakia (n 243); Ukraine (n 410).

## 252 SUCCESSION AND NATIONALITY

national who lacks a local citizenship (e.g.—an expatriate) is determined according to his last place of permanent residence in the territory of the predecessor. If he had never resided permanently in its territory, then it is identified by his place of birth; if he was neither born nor permanently resident in its territory, then it follows the rule of descent.

### (b) Indigeneity

By a succession agreement or nationality law enacted no later than the date of succession,[121] a requirement of indigeneity may be enacted as membership of a race[122] or ethnicity.[123] To identify the ethnicities qualifying as indigenous, successors have expressly designated a list of recognized groups[124] or a historical date by which groups were required to be 'settled' in the transferred territory.[125] To directly determine the membership of an individual in a qualifying group, requirements of linguistic competence, religious membership, and adherence to prevailing social custom have been stipulated.[126] Indirectly, descent[127] from persons born in the transferred territory over one or more generations has also been applied.[128] In certain cases, no definition has been specified,[129] with a wide margin of discretion exercised by authorities.[130]

Amid wide diversity on the criteria applied by successors, indigeneity is not a general principle of law.[131] The right of a predecessor or successor to discriminate on ethnic grounds may be displaced by its participation in a treaty:

- the 1961 Convention on the Reduction of Statelessness ('1961 Statelessness Convention');[132]
- the 1999 European Convention on Nationality;[133] or

---

[121] E.g. – Burma (n 311); Malaya (notes 320–23); Equatorial Guinea (n 382); South Sudan (n 439).

[122] E.g. – Burma (n 316); Palau (n 486).

[123] E.g. – Malaya (notes 320–23); South Sudan (n 439).

[124] E.g. – Burma (n 316); Laos (n 352).

[125] E.g. – Malaya (n 316); DRC (n 373); South Sudan (n 437); Eritrea (n 421).

[126] E.g. – Treaty of Peace with Italy (n 47) annexe XIV (s 9); Malaya (notes 320–23); Somaliland Nationality and Citizenship Ordinance 1960 (n 105) s 4. On 'Poles who are German nationals', see: Günther Jaenicke, Karl Doehring, and Erich Zimmermann (eds) *Fontes Iuris Gentium: Decisions of the German Supreme Court relating to Public International Law* (Carl Heymanns Verlag KG 1960) 58.

[127] On adoption, see: Malaya (n 345). On 'mixed ancestry', see, e.g. – Burma (n 312); South Sudan (notes 441–42); Israel (n 462).

[128] E.g. – *UN Materials* (n 321) 174 (Cyprus), 307 (Malawi). On Sri Lanka, see: Citizenship Act No 18 (15 November 1948) ss 2, 4–5; *Mudanayake v Sivagnanasunderam*, Supreme Court of Ceylon (28 September 1951) 16 CILC 163; *Asary v Vanden Dreesen (Inspector of Police)* Supreme Court of Ceylon (22 February 1962) 16 CILC 183.

[129] E.g. – Eritrea (n 255) Burma (n 311) Indonesia (nn 332–33) Hong Kong (n 271); Macao (n 279). See also: AN Makarov and Ernst Schmitz (eds) *I Fontes Juris Gentium: Digest of the Diplomatic Correspondence of the European States (1871–1878)* (Heymann 1937) 280–86.

[130] E.g. – Croatia (n 231); Madagascar (nn 361 & 365). This can result in error, e.g. – *Hasan Ali* (n 316).

[131] E.g. – *Weber v Nederlands Beheer-Instituut* (n 251).

[132] Note 65, art 9.

[133] Note 68, art 5.

THE GENERAL PRINCIPLE OF AUTOMATICITY    253

- the 2006 Council of Europe Convention on the Avoidance of Statelessness in relation to State Succession ('Council of Europe Convention').[134]

Citing these treaties, Article 15 of the ILC Articles states that discrimination is not permitted 'on any ground', which does not reflect State practice[135] and so is *lex ferenda*.[136]

### (c) Permanent Residence

In default of any other criterion specified in a succession agreement or nationality law, a national of the predecessor who is permanently resident in the transferred territory on the date of succession is included in the affected body of nationals.[137] Originating in the peace treaties of the First World War,[138] 'habitual residence' has been used alongside 'ordinary residence'[139] in succession agreements and nationality laws to denote the establishment of habitual life in a locality.[140] The proposed default period for the establishment of 'residence' is five years, which reflects the most common period applied in practice.[141] To qualify for inclusion, a national must generally have resided in the transferred territory for a continuous (not cumulative[142]) period concluding on the date of succession. Absences do not break the 'continuous' period of residence if its 'essential continuity' be maintained.[143] Continuity can be maintained if absences are caused by extraneous events, such as electoral violence.[144]

Used in many succession agreements[145] and nationality laws,[146] the term 'domicile' denotes the intention of a resident (*établi*) person to 'permanently' reside in one or more localities.[147] A locality can differ from other places of 'habitual'

---

[134] Note 72, art 4. The 'legal provisions of State Parties concerning nationality' are excluded: Convention on the Elimination of All Forms of Racial Discrimination (adopted 7 March 1966, entered into force 4 January 1969) 660 UNTS 195, arts 1(3) 5(d)(iii).

[135] ILC Articles (n 29) 40 (n 113).

[136] 2483rd meeting (n 94) paras 41–43, 46, 47, 48, 49; 2484th meeting (n 94) paras 6, 24, 25, 33, 43; Comments and observations from Governments (n 37) 168–69.

[137] ILC Articles (n 29) art 5.

[138] O'Connell (n 3) 512–13. E.g. – Treaty of Versailles (n 474) art 84; Convention concerning Questions of Option and Nationality (adopted 30 August 1924, entered into force 31 January 1925) 32 LNTS 333, art 4.

[139] E.g. – Walvis Bay (n 266); Hong Kong (n 276); Namibia (n 478).

[140] E.g. – Slovenia (n 229). On *pertinenza*, see: Treaty of Saint-Germain-en-Laye (n 91) arts 64, 70–77.

[141] E.g. – India (n 302); Georgia (n 415); Namibia (n 478); Northern Mariana Islands (n 481); *UN Materials* (n 321). Other periods ranging from 6 months to 15 years have been stipulated, e.g. – Indonesia (n 332); Portuguese India (n 256); Czechia (n 242); *UN Materials* (n 321) 124 (Barbados), 472–73 (Zambia); Treaty of Versailles (n 474) annex, para 3 (Alsace-Lorraine); Eritrea (n 255); Libya (n 340); Malaya (nn 320–23).

[142] *UN Materials* (n 321) 144 (Guyana).

[143] E.g. – Malaya (nn 320–23).

[144] E.g. – Bangladesh (notes 387–89); Timor-Leste (n 398).

[145] E.g. – Treaty of Peace with Italy (n 47) art 19.

[146] E.g. – South Viet Nam (n 355); South Sudan (n 439).

[147] E.g. – Syria and the Lebanon (n 451); South West Africa (n 474); Northern Mariana Islands (n 481). See also: *Acquisition of Polish Nationality* (Advisory Opinion) (15 September 1923) PCIJ Series B No 7, 20; *Acquisition of Polish Nationality* (Germany v Poland) Arbitrator Kaeckenbeeck (10 July 1924) I RIAA 403, 408–09, 413–14 (French).

# 254  SUCCESSION AND NATIONALITY

residence,[148] such as study or employment[149] and civil servants with a residential requirement, such as diplomats and military personnel.[150] In the absence of specified criteria,[151] the intention of a person to reside permanently is a question of fact to be answered by reference to his conduct with respect to economic and personal affairs.[152]

### (d) Birthplace
When a national lacks a permanent residence in any territory of the predecessor, it is suggested that birthplace apply to identify his dominant connection.[153] For example, birthplace can be pertinent for a national who is permanently resident outside the territory of the predecessor. It has also been used for civil servants with a residential requirement of service, such as soldiers and diplomats, when permanent residence in a particular territory has not been possible to determine.

### (e) Descent
A national of the predecessor who was neither born nor permanently resident in the transferred territory at the date of succession is included in the affected body of nationals if one of his parents was born or permanently resident therein.[154] This might apply, for example, to a national who was born outside the territory of the predecessor to a civil servant.[155] Should the nationalities of his parents differ, the applicable laws of the predecessor determine which parent applies—including on questions of dual nationality.

## 7.2.3  The Right of Option

A right of option may be granted to some or all of the affected body of nationals by a succession agreement[156] or nationality law.[157] Such options are exercised by

---

[148] E.g. – Portuguese India (n 256); India (n 301); Pakistan (n 305).

[149] E.g. – India (n 302); Pakistan (n 305).

[150] E.g. – FRY (n 237).

[151] E.g. – Moldova (n 404); Ukraine (n 410); Belarus (n 412); Kazakhstan (n 407); Turkmenistan (n 409); Uzbekistan (n 408).

[152] E.g. – Treaty of Versailles (n 474) arts 36–37; Arrangement relating to Option (11 September 1922) 41 LNTS 141, s 2.

[153] E.g. – Portuguese India (n 257); South Yemen (n 327); Timor-Leste (notes 393–94); Namibia (n 478).

[154] E.g. – South Yemen (n 327); Timor-Leste (nn 393 and 394); Tanganyika (n 472).

[155] E.g. – Namibia (n 478).

[156] E.g. – French India (n 255); Portuguese India (n 257); Indonesia (n 335); Libya (n 339). On the classical practice following the First World War, see: JL Kunz, *Die Völkerrechtliche Option* vol I (Ferdinand Hist 1925) 100–300; JL Kunz, 'L'Option de Nationalité', 31 RdC 108, 133–172; Charles Rousseau, *Droit international public* vol III (Sirey, Paris, 1977) 368–372; Makarov and Schmitz (n 464) 586.

[157] E.g. – *UN Materials*, 307–08 (Malawi).

THE GENERAL PRINCIPLE OF AUTOMATICITY    255

declaration before designated national authorities under specified procedures.[158] In default of an agreement or law regulating the option, the general principle of collective nationalization is subject to a limited right of option by conduct for the affected body of nationals.[159]

The right of option is confined to the classes of cession and secession to choose between the nationality of the predecessor or the successor.[160] In contrast, there is no default right to choose the nationality of one of multiple successors in dismemberments or rare cases of multiple territories seceding concurrently.[161] While the involvement of more than two States increases factual complexity, there is no difference in principle between these scenarios.

The exercise of an option does not retroactively negate the collective nationalization of the optant.[162] Rather, the optant acquires the nationality of the predecessor and loses that of the successor on the effective date of the option.[163] This rule can be displaced by a succession agreement providing for retroactive effect.[164]

The right of option takes two forms: (1) a positive option to select a nationality; and (2) a negative option to renounce a nationality. In cessions and secessions, an option generally features both forms because it entails the retention of the nationality of the predecessor to replace that of the successor.[165] In rare cases,[166] an option can permit dual nationality by exercising a positive option without requirement to exercise a negative option.

## (a)  Declaration

When prescribed in a succession agreement or nationality law enacted no later than the date of succession,[167] the exercise of the right of option is governed by its procedural provisions.[168] Substantive requirements might also be imposed, such as a condition that an optant migrate to the territory of the opted State.[169] An option may also be granted to all persons who would otherwise become stateless.[170]

---

[158] E.g. – Treaty of Peace with Italy (n 47) art 19. See also: Kunz (n 93) 627.
[159] *Contra*: ILC Articles (n 29) 33–34 (art 10(2)).
[160] E.g. – USSR (n 402).
[161] E.g. – SFRY (n 228); North Macedonia (n 233); Bosnia (n 234). *Contra*: ILC Articles (n 42) 45 (n 135).
[162] *Contra*: ILC Articles (n 29) 30, 41 (art 7).
[163] E.g. – Burma (n 308); Indonesia (n 336); Syria and the Lebanon (n 451).
[164] E.g. – Treaty of Peace with Italy (n 47) art 19.
[165] Infrequently, an option for the nationality of the successor has been provided, e.g. – Indonesia (n 332); Madagascar (n 364); Algeria (n 369).
[166] E.g. – Montenegro (notes 434–35); Timor-Leste (notes 395–98).
[167] E.g. – Indonesia (n 333); Burma (n 308).
[168] E.g. – Ifni (n 262); Burma (n 314).
[169] E.g. – Treaty of Versailles (n 474) art 85.
[170] On Burma, Czechia, and the FRY, see: ILC Articles (n 29) 28.

256  SUCCESSION AND NATIONALITY

The time limit for the exercise of an option by declaration is specified in the enabling instrument.[171] There is no default time limit[172]—a wide range have been adopted in practice from one month[173] to three years.[174] The calculation of the time limit follows the law of the opted State.[175]

## (b) Conduct

In default of an option by declaration, the rule is that an option may be exercised by the establishment of permanent residence in the territory of the opted State. The option by conduct is based primarily upon the acceptance of optants by opted States, whether within[176] or without[177] a treaty framework. In particular, the right of option by conduct has occurred in circumstances in which optants have transferred their residence to opted States amidst armed conflict and population displacement. While the procedure to claim nationality is a matter of internal law, it is likely to be solicited by an application for judicial declaration.[178]

The intention of an optant to establish permanent residence is a question of fact to be answered by his circumstances and conduct. Neither continued residence in the territory of the predecessor nor the solicitation of a passport to enable migration necessarily manifests an intention to opt. However, a proven option by declaration for another State is decisive.[179]

The time limit is a question of fact with respect to the circumstances of a particular optant.[180] Taking into account that the option has frequently been exercised in times of national crisis, it is suggested that time begins to run from the date of succession or such subsequent date as its free exercise became possible.

---

[171] E.g. – Treaty of Peace with Italy (n 47) art 19.

[172] ILC Articles (n 29) 34–35 (art 11(5)); Third Mikulka Report (n 8) 36.

[173] Portuguese India (n 257).

[174] Treaty between the United States and Russia (30 March 1867) 24 BFSP 1269, art 3. For a mixture of time-limits between three months and two years, see, e.g. – Burma (n 312); Indonesia (nn 334 and 336); Ifni (n 262); Micronesia (n 483); Czechia (nn 242 and 243).

[175] E.g. – Ifni (n 262).

[176] E.g. – Definitive Treaty of Peace (France–Spain–Great Britain) (10 February 1763) 42 CTS 279, arts IV, IX, XX; Convention between Great Britain and the Orange River Territory (23 February 1854) 111 CTS 313, art IV; Treaty of Peace (France–Spain) (22 July 1795) 52 CTS 411, art 9.

[177] E.g. – Burma (n 312); Bangladesh (nn 387–89); Portuguese Timor (n 390) USSR (n 417). See also: *Emperor v Jagardeo*, Supreme Court of Bombay (18 June 1925) 15 CILC 190.

[178] E.g. – Indonesia (n 335). Persons convicted of treason against Malawi were found not to have been 'citizens of Malawi' under nationality legislation for lack of evidence of birth and descent in Malawi; however, evidence indicated that the accused had been 'temporarily absent' from homes in Malawi while accommodated as 'refugees from Malawi' at a refugee camp in Tanzania – *Mwakawanga and Others v Malawi*, Supreme Court of Appeal (23 October 1968) (1968–1970) ALR Mal. 14, 38–40, 48–50, 58–67.

[179] E.g. – Burma (n 312).

[180] Third States have recognized travel documents issued by predecessors – ILC, Summary Record of the 2490th Meeting, UN Doc A/CN.4/SR.2490 (10 June 1997) paras 21, 23–24; ILC, Summary Record of the 2486th Meeting, UN Doc A/CN.4/SR.2486 (30 May 1997) para 64.

## 7.2.4 Legal Persons

Legal persons are artificial or abstract entities (e.g.—private companies, charter companies, and charitable associations) that are vested by internal law with limited legal personality.[181] The most common situation in which a succession impacts on the nationality of a legal person is diplomatic protection,[182] which succession agreements[183] and nationality laws have rarely addressed.[184] In practice, the law of the predecessor as provisionally retained by the successor[185] has addressed the matter, whether based on the common law principle of incorporation or the civil law concept of the 'seat' (*siège social*).[186]

As legal persons can have complex structures with links to multiple jurisdictions,[187] recourse to a general principle of law is necessary in the absence of an applicable rule of internal law. According to the limited State practice to date, the test has been the location of the seat; this is presumed to be the location of its head office unless the seat of management and financial control are both elsewhere.[188] Legal persons may accordingly opt for the nationality of another State by changing their seats.[189]

A rare example of succession practice took place with respect to the replacement by Algeria of French nationals on the boards of directors of mining and agricultural companies that had had their head offices in French Algeria. While the judgments of the French and Algerian courts differed on effectiveness of the relocations of registered offices to France, they both applied the test of the seat.[190] Although the 'lifting of the corporate veil' under the law of diplomatic protection is permissible

---

[181] E.g. – Ignaz Seidl-Hohenveldern, *Corporations in and under International Law* (CUP 1987) 1–6, 55–66; Lucius Caflisch, 'La nationalité des sociétés commerciales en droit international privé' (1967) 24 ASDI 119–160, 119–21, 127–30; Lucius Caflisch, *La Protection des Sociétés Commerciales et les Intérêts Indirects en Droit International Public* (Martinus Nijhoff 1969) 3–10.

[182] E.g. – *National Bank of Egypt v Austro-Hungarian Bank* (n 444). See also: Seidl-Hohenveldern (n 181) 7–8; Paul de Visscher, 'La protection diplomatique des personnes morales' (1961-I) 102 RdC 395, 427–79.

[183] E.g. – Treaty of Peace with Italy (n 47) annex XIV (paras 11–12); Treaty of Versailles (n 474) art 54(3); Saint-Germain-en-Laye (n 91) art 75.

[184] Seidl-Hohenveldern (n 181) 29–38, 51–54.

[185] Ibid, 113–118; Caflisch (n 181) 119.

[186] Dumberry (n 14) 362.

[187] E.g. – ILC, 2388th Meeting (n 22) paras 21, 41.

[188] ILC Articles on Diplomatic Protection (n 13) art 9; *Barcelona Traction, Light and Power Company, Limited, Second Phase* [1970] ICJ Rep 3, para 70; *Italy v Libya*, UN Tribunal for Libya (27 June 1955) 22 ILR 103, 107–08. See also: Guilia d'Agnone, 'Determining the Nationality of Companies in ICSID Arbitration' in Annoni and Forlati (n 13) 153–68, 154–63.

[189] E.g. – Wolf Radmann, 'The Nationalization of Zaire's Copper: from Union Minière to GECAMINES' (1978) 25(4) Africa Today 25.

[190] E.g. – *SONAREM v Genebrier and Others*, Court of Annaba (26 December 1968) 41 ILR 384, 389–90, 33–394; *Caisse centrale de Réassurance des Mutuelles agricoles v Mutuelle Centrale d'Assurance et de Réassurance*, France Court of Cassation (30 March 1971) 72 ILR 565, 566–68; *Assicurazioni Generali v Selim Cotran*, Judicial Committee of the Privy Council (27 November 1931) 6 BILC 695, 697; *Bakalian and Hadjithomas v Ottoman Bank*, Court of Appeal of Paris (19 March 1965) 47 ILR 216, 220, 224.

258 SUCCESSION AND NATIONALITY

in limited circumstances,[191] there is no example of such a circumstance applying in the context of a succession save by specific agreement.[192]

## 7.3 Application to the Classes of Succession

In a total succession,[193] the extinction of the predecessor automatically terminates its nationality without right of option.[194] Due to the extinction of the predecessor and the existence of a single successor, it is proposed that a general principle of law for mergers and absorptions is that the nationality of each predecessor is automatically converted to the nationality of the successor at the date of succession.[195] To identify the affected body of nationals, the applicable laws of the predecessor are determinative.[196] Successors may derogate from this general principle of law by enacting a succession agreement or nationality law no later than date of succession.

For the more complex class of dismemberment,[197] a general principle of law is advanced for the automatic conversion of each national of the predecessor into the nationality of one of the successors. As for mergers and absorptions, the affected body of nationals comprises each of the nationals of the predecessor. Due to the existence of multiple successors, the critical issue is the allocation of the affected body for which no right of option applies for individuals to select their preferred nationality.

In a partial succession,[198] a proportion of the nationals of the predecessor are affected by its transfer of territorial title to a successor.[199] The three principal issues that arise are:

1. identification of the affected body of nationals for collective nationalization;
2. a right of option to retain the nationality of the predecessor for the affected body of nationals; and
3. dual nationality resulting from the retention of the nationality of the predecessor along with collective nationalization of the affected body of nationals.

It is suggested that the default rule in cessions and secessions is that the nationality of the affected body of nationals is automatically converted to that of the successor

---

[191] *Barcelona Traction* (n 188) paras 56–58.

[192] E.g. – Agreement intended to Settle the Financial Consequences of Nationalization and Expropriation Measures taken between 1975 and 1978 by Madagascar (1 October 1998) 2179 UNTS 43.

[193] See Chapter 2.

[194] First Mikulka Report (n 8) paras 99–100.

[195] See Chapter 1.

[196] Ibid.

[197] First Mikulka Report (n 8) para 101.

[198] See Chapter 2.

[199] First Mikulka Report (n 8) para 99.

according to the principle of territoriality, subject to a right to opt by conduct for the nationality of the predecessor. In accessions to independence, the nationals of the protected State or territory retain its nationality and automatically lose the nationality of the predecessor (i.e.—the status of 'protected person') without a right of option.

### 7.3.1 Merger

When one State merges with another State to create a new State, the default rule is that the nationalities of the merging States automatically terminate and the nationality of the merged State is automatically acquired by all nationals of the merging States with effect from the date of succession.[200] To identify the affected body of nationals, the nationality laws of the predecessors are determinative. Due to the extinction of the merged States, no right of option to retain their nationalities applies.

This proposed general principle of law derives from the State practice of the successors in respect of the mergers of:

- Syria and Egypt to create the United Arab Republic ('UAR') in 1958;
- British Somaliland with the Trust Territory of Somaliland to form the Republic of Somalia ('Somalia') in 1960;
- Tanganyika and Zanzibar to make the United Republic of Tanganyika and Zanzibar ('Tanzania') in 1964;
- the Democratic Republic of Viet Nam ('North Viet Nam') and the Republic of Viet Nam ('South Viet Nam') to found the Socialist Republic of Viet Nam ('Viet Nam') in 1976; and
- the Yemen Arab Republic ('North Yemen') and the People's Democratic Republic of Yemen ('South Yemen') to establish the Republic of Yemen ('Yemen') in 1990.

While their constitutions were adopted with effect from the date of succession, their nationality laws were subsequently enacted with prospective rather than retroactive effect. The successors enacted their nationality laws after the date of succession, which retrospectively affirmed the conversion of nationality from that date.

Entering into force four days after the date of succession, the provisional constitution of the UAR declared all Syrian and Egyptian nationals to be its nationals, as well as all persons 'who are entitled to it by laws or statutes in force in Syria or

---

[200] ILC Articles (n 29) 32 (art 21); First Mikulka Report (n 8) para 93.

260   SUCCESSION AND NATIONALITY

Egypt.[201] This was affirmed in its nationality law of 22 June 1958.[202] All of the nationals of the predecessors were thus retrospectively declared to have been collectively nationalized.

Enacted four days before the date of succession by British Somaliland and the Trust Territory of Somalia, their law of merger declared: 'All persons who upon the date of this Union possess the citizenship of Somaliland and Somalia respectively shall by this Union now become citizens of the Somali Republic.'[203] The law also provided that all persons who would have acquired their respective citizenships under their nationality laws would become citizens of Somalia.[204] In 1962, Somalia adopted a nationality law that repealed the nationality laws of the predecessors and affirmed the nationality of any person who had acquired the nationality of the predecessors under the repealed laws.[205]

For the merger of Tanganyika and Zanzibar on 26 April 1964, the predecessors had not expressly addressed the question of nationality in their succession agreement and provisional constitution but provided for the retention in force of their respective nationality laws.[206] In November 1964, Tanzania retrospectively declared the nationals of its predecessors under those nationality laws in force on the date of succession to be its nationality.[207] This included all persons who acquired nationality under the laws before their replacement in 1961.

When North Viet Nam and South Viet Nam merged on 2 July 1976, the impact of the succession on their bodies of nationals was obscure.[208] By its 1988 nationality law, Viet Nam retrospectively declared its nationals to be 'persons holding Vietnamese nationality up to the effective date of this Law and persons of Vietnamese nationality in accordance with this Law'.[209] It superseded the nationality laws of North Viet Nam, which had been extended to South Viet Nam since the merger.[210] The existing nationals of South Viet Nam were thus collectively nationalized at the date of succession but new nationals (e.g.—by birth) were designated under the North Vietnamese legislation.

---

[201] Provisional Constitution of the United Arab Republic (5 March 1958) in Eugene Cotran, 'Some Legal Aspects of the Formation of the United Arab Republic and the United Arab States' (1959) 8(2) ICLQ 346, 372 (art 2).

[202] Law No 82 of 1958 in Cotran (n 201) 380 (arts 2–3, 10).

[203] Law of Union between Somaliland and Somalia (27 June 1960) 164 BFSP 697, s 3(1).

[204] Ibid, s 3(2).

[205] Somali Citizenship Law No 28 (22 December 1962) Official Bulletin of the Somali Republic Supplement No 4 to No 12 (1962) art 18.

[206] Acts of Union (1 May 1964) 3(4) ILM 763, arts 5(a)(vi) 8.

[207] Extension and Amendment of Laws Decree No 5 1964, GN No 652 (13 November 1964); Tanzania, Citizenship Act 1961 (CAP52) ss 1–2, 6, 10(1).

[208] Constitution of Viet Nam (18 December 1980) <https://vbpl.vn/TW/Pages/vbpq-toanvan. aspx?ItemID=1534> accessed 16 February 2024, art 53 (Vietnamese); Bernard Dutoit, Daniel Gay, and Terrence Vandevelde, *La nationalité de la femme mariée* vol 3 (Droz 1980) 200.

[209] 'Law on Vietnamese Nationality, 1988' (1988) 15(3) RSL 287, art 1.

[210] Ibid, art 17.

For the creation of Yemen on 22 May 1990, nationality was omitted from the succession agreement[211] but the constitution of Yemen provisionally retained in force the nationality laws of the predecessors.[212] Consequently, the nationals of the predecessors under those laws automatically became nationals of Yemen on the date of succession.[213] On 26 August, Yemen replaced those laws with a new nationality law having prospective effect.[214]

## 7.3.2 Absorption

When one State absorbs another State, the default rule is that the nationality of the absorbed State automatically terminates and the nationality of the absorbing State is automatically acquired by all nationals of the absorbed State with effect from the date of succession.[215] To identify the affected body of nationals, the nationality laws of the predecessor are determinative. Due to the extinction of the absorbed State, no right of option to retain its nationality applies.

This proposed general principle of law derives from the practice of the successors in respect of the absorptions of:

- Austria by Germany (1938);
- Hyderabad by India (1950) and Kalat by Pakistan (1955);[216] and
- the German Democratic Republic ('East Germany') by the Federal Republic of Germany ('West Germany') in 1990.

These cases are also consistent with classical practice on the absorptions of Texas (1845)[217] and Hawai'i (1898).[218]

Following the absorption of Austria on 14 March 1938, Germany retrospectively acknowledged all Austrian nationals as its nationals on 3 July and replaced the Austrian law on nationality with its own nationality law on 30 July 1939.[219]

---

[211] Agreement proclaiming the Republic of Yemen (North Yemen–South Yemen) (adopted 22 April 1990, entered into force 22 May 1990) 2373 UNTS 131, arts 1, 8.

[212] Constitution of Yemen (22 May 1990) (1992) 7(1) ALQ 70, art 130.

[213] Andreas Zimmermann, 'State Succession and the Nationality of Natural Persons: Facts and Possible Codification' in Pierre Eisemann and Martti Koskenniemi (eds) *State Succession: Codification Tested against the Facts* (Martinus Nijhoff 2000) 611, 618.

[214] UNHCR, Law No 6 on Yemeni Nationality (26 August 1990) <https://www.refworld.org/docid/3ae6b57b10.html> accessed 9 January 2024, arts 1, 3.

[215] ILC Articles (n 29) 32; ILC, 2489th Meeting (n 27) paras 44, 48, 50, 51.

[216] TSN Santry, *State Succession in Indian Context* (Dominant Pub 2004) 195–96; 4 CILC 145–73; Pakistan Citizenship Act (n 306) s 13.

[217] JB Moore, *A Digest of International Law* vol I (US Government Printing Office 1906) vol III, 314–15; Treaty of Peace (Mexico–United States) 2 February 1848 (30 May 1848) 37 BFSP 567, arts VIII, IX.

[218] Organic Act of 30 April 1900, 31 United States Stat 141, 8 USC A, ss 4, 100. See also: *United States et al. v Rodiek*, United States Circuit Court of Appeals (17 February 1941) 10 ILR 279, 281.

[219] RE Clute, *The International Legal Status of Austria 1938–1955* (Springer 1962) 64.

262  SUCCESSION AND NATIONALITY

The courts of Switzerland, Belgium, and the Netherlands considered Austrian nationals to have been collectively nationalized and thus subject to enemy alien detention measures.[220] While the American courts recognized the existence of a right of option for nationals of absorbed States by quitting the territory of the absorbing State,[221] the English courts held the extinction of Austria to have extinguished the right of option.[222]

Prior to absorbing East Germany on 3 October 1990,[223] West Germany had considered the nationals of East Germany to be its own nationals under the 1913 nationality law of the German Reich due to its longstanding policy of pursuing reunification.[224] Whereas East Germany had initially retained the same law, it replaced it with a new nationality law in 1967.[225] Upon the absorption of East Germany, all its nationals had thus already been designated nationals of West Germany—rendering collective nationalization superfluous.

### 7.3.3  Dismemberment

When a State is dismembered so that parts of its territory are transferred to existing States or new States, the default rule is that each national of the dismembered State automatically loses its nationality and acquires the nationality of that successor with whose territory he has a dominant connection with effect on the date of succession.[226] Due to the extinction of the dismembered State, no right of option to retain its nationality applies and no general right exists to opt for the nationality of a preferred successor.

This proposed general principle of law derives from the State practice of the successors for the dismemberments of the Socialist Federal Republic of Yugoslavia ('SFRY') between 1990 and 1992 and Czecho-Slovakia in 1993. The State practice of the successors principally comprises their nationality laws, which were usually enacted after the date of succession.

No succession agreement on nationality was struck by the successors to the SFRY, which had provided for citizenship of the federation as well as local citizenship of a constituent republic.[227] The general principle applied by each of the

---

[220]  Ibid, 66.

[221]  *Schwarzkopf v Uhl*, US Second Circuit Court of Appeals, 12 ILR 188, 194 ('Austria').

[222]  *R. v Home Secretary, ex parte L.* [1945] KB 7, 10; *Mangold's Patent*, High Court of Justice (9 October 1950) 18 ILR 244, 246.

[223]  Treaty on German Unity (adopted 30 August 1990, entered into force 3 October 1990) 30 ILM 463, arts 1, 3–4.

[224]  Zimmermann (n 213) 617. See also, e.g. – *Single German Nationality (Teso) Case*, Federal Constitutional Court (21 October 1987) 91 ILR 211, 222–27, 229–30.

[225]  *Eastern Treaties Constitutionality Case*, Federal Constitutional Court (7 July 1975) 78 ILR 177, 188.

[226]  ILC Articles (n 29) 43–44 (art 22); 2492nd Meeting (note) paras 2–35; ILC Report (n 31) paras 209–11, 222.

[227]  Zimmermann (n 213) 634.

successors in their nationality laws was to designate the local citizens of the respective constituent republics as their nationals, which resulted in hundreds of thousands of permanent residents in one successor who held the local citizenship of another successor becoming foreigners in the territory of residence.[228] The principal difference was the criteria for local citizens of other constituent republics to naturalize in the State of residence.

Enacted on its declaration of independence (25 June 1991), the nationality law of Slovenia permitted local citizens of other SFRY republics with permanent residence to apply for naturalization within six months.[229] Also adopted on its declaration of independence (8 October 1991), the nationality law of Croatia provided for a right of option for ethnic Croats with registered residence.[230] In its nationality law adopted six weeks after its declaration of independence on 12 November 1991, North Macedonia permitted local citizens of other constituent republics to apply within one year for naturalization who were adult with registered residence of 15 cumulative years and a permanent source of finance.[231]

Amid the Bosnian War after its declaration of independence of 3 March 1992, Bosnia-Herzegovina ('Bosnia') enacted a nationality law on 6 October providing a six-month right of option for local citizens of other constituent republics who had been permanently resident in its territory for ten years (or five years, if born in Bosnia) at the start of the War on 6 April.[232] Due to a need for military conscription, the law was amended on 23 April 1993 to retroactively remove the additional criteria so that all local citizens of the SFRY who were resident in Bosnia on 6 April 1992 were declared to be Bosnian nationals automatically.[233]

In claiming to be the continuing State of the SFRY, the FRY initially preserved the 1974 SFRY nationality law.[234] By Article 17 of its constitution of 27 April 1992, however, it declared that it would 'confer Yugoslav citizenship on its inhabitants' and that '[a] Yugoslav citizen shall be simultaneously a citizen of one of its member

---

[228] UNHCR, 'Citizenship and Prevention of Statelessness Linked to the Disintegration of the Socialist Federal Republic of Yugoslavia' (1997) 3(1) *European Series* 40.

[229] Ibid, 11. See further: Slovene Citizenship Act, No 1/91 Uradni list (25 June 1991) arts 39–40; Constitution of Slovenia (23 December 1991) in *World Constitutions Illustrated Database* < https://home.heinonline.org/content/world-constitutions-illustrated/> accessed 9 January 2024, art 12.

[230] Ibid, 11–12. See further: Croatia Citizenship Law No 53 (8 October 1991) art 30 in *Nationality & Statelessness: A Collection of Nationality Laws* vol I (Independent Bureau for Humanitarian Issues 1996) 275.

[231] North Macedonia Law on Citizenship (adopted 27 October 1992, entered into force 12 November 1992) arts 7, 26 in UNHCR, 'Citizenship and Prevention of Statelessness' (n 228) 22–26.

[232] Bosnia-Herzegovina Law on Citizenship (6 October 1992) <https://www.refworld.org/docid/3ae6b4d828.html> accessed 9 January 2024, ss 27, 29–30, 36. On the issue whether the Bosnian Serb victims were 'protected persons' with respect to the Bosnian State for the purposes of the Fourth Geneva Convention in the Bosnian War, a duty of States to recognize a general right of option in international law was rejected by the ICTY – *Delalić* (n 43) paras 245–56.

[233] UNHCR, 'Citizenship and Prevention of Statelessness' (n 228) 32–35. See also: Constitution of Bosnia (14 December 1995) <http://www.ccbh.ba/public/down/USTAV_BOSNE_I_HERCEGOVINE_engl.pdf> accessed 28 December 2023, art I(7).

[234] Zimmermann (n 213) 635–36.

## 264 SUCCESSION AND NATIONALITY

republics'.[235] The FRY thus designated the local citizens of the constituent republics of Serbia and Montenegro as well as SFRY citizens resident abroad who lacked a local citizenship.[236]

On 1 January 1997, the FRY enacted a new nationality law whereby it provided a right of negative option for former local citizens of other SFRY republics who were permanently resident in the FRY on 27 April 1992.[237] Though applied retroactively,[238] a conflict with the legal situation between 27 April 1992 and 1 January 1997 did not arise because the new law did not deprive persons of nationality but rather extended the scope of collective nationalization with dual nationality addressed by the negative option.[239]

Like the SFRY, Czechoslovak nationality had comprised both a federal citizenship and a local citizenship of the two constituent republics.[240] Enacted on the date of succession (1 January 1993), the nationality law of Czechia designated local citizens as its nationals.[241] A one-year right of option was provided to local citizens of the other republic who had been permanently resident for at least two years, had no criminal conviction in the previous five years and renounced Slovak nationality.[242] On 19 January, Slovakia enacted its nationality law whereby it retrospectively recognized the local citizens of the Slovak constituent republic as its nationals and all other Czecho-Slovak nationals to opt for Slovak nationality by a simple declaration within one year.[243]

### 7.3.4 Cession

When one State cedes territory to another, the nationality of the ceding State is automatically lost and the nationality of the cessionaire acquired by those nationals of the predecessor with a dominant connection to the transferred territory.[244] The default test of dominant connection is determined primarily by permanent

---

[235] Ibid.

[236] Ibid.

[237] FRY Citizenship Act (accessed 16 July 1996, entered into force 1 January 1997) <https://www.refworld.org/docid/3ae6b4d44.html> accessed 9 January 2024, arts 46–48.

[238] Ibid, arts 52, 54–55.

[239] UNHCR, 'Citizenship and Prevention of Statelessness' (n 228) 33–36.

[240] Victor Knapp, 'Czechoslovakia', I International Encyclopaedia of Comparative Law Online (1980).

[241] Czechia Act No 40/1992 (1 January 1993) <https://www.refworld.org/docid/3ae6b51a8.html> accessed 31 December 2023, art 1.

[242] Ibid, art 6. See also: *Acquisition of Czech Citizenship by Slovak Citizens*, Pl ÚS 9/94 Czechia Constitutional Court (13 September 1994) paras I–III (Czecho-Slovak).

[243] Slovakia Law No 40 (19 January 1993) <https://www.legislationline.org/documents/action/popup/id/3848> accessed 31 December 2023, arts 2–3.

[244] ILC Articles (n 29) art 20; Third Mikulka Report (n 8) paras 1–27.

APPLICATION TO THE CLASSES OF SUCCESSION    265

residence or alternatively by birth.[245] The affected body of nationals may opt by conduct for the nationality of the ceding State.

This proposed general principle of law may be displaced by a succession agreement or by national legislation enacted with prospective effect no later than the date of succession. It derives from State practice with respect to dozens of cessions in the modern era, including:

- Newfoundland (1949);[246]
- Eritrea (1952);[247]
- French India (1952 and 1963);
- Portuguese India (1961 and 1962);
- West New Guinea ('West-Irian') (1962);[248]
- North Borneo, Sarawak, and Singapore (1963);
- Ifni (1971);
- Walvis Bay (1994);
- Hong Kong (1997); and
- Macao (1999).

Classical practice also generally supported the basic principle, such as the cessions of the Philippines (1899),[249] Eupen-Malmédy (1925),[250] the Sudetenland (1938),[251] Alexandretta (1939),[252] and certain border territories by Thailand to France (1946).[253] As cessions have generally been done by treaty, succession agreements have been a highly significant source of practice. Less commonly, the

---

[245] On Cyprus, see, e.g. – Treaty of Lausanne (n 451) arts 17, 20–21; *Agapios v Sanitary and Quarantine Council of Egypt*, Egypt Mixed Court of Appeal (21 January 1920) 1 ILR 201, 202; *Parounak and Bedros Parounakian v Turkish Government*, Anglo–Turkish Mixed Arbitral Tribunal (16 December 1929) 5 ILR 25, 27; *Messih v Minister of the Interior*, Conseil d'État of Egypt (26 December 1950) 28 ILR 291, 292.

[246] Note 291; British North America Act 1949 (23 March 1949) 153 BFSP 130, ss 1–2, sch (para 43).

[247] UNGA Res 390(V) (2 December 1950) 6.

[248] Round-Table Conference Agreements (Netherlands–Indonesia) (adopted 2 November 1949, entered into force 27 December 1949) 69 UNTS 200, 280 (note).

[249] Treaty of Peace (Spain–United States) (adopted 10 December 1898, entered into force 11 April 1899) 90 BFSP 382, art IX; Moore (n 217) vol III, 321.

[250] Treaty of Versailles (n 474) arts 32–24, 36, 84, 91, 105–106, 113, 278. See also: *In re Stoffels*, Court of Cassation of Belgium (9 March 1936) 9 ILR 339, 340; *Schumacher v Office des séquestres*, Court of Cassation of Belgium (16 January 1954) 21 ILR 177, 178.

[251] Munich Agreement (29/30 September 1938) 142 BFSP 438, art 7; Treaty regarding Nationality and Option Questions (adopted 20 November 1938, entered into force 26 November 1938) 142 BFSP arts 1–4; Law on the Reunion of the Sudeten German Districts (21 November 1938) 142 BFSP 585, arts 1–4; *Weber v Nederlands Beheer-Instituut*, Council for the Restoration of Legal Rights in The Hague (4 July 1955) 24 ILR 431, 432; *Amato Narodni Podnik v Julius Keilwerth Musikinstrumentenfabrik*, District Court of The Hague (11 December 1956) 24 ILR 435, 437.

[252] Settlement of Territorial Questions between Turkey and Syria (France–Turkey) (23 June 1939) 143 BFSP 477, arts 2–4 (French); ibid, Protocol (art 1).

[253] Settlement Agreement (Thailand–France) (17 November 1946) 344 UNTS 59; ibid, Exchange of Letters (17 November 1946) para 5; Peace Convention (adopted 9 May 1941, entered into force 5 July 1941) 144 BFSP 805, art 8.

266   SUCCESSION AND NATIONALITY

consequences of succession for nationality were addressed entirely by internal law (e.g.—Portuguese India, Walvis Bay, Hong Kong).

For the cession of Chandernagore on 9 June 1952, France and India agreed that 'French subjects' and 'citizens of the French Union'[254] who were 'domiciled' in Chandernagore were to lose the nationality of France and acquire the nationality of India by operation of law.[255] This was subject to a right of option to be exercised within six months of entry into force of the treaty of cession.

After annexing Dadra and Nagar Haveli on 11 August 1961, India legislated in 1962 for the collective nationalization of 'every person' who had his 'domicile' in the annexed territories and was either born therein or had been 'ordinarily resident' therein for at least two years preceding the date of annexation.[256] Following annexation of the remaining territories of Portuguese India on 5 March 1962, India collectively nationalized all persons who had been born therein on or before the commencement of its occupation on 20 December 1961 as well as those whose parents or grandparents had been born therein, subject to a one-month right of option.[257] In ceding Portuguese India with retroactive effect from the dates of annexation, Portugal and India left nationality to be regulated by internal law.[258]

For the cession of the Crown Colonies of North Borneo, Sarawak, and Singapore to Malaysia on 16 September 1963, a 'Citizen of the United Kingdom and Colonies' who was born, naturalized, or registered therein[259] automatically lost that status and became a Malaysian national on the date of succession.[260] Each person collectively nationalized became a federal citizen of Malaysia and a local citizen of the Borneo states or the state of Singapore, respectively.[261]

Prior to the retrocession of Ifni on 9 January 1971, Spain and Morocco awarded a three-month right to opt for Spanish nationality to Spanish nationals who had been born therein.[262] Optants were obliged to first renounce Moroccan nationality.[263] However, those who had 'acquired' Spanish nationality

---

[254] Notes 346–347.

[255] Treaty of Cession of Chandernagore (France–India) (adopted 2 February 1951, entered into force 9 June 1952) 158 BFSP 599, arts II–III. See also: Treaty ceding the French Establishments to India (France–India) (adopted 28 May 1956, entered into force 16 August 1962) 162 BFSP 848, arts 3–10.

[256] Goa, Daman and Diu (Citizenship) Order (28 March 1962) < https://www.refworld.org/docid/3ae6b51d1c.html> accessed 30 December 2023. See also: India Citizenship Act 1955 (n 300) s 7.

[257] Ibid, s 2. See also: *Rev. Mons Sebastiao Francesco Xavier dos Remedios Monteiro v Goa*, Supreme Court of India (26 March 1969) 8 CILC 306, 310, 320–322.

[258] Treaty on Recognition of India's Sovereignty (Portugal–India) (adopted 31 December 1974, entered into force 3 June 1975) 982 UNTS 153, art I.

[259] Note 293.

[260] Malaysia Act 1963 c 35, s 2, sch 1.

[261] Agreement (Malaya–United Kingdom) Cmd 2094 (July 1963) annex A (arts 23–34); sch 3, part I (s 2), part III (ss19A, 19B), annex D (arts 53–61, 69).

[262] Treaty on the Retrocession of Ifni (Spain–Morocco) (adopted 4 January 1969, entered into force 9 January 1971) BOE (5 June 1969) 8805, art 3 (Spanish). See also: Dirreción General de los Registros y del Notariado, 'Resolución de 19 de mayo de 1972', 1 ADI (1974) 510–13 (Spanish).

[263] Ibid, Additional Protocol (art 1). See also: Decree 1347/1969 on the Nationality Option (26 June 1969) 158 BOE (3 July 1969) 1044.

APPLICATION TO THE CLASSES OF SUCCESSION    267

by one of the means specified in the Spanish Civil Code automatically retain it.[264]

Preceding the retrocession of Walvis Bay on 1 March 1994,[265] South Africa had legislated on 23 February that any South African national 'ordinarily resident' in Walvis Bay at the date of succession could opt for South African nationality.[266] As Namibia had designated Walvis Bay as its territory in its constitution,[267] it regarded persons born in Walvis Bay as 'Namibian citizens by birth' if one parent was also a 'Namibian citizen by birth'.[268] On 28 February 1994, Namibia legislated that any other person who was continuously resident for a minimum of five years in Walvis Bay could apply for naturalization.[269]

Annexed to the succession agreement concluded for the retrocession of Hong Kong on 1 July 1997,[270] the Basic Law of Hong Kong provided for the extension of the Chinese nationality law to the Hong Kong SAR whereby Hong Kong residents 'of Chinese descent' and born in China (including Hong Kong) or otherwise meeting the criteria prescribed by the law were designated Chinese nationals,[271] regardless of the type of British nationality held.[272] Although the Chinese nationality law designated all ethnic groups in China as Chinese nationals,[273] China did not elaborate upon the meaning of 'Chinese descent'.[274]

The Chinese nationality law did not permit dual nationality but Hong Kong residents of Chinese descent could apply to renounce Chinese nationality if a near relative of a foreign national or having other 'legitimate reasons'.[275] On 19 March 1997, the United Kingdom legislated for the acquisition of 'British citizenship' by application of British Dependent Territories citizens who were 'ordinarily resident' in Hong Kong and would otherwise be stateless.[276] Its aim was to avoid the

---

[264] Ibid.

[265] Walvis Bay Agreement (adopted 28 February 1994, entered into force 1 March 1994) 2548 UNTS 17, art 4.

[266] Transfer of Walvis Bay to Namibia Act No 203 1993 (South Africa) 33 ILM 1573, s 5(1).

[267] Constitution of Namibia (21 March 1990) UN Doc S/10967/Add.2, arts 1(4), 4.

[268] Note 478.

[269] Walvis Bay Act No 1 1994, 28 SAGG (28 February 1994) s 3.

[270] Joint Declaration on the Question of Hong Kong (China–United Kingdom) (19 December 1984) 1399 UNTS 33, arts 1–2, annex I (art XIV).

[271] Basic Law of the Hong Kong SAR (May 2021 edition) <https://www.basiclaw.gov.hk/filemana ger/content/en/files/basiclawtext/basiclaw_full_text.pdf> accessed 31 December 2023, annex III (instruments 5, 13).

[272] China Nationality Law (10 September 1980) <https://www.immd.gov.hk/eng/residents/immi gration/chinese/law.html> accessed 31 December 2023, arts 3–6, 9–11, 14. See also: British Nationality Act 1981 c 61, s 15; British Nationality (Hong Kong) Act 1990 c 34, s 1, sch 1.

[273] Ibid, art 2.

[274] Explanations of the Implementation of the Nationality Law in the Hong Kong SAR (15 May 1996) <https://www.immd.gov.hk/eng/residents/immigration/chinese/law.html> accessed 9 January 2024, s 1.

[275] Immigration Ordinance of the Hong Kong SAR (1 April 1972) < https://www.elegislation.gov.hk/ hk/cap115> accessed 17 February 2024, s 6(2).

[276] British Nationality (Hong Kong) Act 1997 c 20, s 1, sch 1.

## 268  SUCCESSION AND NATIONALITY

potential statelessness of ethnic minorities in Hong Kong who might not be recognized by China as its nationals.

Prior to the retrocession of Macao on 20 December 1999,[277] Portugal had designated as Portuguese nationals persons who were born to Portuguese nationals after 3 October 1981 in Macao or elsewhere in Portugal as well as persons born abroad to a Portuguese national by registration.[278] In extending its nationality law to the Macao SAR, China designated Macao residents 'of Chinese descent' as Chinese nationals but permitted residents of 'both Chinese and Portuguese descent' to opt for Portuguese or Chinese nationality.[279]

### 7.3.5  Secession

When a part of the territory of a State secedes to create a new State, the default rule is that the nationality of the parent State is automatically lost and the nationality of the new State acquired on the date of succession by nationals of the predecessor with a dominant connection to the seceding territory.[280] The test of dominant connection is determined primarily by permanent residence or alternatively by birthplace. The affected body of nationals may opt for the nationality of the predecessor by conduct.

This proposed general principle of law derives from State practice on dozens of secessions in the modern era, such as:

- the Philippines from the United States of America (1946);
- India and Pakistan (1947), Myanmar ('Burma', 1948), Sri Lanka ('Ceylon', 1948), Malaya (1957), South Arabia ('South Yemen', 1967), and Mauritius (1968)[281] from the United Kingdom;
- Indonesia from the Netherlands (1949);
- Libya from Italy (1951);

---

[277] Joint Declaration on Macao (Portugal–China) (adopted 13 April 1987, entered into force 15 January 1988) 1498 UNTS 228, arts 1–2.

[278] Portugal Nationality Law No 37/81 (3 October 1981) 228 Diário da República Series I, art 1(d) (Portuguese).

[279] Basic Law of the Macao SAR (31 March 1993) <https://bo.io.gov.mo/bo/i/1999/leibasica/index.asp> accessed 31 December 2023 (Portuguese) art 18, annex III; China, Law No 7/1999 on Nationality Requirements for Residents of the Macao SAR, <https://bo.io.gov.mo/bo/i/1999/01/lei07.asp> accessed 31 December 2023, arts 5, 7 (Portuguese) arts 5, 7 (Portuguese); Clarifications by the Standing Committee of the National People's Congress (29 December 1998) <https://bo.io.gov.mo/bo/i/1999/01/aviso05.asp#7> accessed 9 January 2024, ss 1–2 (Portuguese).

[280] *Contra*: ILC Articles (n 29) art 24.

[281] Mauritius Independence Act 1968, 16 & 17 Eliz II c 8, ss 2(2) 3; Mauritius Independence Order 1968, Government Notice No 54 (6 March 1968) sch, paras 20–26, 111(1). See also: *Panjanadum v Prime Minister*, Supreme Court of Mauritius (19 July 1995) 248 SCJ (1995) 93, 96–98.

APPLICATION TO THE CLASSES OF SUCCESSION   269

- Laos (1953), Cambodia (1953), North Viet Nam and South Viet Nam (1955), Guinea (1958), the Malagasy Republic ('Madagascar', 1960), and Algeria (1962) from France;
- the Democratic Republic of the Congo from Belgium (1960);
- Syria from the UAR (1961);[282]
- Singapore from Malaysia (1965);[283]
- Equatorial Guinea from Spain (1968);
- Bangladesh from Pakistan (1971);
- East Timor ('Timor-Leste') from Portugal (1975);
- Belarus, Ukraine, Armenia, Azerbaijan, Georgia, Kazakhstan, Turkmenistan, Tajikistan, Uzbekistan, Kyrgyzstan, and Moldova from the Soviet Union (1991);
- Eritrea from Ethiopia (1993);
- Montenegro from the FRY (2006); and
- South Sudan from the Sudan (2011).[284]

Though including succession agreements, State practice principally comprises the constitutions and nationality laws of successors. In certain cases (e.g.—East Timor, Eritrea, Montenegro and South Sudan) the enabling laws for referenda are also significant because they defined the body of eligible voters.

On 8 February 1935, a local citizenship for the Commonwealth of the Philippines was created.[285] The United States designated local citizens as 'U.S. nationals' rather than 'aliens' for international law purposes (e.g.—consular protection)[286] and 'U.S. citizens' for certain internal law purposes.[287] By the retention in force of their constitution,[288] the Philippines collectively nationalized their local citizens automatically at the date of succession. Whereas the Supreme Court of the Philippines found an ethnic Chinese person born in the Philippines to Chinese parents not to be a 'citizen by birth' under nationality legislation, it held the courts

---

[282] UAR, Law No 82 (1958) cited in Dalia Malek, 'Report on Citizenship Law: Egypt', EUI Country Report 2021/16 (July 2021) 5; Legislative Decree No 67 of 31 October 1961 (JO 1961, 1090).

[283] Independence of Singapore Agreement (Malaysia–Singapore) (7 August 1965) 4 ILM (1965) 928, art II; Constitution and Malaysia (Singapore Amendment) Act 1965, ibid, 938, ss 3, 6; Singapore Independence Agreement (n 283) arts 10, 12; Constitution of Singapore (9 August 1965) <https://sso. agc.gov.sg/Act/CONS1963> accessed 9 January 2024, art 122.

[284] On classical practice, see, e.g. – Constitution for the Empire of Brazil (25 March 1826) 13 BFSP 936, art VI (French); Moore (n 217) vol III, 314–15.

[285] Constitution of the Philippines (8 February 1935) in AJ Peaslee, *Constitutions of Nations* (Martinus Nijhoff 1950) 789, art IV.

[286] *Del Guercio v Gabot*, US Ninth Circuit Court of Appeals (13 May 1947) 14 ILR 20.

[287] *Suspine et al. v Compañía Transatlantica CentroAmericana, S A.,* et al., US District Court for the Southern District (New York) (13 February 1941) 9 ILR 38–43.

[288] Proclamation of Philippine Independence (4 July 1946) 146 BFSP 899, s 15; Treaty of General Relations (Philippines–United States) (adopted 4 July 1946, entered into force 22 October 1946) 7 UNTS 3, arts V–VI, X.

270 SUCCESSION AND NATIONALITY

to lack the power under the principle of *res judicata* to deprive persons of citizenship who had been recognized as local citizens prior to the succession.[289]

For the British Empire, the law of the United Kingdom had recognized a unitary nationality of 'British subject' for the metropolitan territories, Dominions, and colonies with plenary rights.[290] Following the creation by Canada of a separate nationality in 1947,[291] the other Dominions followed suit.[292] By the 1948 British Nationality Act, the United Kingdom created the status of 'Citizen of the United Kingdom and Colonies' ('CUKC') for specified categories of British subject on the basis of territorial connection through birth, naturalization, descent, or marriage.[293] Persons collectively nationalized by a Dominion under the applicable nationality law (e.g.—Canada, Australia, New Zealand, South Africa, India, Pakistan, or Ceylon) and their children could apply for the status of CUKC if descended in the male line from a qualifying person and intending 'to make his ordinary place of residence within the United Kingdom and Colonies'.[294]

Also provided in the 1948 Act, was the nationality of 'British protected person' for any person with a 'connection' to a colonial protectorate (e.g.—Zanzibar), Mandatory Territory, or Trust Territory (e.g.—Tanganyika).[295] Previously existing by royal prerogative, it provided such nationals with limited rights to British consular protection and passports but not entry, residence, or voting to other British territories.[296] As territories seceded or acceded to independence, the status of CUKC or British protected person was terminated with specified classes of persons automatically retaining British nationality or receiving a time-limited right of option.[297] The practice of secession by territories of the British Empire was generally consistent with the following cases.[298]

Prior to the secessions of India and Pakistan on 15 August 1947, no succession agreement on nationality was reached between the two successors and neither had

---

[289] *José Tan Chong v Secretary of Labor*, GR No 47616, Supreme Court of the Philippines (16 September 1947).

[290] British Nationality and Status of Aliens Act 1914 4 & 5 Geo c 17, ss 1–2, 10–14.

[291] Canadian Citizenship Act 1946 10 Geo VI c 15, s 4.

[292] Clive Parry, *Nationality and Citizenship Laws of the Commonwealth and the Republic of Ireland* vol I (CUP 1957) 431–996.

[293] Ibid, 217–351. See also: British Nationality Act 1948, 11 & 12 Geo 6 c 56, s 12; Mervyn Jones, *British Nationality Law and Practice* (OUP 1947) 135–89.

[294] Ibid, ss 1(3), 12(4), 12(6).

[295] Ibid, ss 30, 32(1). See further: British Protectorates, Protected States and Protected Persons Order in Council, SI 1949 No 140, para 2, schs 1, 3.

[296] E.g. – Mervyn Jones, 'Who Are British Protected Persons?' (1945) 22 BYIL 122, 123–127; Parry (n 292) 352–385.

[297] E.g. – Uganda Independence Act 1962, 10 & 11 Eliz II, c 57, s 2(4); *Ex parte Thakrar*, Court of Appeal of England (4 February 1974) 59 ILR 450, 464–66. For a rare example of persons in Zambia who were both CUKC and British protected persons, see: *Motala v Attorney-General*, House of Lords (7 November 1991) [1992] 1 AC 281, 290–92.

[298] For 20 examples, see: *UN Materials* (n 321) 124–126; *UN Materials on Succession of States in respect of Matters other than Treaties*, UN Doc ST/LEG/SER.B/17 (1978) 124–26; 135–39; 179–80; 189; 194; 203–04; 239, 241, 247; 307–309; 389–390; 404; 424; 425, 429; 432; 472–73; 475–76; Parry (n 292) 363–385.

APPLICATION TO THE CLASSES OF SUCCESSION    271

adopted a nationality law.[299] Though no local citizenship had existed for British India, they provisionally retained the 1914 British Nationality and Status of Aliens Act in their internal law.[300] Following the 'great upheaval' of mass migration during the Partition of British India, India legislated in 1950 and Pakistan in 1955 to recognize a right for persons 'domiciled' in British India and born therein and persons domiciled outside British India but descended from a person born therein to opt for a single nationality on the basis of 'migration' to their respective territories after 1 March 1947.

India designated its nationals by a combination of 'domicile'[301] and birthplace, descent, or 'ordinary residence' for five years.[302] Migrants from Pakistan were also recognized as nationals on the basis of birthplace or descent plus ordinary residence or registration by 1 March 1947.[303] No person was a national if he 'voluntarily acquired the citizenship of any foreign State.'[304]

Pakistan designated its initial body of nationals by similar criteria[305] but adopted a broader policy to register migrants from any territory in the 'Indo-Pakistan sub-continent' with the intention of permanently residing in Pakistan.[306] Persons migrating to India from Pakistan on 1 March 1947 were not to be considered Pakistani nationals unless they should return to Pakistan under a permit for resettlement or permanent return.[307]

For the secession of Burma on 4 January 1948, Burma and the United Kingdom agreed to a right of option for any person designated a national under Burmese law and a CUKC under United Kingdom law.[308] On 10 December 1947, the United Kingdom legislated with effect from the date of succession that persons would cease to be British nationals unless patrilineally descended from persons born outside Burma or married to a man born a British subject.[309] It also provided for a

---

[299] E.g. – Parry (n 292) 836–924.

[300] Indian Citizenship Act 1955, 23 GIE (2 May 1955) ss 3–5, 11, 19.

[301] *Central Bank of India Ltd v Ram Narain*, Supreme Court of India (12 October 1954) 21 ILR 92, 94; *State v Ghoraishi (Qureshi) Sayed Mahomed*, High Court of Bombay (24 July 1963) 16 CILC 451, 468–70.

[302] Constitution of India (26 November 1949) 157 BFSP 34, arts 5, 8.

[303] Ibid, arts 6–7.

[304] Ibid, art 9. Solicitation of a Pakistan passport was evidence of option; e.g. – *Nazirambai v State*, High Court of Masdhya Bharat (7 May 1957) 16 CILC 285, 289, 292–94; *State v Sharifbhai Jamalbhai*, High Court of Bombay (23 April 1958) 16 CILC 299, 304–08. However, the use of a passport to return to India was rebuttable evidence; e.g. – *Andhra Pradesh v Abdul Khader*, Supreme Court of India (4 April 1961) 16 CILC 343, 347–51; *Izhar Ahmad Khan v India*, Supreme Court of India (16 February 1962) 16 CILC 379, 392–96, 426–28.

[305] 'Domicile' required an intention to adopt the country of residence as permanent home – *Nazir* (n 299) 3.

[306] Pakistan Citizenship Act No 2 1951, 158 BFSP 609, ss 2, 4–6, 8.

[307] Ibid, s 7.

[308] Treaty on Burmese Independence (Burma–United Kingdom) (adopted 17 October 1947, entered into force 4 January 1948) 70 UNTS 183, art 3.

[309] Burma Independence Act 1947, 11 Geo 6 c 3, s 2(1) sch 1.

## 272 SUCCESSION AND NATIONALITY

two-year right of option for such persons who were 'immediately before that day domiciled or ordinarily resident' in any other British territory.[310]

In its constitution effective from the date of succession, Burma designated a national as any person who was:

- a descendant of two parents belonging to an indigenous race of Burma;[311] or
- born in Burma and descended from a grandparent belonging to an indigenous race;[312] or
- born in any British territory[313] and resident in Burma for at least eight of the preceding ten years, intending to permanently reside and signifying his option by declaration.[314]

The Parliament of Burma had the power to subsequently alter these categories but not to retroactively deprive nationals of citizenship.[315] However, its 1948 nationality law clarified that the expression 'any of the indigenous races of Burma' would mean 'the Arakanese, Burmese, Chin, Kachin, Karen, Karenni, Mon or Shan race and such racial group as has settled in an of the territories included within [Burma] as their permanent home from a period anterior to 1823 A.D. (1185 B.E.)'.[316]

As Burma did not address persons who had been naturalized as British subjects in Burma and repealed the Burma Nationalization Act in 1948, such persons were neither collectively nationalized as Burmese nationals nor entitled to opt for Burmese nationality.[317] Though China designated all ethnic Chinese as its nationals and neither China nor Burma permitted dual nationality, ethnic Chinese in Burma were nonetheless treated as Burmese nationals with respect to civic and political rights.[318] In 1954, Burma amended its nationality law to enable such persons to naturalize as Burmese by a simplified procedure.[319]

Prior to the secession of Malaya on 31 August 1957, the subjects of the nine Malay State colonial protectorates were British protected persons[320] while the

---

[310] Ibid, para 2(2). See also: *Bulmer v Attorney-General*, High Court of Justice (21 June 1955) 7 BILC 979, 981–82.

[311] Maung Maung, *Burma's Constitution* (Springer 1961) 93–94.

[312] An option by conduct applied to non-indigenous persons born in Burma – *Karam Singh v Controller of Immigration*, Supreme Court of Burma (25 June 1956) [1956] BLR 25, 27–28, 30–31; *Maung Ko Gyi v Burma*, High Court of Burma (10 September 1959) [1959] BLR 268, 269.

[313] E.g. – *Burma v U Ah Tun*, Supreme Court of Burma (8 June 1949) [1949] BLR 541, 542.

[314] Constitution of Burma (adopted 24 September 1947, entered into force 4 January 1948) in Maung (n 311) s 11; *Ko Mya Din v Koby Bin Nga*, High Court of Burma (29 November 1951) [1951] BLR 240, 244; *Burma v Ebrahim Suleman Variava*, High Court of Burma (19 November 1951) [1952] BLR 6, 7.

[315] Ibid, s 12.

[316] Union Citizenship Act No LXVI 1948 < https://www.mlis.gov.mm/mLsView.do;jsessionid= 8AA7974B82F6039DAFFFA1B4379C7424?lawordSn=660> accessed 16 February 2024, s 3(1). See also: *Hasan Ali v Secretary, Ministry of Immigration*, Supreme Court of Burma (4 November 1959) [1959] BLR 187, 194–95.

[317] *Saw Chain Poon v Burma*, Supreme Court of Burma (1 March 1949) [1949] BLR 408, 409–10.

[318] Maung (n 311) 94.

[319] Ibid, 93.

[320] Parry (n 292) 386–430.

APPLICATION TO THE CLASSES OF SUCCESSION    273

populations of the two Straits Settlement colonies of Penang and Malacca were CUKC. Malaya and the United Kingdom agreed to the collective nationalization of the subjects of the Malay States,[321] CUKC born and permanently resident in the Straits Settlements, and 'Malay persons' born in Malaya, as well as CUKC born in Malaya of a father also born therein.[322] Malaya adopted a special provision in its constitution enabling those of its nationals who also qualified for British nationality to possess dual nationality, albeit restricting its use in Malaya.[323]

Prior to the secession of the colonial protectorate of South Yemen on 30 November 1967, inhabitants of the Crown Colony of Aden were CUKC while those of the colonial protectorate of South Arabia were British protected persons. There is no record of a succession agreement on nationality[324] and the United Kingdom deprived all persons possessing its nationality in connection with South Yemen from 14 August 1968,[325] except for persons born, naturalized, or registered in another British territory or patrilineally descended from such a person.[326] On 4 August 1968, South Yemen retrospectively designated its nationals as persons who were born to a South Yemeni father before 30 November 1968.[327] In 2018, the English courts held ethnic Somalis born in Aden before or on the date of succession who had not acquired South Yemen nationality to have remained CUKC by default.[328]

Prior to the secession of Indonesia on 27 December 1949, Dutch law had defined persons born in the Netherlands East Indies of parents established therein as 'Dutch subjects' (*Nederlandse onderdanen-niet Nederlanders*) but not 'Dutch citizens' of the metropolitan Netherlands.[329] After the secessionist government adopted a nationality law in 1946,[330] Indonesia agreed with the Netherlands with prospective effect from the date of succession that persons designated as its nationals under that law were to be 'converted into Indonesian nationality'.[331]

[321] Order in Council regarding the Federation of Malaya (26 January 1948) 150 BFSP 30, art 124(3)(a).

[322] Ibid, art 124.

[323] Ibid, sch I ('Constitution of Malaya') arts 14–15, 167(1). See also: *Public Prosecutor v Oie Hee Koi*, Judicial Committee of the Privy Council (4 December 1967) 9 BILC 235, 252; *Lim Lian Geok v Minister of the Interior*, Judicial Committee of the Privy Council (23 March 1964) 8 BILC 444, 450–53.

[324] Memorandum on Independence for South Arabia (National Front for the Liberation of Southern Yemen–United Kingdom) (29 November 1967) 169 BFSP 136, para 14.

[325] Aden, Perim and Kuria Muria Islands Act 1967, 15 & 16 Eliz 2 c 71, sch 1, s 1; British Nationality (People's Republic of Southern Yemen) Order SI 1968/1310.

[326] Ibid, sch 1, s 3.

[327] People's Republic of Southern Yemen Law of Nationality No 4 (1968) ch 2, art 2.

[328] E.g. – *R (Nooh) v Home Secretary*, High Court of England and Wales (27 June 2018) [2018] WHC 1572 (Admin) paras 13–22; *R (Hassan) v Home Secretary*, High Court of England and Wales (24 May 2019) [2019] EWHC 1288 (Admin) paras 1–42, 119–39.

[329] Act regulating the Nationality of the Dutch East Indies, 296 Staatsblad van Nederlandsch-Indië (1 March 1910) art 1 (Dutch).

[330] Act No 3 concerning Citizens and Residents of Indonesia (10 April 1946) in UN Legislative Series, *Laws Concerning Nationality* (1954) 230 (arts 1–4).

[331] Agreement concerning the Assignment of Citizens in Round-Table Conference Agreements (Netherlands–Indonesia) (adopted 2 November 1949, entered into force 27 December 1949) 69 UNTS 272, art 2.

274 SUCCESSION AND NATIONALITY

Dutch subjects belonging to the indigenous population (*orang jang asli*) had a right of option for Dutch nationality if born outside of Indonesia and resident in the Netherlands or a third territory while Dutch citizens had a right of option for Indonesian nationality if born in Indonesia and resident therein for at least six months.[332] Dutch subjects 'of foreign origin' and born in Indonesia would acquire Indonesian nationality with a right of option to retain Dutch Netherlands nationality.[333]A time limit of two years was stipulated for declarations of option.[334]

In dismissing an application for Dutch nationality by an Ambonese resident of the Netherlands in 1952, the Dutch courts held international law to provide for a right of option in cases of silence or obscurity but not when the matter was unambiguously addressed in the 'instrument of cession of sovereignty' whereby the indigenous population of Indonesia who had been born therein had not been granted the right.[335] By agreement with the Netherlands, Indonesia enacted a special nationality law (the 'Moluccans Law') in 1976 enabling optants for Dutch nationality to opt for Indonesian nationality within two years.[336] In 1955, Indonesia and China agreed that ethnic Chinese in Indonesia who had been dual nationals of China and the Netherlands before being collectively nationalized as Indonesian nationals would be required to choose a single nationality within two years from 20 January 1960.[337]

Prior to the secession of Libya on 24 December 1951, Italian law had designated persons born in Italian Libya as 'Italian Libyan citizens' rather than 'Italian citizens'.[338] In deciding that Libya would become independent, the UN General Assembly had assumed that collective nationalization with a right of option would take place.[339] The Libyan constitution of 7 October 1951 designated Libyan nationals as every person 'normally resident' for at least ten years in Libya without any other nationality and born in Libya of a parent born in Libya.[340] While Italy initially considered former Italian Libya citizens who failed to qualify for Libyan nationality by reason of their residence in Italy to be stateless,[341] the Italian courts applied the provisions of the Peace Treaty concerning cessions of territory by analogy to Libya as a general principle of Italian law[342] in holding 'Italian Libyan'

---

[332] Ibid, arts 3–4. See also: *Ameyund*, Surrogate's Court of Kings County (23 November 1951) 1 AILC 94, 95.

[333] Ibid, arts 5, 10. See further, e.g. – *In re B*, District Court of The Hague (26 May 1952) 19 ILR 318.

[334] Ibid, arts 12–13.

[335] *In re Hehanussa*, Court of Appeal of The Hague (6 November 1952) 19 ILR 337, 338; *Amboinese Soldiers' Case*, Supreme Court of the Netherlands (2 March 1952) 17 ILR 199, 201–02.

[336] ILC, 2390th Meeting (n 28) para 43.

[337] SD Harijanti, 'Report on Citizenship Law: Indonesia', EUI Country Report No 2017/04 (February 2017) 7–9.

[338] *Ministry of Home Affairs v Kemali*, Court of Cassation of Italy (1 February 1962) 40 ILR 191, 193.

[339] UNGA Res 388(V)(A) (15 December 1950) art VI.

[340] Constitution of Libya (7 October 1951) in *Laws concerning Nationality* (n 330) 293 (art 8).

[341] *Kemali* (n 338) 193.

[342] Ibid, 194.

APPLICATION TO THE CLASSES OF SUCCESSION    275

citizenship to be a form of Italian nationality (*status civitatis*) in recognizing them as Italian nationals.[343]

The 1945 French nationality law provided that when a relevant treaty was silent or ambiguous, the default rules were that persons born or 'domiciled' in territory acquired by France by treaty were to acquire French nationality while such persons were to lose French nationality in a cession of territory unless establishing domicile in another French territory.[344]

Whereas residents of colonies, protectorates, and Mandatory Territories qualified for French 'nationality' (*la nationalité française*),[345] they could only acquire metropolitan French 'citizenship' (*la qualité de Français*) by birthplace, marriage, or naturalization.[346] The personal status laws first enacted in Algeria in 1881 (*les codes de l'indigénat*) were preserved whereby the nationality laws of the respective colonial territories divided the populations into 'subjects' (*sujets*) governed by indigenous law and 'citizens' (*citoyens*) regulated by French law. While citizens had political rights not granted to the former, both groups were persons under the protection of France with respect to third States (*ressortissants*).[347]

As colonies were converted into 'overseas territories' or 'overseas departments' and 'protectorates' into 'Associated States' in the 1946 constitution of the Fourth Republic, all French nationals were designated 'citizens of the French Union'.[348] In converting overseas territories into 'Member States of the French Community', the 1958 constitution of the Fifth Republic preserved local citizenships.[349] Whereas the distinctions between categories of French national were rescinded in metropolitan France, they were not fully eliminated elsewhere in the French Community until 1974.[350] The secessions from the French Empire were generally consistent with the following examples.

Prior to becoming 'Associate States' of the French Union, persons originating from Laos and the territories directly administered by France in Viet Nam were defined as 'French subjects' while persons originating from the rest of French Indochina were protected persons (*protegés français*).[351] Defining its local citizens

---

[343] Ibid, 195–98.

[344] French Nationality Code (19 October 1945) 247 JORF (20 October 1945) 6700, art 11–15 (French).

[345] Ibid, arts 6–7, 10.

[346] Ibid, arts 25, 37, 44, 52, 63–64.

[347] E.g. – Decree on the Reorganisation of Justice in the Colonies of West Africa (10 November 1903) 309 JORF (24 November 1903) 7094, arts 1–2, 29–34, 46–60 (French). See also, e.g. – Emannuelle Saada, 'Citoyens et sujets de l'Empire français', 53 Dans Genèses (2003/4) 4–24, 17–18, 21–22.

[348] Constitution of France (27 October 1946) Arts 60–61, 73–74, 80–81, <https://www.elysee.fr/la-presidence/la-constitution-du-27-octobre-1946> accessed 9 January 2024 (French).

[349] PF Gonidec, 'Note sur la nationalité et les citoyennetés dans la Communauté' (1959) 5 AFDI 748–61, 749.

[350] Decree No 53-161 (24 February 1953) JORF (27 February 1953) 1984, arts 1–4, 8–13, 15–19 (French). See also: Richard Plender, 'The New French Nationality Law' (1974) 23(4) ICLQ 709, 718–19.

[351] HT Nguyen, *Quelques problèmes de succession d'États concernant le Viet-Nam* (Bruylant 1970) 47.

276    SUCCESSION AND NATIONALITY

as persons belonging to races definitively settled on Lao territory unless possessing French citizenship,[352] Laos collectively nationalized its local citizens in seceding on 22 October 1953. In seceding on 9 November, Cambodia did likewise for its local citizens, who were defined according to descent from a Cambodian parent or membership of a recognized ethnic group.[353] Having designated French subjects 'originating' from its territory as local citizens of South Viet Nam[354] while French citizens originating therefrom were granted a six-month right of option,[355] South Viet Nam also collectively nationalized its local citizens when it seceded on 26 October 1955.[356]

As the sole Overseas Territory to refuse to join the French Community, French Guinea seceded on 2 November 1958 while provisionally retaining its laws in force.[357] French Guinea had lacked a written nationality law, while the law of the colonial federation of French West Africa had defined 'natives' (*indigènes*) only by implication.[358] While its first constitution did not define its initial body of nationals,[359] Guinea retrospectively recognized natives under the colonial law as its nationals.[360]

Before seceding on 3 August 1960, Madagascar enacted its nationality law on 22 July, in which it defined its local citizens as all persons with one parent of Malagasy origin.[361] However, it also stipulated that such persons 'whose civil status was on that date governed by modern law may, until 31 December 1960, refuse Malagasy nationality if they have retained French nationality according to French law.'[362]

Persons with one parent of Malagasy origin were designated Malagasy nationals regardless of legitimate birth or recognition by a parent who was a French national, subject to a right to refuse it within one year of 22 June 1960.[363] A six-month right to opt for Malagasy was also granted to French nationals married to a Malagasy national, naturalized and domiciled in Madagascar, or otherwise resident in Madagascar for five years.[364] The nationality law did not define the term 'Malagasy

---

[352] Constitution of Laos (11 May 1947) in AJ Peaslee and DX Peaslee, *Constitutions of Nations* (Martinus Hijhoff 1965) 624–25, art 4; Law No 138 on Laotian Nationality (6 April 1953) in *Laws Concerning Nationality* (n 330) 283–84, art 6 (French).

[353] Cambodia Civil Code (1 July 1920) in *Laws Concerning Nationality* (n 330) 67, arts 22–26 (French). Decree No 913-NS (30 November 1954) in UN Legislative Series, *Supplement to the Laws Concerning Nationality* (1959) 10, art 2 (French). Ethnic Chinese and Vietnamese were thus excluded – Christoph Sperfeldt, 'Report on Citizenship Law: Cambodia', EUI Report 2017/02 (January 2017) 4.

[354] Tonkin Civil Code 1931 in: *Laws Concerning Nationality* (n 330) 549–52 (arts 13–14).

[355] Nationality Convention (adopted 16 August 1955, entered into force 17 August 1965) JORF (3 May 1959) 4767, arts 1–18 (French).

[356] Provisional Act constituting the Republic in South Vietnam (26 October 1955) 161 BFSP 539.

[357] MM Whiteman, *Digest of International Law* vol II (Government Printing Office 1964) 878.

[358] Note 347.

[359] Constitution of Guinea (10 November 1958) in Peaslee and Peaslee (n 352) 229–38.

[360] Ordinance No 11 (1 March 1960) (unpublished) in Faciala Keita, 'Guinea' in *International Encyclopaedia of Comparative Law Online* (1979).

[361] Ordinance No 60-064 (22 July 1960) (1960) UNYBHR 227, arts 90–91.

[362] Ibid.

[363] Ibid, art 91.

[364] Ibid, art 92.

origin',[365] though it was interpreted to denote 'blood origin' to the exclusion of the Indian ('Karana') and Chinese minorities.[366] France also denied French nationality to ethnic Indians who had not been recognized by India and Madagascar as nationals, yet were ignorant of the French language.[367]

Prior to the secession of the metropolitan territory of French Algeria on 4 July 1962,[368] France and Algeria agreed that French citizens of 'ordinary civil status' born in Algeria with ten years' permanent residence therein were to be treated for three years as 'French nationals exercising Algerian civil rights' with the right to opt for Algerian nationality by registration at the end of the transitional period.[369] In disputes concerning the nationalization by Algeria of mining and agricultural companies, the Algerian courts considered the companies to have become Algerian nationals on the secession of Algeria by re-registration of the corporate seat (*siège social*) and compliance with Algerian taxation laws.[370] While the French courts concurred with the principle of nationality according to the seat, they held it not to apply to a company whose directors transferred its head office to preserve nationality when the territory on which the seat was established came under the sovereignty of another State.[371]

When the DRC seceded on 30 June 1960, its interim constitution provided for the provisional continuity of existing law, but no local citizenship had existed for the Belgian Congo.[372] Its 1964 constitution prohibited dual nationality and retroactively designated its nationals from the date of succession as anyone with a forefather who 'was a member of a tribe or a part of a tribe established on Congolese territory' before the absorption of the Independent State of the Congo in 1908.[373] In the context of approximately 450 ethnic groups in the DRC, a series of retroactive amendments to the designation of Congolese nationals according to 'establishment' in Congolese territory on various historical dates was enacted in 1971,[374] 1972,[375] 1981,[376] and

---

[365] Ibid, art 11.

[366] E.g. – AL Razafiarison, LA Ratsimatahotrarivo, Richmond Zafera, and Noro Ravaozanany, 'Rapport sur le droit de la nationalité: Madagascar', EUI Country Report No 2022/04 (July 2022) 1–5.

[367] *Procureur v Gova*, Court of Appeal of Paris (13 April 1972) 73 ILR 565, 566.

[368] Note 345.

[369] Declarations drawn up in Common Agreement at Evian (France–Algerian National Liberation Front) (18 March 1962) 1(2) ILM 214, ch II(A)(2)(a).

[370] *SONAREM v Genebrier*, Court of Annaba (26 December 1968) 41 ILR 384, 389–90, 33–94.

[371] *Caisse centrale v Mutuelle Centrale*, Court of Cassation of France (30 March 1971) 72 ILR 565, 566–68.

[372] E.g. – Basic Law of the Congo (19 May 1960) in TM Franck, John Carey, and LM Tondel, *Legal Aspects of the United Nations Action in the Congo* (Oceana Publications, 1963) 108–116 (arts 2, 189, 263); Civil Code (1892) ss 1–5 in Flournoy, *Collection of Nationality Laws of Various Countries* (1929) 42.

[373] Constitution of the Congo (30 May 1964) in Peaslee and Peaslee (n 352) 98, art 6.

[374] Ordinance-Law No 71-020 (26 March 1971) art 1 (French).

[375] Law No 1972-002 on Zairoese Nationality (5 January 1972) JOZ (15 January 1972) art 15 (French).

[376] Law No 1981-002 (29 June 1981) 13 JOZ (1 July 1981) art 4 (French).

278 SUCCESSION AND NATIONALITY

2004.[377] These particularly affected the status of the *Banyarwanda* population (Hutu and Tutsi speakers of Rwanda) in North and South Kivu,[378] which was a prominent issue in the context of a prohibition of dual nationality in Congolese law and multiple tribes inhabiting territories that straddle boundaries with seven States.[379]

Before the secession of Equatorial Guinea on 12 October 1968, the indigenous inhabitants (mainly Bubis and Fangs) of Spanish Guinea were Spanish subjects (*súbditos no nacionales*) of equal status with citizens of metropolitan Spain.[380] These local citizens of Spanish Guinea were eligible to vote in the independence referendum on 11 August 1968 but the non-indigenous temporary workers from Nigeria were not.[381]

Enacted with prospective effect from the date of succession, the constitution of Equatorial Guinea defined its nationals as persons born in the territory of 'African' ancestry.[382] Spain thereafter denied Spanish nationality to persons born in Equatorial Guinea[383] or metropolitan Spain of parents born in Spanish Guinea because the right to Spanish nationality had ceased on the date of succession while metropolitan Spanish law had defined the inhabitants of Spanish Guinea, Ifni, and the Spanish Sahara as 'nationals not by origin'.[384]

Prior to the secession of East Pakistan on 22 February 1974 with retroactive effect from 10 April 1971, Bangladesh provisionally preserved the laws of Pakistan, that had lacked a local citizenship.[385] In the context of mass displacement during its war of secession, Bangladesh legislated on 15 December 1972 to retroactively designate its nationals from 26 March 1971 as persons born (or descended from a father or grandfather born) and permanently resident in East Pakistan on 25 March or born elsewhere and permanently resident continuously.[386]

---

[377] Law No 04/024 (12 November 2004) in Franck Kamunga, 'Report on Citizenship Law: Democratic Republic of Congo', EUI Country Report 2022/1 (2022) 10.

[378] Ibid, 2, 11.

[379] Ibid, 14–15.

[380] E.g. – Basic Law No 191/1963 (20 December 1963) in 'Declaration on the Granting of Independence to Colonial Countries and Peoples' (6 May 1964) UN Doc A/AC.109/71, annex.

[381] E.g. – Decree No 1/748-68 (27 July 1968) 181 BOE (29 July 1968) (Spanish); 'Report of the Special Committee on the Situation with regard to the Implementation of the Declaration on the Granting of Independence to Colonial Countries and Peoples' (30 November 1966) UN Doc A/6300/Rev.1, 15–16.

[382] Constitution of Equatorial Guinea BOGE (24 July 1968) 'Transitional Provisions', ss1ª, 2(1) (Spanish).

[383] Resolutions of 28 January 1989 and 18 May 1989 (1989) 41(2) REDI 276–77, 587–90 (Spanish).

[384] Castelucci Paoloni, 'Comentario a la sentencia del Tribunal Supremo de 20 de julio de 2020' (2021) 13(1) CDT 799, paras 6–23, 27.

[385] Pakistan Citizenship Act (n 306) ss 3–8; Proclamation of Independence (10 April 1971) 24 DLR (1972) 1; Provisional Constitution of Bangladesh Order 1972 (11 January 1972) 24 DLR (1972) 29.

[386] Persons studying or working abroad were 'resident' in Bangladesh – Bangladesh Citizenship (Temporary Provisions) Order 1972, 25 DLR (1973) 57, art 2; *Mirza Shahab Ispahani v Bangladesh*, Supreme Court of Bangladesh (1988) 40 DLR (AD) 87, paras 2–3, 7–23. Habitual residence in West Pakistan and acquisition of a Pakistan passport did not disqualify unless 'owing allegiance' by conduct, e.g. – *Mokhtar Ahmed v Bangladesh*, Supreme Court of Bangladesh (7 June 1979) (1982) 34 DLR (HCD) 29.

In 1974, Bangladesh agreed to the 'repatriation' of hundreds of thousands of Urdu-speaking, non-Bengali Muslims (*Biharis*) who had migrated to Pakistan during the war of secession.[387] In March 1978, Pakistan revoked its nationality from nationals continually resident 'voluntarily or otherwise' in Bangladesh from 16 December 1971.[388] In 2008, the High Court of Dhaka held some 300,000 *Biharis*, including 160,000 residents of ICRC refugee camps, to be entitled to Bangladeshi nationality.[389]

On 29 November 1975, Indonesia annexed the Overseas Territory of Portuguese Timor and collectively nationalized its population while requiring optants for Portuguese nationality to emigrate.[390] Portugal continued to recognize descendants of nationals born in Timor-Leste as its nationals by declaration or registration.[391] From 1992, Australia considered the Timorese to be Portuguese nationals unable to exercise their nationality in Portugal for asylum purposes.[392]

For a plebiscite convened on 30 August 1999 to determine the status of East Timor, eligible voters were persons born in East Timor or descended from a parent born therein.[393] Considering itself to have seceded from Portugal on 28 November 1975, the constitution of Timor-Leste designated as 'original citizens' persons descended from a parent born therein, unknown or stateless parents or a foreign parent declaring for Timorese nationality.[394] While Timor-Leste neither authorized nor prohibited dual nationality,[395] Indonesia offered Timorese inhabitants the option to retain its nationality but applied its ban on dual nationality.[396] In disputes concerning land ownership for which Timorese nationality was a requirement,[397] the Timorese courts upheld the Timorese nationality of two claimants who also held Indonesian nationality because they had been 'habitually resident' in East Timor despite having migrated to Indonesia as refugees from electoral violence in East Timor.[398]

---

[387] TS Cheema, *Pakistan Bangladesh Relations* (Unistar 2013) 56–62, 95–97; Agreement on the Repatriation of Prisoners of War (9 April 1974) 13 ILM 501, arts 11–12.

[388] Pakistan Citizenship (Amendment) Ordinance 1978 in Ridwanul Hoque, 'Report on Citizenship Law: Bangladesh', EUI Country Report No 2016/14 (December 2016) 7, 10.

[389] *Md. Sadaqat Hossain Khan (Fakku) v Chief Election Commissioner*, Supreme Court of Bangladesh (2008) 60 DLR (HCD) 407.

[390] Patricia Jerónimo, 'Report on Citizenship Law: East Timor (Timor-Leste)' EUI Country Report No 2017/07 (March 2017) 10 (n 38).

[391] Portugal Nationality Law No 37/81 (3 October 1981) 228 Diário series I, art 1(d); Portugal Decree-Law No 308-A/75 (24 June 1975) 143 Diário Series I 862, arts 1–2, 4.

[392] Jerónimo (n 390) 12.

[393] Agreement regarding the East Timorese (5 May 1999) 2062 UNTS 39.

[394] Constitution of Timor-Leste (adopted 22 March 2002, entered into force 25 May 2002) art 3 <http://timor-leste.gov.tl/wp-content/uploads/2010/03/Constitution_RDTL_ENG.pdf> accessed 31 December 2023.

[395] Timor-Leste Nationality Law No 9/2002, Jornal da República series I, arts 8, 19, 23, 29 (Portuguese & Tetum).

[396] Jerónimo (n 390) 19.

[397] See Chapter 8.

[398] *Gaspar de Oliveira Amaral Sarmento v Maria Lígia A. Sarmento*, Case No AC-10-03-2010-P-12-CIV-09-TR Court of Appeal of Timor-Leste (3 October 2010) para 3 (Portuguese); *Norberta Belo v*

# 280  SUCCESSION AND NATIONALITY

Prior to the secessions of 11 constituent republics of the USSR on 20 December 1991, Soviet law had provided for a federal citizenship and a local citizenship.[399] As local citizenship was of minor importance, few laws were adopted by the republics to regulate its acquisition and loss, which was done in practice by civil registries for births and passport authorities for permanent residents.[400] The successors struck no succession agreement concerning nationality with the Russian Federation or one another.[401]

The Russian Federation designated Soviet citizens as its nationals who were permanently resident, born in its territory to one parent also born therein or permanently resident in another constituent republic and opting for its nationality.[402] Azerbaijan,[403] Moldova,[404] Tajikistan,[405] and Kyrgyzstan[406] recognized their nationals on the basis of local citizenship. Kazakhstan,[407] Uzbekistan,[408] Turkmenistan,[409] and the Ukraine[410] enacted new nationality laws either prospectively from the date of succession or retrospectively recognizing their nationals on the basis of permanent residence[411] with a right of option for non-resident local citizens or persons born in their territories.

---

*Libert Soares* Case No AC-10-03-2010-P-23-CIV-01-TR (3 October 2010) Court of Appeal, para 17 (Portuguese).

[399] George Ginsburgs, 'From the 1990 Law on the Citizenship of the USSR to the Citizenship Laws of the Successor Republics (Part I) (1992) 18 RCEEL 1, 7–8.

[400] E.g. – UNHCR, 'Questions of Nationality and Statelessness in Armenia' (March 2013) 5.

[401] Zimmermann (n 213) 627–32, 654.

[402] E.g. – Law on Citizenship of the RSFSR, 28 November 1991, 19(3) RCEEL (1993) 293, arts 2, 4, 7, 10, 12–18; Ineta Ziemele, *State Continuity and Nationality: The Baltic States and Russia* (Martinus Nijhoff 2005) 184–87.

[403] UNHCR, 'Nationality Laws of the Former Soviet Republics' (1 July 1993) para 2, <https://www.refworld.org/docid/3ae6b31db3.html> accessed 9 January 2024.

[404] Moldova Law on Nationality (5 June 1991) in Nationality Laws of the Former Soviet Republics (n 399) art 2.

[405] UNHCR, 'Nationality Laws of the Former Soviet Republics (n 399).

[406] Kyrgyzstan Law on Citizenship No 130 (adopted 18 December 1993, entered into force 18 February 1994) <https://www.refworld.org/docid/40fe4f3e4.html> art 1(1), accessed 31 December 2023.

[407] Kazakhstan Law on Citizenship (20 December 1991) art 3 in Hazard and Pechota (n 412) binder 1, <https://www.legislationline.org/download/id/6559/file/Kazakh_Citizenship_law_1991_am2013_en.pdf> accessed 9 January 2024.

[408] Uzbekistan on Citizenship Law No 632-XII (2 July 1992) 9 Gazette of the Supreme Council of the Republic of Uzbekistan 338, art 4.

[409] Turkmenistan Law on Citizenship (30 September 1992) arts 9, 49–50, Turkmenskaya Iskra (11 October 1992) <https://www.legislationline.org/documents/action/popup/id/7023> accessed 9 January 2024, arts 9, 49–50.

[410] Law on Legal Succession of Ukraine No 1543-XII (12 September 1991) in Hazard and Pechota (n 412) Binder 2, art 9; Law on Citizenship of Ukraine (October 1991) art 2 in Second Mikulka Report (n 33) para 79.

[411] Evidence of residence was a permit (*propiska*) – Decree of the Supreme Soviet concerning the coming into force of the Law on Citizenship in Hazard and Pechota (n 412) arts 1–3.

APPLICATION TO THE CLASSES OF SUCCESSION 281

Belarus recognized local citizenship, permanent residence, and option for non-residents born in its territory.[412] While the state of Georgian law was 'chaotic',[413] Georgia treated its local citizens as its nationals[414] and retrospectively recognized all residents for the preceding five years in 1993.[415] Armenia retrospectively recognized on the basis of local citizenship plus permanent residence or ethnicity for residents of other constituent republics.[416] The last criterion of ethnicity was also applied by Azerbaijan and Kazakhstan.[417]

On 15 December 2021, an investor-State arbitral tribunal rendered an award in the *Khudyan v Armenia* arbitration in which it examined the inadmissibility of a claim due to holding the nationality of the Respondent.[418] In observing that great weight must be given to the interpretation and application of nationality law by the authorities, the Arbitral Tribunal reportedly held the Claimant, who had held the local citizenship of the Armenian SSR when he emigrated in August 1989 to the United States, to have become a national of Armenia in virtue of the 1978 Soviet nationality law that had remained in force and the practice of the authorities in automatically recognizing any Soviet national resident abroad who held local citizenship.[419] The omission of the Claimant to register at the consulate did not deprive him of its nationality because this would have rendered him stateless in breach of the 1961 Statelessness Convention, which Armenia had ratified before adopting its nationality law.[420]

Prior to the secession of Eritrea on 24 May 1993, no local citizenship had existed after the abolition of the federation by Ethiopia in 1962. Enacted on 6 April 1992 by the Eritrean People's Liberation Front, the nationality law of Eritrea designated a person 'born to a father or a mother of Eritrean origin in Eritrea or abroad' as an 'Eritrean national by birth'.[421] Eritreans by birth could obtain a certificate of nationality from government bodies in Eritrea or abroad; those resident abroad

---

[412] Belarus Law on Citizenship (adopted 18 October 1991, entered into force 12 November 1991) in JN Hazard and Vratislav Pechota (eds) *Russia and the Republics: Legal Materials* binder 1 (Juris 1993) arts 2, 8–12.

[413] E.g. – FJM Feldbrugge, 'The Law of the Republic of Georgia' (1992) 18(4) RCEEL 367, 373–75; Constitution of Georgia (24 August 1995) in *World Constitutions Illustrated Database*, art 15.

[414] George Ginsburgs, 'From the 1990 Law on the Citizenship of the USSR to the Citizenship Laws of the Successor Republics (Part II)' (1993) 19(3) RCEEL 233, 251.

[415] Law on Citizenship (25 March 1993) <https://www.legislationline.org/documents/id/5498> accessed 9 January 2024, art 2.

[416] Constitution of the Republic of Armenia (5 July 1995) in European Commission for Democracy through Law ('Venice Commission') Opinion No 313/2004 (29 November 2004) art 14; Armenia Law on Citizenship (28 November 1995) <https://www.refworld.org/pdfid/51b770884.pdf> accessed 31 December 2023, art 10.

[417] E.g. – 'Questions of Nationality and Statelessness in Armenia' (n 400) 49–50, 52–53, 89–90.

[418] Convention on the Settlement of Investment Disputes between States and Nationals of other States (adopted 18 March 1965, entered into force 14 October 1966) 575 UNTS 159, art 25(2)(a).

[419] *Khudyan v Armenia* (Award) ICSID Case No ARB/17/36 (15 December 2021) paras 203-244..

[420] Ibid.

[421] Eritrea Nationality Proclamation No 21/1992 (6 April 1992) <https://www.refworld.org/legal/legislation/natlegbod/1992/en/14094> accessed 17 February 2024, s 2.

## 282  SUCCESSION AND NATIONALITY

were to renounce foreign nationality or to make a justified request to retain dual nationality.[422]

For the independence referendum held in Eritrea in 1993, the eligibility of the electorate was determined by the issuing of identification cards on the basis of Ethiopian passports and other documents.[423] Eritrea and Ethiopia made no succession agreement on nationality, though they jointly declared in 1993 that 'until the issue of citizenship is settled in both countries, the traditional right of citizens of one side to live in the other's territory shall be respected'.[424] They agreed in 1996 that 'Eritreans who have so far been enjoying Ethiopian citizenship should be made to choose and abide by their choice' but delayed implementation.[425]

During their armed conflict from May 1998 to June 2000, Ethiopia denationalized and expelled hundreds of thousands of persons of Eritrean origin who were deemed to be security threats on the ground that they had acquired Eritrean nationality by participating in the independence referendum.[426] In their arbitration agreement, Ethiopia and Eritrea agreed that each might file claims '[i]n appropriate cases ... on behalf of persons of Eritrean or Ethiopian origin who may not be its nationals ... on the same basis as claims submitted on behalf of that party's nationals'.[427] In rejecting their respective arguments that registration for the referendum and the continued issuance of Ethiopian passports did not evince nationality, the Claims Commission held:

> Taking into account the unusual transitional circumstances associated with the creation of the new State of Eritrea and both Parties' conduct before and after the 1993 Referendum, the Commission concludes that those who qualified to participate in the Referendum in fact acquired dual nationality. They became citizens of the new State of Eritrea pursuant to Eritrea's Proclamation No. 21/1992, but at the same time, Ethiopia continue to regard them as its own nationals.[428]

The status of persons in Eritrea of Ethiopian origin as Ethiopian nationals was not in dispute.[429]

Prior to the secession of Montenegro on 15 June 2006, the nationality law of the FRY provided for a local citizenship of its two constituent republics.[430] For the

---

[422] Ibid.

[423] Eritrean Referendum Proclamation No 22/1992 (7 April 1992) <https://www.loc.gov/item/eritrean-proc-22-1992/> accessed 17 February 2024; *Civilians Claims: Eritrea's Claims 15, 16, 23 & 27–32* (Partial Award) Eritrea–Ethiopia Claims Commission (17 December 2004) paras 48–49.

[424] GF Treverton, *Dividing Divided States* (University of Pennsylvania Press 2014) 13–15.

[425] Eritrea's Claims 15, 16, 23, & 27–32 (n 423) s 52.

[426] Ibid, ss 10–11.

[427] Agreement for the Settlement of Displaced Persons (12 December 2000) 2138 UNTS 93, art 5(9).

[428] Civilians Claims (n 425) para 51.

[429] *Civilians Claim: Ethiopia's Claim 5* (Partial Award) Eritrea–Ethiopia Claims Commission (17 December 2004).

[430] FRY Citizenship Act (16 July 1996) (n 237) art 5; 'Constitutional Charter of the State Union of Serbia and Montenegro' (2003) 70(2) Rivista di studi politici internazionali 292, art 8.

APPLICATION TO THE CLASSES OF SUCCESSION    283

independence referendum held on 21 May 2006, electors were required to register to vote in the constituent republic of Montenegro pursuant to the electoral law.[431] On 3 June, Montenegro adopted a declaration of independence whereby it provisionally retained the laws of the FRY.[432]

In February 2008, Serbia amended its nationality law to permit Montenegrins who held registered residence in Serbia on 3 June 2006 to apply for Serbian nationality, including as dual citizens.[433] By its 2008 nationality law, Montenegro repealed the 1999 local citizenship law but affirmed the nationality of local citizens and permitted other person to apply for nationalization.[434] While nationals were to lose Montenegrin nationality if voluntarily acquiring the nationality of another State, those who were granted another nationality after 3 June 2006 were permitted to retain Montenegrin nationality for one year.[435]

Prior to the secession of South Sudan on 9 July 2011, the nationality law of the Sudan did not provide for a local citizenship and nationality questions were omitted from the succession agreements.[436] For the independence referendum held in January 2011, eligible persons were determined under the enabling legislation.[437] On 7 July 2011, the transitional government of South Sudan adopted a nationality law with criteria similar to those used for the independence referendum in declaring any person to be a national of South Sudan by birth if descended from one person in three generations who was born in South Sudan, belonging to an indigenous ethnic community, or domiciled[438] in South Sudan from 1 July 1956.[439]

Adopted with prospective effect on the date of succession, amendments to the 1994 Sudanese nationality law provided that a person would automatically lose Sudanese nationality when he 'has acquired, *de jure* or *de facto*' the nationality of South Sudan.[440] The Sudanese courts and the African Committee of Experts on the Rights and Welfare of the Child held Sudan to have breached the rights of persons

---

[431] Law on State-Legal Status of the Republic of Montenegro, <http://www.rtcg.org/referendum/reg ulativa/zakon_o_referendumu.pdf#search=%22zakon%20o%20referendumu%> accessed 9 January 2024, art 3 (Montenegrin).

[432] Declaration of Independence of Montenegro (3 June 2006) in Jure Vidmar, 'Montenegro's Path to Independence: A Study of Self-Determination, Statehood and Recognition' (2007) 3(1) HLR 73, 99 (art 4).

[433] Serbia Citizenship Law 2008 <https://www.refworld.org/pdfid/4b56d0542.pdf> accessed 31 December 2023, arts 51–52.

[434] Montenegrin Citizenship Act No 13/08 2008, Crne Gore (26 February 2008) arts 39, 40, 43, 46–47 (Montenegrin).

[435] Ibid, arts 18, 39, 41.

[436] Sudanese Nationality Act 1994/5/17 (17 May 1994) <https://www.refworld.org/docid/503492 892.html> accessed 31 December 2023, s 15.

[437] Francesca Marzatico, 'Southern Sudan Referendum on Self-Determination: Legal Challenges and Procedural Solutions' (2011) 10(1) JAE 1, 12–15.

[438] 'Domicile' was defined as 'permanent residence' – Sudanese Nationality Act (Amendment) 2018 <https://www.refworld.org/docid/503492892.html> accessed 31 December 2023, s 2.

[439] South Sudan Nationality Act 2011 <https://www.refworld.org/country,LEGAL,NATLEG BOD,LEGISLATION,SSD,,4e94318f2,0.html> accessed 31 December 2023, s 8.

[440] Sudanese Nationality Act (Amendment) 2011, <https://www.refworld.org/docid/503492892. html> accessed 31 December 2023, s 10.

284　SUCCESSION AND NATIONALITY

born to a South Sudanese father by denying Sudanese nationality in wrongly assuming that such persons would be granted nationality by South Sudan.[441] It has been claimed that thousands of persons belonging to a tribe of one State but permanently resident in the other, as well as persons of mixed heritage, had been left stateless after the succession.[442]

### 7.3.6 Accession to Independence

When a protected State or territory accedes to independence, its nationals retain its nationality and automatically lose the nationality of the predecessor without right of option on the date of succession.[443] During a protectorate, the protected State or territory has its own nationality and its nationals also hold the nationality of the predecessor as 'protected persons' (*ressortissants*; *protégés*; *Staatsangehöriger*) without the rights in internal law of its other nationals (e.g.— 'citizens').[444] To identify the affected body of nationals, the applicable laws of the protected State or territory are determinative.[445]

The general principle of law derives from State practice with respect to the accessions to independence of Mandatory and Trusteeship Territories and protected States, including:

- Syria and the Lebanon from France on 1 January 1944;
- Israel ('Mandatory Palestine') from the United Kingdom on 15 May 1948;
- Morocco from France on 28 May 1956;
- Tanganyika from the United Kingdom on 9 December 1961;
- Namibia ('South West Africa') from South Africa on 21 March 1990; and
- Micronesia and the Marshall Islands (21 October 1986) plus Palau (1 October 1994) from the United States ('Pacific Islands').[446]

---

[441] *Ramadan v Ministry of Interior* Case No 223/2017 Supreme Court of the Sudan (7 September 2017) <https://www.refworld.org/cases,SDN_SC,59bfc5654.html> accessed 31 December 2023; Decision No 002/2018, African Committee of Experts on the Rights and Welfare of the Child (May 2018) 10–89, 104–05, https://cadmus eui.eu/bitstream/handle/1814/74634/RSC_GLOBALCIT_CR_2022_05.pdf?sequence=1&isAllowed=y.

[442] E.g. – MA Babiker, 'Report on Citizenship Law: Sudan', EUI Country Report No 2022/05 (July 2022) 13–16.

[443] E.g. – *UN Materials* (n 321) 194 (Ghana); 472 (Tanganyika); 523 (Zambia). The ILC considered Articles 24 to 26 on secession to apply to newly independent States: ILC Articles (n 29) 23, 46; First Mikulka Report (n 8) paras 92–93; ILC, 2488th Meeting (n 32) paras 8–52.

[444] E.g. – United Kingdom (n 296); France (nn 345 and 347). See also: Elihu Lauterpacht, 'Nationality of Denationalized Persons' (1948) 1 JYIL 164, 165–66. On the Peace Treaty of Versailles, see, e.g. – *National Bank of Egypt v Germany and Bank für Handel und Industrie*, Anglo-German Mixed Arbitral Tribunal (31 May 1924) 2 ILR 21, 22–23.

[445] E.g. – Tanganyika (n 471).

[446] On New Guinea, see: *Wong Man On v The Commonwealth*, High Court of Australia (6 June 1952) 19 ILR (1952) 327.

APPLICATION TO THE CLASSES OF SUCCESSION    285

Inter-State practice underpinning this general principle of law comprises Mandatory and Trusteeship Agreements and implementing decisions while State practice includes the nationality laws and judicial decisions of the predecessor, successor, and third States.

The decision concerning dual nationality for the inhabitants of Mandatory Territories was taken in 1923 by the League of Nations,[447] which consistently maintained the distinct nationality of Mandatory Territories.[448] The rule of continuity for the nationality of the protected Territory with termination of protected person status was shown in 1936 with the first accession to independence of a Mandatory Territory (Transjordan).[449]

For the accessions to independence of Syria and the Lebanon[450] in 1944 when the League of Nations was inoperative, the nationality laws of each territory designated their respective nationals as those 'Turkish nationals' who had been 'established' in their territories on 30 August 1924, subject to the two-year right of option provided under the Peace Treaty of Lausanne.[451] In acceding to independence, Syria and the Lebanon retained their nationality laws in force[452] and France rescinded the status of protected person.

Following the accession to independence of Israel on 15 May 1948 amid the 1947–49 Palestine War,[453] the United Kingdom terminated the status of protected person for all nationals of Mandatory Palestine.[454] Provisionally retaining existing laws in force,[455] the District Court of Tel Aviv held all nationals of Mandatory Palestine to have become Israeli nationals by international law in the absence of an internal law to the contrary.[456] Intended to 'remove a source of confusion ... affecting every person in the country', Israel issued 'travel documents' (*laissez-passer*) stating its bearers to have 'Israeli nationality' but 'a sharp conflict of judicial opinion' existed concerning the status of former nationals of Mandatory Palestine (particularly those not resident in Israel) after the termination of the

---

[447] Norman Bentwich, 'Nationality in Mandated Territories Detached from Turkey' (1926) 7 BYIL 97, 99–102; Quincy Wright, 'Status of the Inhabitants of Mandated Territory' (1924) 18(2) AJIL 306, 310–15.

[448] On the Cook Islands and Western Samoa, see: *Levave v Immigration Department*, Court of Appeal of New Zealand (20 July, 31 August 1979) 16 CILC 141.

[449] Lillian Frost, 'Report on Citizenship Law: Jordan', EUI Country Report RSC/GLOBALCIT-CR 2022/2 (February 2022) 7–8.

[450] 'Text of "A" Class Mandates: French Mandate for Syria and the Lebanon' (24 July 1922) (1922) 3 YLN 410, arts 3, 11.

[451] Decision No 2825 (30 August 1924) arts 1–4 (French) in *Laws Concerning Nationality* (n 330) 284.

[452] Decision No 15/S (19 January 1925) in *Laws Concerning Nationality* (n 330) 285–87.

[453] Palestine Act 1948 (11 & 12 Geo. 6) c 27, s 1.

[454] Palestinian Citizenship Order (24 July 1925) Official Gazette (16 September 1925), ss 1–17. See also: 'Text of "A" Class Mandates: British Mandate for Palestine' (24 July 1922) (1922) 3 YLN 402, art 7.

[455] Law and Administration Ordinance 5708-1948, I Laws of the State of Israel 7, ss 11, 15, 17, 21.

[456] *A.B. v M.B.*, District Court of Tel Aviv (6 April 1950) 17 ILR (1950) 110, 111.

286　SUCCESSION AND NATIONALITY

Mandate, as well as that of illegal Jewish immigrants qualifying for Israeli nationality under the Law of Return.[457]

Enacted on 14 July 1952, the nationality law of Israel repealed the Palestine Citizenship Orders 1925–42 with effect from the 'date of establishment of Israel' (14 May 1948) and declared any national of Mandatory Palestine to have become an Israeli national if:

- registered on 1 March 1952;[458]
- an inhabitant of Israel on the entry into force of the Law; and
- present in Israel from the establishment of the State to the entry into force of the Law, or lawfully entering[459] Israel during that period.[460]

While scholarly opinion considered the nationality law not to have had retroactive effect in clarifying that the Palestine Citizenship Orders had remained in force, the Supreme Court of Israel held on 6 November 1952 that nationals of Mandatory Palestine had become not Israeli nationals but stateless between the establishment of Israel and the entry into force of the nationality law.[461] The effect of the nationality law was to deny Israeli citizenship to hundreds of thousands of Mandatory Palestine nationals of non-Jewish ethnicity[462] who had been resident in Israeli territory on the date of succession but emigrated during the War.[463]

Like Tunisia,[464] the subjects of the Sultan of Morocco[465] were not French citizens or citizens of the French Union but protected persons.[466] In acceding to independence on the termination of the French protectorate in 1956, the subjects of the Sultan continued to hold Moroccan nationality while ceasing to be French protected persons. The 1958 nationality law of Morocco did not apply with retroactive effect.[467]

As for British Togoland and British Cameroons, the inhabitants of the Mandatory Territory for Tanganyika had their own nationality while also

---

[457] Rosenne (n 460) 4 (n 3) 31, 41–42.

[458] Registration of Inhabitants Ordinance 5709-1949 (3 February 1949) II Laws of the State of Israel 103, ss 2–4.

[459] *Naqara v Minister of the Interior*, Supreme Court of Israel (16 October 1953) 20 ILR (1953) 49, 50.

[460] Nationality Law 5712-1952 VI Israel Laws 50, ss 2–9; Haim Margarith, 'Enactment of a Nationality Law in Israel' (1953) 2(1) AJCL 63, 64–66; Shabtai Rosenne, 'La Loi israélienne sur la nationalité 5712-1952 et la loi du retour, 5710-1950' (1954) 81 JDI 4, 61.

[461] *Hussein v Governor of Acre Prison*, Supreme Court of Israel (6 November 1952) 17 ILR 111.

[462] Israeli Nationality Law (n 460) s 2; Law of Return 5710-1950 (5 July 1950) V Israel Laws 114, ss 1, 4. Some Arab nationals were granted Jordanian nationality when Jordan annexed the West Bank – Frost (n 449).

[463] E.g. – Victor Kattan, 'The Nationality of Denationalized Palestinians' (2005) 74(1) NJIL 67.

[464] AN Makarov and Ernst Schmitz (eds) *Fontes Juris Gentium: Digest of the Diplomatic Correspondence of the European States (1871–1878)* (Carl Heymanns Verlag KG 1937) 279–80.

[465] Pierre Guiho, *La Nationalité Marocaine* (La Porte 1961) 9–12. See also: *Nationality Decrees issued in Tunisia and Morocco* (Advisory Opinion) PCIJ Series B (7 February 1923) 7, 28–32.

[466] E.g. – *Re Hamou Ben Brahim Ben Mohamed*, Conseil d'État (18 March 1955) 22 ILR (1955) 60.

[467] Decree No 1-58-250 (6 September 1958) 2394 BORM (12 September 1958) 1492, art 2 (French).

APPLICATION TO THE CLASSES OF SUCCESSION    287

designated British protected persons.[468] Preserved on its conversion into a Trusteeship Territory,[469] Tanganyikan nationality was governed by its customary laws unless a person otherwise qualified as a CUKC under United Kingdom law.[470] Acceding to independence on 9 December 1961, every CUKC and protected person born in Tanganyika lost such status but retained the nationality of Tanganyika unless neither parent had been born there.[471] Residents who were not nationals of Tanganyika were provided a time-limited window in which to apply for Tanganyikan nationality,[472] which seemingly rendered 'stateless a large number of Asians who failed to apply for Tanzanian citizenship in the requisite time'.[473]

The case of Namibia was unique due to the revocation of the Mandate by the General Assembly in 1967 and the occupation of South Africa until 1990. On assuming the Mandate for South West Africa, South Africa agreed with Germany to collectively nationalize as 'Union citizens' all German subjects 'domiciled' therein.[474] The South African courts held German nationals resident in the Mandatory Territory not to have become 'British subjects' due to their specific status as protected persons.[475] When South Africa created its own nationality in 1949, it designated all persons born in South West Africa since 1923 as 'citizens of South Africa by birth'.[476]

Following its revocation of the Mandate, the United Nations issued travel and identity documents to refugees from South West Africa.[477] In acceding to independence on 21 March 1990, Namibia recognized as its nationals all persons born in Namibia to a parent also born in Namibia or 'ordinarily resident' for a minimum of five years.[478] On the same date, South Africa revoked the nationality of persons with respect to South West Africa.[479]

In the unusual circumstances of the 'dismemberment' of the Trust Territory for the Pacific Islands, its inhabitants had had their own nationality and were also

---

[468] Tanganyika Order in Council 1920, SI 1920/1583.

[469] Note 295; Trusteeship Agreement for the Territory of Tanganyika (13 December 1946) Cmd 7015.

[470] Nalule and Nambooze (n 207) 3.

[471] Tanganyika Independence Act 1961 c 1, s 2; Tanganyika (Constitution) Order in Council 1961, sch II (art 1).

[472] Ibid, art 2.

[473] O'Connell (n 3) 522; Nalule and Nambooze (n 207) 8, 25–26.

[474] Memorandum (23 October 1923) 28 LNTS 418, s 1; Treaty of Versailles, 28 June 1919 (10 January 1920) 225 CTS 188, art 122.

[475] *Rimpelt v Clarkson*, Transvaal Provincial Division (1947) 14 ILR (1947) 32, 33; *Westphal v Conducting Officer of Southern Rhodesia*, Cape Provincial Division (24 January 1948) 15 ILR (1948) 211, 212.

[476] Note 292.

[477] UNGA Res 2372 (XII) (12 June 1968) para 4(c). See also: *Re Bartholomeus T.*, District Court of Cracow (21 December 1970) 52 ILR 28, 29; *Shipanga v Attorney-General*, Supreme Court of Zambia (5 January 1978) 79 ILR 18.

[478] Constitution of Namibia (n 267) arts 4, 16; Namibian Citizenship Act 14 1990, Government Gazette 65, ss 2–5.

[479] Act No 74 1990, 300 SAGG (29 June 1990) 2.

# 288 SUCCESSION AND NATIONALITY

under protected persons of the United States.[480] When the Northern Mariana Islands were ceded to the United States in 1978, they collectively nationalized as United States citizens all Trust Territory citizens born in the Islands and domiciled therein or in the United States as well as other citizens domiciled in the Islands for at least five years.[481]

In acceding to independence in 1986, Micronesia collectively nationalized all Trust Territory nationals who were 'domiciled'[482] in its territory[483] with a six-month right of option for Trust Territory nationals of other districts.[484] The Marshall Islands based its collective nationalization on land rights in acceding to independence[485] while Palau designated its nationals on the basis of ethnicity.[486]

## 7.4 Conclusions

Uniquely in the law of succession, the field of nationality is principally governed by rules that principally derive from State practice not at the international but the national level. Although the central objective of the ILC Articles is the prevention of statelessness resulting from a succession, their hortatory character and policy basis means that the text very largely represents progressive development. This is due to a combination of the limited State practice investigated during the project and the methodological choice to prioritize the policy objectives of avoiding state-lessness and promoting the freedom of choice of the individual. Most significantly, the ILC Articles represent a bold attempt to persuade States for the purposes of their internal law to accept positive duties to grant and deprive nationality by these policies.

However, State practice shows the traditional dualism of the field to persist whereby nationality remains principally the prerogative of States in their internal law. While default rules deriving from State practice at the national level have been proposed, they only regulate the consequences of nationality from a succession for the limited purposes of international law. In contrast to the approach taken by the

---

[480] Trusteeship Agreement for the Former Japanese Mandated Islands, 2 April 1947, 8 UNTS 189 (1947) art 11(1); 'Trust Territory of the Pacific Islands' (1963) 1 DIL 769, 819–20.

[481] Covenant to establish a Commonwealth of the Northern Mariana Islands (adopted 15 February 1975, entered into force 24 March 1976) 14 ILM 344, art III (s 301).

[482] AB Burdick, 'The Constitution of the Federated States of Micronesia' (1986) 8(2) UHLR 419, 436–37. See also: Federated States of Micronesia Annotated Code 2014, Title 7 ('Citizenship') ch 2, s 202; *In re Sproat*, Supreme Court of Micronesia (6 February 1985) 2 FSM Intrm. 1.

[483] Constitution of the Federated States of Micronesia (adopted 1 October 1978, entered into force 10 May 1979) in BM Turcott, 'The Beginnings of the Federated States of Micronesia Supreme Court' (1983) 5 UHLR 361, art III(1).

[484] Ibid, art III.

[485] Constitution of the Republic of the Marshall Islands (1 May 1979) <http://paclii.org/mh/legis/consol_act/cotrotmi490/> accessed 31 December 2023, art XI(1).

[486] Constitution of the Republic of Palau (adopted 2 April 1979, entered into force 1 January 1981) <http://paclii.org/pw/constitution.html> accessed 31 December 2023, art III(1).

ILC, these default rules thus apply only to specific situations in which a succession agreement or nationality law has not determined the status of nationals at the date of succession (e.g.—expatriates).

Whereas a State concerned can subsequently legislate for its internal law to retroactively grant or deprive its nationality, such retroactivity is ineffective in international law. If regulating its nationality prospectively from the date of succession, the general rules apply to any omission.[487] Persons who are collectively nationalized may thus be afforded diplomatic and consular protection by that State and be designated its national for the purposes of investor-State arbitration[488] and international claims.[489] This means that a State may grant or deprive nationality with effect from the date of decision but not retroactively from the date of succession: in international law, the affected national was a national of the State concerned in the interim period.

The prerogative of the States concerned to designate their nationals also extends to the selection of criteria for nationality and the question of statelessness. Whereas the default principle of territoriality for the application of collective nationalization is proposed to be based on permanent residence and birthplace as objective criteria, State practice is clear in permitting local citizenship and indigeneity to be applied; subject to participation in the relevant treaties, this also permits discrimination and statelessness to occur.

The weak authority of default rules and these effects on individuals means that nationality is arguably the least satisfactory field in the law of succession. In the absence of interest among most States to regulate the field by relinquishing some of their prerogative to designate nationals, its future is likely to emphasize the need for clear elaboration and consistent application of succession agreements and nationality laws alongside the gradual consolidation of the proposed general principles of law as secondary rules. While this evolutionary dynamic will not preclude the problems seen in the desovietization era and beforehand (e.g.—permanent residents becoming foreigners,[490] evidentiary deficiencies,[491] statelessness, and dual nationality conflicts), it will provide a settled foundation for the orderly and consistent management of nationality. This in turn will reduce the scope for such problems to arise, and mitigate their effects.

On this basis, the following conclusions are offered in summary for the general principles of law regulating the effects of State succession on nationality to apply in default of a succession agreement or nationality law in force at the date of succession:

---

[487] E.g. – Burma (n 319); South Sudan (n 442).
[488] E.g. – Armenia (n 419).
[489] E.g. – Eritrea (n 428).
[490] E.g. – Portuguese India (n 257); Walvis Bay (n 266); Hong Kong (nn 270 and 275).
[491] E.g. – South Sudan (nn 439–42).

- in total successions, the nationality of the predecessor is automatically terminated due to its extinction;
- in mergers and absorptions, the affected body of nationals automatically acquire the nationality of the successor;
- in dismemberments, the affected body of nationals automatically acquire the nationality of one of the successors according to the principle of territoriality;
- in cessions and secessions, the affected body of nationals automatically lose the nationality of the predecessor and acquire the nationality of the successor under the principle of territoriality;
- for accessions to independence, the affected body of nationals automatically lose the nationality of the predecessor as protected persons and continue the nationality of the successor;
- the affected body of nationals comprises all persons holding the nationality of the predecessor in its internal law with a dominant connection to the transferred territory, with wives and widows holding independent status but not minors and wards;
- the test of dominant connection for the principle of territoriality is determined by permanent residence of five years at the date of succession or place of birth for nationals not permanently residence in the territory of the predecessor;
- a right of option by conduct exists for cessions and secessions whereby an affected national may opt for the nationality of the predecessor through permanent residence in its territory within a reasonable time of the date of succession;
- the nationality of legal persons is determined by its seat at the date of succession with the right to change its nationality by transferring the seat to another State.

# 8

# Succession and Private Property

## 8.1 Introduction

A longstanding doctrinal question in the law of State succession has been whether a 'doctrine of acquired rights'[1] obliges a successor to recognize and respect the private rights of individuals, companies, and other legal persons that were granted by the predecessor.[2] While the debate concerning the existence and scope of such a doctrine was conducted from the beginnings of the intellectual construction of the field in the nineteenth century, it was infused with particular controversy during the decolonization era. This was due to the phenomenon of certain decolonized States taking confiscatory measures against assets held by certain foreign nationals (particularly those of the predecessor) pursuant to nationalization.

In 1969, the Special Rapporteur of the International Law Commission ('ILC') for its project 'State succession in matters other than treaties', Mohammed Bedjaoui, devoted his second report to the topic of 'acquired rights'. A proponent of the 'new international economic order' for the attainment of 'economic sovereignty' for newly decolonized States,[3] he opined that no rule of international law existed for respect for such rights unless the successor specifically consented.[4] The ILC decided not to deal with the 'extremely controversial' topic of acquired rights 'until the Commission had made sufficient progress, or perhaps had even exhausted the entire subject' of State succession.[5]

---

[1] E.g. – PA Lalive, 'The Doctrine of Acquired Rights' in Bender (ed.) *Rights and Duties of Private Investors Abroad* (Southwestern Legal Foundation 1965) 145; S Friedmann, *Expropriation in International Law* (Stevens & Sons 1955) 120; Amerasinghe, *State Responsibility for Injuries to Aliens* (OUP 1967) 145; FV García-Amador, *The Changing Law of International Claims* (Oceana 1984) 263; Antoine Pillet, 'La théorie générale des droits acquis', (1925-III) 8 RdC 489, 496–502.

[2] DP O'Connell, *State Succession in Municipal Law and International Law* vol I (OUP 1968) 263. For a recent survey, see: Daniel Costelloe, 'The Enforceability of Private Property and Contract Rights against a Successor State in International Law' (2023) 56 Vanderbilt Journal of International Law 1213.

[3] Note 103. See also, e.g. – Mohammed Bedjaoui, 'Problèmes récents de succession d'états dans les états nouveaux' (1970–II) 130 RdC 454, 544–61.

[4] Mohammed Bedjaoui, 'Second report on succession in respect of matters other than treaties' (18 June 1969) UN Doc A/CN.4/216/REV.1 (1969) ILC Yearbook vol II, paras 80, 148–56.

[5] 'Report of the International Law Commission on the work of its twenty-first session, 2 June – 8 August 1969', UN Doc A/7610/Rev.1, paras 43–62.

---

*The Law of State Succession.* Arman Sarvarian, Oxford University Press. © Arman Sarvarian 2025.
DOI: 10.1093/oso/9780198817956.003.0008

## 292   SUCCESSION AND PRIVATE PROPERTY

As the phenomenon of large-scale appropriation of foreign nationals' assets did not recur during the desovietization era, the bulk of State practice took place prior to the expansion of the investor-State arbitration system from 1990.[6] In those successions to have subsequently taken place, the substantive rules of customary international law on foreign nationals' property have not yet featured in any investment arbitration.[7] Rather, the 'threshold' problem has been the jurisdiction of an investor-State arbitral tribunal based on succession to a bilateral investment treaty.[8]

Before the advent of the modern investor-State arbitration system, the international minimum standard of treatment of aliens had evolved into a rule of customary international law during the 1930s.[9] Closely linked to the 'legal fiction' of injury to the home State in diplomatic protection (e.g.—on nationality, local remedies, and other admissibility issues) it is inapplicable to expropriatory measures by a successor of its nationals (e.g.—in creating a socialist economy). Although the investor-State dispute settlement system are the primary means of resolving disputes concerning the deprivation of assets belonging to foreign nationals, the system of diplomatic protection continues to exist as well.[10]

In this chapter, it is argued that the State practice does not support a 'doctrine of acquired rights' as a freestanding rule of the law of State succession. Apart from the conceptual vagueness and superfluity of the term 'acquired'[11] and the opacity of the claimed 'rights' (e.g.—contractual, proprietary, statutory, or other),[12] the essential point is that State practice has been coherent in applying the criteria prescribed for the protection of proprietary rights under the international minimum

---

[6] *Asian Agricultural Products Ltd (APPL) v Sri Lanka* (Award) ICSID Case No ARB/87/3 (27 June 1990) 30 ILM 557. See further, e.g. – Arnaud de Nanteuil, *International Investment Law* (Elgar 2021) 32–39.

[7] E.g. – Patrick Dumberry, *A Guide to State Succession in International Investment Law* (Elgar 2018) 3–8, 33–42.

[8] E.g. – Arman Sarvarian, 'The Protection of Foreign Investment in the Law of State Succession' in Andreas Kulick and Michael Waibel, *General International Law in International Investment Law: A Commentary* (OUP 2024) 450.

[9] Martins Paparinskis, *The International Minimum Standard and Fair and Equitable Treatment* (OUP 2013) 54–63, 83–98, 223–28.

[10] E.g. – *Ahmadou Sadio Diallo (Guinea v Democratic Republic of the Congo)* (Preliminary Objections) [2007] ICJ Rep 582, paras 89–94; *Ahmadou Sadio Diallo (Guinea v Democratic Republic of the Congo)* (Merits) [2010] ICJ Rep 639, paras 149–59; *Ahmadou Sadio Diallo (Guinea v Democratic Republic of the Congo)* (Compensation) [2012] ICJ Rep 324. See also, e.g. – Rodrigo Polanco, *The Return of the Home State to Investor-State Disputes: Bringing Back Diplomatic Protection?* (CUP 2019) 215–73; Christoph Schreur, 'Investment Protection and International Relations' in August Reinisch and Ursula Kriebaum (eds) *The Law of International Relations: Liber amicorum Hanspeter Neuhold* (Eleven International 2007) 345–58.

[11] E.g. – O'Connell (n 2) 242–44.

[12] For example, it has been invoked with respect to concessionary rights 'acquired' before another concession was granted on the same subject-matter to justify the right to exclusivity of the former – *Aramco v Saudi Arabia*, Award (23 August 1958) 27 ILR 117, 168.

standard of treatment in the context of State succession. As general international law before national courts or in diplomatic protection, the international minimum standard of treatment thus applies in default of specific rules for the protection of foreign investment and informs the interpretation of provisions on expropriation contained in an investment treaty, contract, or statute.[13]

As for succession to territorial rights and obligations,[14] there has been no variegation in practice among the classes of succession. Unlike other fields of succession, it is not a question of the existence of a general rule that is peculiar to the phenomenon of State succession but rather one of the applicability of a rule of general international law on the treatment of foreign nationals ('aliens') in the context of succession. Since the international minimum standard of treatment for the protection of aliens applies to all States regardless of their condition, its inapplicability to a particular situation is a matter of exception. Consequently, the doctrinal issue is whether State practice supports such an exception in the context of State succession.

Whereas the terms 'nationalization' and 'expropriation' are often used interchangeably,[15] the distinction between them is that nationalization denotes the taking into public ownership of a company or sector of economic activity while an expropriation is a deprivation by the State of specific property from an owner.[16] The former may be considered to be of greater scale and to encompass the latter: while nationalization entails expropriation, not every expropriation is a nationalization.[17] A 'transfer of ownership' by the host State from a foreign owner to another private person, such as a national of the host State, also entails an expropriation. Consequently, this chapter refers exclusively to expropriation, though the deprivation of property—the essential element—occurs during nationalization and transfer of ownership as well.

---

[13] An unresolved question is whether the fair and equitable treatment standard as an autonomous standard based on treaty law or has replaced the international minimum standard of treatment as the basic standard under customary international law; e.g. – *Diallo (Preliminary Objections)* (n 10) paras 89–90; Rudolph Dolzer and Christoph Schreuer, *Principles of International Investment Law* (OUP 2012) 130–42; Paparinskis (n 9) 160–67; de Nanteuil (n 6) 283–89.

[14] See Chapter 2.

[15] The terms are included together in the vast majority of lump-sum compensation agreements – RB Lillich and BH Weston, *International Claims: Their Settlement by Lump Sum Agreements* vol I (University Press of Virginia 1975) 106–10 175–76. For an example of the confusion that can result, see: *Case No 3 Benin v Whimster*, Court of Appeal of England and Wales (1975) 47 BYIL 345, 346. See further, e.g. – Fritz Münch, 'Les effets d'une nationalisation à l'étranger' (1959-III) 98 RdC 411, 418–22; MS Petrén, 'La confiscation des biens étrangers et les réclamations internationales' (1963-II) 109 RdC 487, 493–510.

[16] E.g. – de Nanteuil (n 6) 310–11; Irmgard Marboe, *Calculation of Compensation and Damages in Investment Law* (OUP 2017) 44–45.

[17] For example, a nationalization of a concession encompasses expropriation not only of proprietary rights held by the concessionaire in specific assets but also of the contractual rights arising from the concession itself.

294   SUCCESSION AND PRIVATE PROPERTY

## 8.2 The International Minimum Standard of Treatment

Rooted in diplomatic protection, the international minimum standard of treatment is a rule of customary international law that obliges States to respect, *inter alia*, property belonging to foreign nationals.[18] While the 'fair and equitable treatment' standard – developed in the latter half of the twentieth century through bilateral investment treaty practice – is based on the minimum standard of treatment, the two are distinct.[19] The crystallization of the international minimum standard of treatment is likely to have taken place during the 1930s.[20]

During the nineteenth century, State practice and *opiniones juris* gradually accumulated in favour of a duty in customary international law for successors to respect the private property of foreign nationals. While the practice of the United States with respect to their various territorial acquisitions was the most affirmative, that of other successors was largely consistent. Whereas the 'act of State' doctrine constrained the jurisdiction of the municipal courts in the British Empire to enforce proprietary rights, the United Kingdom nonetheless acknowledged the existence of an *international* duty to respect them.[21] Similar policies were applied by France, Russia, Japan, Spain, and the Central and South American States in their treatment of aliens' property in State succession.[22]

While considerable support existed for the international minimum standard of treatment of foreign nationals on procedural rights (e.g.—non-discrimination on the basis of nationality and 'denial of justice'), the protection of aliens' private property remained contentious at the 1930 League of Nations Codification Conference. In the abundant arbitral practice that arose after the First World War, tribunals did

---

[18] E.g. – de Nanteuil (n 6) 13, 94, 284. On the 'Calvo Doctrine', see: Marboe (n 16) 17.

[19] Ibid, 285–307.

[20] Paparinskis (n 9) 39–64. See also, e.g. – Hartley Shawcross, 'The Problems of Foreign Investment in International Law' (1961-I) 102 RdC 335, 344–46; Alfred Verdross, 'Les règles internationales concernant le traitement des étrangers' (1931-III) 37 RdC 323, 357–88.

[21] E.g. – *Sirdar Bhagwan Singh v Secretary of State for India in Council*, Judicial Committee of the Privy Council (12 November 1874) 2 BILC 582, 586–88; *Secretary of State for India v Bai Rajbai*, 2 BILC 631, 633–40; *Vajesingji Joravarsingji and Others v Secretary of State for India in Council*, Judicial Committee of the Privy Council (26 June 1924) 2 BILC 642, 643–47; *Secretary of State for India v Sardar Rustam Khan*, Judicial Committee of the Privy Council (28 April 1941) 8 CILC 66, 71–82. The rule did not apply to claims by British subjects but only to those of foreign nationals at the date of succession; e.g. – *Ram v Secretary of State in Council of India*, Judicial Committee of the Privy Council (1872) LR Ind App Suppl 119; *Doss v Secretary of State for India* Judicial Committee of the Privy Council (1875) LR 19 Eq 509.

[22] E.g. – Treaty concerning the Recognition of the Empire of Brazil (Portugal-Brazil) (adopted 29 August 1825, entered into force 15 November 1825) 12 BFSP 674, art V; Treaty of Peace and Friendship (Spain–Mexico) (adopted 28 December 1836, entered into force 7 December 1837) 24 BFSP 864, arts VI–VII; JB Moore, A Digest of International Law vol I (US Government Printing Office 1906) 422; EH Feilchenfeld, *Public Debts and State Succession* (Macmillan 1931) 369–72; Convention regulating various questions arising from the Reunion of Savoy and Nice to France (France–Sardinia) (adopted 23 August 1860, entered into force 4 October 1860) 17(2) MNRG (2nd Series) 22, arts 1–5, 8–10 (French); Treaty concerning the incorporation of Korea into the Japanese Empire (Japan–Korea) 103 BFSP 992, art VI.

not invoke it as an autonomous rule, but only to interpret a treaty obligation for a successor to respect private property.[23]

In the *Certain German Interests in Upper Silesia Case*, Germany applied to the Permanent Court of International Justice ('PCIJ') for a declaration that a Polish law of 14 July 1920 purporting to nullify any conveyances of real property taking place after 11 November 1918 and belonging to German nationals constituted liquidation of their proprietary and contractual rights in breach of the 1922 German–Polish Accord on East Silesia ('Geneva Convention')[24] and the Treaty of Versailles.[25]

The PCIJ held the expropriation provisions of the Geneva Convention to be 'a derogation from the rules generally applied in regard to the treatment of foreigners and the principle of respect for vested rights'.[26] It considered the 'transfer of sovereignty' of Upper Silesia to have resulted from the entry into force of the Treaty of Versailles, Article 256 of which did not prohibit the alienation by Germany of real property up to the date of succession.[27] Consequently, the accuracy of the conclusion of the PCIJ, as a statement of the law as it stood at the time, is doubtful.[28]

Although the international minimum standard of treatment on respect for the property of aliens crystallized into a rule of customary international law some time before the founding of the United Nations, it was an open question whether an exception existed for State succession. In 1962 the General Assembly adopted its resolution on 'permanent sovereignty over natural resources', which articulated a right to nationalize, expropriate, or requisition private property for specified purposes and subject to compensation.[29] Noting, however, that the topic of State succession was being examined as a matter of priority by the ILC, the General Assembly added: 'nothing in [the aforementioned paragraph] in any way prejudices the position of any Member State on any aspect of the question of the rights and obligations of successor States and Governments in respect of property acquired before the accession to complete sovereignty of countries formerly under colonial rule.'[30]

---

[23] E.g. – *Goldenberg (Romania v Germany)* (Award) Sole Arbitrator Robert Fazy (27 September 1928) 2 RIAA 903, 906–08.

[24] Convention relating to Upper Silesia (15 May 1922) 9 LNTS 465. See also *Hausen v Polish State*, Upper Silesian Arbitral Tribunal (16 November 1934) 7 ILR 102, 104.

[25] *Certain German Interests in Upper Silesia* (Merits) (Judgment of 25 May 1926) PCIJ Series A (No 7) 6–7, 9–11. See also: *Factory at Chórzow (Germany v Poland)* (Jurisdiction) (Judgment of 26 July 1927) PCIJ Series A No 7, 27.

[26] Ibid, 22.

[27] Ibid, 29–30, 39–40. See also: *Office Français v Office Allemand (Zinc de Silésie)* French-German Mixed Arbitral Tribunal (9 April 1926) 3 ILR 108, 109. *Contra*: *Polish State Treasury v von Bismarck*, Supreme Court of Poland (28 April 1923) 2 ILR 80, 81.

[28] Paparinskis (n 9) 54–63, 83–98, 223–28.

[29] 'Permanent Sovereignty over Natural Resources' UNGA Res 1803(XVII) (14 December 1962) art 4. The resolution was adopted by a vote of 87-2-12-9 of a voting membership of 110.

[30] Ibid, preamble.

296   SUCCESSION AND PRIVATE PROPERTY

However, extensive State practice preceding and succeeding the adoption by the General Assembly of its resolution of 1962 saw successors respect the property of aliens validly acquired before the date of succession. Examples include:

- the accessions to independence of Syria and the Lebanon in 1945;[31]
- the cession of Carpatho-Ukraine by Czecho-Slovakia to the Soviet Union in 1945;[32]
- the secession of the Philippines in 1946;[33]
- the secessions of India and Pakistan from the United Kingdom in 1947;[34]
- the accession to independence of Israel in 1948;[35]
- the secession of Libya from Italy in 1950;[36]
- the merger of Egypt and Syria in 1958;[37]
- the secession of Gabon from France in 1960;[38]
- the cession of West New Guinea by the Netherlands to Indonesia in 1962;[39]
- the cession of French India by France to India in 1963;[40] and
- the cession of Ifni by Spain to Morocco in 1969.[41]

While most of the practice during the decolonization era saw the acceptance by successors of a duty to respect the private property of aliens in succession agreements and internal law, the most significant examples to determine the applicability of the international minimum standard of treatment concern expropriatory measures taken by a minority of successors.

[31] AJ Peaslee, *Constitutions of Nations* (Martinus Nijhoff 1950) 152–53 (art 13), 353 (art 15).

[32] Treaty concerning the Trans-Carpathian Ukraine (Czechoslovakia–USSR) (adopted 29 June 1945, entered into force 30 January 1946) 504 UNTS 310, arts 1, 2; ibid, Protocol (arts 2–4).

[33] Constitution of the Philippines (23 March 1935) in Peaslee (n 31) 789–809, arts III(I)(2) XII(I) XVI(I)(3); Treaty of General Relations (Philippines–United States) (adopted 4 July 1946, entered into force 22 October 1946) 7 UNTS 3, arts IV, VI, Protocol.

[34] Indian Independence Act 1947 c 30, para 18(3); India (Adaptation of Existing Laws) Order 1947 (14 August 1947) G.G.O. 16, Gazette of India Extraordinary (14 August 1947) 904, art 7; Indian Independence (Rights, Property and Liabilities) Order 1947 3 CILC 134, arts 3, 8–9.

[35] Absentee Property Law 1950 4 Israel Laws 68, paras 1, 4, 7–8, 11, 19–21, 27–28. See also: *Jabbour v Custodian of Israeli Absentee Property*, Queen's Bench Division (27 November 1953) 7 BILC 219, 221–32.

[36] UNGA Res 388(V)(A) (15 December 1950) arts I–IV, VI(1) IX(1).

[37] Provisional Constitution of the United Arab Republic (5 March 1958) in Eugene Cotran, 'Some Legal Aspects of the Formation of the United Arab Republic and the United Arab States' (1959) 8(2) ICLQ 346, art 5.

[38] Constitution of Gabon (21 February 1961) in Peaslee and Peaslee, *Constitutions of Nations* vol I (Springer 1968) 191, art 1(6); *Re Draft Ordinance Modifying Law 6/61 Governing Expropriation*, Supreme Court of Gabon (14 August 1970) 48 ILR 151, 153.

[39] Agreement concerning West New Guinea (West Irian) (Netherlands–Indonesia) (15 August 1962) 437 UNTS 273, arts I–III, XII, XIV, XXII.

[40] Agreement concerning the French Establishments in India (France–India) (21 October 1954) 161 BFSP 533, arts 13–15; Treaty ceding the French Establishments to India (France–India) (adopted 28 May 1956, entered into force 16 August 1962) 162 BFSP 848, arts 4–8, 17–18.

[41] Treaty on the Retrocession of Ifni (Spain–India) (adopted 4 January 1969, entered into force 9 January 1971) BOE (5 June 1969) 8805, art 4 (Spanish).

THE INTERNATIONAL MINIMUM STANDARD OF TREATMENT    297

In seceding from the United Kingdom in 1948, Burma had expropriated all large agricultural landholdings and banned foreigners from purchasing real property from 1947. However, it agreed with the United Kingdom to mutual respect of the proprietary rights of their nationals and to equitable compensation for expropriation, with any residual question to be decided by the Parties 'in accordance with the generally accepted principles of international law and with modern international practice'.[42] Several British-owned enterprises were nationalized, with special tribunals to assess equitable compensation; Burma undertook to pay compensation not exceeding twelve times the land revenue to be determined according to the nature of the tenure, the duration of possession, the benefits arising from possession, and the losses sustained in respect of the land.[43]

When Poland absorbed the Free City of Danzig in June 1945, it expelled the German inhabitants and confiscated their property.[44] In 1948, Poland reached compensation agreements for measures affecting French and British nationals. Whereas the British agreement was based upon 'adequate compensation' to be fixed relative to the value of investment by a mixed commission,[45] the French agreement was premised on 'fixed and total compensation' (*indemnisation globale et forfaitaire*) for specified French property.[46]

In seceding from the Netherlands in 1949, Indonesia undertook to safeguard proprietary rights, concessions, and licences of aliens while pursuing a general policy of 'the economic building up of the Indonesian community as a whole'.[47] It also specified the conditions for lawful expropriation applicable to 'all persons' in

---

[42] Treaty on Burmese Independence (Burma–United Kingdom) (adopted 17 October 1947, entered into force 4 January 1948) 70 UNTS 183, art 7; Exchange of Notes (Burma–United Kingdom) (17 October 1947) 70 UNTS 196, 198; Constitution of Burma (adopted 24 September 1947, entered into force 4 January 1948) in Maung Maung, *Burma's Constitution* (1961) 258, arts 23, 30; Burma Transfer of Immoveable Property (Restriction) Act No 86 (31 December 1947) <https://www.burmalibrary.org/en/government-of-the-union-of-burma-law-no-861947-the-transfer-of-immoveable-property-restriction-act> accessed 12 January 2024, para 3; Burma Land Nationalization Act No LX 1948 (Burma Government Printing and Stationery 1950) s 3; *Ko Aung v Abdul Latiff*, High Court of Burma (17 June 1958) [1958] BLR 216, 219.

[43] Land Nationalization Act (n 42) s 7, sch II. India discontinued a claim on behalf of the South Indian Chettyars after Burma paid compensation – DP O'Connell, *State Succession in Municipal Law and International Law* vol I (OUP 1968) 287.

[44] 'Report of Tripartite Conference of Berlin' (1945) 39 AJIL 245, 253–55; Poland Decree on the Administration of the Recovered Territories (13 November 1945) 51 Dziennik Ustaw 295, art 2 (Polish); *Eastern Treaties Constitutionality Case*, Federal Constitutional Court of the Federal Republic of Germany (7 July 1975) 78 ILR 177, 180, 186–89, 192–93.

[45] Exchange of Notes concerning Compensation for British Interests affected by the Polish Nationalisation Law of 3rd January, 1946 (Poland–United Kingdom) (24 January 1948) 151 BFSP 67, Minute (arts 1(c) 3, 10, 13). Poland subsequently agreed to pay compensation – Agreement regarding the Settlement of Financial Matters (Poland–United Kingdom) (11 November 1954) 161 BFSP 147, art 1(a), sch.

[46] Agreement for the Settlement of French Claims for Compensation due to Nationalisation in Poland (France–Poland) (19 March 1948) 152 BFSP 369, arts 2, 3, 4, 6, 8.

[47] Round-Table Conference Agreement (Indonesia–Netherlands) (2 November 1949) 69 UNTS 200, appendix ('Union Statute') art 2; ibid, Financial and Economic Agreement, art 6.

## 298  SUCCESSION AND PRIVATE PROPERTY

its internal law.[48] In expropriating assets belonging to Dutch nationals from 1958 to promote Indonesian claims to Irian Barat (West New Guinea), Indonesia legislated for the payment of compensation by a government-appointed committee.[49] In 1969, Indonesia concluded a lump-sum compensation agreement for the proprietary rights of the Dutch nationals concerned, including in West New Guinea.[50]

Both the Republic of Viet Nam ('South Viet Nam')[51] and the Democratic Republic of Viet Nam ('North Viet Nam')[52] undertook to respect the property of aliens in their territories.[53] However, the constitution of North Viet Nam guaranteed property rights of Vietnamese nationals alone.[54] In 1953, it adopted laws for the confiscation without compensation of land belonging to 'French colonialists and other invading countries'.[55] France protested the confiscation of land belonging to French nationals and the Catholic Church in 1955 and 1956.[56] Save in the case of the *Société des Charbonnages du Tonkin*, no reparation is known to have been made.[57]

In acceding to independence in 1956, Morocco pledged to respect the rights of French and Spanish nationals[58] and guaranteed the private property of all persons in its internal law.[59] From 1963, Morocco expropriated agricultural property belonging to aliens,[60] but it subsequently agreed to compensate the nationals of

---

[48] Provisional Constitution of Indonesia (15 August 1950) in AJ Peaslee, *Constitutions of Nations* vol 2 (Martinus Nijhoff 1956) 368, arts 8, 26(2), 27(1).

[49] Indonesia Nationalization of Dutch Enterprises Act No 86 (31 December 1958) (1959) 6 NTIR 291, arts 1–2. See also *N.V. Verenigde Deli-Maatschappijen and N.V. Senembah Maatschappij v Deutsch-Indonesische tabak-Handelsgesellschaft m.b.H.*, Court of Appeal of Bremen (21 August 1959) 28 ILR 16, 17, 22, 28–29.

[50] Financial Agreement (Indonesia–Netherlands) (adopted 7 September 1966, entered into force 21 May 1969) 686 UNTS 122, arts 1–3.

[51] Constitution of Viet Nam (26 October 1956) BFSP 1056, art 20.

[52] North Viet Nam had adopted laws respecting the property of foreign firms and nationals – Law No 48 (9 October 1945) <http://vbpl.vn/TW/Pages/vbpq-toanvan.aspx?ItemID=804> accessed 12 January 2024, art 1 (Vietnamese); Law No 29 (10 September 1945) <http://vbpl.vn/TW/Pages/vbpq-toanvan.aspx?ItemID=804> accessed 12 January 2024, art 2 (Vietnamese).

[53] North Viet Nam agreed to restore requisitioned property to French nationals: Convention recognising the Independence of Viet-Nam (France–North Viet Nam) (6 March 1946) 149 BFSP 657 (French); *Modus Vivendi* Agreement (France–North Viet Nam) (adopted 14 September 1946, entered into force 30 October 1946) 149 BFSP 659, arts 2, 8 (French).

[54] Constitution of North Viet Nam (9 November 1946) <http://vbpl.vn/TW/Pages/vbpq-toanvan.aspx?ItemID=535> accessed 12 January 2024, art 12 (Vietnamese). See also: Constitution of the Vietnam Democratic Community (31 December 1959) ibid, arts 11–18 (Vietnamese).

[55] North Viet Nam Law on Land Reform (4 December 1953) <http://vbpl.vn/TW/Pages/vbpq-toanvan.aspx?ItemID=535> accessed 12 January 2024, arts 1–2 (Vietnamese).

[56] 'Pratique française du droit international' (1956) 2(1) AFDI 838–39.

[57] Pierre Brocheux, 'Les relations économiques entre la France et le Vietnam, 1955–1975' (2017) 2 Outre-Mers 193, 194–96, 199–200.

[58] Joint Declaration on Moroccan Independence (Morocco–Spain) (7 April 1956) 162 BFSP 1017; Joint Declaration on Moroccan Independence (Morocco–France) (2 March 1956) 162 BFSP 958 (French); Agreement on the Withdrawal of the Peseta (Spain–Morocco) (7 July 1957) 1353 UNTS 287, art X.

[59] Constitution of Morocco (14 December 1962) in AJ Peaslee and DX Peaslee, *Constitutions of Nations* (Martinus Hijhoff 1965) 563 (art 15).

[60] Decree No 1-63-289 fixing the Conditions for the Recovery by the State of Colonisation Lots (26 September 1963) 2657 BORM (27 September 1963) 1527, arts 1–3 (French); Joint Ordinance No

France,[61] Spain,[62] Italy,[63] and Switzerland.[64] Following numerous proceedings brought by former landowners before the Moroccan courts and those of other States, Morocco enacted a procedure for restitution in 2006.[65]

In ceding the Cocos (Keeling) Islands to Australia in 1955, the United Kingdom transferred all of its rights, liabilities and property 'in or in connection with the Islands'.[66] This archipelago in the Indian Ocean was settled by the Clunies-Ross family in 1827; the United Kingdom had annexed the islands in 1857, and granted perpetual title to the land to the family in 1886.[67] Australia compulsorily purchased title to all land on the islands on 31 August 1978 with compensation.[68]

For the secession of Madagascar in 1956, France and Madagascar had agreed to mutual respect for the proprietary rights of their nationals and Madagascar had affirmed respect for proprietary rights of its nationals and aliens in its 1959 constitution.[69] France successfully objected, on the basis of their succession agreement, to the application to French nationals of a 1962 law on reclamation of unproductive land without compensation. While Madagascar initially argued that the laws implemented a constitutional duty to develop natural resources, it agreed to pay 'fair and equitable compensation, in accordance with international law'.[70] Guinea likewise reached a lump-sum compensation agreement with France in 1976[71] for expropriations of property belonging to French nationals in 1965.[72]

---

500-63 of 26 September 1963, ibid, 1528, art 1 (French); Decree pursuant to Law No 1-73-213 (2 March 1973) 3149 BORM (7 March 1973) 391, arts 1, 3, 8 (French).

[61] Agreement for the Settlement of the Financial Consequences of Measures taken by the Moroccan Government with respect to Agricultural Property owned by French Nationals (France–Morocco) (2 August 1974) 962 UNTS 49, arts 1–4.

[62] Agreement concerning Compensation for the Lands Recovered by the Moroccan State under the Dahir of 2 March 1973 (Spain–Morocco) (8 November 1979) 1410 UNTS 195, arts 1–4.

[63] BH Weston, RB Lillich and DJ Bederman, *International Claims: Their Settlement by Lump Sum Agreements, 1975–1995* (HOTEI Pub. 1999) 277, arts I–IV.

[64] Agreement concerning the Settlement of the Financial Consequences resulting from the Transfer to the Moroccan State of Agricultural Estates (Switzerland–Morocco) (adopted 6 June 1978, entered into force 5 February 1981) 1226 UNTS 120, arts 1–4.

[65] Law No 42-05 (14 February 2006) 5400 BORM (2 March 2006) 347, art 1 (French).

[66] Cocos Islands Order in Council 1955 (United Kingdom) (adopted 28 October 1955, entered into force 23 November 1955) SI 2435, paras 1–5; Cocos (Keeling) Islands Act 1955 (Australia) paras 5–7, annex.

[67] UN Department of Political Affairs, Trusteeship and Decolonization, 'Issue on Cocos (Keeling) Islands', No 11 (April 1978) 2, annex I.

[68] *Clunies-Ross v Commonwealth of Australia and Others*, High Court of Australia (25 October 1984) 118 ILR 311, 312–15.

[69] Convention on Establishment (France–Madagascar) (adopted 27 June 1960, entered into force 18 July 1960) 820 UNTS 364, art 11. See also: Constitution of Madagascar (29 April 1959) in Peaslee and Peaslee (n 59) 453, preamble; Daniel Bardonnet, *La Succession d'États à Madagascar* vol II (Libraire Générale de Droit et de Jurisprudence 1970) 632–44.

[70] Agreement intended to Settle the Financial Consequences of Nationalization and Expropriation Measures taken between 1975 and 1978 (France–Madagascar) (1 October 1998) 2179 UNTS 43, arts 2–3.

[71] Agreement concerning the Settlement of Financial Disputes (Guinea–France) (26 January 1977) JORF (14 February 1978) 711, art II (French).

[72] Peaslee and Peaslee (n 59) 229–38.

# 300    SUCCESSION AND PRIVATE PROPERTY

For the secession of the Democratic Republic of the Congo ('DRC') from Belgium in 1960, the DRC recognized rights of property, including those of aliens, subject to specified conditions for lawful expropriation.[73] While Belgium and the DRC also agreed in 1960 to the protection of investments from expropriation save in the public interest and with fair compensation,[74] the DRC refused to ratify the succession agreements and instead nationalized the Belgian companies ('para-statal entities') operating in the crucial mining sector with interlocking boards in 1964.[75] In a detailed explanatory statement, the DRC declared its refusal to pay compensation to be based on UN decolonization principles and asserted the affected companies to have acquired their rights not by purchase but rather at the expense of the native population.[76] It concluded:

> [T]he Congo Republic wishes to stress that in taking this position it by no means intends to injure in any way the legitimate rights of aliens residing in the country or having capital invested there. The property and rights of aliens will still be safe-guarded by the Government. But it intends to put an end to ownership of colonial origin which was exemplified by the substance of Congolese soil at the dispos-ition of the Compagnie du Katanga, the C.S.K., the C.F.L., and the C.N.K.I.[77]

After expropriating land belonging to foreign companies without compensation in 1966,[78] the DRC paid compensation in settlement agreements with the para-statal entities and other affected owners between 1965 and 1973.[79]

For its secession from France in 1962, Algeria undertook to respect the pro-prietary rights of French nationals with specified conditions for lawful expropri-ation.[80] For agrarian reform, France was to grant Algeria financial aid with a view

---

[73] Constitution of the Congo (Leopoldville) (30 May 1964) in Peaslee and Peaslee (n 59) 98, arts 43, 46, 195. See also: Pierre Piron and Philippe Piron, 'Zaïre', I International Encyclopaedia of Comparative Law Online (1977). See also: Congo Investment Code, Decree-Law (30 August 1965) 19 Moniteur congolais (15 October 1965) in CRISP, *Congo 1965: Political Documents of a Developing Nation* (Princeton University Press 1967) 252–53 (French).

[74] Wolf Radmann, 'The Nationalization of Zaire's Copper: from Union Minière to GECAMINES' (1978) 25(4) Africa Today 25–47, 26–27, 30–31; *La Conférence Belgo-Congolaise Economique, Financière et Sociale* (26 April–16 May 1960) 46–47, 54–55.

[75] *La Conférence Belgo-Congolaise Economique, Financière et Sociale* (26 April–16 May 1960) 42–44.

[76] Congo Decree cancelling Belgian Companies' Rights to Grant Mining Concessions (29 November 1954) 4(2) ILM 232, arts 1–3; ibid, Explanatory Statement, paras 16–18.

[77] Ibid, Explanatory Statement, para 21.

[78] Ordinance-Law No 66-341, I Moniteur Congolais (15 August 1966) 523, art 2; Ordinance-Law No 66-343 guaranteeing all Rights of Property in the Democratic Republic of the Congo, I Moniteur Congolais (15 August 1966) 560, arts 1–2 (French); Ordinance-Law No 67-01bis, I Moniteur Congolais (1967) 29, arts 1–2 (French); Ordinance-Law No 67-55 relating to the Devolution of Ownership of the Properties and Holdings of Union Minière du Haut-Katanga on the Democratic Republic of the Congo (28 January 1967) 6(5) ILM 915, arts 1–3.

[79] 'Announcement of Settlement between the Congo and the Compagnie du Katanga', 4(2) ILM 239; Radmann (n 74) 40, 42, 45; Agreement concerning the Indemnification of Zaireanized Property (adopted 28 March 1976, entered into force 16 July 1976) in Weston et al (n 63) 229, arts 1, 3–5.

[80] Declarations drawn up in Common Agreement at Evian (France–Algerian National Liberation Front) (18 March 1962) 1(2) ILM 214, ch II(A)(2)(b), ch II(B)(2)(b); ibid, Declaration of Principles

THE INTERNATIONAL MINIMUM STANDARD OF TREATMENT 301

to the repurchase in whole or in part of property owned by French nationals.[81] After Algeria expropriated without compensation agricultural property from 1963, the French courts invoked the succession agreements as public policy (*ordre public*) in refusing to recognize those acts. Algeria conceded that the seized property was to be regarded as legally in the possession of absent French owners.[82] The French courts reached divergent conclusions as to whether immediate nationalization that left the fixing of compensation to the executive within an undetermined and discretionary period was compatible with French public policy.[83]

For the secession of Equatorial Guinea from Spain in 1968, its constitution guaranteed the proprietary rights of all persons and it also concluded a succession agreement providing for respect for concessions awarded by Spain and mutual respect for the proprietary rights of aliens 'in application of international law'.[84] Amid civil disturbances in February 1969, the majority of the Spanish population quit the country and the constitution was suspended in 1971.[85] In 1980, Equatorial Guinea agreed to the restitution of farms confiscated from Spanish nationals and compensation for damages caused by riots and government seizures.[86]

For the secession of Bangladesh from Pakistan in 1971 amid a war of independence, Bangladesh provisionally preserved existing laws in force[87] but empowered its officials to seize without compensation any industrial or commercial concern whose owner, director, or manager had left Bangladesh or who, in the view of the government, could not, in the public interest, be allowed to manage it.[88] In awarding disputed assets to Pakistani claimants, the United States rejected these measures as contrary to public policy due to their confiscatory nature.[89]

---

concerning Economic and Financial Cooperation, preamble (para 1), arts 12, 14, 17; ibid, Declaration of Principles on Cooperation for the Exploitation of the Wealth of the Saharan Subsoil, title I(A)(I). The first constitution omitted private property: Constitution of Algeria (10 September 1963) in Peaslee and Peaslee (n 59) arts 12–22.

[81] Ibid, art 13.

[82] O'Connell (n 2) 295.

[83] e.g. – *Crédit du Nord v Ribes-Brossette,* Court of Appeal of Aix (12 July 1966) 47 ILR 60, 61–62. *Banque Nationale pour le Commerce et l'Industrie Afrique v Narbonne,* Court of Appeal of Aix-en-Provence (2 December 1965) 47 ILR 120, 125–126; *Cohen v Crédit du Nord,* Court of Appeal of Paris (14 March 1967) 48 ILR 82, 83.

[84] First Constitution of Equatorial Guinea, BOGE (24 July 1968) art 3; 'Transitional Provisions', para 2ª (Spanish); Convention establishing a Transitional Regime (Spain–Equatorial Guinea) (14 February 1972) 50 BOE (28 February 1972) 3511, arts III–VI, VIII–XII (Spanish).

[85] Peaslee and Peaslee (n 59) 176.

[86] Treaty of Friendship (Spain–Equatorial Guinea) (adopted 23 October 1980, entered into force 14 April 1982) 1322 UNTS 66, Exchange of Letters, Final Act. See also: *Comercial F SA v Council of Ministers* Case No 516 Supreme Court of Spain (6 February 1987) 88 ILR 691, 694, 696.

[87] Laws Continuance Enforcement Order (10 April 1971) 24 DLR (1972) 1, 3; Provisional Constitution of Bangladesh Order 1972 (11 January 1972) 24 DLR 29.

[88] Bangladesh (Taking over Control and Management of Industrial and Commercial Concerns) Order 1972, 24 DLR 8, arts 2, 5–6.

[89] *United Bank Ltd* et al *v Cosmic International, Inc.,* US Southern District Court of New York (31 March 1975) 22 AILC 279, 280–86; *Rupali Bank v Provident National Bank,* US Eastern District Court (22 September 1975) 66 ILR 192, 194–96.

## 302  SUCCESSION AND PRIVATE PROPERTY

Whereas provision was made for the restoration of the immovable property of evacuees, the government was empowered to confiscate the property of persons collaborating with Pakistan or absent from Bangladesh.[90] In 1977 the Supreme Court of Bangladesh held the government not to have acquired any beneficial interest in seized property, as the purpose of the legislation had been to prevent payment to an enemy firm so that such properties were to be restored to the owners after the war.[91] In 2013, Bangladesh adopted the Vested Properties Return (Amendment) Act to provide for the restitution of confiscated properties.

State practice concerning successions occurring after the adoption by the General Assembly of its Resolution on Permanent Sovereignty over Natural Resources is consistent in rejecting an exception for State succession of the international minimum standard of treatment for property. This is shown by the widespread adoption of succession agreements and the internal laws of successors of protections for aliens. While a minority of successors challenged the application of the standard to the nationals of predecessors that had acquired property during colonial rule, they generally accepted a duty to compensate for their expropriations in dispute settlement and did not stipulate a 'without prejudice' clause to preserve their initial legal positions.

This coherence in the State practice concerning succession is reflected in the resolution of the General Assembly adopted in 1974 on the 'Charter of Economic Rights and Duties of States' in which it affirmed the right of each State to expropriate foreign property, subject to 'appropriate compensation'.[92] Unlike in 1962, the resolution omitted any qualifier to keep open the question of its applicability to State succession.[93] It accordingly marked a decisive moment in the applicability of the international minimum standard of treatment to the property of aliens, including nationals of the predecessor, in State succession.

Subsequent practice has affirmed this interpretation, largely through the recognition in succession agreements and internal laws of the proprietary rights of aliens by successors without dispute. These are the following:

- the merger of the Socialist Democratic Republic of Yemen ('South Yemen') with the Arab Yemen Republic ('North Yemen') in 1990;[94]

---

[90] Bangladesh (Restoration of Evacuee Property) Order 1972, 24 DLR, art 2(c); Bangladesh Collaborators (Special Tribunal) Order, 24 DLR, art 2(b) 12.

[91] *Benoy Bhusan v Sub-Divisional Officer, Brahmanbaria*, Supreme Court of Bangladesh (29 November 1977) 30 DLR 139, 145, 147, 151–55, 158.

[92] Charter of Economic Rights and Duties of States, UNGA Res 3281 (XXIX) (12 December 1974) art 2(2)(c). The resolution was adopted by a vote of 120-6-10-2 of a voting membership of 138. See also: Declaration on the Establishment of a New International Economic Order, UNGA Res 3201 (S-VI) (1 May 1974) art 4(e).

[93] E.g. – Rosalyn Higgins, 'The Taking of Property by the State: Recent Developments in International Law' (1982-III) 176 RdC 259, 286–87.

[94] Constitution of Yemen (22 May 1990) (1992) 7(1) ALQ 70, art 6(4); Yemen Law No 22 of 1991 in Abdulla Maktari and John McHugo, *Business Laws of Yemen* (1995) 37–82, arts 1–5, 13.

## THE INTERNATIONAL MINIMUM STANDARD OF TREATMENT   303

- the absorption of the Democratic Republic of Germany ('East Germany') by the Federal Republic of Germany ('West Germany') in 1990;[95]
- the accession to independence of Namibia in 1990;[96]
- the secessions of eleven constituent republics from the USSR in 1991;[97]
- the dismemberment of the Socialist Federal Republic of Yugoslavia ('SFRY') from 1991;[98]
- the dismemberment of Czecho-Slovakia in 1992;[99]
- the secession of Eritrea from Ethiopia in 1993;[100]
- the retrocession of Hong Kong by the United Kingdom to China in 1997;[101]
- the retrocession of Macao by Portugal to China in 1999;[102]
- the secession of Montenegro from the Federal Republic of Yugoslavia ('State Union of Serbia and Montenegro') in 2006;[103] and
- the secession of South Sudan from the Sudan in 2011.[104]

The rarity of expropriatory measures is even shown by the special case of Timor-Leste, which seceded from Portugal in 2002 with retroactive effect to 1975 after a transitional period of UN administration from the occupation of Indonesia.

---

[95] Treaty on the Establishment of German Unity (West Germany–East Germany) (adopted 30 August 1990, entered into force 3 October 1990) 30 ILM 463, arts 1, 41, annex III.

[96] Constitution of Namibia (21 March 1990) UN Doc S/10967/Add.2, arts 16, 140, 146, annex I, sch 5. See also, e.g. – *De Roeck v Campbell and Others (1)* High Court of Namibia (15 June 1990) [1990] NR 28 (HC); *De Roeck v Campbell and Others (2)* High Court of Namibia (14 September 1990) [1990] NR 126 (HC); SK Amoo and SL Harring, 'Namibian Land: Law, Land Reform, and the Restructuring of Post-apartheid Namibia' (2009) 9 UBLJ 87, 98–120; *Namibia v Cultura 2000*, Supreme Court of Namibia (15 October 1993) 103 ILR 104.

[97] E.g. – Kyrgyzstan Law on General Principles of Entrepreneurship in JN Hazard and Vratislav Pechota (eds) *Russia and the Republics: Legal Materials* (1993) binder 1, arts 5, 37; Armenia Law on Ownership (31 October 1990) ibid, arts 1–2, 4–6, 8–9, 11–15, 59–61; Georgia Law on Principles of Entrepreneurial Activity (25 July 1991) ibid, binder 1, arts 1–11; Moldova Law on Property (22 January 1991) in Hazard and Pechota ibid, arts 1–3, 12, 38, 41, 43–44; Ukraine Law on Property (7 February 1991) ibid, arts 2–4, 8, 11–24, 31, 48, 55–57; Ukraine Law on the Protection of Foreign Investments in Ukraine (10 September 1991) ibid, arts 1–4.

[98] E.g. – Agreement on Succession Issues between the Five Successor States of the former State of Yugoslavia (adopted 29 June 2001, entered into force 2 June 2004) 2262 UNTS 251, annex G, arts 1–2. See also: Milica Uvalić, *Investment and Property Rights in Yugoslavia* (CUP 1992) 176–209.

[99] E.g. – Constitutional Law No 4/1993 Coll Zákony Prolidi (15 December 1992) arts 1(1), 2 (Czecho–Slovak); Constitution of Slovakia (1 September 1992) No 460/1992 Coll Pravne Predpisy, art 20 (Czechoslovak).

[100] Eritrea Law on Investment (31 December 1991) Proclamation No 18/1991 4 Gazette of Eritrean Laws (1991) s 11(1); Eritrea, Investment Proclamation No 59/1994 4 Gazette of Eritrean Laws (1994) para 13.

[101] Joint Declaration on the Question of Hong Kong (China–United Kingdom) (19 December 1984) 1399 UNTS 33, art 3(5), annex I (art VI), annex III.

[102] Joint Declaration on Macao (Portugal–China) (adopted 13 April 1987, entered into force 15 January 1988) 1498 UNTS 228, arts 2–3; annex I (arts I, III–IV, VI, VIII–IX, XI–XII, XIV).

[103] Foreign Investment Law of Montenegro (25 March 2011) <https://investmentpolicy.unctad.org/investment-laws/laws/121/montenegro-foreign-investment-law> accessed 31 December 2023, arts 11, 33.

[104] Transitional Constitution of South Sudan (9 July 2011) <https://www.wipo.int/edocs/lexdocs/laws/en/ss/ss013en.pdf> accessed 13 January 2024, art 28.

## 304    SUCCESSION AND PRIVATE PROPERTY

Timor-Leste recognized the private property of all persons in its internal law with protections against unlawful expropriation.[105] While Timor-Leste has since taken measures to restore real estate that had been confiscated from Portuguese Timorese nationals during the occupation,[106] these measures did not concern the expropriation of property owned by aliens but rather the identification of true owners to title held at the start of the occupation.[107]

Since 1962, the weight of State practice has thus recognized no exception to the international minimum standard of treatment for State succession. While much of it comprises the undertakings of successors in internal law and succession agreements with predecessors, which could be interpreted as voluntary acts, expropriatory measures taken by certain successors concerning the property of aliens have also tested the existence and scope of a general rule of customary law. In exercising their right to expropriate the property of aliens, Burma, Australia, and Madagascar accepted a duty to compensate them. Indonesia, Morocco, Guinea, Equatorial Guinea, and the DRC agreed to reparation by agreement with the home States of affected aliens without stipulating an *ex gratia* or 'without prejudice' clause as to their positions on the lawfulness of the measures taken.

While treaty provisions were invoked in a few cases, such as those of Burma and Madagascar, successors nonetheless consistently recognized a duty to compensate 'in international law' irrespective of the existence of a special agreement. In no case was an *ex gratia* or 'without prejudice' clause stipulated to deny the existence of a legal duty concerning lawful expropriation—even in that of the DRC, in which a detailed explanatory memorandum of its legal position was published. Only in the cases of North Viet Nam and Algeria was no reparation made for their seizures of property belonging to French nationals, while Bangladesh has adopted legislation for the restitution of confiscated property remaining in its possession.

There is no evidence in State practice of international investment law, as developed principally through the jurisprudence of investor-State arbitration, impacting on the application of the customary rule of the international minimum standard in State succession. Conversely, there is no proof that the customary rule has influenced the interpretation of the specific rules on foreign investment protection in bilateral investment treaties,[108]

---

[105] UNTAET Regulation No 2000/27 (14 August 2000) paras 1–2, 54.

[106] Timor-Leste Law on Real Estate Property No 1/2003 Jornal da República Series I, preamble, arts 5–6, 12 (Portuguese & Tetum).

[107] Patrícia Jerónimo, 'Report on Citizenship Law: East Timor (Timor-Leste)' (March 2017) EUI Country Report 2017/07, paras 6–8, 12–14, 17. See also: *Gaspar de Oliveira Amaral Sarmento and Gaspar Sarmento v Maria Lígia A. Sarmento* Case No AC-10-03-2010-P-12-CIV-09-TR, Court of Appeal of Timor-Leste (3 October 2010) para 3 (Portuguese); *Norberta Belo v Libert Soares and Clara Ana Augusta Freitas,* Case No AC-10-03-2010-P-23-CIV-01-TR, Court of Appeal (3 October 2010) para 17 (Portuguese).

[108] E.g. – *Frontier Petroleum Services Ltd v Czech Republic* (Final Award) PCA Case No 45035 (12 November 2010) paras 28, 278–79, 306–07, 729; *InterTrade Holding GmbH (Germany) v Czech Republic* (Final Award) PCA Case No 2009-12 (29 May 2012) 62–76; *Voecklinghaus v Czech Republic* (Final Award) Arbitral Tribunal (UNCITRAL) (19 September 2011) <https://jusmundi.com/en/

contracts,[109] and statutes. For example, the definition of 'investment' has not influenced the definition of 'property', while the duties of protection for foreign nationals' investments in bilateral investment treaties have not affected the application of the customary rule in State succession.

Nevertheless, it is suggested that arbitral jurisprudence on the application of other principles (e.g.— 'transparency' or 'legitimate expectations') should not be considered in the application of the customary rule.[110] For example, a treaty rule might not comprehensively define the content or standard of obligation but refer to general international law.[111] While there is no example of the general rule of treaty interpretation[112] being applied to the investment treaties in a case of State succession since the 1990s, it is possible that it will occur in future arbitral practice.[113]

In this context, the key doctrinal issues for the application of the international minimum standard of treatment to State succession are twofold: (1) the nature of the rights that qualify for protection; and (2) the 'foreign' status of the owner, particularly when his nationality changes in consequence of the succession. In other words, the questions are *which* rights and *whose* rights qualify for the protection of the customary rule. As State practice has settled on the basic principle of respect for the private property of aliens, this is not a simple and binary choice but rather a sophisticated analysis of the character of each asset and owner claiming to benefit from the protection of the rule.

### 8.2.1 Property

To qualify for the protection of the customary rule, the claimed proprietary rights must have been validly 'acquired' prior to the date of succession under the law of the predecessor in force at the relevant time.[114] The property must also be

document/decision/en-peter-franz-vocklinghaus-v-czech-republic-final-award-monday-19th-septem ber-2011#decision_340> accessed 13 January 2024; *Binder v Czech Republic* (Final Award) Arbitral Tribunal (UNCITRAL) (15 July 2011) <https://www.italaw.com/cases/151> accessed 13 January 2024, paras 165, 351, 372–73, 437–67; *Achmea B.V. v Slovak Republic* (Final Award) PCA Case No 2008-13 (7 December 2012) paras 287–95; *MNSS B.V. v Montenegro* (Award) ICSID Case No ARB(AF)/12/8 (4 May 2016) paras 230, 323–28; *Sanum Investments Limited v Laos* (Award) Arbitral Tribunal (UNCITRAL) (6 August 2019) paras 178–250.

[109] *Yucyco Ltd. v Slovenia*, US Southern District Court for New York (18 November 1997) 984 F Supp 209 (SDNY 1997).

[110] E.g. – *Obligation to Negotiate Access to the Pacific Ocean (Bolivia v Chile)* [2018] ICJ Rep 507, para 162.

[111] Treaty concerning Investment (adopted 14 November 1991, entered into force 20 October 1994) UNTS I-54935, art II(2)(a).

[112] Vienna Convention on the Law of Treaties (adopted 23 May 1969, entered into force 27 January 1980) 1155 UNTS 331, art 31(3)(c).

[113] On the interpretation of bilateral investment treaties, see, e.g. – Paparinskis (n 9) 141–50.

[114] E.g. – *Vrajlal Narandas v Collector of Rangoon*, Supreme Court of Burma (21 July 1952) [1952] BLR 118, 120–23; *Damodhar Bapu, Laxman Bapu v Central Provinces and Berar*, High Court of Nagpur (7 April 1955) 3 CILC 475; *U Tun Hla v Daw Sein*, High Court of Burma (18 March 1959) [1959] BLR

## 306   SUCCESSION AND PRIVATE PROPERTY

owned by private persons (e.g.—individuals, companies, charities, or other non-governmental entities). In general, the applicable law to determine the character of the property is the internal law of the predecessor.[115]

No universal definition exists in international law for 'property', which also concerns succession to State property.[116] Rather, the term is used to cover a wide range of rights founded in title, contract, statute, or executive grant (e.g.—a tenancy of land).[117] In the absence of a bespoke treaty definition, the internal law of the predecessor in force at the time of the acquisition of the claimed right determines whether it qualifies for the protection of the rule on procedural[118] or substantive[119] grounds.

However, this can be displaced by a special definition in a treaty or international resolution.[120] In 1951, for example, Italy and the United Kingdom agreed that the United Kingdom would release the property of Italian institutions, companies, and associations.[121] Libya challenged this agreement on the basis that the property to

95, 98–99; *Shripatrao Patwardhan v Bombay*, High Court of Bombay (14 December 1960) 49 ILR 468, 473–74, 476–80.

[115] E.g. - *Asrar Ahmed v Durgah Committee, Ajmer*, Judicial Committee of the Privy Council (29 July 1946) 8 CILC 112, 117–19; *Germany v Elicofon (Grand Duchess of Saxony-Weimar intervening) and Kunstsammlungen Zu Weimar v Elicofon*, US Second Circuit Court of Appeals (25 April 1973) 61 ILR 143, 146–47, 149, 153–54; *Kuntstsammlungen zu Weimar v Elicofon*, US Second Circuit Court of Appeals (5 May 1982) 94 ILR 135, 178–81, 192–93.

[116] See Chapter 4. For a recent example outside the context of succession, see: *Koch Industries, Inc. and Koch Supply & Trading, LP v Canada*, ICSID Case No ARB/20/52, Award (13 March 2024) paras 159–63.

[117] In lump-sum compensation treaties, for example, broad terms such as 'property, rights and interests' have been interpreted to encompass debts and intangible property – Lillich and Weston (n 15) 180–86.

[118] E.g. - *Firm Bansidar Premsukhdas v Rajasthan*, Supreme Court of India (29 March 1966) 4 CILC 453, 455–58; *Simon v Administrator-General, South West Africa*, High Court of Namibia (3 April 1991) 1991 NR 151 (HC); Yemen Law No 22 (n 94) arts 1–5, 13.

[119] E.g. - Covenant to establish a Commonwealth of the Northern Mariana Islands (adopted 15 February 1975, entered into force 24 March 1976) 14 ILM 344, arts V (s 505), VIII (s 806); Constitution of Micronesia, ibid, arts IV(3) XV(1); Constitution of the Marshall Islands, ibid, arts I(2) X, XIII(1)(1); Constitution of Palau, ibid, arts V(1) XV(3). In construing a constitutional provision for the protection of private property from unlawful expropriation, a 'generous rather than a legalistic interpretation' is to be given in light of the legal traditions of the successor (e.g. - the mixed French and English traditions of Mauritius): *La Compagnie Sucrière de Bel Ombre Ltée and Others v Mauritius*, Judicial Committee of the Privy Council (13 December 1995) [1995] MR 223, 227–30. Unless otherwise shown, constitutional provisions are to be interpreted as retaining legal freedoms from unlawful expropriation that were enjoyed prior to the succession: *Société United Docks v Mauritius & Desmarais Brothers Ltd and Others v Mauritius*, Supreme Court of Mauritius (7 December 1981) (1981) MR 500, 503–11, 521–23.

[120] E.g. - Treaty on German Unity (n 108) art 41, annex III. See also: *Unification Treaty Constitutionality Case (Merits)* Constitutional Court of the Federal Republic of Germany (23 April 1991) 94 ILR 42, 48–53, 59–66. See also: Treaty on Intra-German Relations (West Germany–East Germany) (21 December 1973) 12 ILM 16, preamble, arts 2, 3, 4, 6, 8, 9; ibid, Supplementary Protocol (note).

[121] Agreement concerning the Disposal of Italian Private Property in Cyrenaica and Tripolitania (Italy–United Kingdom) (28 June 1951) 118 UNTS 115, annex (arts 1–2, 4–5); Agreement concerning the Disposal and Future Administration of Italian Private Property in Cyrenaica (Italy–United Kingdom) (7 November 1951) ibid, annex (arts 1–2).

THE INTERNATIONAL MINIMUM STANDARD OF TREATMENT    307

be restored was patrimonial State property of Italy rather than private property of Italian nationals.

The Arbitral Tribunal held the term 'public institutions' (*établissements publics*) to reflect a deliberate decision by the drafters of the General Assembly resolution in question to employ an expression having a broader meaning than the term *ente pubblico* in Italian law; consequently, the Tribunal was not bound by Italian legislation or judicial precedent but rather examined each asset in its own factual context.[122] In 1956, Italy agreed with Libya to transfer its movable and immovable property in Libya of alienable character with detailed provisions for the protection of the private property of Italian nationals formerly resident in Libya.[123]

In deciding that Eritrea was to be ceded by Italy to Ethiopia in 1952, the General Assembly resolved to apply the provisions of the Treaty of Peace with Italy relating to ceded territories.[124] Pursuant to its federal arrangement in Ethiopia, the region of Eritrea was to receive without payment all Italian 'State property' located therein.[125] State property was defined as including property held by the Fascist Party, four 'autonomous agencies' of the State, and companies and public associations having their seat in Eritrea.[126] The property of Italian nationals 'acquired in accordance with the laws prevailing at the time of acquisition' was to be respected, while those persons quitting Eritrea were entitled to convey or to sell their movable and immovable property free of duty.[127]

Whether based on a special definition provided by an international instrument or the default definition under the internal law of the predecessor, the doctrinal question is thus whether a particular form of right qualifies as 'private'. Examples of problematic areas have been aboriginal title of a communal character,[128] hybrid entities with private and statal characteristics,[129] Crown property as State property

---

[122] *Libya v Italy*, UN Tribunal for Libya (27 June 1955) 22 ILR 103, 106, 108; *Italy v United Kingdom and Libya*, UN Tribunal for Libya (31 January 1953) 25 ILR 2, 12; *Italy v Libya*, UN Tribunal for Libya (3 July 1954) 25 ILR 13. See further: Agreement on Economic Cooperation and Settlement of Issues arising from Resolution 388(V) of 15 December 1950 (Italy–Libya) (adopted 2 October 1956, entered into force 7 December 1957) 2328 UNTS 149, arts 3–8, 13, 15–16; ibid, Exchange of Notes dated 2 October 1956.

[123] Agreement on Economic Cooperation (n 122) arts 3–8, 13, 15–16; Exchange of Notes (2 October 1956). See also: *Società Anonima Principe di Paternò Moncada v INPS*, Court of Appeal of Palermo (18 June 1966) 71 ILR 219, 220.

[124] UNGA Res 530(VI) (29 January 1952) preamble.

[125] Ibid, art I.

[126] Financial Agreement regarding the Establishment of the Federation of Eritrea with Ethiopia (Ethiopia–United Kingdom) (5 & 6 September 1952) 149 UNTS 57, paras 1–2.

[127] UNGA Res 530(VI) (n 124) arts VII(1) VII(2).

[128] On Fiji, see: *Burt (George Rodney) Case*, British-American Claims Arbitral Tribunal (26 October 1923) 2 ILR 78, 79; *Isaac M. Brower Case (United States v Great Britain)* British-American Claims Arbitral Tribunal (1923) VI RIAA 109. On New Zealand, see: *Webster Claim (United States v Great Britain)* British-American Claims Arbitral Tribunal (1925) VI RIAA 166. On Malaya, see: *Adolph G. Studer Claim (United States v Great Britain)* British-American Claims Arbitral Tribunal (1925) VI RIAA 149, 152, 168. On Kenya, see: *Endorois Case*, African Commission on Human and Peoples' Rights (4 February 2010) 142 ILR 1, 7, 18–19, 23–31, 51–70.

[129] For example, the gold holdings of the *Banque d'État du Maroc* (a private bank owned by the French State) were transferred to the newly-established central Bank of Morocco on 1 July 1959 – '1959

308    SUCCESSION AND PRIVATE PROPERTY

or private property,[130] and 'para-statal property' owned by entities partially or wholly owned by the State.[131]

## 8.2.2 Concessions

A classical question in doctrine has been whether the conceptual distinction recognized in systems of internal law between contractual rights as 'personal' to the party (*in personam*) and proprietary rights as 'real' to the asset (*in rem*) applies to exclude the former from the scope of the protection of the international minimum standard of treatment. This has had particular importance for contracts concluded by a State with a private person for the provision of goods or services.[132] In the field of State succession, it has usually had even more specific application to concessions as a form of State contract transferring State property to the concessionaire in exchange for the performance of contractual obligations concerning the transferred property.[133]

In doctrine, a concession was generally considered to have 'no fixed legal meaning' but was considered to be 'usually a licence granted by the State to a

---

Consultations: Morocco' IMF Archives Doc SM/59/57, supplement 1 (15 October 1959) 2–3. See also: Final Declaration and Annexed Protocol of the International Conference of Tangier (29 October 1956) (1957) 51(2) AJIL 460, art 2.

E.g. – *Rahimtoola v Nizam of Hyderabad*, House of Lords (7 November 1957) 24 ILR 175, 182–84; *State of Rajasthan v Sawai Tejsinghi Maharaja of Alwar*, High Court of Rajasthan (29 April 1968) 5 CILC 464, 472–73; *Ahmadunnissa Begum v India*, High Court of Andhra Pradesh (29 January 1968) 4 CILC 463, 469–75.

[130] E.g. – *Secretary of State in Council of India v Kamachee Boye Sahaba*, Judicial Committee of the Privy Council (9 July 1859) 1 BILC 543; *Salaman v Secretary of State in Council for India*, Court of Appeal (20, 21, 27 February 1906) 1 BILC 594; *Ex-Rajah of Coorg (Veer Rajunder Wadeer) v East India Company*, Court of Chancery (1314 November, 8 December 1860) 1 BILC 571; *Rahimtoola v Nizam of Hyderabad*, House of Lords (7 November 1957) 24 ILR 175, 182-184; *Rajasthan v Sawai Tejsinghi Maharaja of Alwar*, High Court of Rajasthan (29 April 1968) 5 CILC 464, 472–73; *Ahmadunnissa Begum v India*, High Court of Andhra Pradesh (29 January 1968) 4 CILC 463, 469–75; *Na'Oroji Bera'mji v Henry Roberts and Others, trading in Bombay and Puna as Rogers and Co.*, High Court of Bombay (1 August 1867) 7 CILC 142; *Tunku Mahmoud bin Sultan Ali et al v Tunku Ali bin Tunku Allum et al*, Straits Settlements Court of Appeal (23 December 1897) 7 CILC 429, 447–48; Treaty of Cession (Johore-East India Company) (2 August 1824) 74 CTS 379, art 7; *Kuntstsammlungen zu Weimar and Others v Elicofon* (n 115) 178–81, 192–93; *Federal Republic of Germany v Elicofon* (n 115) 146–47, 149, 153–54.

[131] E.g. – Treaty of Peace with Italy (10 February 1947) 49 UNTS 3, art 29, annexe XIV (para 1). See also: *Frontier (Local Authorities) Award*, Franco-Italian Conciliation Commission (1 December 1953) 20 ILR 63, 67–68, 74–76.

[132] E.g. – Christopher Greenwood, 'State Contracts in International Law – The Libyan Oil Arbitrations' (1982) 53 BYIL 27, 28.

[133] Doctrinal definitions have focused upon the grant to a private person of rights affecting the 'public interest' with typical characteristics being the conclusion of a contract with the concessionaire, the investment of capital, the execution of public works or exploitation of the State domain, the right of the concessionaire to profit from the activity subject to taxation or royalties to the State, and the mixed public–private character of the legal relationship: Charles Rousseau, *Droit international public* vol III (Sirey 1977) 404–05.

THE INTERNATIONAL MINIMUM STANDARD OF TREATMENT  309

private individual or corporation to undertake works of a public character extending over a considerable period of time, and involving the investment of more or less large sums of capital ... [with] the grant of ... rights over State property.'[134] Though rarely defined in State practice, an exception was the resolution adopted for the succession of Eritrea:

> (a) 'Concession' means a grant by the former Italian administration or by the Administering Power or by a municipal authority of the enjoyment in Eritrea of specific rights and assets in exchange for specific obligations undertaken by the concessionaire with regard to the use and improvement of such assets, such grant being made in accordance with the laws, regulations and rules in force in Eritrea at the time of such grant.
>
> (b) 'Contract in the nature of a concession' means a lease for a period of years by the former Italian administration or by the Administering Power or by a municipal authority of land in Eritrea by the terms of which lease the tenant undertakes obligations similar to those of a concessionaire in the case of a concession, such lease not being made under any specific law, regulation or rule containing provisions for such leases.[135]

Typical examples of concessions include the construction, operation, or maintenance of public utilities (e.g.—railways); the provision of public services (e.g.—transport); and the exploitation of natural resources (e.g.—mining).[136]

Classical practice consistently recognized a duty for the successor to respect the rights of foreign concessionaries.[137] A wide range of treaties in the nineteenth century made express provision for concessions.[138] Though having both contractual

---

[134] O'Connell (n 2) 304.

[135] UNGA Res 530(VI) (n 150) art VIII(1)(a)-(b).

[136] On 'the grant by a public authority of a perpetual or temporary right of exploitation of a mine to the beneficiary', see: *Affaire des réparations allemandes selon l'article 260 du traité de Versailles Réparation (Allemagne c. Commission des Réparations)* (1948) I RIAA 429, 473–74.

[137] An exceptional treaty rule was agreed by the successors to the SFRY, whereby they undertook to protect private property and acquired rights of 'citizens and other legal persons of the SFRY', including contracts concluded with public enterprises: Agreement on Succession Issues (n 98) annex G (arts 1–2).

[138] Moore (n 22) 385. For examples, see: Act for the Cession of Sicily (Spain–Savoy) (10 June 1713) 28 CTS 204, arts VI–VII; Treaty of Peace (Austria–France) (17 October 1797) 54 CTS 158, art 9; Definitive Treaty of Peace and Amity (Austria–Portugal–Prussia–Russia–Sweden–France–Great Britain) (30 May 1814) 63 CTS 171, arts XIX, XXI, XXX–XXXI; Convention regulating various questions arising from the Reunion of Savoy and Nice to France (France–Sardinia) (adopted 23 August 1860, entered into force 4 October 1860) 17(2) MNRG (2nd Series) 22, arts 1–5, 8–10 (French); Treaty respecting the Union of the Ionian Islands to the Kingdom of Greece (France–Russia–Greece–United Kingdom) (29 March 1864) 129 CTS 97, art VII; Treaty of Peace (Austria–Italy) (adopted 3 October 1866, entered into force 12 October 1866) 56 BFSP 700, arts III–IV, VI, VIII–X (French). See also: *Comune di Belgioioso c. Ministeri delle finanze*, Tribunale di Pavia (16 maggio 1879) Giurisprudenza 944, 947; *Comune di Bramans c. Comune di Ferrera*, Corte di cassazione di Torino (23 aprile 1880) I Giruisprudenza 1054, 1056. Switzerland had requested Sardinia to ensure the preservation of Swiss concessions as 'les droits bien acquis soient sauvegardés comme l'exige le droit international': AN Makarov and Ernst Schmitz

310 SUCCESSION AND PRIVATE PROPERTY

and proprietary dimensions, concessions were also commonly included within the definition of 'property' for the customary duty to respect the private property of aliens.[139] Following the First World War, arbitral tribunals held there to be a 'principle of public international law that concessionary rights of a private company were not affected by a transfer of territory on which the concession was to be performed' as adjusted to the altered circumstances.[140]

In modern practice, successors have also widely recognized a duty to respect concessions granted by the predecessor to aliens. Examples of successions in which this duty was recognized by the successor without dispute include:

- the cession of territory by Finland to the Soviet Union in 1944;[141]
- the accessions to independence of Syria and the Lebanon in 1944;[142]
- the secession of the Philippines from the United States in 1946;[143]
- the secession of Libya from Italy in 1950;[144]
- the accession to independence of Somalia in 1960;[145]
- the accession to independence of Kuwait from the United Kingdom in 1961;[146]
- the secession of Singapore from Malaysia in 1965;[147]
- the secession of Mozambique from Portugal in 1975;[148] and

(eds) *Fontes Juris Gentium (1856–1871): Digest of the Diplomatic Correspondence of the European States* vol II (Verlag 1933) 583; Makarov and Schmitz (n 139) 587–88.

[139] E.g. – *Raibl Claim*, Anglo-Italian Conciliation Commission (19 June 1964) 40 ILR 260; *Collas & Michel Claim*, Franco-Italian Conciliation Commission (21 January 1953) 20 ILR 628, 632.

[140] *Zetweg-Wolfsberg and Unterdrauburg-Woellan Railway Case (Austria, Yugoslavia, Railway Company Zeltweg-Wolfsberg and Unterdrauburg-Woellan)* Arbitral Tribunal (1933, 1934, 1938) III RIAA 1795, 1803; *Sopron-Köszeg Railway Case (Sopron-Köszeg Railway v Austria and Hungary)* Arbitral Tribunal (1929) II RIAA 961, 967. See also: *Barcs-Pakrac Railway Case (Hungary v Yugoslavia)* (Award) Arbitral Tribunal (5 October 1934) III RIAA 1569; *Watercourses in Katanga Case (Compagnie du Katanga v Colony of the Belgian Congo)* (Award) Arbitral Tribunal in JG Wetter and SM Schwebel, 'Some Little-Known Cases on Concessions' (1964) 40 BYIL 183, 184–94.

[141] MM Whiteman, *Digest of International Law* vol I (Government Printing Office 1964) 828.

[142] Agreement concerning Monetary and Financial Relations (Lebanon–France) (adopted 24 January 1948, entered into force 16 February 1949) 173 UNTS 99, Exchange of Letters dated 24 January 1948; Isaac Paenson, *Les conséquences financières de la succession d'États* (Éditions Domat-Montchrestien 1954) 37. See also: *Électricité de Beyrouth Company Case (France v Lebanon)* (Order of 29 July 1954) [1954] ICJ Rep 107; *Compagnie du Port, des Quais et des Entrepôts de Beyrouth and the Société Radio-Orient (France v Lebanon)* (Order of 31 August 1960) [1960] ICJ Rep 186.

[143] Treaty of General Relations (n 32) art VII; Treaty of Peace (adopted 10 December 1898, entered into force 11 April 1899) Malloy vol II 1690, art III. See also: Convention regarding the Boundary between the Philippine Archipelago and the State of North Borneo (United States–United Kingdom) (2 January 1930 & 6 July 1932, entered into force 13 December 1932) Treaty Series No 2 (1933) Cmd 4241.

[144] UNGA Res 388(V)A-B (15 December 1950) art IX.

[145] E.g. – *The Ditta Luigi Gallotti v The Somali Government* (Award) Arbitral Tribunal (5 December 1964) 40 ILR 158, 160.

[146] *Kuwait v Aminoil* (Award) Arbitral Tribunal (24 March 1982) 66 ILR 518, 546–48.

[147] Independence of Singapore Agreement (Malaysia–Singapore) (7 August 1965) 4 ILM (1965) 928, annex B (para 9).

[148] Exchange of Letters between Lourenço Marques and Victor Manuel Trigueiros Crespo (24 March, 24 & 28 April 1975) in 'Alto Comissão Moçambique', Portugal Archives Box 40603 (Portuguese).

- the secession of South Sudan from the Sudan in 2011.[149]

The most significant instances of State practice have featured disputes as to the existence and application of a rule requiring a successor to respect concessions granted to aliens.

After acceding to independence in 1948, the Supreme Court of Israel held that, while Israel had elected to recognize certain types of rights granted by Mandatory Palestine, it could lawfully refrain from recognizing a concession to operate kiosks in railway stations because 'there [was] no accepted rule of international law requiring an occupying State, or an emancipated State, to recognize, in its domestic legislation, any action performed by the previous authority—including acts creating private rights for the individual'.[150] However, the *opinio juris* of Israel changed in 1958 when, responding to a complaint by Syria at the UN Security Council concerning certain works in the demilitarized zone, it asserted that they were done pursuant to a concession granted by Mandatory Palestine to the Palestine Electric Corporation in 1926 as 'a legally established private right, deriving from the period before Israel's establishment ... a right which, according to the principles of international law, any government would be obliged to respect and to uphold'.[151]

In seceding from France in 1962, Algeria pledged to respect the economic interests and vested rights of French nationals, including concessions granted by France in the mining, exploration, and transport sectors.[152] From 1963, Algeria expropriated without compensation agricultural property belonging to French nationals, which the French courts refused to recognize.[153] In nationalizing concessionaries in the mining sector and others, Algeria accepted a duty to compensate shareholders on the basis of the average price of shares during the preceding two years.[154] The French courts denied an obligation of France to pay compensation for nationalized concessions.[155]

Prior to the secession of the DRC in 1960, Belgium and the DRC agreed to the protection of foreign investments from expropriation but specially agreed to the early termination of the concessions of the *Comité Spécial du Katanga* in the mining

---

[149] 'The Cooperation Agreement between the Republic of the Sudan and the Republic of South Sudan – A Legal Analysis' (8 November 2012) <https://www.allenovery.com/en-gb/global/news-and-insights/publications/the-cooperation-agreement-between-the-republic-of-the-sudan-and-the-repub lic-of-south-sudan--a-legal> accessed 13 January 2024. See also: *Active Partners Group Limited v South Sudan* (Final Award) PCA Case No 2013/4 (27 January 2015) paras 5, 48, 114, 122, 140, 144.

[150] *Pales v Ministry of Transport*, Supreme Court of Israel (17 March 1955) 22 ILR 113, 119.

[151] UNSC 633rd Meeting (30 October 1958) Off Rec 8th Year 16 (para 81).

[152] Evian Agreements (n 80) ch II(B)(2)(b); ibid, Declaration of Principles concerning Economic and Financial Cooperation, Preamble (para 1), arts 14, 17; ibid, Declaration of Principles on Cooperation for the Exploitation of the Wealth of the Saharan Subsoil, title I(A)(I). See also: *Re Algiers Land and Warehouse Company Ltd.*, Conseil d'État (13 July 1967) 48 ILR 58.

[153] Notes 79–81.

[154] *SONAREM v Genebrier and Others*, Court of Annaba (26 December 1968) 41 ILR 384, 393–94.

[155] *Re Job*, Administrative Tribunal of Paris (31 January 1967) 48 ILR 59, 60; *Re Algiers Land and Warehouse Company Ltd.*, Conseil d'État (13 July 1967) 48 ILR 58.

sector.[156] Belgium also concluded agreements with three other concessionaries for the early termination with compensation of concessions for public land, mining, forestry, and railway management.[157] After the DRC nationalized the remaining foreign concessions, settlement agreements were reached with the concessionaires in 1969 and 1974.[158]

After the accession to independence of Tanganyika in 1961, it proposed in 1962 that the Belbases concession at the port of Dar-es-Salaam be taken over by the East Africa Common Services Organization with compensation awarded for capital investment.[159] Upon receipt of notes from the DRC, Rwanda, and Burundi asserting succession to the 1921 treaty under which the United Kingdom had granted the concession, Tanganyika proposed a new arrangement for the facilities and that the three States determine the apportionment of compensation *inter se*.[160] However, the concessionaire continued to general satisfaction until the expiry of the concession in 1971, whereupon Tanzania granted a fresh concession until the concessionaire concluded 70 years of service on 1 January 1996.[161]

Prior to its secession from the United Kingdom in 1964, Northern Rhodesia ('Zambia') adopted an initial position of rejecting a duty to respect the concession granted the British South Africa Company (founded by Cecil Rhodes in 1889) that was due to expire in 1986.[162] Hours before its secession, however, Zambia and the United Kingdom agreed with the concessionaire to joint compensation for early termination in equal shares of four million pounds rather than the eighteen million pounds claimed by the concessionaire.[163]

For the retroactive cession of Portuguese India by Portugal to India in 1961 and 1962, the Supreme Court of India denied a duty in international law to recognize mining concessions granted by Portugal and asserted a prerogative of the successor to accept them by contract, executive act, or legislation.[164] In 1987, India retroactively declared the abolition of such concessions with effect from 20 December 1961 and their conversion into mining leases with cash compensation to the concession-holders.[165]

---

[156] Radmann (n 74) 26–27, 30–31; *La Conférence Belgo-Congolaise* (n 74) 46–47, 54–55. See also Congo Investment Code (n 73) 252–53 (French); Constitution of the Congo (n 73) 98, arts 43, 46, 195.

[157] Congo Decree cancelling Belgian Companies' Rights (n 76) Explanatory Statement (paras 16–18).

[158] Note 87.

[159] O'Connell (n 43) vol I, 242.

[160] Ibid, 243. See also Chapter 5.

[161] Léon Darcis, 'Les Belbase: une réalisation peu connue de l'expansion belge en Afrique de l'Est' (2007) 53(2) Bulletin des séances 143.

[162] Rousseau (n 134) 418.

[163] Ibid.

[164] Mines and Minerals (Regulation and Development) Act No 67 1957 <https://ibm.gov.in/writer eaddata/files/07102014115602MMDR%20Act%201957_10052012.pdf> accessed 30 December 2023, s 4; *Gosalia v Agarwal and Others*, Supreme Court of India (26 August 1981) 118 ILR 429, 443–46.

[165] Goa, Daman and Diu Mining Concessions (Abolition and Declaration as Mining Leases) Act No 16 of 1987 <https://www.indiacode.nic.in/handle/123456789/1884?view_type=browse&sam_han dle=123456789/1362> accessed 30 December 2023, ss 2, 4–7.

THE INTERNATIONAL MINIMUM STANDARD OF TREATMENT    313

Following the merger of North Yemen with South Yemen in 1990, Yemen replaced North Yemen in a concession granted to an American company for the Marib sector in 1985 as well as South Yemen in a concession awarded to a Soviet agency for the Shabwah sector in 1986.[166] In one arbitration, Yemen unsuccessfully challenged a duty to respect a concession granted by North Yemen to a Belgian concessionaire for the construction and maintenance of a port. Upheld by the Supreme Court of Cyprus, an arbitral tribunal found that Yemen was party to the concessionary contract because it took the burden of the contract alongside the territorial benefit.[167]

While successors have recognized in the great majority of cases a duty to respect concessions granted by predecessors to aliens, including its own nationals, a minority have challenged such a duty by revoking concessions without compensation. In rare cases such as the secession of North Viet Nam, the concessionaires received compensation neither from the successor nor the predecessor.[168] More frequently, however, the successor adopted an initial position of rejecting a duty to compensate in a dispute but eventually accepted such a duty in settlements reached with the concessionaire or the predecessor. This occurred in the cases of Israel, Algeria, Tanganyika, Portuguese India, and Yemen.

While concessions have thus been widely recognized as a form of private property that comes within the protection of the international minimum standard of treatment, they have two special features. First, their contractual basis means that they are usually time-limited rather than perpetual, which prompts special consideration concerning the potential interruption to an ongoing project or service. Second, they entail not only a duty to respect the real property conveyed to the concessionaire (e.g.—land for the purposes of the project) but also the substitution of the successor for the predecessor as party to the concessionary contract to ensure its performance.

The successor may thus either accept substitution or terminate the concession upon payment of compensation to the concessionaire. Unless otherwise stipulated by treaty law,[169] the governing law of the concession is determined by its own

---

[166] World Bank, 'The Republic of Yemen: Unlocking the Potential for Economic Growth' (October 2015) paras 222, 227, 244; Moustafa As-Saruri and Rasul Sorkhabi, 'Petroleum Basins of Yemen' (2016) 13(2) GEOExPro <https://www.geoexpro.com/articles/2016/04/petroleum-basins-of-yemen> accessed 13 January 2024.
[167] *Compagnie d'Enterprises CFE SA v Yemen* (Award) Sole Arbitrator ICC Case No 7748/BGD/OLG (26 September 1997) (unpublished) in *Yemen v Compagnie d'Enterprises CFE SA*, Supreme Court of Cyprus (28 June 1992) ORIL, paras F1–F4.
[168] Note 61. See also: *Re Compagnie des Eaux d'Hanoi*, Conseil d'État of France (19 June 1963) 44 ILR 37, 38; *In re Société des Transports en Commun de la Région d'Hanoi*, Conseil d'État of France (28 June 1967) 52 ILR 5, 6.
[169] E.g. – Tangier Declaration (n 128) arts 14–19; Joint Declaration on Macao (n 102) art 3; Basic Law of Macao in Joint Declaration on Macao (Portugal–China) (adopted 13 April 1987, entered into force 15 January 1988) 1498 UNTS 228, annex I, art 145; Joint Declaration on Hong Kong (n 101) art 4; Basic Law of the Hong Kong SAR (May 2021 edition) <https://www.basiclaw.gov.hk/filemanager/content/en/files/basiclawtext/basiclaw_full_text.pdf> accessed 31 December 2023, art 160.

314    SUCCESSION AND PRIVATE PROPERTY

terms. A successor is not bound by concessions that were granted in breach of the laws of the predecessor[170] or by an occupier (e.g.—Austria,[171] Namibia,[172] and Timor-Leste[173]).

The abundant practice in support of concessions does not apply to every form of State contract. In particular, there is scant evidence to support a duty of a successor to respect contractual rights of civil servants employed by the predecessor on its territory.[174] It may nevertheless elect to do so, such as on the basis of nationality[175] with provisional,[176] existing,[177] or new[178] terms. Although contractual debts owed to private creditors of foreign nationality (e.g.—bondholders, pension claimants, judgment-creditors) come within the scope of succession to State debt,[179] the critical issue there is the succession of the successor to a particular debt.

---

[170] Tangier Declaration (n 128) arts 14–19.

[171] E.g. – *Kleihs v Republic of Austria*, Supreme Court of Austria (24 January 1948) 14 ILR 51; *Schäcke and another v Austria*, Supreme Restitution Commission of Austria (23 September 1950) 17 ILR 34, 35; *Schleiffer v Directorate of Finance for Vienna, Lower Austria and Burgenland*, Administrative Court of Austria (23 May 1958) 26 ILR 609, 610; *German Railways (Austria) Case*, Court of Appeal (Landesgericht) of Vienna (16 August 1949) 16 ILR 61, 62; *Tax Legislation (Austria) Case*, Administrative Court of Austria (4 February 1949) 16 ILR 66.

[172] Constitution of Namibia (21 March 1990) UN Doc S/10967/Add.2, arts 140, 145; *Minister of Defence, Namibia v Mwandinghi*, Supreme Court of Namibia (25 October 1991) 91 ILR 341, 360, 368–69; *Limbo v President of the Republic of Namibia and Another*, High Court of Namibia (4 June 1992) [1992] NR 102 (HC) 104–08; UNSC Res 301 (1971) 12.

[173] Agreement concerning the continued Operation of the Treaty between Australia and Indonesia on the Zone of Cooperation (UNTAET–Australia) (10 February 2000) 29 ILM 469, arts 2, 4; Constitution of Timor-Leste (adopted 22 March 2002, entered into force 25 May 2002) <http://timor-leste.gov.tl/wp-content/uploads/2010/03/Constitution_RDTL_ENG.pdf> accessed 31 December 2023, art 158(3); Timor Sea Treaty (Australia–Timor Leste) (adopted 20 May 2002, entered into force 2 April 2003) 2258 UNTS 3, arts 2, 4. See also: Agreement relating to the Sunrise Troubadour Fields (Australia–Timor Leste) (adopted 6 March 2003, entered into force 23 February 2007) 2483 UNTS 317, art 2.

[174] See Chapter 4. On Uganda, see: *Attorney-General v Godfrey Katondwaki*, High Court of Uganda (10 January 1963) 51 ILR 1, 7. On Mandatory Palestine, see: *Sifri v Attorney-General*, Supreme Court of Israel (20 July 1950) 17 ILR 92; Financial Agreement (Israel–United Kingdom) (15 April 1965) 551 UNTS 19. On Morocco, see: Judgment of the Supreme Court of Spain (30 June 1975) (1981) 33(1) REDI 224–25.

[175] On Mauritius, for example, see: Mauritius Independence Order 1968, Government Notice No 54 (6 March 1968) arts 13(1) 15–16; sch, (arts 89, 94–95); Public Officers Agreement (Mauritius–United Kingdom) (12 March 1968) 648 UNTS 44, arts 1–4, 7.

[176] On Bangladesh, see: Law Continuance Enforcement Order, 24 DLR (1972) 1; *Governor, Bangladesh Bank v Shamsul Huda Khan*, Supreme Court of Bangladesh (1975) 27 DLR (1975) 71, 73, 74, 78; Bangladesh Public Servants' (Retirement) Order 1972, 24 DLR (1972) 35, arts 4(b) 5(1) 8). On Namibia, see: *Courtney-Clarke v Bassingthwaighte*, High Court of Namibia (7 September 1990) [1990] NR 89 (HC); *Namibian Broadcasting Corporation v Kruger*, Supreme Court of Namibia (12 June 2009) [2009] (1) NR 196 (SC).

[177] On Indonesia, see: Round-Table Conference Agreement (n 47) Agreement concerning Civil Government Officials, arts 1–2; Indonesia Civil Service Personnel Guarantee Act 1950, 268 Staatsblad (1950) arts 1–4 (Dutch).

[178] E.g. – Treaty on German Unity (n 108) art 20, annex I; Protocol (art 11).

[179] Ibid. See also: Lillich and Weston (n 15) 186–96; FA Mann, 'The Law Governing State Contracts' (1944) 21 BYIL 11, 13–15.

## 8.2.3 Nationality

Since the international minimum standard of treatment applies only to aliens, an owner must hold foreign nationality after the succession to benefit from it.[180] While nationals of third States owning property in the territory of the successor clearly do so, nationals of the predecessor owning property in the territory of the successor are potentially eligible if they retain its nationality. There is likely to be a temporal overlap between the collective nationalization of the affected body of nationals in consequence of a succession and the admissibility of the claim of an injured national. However, the former logically precedes the latter: the question of the nationality of the injured person must first be determined before addressing the admissibility of a claim of the State purporting to exercise diplomatic protection on behalf of that person.

In a case of partial succession, the critical issue in the majority of cases is whether the injured person retains the nationality of the predecessor from the date of succession. As the rule of continuous nationality in the law of diplomatic protection does not apply in State succession,[181] an owner can qualify for diplomatic protection until the date when collective nationalization is effected (if not the date of succession). If exercising an option in favour of the predecessor's nationality, the period in which the owner ceased to hold foreign nationality is inadmissible in a claim for breach of the international minimum standard of treatment.

Whereas any State of which an injured person is a national may prosecute his claim singly or jointly with another State of nationality,[182] the law of diplomatic protection disqualifies a State from claiming on behalf of a national of the responding State unless the predominant nationality of the injured person be that of the claiming State.[183] In the context of succession, this applies when the injured person acquires the nationality of the successor between the date of succession and the date of injury. The factors to be considered to determine the predominant nationality include permanent residence, time spent in each country of nationality, taxation, familial ties, and education.[184]

State practice in cases of succession is consistent with the customary rule that diplomatic protection may be exercised on behalf of a legal person (i.e.—company or corporation) incorporated in the territory of the claiming State. It is not yet clear whether an exception proposed by the ILC has been taken up by States in favour of the eligibility of a State to bring a claim on the basis of its location of business activity, seat of management, and financial management.[185] Although State practice

---

[180] See Chapter 7.
[181] See Chapter 7.
[182] ILC Draft Articles on Diplomatic Protection with Commentaries (2006) ILC Yearbook vol II Part Two, 33–34 (art 6). See, however, Amerasinghe (n 1) 112–13.
[183] Ibid, 34–35 (art 7). See, however, Amerasinghe (n 1) 106–13.
[184] Ibid, 35 (para 5).
[185] Ibid, 37–38 (art 9); Amerasinghe (n 1) 122–38.

316 SUCCESSION AND PRIVATE PROPERTY

in exercising diplomatic protection on behalf of entities vested by a national juris-diction with legal personality (e.g.—universities, charities, and churches) is scant, the ILC proposed that such legal persons also qualify.[186]

## 8.3 The Criteria for Lawful Expropriation

The customary rule of the international minimum standard of treatment requiring successors to respect the private property of aliens from the date of succession does not forbid them from expropriating such property. The right of a State to ac-quire private property without the consent of the owner is widely recognized in national laws[187] and bilateral investment treaties.[188] For an expropriation of pri-vate property owned by an alien to be lawful, States have accepted that it must be done: (1) according to a prescribed law; (2) pursuant to a public interest; (3) without discrimination towards or among aliens; and (4) with payment of ad-equate compensation.[189]

In the interpretation and application of the international minimum standard, State practice has shown there to be no substantive difference between an expro-priation done in a succession and one done in other contexts. The interpretation of the international minimum standard in international jurisprudence outside the field of succession[190]—particularly by investment arbitral tribunals—is therefore relevant to the elaboration of the standard in cases of succession. An exception is the extent to which a finding in a particular award is based on the interpretation of an instrument that differs in significant respect from the standard.

---

[186] Ibid, 43–44 (art 13); Amerasinghe (n 1) 138–41.

[187] E.g. – *Norwegian Shipowners Claims (Norway v United States)* (Award) Arbitral Tribunal (13 October 1922) 1 RIAA 307, 322. For a comparative study of 16 States, see: GM Erasmus (ed.) *Compensation for Expropriation: A Comparative Study* (United Kingdom Committee of Comparative Law 1990) vol I, 1–5 (United Kingdom), 33–40 (France), 81–88 (Germany), 104–09 (Italy), 121–31 (Sweden), 153–65, 187–91, 232–43 (United States), 263–74 (Mexico), 289–96 (Australia), 321–26 (Canada), 358–61 (Kenya), 373–77 (South Africa); ibid, vol II, 1–10 (Malaysia, Singapore), 34–44 (India), 58–62 (Japan), 75–81 (Romania). On the jurisprudence of the European Court of Human Rights, see: Suetens, 'Property Rights and Expropriation: The European Dimension' in Erasmus, ibid, 216–44; European Court of Human Rights, 'Guide on Article 1 of Protocol No 1 to the European Convention on Human Rights' (31 December 2021) 19–37. For a comparison of the Inter-American and European human systems, see: Albrecht Randelzhofer and Christian Tomuschat (eds) *State Responsibility and the Individual* (Kluwer 1999) 63–148. For a comparison of the USA, Germany, France, the ECtHR, and the IACtHR, see: Borzu Sabahi and NJ Birch, 'Comparative Compensation for Expropriation' in Stephan Schill (ed.) *International Investment Law and Comparative Public Law* (OUP 2010) 755.

[188] E.g. – de Nanteuil (n 6) 312. State practice in concluding provisions on expropriation in inter-national investment treaties is consistent with these criteria; see, e.g. – David Khachvani, 'Compensation for Unlawful Expropriation: Targeting the Illegality' (2017) 32(2) ICSID Review 385, 385–87.

[189] Marboe (n 16) 45. E.g. – Philippines, Constitution (n 33) art III(I)(2); Constitution of Burma (n 42) art 23; Netherlands Note regarding Nationalization of Dutch-Owned Enterprises (18 December 1959) (1960) 54 AJIL 484, 485–89; Constitution of Yemen (n 94) art 6(4); Yemen Law No 22 (n 94) 37–82, arts 1–5, 13.

[190] ICJ Statute, art 38(1)(d).

THE CRITERIA FOR LAWFUL EXPROPRIATION    317

In practice, the requirement to compensate has been the most significant and contentious criterion. While some States have stipulated that the lawfulness of the expropriation and the adequacy of the compensation must be determined prior to the seizure of the assets,[191] the practice is insufficiently general on this point. Amid long debate concerning whether a failure to pay compensation might render an expropriation unlawful, investment arbitration jurisprudence has coalesced around the position that acceptance by the expropriating State of the duty to compensate (e.g.—by creating a mechanism for that purpose) suffices to satisfy the criterion.[192] A dispute concerning the 'adequacy' of the compensation offered by the expropriating State does not render unlawful the expropriation.[193]

While the bulk of practice in the field of succession concerns expropriation, the international minimum standard also embraces lesser infringements, such as sequestration,[194] which have also featured in successions. There are no clear examples of 'indirect' or 'creeping' expropriations[195] in succession practice but there is also no indication that such interferences in proprietary rights would be exempted from the application of the standard.

### 8.3.1 Prescribed Law

An expropriation may only be performed on the basis of a law enacted and published beforehand for the purpose. Bilateral investment treaties frequently provide for a broader duty of 'due process', such as a requirement of transparency.[196] Insofar as these criteria differ, the requirement to expropriate in accordance with prescribed law does not impose extraneous requirements on that law. Rather, the State is required to have provided for a legal framework for the expropriation to be done, thus serving notice to foreign nationals potentially affected by it and adhering to the procedural requirements under that framework.

---

[191] On Algeria, for example, see: *Crédit du Nord v Ribes-Brossette,* Court of Appeal of Aix (12 July 1966) 47 ILR 60, 61–62; *Banque Nationale pour le Commerce et l'Industrie Afrique v Narbonne,* Court of Appeal of Aix-en-Provence (2 December 1965) 47 ILR 120, 125–26; *Cohen v Crédit du Nord,* Court of Appeal of Paris (14 March 1967) 48 ILR 82, 83; *Cie. Française de Credet et de Banque v Atard,* Court of Cassation of France (23 April 1969) 52 ILR 8, 10.

[192] Marboe (n 16) 46–65.

[193] Ibid.

[194] A variety of terms have been used in lump sum compensation treaties, such as 'collectivization', 'confiscation', 'dispossession', 'liquidation', 'other taking', 'public control', 'receivership', 'requisition', and 'State administration' – Lillich and Weston (n 15) 178–79.

[195] Marboe (n 16) 65–67; Lillich and Weston (n 15) 167–73.

[196] De Nanteuil (n 6) 314–15. On the application of the international minimum standard of treatment in investment disputes as customary international law, see, e.g. – Ursula Kriebaum, 'Article 41' in Stephan Schill et al. (eds) *Schreur's Commentary on the ICSID Convention* (CUP 2022) 797, 842–49, 870–71.

318   SUCCESSION AND PRIVATE PROPERTY

## 8.3.2  Public Interest

An expropriation must be done in pursuit of a public interest,[197] such as the completion of an infrastructure project. While there is broad discretion for a State to define that interest, there are known examples of purposes that would not qualify, such as exerting pressure on another State by targeting its nationals[198] or targeting a foreign national that had lost its favour.[199] A potential example of the former in the succession context were the expropriations of property belonging to Dutch nationals by Indonesia for the purpose of pressuring the Netherlands to cede the territory of West Irian.[200] A possible example of the latter in the succession context was a decision to compulsorily acquire the private property of the Clunies-Ross family in the Cocos Islands after the sale of title to all other lands in the Islands to Australia in 1978.[201]

## 8.3.3  Discrimination

An expropriation may not be done by targeting the assets on the basis of the nationality of their owner.[202] The extent to which the standard of the obligation to refrain from discriminating against foreign nationals is influenced by other principles of international investment law (i.e.—most-favoured-nation clause, national treatment clause, and the fair and equitable treatment standard) is an open question. In practice, establishing that an expropriation was based on nationality presents evidentiary issues. Claims asserting that expropriations were discriminatory against the nationals of a home State in succession practice were made by the Netherlands against Indonesia in 1959.[203]

## 8.3.4  Compensation

Though different terms have been employed, States have consistently recognized a duty to provide 'fair', 'just', 'equitable', or 'adequate' compensation. The 'Hull formula' of 'adequate, effective and prompt' compensation was contested by many

---

[197]  Ibid, 312–13.
[198]  E.g. – *BP Exploraiton Co. Ltd v Libya* (Award) Arbitral Tribunal (1 August 1974) 53 ILR 297, 329.
[199]  E.g. – *Caratube International Oil Co. LLP v Kazakhstan* (Award) ICSID Case No ARB/13/13 (27 September 2017) paras 935–36, 940–43.
[200]  Note 47. E.g. – Netherlands Note (n 190) 484, 485–89.
[201]  Note 77.
[202]  De Nanteuil (n 6) 313–14. E.g. – *Compañia de aguas del Aconquija S.A. v Argentina* (Award) ICSID Case No ARB/97/3 (20 August 2007) paras 7.5.23–7.5.34.
[203]  Indonesia (n 201).

THE CRITERIA FOR LAWFUL EXPROPRIATION   319

host States during much of the twentieth century.[204] However, the substantive change introduced by the 1962 Resolution on Permanent Sovereignty over Natural Resources[205] and the 1974 Charter of Economic Rights and Duties of States[206] was not the substitution of a different standard of 'appropriate compensation' but rather its linkage to the internal law of the expropriating State.[207] Although substantive differences between the Hull formula and the alternative of 'appropriate' compensation are slight in practice,[208] modern treaty and arbitral practice on expropriation has coalesced around the latter.[209]

The level of compensation must be commensurate to the 'fair market value' of the property at the time of its taking or the publication of the decision to expropriate.[210] This is typically defined as the 'highest and best use' of the asset:

> [T]he price, expressed in terms of cash equivalents, at property would change hands between a hypothetical willing and able buyer and a hypothetical willing and able seller, acting at arm's length in an open and unrestricted market, when neither is under an obligation to buy or sell and when both have reasonable knowledge of the relevant facts.[211]

It is an open question whether 'loss of profit' (*lucrum cessans*) as distinct from 'actual loss' (*damnum emergens*) is omitted from the duty to compensate for lawful expropriations in contradistinction to the duty to repair for unlawful expropriations. As investment arbitral jurisprudence has employed modern methods of economic valuation concerning the capacity of assets to generate future income, the issue has arguably diminished in importance.[212]

---

[204] 'Promptness' refers to payment as soon as is reasonable in the circumstances, 'effectiveness' to payment in the currency of the foreign national or in an internationally convertible currency and 'adequacy' to equivalency to the full value of the property taken together with interest to the date of payment; e.g. – Marboe (n 15); Sergey Ripinsky and Kevin Williams, *Damages in International Investment Law* (British Institute of International and Comparative Law 2015).

[205] Note 27 (para 4).

[206] Note 104 (art 2(c)).

[207] In identifying the applicable general rules deriving from the resolution of the General Assembly on the identification of compensation for the lawful nationalization of oil concessions by Kuwait, an arbitral tribunal held the meaning of the term 'appropriate' compensation to be carried out by means of enquiry into all the circumstances relevant for a concrete case, rather than through abstract theoretical discussion, particularly the 'legitimate expectations' of the Parties with respect to their long-term contractual equilibrium, which included their positions with respect to the establishment of a 'reasonable rate of return' in a renegotiated concession – *Aminoil* (n 196) 599–613.

[208] Marboe (n 15) 28–29; de Nanteuil (n 6) 317–318. In certain cases, successors have defined 'fair compensation' according to the market value of immovable property; e.g. – Yemen Law No 22 (n 107) 37–82 (arts 1–5, 13).

[209] E.g. – *CME Czech Republic B.V. (The Netherlands) v Czech Republic* (Final Award) UNCITRAL ad hoc Arbitral Tribunal (14 March 2003) 9 ICSID Reports 412 para 497; World Bank, 'Legal Framework for the Treatment of Foreign Investment, vol 2, Report to the Development Committee and Guidelines on the Treatment of Foreign Direct Investment', 31 ILM (1992) 1363.

[210] Marboe (n 16) 19–29.

[211] Ibid, 27 (n 100) 176–77.

[212] Ibid, 67–73.

## 320  SUCCESSION AND PRIVATE PROPERTY

In a financial sense, the question of dating can be the most significant issue in the valuation exercise. A distinction has been drawn between lawful and unlawful expropriation in international jurisprudence whereby the former is generally valuated according to the date of expropriation and the latter by the date of reparation (i.e.—judgment or award).[213] This difference affects the calculation of both principal claims (e.g.—fluctuations in market value) and interest. While a degree of discretion has been exercised by investment arbitral tribunals in the fixing of the date for indirect or 'creeping' expropriations, they have tended to opt for a later rather than an earlier date in setting the lower limit of damages.[214] As for reparation, investment awards for contractual damages have generally been linked to the date of award.[215]

Although certain national jurisdictions (e.g.—France) require compensation to be paid before an expropriation to render it lawful, this criterion has not been adopted in general international law. Rather, general international law requires payment of compensation 'promptly' (i.e.—without delay), whether before or after the expropriation. The duty is discrete from the adequacy of the sum and its precise application is necessarily dependent on the factual circumstances of a particular expropriation.

## 8.4  The Principles of Reparation

If a State unlawfully expropriate property belonging to foreign nationals, it is obliged to make 'full reparation' under the law of international responsibility.[216] Customary international law, as expressed by Article 36 of the International Law Commission Articles on the Responsibility of States for Internationally Wrongful Acts 2001 ('ARSIWA'),[217] provides:

1. The State responsible for an internationally wrongful act is under an obligation to compensate for the damage caused thereby, insofar as such damage is not made good by restitution.
2. The compensation shall cover any financially assessable damage including loss of profits insofar as it is established.

---

[213] Ibid, 129–39, 147–50.
[214] Ibid, 142–47.
[215] Ibid, 147–53.
[216] Marboe (n 16) 29–32.
[217] 'Draft articles on Responsibility of States for Internationally Wrongful Acts, with commentaries' (2001) ILC Yearbook vol II Part Two.

THE PRINCIPLES OF REPARATION 321

The commentaries to Articles 34 and 36 of the ARSIWA neutrally describe the valuation methods applied in international arbitration and adjudication.[218] To distinguish from the duty to compensate for a lawful expropriation, the alternative term 'damages' has been applied by investment arbitral tribunals to the compensation owed from an unlawful expropriation.[219]

They have recognized two practical differences between the duty to compensate for lawful expropriations and the duty to repair for unlawful expropriations: (1) the availability of the remedy of restitution for unlawful expropriations only; and (2) an increase in the value of the expropriated assets between the date of expropriation and the date of award may be taken into account for unlawful expropriations only.[220]

When a claim is pursued by means of diplomatic protection, however, the claiming State may claim for damages owed to itself (e.g.—satisfaction) in addition to those owed to the injured national.[221] While a State is obliged to 'adequately' compensate for the objective (market) value of lawfully expropriated property, it must make 'full' reparation for the subjective (actual) losses sustained by the claimant from an unlawful expropriation.[222] Consequential damages can accrue for unlawful expropriation.[223]

The 'differential method' between the actual and the hypothetical financial situation of the injured person has been applied most frequently by international courts and tribunals, though 'fair market value' has also been used by some investment arbitral tribunals to calculate full reparation.[224] The standard of full reparation may be modified by agreement: for example, Poland paid damages to the United Kingdom from confiscatory measures affecting British nationals in former German territories according to 'adequate compensation' to be fixed relative to the value of investment by a mixed commission, while it paid damages to France for injuries to French nationals based on 'fixed and total compensation' (*indemnisation globale et forfaitaire*) for specified property.[225]

---

[218] Ibid, 95–96, 98–105 (arts 34, 36). In the first stage of the codification project, the notion of 'injury' as 'material or moral damage' was integral to the notion of responsibility itself; this approach was subjected to fierce criticism in the Commission and the Sixth Committee and ultimately discarded when the project was restarted in 1969 – FV García Amador, 'International Responsibility: Third Report', UN Doc A/CN.4/111 (2 January 1958) 67–70, 72 (Art 13) 73 (Art 24(3)); FV García Amador, 'International Responsibility: Fourth Report', UN Doc A/CN.4/119 (26 February 1959) paras 75–92; Roberto Ago, 'First report on State responsibility', UN Doc A/CN.4/217 and Add. 1 (7 May 1969 and 20 January 1970) paras 59–90; Alain Pellet, 'The ILC's Articles on State Responsibility' in James Crawford, Alain Pellet and Simon Olleson (eds) *The Law of International Responsibility* (OUP 2010) 75–94, 76.

[219] E.g. – Marboe (n 16) 10–15, 82–84.

[220] Ibid, 81.

[221] Ibid, 87, 315–26; Lillich and Weston (n 15) 106–10. See, however: *Diallo* (Compensation) (n 10) paras 10, 13, 57–60.

[222] Ibid, 40–41.

[223] Ibid, 306–15.

[224] Ibid, 88–100.

[225] Agreement providing for the Settlement of French Claims for Compensation due to Nationalisation in Poland (France-Poland) (19 March 1948) 152 BFSP 369, arts 2, 3, 4, 6. 8.

# 322   SUCCESSION AND PRIVATE PROPERTY

Successors that have made reparation for unlawful expropriations of alien property include Indonesia,[226] Poland,[227] Morocco,[228] the DRC,[229] Equatorial Guinea,[230] and Bangladesh.[231] Due to the general popularity of lump-sum compensation treaties in post-War practice,[232] many of the disputes concerning the treatment by a successor of foreign nationals' property were settled by those means rather than by adjudication or arbitration.

In most cases, they stipulated the payment of a lump sum by the successor to the predecessor to be distributed to its injured nationals without specifying the techniques used to calculate it.[233] This task was consequently discharged by compensation commissions established by the home States, which typically relied on methods of valuation known to their national jurisdictions (e.g.—estimated net income and reasonable rate of interest in the United Kingdom).[234] As these commissions frequently exercised broad discretion to assess losses according to equity, the opacity of valuation methods has produced outcomes in which aliens have claimed to have received significantly reduced payments in relation to the 'book value' or market value of their assets.[235]

While damages for breach of contract are generally governed by the national law governing the contract, it is possible for a choice-of-law clause to refer to 'international law'.[236] If so, national laws indicate that contractual damages are to place the claimant in the position he would have been in had the contract been performed.[237] There is no clear practice on the question of violation of stabilization

---

[226] Notes 57–58.

[227] Note 289.

[228] Note 297.

[229] Notes 86–87.

[230] Note 96.

[231] Note 102.

[232] One study covered 126 of approximately 170 known treaties between 1945 and 1971 – RB Lillich and BH Weston part I (n 15) 3; ibid, part II, v. On the treatment of such treaties for the identification of customary international law, see: Lillich and Weston, ibid, 247–56, 259–60.

[233] For example, Morocco agreed in 1974 to pay to France an all-inclusive lump sum of DH 104,500,000 (F 113,357,592) to be distributed to the French nationals affected by the Moroccan legislation of 1973; the calculation was based on equipment, livestock, stocks, costs of cultivation, land, plantings, dwellings, farm building, shares in cooperatives, and debts owed by French farmers and legal persons to the Moroccan State up to specified limits – Settlement Agreement on Agricultural Property (n 61) arts 1–4. On the valuation of property, see also: Morocco Law No 70-632 (15 July 1970) and Decree on the Determination and Valuation of Compensable Properties located in Morocco (21 April 1971) in Administrative Court of Appeal of Lyon Case Nos 96LY02491 (6 November 1998), 93LY00210 (29 June 1994) & 92LY00730 (16 March 1994) (French).

[234] RB Lillich, *International Claims: Postwar British Practice* (CUP 1967) 112–28; RB RB Lillich, *International Claims: Contemporary European Practice* (OUP 1982) 53–63 (Austria) 84–89 (Belgium) 124–28 (Italy) 171–80 (Switzerland).

[235] This was the case with respect to the compensation paid by the DRC to the *Union Minière du Haut-Katanga* in 1973, which the latter estimated to be 7.75 billion francs as compared with the estimated book value of 16.2 billion francs and the market value in December 1966 of 40 billion francs – Radmann (n 74) 27–29.

[236] Marboe (n 16) 32.

[237] Ibid, 33.

THE PRINCIPLES OF REPARATION    323

clauses providing for the preservation of national laws applicable at the conclusion of the contract over its duration, which also remains an open question in international investment law.[238] Investment arbitral tribunals have tended to evaluate damages for concessions according to contractual principles.[239]

A critical issue is the methodology to be employed for the valuation of property for the provision of compensation for lawful expropriation and damages for unlawful expropriation on which arbitral jurisprudence has been variegated.[240] As there is no universal framework for the valuation of property in international law, including international investment law, techniques employed in national legal systems have often been applied in international dispute settlement.[241] However, guidelines have been developed by a number of bodies that have influenced investment arbitral jurisprudence; notably, the 2013 International Valuation Standards and the 1992 World Bank Guidelines on the Treatment of Foreign Direct Investment.

A degree of judgement is exercised by investment arbitral tribunals in considering, for example, the economic situation of the respondent.[242] However, the general lack of detailed reasoning in some 261 arbitral awards addressing claims for compensation between 1794 and 1972, coupled with the general absence of explanation in lump-sum compensation agreements, has often left opaque the methods employed in an abundant State practice on damages.[243] In modern arbitral jurisprudence, a combination of valuation methods is often employed in a

---

[238] Ibid, 67–73.

[239] Ibid, 118–21. On the Libyan oil concessions, for example, see: Christopher Greenwood, 'State Contracts in International Law – The Libyan Oil Arbitrations' (1982) 53 BYIL 27, 28.

[240] Marboe (n 16) 33–34, 40, 100–18. E.g. –Pieter Bekker and Fatima Bello, 'Reimagining the Damages Valuation Framework Underlying Fair and Equitable Treatment Standard Violations through a Three-Stage Contextual Approach' (2021) 36(2) ICSID Review 339, 343–50; Jonathan Bonnitcha and Sarah Brewin, 'Compensation under Investment Treaties', International Institute for Sustainable Development Best Practice Series (November 2020) 6–23; MA Bahmaei and HF Mehrabi, 'The Valuation Date of an Unlawfully Expropriated Property in International Investment Arbitration: A Critique of Acquisitive Valuation' (2021) 36(2) ICSID Review 441; UNCITRAL Secretariat, 'Possible Reform of ISDS: Damages and Valuation' (26 August 2021) <https://uncitral.un.org/sites/uncitral.un.org/files/note_by_the_secretariat_-_assessment_of_damages_and_compensation_.pdf> accessed 13 January 2024; Jonathan Bonnitcha, Malcolm Langford, JM Alvarez-Zarate and Daniel Behn, 'Damages and ISDS Reform: Between Procedure and Substance', UNCITRAL Working Group III Academic Forum Paper (26 August 2021) <https://uncitral.un.org/sites/uncitral.un.org/files/media-documents/uncitral/en/damages_and_isds_-_uncitral_af_paper.pdf> accessed 13 January 2024.

[241] Karl Meessen, 'Domestic Law Concepts in International Expropriation Law' in RB Lillich (ed.) Valuation of Nationalized Property in International Law vol IV (University Press of Virginia 1987) 157–72. See, e.g. – Certain Phosphate Lands in Nauru (Nauru v Australia) (Preliminary Objections) (Counter-Memorial) [1992] ICJ Rep 240, para 371; ibid (Memorial) para 429.

[242] Marboe (n 16) 155–62.

[243] Though official exchanges concerning valuation are rarely published, a certain amount of data has been deduced – NM Mintz, 'Economic Observations on Lump Sum Agreements' in Lillich and Weston (n 15) 264–82. See further, e.g. – Christine Gray, Judicial Remedies in International Law (OUP 1990) 11, 18–30, 38–41, 77–92. On the Aminoil award, see: n 196; FA Mann, 'The Aminoil Arbitration' (1983) 54 BYIL 213; Alan Redfern, 'The Arbitration between the Government of Kuwait and Aminoil' (1984) 55 BYIL 65; R Young and WL Owen, 'Valuation Aspects of the Aminoil Award' in RB Lillich, Valuation of Nationalized Property in International Law vol IV (University Press of Virginia 1987) 3–30.

324 SUCCESSION AND PRIVATE PROPERTY

single proceeding for different types of assets, particularly when the existence of a 'market' in which to place an asset proves to be elusive.[244]

A commonplace 'basis of value' (i.e.—assumptions as to value to whom and under what conditions) is the 'market value' basis, which seeks to identify the exchange value of the asset in an open and competitive market.[245] The 'market approach' is frequently used to provide an indication of objective value by comparing the subject asset (e.g.—real estate) with identical or similar assets for which price information is available (e.g.—public stock markets, acquisition market, and prior transactions in the ownership of the subject business).[246]

The 'income approach' provides an indication of objective value in terms of the ability of an asset (e.g.—a going concern) to yield financial benefit to its owner by converting future cash flows to a single current capital value: the most significant methods are the 'earnings method' and the 'discounted cash flow' method.[247] The 'cost approach' indicates the replacement value of an object (e.g.—a company) according to the aggregate values of its component parts: the most commonplace methods are book value, replacement value, and liquidation value.[248]

Alternative bases of value seek to identify the use value of the property to the holder, rather than its exchange value in a marketplace.[249] In contrast to the objective purpose of the market value basis, the alternative bases of value may be subjective in identifying the relationship between the asset and the owner. The 'investment value method' estimates the value of an asset to an owner for investment or operational objectives, the 'fair value method' assesses a price considered to be fair by the identified parties, and the 'contractual value method' applies valuations defined in a contract.[250]

An exercise primarily concerned with the application of economic and financial criteria, valuation is of great importance to the determination of the size of an award. Though expert evidence can be pivotal, there remains considerable discretion to arbitrators or to the disputing parties to select methods to suit the facts of a given dispute. The principal difference between the duty to compensate for a lawful expropriation and the duty to repair for an unlawful expropriation is the dates for admissibility of claims (i.e.—the date of expropriation versus the date of award), with scope for consequential damages to be claimed for the latter. Consequently, there is more room for subjective methods of valuation to be applied in cases of unlawful expropriation due to the nature of the claims for damages that might be brought; notably, disruptions to market value in the many years

---

[244] Marboe (n 16) 294–98; Lillich (n 308) vii–ix.
[245] Ibid, 174–76.
[246] Ibid, 185–89, 214–34.
[247] Marboe (n 16) 190–201, 234–77; Ripinsky and Williams (n 205) 53.
[248] Ibid, 201–07, 278–94.
[249] Ibid, 174–75.
[250] Ibid, 179–83, 298–302.

between date of expropriation and date of award, as well as anticipated profits over long-term contracts.

## 8.5 Conclusions

The duty of a successor to respect property owned by foreign nationals at the date of succession has been traditionally expressed in legal scholarship as the 'doctrine of acquired rights'. This vague concept became a source of considerable debate in the General Assembly and the ILC, reflecting political tensions among colonial and decolonized States. Such was the scale of polarization that the ILC revised its project on State responsibility to detach it from the concept of injury to aliens and abandoned consideration of the topic in its project on State succession in matters other than treaties.

It is suggested that the true question was not the creation of a new rule of customary international law within the field of State succession but rather the existence of an exception from the application of the customary rule of the international minimum standard of treatment. While the question had been kept open in the early years of decolonization, the bulk of State practice and *opiniones juris* did not subsequently support such an exception. Most notably, the majority of successors expropriating the property of aliens without compensation came to eventually accept a duty to compensate with reference to general international law expressed in certain cases. This cohesive practice underpinned the recognition of the standard by the General Assembly on 12 December 1974 with the adoption of the Charter of Economic Rights and Duties of States without reservation for the field of State succession in contrast to its position when it adopted the Resolution on Permanent Sovereignty over Natural Resources in 1962. No successor has since challenged the applicability of the standard in State succession.

In most modern cases, the application of the international minimum standard to State succession does not occur in dispute settlement. Rather, it is manifested in negotiations between the successor and other States (in particular, the predecessor) concerning the treatment of the property of aliens in its territory, alongside the enactment by the successor of legislation for that purpose. Apart from investment treaties, contracts, and laws, the application of the international minimum standard retains relevance when a foreign national need to seek redress before the national courts of a successor or by diplomatic protection through his home State. The jurisprudence of international courts and tribunals, particularly investment arbitral tribunals, concerning the scope of the international minimum standard is directly applicable to determine the lawfulness of expropriations in application of the rule in a case of succession.

Opponents of the applicability of a 'doctrine of acquired rights' in State succession—such as the ILC Special Rapporteur on the 'State succession in matters

## 326 SUCCESSION AND PRIVATE PROPERTY

other than treaties' project, Mohammed Bedjaoui—focused their criticism on the duty to compensate foreign nationals for expropriation of their property. The resolution in the affirmative of the applicability of the international minimum standard to State succession has shifted the field of debate in dispute settlement to the scope of the duty to compensate for expropriation. The compromise in the Charter of Economic Rights and Duties of States was to recognize a duty to provide 'appropriate compensation'—rather than the 'Hull formula' favoured by home States—while tying it to the terms defined by the expropriating State in its legislation. Consequently, the legal question is no longer whether or when a successor must compensate to lawfully expropriate but rather how to determine the adequacy of the compensation amount.

Substantive differences have been identified in arbitral jurisprudence between the duty to compensate for lawful expropriations and the duty to repair for unlawful expropriations (i.e.—the availability of restitution and the admissibility of claims up to the date of award). However, two inter-related areas of vagueness in the modern law are: (1) the admissibility of claims for losses in cases of lawful versus unlawful expropriation; and (2) the selection of 'objective' versus 'subjective' bases of valuation for different types of claims. In their considerable importance for the ultimate size of the financial payments to be made to a foreign national by a host State, they are the latest manifestation of earlier debates concerning the higher standard of proprietary protection provided by international law for foreign nationals in comparison with the nationals of the host State.

# 9

# Conclusion: The Future of State Succession

When the 1978 Vienna Convention on Succession of States in respect of Treaties ('VCSST') was adopted, DP O'Connell appraised the result of the codification project of the International Law Commission ('ILC') and the UN Diplomatic Conference. Opening his essay, he noted the 'unique' nature of the UN Diplomatic Conference in treating the ILC text 'as so sacred that [it] could not be challenged'.[1] Observing that this attitude posed 'serious questions for the future methodology of international law', he wrote of

> a new mythology about State succession, and when the doctrine of international law is built upon myth its ultimate content, as well as its stability, is questionable. State succession is a subject altogether unsuited to the processes of codification, let alone of progressive development, but this particular essay in refashioning the law was marred from its inception by a preoccupation with the special problem of decolonisation, around which myth and emotion have accumulated like mists in the marsh, so that the whole context became intellectually distorted; and, furthermore, it might be said that it has come too late to serve any practical purpose in that matter.[2]

The record of the four ILC projects on State succession supports the criticism of O'Connell concerning the timeliness and political perceptions of the subject. For differing reasons, the projects have largely failed to achieve their primary goal to provide States with sets of objective rules capable of wide application in their succession practice.

Nevertheless, the larger objection of O'Connell that State succession is intrinsically unsuited to codification is dubious. To the contrary, the fact that three texts have been produced by the ILC in addition to those of the Institut de droit international ('IDI') and International Law Association shows at an actuarial level that the compilation of written rules on State succession in a cohesive compendium is achievable. In evaluating the legacy of the ILC projects, the question is not whether State succession cannot be codified but rather whether the necessary conditions are present for a successful codification.

---

[1] DP O'Connell, 'Reflections on the State Succession Convention' (1979) 39 ZaöRV 725.
[2] Ibid, 726.

*The Law of State Succession*. Arman Sarvarian, Oxford University Press. © Arman Sarvarian 2025.
DOI: 10.1093/oso/9780198817956.003.0009

328   CONCLUSION

The record shows timing to be of the essence. This is not only to avoid the excessive intrusion of political perceptions into the process, which was an oft-observed feature of the projects that led to the VCSST[3] and 1983 Vienna Convention on Succession of States in respect of State Property, Archives and Debts ('VCSSP').[4] It is also necessary to facilitate a study of the necessary breadth and depth to adequately inform the project of the rich and intricate array of practice to have taken place. In this respect, a chronic problem in the various codification projects has been insufficient time, resources, and scope to survey the field.[5] This in turn has led to a strong, even myopic focus on reacting to the problems and practice to have taken place in the recent past.

An example is the overweening influence of the Socialist Federal Republic of Yugoslavia case study on general perceptions of the field in doctrine during the desovietization era. Though an important example, it is not representative of the wide and diverse range of successions to have taken place in practice—not only as a rare case of dismemberment but also as an even rarer example of a prolonged dispute concerning legal identity overlapping with succession practice in the same period.

Albeit to a lesser degree, this comment may also be applied to the absorption of the German Democratic Republic and the 11 secessions from the Union of Soviet Socialist Republics. Doctrinal interest in other successions in the same period (e.g.—the secession of Eritrea, the merger of North Yemen and South Yemen, the accessions to independence from the Trust Territory for the Pacific Islands, or the retrocessions of Hong Kong and Macao) was far less pronounced.

While none of the texts resulting from the ILC projects has gained general acceptance by States, this does not mean that they are to be dismissed. Not directly applied to any succession as treaty law, some provisions of the VCSST and VCSSP nonetheless accurately express customary international law in reference to prior State practice as affirmed in subsequent practice and jurisprudence. This applies to a lesser extent to the 1999 Articles on Nationality of Natural Persons in relation to the Succession of States ('ILC Articles') because they were primarily elaborated to promote certain policy objectives, such as the prevention of statelessness, as progressive development. Nonetheless, even the provisions of the ILC texts that do not accurately reflect State practice perform a useful function as a point of comparison in the development of doctrine with reference to emerging practice.

The call of O'Connell for the organic gestation of a 'common law' of succession through State practice was largely not heeded by the community of international

---

[3] Vienna Convention on the Succession of States with respect to Treaties 1978 (adopted 23 August 1978, entered into force 6 November 1996) 1946 UNTS 3 ('VCSST').

[4] Vienna Convention on Succession of States in respect of State Property, Archives and Debts 1983 (adopted 8 April 1983, not in force) 22 ILM 306.

[5] E.g. – Arman Sarvarian, 'Codifying the Law of State Succession: A Futile Endeavour?' (2016) 27(3) EJIL 789.

CONCLUSION 329

lawyers, yet the historical record over the past 40 years has proven its worth. Even as doctrine has struggled to reconcile the codification conventions with the practice that has taken place,[6] the degree of coherence to have emerged from that practice shows how the officials, legislators, and judges of States have found pragmatic solutions to practical problems in an evolutionary way. Far from a sweeping and binary question of 'succession versus non-succession' on a given point,[7] general principle and specific rule alike address the consequences of a succession in a sophisticated and nuanced fashion with a variety of potential outcomes.

The construction of a legal order providing clarity and cohesion is not to be confused with a policy objective of continuity. In this respect, the call of O'Connell for a 'presumption of continuity which concrete analysis may rebut ... in relation to specific issues'[8] is to be resisted. Whatever the merits of the normative argument, the practice has shown 'continuity' (transfer) of rights and obligations not to be regarded by States as an intrinsic good: the basic principle of consent admits the possibility of non-succession to treaties, for example, while State practice points to default rules of non-succession to most forms of territorial obligation, international claims and responsibility, and odious debts. The overarching policy of the law of succession is neither to foist rights and obligations upon successors in the name of continuity nor to vest them with untrammelled discretion to 'pick and choose'. Rather, it is to provide them with a lucid and objective framework of principles and legal tests (e.g.—the principle of territoriality) to inform and guide their negotiations and to decisively address residual issues not otherwise addressed by agreement.

The most consequential error made by the ILC in the doctrinal development of the field was its abandonment of the traditional understanding of a succession as a transfer of territorial title (or 'territorial sovereignty') in favour of its newfangled definition.[9] Though lacking a clear basis in prior practice or theory, the prime catalyst for the conceptualization of a succession as a 'factual replacement' was a misconception of the law of decolonization as nullifying the territorial titles of colonial States. As acknowledged in the ILC debates of the time, the premise was a political one to accommodate the perspective of colonial titles as illegitimate rather than a technical one grounded in empirical study or grand theory.

This mistake was to have profound consequences not only for the two codification projects at hand but also the subsequent decades of intellectual thought.[10]

---

[6] E.g. – Matthew Craven, *The Decolonization of International Law: State Succession and the Law of Treaties* (OUP 2007) 256.

[7] E.g. – O'Connell (n 1) 727–29; CJ Tams, Giovanni Distefano, Gloria Gaggioli, and Aymeric Hêche (eds) *La convention de Vienne de 1978 sur la succession d'États en matière des traités: Commentaire article par article et études thématiques* (Bruylant 2016).

[8] Ibid, 35.

[9] See Chapter 2.

[10] For example, the perception of State succession as being 'above all, a political phenomenon' incapable of objective classification and the false dichotomy between 'legality' and 'pragmatism' – Pierre Michel Eisemann, 'Rapport du directeur d'études de la section de langue française du Centre' in

330    CONCLUSION

Whether it was the abandonment of an early proposal to codify the effect of a succession on 'acquired rights',[11] the exclusion of State debt owed to private creditors from the VCSSP,[12] or succession to treaties as a false choice between 'automatic continuity' versus 'clean slate',[13] the notion of a succession as a mere factual event had the persistent and pernicious effect of polarizing debate into binary choices at a high level of generality. Compounding this tendency has been insufficient attention paid to the intricate positions taken by States in succession practice when their tangible interests are at stake, as opposed to the rather abstract and generic debates in the Sixth Committee and UN codification conferences.

For that practice has shown States—in particular, decolonized States—to have consistently regarded successions for the purposes of international law not as factual replacements of their predecessors as 'occupiers' with their own, original title but rather as transfers of territorial rights and obligations. This has been based not on a grand theory of universal succession from which can be extrapolated all of the various legal effects of a succession but rather on the practice of States on territorial claims for which they have unequivocally asserted automatic succession to the rights of their predecessors.[14] By implication, this shows successors to have regarded the source of their territorial rights and obligations (e.g.—maritime entitlements) to be based not on original but derivative title.

This definition of a succession as a *legal* event entailing a transfer of territorial rights and obligations does not determine succession to other rights and obligations (e.g.—State property) to which the respective rules apply. While the principle of territoriality is a prominent theme across the field, the definition in itself serves to distinguish a succession from other legal events; notably, belligerent occupation.[15] The practice also shows O'Connell's conception of State succession as a 'sociological fact'—however well-founded in historical science—to be only partially seen in States' approaches to the phenomenon.

On the one hand, States have at times described a succession in ambiguous or vague terms in succession agreements or dispute settlement to accommodate different positions on the lawfulness of the *acquisition* of territorial title by the predecessor. Examples include the differing positions of the United Kingdom and China concerning the cession of Hong Kong under the 'unequal treaties' era as

---

Pierre Eisemann and Martti Koskenniemi (eds), *State Succession: Codification Tested against the Facts* (Martinus Nijhoff 2000) 1, 33.

[11] See Chapter 8.
[12] See Chapter 4.
[13] See Chapter 5.
[14] See Chapter 2.
[15] On Cyprus, for example, see: James Crawford, *The Creation of States in International Law* (OUP 2006) 131–32. On the Crimea, see: Patrick Dumberry, 'Requiem for Crimea: Why Tribunals Should Have Declined Jurisdiction over the Claims of Ukrainian Investors against Russia under the Ukraine-Russia BIT' (2018) 9(3) JIDS 506.

well as those of Portugal and India on the lawfulness of the latter's annexations of Portuguese India in denying Portuguese colonial title. Such ambiguity can be compounded by constitutional positions taken by successors in their internal law, such as the rejection by Austria of any succession to the dismembered Austria–Hungary (e.g.—on administrative debt) or the conflicting positions taken by Israel concerning its legal identity with Mandatory Palestine.

To construct a typology of succession that compares like cases with like in order to enable coherent answers to be provided to doctrinal questions, it is necessary to interpret the practice with reference not simply to a (sometimes ambiguous) description of the event. More widely, the substantive treatment by the States concerned of the range of issues provides a complete picture of its nature. The special decision of the General Assembly to revive the defunct membership of Syria rather than require its admission to the United Nations under the usual procedure, for example, is an aberrant factor in the broader context of the consistent treatment by the States concerned of the event as a secession from the United Arab Republic.

Apart from unitary concepts such as the definitions of a succession of States and the date of succession, the dynamics arising in different classes of succession show the integral character of the field as general international law. Far from each sub-field of succession (State property and debt, treaties, etc.) being separate and distinct from one another, the conceptual distinction between total succession and partial succession is critical to determine the legal consequences of the event. Furthermore, the specific aspects of a class of succession (e.g.—the existence of one successor after a merger or absorption versus multiple successors in dismemberment) shapes the essence of the conceptual problems in each field of activity.

Its cohesive character is also demonstrated by the inter-relationship between its various sub-fields as well as general international law at large. For example, determination of the effect of a succession on the nationality of a natural or legal person is necessary for a potential claimant to qualify as a foreign national for the protection of the law of diplomatic protection or international investment law. The claimant can invoke an international law claim against the successor in its national judicial system for tortious debts committed by the predecessor that have a dominant connection to the transferred territory but a claim against the successor by the home State in diplomatic protection through succession to international responsibility can only be brought in certain circumstances. However, succession to a treaty (e.g.—a bilateral investment treaty) can provide a basis for a direct claim against the successor for any continuing breach of the rights of the national as a foreign investor.

Although the formalism underpinning a system of classification that O'Connell deplored is necessary to facilitate comparison, it is thus informed not merely by a superficial reading of text—for example, the 'union' of Newfoundland with Canada, the 'incorporation/reintegration' of Walvis Bay into Namibia, or the 'unification' of East Germany with West Germany—but rather by substantive treatment of the practical issues. This approach does not obviate political narratives of the event that might well exist in parallel and underpin ambiguous descriptions in succession agreements, such as those for the cessions of Portuguese India, Hong Kong, and Macao. By classifying the cases in an objective way for the purposes of international law, accurate comparison of practice is nevertheless facilitated to identify default rules that apply to similar cases.

While the typology developed by the ILC had other flaws, such as the conflation of mergers and absorptions and the assumption that only new States could emerge from a dismemberment, its wide definition of newly independent States had the most profound implications for subsequent doctrinal development. Beyond the adoption of preferential rules for newly independent States that undermined the VCSST and VCSSP, the inclusion of Non-Self-Governing Territories and other 'colonies' in the definition led to persistent difficulties in treating with decolonization practice. While the motivations for decolonized States' lack of interest in participation in the VCSST and VCSSP are not known, it can be speculated that the breadth of the definition of newly independent States and the preferential rules are not attractive to decolonized States as potential predecessors in future successions.

The most immediate doctrinal consequence of the misclassification of a wide variety of decolonization practice was the failure to identify the important rule of continuity for the 'special cases' of protected States and Territories. The perception of decolonization as a 'unique phenomenon' has resulted in enduring difficulty in engaging with this most rich and sophisticated source of State practice in the field. Far from being a 'self-contained era' (e.g.—the secession of the Philippines in 1945 to the accession to independence of Namibia in 1990) the secessions of the various colonial territories (overseas territories, colonies, colonial protectorates, etc.) are legally comparable to the secessions of other forms of territory from a metropolitan State across historical eras. Close engagement with the succession agreements and subsequent practice of the States concerned during the decolonization era furnishes a wealth of pertinent information not only on secessions but also on other classes of succession.

In this respect, succession to treaties has played an overweening role in doctrinal perceptions of the field. Despite the fact that treaties are typically not the immediate priority for successors in comparison with areas such as State property, debt, and nationality,[16] treaties have nevertheless dominated the intellectual thinking in the field. Due to time delays and logistical difficulties in obtaining information on State practice,[17] a partial picture frequently emerges from studies of the practice that focus on a limited time period. Though the relative accessibility of information on treaties has facilitated its study, the perceived 'confusion' in the practice[18] is attributable to a focus upon the application of automatic outcomes

[16] O'Connell (n 1) 726.
[17] See Chapter 1.
[18] Eisemann (n 8) 48–51.

CONCLUSION   333

prescribed by the VCSST as well as the limited time window and data (especially on bilateral treaties) available during the study.

Although the possibility of a return to the codification enterprise cannot be definitively excluded, the doctrinal future of the field is suggested to be a renewed focus on its progressive evolution through comparative analysis of practice. This includes not only the inevitable emergence of new cases of succession but also continuing research into historical cases. In shifting the focus of the profession from the ILC texts in 'testing codification against the facts' to the derivation of general rules through sustained study of evolving practice, the codification projects will no longer be the primary point of reference. Though retaining residual relevance as points of comparison, the focus of international lawyers in the provision of advisory and representational services to parties should be on detailed and forensic engagement with precedent to extrapolate the applicable rules for the case at hand.

General rules of the law of succession do not require the parties to a succession to conform to preordained outcomes. Rather, they serve to guide the parties to conclude succession agreements as well as disputing parties to interpret its provisions and to regulate questions omitted from such agreements. While these functions necessarily mean that a particular succession agreement can derogate from a general rule or apply it, the practical importance of such agreements in the field amplifies their cumulative importance for the identification of default rules.

Despite the considerable logistical obstacles,[19] the fact that much of the implementing practice for State succession is found not at the international but the national level demands close engagement with detail to form an accurate picture of a given case study. The jurisprudence of inter-State arbitration, the Permanent Court of International Justice, and mixed arbitral tribunals in classical practice furnished a number of important international decisions on a variety of questions; in particular, questions of State property, nationality, and private property. In contrast, the influence of international courts and tribunals in the modern era has been much more limited aside from the field of territorial rights and obligations. These limited contributions of international courts and tribunals are dwarfed by the mass of jurisprudence produced by national courts dealing with the consequences of succession—even on quintessentially 'international' fields like succession to treaties.

International legal argument in dispute settlement before international courts and tribunals during the desovietization era—for example, the *Gabčikovo-Nagymaros Project Case*, *Bosnia Genocide Case*, and *Croatia Genocide Case* at the ICJ—reflected the focus of the profession on the VCSST. However, cases in investor-State arbitration and national courts over the past 15 years (e.g.—*Gold Pool v Kazakhstan*, *Deripaska v Montenegro*, *Sudapet v South Sudan*, and *Khudyan*

---

[19]  See Chapter 1.

334 CONCLUSION

*v Armenia*) have seen a greater willingness to disregard the ILC products in favour of a forensic approach. This renewed focus upon the detail of party conduct in a succession is a welcome shift away from a focus upon the application of prescribed outcomes in the ILC texts.

To continue this evolution in legal technique, it is suggested that the next step is to move beyond the narrow confines of interpretation of party conduct in a specific case towards direct comparison with applicable precedent. In cases in which a succession agreement and implementing conduct provides vague guidance or no guidance at all as to the parties' intent, the *application* of default rules on the basis of systemic classification will mark the maturity of the field as general international law for the interpretation and augmentation of specific agreements. This in turn will promote the gradual maturity of doctrine through accurate and comprehensive treatment of State practice on a settled theoretical foundation.

Across the field of State succession, the role of automaticity in the default rules distilled from State practice is variegated. On succession to territorial rights and obligations, the old doctrinal debate concerning their parasitic relationship with the treaty that created them has been resolved with the successful codification of Articles 11 and 12 of the VCSST. Subsequent State practice on territorial claims and boundaries has shown their doctrinal foundation to be a 'real' character independent from treaty. Unlike the basic principle of consent for succession to treaties, succession to territorial rights and obligations thus occurs automatically as the intrinsic feature of the very definition of a succession.

This form of 'absolute' automaticity is contrasted by the conditional automaticity of the default rules on succession to State property and debt. Unlike territorial rights, these default rules are displaced by specific rules adopted by the parties to the succession. The VCSSP accurately reflects some of the default rules of customary international law on the basis of the principle of territoriality, yet they are sustained by a high degree of consistency and coherence in State practice. While open questions remain on points of detail (e.g.—default criteria on equitable apportionment), practical questions concern not the application of vague principles of 'equity' but the application of definitions to specific assets and debts and the principle of territoriality to their factual circumstances.

Similarly, the voluminous practice on succession to treaties that has occurred shows the falsity of the simplistic paradigm between a 'rule of automaticity' versus a 'clean slate principle'. Despite the mistake made by the ILC in confining the principle of consent to the privileged class of newly independent States (as wrongly defined) while overlooking the principle of continuity for protected States and Territories as the true newly independent States, the provisions of the VCSST on the principle of consent largely reflect State practice across the classes of succession. The high degree of technical detail in the rules of succession shows the coherence of the basic principle of succession by notification for multilateral treaties and agreement for bilateral treaties, subject to automatic rules on eligibility.

CONCLUSION    335

For treaties, automaticity is thus manifested in a third way by performing a negative function to determine not whether a successor must succeed but whether it may succeed. Though intersecting with the law of treaties at several points (e.g.—the rule of territorial application) the rules governing succession to treaties remain distinct because succession as a means of participation in a treaty is a unique treaty action. Far from a binary question concerning succession or non-succession to all treaties of the predecessor, the technical sophistication of the field is shown by the current questions in practice on the identification of consent amid silence and the temporal applicability of a treaty during the 'twilight period' between the date of succession and the effective date of notification or agreement.

In stark contrast to other fields, succession to international claims and responsibility is marked by a dearth of State practice in most classes of succession. More than any factor, this inhibited the ability of the ILC to successfully execute its codification project. The considerable reliance of the IDI on a false analogy with tortious debts as well as normative considerations was in no small part due to the scarcity of practice, much of it preceding the Charter era. While a sufficient evidentiary foundation can be identified for a default rule of succession in cases of merger and secession as well as a rule of continuity for accessions to independence, this field is likely to undergo considerable development in the coming century. As new practice emerge and the need to invoke classical practice accordingly diminish, the task of international lawyers will be to articulate the doctrinal rationales for default rules through rigorous treatment of State practice while avoiding preoccupation with normative argument (e.g.—unjust enrichment).

As O'Connell noted, the secondary consequences for nationality are 'one of the most difficult problems of State succession'.[20] In attempting to surpass the 'intractable dualism' between nationality in internal law and nationality in international law, the ILC Articles were a valiant attempt to persuade States to accept *obligations* to deprive and to grant nationality in their internal law according to overarching policy aims on human rights, the will of the individual, and the avoidance of statelessness. As the dualism has remained intractable amid the indifference of most States to this attempt at progressive development, the prerogative of States concerning nationality has meant that the consequences of succession have—more than in any other field—been largely determined at the national level. More than in any other field, it is nationality that has a claim to be the least regulated and most problematic in the law of State succession.

While general principles of law have been proposed that are principally derived from State practice in their internal laws and national jurisprudence, the 'radical' nature of general principles of law as a basis for substantive rules of international law is a secondary concern. As these proposed rules would only apply to the

[20] DP O'Connell, *State Succession in Municipal Law and International Law* vol I (CUP 1967) 503–04.

336 CONCLUSION

limited purposes of international law, leaving the prerogative of States intact, the wider challenge of persuading States to cede a degree of their prerogative over nationality remains. As for other areas of succession, the solution is suggested to lie in the organic gestation into settled practice by influencing States—in particular, national courts—to accept the application of general principles of international law (e.g.—the objective criterion of permanent residence) to questions of nationality under their internal law.

Unlike the other fields, succession to territorial rights applies uniformly across the classes of succession because it is intrinsic to the very definition of a succession. While there is also no variegation on the substantive rule concerning respect for private property, the reason differs in that the rule is not one of the law of succession. Rather, it is the application to a succession of the international minimum standard of treatment as a wider rule of general international law. Despite the fact that the 'doctrine of acquired rights' proved to be so controversial in the early decolonization era that the ILC declined to take up the topic, the application of the international minimum standard of treatment to State succession has become settled. Early controversy concerning seizures of property by certain decolonized States without compensation has shifted towards an acceptance of the basic rule of respect for private property with modern questions now concerning (as in international investment law) the foreign nationality of the owner and the scope of the duty to compensate, particularly the methodology for valuation of assets.

Overall, this account generally shows the degree of cohesion and sophistication reached in State practice to exceed the impression rendered by the status of the ILC products. As future successions are inevitable and legacy issues can spontaneously arise decades after a succession, the challenge for international lawyers in the interim—whether in advising and representing clients or commenting upon the law—will be to depart from the divisive debates of the past by coalescing around a settled consensus concerning the fundamentals of the field. As the experience of the ILC has shown, States will accept general rules of State succession if they are grounded in a compelling and painstaking account of their practice with a conceptual foundation that treats with that practice in a consistent and objective manner.

In orderly and chaotic succession alike, the role of international law is not to deny the politics of the historical event but rather to be blind to them. While this approach leaves room for normative argument concerning the limitations and weaknesses of the positive law, the experience of State succession has amply demonstrated the dangers of normativity assuming pride of place in relation to actual practice. For progressive development to take place, consensus on the current state of the law is necessary. So too is a recognition of the limits of the substantive law: default rules can guide the States concerned and deal with matters not regulated by a succession agreement but they cannot avert the procedural and practical problems that can arise, such as the destruction of documents. Whether a succession was planned or not, its consequences must be faced for the necessities that they are.

# Illustrative List of Successions
# (Chronological)

| Transferred Territory | Date of Succession | Class of Succession | Predecessor(s) | Successor(s) |
|---|---|---|---|---|
| Canada, Dominica, Grenada, Saint Vincent and the Grenadines, Tobago | 10 February 1763[1] | Cession | France | United Kingdom |
| The Thirteen Colonies | 14 January 1784[2] | Secession | United Kingdom | United States of America |
| Louisiana | 21 March 1801 | Cession | Spain | France |
| Louisiana | 20 December 1803[3] | Cession | France | United States |
| West Florida | 22 February 1821[4] | Cession | Spain | United States of America |
| Empire of Brazil | 15 November 1825[5] | Secession | Portugal | Brazil |
| Beylik of Algiers | 5 July 1830 | Absorption | Algiers | France |
| Union of Colombia | 19 November 1831 | Dismemberment | Union of Colombia | New Grenada (Colombia) Venezuela Ecuador |
| Viceroy of Mexico | 28 December 1836[6] | Secession | Spain | Mexico |

---

[1] Definitive Treaty of Peace (France–Spain–Great Britain) (10 February 1763) 42 CTS 279, art XXII.

[2] Definitive Treaty of Peace (Great Britain–United States) (3 September 1783) 48 CTS 487, arts I, V, VII. See also: *Barclay v Russell*, Court of Chancery (27 June 1797) 2 BILC 207, 212–13; *North Carolina v B.C. West, Jr*, North Carolina Court of Appeal (November 1976) 22 AILC 268, 272–73. The latter ruling was upheld by the state supreme court: WS Price, '*N.C. v B.C. West, Jr*', (1978) 41(1) American Archivist 21, 23.

[3] Treaty for the Cession of Louisiana (France-United States) (adopted 30 April 1803, entered into force 21 October 1803) I Malloy 508, arts I–III, VI.

[4] Treaty of Friendship, Cession of the Floridas, and Boundaries (Spain–United States) (adopted 22 February 1819, entered into force 22 February 1821) II Malloy 1651, arts II–III, VI, VIII.

[5] Treaty concerning the Recognition of the Empire of Brazil (Portugal–Brazil) (adopted 29 August 1825, entered into force 15 November 1825) 12 BFSP 674, arts I–IV.

[6] Treaty of Peace and Friendship (Spain–Mexico) (adopted 28 December 1836, entered into force 7 December 1837) 24 BFSP 864, art I.

338    ILLUSTRATIVE LIST OF SUCCESSIONS

| Transferred Territory | Date of Succession | Class of Succession | Predecessor(s) | Successor(s) |
| --- | --- | --- | --- | --- |
| Southern Netherlands | 19 April 1839 | Secession | Netherlands | Belgium |
| New Zealand | 6 February 1840 | Absorption | Aotearoa | United Kingdom |
| Hong Kong | 26 June 1843[7] | Cession | China | United Kingdom |
| Texas | 29 December 1845[8] | Absorption | Texas | United States of America |
| Grand Duchy of Tuscany Duchy of Parma Duchy of Modena and Reggio | 22 March 1860 | Absorptions | Grand Duchy of Tuscany Duchy of Parma Duchy of Modena and Reggio | Sardinia (Italy) |
| Nice and Savoy | 24 March 1860 | Cession | Sardinia | France |
| Kingdom of the Two Sicilies | 18 February 1861 | Absorption | Two Sicilies | Sardinia (Italy) |
| Angor and Battambang | 11 August 1863[9] | Cession | Cambodia | Thailand |
| Kingdom of Hanover Electorate of Hesse Duchy of Nassau Free City of Frankfurt Duchy of Saxe-Lauenburg | 1866 | Absorptions | Kingdom of Hanover Electorate of Hesse Duchy of Nassau Free City of Frankfurt Duchy of Saxe-Lauenburg | Prussia |
| Venetia-Lombardy | 22 October 1866 | Cession | Austria-Hungary | Italy |
| Alaska | 30 March 1867[10] | Cession | Russia | United States of America |
| Papal States | 20 September 1870 | Absorption | Papal States | Sardinia (Italy) |

[7] Treaty of Nanking (China–United Kingdom) (29 August 1842) in WM Mayers, *Treaties between the Empire of China and Foreign Powers* (4th edn, North-China Herald Office 1902) 1–3 (art 4).

[8] Treaty of Peace (Mexico–United States) 2 February 1848 (30 May 1848) 37 BFSP 567, art V.

[9] Treaty of Amity and Commerce (France–Cambodia) (11 August 1863) Recueil des traités 98–134 (French).

[10] Treaty between the United States and Russia (30 March 1867) 24 BFSP 1269, arts II–III, VI (inventories A, B, C, E).

## ILLUSTRATIVE LIST OF SUCCESSIONS 339

| Transferred Territory | Date of Succession | Class of Succession | Predecessor(s) | Successor(s) |
| --- | --- | --- | --- | --- |
| Kingdom of Bavaria Kingdom of Württemberg Grand Duchy of Baden Kingdom of Saxony Grand Duchy of Hesse | 18 January 1871 | Absorptions | Kingdom of Bavaria Kingdom of Württemberg Grand Duchy of Baden Kingdom of Saxony Grand Duchy of Hesse | Prussia (Germany) |
| Kingdom of Fiji | 10 October 1874 | Absorption | Fiji | United Kingdom |
| Principality of Bulgaria | 13 July 1878[11] | Secession | Turkey | Bulgaria |
| Tarapacá | 28 March 1884[12] | Cession | Peru | Chile |
| Empire of Viet Nam | 23 February 1886[13] | Absorption | Viet Nam | France |
| Kingdom of Laos | 7 May 1886[14] | Absorption | Laos | France |
| Kingdom of Pondoland | 7 June 1894[15] | Absorption | Pondoland | United Kingdom |
| Kingdom of Madagascar | 6 August 1896[16] | Absorption | Madagascar | France |
| Hawai'i | 12 August 1898[17] | Absorption | Hawai'i | United States of America |
| Puerto Rico Guam The Philippines | 11 April 1899[18] | Cession | Spain | United States of America |

[11] Treaty of Berlin (13 July 1878) 3 MNRG (2nd Series) 449.

[12] Treaty of Peace and Friendship (Chile–Peru) (adopted 20 October 1883, entered into force 28 March 1884) 74 BFSP 349, arts II–III.

[13] Protectorate Treaty (France–Annam) (adopted 6 June 1884, entered into force 23 February 1886) 12 MNRG (2nd Series) 634, arts 1, 6–7, 12–13, 15, 17 (French).

[14] Trade Convention (France-Siam) (7 May 1886) Recueil des traités 252–58, 315–16 (French). See also: Martin Stuart-Fox, 'The French in Laos, 1887-1945' (1995) 29(1) MAS 111, 116, 118–21.

[15] British Letters Patent for the Annexation of the British Possession of Pondoland (7 June 1894) 86 BFSP 131.

[16] Treaty respecting the Relations between Madagascar and France (18 January 1896) 88 BFSP 1223, arts I–IV. For an overview, see: Daniel Bardonnet, *La Succession d'États à Madagascar* vol I (Librairie Générale de Droit et de Jurisprudence 1970) 23–46.

[17] Joint Resolution annexing the Hawaiian Islands (7 July 1898) 90 BFSP 1250, s 1. See also: Moore (note 2) vol I, 309, 336–38.

[18] Treaty of Peace (Spain–United States) (adopted 10 December 1898, entered into force 11 April 1899) 90 BFSP 382, arts I–III. See further: Moore (note 2) vol I, 520–32.

340   ILLUSTRATIVE LIST OF SUCCESSIONS

| Transferred Territory | Date of Succession | Class of Succession | Predecessor(s) | Successor(s) |
|---|---|---|---|---|
| Cuba | 11 April 1899[19] | Secession | Spain | Cuba |
| Transvaal Republic | 31 May 1902[20] | Absorption | Transvaal Republic | United Kingdom |
| Panama | 3 November 1903 | Secession | Colombia | Panama |
| Atacama | 10 March 1905[21] | Cession | Bolivia | Chile |
| Port Arthur | 15 October 1905[22] | Cession (Administrative) | Russia | Japan |
| Independent State of the Congo | 15 November 1908[23] | Absorption | Independent State of the Congo | Belgium |
| Kingdom of Korea | 22 August 1910[24] | Absorption | Korea | Japan |
| Various territories in Europe | 29 September 1913[25] | Cession | Turkey | Bulgaria |
| Various territories in Europe | 12 August 1913[26] | Cession | Turkey | Serbia |
| Various Mediterannean Islands | 1913[27] | Cession | Turkey | Greece |
| Various Mediterranean Islands | 1913[28] | Cession | Turkey | Italy |
| Various territories in Europe | 1914[29] | Cession | Turkey | Greece |

[19] Treaty of Peace (Spain–United States) (adopted 10 December 1898, entered into force 11 April 1899) 90 BFSP 382, arts I–III. See further: Moore (note 2) vol I, 520–32.

[20] *Madzimbamuto v Lardner-Burke*, Judicial Committee of the Privy Council (23 July 1968) 39 ILR 61, 102–03. E.g. – *Halder v Ministry of Defence and the Provost Marshal of Pretoria*, Supreme Court of South Africa, Transvaal Provincial Division (1 October 1915) 15 CILC 102.

[21] Treaty of Peace (Bolivia–Chile) (adopted 20 October 1904, entered into force 10 March 1905) 98 BFSP 763, art II.

[22] Treaty of Peace (Japan–Russia) 23 August and 6 September 1905 (entered into force 15 October 1905) 98 BFSP 735, arts V–VI (French).

[23] Treaty for the Cession of the Independent State of the Congo to Belgium, 28 November 1907 (15 November 1908) 100 BFSP 705, art 1 (French).

[24] Treaty concerning the incorporation of Korea into the Japanese Empire (Japan–Korea) 103 BFSP 992, arts 1–2 (English). See also: 'The Annexation of Korea to Japan' (1910) 4(4) AJIL 923–25.

[25] Treaty of Peace (Bulgaria–Turkey) (29 September 1913) (1914) 8(1) AJIL 27, arts I, VII, X, XIII; Treaty of Peace between Turkey and the Balkan Allies (30 May 1913) (1914) 8(1) AJIL 12, arts 2, 4; Treaty of Peace between Bulgaria and Roumania, Greece, Montenegro and Servia (1914) 8(1) AJIL 13, arts I–V.

[26] Treaty of Peace between Bulgaria, Greece, Montenegro, Roumania and Serbia (adopted 28 July 1913, entered into force 12 August 1913) 107 BFSP 658, arts I–III (French); Treaty of Peace between Turkey and the Balkan Allies (30 May 1913) (1914) 8(1) AJIL 12, arts 2, 4; Treaty of Peace between Bulgaria and Roumania, Greece, Montenegro and Servia (1914) 8(1) AJIL 13, arts I–V.

[27] Peace Treaty of Lausanne (adopted 24 July 1923, entered into force 6 August 1924) 28 LNTS 11, art 12.

[28] Ibid, art 15.

[29] Treaty of Peace (Turkey–Greece) (11 November 1913) (1914) 8(1) AJIL 46, arts 4–7, 14; Treaty of Peace between Turkey and the Balkan Allies (30 May 1913) (1914) 8(1) AJIL 12, arts 2, 4; Treaty of Peace between Bulgaria and Roumania, Greece, Montenegro and Servia, (1914) 8(1) AJIL 13, arts I–V.

## ILLUSTRATIVE LIST OF SUCCESSIONS 341

| Transferred Territory | Date of Succession | Class of Succession | Predecessor(s) | Successor(s) |
| --- | --- | --- | --- | --- |
| Cyprus, Egypt, Soudan | 5 November 1914[30] | Cession | Turkey | United Kingdom |
| Congress Kingdom of Poland | 30 March 1917[31] | Secession | Russia | Poland |
| Danish West Indies | 31 March 1917[32] | Cession | Denmark | United States of America |
| Iceland | 1 December 1918[33] | Secession (as protected State) | Denmark | Kingdom of Iceland |
| Moresnet, Eupen and Malmédy | 10 January 1920[34] | Cession | Germany | Belgium |
| Alsace-Lorraine | 10 January 1920[35] | Cession | Germany | France |
| Hlučín Region, Upper Silesia | 10 January 1920[36] | Cession | Germany | Czecho-Slovakia |
| Memelland | 10 January 1920[37] | Cession | Germany | Allied Powers (as international protectorate) |
| Danzig | 10 January 1920[38] | Secession | Germany | Free City of Danzig (as international protectorate) |
| Shantung (Kiachow) Lease | 10 January 1920 | Cession (Administrative) | Germany | Japan |
| Estonia | 2 February 1920[39] | Secession | Russia | Estonia |
| Empire of Austria | 16 July 1920[40] | Dismemberment | Austria-Hungary | Austria |
| Kingdom of Hungary | 16 July 1920[41] | Dismemberment | Austria-Hungary | Hungary |

[30] Ibid, arts 17, 20–21.

[31] Krystyna Marek, *Identity and Continuity of States in International Law* (Droz 1968) 417–25.

[32] Convention providing for the Cession of the West Indies (Denmark-United States) (adopted 4 August 1916, entered into force 17 January 1917) (1917) 11(2) AJIL 15, Art 1.

[33] Danish Law providing for the Union of Denmark and Iceland (30 November 1918) 111 BFSP 703, ss 1, 7, 19.

[34] Treaty of Versailles, 28 June 1919 (10 January 1920) (1919) 225 CTS 188, arts 32 Peaslee 34, 36.

[35] Ibid, art 51.

[36] Ibid, arts 81, 83.

[37] Ibid, art 99.

[38] Ibid, arts 100, 102.

[39] Peace Treaty (Russia-Estonia) (2 February 1920) 11 LNTS 29.

[40] Treaty of Saint-Germain-en-Laye, 10 September 1919 (16 July 1920) (1919) 226 CTS 8, preamble; Treaty of Trianon, 4 June 1920 (26 July 1921) 3 Malloy 3539, preamble.

[41] Treaty of Trianon, 4 June 1920 (26 July 1921) 3 Malloy 3539, preamble.

## 342 ILLUSTRATIVE LIST OF SUCCESSIONS

| Transferred Territory | Date of Succession | Class of Succession | Predecessor(s) | Successor(s) |
|---|---|---|---|---|
| Bohemia and Moravia | 16 July 1920[42] | Dismemberment | Austria-Hungary | Czecho-Slovakia |
| Bukovina and Transylvania | 16 July 1920[43] | Dismemberment | Austria-Hungary | Roumania |
| Vojvodina, Montenegro, State of the Slovenes, Croats and Serbs | 16 July 1920[44] | Dismemberment | Austria-Hungary | Serbia |
| Western Thrace | 16 July 1920[45] | Cession | Bulgaria | Greece |
| Latvia | 16 December 1920[46] | Secession | Russia | Latvia |
| Grand Duchy of Finland | 31 December 1920[47] | Secession | Russia | Finland |
| Kaiser-Wilhelmsland | 17 December 1920 | Cession | Germany | League of Nations (as Mandatory – United Kingdom (Dominion of Australia)) |
| Colony of German Samoa | 17 December 1920 | Cession | Germany | League of Nations (as Mandatory Territory – United Kingdom (Dominion of New Zealand)) |
| Colony of Nauru | 17 December 1920 | Cession | Germany | League of Nations (as Mandatory Territory – United Kingdom) |

---

[42] Treaty of Saint-Germain-en-Laye, 10 September 1919 (16 July 1920) (1919) 226 CTS 8, preamble.

[43] Ibid, arts 59, 210.

[44] Treaty of Neuilly-sur-Seine, 27 November 1919 (9 August 1920) (1919) 226 CTS 332, preamble, arts 37, 40–41, 141–42, 177.

[45] Ibid, arts 42, 48.

[46] Peace Treaty (Russia–Latvia) (adopted 11 August 1920, entered into force 16 December 1920) 2 LNTS 195.

[47] Treaty of Peace (Russia–Finland) (adopted 14 October 1920, entered into force 31 December 1920) 12 MNRG (3rd Series) 37, preamble, arts 9, 11, 27–28 (French).

## ILLUSTRATIVE LIST OF SUCCESSIONS 343

| Transferred Territory | Date of Succession | Class of Succession | Predecessor(s) | Successor(s) |
| --- | --- | --- | --- | --- |
| Colony of South West Africa | 17 December 1920 | Cession | Germany | League of Nations (as Mandatory Territory – United Kingdom (Dominion of South Africa)) |
| South Seas Colony | 17 December 1920 | Cession | Germany | League of Nations (as Mandatory Territory – Japan) |
| Territories in Belarus and the Ukraine | 25 September 1921[48] | Cession | Russia | Poland |
| Lithuania | 14 October 1921[49] | Secession | Russia | Lithuania |
| Shantung (Kiachow) Lease | 4 February 1922[50] | Cession | Japan | China |
| Sultanate of Egypt | 28 February 1922[51] | Accession to Independence | United Kingdom | Kingdom of Egypt |
| Territory in Schleswig-Holstein | 10 April 1922[52] | Cession | Germany | Denmark |
| Territories in East Prussia and Upper Silesia | 15 May 1922[53] | Cession | Germany | Poland |
| Colony of East Africa | 19 July 1922 | Cession | Germany | League of Nations (as Mandatory Territories – Belgium,United Kingdom) |

[48] Peace Treaty (Russia–Poland) (adopted 18 March 1921, entered into force 25 September 1921) LNTS 52, art 2.

[49] Peace Treaty (Lithuania–Russia) (adopted 12 July 1920, entered into force 14 October 1920) 3 LNTS 121, arts 1–2.

[50] Treaty for the Settlement of Outstanding Questions Relative to Shantung (Japan–China) (4 February 1922) 10 LNTS 310, art 1.

[51] Circular Despatch stating the decision of His Majesty's Government to terminate the Protectorate and to recognise Egypt as an independent sovereign States (15 March 1922) 116 BFSP 84.

[52] Ibid, art 109. See further: Treaty .concerning the settlement of questions arising out of the transfer to Denmark of North Schleswig (10 April 1922) 10 LNTS 73.

[53] Ibid, art 88. See further: Upper Silesia Convention (15 May 1922) 16 MNRG 645, arts 1, 2(3) 6, 25–39, 207–08, 396, 562, 587 (French); Final Protocol art IV (French).

# 344 ILLUSTRATIVE LIST OF SUCCESSIONS

| Transferred Territory | Date of Succession | Class of Succession | Predecessor(s) | Successor(s) |
|---|---|---|---|---|
| Togoland Protectorate | 20 July 1922 | Cession | Germany | League of Nations (as two Mandatory Territories – France and United Kingdom) |
| Palestine | 24 July 1922[54] | Cession | Turkey | League of Nations (as Mandatory Territory – United Kingdom) |
| Transjordan | 24 July 1922[55] | Cession | Turkey | League of Nations (as Mandatory Territory – United Kingdom) |
| Syria | 24 July 1922[56] | Cession | Turkey | League of Nations (as Mandatory Territory – France) |
| Lebanon | 24 July 1922[57] | Cession | Turkey | League of Nations (as Mandatory Territory – France) |
| Memel Territory | 16 February 1923[58] | Absorption | International Protectorate (France) | Lithuania |

[54] Covenant of the League of Nations (28 June 1919) 108 LNTS 188, art 22. The respective Mandates were published in: (1922) 3 YLN 402.

[55] Ibid.

[56] Ibid.

[57] Ibid.

[58] 'The Status of the Memel Territory' (1924) 5 LNOJ 121, 122–23; Convention concerning the Territory of Memel (adopted 8 May 1924, 27 September 1924) 29 LNTS 86, art 2.

# ILLUSTRATIVE LIST OF SUCCESSIONS   345

| Transferred Territory | Date of Succession | Class of Succession | Predecessor(s) | Successor(s) |
|---|---|---|---|---|
| Mesopotamia | 25 September 1924[59] | Cession | Turkey | League of Nations (as Mandatory Territory – United Kingdom) |
| Dominion of Australia | 15 November 1926* | Secession | United Kingdom | Australia |
| Dominion of New Zealand | 15 November 1926 | Secession | United Kingdom | New Zealand |
| Dominion of Canada | 15 November 1926 | Secession | United Kingdom | Canada |
| Dominion of South Africa | 15 November 1926* | Secession | United Kingdom | South Africa |
| Ireland | 15 November 1926* | Secession | United Kingdom | Irish Free State |
| Vatican City | 7 June 1929 | Cession | Italy | Holy See |
| Mandatory Territory for Mesopotamia | 3 October 1932 | Accession to Independence | United Kingdom | Iraq |
| Republic of Austria | 14 March 1938[60] | Absorption | Austria | Germany |
| Sudetenland | 30 September 1938[61] | Cession | Czecho-Slovakia | Germany |
| Alexandretta | 23 June 1939[62] | Cession | Syria | Turkey |
| Mandatory Territory for Syria and the Lebanon | 1 January 1944[63] | Accession to Independence | France | Syria Lebanon |

[59] Treaty of Alliance (Iraq–United Kingdom) (adopted 10 October 1922, entered into force 19 December 1924) 35 LNTS 14; Council of the League, Fourteenth Meeting (27 September 1924) (1924) 5 LNOJ 1346, 1347.

[60] German Law regarding the Incorporation of Austria in the Reich, 13 March 1938, 142 BFSP (1938) 583, arts 1, 3; German Decree on the Introduction into Austria of Laws of the German Reich, 15 March 1938, 142 BFSP (1938) 584, arts 1, 2, 4; Records of the Nineteenth Ordinary Session of the Assembly, annex 8, Special Supplement No 185 LNOJ 140. Retroactively annulled in: Declaration of Four Powers on General Security (1 November 1943) I FRUS (1943) 761 (annex 6).

[61] Munich Agreement, 29/30 September 1938, 142 BFSP 438, Preamble, arts 1, 7. Retroactively annulled in: Treaty on Mutual Relations (Federal Republic of Germany–Czechoslovakia) (adopted 11 December 1973, entered into force 19 July 1974) 951 UNTS 355, art I.

[62] Settlement of Territorial Questions between Turkey and Syria (France–Turkey) (23 June 1939) 143 BFSP 477, arts 1–4 (French); Protocol, ibid, arts 1–2 (French).

[63] France–Syria–Lebanon, Convention concernant le transfert des Services, 22 December 1943, France Treaty Database, No TRA19430008; IV *Foreign Relations of the United States* (1943), 1055.

## 346  ILLUSTRATIVE LIST OF SUCCESSIONS

| Transferred Territory | Date of Succession | Class of Succession | Predecessor(s) | Successor(s) |
| --- | --- | --- | --- | --- |
| Kingdom of Iceland | 17 June 1944 | Accession to Independence | Denmark | Iceland |
| Free City of Danzig | 2 August 1945[64] | Absorption | Danzig | Poland |
| Mandatory Territory of Transjordan | 25 May 1946 | Accession to Independence | United Kingdom | Jordan |
| Commonwealth of the Philippines | 4 July 1946[65] | Secession | United States of America | Philippines |
| British India | 15 August 1947[66] | Secession | United Kingdom | India, Pakistan, Hyderabad, Khalat |
| Multiple Adriatic islands, Zadar, Istria, Rijeka, Julian March | 15 September 1947[67] | Cession | Italy | Yugoslavia |
| Dodacanese Islands | 15 September 1947[68] | Cession | Italy | Greece |
| Briga and Tenda | 15 September 1947[69] | Cession | Italy | France |
| Saar Territory | 17 December 1947[70] | Cession | Germany | Principal Allied Powers (as international protectorate – France) |
| Province of Burma | 4 January 1948[71] | Secession | United Kingdom | Burma ('Myanmar') |
| Dominion of Ceylon | 4 February 1948 | Secession | United Kingdom | Sri Lanka |

[64] United States–Great Britain–Soviet Union Report of Tripartite Conference of Berlin, 17 July–2 August 1945 (1945) 39 AJIL Sup 245, art XIII.

[65] Proclamation of Philippine Independence, 4 July 1946, 146 BFSP (1946) 899; Treaty of general relations, 4 July 1946 (22 October 1946), 7 UNTS (1947) 3, art I.

[66] Indian Independence Act 1947 c.30, ss 1–2, 7.

[67] Treaty of Peace with Italy (10 February 1947) 49 UNTS 3, arts 2–3, 6, 11, 14.

[68] Ibid.

[69] Ibid.

[70] MM Whiteman, *Digest of International Law* vol III (Government Printing Office 1964) 393–95.

[71] Treaty on Burmese Independence, 17 October 1947 (4 January 1948), 70 UNTS 183, art 1; Burma Independence Act 1947, 11 Geo 6 C 3 (10 December 1947), s 1.

# ILLUSTRATIVE LIST OF SUCCESSIONS 347

| Transferred Territory | Date of Succession | Class of Succession | Predecessor(s) | Successor(s) |
|---|---|---|---|---|
| Mandatory Territory for Palestine | 14 May 1948[72] | Accession to Independence | United Kingdom | Israel |
| Dominion of Newfoundland | 1 April 1949[73] | Cession | United Kingdom | Canada |
| Netherlands East Indies | 27 December 1949[74] | Secession | Netherlands | Indonesia |
| Hyderabad State | 26 January 1950 | Absorption | Hyderabad | India |
| Colony of Libya | 24 December 1951[75] | Secession | Italy | Libya |
| Free Town of Chandernagore | 9 June 1952[76] | Cession | France | India |
| Colony of Eritrea | 15 September 1952[77] | Cession | Italy | Ethiopia |
| Kingdom of Laos | 22 October 1953[78] | Secession | France | Laos |
| Kingdom of Cambodia | 9 November 1953[79] | Secession | France | Cambodia |
| Protectorate of Tonkin | 21 July 1954[80] | Secession | France | Democratic Republic of Viet Nam ('North Viet Nam') |
| Protectorate of Annam, Colony of Cochinchina | 21 July 1954[81] | Secession | France | Republic of Viet Nam ('South Viet Nam') |

[72] Proclamation of Independence of the State of Israel, 14 May 1948, I *Laws of the State of Israel*, 3; Palestine Act 1948 c.27, ss 1–2.

[73] British North America Act 1949, 153 BFSP (1949) 130, ss 1–2; Schedule ('Terms of Union of Newfoundland with Canada'), para 50.

[74] Round-Table Conference Agreement (2 November 1949) (Indonesia-Netherlands) 69 UNTS 200; Act of Transfer of Sovereignty and Recognition (27 December 1949) ibid, 392.

[75] UNGA Res 387(V) (17 November 1950); UNGA Res 995(X) (14 December 1955).

[76] Indo-French Treaty of Cession of the Free Town of Chandernagore, 2 February 1951 (9 June 1952), 158 BFSP (1951) 599, art I.

[77] UNGA Res 390(V) (2 December 1950) 1.

[78] France–Laos, Treaty of Friendship and Association, 22 October 1953, 160 BFSP (1953) 658, art I (French).

[79] E.g. – Cambodia–France, Protocol regarding the transfer of Military Control, 17 October 1953, 160 BFSP (1953) 623, art 1 (French).

[80] Final Declaration of the Geneva Conference on Indo-China, 21 July 1954, 161 BFSP (1954) 359, paras 1–2, 5–7, 10–11, Annex F (French).

[81] Final Declaration of the Geneva Conference on Indo-China, 21 July 1954, 161 BFSP (1954) 359, paras 1–2, 5–7, 10–11, Annex F (French).

## 348 ILLUSTRATIVE LIST OF SUCCESSIONS

| Transferred Territory | Date of Succession | Class of Succession | Predecessor(s) | Successor(s) |
|---|---|---|---|---|
| Khanate of Khalat | 14 October 1955 | Absorption | Khalat | Pakistan |
| Condominium of the Sudan | 1 January 1956 | Secession | Egypt United Kingdom | Sudan |
| Kingdom of Tunisia | 20 March 1956[82] | Accession to Independence | France | Kingdom of Tunisia |
| Spanish Protectorate in Morocco | 7 April 1956[83] | Cession | Spain | Morocco |
| French Protectorate in Morocco | 28 May 1956[84] | Accession to Independence | France | Morocco |
| Saar Territory | 1 January 1957[85] | Absorption | International Protectorate (France) | West Germany |
| Dominion of Ghana | 5 March 1957 | Secession | United Kingdom | Ghana |
| Federation of Malaya | 31 August 1957[86] | Secession | United Kingdom | Malaya |
| Arab Republic of Egypt, Arab Republic of Syria | 1 March 1958[87] | Merger | Egypt, Syria | United Arab Republic |
| Overseas Territory of French Guinea | 2 October 1958[88] | Secession | France | Guinea |
| Trust Territory of French Cameroon | 1 January 1960 | Accession to Independence | France | Cameroon |

[82] Treaty of Friendship (France–Tunis) (12 May 1881) 72 BFSP 247, arts I–VII. See further, e.g. – *Orsini v Ferrovecchio*, Court of Cassation of France (28 July 1925) 3 ILR 39 (note); *Falla-Nataf and Brothers v Germany*, Franco-German Mixed Arbitral Tribunal (30 December 1927) 4 ILR 44; *Nationality Decrees Issued in Tunis and Morocco (French Zone) on November 8, 1921* (Advisory Opinion) PCIJ Series B No 4.

[83] Morocco–Spain, Joint Declaration on Moroccan Independence, 7 April 1956, 162 BFSP (1955–1956) 1017.

[84] Morocco–France, Joint Declaration on Moroccan Independence, 2 March 1956, 162 BFSP (1955–1956) 958 (French).

[85] Treaty for the Settlement of the Question of the Saar (adopted 27 October 1956, entered into force 1 January 1957) 1053 UNTS 3, art 1.

[86] Federation of Malaya Independence Act 1957, 5 & 6 Eliz. II (c.60), s.1(1); Agreement on the independence of Malaya, 5 August 1957, 163 BFSP (1957–58) 46, art 3; UNSC Resn 125 (5 September 1957); UNGA Resn 1134 (XII), 17 September 1957.

[87] Young, 'State of Syria: Old or New?', AJIL (1962) 482, 484; Cotran, 'Some Legal Aspects of the Formation of the United Arab Republic and the United Arab States', 8(2) *ICLQ* (1959) 346, 347.

[88] Fischer, 'L'indépendance de la Guinée et les accords franco-guinéens', 4 *AFDI* (1958) 711–22.

## ILLUSTRATIVE LIST OF SUCCESSIONS    349

| Transferred Territory | Date of Succession | Class of Succession | Predecessor(s) | Successor(s) |
|---|---|---|---|---|
| Federation of Mali | 20 June 1960 | Secession | France | Federation of Mali |
| Colony of the Belgian Congo | 30 June 1960[89] | Secession | Belgium | Democratic Republic of the Congo |
| Trust Territory for Somalia | 1 July 1960[90] | Accession to Independence | Italy | Somalia |
| Somaliland Protectorate, Trust Territory for Somalia | 1 July 1960[91] | Merger | Somaliland, Trust Territory for Somalia | Somalia |
| Autonomous Republic of Mauritania | 28 July 1960 | Secession | France | Mauritania |
| Autonomous Republic of Dahomey | 1 August 1960 | Secession | France | Benin |
| Overseas Territory of Madagascar | 3 August 1960[92] | Secession | France | Madagascar |
| Autonomous Republic of Niger | 3 August 1960 | Secession | France | Niger |
| Autonomous Republic of Upper Volta | 5 August 1960 | Secession | France | Burkina Faso |
| Autonomous Republic of Côte d'Ivoire | 7 August 1960 | Secession | France | Côte d'Ivoire |
| Crown Colony of Cyprus | 9 August 1960 | Secession | United Kingdom | Cyprus |
| Autonomous Republic of Chad | 11 August 1960 | Secession | France | Chad |

[89] Loi fondamentale relative aux structures du Congo du 19 mai 1960, *Moniteur congolais* (27 mai 1960), 1535–83, arts 2, 189, 263, in Lyman et al, *Legal Aspects of the United Nations Action in the Congo* (Oceana Publications 1963), 108–16; Constitution of the Congo (Leopoldville), 30 May 1964, art 195.

[90] E.g. – Cotran, 'Legal Problems Arising Out of the Formation of the Somali Republic', 12 ICLQ (1963), 1010–26, 1011.

[91] Law of Union between Somaliland and Somalia, 27 June 1960, 164 BFSP 697, ss 2–3, 11.

[92] Accord particulier portant transfert à la République Malgache des compétences de la Communauté, 153 *JORF* (2 juillet 1960) 5968, art 1.

350 ILLUSTRATIVE LIST OF SUCCESSIONS

| Transferred Territory | Date of Succession | Class of Succession | Predecessor(s) | Successor(s) |
| --- | --- | --- | --- | --- |
| Autonomous Republic of Central Africa | 13 August 1960 | Secession | France | Central African Republic |
| Autonomous Republic of the Congo | 15 August 1960 | Secession | France | Republic of the Congo |
| Federation of Mali | 20 August 1960 | Dismemberment | Federation of Mali | Senegal Mali |
| Colony and Protectorate of Nigeria | 1 October 1960 | Secession | United Kingdom | Nigeria |
| Autonomous Republic of Gabon | 17 October 1960 | Secession | France | Gabon |
| Syria Region | 29 September 1961 | Secession | United Arab Republic | Syria |
| Colony and Protectorate of Sierra Leone | 27 April 1961 | Secession | United Kingdom | Sierra Leone |
| Trust Territory for the British Cameroons | 1 June & 1 October 1961 | Dismemberment | Trust Territory for the British Cameroons | Nigeria Cameroon |
| Emirate of Kuwait | 19 June 1961 | Accession to Independence | United Kingdom | Kuwait |
| Dadra and Nagar Haveli | 11 August 1961[93] | Cession | Portugal | India |
| Trust Territory for Tanganyika | 9 December 1961[94] | Accession to Independence | United Kingdom | Tanganyika |
| Trust Territory for Western Samoa | 1 January 1962 | Accession to Independence | New Zealand | Samoa |
| Overseas Territory of Portuguese India | 1961 and 1962[95] | Cession | Portugal | India |

[93] Dadra and Nagar Haveli Act 1961 (Act 35 of 1961), ss 6–8; Treaty on recognition of India's sovereignty over Goa, Daman, Diu, Dadra and Nagar Haveli, 31 December 1974 (3 June 1975), 982 UNTS 153, art I.

[94] Tanganyika Independence Act 1961 c.1, s.1(1); Tanganyika (Constitution) Order in Council 1961, S.I. 1961, no 2274, Sch II.

[95] Treaty on Recognition of India's Sovereignty over Goa, Daman, Diu, Dadra and Nagar Haveli (adopted 31 December 1974, entered into force 3 June 1975) 982 UNTS 153, art I.

## ILLUSTRATIVE LIST OF SUCCESSIONS    351

| Transferred Territory | Date of Succession | Class of Succession | Predecessor(s) | Successor(s) |
| --- | --- | --- | --- | --- |
| Trust Territory for Ruanda-Urundi | 1 July 1962 | Accession to Independence | Belgium | Rwanda Burundi |
| Crown Colony of Trinidad and Tobago | 31 August 1962 | Secession | United Kingdom | Trinidad and Tobago |
| Uganda Protectorate | 9 October 1962 | Secession | United Kingdom | Uganda |
| Goa, Daman and Diu | 5 August 1962[96] | Cession | Portugal | India |
| Crown Colony of Jamaica | 6 August 1962 | Secession | United Kingdom | Jamaica |
| Colony of West New Guinea (West Irian) | 1 May 1963[97] | Cession | Netherlands | Indonesia |
| French Settlements in India | 1 July 1963[98] | Cession | France | India |
| Crown Colonies of Singapore, North Borneo ('Sabah'), Sarawak | 16 September 1963[99] | Cession | United Kingdom | Malaysia |
| Colony and Protectorate of Kenya | 12 December 1963 | Secession | United Kingdom | Kenya |
| Sultanate of Zanzibar | 10 December 1963[100] | Secession | United Kingdom | Zanzibar |
| Republic of Zanzibar, Republic of Tanganyika | 26 April 1964[101] | Merger | Zanzibar, Tanganyika | Tanzania |

[96] Goa, Daman and Diu (Administration) Act, 27 March 1962, ss 4–5; Treaty on recognition of India's sovereignty over Goa, Daman, Diu, Dadra and Nagar Haveli, 31 December 1974 (3 June 1975), 982 UNTS 153, art I.

[97] Agreement concerning West New Guinea (West Irian), 15 August 1962, 437 UNTS (1962) 273, 1(2) ILM (1962) 231.

[98] Indo–French Treaty ceding the French Establishments to India, 28 May 1956 (16 August 1962), 162 BFSP (1955–1956) 848, arts 1, 3–10, 14, 19, 26–27; Protocol, art 8.

[99] Agreement concerning the Federation of Malaysia, 9 July 1963, Cmnd 2094, art I; Malaysia Act 1963 c.35, s.1.

[100] Zanzibar–United Kingdom, Exchange of letters terminating the 1890 Agreement as respects the dominions of the Sultan (2 & 12 November 1963), Cmd. 2218 (December 1963).

[101] Acts of Union of Tanganyika and Zanzibar 1964, 3(4) ILM (July 1964) 763, s 4.

## 352  ILLUSTRATIVE LIST OF SUCCESSIONS

| Transferred Territory | Date of Succession | Class of Succession | Predecessor(s) | Successor(s) |
|---|---|---|---|---|
| Protectorate of Nyasaland | 4 July 1964 | Secession | United Kingdom | Malawi |
| Crown Colony of Malta | 21 September 1964 | Secession | United Kingdom | Malta |
| Protectorate of Northern Rhodesia | 24 October 1964 | Secession | United Kingdom | Zambia |
| Singapore state | 9 August 1965[102] | Secession | Malaysia | Singapore |
| Colony of British Guiana | 26 May 1966 | Secession | United Kingdom | Guyana |
| Protectorate of Bechuanaland | 30 September 1966 | Secession | United Kingdom | Botswana |
| Crown Colony of Basutoland | 4 October 1966 | Secession | United Kingdom | Lesotho |
| Crown Colony of Barbados | 30 November 1966 | Secession | United Kingdom | Barbados |
| Federation of South Arabia Protectorate of South Arabia | 30 November 1967 | Secession | United Kingdom | South Yemen |
| Crown Colony of Mauritius | 12 March 1968[103] | Secession | United Kingdom | Mauritius |
| Overseas Territory of Spanish Guinea | 12 October 1968[104] | Secession | Spain | Equatorial Guinea |
| Overseas Territory of Ifni | 4 January 1969[105] | Cession | Spain | Morocco |
| Kingdom of Tonga | 4 June 1970 | Accession to Independence | United Kingdom | Tonga |
| Province of East Pakistan | 10 April 1971 | Secession | Pakistan | Bangladesh |

[102] Independence of Singapore Agreement, 7 August 1965, 4 ILM (1965) 928, 933 (art II); Constitution and Malaysia (Singapore Amendment) Act 1965, ibid, ss 3, 6.

[103] Mauritius Independence Act 1968, 16 & 17 Eliz. II c.8, s.1(1); Mauritius Independence Order 1968, GN No 54 of 1968 (6 March 1968), art 3(1).

[104] Decree No 2467/1968 of 9 October 1968.

[105] Spain-Morroco, Tratado sobre retrocesión de Ifni, firmado 4 de enero de 1969 (9 de enero de 1971), BOE (5 junio 1969) 8805, art 1.

## ILLUSTRATIVE LIST OF SUCCESSIONS    353

| Transferred Territory | Date of Succession | Class of Succession | Predecessor(s) | Successor(s) |
| --- | --- | --- | --- | --- |
| Emirate of Bahrain | 15 August 1971 | Accession to Independence | United Kingdom | Bahrain |
| Emirate of Qatar | 3 September 1971 | Accession to Independence | United Kingdom | Qatar |
| East Germany | June 1973 | Secession | Germany | East Germany |
| Crown Colony of the Bahamas | 10 July 1973 | Secession | United Kingdom | Bahamas |
| Overseas Territory of Portuguese Guinea | 10 September 1974 | Secession | Portugal | Guinea-Bissau |
| Overseas Territory of Mozambique | 25 June 1975 | Secession | Portugal | Mozambique |
| Suriname | 25 November 1975 | Secession | Netherlands | Suriname |
| Trust Territory for New Guinea | 16 September 1975 | Accession to Independence | Australia | Papua New Guinea |
| Overseas Territory of Portuguese Angola | 11 November 1975 | Secession | Portugal | Angola |
| Northern Mariana Islands | 24 March 1976[106] | Cession | Trust Territory for the Pacific Islands | United States of America |
| Crown Colony of the Seychelles | 29 June 1976 | Secession | United Kingdom | Seychelles |
| Democratic Republic of Viet Nam ('North Viet Nam'), Republic of South Viet Nam | 2 July 1976[107] | Merger | North Viet Nam, South Viet Nam | Viet Nam |
| Gilbert Islands | 12 July 1979 | Secession | United Kingdom | Kiribati |
| Crown Colony of Rhodesia | 18 April 1980 | Secession | United Kingdom | Zimbabwe |
| New Hebrides Condominium | 30 July 1980 | Secession | France, United Kingdom | Vanuatu |

[106] Covenant to establish a Commonwealth of the Northern Mariana Islands (adopted 15 February 1975, entered into force 24 March 1976) 14 ILM 344, art I.

[107] The 1959 Constitution of North Viet Nam was adopted for Viet Nam – Resolution of the National Assembly of the Socialist Republic of Vietnam on the Organization and Operation of the State (2 July 1976) (Vietnamese), §1.

## 354 ILLUSTRATIVE LIST OF SUCCESSIONS

| Transferred Territory | Date of Succession | Class of Succession | Predecessor(s) | Successor(s) |
| --- | --- | --- | --- | --- |
| Colony of British Honduras | 21 September 1981 | Secession | United Kingdom | Belize |
| Sultanate of Brunei | 1 January 1984 | Accession to Independence | United Kingdom | Brunei |
| District of the Northern Mariana Islands | 21 October 1986[108] | Cession | Trust Territory for the Pacific Islands | United States of America |
| District of Micronesia | 21 October 1986[109] | Accession to Independence | United States of America | Micronesia |
| District of the Marshall Islands | 21 October 1986[110] | Accession to Independence | United States of America | Marshall Islands |
| Mandatory Territory for South West Africa | 21 March 1990[111] | Accession to Independence | United Nations, South Africa | Namibia |
| Republic of Yemen ('North Yemen'), People's Democratic Republic of Yemen ('South Yemen') | 22 May 1990[112] | Merger | North Yemen, South Yemen | Yemen |
| Federal Republic of Germany ('West Germany'), Democratic Republic of Germany ('East Germany') | 3 October 1990[113] | Absorption | East Germany | West Germany |

---

[108] Proclamation 5564 (3 November 1986), 51 Federal Register 40339.

[109] Ibid.

[110] Ibid.

[111] UNGA Resn S-18/1 (23 April 1990); UNGA Resn 44/243(A)(11 September 1990).

[112] Agreement proclaiming the Republic of Yemen, Sana'a, 22 April 1990 (22 May 1990), arts 1, 8.

[113] Treaty on the Establishment of German Unity, 30 August 1990 (3 October 1990), 30 ILM (1991) 463, art 1; Treaty on Final Settlement, 12 September 1990, 1696 UNTS 123, 29 ILM (1990) 1187, arts 1(1), 7.

## ILLUSTRATIVE LIST OF SUCCESSIONS  355

| Transferred Territory | Date of Succession | Class of Succession | Predecessor(s) | Successor(s) |
|---|---|---|---|---|
| Soviet Socialist Republic of the Ukraine, Soviet Socialist Republic of Belarus, Soviet Socialist Republic of Moldova, Soviet Socialist Republic of | 26 December 1991[114] | Secession | Soviet Union ('Russia') | Ukraine, Belarus, Moldova, Georgia, Armenia, Azerbaijan, Kazakhstan, Kyrgyzstan, Turkmenistan, Tajikstan |
| Georgia, Soviet Socialist Republic of Armenia, Soviet Socialist Republic of Azerbaijan, Soviet Socialist Republic of Kazakhstan, Soviet Socialist Republic of | | | | |
| Kyrgyzstan, Soviet Socialist Republic of Turkmenistan, Soviet Socialist Republic of Tajikstan | | | | |
| Socialist Republic of Slovenia | 25 June 1991[115] | Dismemberment | Socialist Federal Republic of Yugoslavia | Slovenia |
| Socialist Republic of Croatia | 25 June 1991[116] | Dismemberment | Socialist Federal Republic of Yugoslavia | Slovenia |

---

[114] Hamant, *Démembrement de l'URSS et problèmes de succession d'États* (2007), 76–90, 177–78.
[115] Conference on Yugoslavia, Arbitration Commission, Opinion No 1 (29 November 1991), 92 ILR 162, 165.
[116] Ibid.

356   ILLUSTRATIVE LIST OF SUCCESSIONS

| Transferred Territory | Date of Succession | Class of Succession | Predecessor(s) | Successor(s) |
|---|---|---|---|---|
| Socialist Republic of Macedonia | September 1991[117] | Dismemberment | Socialist Federal Republic of Yugoslavia | The Former Yugoslav Republic of Macedonia ('North Macedonia') |
| Socialist Republic of Bosnia and Herzegovina | September 1991[118] | Dismemberment | Socialist Federal Republic of Yugoslavia | Bosnia and Herzegovina |
| Socialist Republic of Serbia, Socialist Republic of Montenegro | 27 April 1992[119] | Dismemberment | Socialist Federal Republic of Yugoslavia | Federal Republic of Yugoslavia |
| Czechoslovak Socialist Republic | 31 December 1992[120] | Dismemberment | Czecho-Slovakia | Czech Republic Slovakia |
| Province of Eritrea | 24 May 1993[121] | Secession | Ethiopia | Eritrea |
| Walvis Bay | 1 March 1994[122] | Cession | South Africa | Namibia |
| District of Palau | 1 October 1994[123] | Accession to Independence | United States of America | Palau |
| British Dependent Territory of Hong Kong | 30 June 1997[124] | Cession | United Kingdom | China |
| Overseas Territory of Macao | 20 December 1999[125] | Cession | Portugal | China |

[117] Bethlehem and Weller, *The Yugoslav Crisis* (1997), xxvii–xxx.

[118] Ibid.

[119] 'Letter dated 6 May 1992 from the Permanent Mission of Yugoslavia to the United Nations', UN Doc A/46/915 (7 May 1992); Application of the FRY for admission to membership in the United Nations, UN Doc A/55/528-S/2000/1043 (30 October 2009).

[120] Czechia Constitutional Act No 542/1992 Zákony Prolidi Coll (25 November 1992) arts 1–2, 6, 8 (Czecho-Slovak).

[121] 'Application of Eritrea for admission to membership in the United Nations', UN Doc A/47/948-S/25793 (18 May 1993), Annex.

[122] Namibia-South Africa, Agreement with respect to Walvis Bay, 28 February 1994 (1 March 1994), 2548 UNTS 17, art 2.

[123] Proclamation 6826 (27 September 1994), 108 Stat 5631, s.1; UN Trusteeship Council Resn 2199 (LXI).

[124] China–United Kingdom, Joint Declaration on Hong Kong, 19 December 1984 (27 May 1985), 1399 UNTS 33, arts 1–2.

[125] Portugal–China, Joint Declaration on Macao, 13 April 1987 (15 January 1988), 1498 UNTS 228, arts 1–2.

| Transferred Territory | Date of Succession | Class of Succession | Predecessor(s) | Successor(s) |
|---|---|---|---|---|
| Overseas Territory of Timor | 25 May 2002 with retroactive effect from 29 November 1975[126] | Secession | Portugal | Timor-Leste |
| Republic of Montenegro | 15 June 2006[127] | Secession | Federal Republic of Yugoslavia ('State Union of Serbia and Montenegro') | Montenegro |
| Southern Sudan | 9 July 2011[128] | Secession | Sudan | South Sudan |

[126] Indonesia–Portugal, Agreement on East Timor, 5 May 1999, 2062 UNTS 7, arts 1, 5–6; Constitution of Timor-Leste, 22 March 2002 (25 May 2002), ss 1(2), 165, http://timor-leste.gov.tl/wp-content/uploads/2010/03/Constitution_RDTL_ENG.pdf; Timor-Leste, Law on the Interpretation of the Law in Force on 19 May 2002 No 2/2002, *Jornal da República*, Series I, art 1 (Portuguese & Tetum).

[127] Vidmar, 'Montenegro's Path to Independence: A Study of Self-Determination, Statehood and Recognition', 3(1) *HLR* (2007), 73–102, 99.

[128] Gray and McConnell, 'Jubilation as South Sudan declares independence', *The Times* (9 July 2011).

# Primary Bibliography

African Union Border Programme, 'Delimitation and Demarcation of Boundaries in Africa: General Issues and Case Studies' (2014) <https://archives.au.int/handle/123456789/5042> accessed 1 January 2024

Ago R, 'First Report on State Responsibility', UN Doc A/CN.4/217 and Add. 1 (7 May 1969 and 20 January 1970)

Aguilar FV, 'Report on Citizenship Law: Philippines', EUI Country Report 2017/01 (January 2017)

Ahmed DM, *Boundaries and Secession in Africa and International Law* (CUP 2015)

Ahmed M, 'Sudan and South Sudan: New Era, New Opportunities' (23 July 2011) <https://www.imf.org/en/News/Articles/2015/09/28/04/54/vc072311> accessed 3 January 2024

Aitchison CU, A Collection of Treaties, Engagements and Sanads relating to India and Neighbouring Countries (Government of India Central Publication Branch 1931)

Akehurst M, 'State Responsibility for the Wrongful Acts of Rebels—An Aspect of the Southern Rhodesian Problem' 43 BYIL (1968–1969) 49

Aktar C and Giragosian R, 'Turkey–Armenia Relations' (October 2013) <https://www.europarl.europa.eu/RegData/etudes/note/join/2013/433710/EXPO-AFET_NT(2013)433710_EN.pdf> accessed 1 January 2024.

Akweenda S, 'The Legal Significance of Maps in Boundary Questions' (1989) 60 BYIL 205

Alan D, 'Chronique des faits internationaux' (1975) 79 RGDIP 165

Amerasinghe CF, *Diplomatic Protection* (OUP 2008)

Amin SH, *Law and Justice in Contemporary Yemen: People's Democratic Republic of Yemen and Yemen Arab Republic* (Royston Limited 1987)

Argudo Périz JL and Pérez Milla JJ, 'Vinculacion Nacional y Nacionalidad de los habitantes de los territorios descolonizados del Africa Española' (1991) 1 Acciones E Investigaciones Sociales 152

Ashesh A and Thiruvengadam A, 'Report on Citizenship Law: India', Country Report 2017/12, European University Institute (July 2017)

As-Saruri M and Sorkhabi R, 'Petroleum Basins of Yemen' (2016) 13(2) GEOExPro <https://www.geoexpro.com/articles/2016/04/petroleum-basins-of-yemen> accessed 13 January 2024

Aufricht H, 'State Succession under the Law and Practice of the International Monetary Fund' (1962) 11 ICLQ 154

Aulakh HS and Asombang WW, *Economic Development Strategies for Independent Namibia* (UN Institute for Namibia 1989)

Aust A, *Modern Treaty Law and Practice* (CUP 2013)

Babiker MA, 'Report on Citizenship Law: Sudan', European University Institute Country Report No. 2022/05 (July 2022)

Bahmaei MA and Mehrabi HF, 'The Valuation Date of an Unlawfully Expropriated Property in International Investment Arbitration: A Critique of Acquisitive Valuation' (2021) 36(2) ICSID Review 441

Baker PJN, *The Present Juridical Status of the British Dominions in International Law* (Longmans, Green & Co 1929)

Ballreich et al (eds), *Fontes Iuris Gentium: Decisions of German Superior Courts relating to International Law* (Carl Heymanns Verlag KG 1956)

Bardonnet D, 'Les minorités asiatiques à Madagascar' (1964) 10 AFDI 127

Bardonnet D, 'La succession aux traités à Madagascar' (1966) 12 AFDI 593

Bardonnet D, *La Succession d'États à Madagascar* vol I and II (Libraire Générale de Droit et de Jurisprudence 1970)

360    PRIMARY BIBLIOGRAPHY

Bartoš T, 'Uti Possidetis. Quo Vadis?' (1997) 18 Australian Yearbook of International Law 37

Batchelor C, Leclerc P, and Schack B, 'Citizenship and Prevention of Statelessness Linked to the Disintegration of the Socialist Federal Republic of Yugoslavia' (1997) 3(1) European Series

Beaudoin A, *Uti possidetis et sécession* (Dalloz 2011)

Bedjaoui A, 'Problemes recents de successions d'Etats dans les Etats nouveaux' (1970-II) 130 RdC 455–586

Bedjaoui M, 'Article 73' in JP Cot and A Pellet (eds) *La Charte des Nations-Unies* vol II (Economica 2005) 1753

Bedjaoui M, 'Eleventh Report on Succession of States in respect of Matters other than Treaties', UN Doc A/CN.4/322 and Corr.1 & Add.1 & 2 (18, 29, and 31 May 1979)

Bedjaoui M, *Law and the Algerian Revolution* (International Association of Democratic Lawyers 1961)

Beemelmans H, 'State Succession in International Law: Remarks on Recent Theory and State Practice' (1997) 15 BUILJ 71

Bekker P, 'Reimagining the Damages Valuation Framework Underlying Fair and Equitable Treatment Standard Violations through a Three-Stage Contextual Approach' (2021) 36(2) ICSID Review 339

Bentwich N, 'Nationality in Mandated Territories Detached from Turkey' (1926) 7 BYIL 97

Bentwich N, 'State Succession and Act of State in the Palestine Courts' (1943) 23 BYIL 330

Bethlehem D and Weller M (eds), *The Yugoslav Crisis in International Law* (CUP 1997)

Billot A, *L'affaire du Tonkin* (Hachette Livre 1886)

Blackstone W, *Commentaries on the Lawes of England* vol I (J.B. Lippincott 1765)

Blumenwitz D, *Staatenachfolge und die Einigung Deutschlands* (Teil I 1992)

Bluntschli JC, *Das moderne Völkerrecht der civilisirten Staten als Rechstbuch Dargestellt* (Beck 1868)

Bodeau-Livinec P and Morgan-Foster J, 'Article 53 Convention of 1969' in Olivier Corten and Pierre Klein (eds) *The Vienna Convention on the Law of Treaties: A Commentary* vol II (OUP 2011)

Bohatá M, 'Privatization in Czechoslovakia' in Koslowski (ed) *Ethics in Economics, Business and Economic Policy* (Springer-Verlag 1992)

Boll AM, *Multiple Nationality and International Law* (Martinus Nijhoff 2007)

Bonnitcha J and Brewin S, 'Compensation under Investment Treaties', International Institute for Sustainable Development Best Practice Series (November 2020)

Bonnitcha J, Langford M, Alvarez-Zarate JM, and Behn D, 'Damages and ISDS Reform: Between Procedure and Substance', UNCITRAL Working Group III Academic Forum Paper (26 August 2021) <https://uncitral.un.org/sites/uncitral.un.org/files/media-documents/uncitral/en/damages_and_isds_-_uncitral_af_paper.pdf> accessed 13 January 2024

Borchard EM, 'Opinion on the Roumanian-Hungarian Dispute before the Council of the League of Nations' (1928) 16(2) CLR 120

Bowett D, 'The Dubai Sharjah Boundary Arbitration of 1981' (1994) 65 BYIL 103

Bracton H, *Tractatus de legibus et consuetudinibus regni Angliae* (c 1188) Fol. 382, 382b

Brandt HH, 'Die Regelung der österreichischen Bundesschulden' (1939) 9 HJIL 127

Brocheux P, 'Les relations économiques entre la France et le Vietnam, 1955–1975' (2017) 2 Outre-Mers 193

Brown DJL, 'The Ethiopia–Somaliland Frontier Dispute' (1956) 5 ICLQ 245

Brown DJL, 'Recent Developments in the Ethiopia–Somaliland Frontier Dispute'(1961) 10 ICLQ 167

Brown PM, 'The Ottoman Public Debt Arbitration'(1926) 20 AJIL 135, 139

Buckland WW, *A Text-Book of Roman Law from Augustus to Justinian* (OUP 1932)

Bühler K, 'State Succession, Identity/Continuity and Membership in the United Nations' in Eisemann and Koskenniemi (eds) *State Succession: Codification Tested against the Facts* (Martinus Nijhoff 2000)

Burdick AB, 'The Constitution of the Federated States of Micronesia' (1986) 8(2) UHLR 419

# PRIMARY BIBLIOGRAPHY    361

Bureau of the Fiscal Service, Unpaid Foreign Claims: Vietnam, <https://www.fiscal.treasury.gov/unpaid-foreign-claims/vietnam-claimshtml> accessed 2 January 2024

Caflisch L, 'La nationalité des sociétés commerciales en droit international privé' (1967) 24 ASDI

Caflisch L, *La Protection des Sociétés Commerciales et les Intérêts Indirects en Droit International Public* (Martinus Nijhoff 1969)

Cahn HJ, 'The Responsibility of the Successor State for War Debts' (1950) 44 AJIL 477

Castelucci P, 'Comentario a la sentencia del Tribunal Supremo de 20 de julio de 2020' (2021) 13(1) CDT 799

Charpentier J, 'La pratique française de droit international' (1963) 9 AFDI1021

Cheema TS, *Pakistan Bangladesh Relations* (Unistar 2013)

Cheng B, *General Principles of Law as Applied by International Courts and Tribunals* (CUP 1953)

Climate Diplomacy, 'Transboundary Water Disagreements between South Africa and Namibia' <https://climate-diplomacy.org/case-studies/transboundary-water-disagreements-betw een-south-africa-and-namibia#:~:text=Since%20Namibia%20gained%20independence%20 and,Highlands%20Water%20Project%20(LHWP)> accessed 1 January 2024.

Clute RE, *The International Legal Status of Austria 1938–1955* (Springer 1962)

Cohen R, 'Legal Problems arising from the Dissolution of the Mali Federation' (1960) 36 BYIL 375

Collins RO, 'The Illami Triangle' (2004) 20 Annales d'Éthiopie 5

Colonial Office, 'Report of the Somaliland Protectorate Constitutional Conference' (May 1960) Cmd 1044, annex VIII ('Draft Somaliland Ordinance')

Commission des réparations, *La répartition de la dette publique d'avant-guerre autrichienne et hongroise* vol VII (1925) 12–13, 39 (annexe D) 45–48 (annexe G)

Commonwealth Relations Office, 'Note of a Meeting held to discuss the rehousing of the India Office Library' (19 January 1961) National Archives, Doc T 296/33

Conference on Yugoslavia Arbitration Commission, Opinion No 1 (29 November 1991) 92 ILR 162, 165

*Consolidated Debt of New Grenada Cases*, US–Colombian Claims Commission (1864) IV Moore 3612.

Constitution of Georgia (24 August 1995) in *World Constitutions Illustrated Database* <https://home.heinonline.org/content/world-constitutions-illustrated/> accessed 1 January 2024

Coret A, *Le Condominium* (Pichon & Durand-Auzias 1960)

Corten O, 'Droit des peuples à disposer d'eux-mêmes et uti possidetis: deux faces d'une même médaille?', 31 Revue Belge de Droit International (1998)

Corten O and Klein P (eds), *The Vienna Convention on the Law of Treaties: A Commentary* (OUP 2011)

Costelloe D, 'The Role of Domestic Law in the Identification of General Principles of law under Article 48(1)(c) of the Statute of the International Court of Justice' in Andendas et al (eds) *General Principles and the Coherence of International Law* (Brill 2019) 185

Cotran E, 'Legal Problems Arising Out of the Formation of the Somali Republic' (1963) 12 ICLQ 1010, 1011

Craven M, 'The European Community Arbitration Commission on Yugoslavia' (1995) 66 BYIL 333

Craven M, *The Decolonization of International Law: State Succession and the Law of Treaties* (OUP 2007)

Craven M, 'Colonial Fragments: Decolonization, Concessions, and Acquired Rights' in J von Bernstorff and P Dann (eds) *The Battle for International Law: South–North Perspectives on the Decolonization Era* (OUP 2019)

Crawford J, 'First Report on State Responsibility', UN Doc A/CN.4/490 (24 April 1998) para 279

Crawford J, *The Creation of States in International Law* (OUP 2006)

Crawford J, *Brownlie's Principles of Public International Law* (OUP 2012)

CRISP, 'Le contentieux Belgo-Congolais' (30 April 1965) 283 Courrier hebdomadaire 3 (French)

Cummins S and Stewart D (eds) *Digest of United States Practice in International Law: 2000* (Office of the Legal Adviser 2001)

362  PRIMARY BIBLIOGRAPHY

Czaplinski W, 'State Succession and State Responsibility' (1990) 28 CYIL 339

Daniels J, 'Ghana', I *International Encyclopaedia of Comparative Law Online* (1979)

Darcis L, 'Les Belbase: une réalisation peu connue de l'expansion belge en Afrique de l'Est' (2007) 53(2) Bulletin des séances 143

Dawson FG and Head I, *International Law, National Tribunals and the Rights of Aliens* (Procedural Aspects of International Law Institute 1971)

de Burlet J, *Nationalité des personnes physiques et décolonisation* (Bruylant 1975)

de Martens GF, *Précis du droit des gens moderne de l'Europe* (Guillaumin 1858)

de Muralt RGW, *The Problem of State Succession with regard to Treaties* (vam Stockum 1954)

de Nanteuil A, *International Investment Law* (Elgar 2021)

Deak F, *The Hungarian-Rumanian Land Dispute* (Columbia University Press 1928)

Declaration of Independence of Montenegro (3 June 2006) in Jure Vidmar, 'Montenegro's Path to Independence: A Study of Self-Determination, Statehood and Recognition' (2007) 3(1) HLR 73, 99 (art 4)

Declaration regarding the Defeat of Germany, 5 June 1949 (1945) 39 AJIL 171

Delcourt B, 'L'application de l'uti possidetis juris au démembrement de la Yougoslavie: Règle coutumière ou impératif politique?' (1998) 31 Revue Belge de Droit International

DGRN Resolutions (28 January 1989 and 18 May 1989) 41(2) REDI (1989)

Días Marques de Oliveira J, *Los Caminhoshistóricos das fronteiras de Angola* (Cefolex 2010)

Distefano G, Gaggioli G, and Hêche A (eds), *La Convention de Vienne de 1978 sur la succession d'États en matière de traités* (Bruylant 2016)

Djanić V, 'Analysis: State succession takes centre-stage in arbitration between Sudan's state-owned oil company and newly-independent South Sudan' (21 October 2022) IAReporter <https://www.iareporter.com/articles/analysis-state-succession-takes-centre-stage-in-arbi tration-between-sudans-state-owned-oil-company-and-newly-independent-south-sudan/> accessed 3 January 2024

Djanić V, 'Kazakhstan fends off claims by Canadian gold miner, as tribunal finds it is not a successor to USSR BIT', IAReporter (4 August 2020)

Dmitrieva GK and Lukashuk IL, 'The Russian Federation Law on Citizenship' (1993) 19(3) RCEEL 267

do Nascimento e Silva E, 'Succession of State Debts' in M Rama-Montaldo (ed) *Liber Amicorum Eduardo Jiménez de Aréchaga* vol II (FCU 1994)

Doehring K et al (eds) *Fontes Iuris Gentium: Decisions of the Superior Courts of the Federal Republic of Germany relating to Public International Law: 1949–1960* (Carl Heymanns Verlag KG 1970)

Dolzer R and Schreuer C, *Principles of International Investment Law* (OUP 2012)

Domke M, 'Indonesian Nationalization Measures before Foreign Courts'(1960) 54 AJIL

Donner R, *The Regulation of Nationality in International Law* (Transnational 1994)

Dörr O and Schmalenbach K, *Vienna Convention on the Law of Treaties: A Commentary* (Springer 2018).

Dörr O, 'Cession', *Max Planck Encyclopaedia of Public International Law* (April 2006)

Draft articles on Responsibility of States for Internationally Wrongful Acts with commentaries 2001 (2001) *ILC Yearbook*, vol II, Part Two

Drakidis P, 'Succession d'Etats et enrichissementssans cause des biens public du Dodécanese' (1971) 24 RHDI 109

Dronova NV, 'The Division of State Property in the Case of State Succession in the Former Soviet Union' in Pierre Eisemann and Martti Koskenniemi (eds) *State Succession: Codification Tested against the Facts* (Martinus Nijhoff 2000)

Dugard J, 'Succession to Federal Treaties on the Dissolution of a Federation' (1967) 84(3) SALJ

Dugard J, 'Addendum to First Report on Diplomatic Protection', UN Doc A/CN.4/506/Add.1 (20 April 2000)

Dugard J, 'Seventh Report on Diplomatic Protection', UN Doc A/CN.4/567 (7 March 2006)

Dumberry P, *State Succession to International Responsibility* (Martinus Nijhoff 2007)

Dumberry P, *A Guide to State Succession in International Investment Law* (Elgar 2018)

PRIMARY BIBLIOGRAPHY    363

Dupuy P and Kerbrat Y, *Droit International Public* (Dalloz 2014)

Durieux A, *Le problème juridique des dettes du Congo belge et de l'Etat du Congo* (AcadémieRoyale des Sciences d'Outre-mer 1961)

Duško Dimitrijević, 'A Review of the Issue of the Border between Serbia and Croatia on the Danube' (2012) 3 Megatrend Revija 1

Dutoit B, Gay D and Vandevelde T, *La nationalité de la femme mariée* vol 3 (Droz 1980)

Duy-Tân N, 'La représentation du Viet Nam dans les institutions spécialisées' (1976) 22(1) AFDI 405, 408

Earle Seaton and ST Maiti, *Tanzania Treaty Practice* (OUP 1973)

Edwards A, 'The Meaning of Nationality in International Law in an Era of Human Rights: Procedural and Substantive Aspects' in Alice Edwards and Laura van Waas (eds) *Nationality and Statelessness in International Law* (CUP 2014)

Eisemann P and Koskenniemi M (eds), *State Succession: Codification Tested against the Facts* (Martinus Nijhoff 2000)

Engers J, 'The United Nations Travel and Identity Documents for Namibians' (1971) 65(3) AJIL 571

Escarra J, *La Chine et le droit international* (Pedone 1931)

Espín Cánovas D, 'Equatorial Guinea', I *International Encyclopedia of Comparative Law Online* (1974)

Explanations of the Implementation of the Nationality Law in the Hong Kong SAR(15 May 1996) <https://www.immd.gov.hk/eng/residents/immigration/chinese/law.html> accessed 9 January 2024, s 1

Faciala K, 'Guinea' in *International Encyclopaedia of Comparative Law Online* (1979)

Falkowska M, Bedjaoui M, and Leidgens T, 'Article 44 Convention of 1969' in Olivier Corten and Pierre Klein (eds) *The Vienna Convention on the Law of Treaties: A Commentary* vol II (OUP 2011) 1046

Fassbender B and Peters A (eds), *The Oxford Handbook of the History of International Law* (2012)

Fastenrath U, 'Chapter XI: Non-Self-Governing Territories: Article 73' in Bruno Simma et al (eds) *The Charter of the United Nations: A Commentary* (OUP 2012)

Fáundez J, *Independent Namibia: Succession to Treaty Rights and Obligations* (UN Institute for Namibia 1989)

Feilchenfeld EH, *Public Debts and State Succession* (Macmillan 1931)

Feldbrugge FJM, 'The Law of the Republic of Georgia' (1992) 18(4) RCEEL 367

Feldbrugge FJM, 'The New Constitution of Georgia' (1996) 22(1) RCEEL 9, 10

Fenge T and Aldridge J, *Keeping Promises: The Royal Proclamation of 1763, Aboriginal Rights, and Treaties in Canada* (McGill-Queen's University Press 2015)

Final Declaration and Annexed Protocol of the International Conference of Tangier (29 October 1956) (1957) 51(2) AJIL 460

Fischer G, 'L'indépendance de la Guinée et les accords franco-guinéens' (1958) 4 AFDI 711

Fischer G, *Un Cas de Décolonisation: Les Etats-Unis et les Philippines* (Librairie générale de droit et de jurisprudence 1960)

Flournoy R, *Collection of Nationality Laws of Various Countries as Contained in Constitutions, Statutes and Treaties* (OUP 1929)

Franck TM, Carey J, and Tondel LM, *Legal Aspects of the United Nations Action in the Congo* (Oceana Publications 1963)

Friedmann S, *Expropriation in International Law* (Stevens & Sons 1955)

Frost L, 'Report on Citizenship Law: Jordan', EUI Country Report RSC/GLOBALCIT-CR 2022/ 2 (February 2022)

*Führer-Erlasse 1939–1945* (Franz Steiner Verlag 1997)

Gabbà CF, *Questioni di diritto civile* (Chiantore e Mascarelli 1882)

Gaebler RF, 'Austria' in RF Gaebler and A Shea (eds) *Sources of State Practice in International Law* (Martinus Nijhoff 2014) 46–50

Gaja G, 'General Principles of Law', *Max Planck Encyclopaedia of Public International Law* (2013)

364  PRIMARY BIBLIOGRAPHY

García Amador FV, 'International Responsibility: Third Report', UN Doc A/CN.4/111 (2 January 1958)

García Amador FV, 'International Responsibility: Fourth Report', UN Doc A/CN.4/119 (26 February 1959)

García-Amador FV, *The Changing Law of International Claims* (Oceana 1984)

Garner JW, 'Questions of State Succession Raised by the German Annexation of Austria' (1938) 32 AJIL 421

Gautier, 'Article 2 Convention of 1969' in O Corten and P Klein, *The Vienna Convention on the Law of Treaties: A Commentary* vol I (OUP 2011)

Gautron JC, 'Sur quelques aspects de la succession d'Etats au Senegal' (1962) 8 AFDI 838

General Framework Agreement for Peace in Bosnia and Herzegovina (14 December 1995) <https://www.osce.org/files/f/documents/e/0/126173.pdf> accessed 31 December 2023

Gerber JL, 'The East India Company and Southern Africa: A Guide to the East India Company and the Board of Control, 1600–1858' (PhD thesis, University College London 1998)

Ginsburgs G, 'From the 1990 Law on the Citizenship of the USSR to the Citizenship Laws of the Successor Republics (Part II)', 19(3) Review of Central and East European Law (1993) 233

Goa, Daman and Diu (Citizenship) Order (28 March 1962) <https://www.refworld.org/docid/3ae6b51d1c.html> accessed 30 December 2023

Goerdeler, Die Staatensukzession in multilaterale Verträge (1970)

Gonçalves Pereira A, *La succession d'États en matière de traité* (Pedone 1969)

Gonçalves Pereira A, *Índia Portuguesa* (Agência Geral do Ultramar Divisão de Publicações e Biblioteca 1953)

Gonidec PF, 'Note sur la nationalité et les citoyennetés dans la Communauté' (1959) 5 AFDI 748–761

Gosselin C, *L'Empire d'Annam* (Perrin 1904)

Gotlieb AE, 'Canadian Practice in International Law during 1967' (1968) 6 CYIL 276

Goy R, 'L'indépendance de la Namibie' (1991) 37 Annuaire Français de Droit International 387

Goy R, 'L'indépendance de l'Érythrée' (1993) 39 AFDI 337

Gradoni L, 'Article 2' in Distefano G, Gaggioli G and Hêche A (eds) *La Convention de Vienne de 1978 sur la succession d'États en matière de traités*, vol 1 (Bruylant 2016)

Gray C, *Judicial Remedies in International Law* (OUP 1990)

Gray S and McConnell T, 'Jubilation as South Sudan declares independence' The Times (9 July 2011)

Grayson CT, *Austria's International Position 1938–1953* (Droz 1953)

Greenwood C, 'State Contracts in International Law—The Libyan Oil Arbitrations' (1982) 53 BYIL 27

Guiho P, *La Nationalité Marocaine* (La Porte 1961)

Günther J, Doehring K, and Zimmermann E (eds) *Fontes Iuris Gentium: Decisions of the German Supreme Court relating to Public International Law* (Carl Heymanns Verlag KG 1960) 109

Hackworth GH, *Digest of International Law* vol I (Government Printing Office 1940) 448 (art 1)

Hafner G and Buffard I, 'Les principales différences entre les propositions de la Commission du Droit International et le résultat de la Conférence des Nations Unies à Vienne sur la succession d'États en matière des traités' in Giovanni Distefano, Gloria Gaggioli, and Aymeric Hêche (eds) *La Convention de Vienne de 1978 sur la succession d'États en matière de traités*, vol 1 (Bruylant 2016)

Hamant H, *Démembrement de l'URSS et problèmes de succession d'États* (Bruylant 2007)

Harijanti SD, 'Report on Citizenship Law: Indonesia', EUI Country Report No 2017/04 (February 2017)

Hazard JN and Pechota V (eds) *Russia and the Republics: Legal Materials* (Juris 1993)

Himsworth K, *A History of the British Mission in Kabul, Afghanistan* (British Embassy 1976)

Hiribarren V, 'Hiding the European Colonial Past: A Comparison of Archival Policies' in James Hong Kong Government Reports Online, <http://sunzi.lib.hku.hk/hkgro/result.jsp?total=536&first=1&no=20> accessed 29 December 2023.

Hong Kong SAR, 'International Agreements' <https://www.doj.gov.hk/en/external/internati onal_agreements.html> accessed 6 January 2024

Hong Thao N, 'Legal aspects of the supplementary treaty to the 1985 treaty on boundary delimitation between Vietnam and Cambodia' (26 January 2006) Vietnam Law & Legal Forum Magazine <https://vietnamlawmagazine.vn/legal-aspects-of-the-supplementary-treaty-to-the-1985-treaty-on-boundary-delimitation-between-vietnam-and-cambodia-3800.html> accessed 31 December 2023

Hopt-Nguyen ND, 'Vietnam', Max Planck Encyclopaedia of Public International Law (2009)

Hoque R, 'Report on Citizenship Law: Bangladesh', European University Institute Country Report No. 2016/14 (December 2016)

Hurst C, 'State Succession in Matters of Tort' (1924) 5 BYIL 163

Huu Tru N, *Quelques problèmes de succession d'États concernant le Viet-Nam* (Bruylant 1970)

Hyde, 'Compensation for Expropriations' (1939) 33(1) AJIL 37

IAEA, Convention on the Physical Protection of Nuclear Material, Status List (21 September 2020)

*ICJ Pleadings, Temple of Preah Vihear* vol II, 161

IDI, Resolution, Les effets des changements territoriaux sur les droits patrimoniaux, 44-II Annuaire de l'Institut de Droit International (1952) 471

IMF Decision No 10248-92/157 (30 December 1992)

IMF Press Release No 92/92 (15 December 1992)

IMF Press Release No 92/92 (15 December 1992)

Immigration Ordinance of the Hong Kong SAR (1 April 1972) <https://www.elegislation.gov.hk/ hk/cap115> accessed 17 February 2024, s 6(2)

Institut de droit international, 'Resolution: State Succession in Matters of Property and Debts', Seventh Commission, Vancouver (2001)

International Bank for Reconstruction and Development, 'The Economy of Mauritius' (10 September 1963) Report No EA-139

International Law Association, 'Final Report: Aspects of the Law of State Succession', Seventy-Third Conference, Rio de Janeiro (2008)

International Law Association Committee, 'Aspects of the Law of State Succession', Draft Final Report, Rio de Janeiro Conference (2008) 59–62

International Law Association, *The Effect of Independence on Treaties* (Stevens & Sons 1965)

Islam MR, 'The Nationality Law and Practice of Bangladesh' in KW Sik (ed) *Nationality and International Law in Asian Perspective* (Martinus Nijhoff 1990)

Jaenicke G, Doehring K, and Zimmermann E (eds) *Fontes Iuris Gentium: Decisions of the German Supreme Court relating to Public International Law* (Carl Heymanns Verlag KG 1960)

James HG, 'The Controversy over Tacna and Arica' (1920) 1(2) SPSQ 155

Janusz-Pawletta B, *The Legal Status of the Caspian Sea* (Springer 2015)

Jerónimo P, 'Report on Citizenship Law: East Timor (Timor-Leste)' EUI Country Report No 2017/07 (March 2017)

Jèze G, *Le partage des dettes publiques au cas de démembrement du territoire (application aux traités de Versailles et de Saint-Germain)* (Giard 1921)

Johnston DM and Valencia MJ, *Pacific Ocean Boundary Problems: Status and Solutions* (Springer 1991)

Jones JM, 'State Succession in the Matter of Treaties' (1947) 14 BYIL 360

Jones M, 'Who are British Protected Persons?' (1945) 22 BYIL 122

Jones M, *British Nationality Law and Practice* (OUP 1947)

Justinian, *Corpus iuris civilis* (c 529–534) 50 17 54; Ulpian, *Libri ad edictum* (c 211) Lib LXVI

Kaikobad KH, 'The Shatt-al-Arab River Boundary: A Legal Reappraisal' (1985) 56 BYIL 49, 52–69

Kamunga F, 'Report on Citizenship Law: Democratic Republic of Congo', EUI Country Report 2022/1 (2022)

Kaneko-Iwase M, *Nationality of Foundlings* (Springer 2021)

Kattan V, 'The Nationality of Denationalized Palestinians' (2005) 74(1) NJIL 67

Keith AB, 'The League of Nations and Mosul' (1926) 8(1) JCLIL 38

## 366 PRIMARY BIBLIOGRAPHY

Keyuan Z, 'The Sino-Vietnamese Agreement on Maritime Boundary Delimitation in the Gulf of Tonkin' (2005) 36(1) ODIL 13

Khachvani D, 'Compensation for Unlawful Expropriation: Targeting the Illegality' (2017) 32(2) ICSID Review 385

Khadduri M, 'The Franco-Lebanese Dispute and the Crisis of November, 1943' (1944) 38 AJIL 601

Kiaochow Convention (6 March 1898) in WF Mayers, *Treaties between the Empire of China and Foreign Powers* (4th edn, North-China Herald Office 1902)

King J, *The Doctrine of Odious Debt in International Law* (CUP 2016)

Kisangani EF and Pickering J, *African Interventions: State Militaries, Foreign Powers, and Rebel Forces* (CUP 2021)

Klemencic M, 'The Border Agreement between Croatia and Bosnia-Herzegovina' (Winter 1999–2000) IBRU Boundary and Security Bulletin 96

Klüber JL, *Droit des gens modern de l'Europe* (Aillaud 1831)

Knapp V, 'Czechoslovakia', I *International Encyclopedia of Comparative Law Online* (1980)

Kohen M and Dumberry P, *The Institute of International Law's Resolution on State Succession and State Responsibility: Introduction, Text and Commentaries* (CUP 2019)

Kohen MG, Possession contestée et souveraineté territoriale (Presses Universitaires de France 1997)

Korman S, *The Right of Conquest* (OUP 1996)

Kunz JL, *Die Völkerrechtliche Option* vol I (Ferdinand Hist 1925)

Kunz JL, 'Nationality and Option Clauses in the Italian Peace Treaty of 1947' (1947) 41(3) AJIL 622

*La Conférence Belgo-Congolaise Economique, Financière et Sociale* (26 April–16 May 1960)

Lalbahadur A, 'A Stitch in Time: Preventative Diplomacy and the Lake Malawi Dispute' (2016) 32 Policy Insights 1

Lamouri M, *Le contentieux relatif aux frontières terrestres du Maroc* (FeniXX 1979)

Lamouri M, 'Article 77' in JP Cot and A Pellet (eds) *La Charte des Nations-Unies* vol II (Economica 2005)

Lampué P, 'L'application des traités dans les territoires et départements d'outre-mer' (1960) 6 AFDI 907, 919 (1902 Hague Convention, Algeria)

Långström T, 'The Dissolution of the Soviet Union in the Light of the 1978 Vienna Convention on Succession of States in Respect of Treaties' in Pierre Eisemann and Martti Koskenniemi (eds) *State Succession: Codification Tested against the Facts* (Martinus Nijhoff 2000)

Lansford T (ed) *Political Handbook of the World* (SAGE Publications 2015)

Lauterpacht H, *Private Law Sources and Analogies of International Law* (Longmans, Green & Co Ltd 1927)

Lauterpacht H, 'Nationality of Denationalized Persons', 1 JYIL (1948) 164

Lauterpacht H, *Oppenheim's International Law* vol I (7th edn, OUP 1948) 519

Lauterpacht H, 'River Boundaries: Legal Aspects of the Shatt-al-Arab Frontier' (1960) 9(2) ICLQ 208

Lauterpacht H, 'The Contemporary Practice of the United Kingdom in the Field of International Law' (1961) 10(3) ICLQ 548

Lazrak R, *Le Contentieux Territorial entre le Maroc et l'Espagne* (Dar el Kitab 1974)

League of Nations, Board of Liquidation Final Report (31 July 1947) League of Nations Doc C 5.M.5. (1947) 40

Legal Obligations of Montenegro (2007) 78 BYIL 673

Leich M (ed) *Digest of United States Practice in International Law 1980* (Office of the Legal Adviser 1986)

Leriche A, 'De l'application à l'Erythrée des obligations résultant des traités conclus par l'Ethiopie antérieurement à la Féderation' (1953) 57 RGDIP 262

Lester AP, 'State Succession to Treaties in the Commonwealth' (1963) 12 ICLQ 475

Lewis M, 'The Free City of Danzig' (1924) 5 BYIL 89

Lillich RB, *International Claims: Postwar British Practice* (CUP 1967)

Lillich RB, *International Claims: Contemporary European Practice* (OUP 1982)
Lillich RB and Weston BH, *International Claims: Their Settlement by Lump Sum Agreements* vol I (University Press of Virginia 1975)
Lin Low C, 'Report on Citizenship Law: Malaysia and Singapore' (February 2017) EUI Country Report 2017/03
Lloyd L and James A, 'The External Representation of the Dominions, 1919–1948: Its Role in the Unravelling of the British Empire' (1996) 67 BYIL 479
Loughead S, 'The End Game: Britain's Role in Afghanistan 1947–50' (21 October 2016) <https://www.historyextra.com/period/second-world-war/the-end-game-britains-role-in-afghanistan-1947-50/> accessed 2 January 2024
Ludwickowski RR, 'Constitution Making in the Countries of Former Soviet Dominance: Current Development' (1993) 23(2) GJICL 155
Lyman et al, *Legal Aspects of the United Nations Action in the Congo* (Oceana Publications 1963)
Macao SAR, 'International Law' <https://www.io.gov.mo/pt/legis/int/> accessed 6 January 2024
Mahony C et al, 'Where Politics Borders Law: The MalawiTanzania Boundary Dispute', New Zealand Centre for Human Rights Law, Policy and Practice: Working Paper 21 (February 2014), <https://www.legal-tools.org/doc/f78000/pdf/> accessed 1 January 2024
Makarov AN and Schmitz E (eds), *Fontes Juris Gentium: Digest of the Diplomatic Correspondence of the European States (1871–1878)* vol I (Carl Heymanns Verlag KG 1937)
Malek D, 'Report on Citizenship Law: Egypt', Country Report 2021/16 (July 2021)
Mälksoo L, 'International Law and the 2020 Amendments to the Russian Constitution' (2021) 115(1) AJIL 78
Manière L, 'Le Code de l'indigénat en Afrique occidentale française et son application: le cas du Dahomey (1887–1946)' (unpublished PhD thesis, Université Paris VII-Denis Diderot 2007)
Mann FA, 'The Liability for Debts of the Former German Protectorates in Africa Considered in the Light of Decisions of the German Supreme Court' (1934) 16 JCLIL 281
Mann FA, 'The Law Governing State Contracts' (1944) 21 BYIL 11, 13–15
Marboe I, *Calculation of Compensation and Damages in Investment Law* (OUP 2017)
Marek K, *Identity and Continuity of States in International Law* (Droz 1968)
Margarith H, 'Enactment of a Nationality Law in Israel' (1953) 2(1) American Journal of Comparative Law 63
Marston G, 'The Anglo-Brazilian Dispute over the Island of Trinidade' (1983) 54 BYIL 222
Martens E, 'Article 102' in Bruno Simma et al (eds) *The Charter of the United Nations: A Commentary* vol II (OUP 2012)
Martin L, *The Treaties of Peace, 1919–1923* (Carnegie Endowment for International Peace 1924)
Marzatico F, 'Southern Sudan Referendum on Self-Determination: Legal Challenges and Procedural Solutions' (2011) 10(1) JAE 1
Matz-Lück N, 'Namibia', Max Planck Encyclopaedia of Public International Law (April 2009)
Maung M, *Burma's Constitution* (Springer 1961)
Maybon CB, *Histoire moderne du pays d'Annam (1592–1820)* (Librairie Plon 1920)
Mayne E, 'Raj-era embassy in Afghanistan to be rebuilt', The Telegraph (11 November 2007)
Mbaye S, *Histoire des institutions coloniales françaises en Afrique de l'Ouest (1816–1960)* (Dakar 1991)
McNair A, *The Law of Treaties* (OUP 1961)
McRae D, 'The Work of the International Law Commission, 2007–2011: Progress and Prospects' (2012) 106 AJIL 322
Meessen K, 'Domestic Law Concepts in International Expropriation Law' in RB Lillich (ed) *Valuation of Nationalized Property in International Law* vol IV (University Press of Virginia 1987)
Mendelson M, 'The *Cameroon–Nigeria* Case in the International Court of Justice: Some Territorial Sovereignty and Boundary Delimitation Issues' (2004) 75 BYIL 223
Mendelson M and Hulton SC, 'The Iraq–Kuwait Boundary: Legal Aspects' (1990) 23(2) RBDI 293
Mendelson M and Hulton SC, 'The Iraq–Kuwait Boundary' (1993) 64 BYIL 135

## 368   PRIMARY BIBLIOGRAPHY

Menon PK, *The Succession of States in respect to Treaties, State Property, Archives and Debts* (E. Mellen Press 1991)

Mériboute Z, *La codification de la succession d'États aux traités* (Presses Universitaires de France 1984)

Mikulka V, 'Introductory Note: Articles on Nationality of Natural Persons in relation to the Succession of States', UN Audiovisual Library of International Law Bibliography

Mikulka V, 'The Dissolution of Czechoslovakia and Succession in Respect of Treaties' in Mojmir M (ed) *Succession of States* (Kluwer 1999)

Millot A, *Les Mandats Internationaux* (Larose 1924)

Monnier JP, 'La succession d'Etats en matière de responsabilité internationale' (1962) 8 AFDI 65

Moore JB, *International Arbitrations to which the United States has been a Party* vol III (1898)

Moore JB, *A Digest of International Law*, vol I (US Government Printing Office 1906)

Mosses M, 'Revisiting the Matthew and Hunter Islands Dispute in Light of the Recent Chagos Advisory Opinion and Some Other Relevant Cases' (2019) 66 NILR 475

Moura J, *Le royaume du Cambodge* (E. Leroux 1883) Vol. II

Moussa J, 'L'indépendance du Soudan du Sud et la Convention de Vienne sur la succession d'États en matière de traités' in Giovanni Distefano, Gloria Gaggioli, and Aymeric Hêche (eds) *La Convention de Vienne de 1978 sur la succession d'États en matière de traités*, vol 2 (Bruylant 2016)

Mozingo D, 'The Sino-Indonesian Dual Nationality Treaty' (1961) 10(1) Asian Survey 25

Mrăk M, 'Succession to the Former Yugoslavia's External Debt: The Case of Slovenia' in Mojmir Mrăk (ed) *Succession of States* (Kluwer 1999)

Mushkat R, 'Hong Kong and Succession of Treaties' (1997) 46 ICLQ 181

Nabil A, 'Boundaries and Boundary Disputes in South Arabia', Gulf Centre for Strategic Studies, Monograph 6 (May 1990)

Nalule C and Nambooze A, 'Report on Citizenship Law: Tanzania' (April 2020) <https://cadmus eui.eu/bitstream/handle/1814/66748/RSC_GLOBALCIT_2020_6.pdf?sequence> accessed 9 January 2024

Nash M (ed) *Cumulative Digest of United States Practice in International Law: 1981–1988* book I (Office of the Legal Adviser 1993)

Nazir F, 'Report on Citizenship Law: Pakistan', Country Report 2016/13, European University Institute (December 2016)

Netherlands Note regarding Nationalization of Dutch-Owned Enterprises (18 December 1959) (1960) 54 AJIL 484

Nguya-Ndila C, *Indépendance de la République Démocratique du Congo et les engagements internationaux antérieurs* (University of Kinshasa 1971)

Nguyen HT, *Quelques problèmes de succession d'États concernant le Viet-Nam* (Bruylant 1970)

Ninth Report of the Special Rapporteur (1977) ILC Yearbook vol II, Part One 45

Noor S, 'Outstanding Issues between Pakistan and Bangladesh' (2005) 58(1) Pakistan Horizon 47

Note on Treaties (Argentina–Slovakia) (13 July 1995) Argentina Treaty Database No 5671 (Spanish)

Note Verbale of the German Minister of Foreign Affairs, UN Doc A/45/567 (3 October 1990)

Notification of Portugal for the 1949 Geneva Conventions (22 November 1999) Switzerland Treaty Database Doc P.242.512.0 (7 July 2000)

Notification of the United Kingdom for the 1949 Geneva Conventions (13 June 1997) Switzerland Treaty Database Doc P.242.512.0 (24 June 1997)

O'Connell DP, 'The British Commonwealth and State Succession after the Second World War' (1949) 26 BYIL 454

O'Connell, 'Economic Concessions in the Law of State Succession', 27 BYIL (1950) 93

O'Connell DP, *State Succession in Municipal Law and International Law* (CUP 1967)

O'Connell DP, *State Succession in Municipal Law and International Law* vol II (OUP 1968)

O'Connell DP, 'The Condominium of the New Hebrides' (1968–1969) 43 BYIL 71

O'Connell DP, 'Reflections on the State Succession Convention' (1979) 39 ZaöRV 725

PRIMARY BIBLIOGRAPHY  369

Oduntan G, 'Why Malawi and Tanzania should stick to mediation to settle lake boundary dispute', *The Conversation* (3 July 2017)

Onory AGM, *La succession d'États aux traités* (Giuffrè 1968)

Onuma Y, 'Nationality and Territorial Change: In Search of the State of the Law' (1981) 8(1) Yale Journal of World Public Order 1

Orlowski LT, 'Direct Transfers between the Former Soviet Union Central Budget and the Republics' (November 1992) Kiel Working Paper No 543.

Paenson I, *Les conséquences financières de la succession d'États* (Éditions Domat-Montchrestien 1954)

Pahis S, 'BITs & Bonds: The International Law and Economics of Sovereign Debt' (2021) 115(2) AJIL 242

Paoloni OBC, 'Comentario a la sentencia del Tribunal Supremo de 20 de julio de 2020. Denegación de nacionalidad española de origen a los nacidos en la antigua Guinea Ecuatorial' (2021) 13(1) Cuadernos de Derecho Transnacional 799

Paparinskis M, *The International Minimum Standard and Fair and Equitable Treatment* (OUP 2013)

Paris Club, 'Restructuring the Debt of the Former Federal Republic of Yugoslavia' (17 November 2001) Press Release <https://clubdeparisorg/en/communications/press-release/restructuring-the-debt-of-the-former-federal-republic-of-yugoslavia-17> accessed 2 January 2024.

Parry C, *Nationality and Citizenship Laws of the Commonwealth and the Republic of Ireland* vol I (CUP 1957)

Peaslee AJ and Peaslee DX, *Constitutions of Nations* (Martinus Hijhoff 1965)

Pellet A, 'Note sur la Commission d'arbitrage de la Conférence Européenne pour la paix en Yougoslavie', 37 Annuaire Français de Droit International (1991)

Pellet A, 'L'activité de la Commission d'arbitrage de la Conférence européenne pour la paix en Yougoslavie' (1992) 38

Pellet A, 'Sixteenth Report on Reservations to Treaties', UN Doc A/CN.4/626 (19 March 2010)

Pellet A, 'The ILC's Articles on State Responsibility' in James Crawford, Alain Pellet and Simon Olleson (eds) *The Law of International Responsibility* (OUP 2010)

Pellet A, 'Article 38' in Zimmerman A et al (eds) *The Statute of the International Court of Justice: A Commentary* (2nd edn, OUP 2012)

Pereira GP, *La succession d'Etats en matière de traité* (Pedone 1969)

Périz A and Pérez M, 'Vinculacion Nacional y Nacionalidad de los habitantes de los territorios descolonizados del Africa Española' (1991) 1 Acciones e Investigaciones Sociales 152

Phillimore R, *Commentaries upon International Law* (Butterworths 1854)

Piotrowicz RW, 'The Polish–German Frontier in International Law: The Final Solution' (1992) 63 BYIL 367

Piron P and Piron P, 'Zaïre', I International Encyclopaedia of Comparative Law Online (1977)

Polanco R, *The Return of the Home State to Investor-State Disputes: Bringing Back Diplomatic Protection?* (CUP 2019)

Posner E, 'Effects of Changes of Sovereignty on Archives' in Ken Munden (ed) *Archives and the Public Interest* (Public Affairs Press 1967)

Radmann W, 'The Nationalization of Zaire's Copper: from Union Minière to GECAMINES' (1978) 25(4) Africa Today 25

Randolph CF, *The Law and Policy of Annexation* (Longmans, Green & Co 1901)

Ratner S, 'Land Feuds and Their Solutions: Finding International Law Beyond the Tribunal Chamber' (2006) 100 American Journal of International Law 71

Razafiarison AL, Ratsimatahotrarivo LA, Zafera R, and Ravaozanany N, 'Rapport sur le droit de la nationalité: Madagascar', EUI Country Report No 2022/04 (July 2022)

Redfern A, 'The Arbitration between the Government of Kuwait and Aminoil' (1984) 55 BYIL 65

Report of the International Committee of Jurists entrusted by the Council of the League of Nations with the task of giving an advisory opinion upon the legal aspects of the Aaland Islands question', League of Nations, Official Journal, Special Supplement No. 3 (October 1920) 3

## 370 PRIMARY BIBLIOGRAPHY

*Restatement of the Law Fourth: The Foreign Relations Law of the United States* (American Law Institute 2017)

Rosenne S, 'La Loi israélienne sur la nationalité 5712–1952 et la loi du retour, 5710–1950' (1954) 81 Journal du Droit International 4

Rousseau C, 'Algérie et France: Conséquences financières de l'accession de l'Algérie à l'indépendance. Succession aux dettes publiques' (1967) 38(3) RGDIP 721

Rousseau C, *Droit international public* vol III (Sirey 1977)

Ryan KW and White MWD, 'The Torres Strait Treaty' (1978) 7 AYBIL 87

Sanderson M, 'The Post-Secession Nationality Regimes in Sudan and South Sudan' [2013] Journal of Immigration, Asylum and Nationality Law 204

Santos VA and Lennhoff CDT, 'The Taganak Island Lighthouse Dispute' (1951) 45(4) AJIL 680

Santry TSN, *State Succession in Indian Context* (Dominant Pub 2004)

Sarvarian A, 'Codifying the Law of State Succession—A Futile Endeavour?' (2016) 27(3) EJIL 789

Sato ET, 'The Commonwealth of the Northern Mariana Islands: A Mass Grant of United States Citizenship' (1975) 8 UCDLR 453

Saxena JN, 'Extradition of a Soviet Sailor' (1963) 57 AJIL 883

Schechtmann, 'The Option Clause in the Reich's Treaties on the Transfer of Population' (1944) 38 AJIL 35

Schneider L, 'The Tanzania National Archives' (2003) 30 *History in Africa* 447

Schofield R, 'Negotiating the Saudi-Yemeni international boundary' (July 2000) <https://al-bab.com/negotiating-saudi-yemeni-international-boundary> accessed 1 January 2024

Schofield R and Blake GH (eds) *Arabian Boundaries: Primary Documents 1853–1957* (Archive Editions 1988) vol 15

Schreur C, 'Investment Protection and International Relations' in August Reinisch and Ursula Kriebaum (eds) *The Law of International Relations: Liber amicorum Hanspeter Neuhold* (Eleven International 2007)

Scott JB (ed) *Official Statements of War Aims and Peace Proposals: December 1916 to November 1918* (Carnegie Endowment for International Peace 1921) 472

Scott L, *The Treaty of Trianon and the Claims of Hungarian Nationals with Regard to their Lands in Transyvlania* (Kraus 1927)

Seaton EE and Maiti ST, *Tanzania Treaty Practice* (OUP 1973)

Seidl-Hohenveldern I, *Corporations in and under International Law* (CUP 1987)

Selassie BH, 'Creating a Constitution for Eritrea' (1998) 9(2) Journal of Democracy 164

Shaw A, 'State Succession Revisited' (1994) 5 FYBIL 34

Shaw M, *Title to Territory in Africa* (OUP 1986)

Shaw M, 'The Heritage of States: The Principle of *Uti possidetis juris* Today' (1996) 67 BYIL 75

Shaw M and Fournet C, 'Article 62 Convention of 1969' in Olivier Corten and Pierre Klein (eds) *The Vienna Convention on the Law of Treaties: A Commentary* vol II (OUP 2011)

Shearer IA, 'La Succession d'Etats et les traites non localises' (1964) 68(1) RGDIP 5

Sheridan LA, 'Federation of Malaya Constitution: Parts Two and Three' (1959) UMLR 175, art 13

Sheridan LA, 'Federation of Malaya Constitution: Parts Five to Thirteen' (1960) 2(2) UMLR 246

Shihata IFI, 'Matters of State Succession in the World Bank's Practice' in Mrǎk M (ed) *Succession of States* (Kluwer 1999) 75, 89

Spens P, 'The Arbitral Tribunal in India 1947–48' (1950) 36 Transactions of the Grotius Society 61

Sperfeldt C, 'Report on Citizenship Law: Cambodia', EUI Report 2017/02 (January 2017)

Stahn C, *The Law and Practice of International Territorial Administration* (CUP 2008)

Stanič A, 'Financial Aspects of State Succession: The Case of Yugoslavia' (2001) 12 EJIL 75

Starke JG, 'The Acquisition of Title to Territory by Newly Emerged States' (1965–1966) 41 BYIL 411

Stern B, 'Responsabilité internationale et succession d'Etats' in Laurence Boisson de Chazournes and Vera Gowlland-Debbas (eds) *The International Legal System in Quest of Equity and Universality, Liber Amicorum Georges Abi-Saab* (Martinus Nijhoff 2001)

Stern WB, 'The Treaty Background of the Italo-Ethiopian Dispute' (1936) 30(2) AJIL 189

Stoyanovsky J, *The Mandate for Palestine* (Longmans, Green & Co 1928)

Strydom HA, 'Namibian Independence and the Question of the Contractual and Delictual Liability of the Predecessor and Successor Governments' in DH Van Wyk, Marinus Wiechers, and Romaine Hill (eds) *Namibia: Constitutional and International Law Issues* (University of South Africa 1991)

Stuart GH, *The International City of Tangier* (SUP 1955)

Stuart-Fox M, 'The French in Laos, 1887–1945' (1995) 29(1) MAS 111

Šturma V, 'First Report on Succession of States in respect of State Responsibility', UN Doc A/CN.4/708 (31 May 2017)

Šturma V, 'Second Report on Succession of States in respect of State Responsibility', UN Doc A/CN.4/719 (6 April 2018)

Šturma V, 'Fourth Report on Succession of States in respect of State Responsibility', UN Doc A/CN.4/743 (27 March 2020)

Switzerland, Depositary Notification Nos p.o.411.61.(5)(25 October 1991) & p.o.411.61.(5)(30 November 1983)

Szasz PC, 'Succession to Treaties under the Namibian Constitution' in DW van Wyck, Marinus Wiechers, and Romaine Hill (eds) *Namibia: Constitutional and International Law Issues* (University of South Africa 1991)

Taha FAA, 'Some Legal Aspects of the Anglo-Egyptian Condominium over the Sudan, 1899–1954' (2005) 76 BYIL 337

Third Bilateral Treaties Study, UN Doc A/CN.4/243/Add.1

Thirlway H, 'The Law and Procedure of the International Court of Justice: Part Seven' (1995) 66 BYIL 1

Thomas DL, 'Western Samoa: Establishment of a National Archive' (11 February 1986) UNESCO Doc RP/1984-1985/VII.2.1

Tichy H, 'Two Recent Cases of State Succession—An Austrian Perspective' (1992) 44 AJPIL 117

Toktomushev K, 'Understanding Cross-Border Conflict in Post-Soviet Central Asia: The Case of Kyrgzstan and Tajikstan' (2018) 17(1) Connections 21

Torres Bernárdez S, 'The "Uti Possidetis Juris Principle" in Historical Perspective' in Konrad Ginther et al (eds) *Völkerrecht zwischen normativem Anspruch und politischer Realität* (Duncker and Humblot 1994)

Touval S, 'The Organization of African Unity and African Borders' (1967) 21(1) International Organization 102

Treverton GF, *Dividing Divided States* (University of Pennsylvania Press 2014)

Trinidad J, 'An Evaluation of Morocco's Claims to Spain's Remaining Territories in Africa' (2012) 61(4) ICLQ 961

Trinidad J, 'The Disputed Waters around Gibraltar' (2015) 86 BYIL 101

Tru NH, *Quelues problèmes de succession d'États concernant le Viet-Nam* (Bruylant 1970)

Trusteeship Agreement for the Mandated Territory of Tanganyika, UN Doc A/152/Rev.2 (12 December 1946) in UNGA Res 63(I)(XIV) (13 December 1946) para 6

Tuerk H, 'Montenegro', Max Planck Encyclopaedia of Public International Law (2015)

Udina M, 'La succession des Etats quant aux obligations internationales autres que les dettes publiques', 44 RdC (1933-II) 767

*UN Materials on Succession of States* (1967) UN Doc ST/LEG/SER.B/14

UNHCR, 'A Study of Statelessness in South Sudan' (2017) 14–19, https://data.unhcr.org/en/documents/download/63857

UNHCR, 'Citizenship and Prevention of Statelessness Linked to the Disintegration of the Socialist Federal Republic of Yugoslavia' (1997) 3(1) *European Series* 40

UNHCR, 'Citizenship and Statelessness in the Member States of the Southern African Development Community' (December 2020) 91, <https://reliefweb.int/sites/reliefweb.int/files/resources/Statelessness_in_Southern_Africa_Dec2020.pdf> accessed 9 January 2024

UNHCR, 'Nationality Laws of the Former Soviet Republics' (1 July 1993) <https://www.refworld.org/docid/3ae6b31db3.html> accessed 31 December 2023

UNHCR, 'Questions of Nationality and Statelessness in Armenia' (March 2013)

372 PRIMARY BIBLIOGRAPHY

UNHCR, 'Submission for the Office of the High Commissioner for Human Rights' Compilation Report – Universal Periodic Review: Montenegro' (July 2012) 1, 6, <https://www.refworld.org/topic,50ffbce524d,50ffbce5268,4ffd355f2,0,,,MNE.html> accessed 10 January 2024

UNHCR, Law No 6 on Yemeni Nationality (26 August 1990) <https://www.refworld.org/docid/3ae6b57b10.html> accessed 9 January 2024, arts 1, 3

United Nations (ed), *Seventy Years of the International Law Commission: Drawing a Balance for the Future* (Brill Nijhoff 2021)

United States Office of the Geographer, 'International Boundary Study No 1: Algeria-Libya Boundary' (28 April 1961) <http://library.law.fsu.edu/Digital-Collections/LimitsinSeas/numericalibs.html> accessed 1 January 1024

United States Office of the Geographer, 'International Boundary Study No 121: Libya-Tunisia Boundary' (7 April 1972) <http://library.law.fsu.edu/Digital-Collections/LimitsinSeas/numericalibs.html> accessed 1 January 2024.

United States Office of the Geographer, 'International Boundary Study No 91: Benin (Dahomey)–Nigeria Boundary' (15 October 1969) <http://library.law.fsu.edu/Digital-Collections/LimitsinSeas/numericalibs.html> accessed 1 January 2024

US Department of State, 'Depositary Information' <https://www.state.gov/depositary-information/> accessed 7 January 2024

Uvalić M, *Investment and Property Rights in Yugoslavia* (CUP 1992)

van der Meersch G, *Fin de la Souveraineté Belge au Congo* (Institut royal des relations internationales 1963)

van Panhuys HF, 'La Succession de l'Indonesie aux Accords Internationaux conclus par les Pays-Bas avant l'Independence de l'Indonesie' (1959) 2 NTVIR 55

van Panhuys HF, *The Role of Nationality in International law* (Sythoff 1969)

Vázquez-Bermúdez M, 'Second Report on General Principles of Law', UN Doc A/CN.4/741 (9 April 2020)

Vázquez-Bermúdez M, 'Third Report on General Principles of Law', UN Doc A/CN.4/753 (18 April 2022)

Vec M, 'From the Congress of Vienna to the Paris Peace Treaties of 1919' in Bardo Fassbender and Anne Peters (eds) *The Oxford Handbook of the History of International Law* (OUP 2012)

Večernji List <https://www.vecernji.hr/vijesti/titov-stan-u-new-yorku-prodan-za-12-milijuna-dolara-1249483> accessed 2 January 2024 (Serbo-Croatian)

Veïcopoulos N, *Traité des Territoires Dépendants* vol I (Larcier 1960)

Vidmar J, 'Montenegro's Path to Independence: A Study of Self-Determination, Statehood and Recognition' (2007) 3(1) HLR 73

Volkovitsch MJ, 'Towards a New Theory of State Succession to Responsibility for International Delicts'(1992) 92 Col LR 2162, 2178–2182

Waibel M, 'Opening Pandora's Box: Sovereign Bonds in International Arbitration' (2007) 101(4) AJIL 711

Waldock H, 'Disputed Sovereignty in the Falkland Islands Dependencies' (1948) 25 BYIL 311

Wallot JP, 'Les grands principes internationales concernant la migration des archives' (1996–1997) 28 Archives 3

Walvis Bay and Offshore Islands Act No. 1 1994, 28 Government Gazette (28 February 1994)

Watts A, 'State Succession: Some Recent Practical Legal Problems' in PC Götz, Peter Selmer, and Rüdiger Wolfrum (eds) *Liber amicorum Günther Jaenicke* (Springer 1998)

Weis P, *Nationality and Statelessness in International Law* (Stevens 1979)

Westlake J, *International Law* (CUP 1910) vol I

Weston BH, Lillich RB, and Bederman DJ, *International Claims: Their Settlement by Lump Sum Agreements, 1975–1995* (Transnational 1999)

Wheaton H, *Elements of International Law* (Little 1857)

Whiteman MM, *Digest of International Law* vol I (Government Printing Office 1964)

Whiteman MM, *Digest of International Law* vol II (Government Printing Office 1964)

Wickersham GW, *Opinion Regarding the Rights of Hungary and certain Hungarian Nationals under the Treaty of Trianon* (Kolligátum 1928)

Wilde R, *International Territorial Administration* (OUP 2008)

Williamson ED and Osborn JE, 'A US Perspective on Treaty Succession and Related Issues in the Wake of the Break-up of the USSR and Yugoslavia' (1992) 33 VJIL 261

Wilson GG, *The Hague Arbitration Cases* (Ginn & Co 1915)

Philip Winter, 'A Border Too Far: The Ilemi Triangle Yesterday and Today', Durham Middle East Paper No 100 (2019)

Wolf, Les Conventions du Travail et la Succession d'Etats, AFDI (1961) 742

Wolfrum R, 'General International Law (Principles, Rules, and Standards)' (December 2010) in Wolfrum R (ed), *Max Planck Encyclopaedia of Public International Law* (online edn)

World Bank, 'The Republic of Yemen: Unlocking the Potential for Economic Growth' (October 2015) paras 222, 227, 244

Wright Q, 'Status of the Inhabitants of Mandated Territory'(1924) 18(2) AJIL 306

Wright Q, 'The Goa Incident' (1962) 56(3) AJIL 617

Wyler É, *La règle dite de la continuité de la nationalité dans le contentieuxinternational* (PUF 1990)

Yakemtchouk R, 'Les conflits de territoire et de frontière dans les États de l'ex-URSS' (1993) 39 AFDI 393

Ydit M, *Internationalised Territories* (AW Sythoff 1961)

Young R, 'State of Syria: Old or New?' (1962) 56(2) AJIL 482

Young R and Owen WL, 'Valuation Aspects of the Aminoil Award' in RB Lillich, *Valuation of Nationalized Property in International Law* vol IV (University Press of Virginia 1987)

Zanardi PL, Luzzatto R, Sacerdoti G, and Santa Maria A, *La Guirisprudenza di Diritto Internazionale (1861–1875)* (Jovene Napoli 1973)

Zemanek K, 'State Succession after Decolonization' (1968–1969) 116 RdC 236

Ziemele I, *State Continuity and Nationality: The Baltic States and Russia* (Martinus Nijhoff 2005)

Zimmermann A, 'State Succession in Respect of Treaties' in Jan Klabbers et al (eds) *State Practice regarding State Succession and Issues of Recognition* (Kluwer 1999)

Zimmermann A, *Staatennachfolge in völkerrechtliche Verträge* (Springer 2000)

Zimmermann A, 'State Succession and the Nationality of Natural Persons: Facts and Possible Codification' in Pierre Eisemann and Martti Koskenniemi (eds) *State Succession: Codification Tested against the Facts* (Martinus Nijhoff 2000)

Zimmermann A, 'The International Court of Justice and State Succession to Treaties: Avoiding Principled Answers to Questions of Principle' in Christian Tams and James Sloan (eds) *The Development of International Law by the International Court of Justice* (OUP 2013)

Zimmermann A, 'La Convention de Vienne sur la succession d'États en matière de traités: codification réussie ou échouée?' in Giovanni Distefano, Gloria Gaggioli, and Aymeric Hêche (eds) *La Convention de Vienne de 1978 sur la succession d'États en matière de traités*, vol 1 (Bruylant 2016)

## Other sources

*International resolutions and documents*

**United Nations Security Council**

UNSC 639th Meeting (18 November 1953)

UNSC Res 242 (1967)

UNSC 1382nd Meeting (22 November 1967)

UNSC Res 264 (20 March 1969)

UNSC Res 301 (1971)

UNSC Res 1864th Meeting (15 December 1975)

UNSC Res 435 (1978)

UNSC 2319th Meeting (17 December 1981)

UNSC 2320th Meeting (18 December 1981)

UNSC Res 643 (1989)

UNSC Res 757 (19 September 1992)

UNSC Res 1272 (1999)

UNSC Res 1310 (2000)

374  PRIMARY BIBLIOGRAPHY

UNSC 5924th Meeting (24 June 2008)
UNSC Res 2548 (2020)
'Report of the Secretary-General on the implementation of Security Council resolutions 425 (1978) and 426 (1978)', UN Doc S/2000/460 (22 May 2000)
'Report on the UNTAET', UN Doc S/2002/432 (17 April 2002)
UN Commission for Indonesia, 'Special Report to the Security Council on the Round Table Conference', UN Doc S/1417 (10 November 1949) 11

## United Nations General Assembly

UNGA Res 24(I) (12 February 1946)
UNGA Res 65(I) (14 December 1946)
UNGA 128th Plenary Meeting (29 November 1947)
UNGA Res 181 (II) (19 November 1947)
UNGA Res 174 (II) (21 November 1947)
UNGA Res 289(IV)(A) (21 November 1949)
UNGA Res 387(V) (17 November 1950)
UNGA Res 390(V) (2 December 1950)
UNGA Res 388(V)A-B (15 December 1950)
UNGA Res 392(V) (15 December 1950)
UNGA Res 387(V) (17 November 1950)
UNGA Res 388(V)A-B (15 December 1950)
UNGA Res 390(V) (2 December 1950)
UNGA Res 392(V) (15 December 1950)
UNGA Res 530(VI) (29 January 1952)
UNGA Res 995(X) (14 December 1955)
UNGA Res 1514 (14 December 1960)
UNGA Res 1541 (15 December 1960)
UNGA Res 1654 (27 November 1961)
UNGA Res 1630th Plenary Meeting (14 December 1967)
UNGA Res 1803(XVII) (14 December 1962)
UNGA 1228th Plenary Meeting (4 October 1963)
UNGA Res 2145 (17 October 1966)
UNGA Res 2676 (XXV) (9 December 1970)
UNGA Res 3295 (XXIX) (13 December 1974)
UNGA Res 31/53 (1 December 1976)
UNGA Res 32/9 D (4 November1977)
UNGA, 33rd Plenary Meeting (13 October 1977)
UNGA 19th Plenary Meeting (3 October 1979) GAOR: 34th Session
UNGA 15th Plenary Meeting (29 September 1980) GAOR: 35th Session
UNGA Res 25-19 (11 November 1980)
UNGA 18th Plenary Meeting (29 September 1981) GAOR: 36th Session
UNGA Res 36/113 (10 December 1981)
UNGA Res 37/11 (15 November 1982)
UNGA 18th Plenary Meeting (5 October 1982) GAOR: 37th Session
UNGA 13th Plenary Meeting (30 September 1983) GAOR: 38th Session
UNGA 38th Session Official Records, 13th Plenary Meeting (30 September 1983)
UNGA Ninth Emergency Special Session, 12th Plenary Meeting (5 February 1982) GAOR
UNGA Res 44/243(A) (11 September 1990)
UNGA Res 47/1 (22 September 1992)
UNGA Res 47/114 (16 December 1992)
UNGA Res 49/91 (26 January1995)
UNGA Res 530(VI) (29 January 1952)
UNGA Res 55/153 (12 December 2000)
UNGA Res 59/34 (2 December 2004)

PRIMARY BIBLIOGRAPHY    375

UNGA Res 60/264 (28 June 2006)
UNGA Res 63/118 (11 December 2008)
UNGA Res 65/308 (25 August 2011)
UNGA Res 66/92 (9 December 2011)
UNGA Res 68/262 (1 April 2014)
UNGA 8th Plenary Meeting (26 September 2018)

**<u>United</u> <u>Nations</u> <u>Sixth</u> <u>Committee</u> <u>(Legal)</u>**

UNGA Sixth Committee, 1317th Meeting (29 September 1972)
UNGA Sixth Committee, 1321st Meeting (4 October 1972)
UNGA Sixth Committee, 1322nd Meeting (5 October 1972)
UNGA Sixth Committee, 1323rd Meeting (5 October 1972)
UNGA Sixth Committee, 1324th Meeting (6 October 1972)
UNGA Sixth Committee, 1325th Meeting (6 October 1972)
UNGA Sixth Committee, 1326th Meeting (9 October 1972)
UNGA Sixth Committee, 1318th Meeting (2 October 1972) GAOR: Twenty-seventh Session
UNGA Sixth Committee, 1320th Meeting (4 October 1972) GAOR: Twenty-Seventh Session
UNGA Sixth Committee, 1322nd Meeting (5 October 1972) GAOR: Twenty-Seventh Session
UNGA Sixth Committee, 1323rd Meeting (5 October 1972) GAOR: Twenty-seventh Session
UNGA Sixth Committee, 1325th Meeting (6 October 1972) GAOR
UNGA Sixth Committee, 1326th Meeting (9 October 1972) GAOR: Twenty-seventh Session
UNGA Sixth Committee, 1328th Meeting (10 October 1972) GAOR: Twenty-seventh Session
UNGA Sixth Committee, 1487th Meeting (29 October 1974) GAOR: Twenty-Ninth Session
UNGA Sixth Committee, 1489th Meeting (31 October 1974)
UNGA Sixth Committee, 1490th Meeting (1 November 1974)
UNGA Sixth Committee, 1492nd Meeting (5 November 1974)
UNGA Sixth Committee, 1493rd Meeting (6 November 1974)
UNGA Sixth Committee, 1494th Meeting (7 November 1974)
UNGA Sixth Committee, 1495th Meeting (8 November 1974)
UNGA Sixth Committee, 1496th Meeting (11 November 1974)
UNGA Sixth Committee, 1528th Meeting (1 October 1975)
UNGA Sixth Committee, 1537th Meeting (13 October 1975)
UNGA Sixth Committee, 1540th Meeting (15 October 1975)
UNGA Sixth Committee, 1543rd Meeting (20 October 1975)
UNGA Sixth Committee, 1545th Meeting (21 October 1975)
UNGA Sixth Committee, 1547thMeeting (23 October 1975)
UNGA Sixth Committee, 1548th Meeting (24 October 1975)
UNGA Sixth Committee, 1549th Meeting (27 October 1975)
UNGA Sixth Committee, 'Summary record of the 17th meeting' (26 October 2021) UN Doc A/
    C.6/76/SR.17 (10 December 2021)
UNGA Sixth Committee, 'Summary record of the 21st meeting' (25 October 2016) UN Doc A/
    C.6/71/SR.21 (16 November 2016)
UNGA Sixth Committee, 'Summary record of the 23rd meeting' (2 November 2021) UN Doc A/
    C.6/76/SR.23 (10 December 2021)
UNGA Sixth Committee, 'Summary record of the 24th meeting' (3 November 2021) UN Doc A/
    C.6/76/SR.24 (9 December 2021)
UNGA Sixth Committee, 'Summary record of the 25th meeting' (3 November 2021) UN Doc A/
    C.6/76/SR.24 (12 April 2022)
UNGA Sixth Committee, 'Summary record of the 28th meeting' (30 October 2018) UN Doc A/
    C.6/73/SR.28 (10 December 2018)
UNGA Sixth Committee, 'Summary record of the 30th meeting' (31 October 2018) UN Doc A/
    C.6/73/SR.30 (6 December 2018)
UNGA Sixth Committee, 'Summary record of the 32nd meeting' (6 November 2019) UN Doc A/
    C.6/74/SR.32 (27 November 2019)

376   PRIMARY BIBLIOGRAPHY

UNGA Sixth Committee, 'Summary record of the 29th meeting' (2 November 2016) UN Doc A/
C.6/71/SR.29 (2 December 2016)
UNGA Sixth Committee, 'Summary record of the 23rd meeting' (26 October 2016) UN Doc A/
C.6/71/SR.23 (14 November 2016)

### United Nations Council for Namibia

UNCN Report (1991) GAOR Fifty-third Session, Supplement No 24 (A/43/24) 228
UNCN, 'Decree on the Natural Resources of Namibia' (1974) UN Doc A/9624/Add.1
UNCN, 'Decree on the Natural Resources of Namibia' (1974) UN Doc A/9624/Add.1
UNCN, 'Implementation of Decree No 1 for the Protection of the Natural Resources of Namibia',
UN Doc A/AC.131.194 (23 October 1985)
UN Council for Namibia, 'Independent Namibia: Succession to Rights and Duties and
Succession to Law', UN Doc A/AC.131/151 (11 January 1985)
UNCN, 'Implementation of Decree No 1 for the Protection of the Natural Resources of
Namibia: Study on the possibility of instituting legal proceedings in the domestic courts of
States', UN Doc A/AC.131.194 (23 October 1985)

### United Nations Special Committee on Decolonization

'Report of the Special Committee on the Situation with regard to the Implementation of the
Declaration on the Granting of Independence to Colonial Countries and Peoples', UN Doc A/
6300/Rev.1 (30 November 1966)
'Report of the Special Committee', UN Doc A/6300/Rev.1 (30 November 1966)

### UN Secretariat Office of Legal Affairs

'Selected Legal Opinions of the Secretariat of the United Nations' (1963) UNJY
'Summary of Practice of the Secretary-General as Depositary of Multilateral Treaties', UN Doc
ST/LEG/7/Rev.1 (1999)
'Summary of the Practice of the Secretary-General as Depositary of Multilateral Agreements', UN
Doc ST/LEG/7 (7 August 1959)
UN Secretariat, 'Succession of States in respect of Bilateral Treaties: Second Study – Air Transport
Agreements', UN Doc A/CN.4/253 (24 March 1971)(1971) ILC Yearbook vol II

*Government Documents*

'Cablegram dated 15 May 1948 addressed to the Secretary-General by Foreign Secretary of Israel',
UN Doc. S/747 (15 April 1948)
Colonial Office, 'The Colonial Territories: 1961–1962', Cmd 1751 (June 1962)
Croatia: Succession. UN Doc C.N.1573.2003.TREATIES-1 (30 December 2003)
Eritrea: Signature. UN Doc C.N.434.1993.TREATIES-3 (13 October 1993)
'Final Act of the UN Conference on Succession of States in respect of State Property, Archives and
Debts, UN Doc. A/CONF.117/15, Official Records on Succession of States in respect of State
Property, Archives and Debts, Vol. II, 137
'Former Italian Colonies, Economic and Financial Provisions Relating to Libya: Report of the Ad
Hoc Political Committee', UN Doc A/1726 (14 December 1950) 9
'Instructions on the Payment of Debts' (30 August 1976) No15/TC/BB <https://vbpl.vn/TW/
Pages/vbpq-toanvan.aspx?ItemID=78139> accessed 2 January 2024, para I (Vietnamese)
Guinea: Succession. UN Doc C.N.217.1965.TREATIES-2 (8 February 1966)
Guinea: Succession UN Doc C.N.79.1962.TREATIES-2 (2 May 1962)
Letter from Cameroon to Switzerland (16 September 1963) and Letter from Switzerland to
the UN Secretariat (11 November 1963) in UN Archives, 'State Succession to Treaty Rights
and Obligations: Federal Republic of Cameroun', Folder No (213 CAMER) (January 1960–
December 1963) (French).
Letter from Consul-General of Switzerland to Prime Minister of the Transitional Government
of Mozambique (9 April 1975) in 'Alto Comissão Moçambique' Portugal Archives Box 40603
(Portuguese)

## PRIMARY BIBLIOGRAPHY   377

Letter from the Prime Minister of the German Democratic Republic (27 September 1990) UN Doc A/45/557

Letter from the UN Secretariat to Dr D.P. O'Connell' (11 December 1957) UN Archives Folder LE 213 ('State Succession to Treaty Rights and Obligations: General') (November 1957–December 1959) (Tunisia)

Letter from the UN Secretariat to Malaya, Doc LE 352/2 (28 November 1961) UN Archives Folder No 213 MALA ('State Succession to Treaty Rights and Obligation: Federation of Malaya') (January 1960–23 January 1963)

Letter from UN Secretariat to Pakistan, Doc LE 222 (13 July 1967) UN Archives Folder No 222 PAKI ('State Succession to Treaty Rights and Obligations: Pakistan') (January 1964–December 1967).

Letters from Rwanda (18 February 1963) and from Burundi (1 February 1963) to the UN Secretariat in UN Archives, 'State Succession to Treaty Rights and Obligations: Kingdom of Burundi', Folder No 213 BURU (January 1960–December 1963)

Letter dated 31 December 1992 from the Permanent Representative of Czechoslovakia to the U.N., UN Doc. A/47/848. 31 Dec. 1992

'Memorandum: Germans in the Mandated Territory of South-West Africa, London, October 23, 1923' 28 LNTS 418

'Mesures consecutives à la liquidation de l'union réelle dano-islandaise : Restitution d'archives' (1967) 121 RGDIP 401

'Minute by the Viceroy of India as to the future Administration of Upper Burma' (17 February 1886) in 'Further Correspondence relating to Burmah', Cmd 4887 (1886) 32

'Mr Adams, Secretary of State, to Mr Anderson, min. to Colombia, May 27, 1823' 13 BFSP 459, 480–481

'Report of the Special Committee on the Situation with regard to the Implementation of the Declaration on the Granting of Independence to Colonial Countries and Peoples', UN Doc. A/6300/Rev.1 (30 November 1966)

Serbia: Succession. UN Doc C.N.241.2019.TREATIES-XIV.7 (11 June 2019)

'State Succession to Treaty Rights and Obligations: Nigeria', UN Doc C.N.78.1961.TREATIES-1 (24 July 1961) UN Archives Folder No 213 NIGE (January 1960–December 1963)

The former Yugoslav Republic of Macedonia: Succession UN Doc C/N/1351/2005.TREATIES-3 (5 September 2007)

Senegal: Succession UN Doc C.N.45.1963.TREATIES-2 (22 March 1963)

Ukraine: Succession. UN Doc C.N.423.1994.TREATIES-7 (12 April 1995)

'United Kingdom–Hong Kong: Selected Issues', IMF Doc SM/97/43 (21 May 1997)

'United Kingdom Materials on International Law 1979' (1979) 50 BYIL 302

'United Kingdom Materials on International Law' (1981) 52 BYIL 378

'United Kingdom Materials on International Law'(1993) 64 BYIL 636

'Viet Nam International Reserves' (January 1975) IMF Archives File Nos 54732 and 96414

1951 Refugees Convention, Succession. UN Doc C.N.152.1957.TREATIES-4 (18 November 1957)

337 Hansard series 5 col 34

645 HC (4 August 1961) col 1801

91 CCFB (1964) 301–302

91 RCCFB (1964) 301–302

'Yemen Arab Republic – Recent Economic Developments' (24 April 1989) IMF Doc SM/78/72

<https://treatiesun.org/Pages/ViewDetailsaspx?src=IND&mtdsg_no=III-12&chapter=3&clang=_en> accessed 16 February 2024

### Paris Club documents

'Sudan – debt treatment – July 15, 2021' <https://clubdeparisorg/en/traitements/sudan-15-07-2021/en> accessed 3 January 2024

'Sudan: Enhanced Heavily-Indebted Poor Countries Initiative – Preliminary Document' (2021)<https://www.elibrary.imf.org/view/journals/002/2021/066/article-A002-en.xml> accessed 3 January 2024

378    PRIMARY BIBLIOGRAPHY

## International Law Commission

'Comments and observations of Governments on the draft articles on succession of States in respect of matters other than treaties', UN Doc A/CN.4/338 (1981) ILC Yearbook vol II

'Digest of Decisions of National Courts relating to Succession of States and Governments: Study prepared by the Secretariat', UN Doc A/CN.4/157 (18 April 1963) II ILC Yearbook(1963)

'International Law Commission: Provisional summary record of the 3374th meeting' (13 July 2017) UN Doc A/CN.4/SR.3374 (14 August 2017)

'Observations of Member States on the draft articles on succession of States in respect of treaties adopted by the Commission at its twenty-fourth session', UN Doc A/CN.4/275 ILC Yearbook (1974) vol II

'Replies from Governments to Questionnaires of the International Law Commission', UN Doc A/CN.4/19 (23 March 1950)

'Report of the International Law Commission on the work of its seventy-second session (2021): Topical summary of the discussion held in the Sixth Committee during its seventy-sixth session', UN Doc A/CN.4/746 (28 February 2022)

'Report of the International Law Commission on the work of its sixty-eighth session (2016): Topical summary of the discussion held in the Sixth Committee of the General Assembly during its seventy-first session', UN Doc A/CN.4/703 (22 February 2017)

'Report of the International Law Commission: Seventy-second session (26 April–4 June and 5 July–6 August 2021)', UN Doc A/76/10

'Report of the International Law Commission: Sixty-eighth session (2 May–10 June and 4 July-12 August 2016)', UN Doc A/71/10

'Report of the International Law Commission: twenty-fourth session', ILC Yearbook (1972) vol II, 231

'Statement by Afzan Abd Kahar, Delegate of Malaysia to the UNGA 73rd Session, Agenda Item 82: Report of the International Law Commission on the Work of its Seventieth Session' (31 October 2018)

'Succession of States in relation to general multilateral treaties of which the Secretary-General is depositary', UN Doc A/CN.4/150 (10 December 1962)

'Succession of States in respect of bilateral treaties: second study – Air transport agreements', UN Doc A/CN.4/253 (24 March 1971)

'Succession of States in respect of bilateral treaties: study prepared by the Secretariat', UN Doc A/CN.4/229 (28 May 1970)

'Succession of States in respect of bilateral treaties: third study – Trade agreements', UN Doc A/CN.4/253/Add.1 (9 April 1971)

'Succession of States to multilateral treaties; seventh study prepared by the Secretariat', UN Doc A/CN.4/225 (24 April 1970) (1970) Yearbook of the International Law Commission vol II

'Succession of States to multilateral treaties: studies prepared by the Secretariat', UN Doc A/CN.4/200 (21 February 1968)

Bedjaoui M, 'Second report on succession in respect of matters other than treaties', UN Doc A/CN.4/216/REV.1 (18 June 1969) ILC Yearbook (1969) vol II

Draft Articles on Nationality of Natural Persons in relation to the Succession of States with commentaries, ILC Yearbook (1999) vol II

Draft articles on Succession of States in respect of State Property, Archives and Debts with commentaries 1981, ILC Yearbook (1981), vol II, Part Two 20, para 4

Govern Report of the International Law Commission on the work of its fiftieth session, 20 April–12 June and 27 July–14 August 1998', UN Doc. A/53/10

ILC Summary Record of the 2486th Meeting, UN Doc A/CN.4/SR.2486 (30 May 1997)

ILC, 'Conclusions of the Work of the Study Group', ILC Yearbook (2006), vol II, Part Two

ILC, 'Digest of Decisions of National Courts relating to Succession of States and Governments: Study prepared by the Secretariat', UN Doc A/CN.4/157 (18 April 1963) ILC Yearbook (1963) vol II

ILC, 'Draft articles on Succession of States in respect of Treaties with commentaries' (1974) ILC Yearbook vol II, part I

PRIMARY BIBLIOGRAPHY 379

ILC, 'Draft articles on Succession of States in respect of Treaties with commentaries', ILC Yearbook (1974) vol 2, Part I (ILC Articles)

ILC, 'Draft Conclusions on Identification of Customary International Law' in 'Report of the International Law Commission: Seventieth Session (30 April–1 June and 2 July–10 August 2018)', UN Doc A/73/10

ILC, 'Draft Conclusions on Identification of Customary International Law' in 'Report of the International Law Commission: Seventieth Session (30 April–1 June and 2 July–10 August 2018)', UN Doc A/73/10

ILC, 'Draft Conclusions on Identification of Customary International Law' in 'Report of the International Law Commission: Seventieth Session (30 April–1 June and 2 July–10 August 2018)', UN Doc A/73/10

ILC, 'First report on State succession and its impact on the nationality of natural and legal persons by Mr. Václav Mikulka, Special Rapporteur', UN Doc A/CN.4/467 (17 April 1995)

ILC, 'First report on succession of States in respect of State responsibility by Mr. Pavel Šturma, Special Rapporteur', UN Doc A/CN.4/708 (31 May 2017)

ILC, 'General principles of law: Consolidated text of draft conclusions 1 to 11 provisionally adopted by the Drafting Committee', UN Doc A/CN.4/L.971 (21 July 2022)

ILC, 'Provisional summary record of the 3375th meeting' (14 July 2017) UN Doc A/CN.4/SR.3375 (7 August 2017) 3–5 (Murphy) 4–6 (Nguyen)

ILC, 'Provisional summary record of the 3376th meeting' (18 July 2017) UN Doc A/CN.4/SR.3376 (17 August 2017)

ILC, 'Provisional summary record of the 3377th meeting' (19 July 2017) UN Doc A/CN.4/SR.3377 (18 August 2017)

ILC, 'Provisional summary record of the 3377th meeting' (19 July 2017) UN Doc A/CN.4/SR.3377 (18 August 2017)

ILC, 'Provisional summary record of the 3378th meeting' (20 July 2017) UN Doc A/CN.4/SR.3378 (18 August 2017)

ILC, 'Provisional summary record of the 3379th meeting' (21 July 2017) UN Doc A/CN.4/SR.3378 (16 August 2017)

ILC, 'Provisional summary record of the 3380th meeting' (25 July 2017) UN Doc A/CN.4/SR.3380 (24 August 2017)

ILC, 'Provisional summary record of the 3381stmeeting' (25 July 2017) UN Doc A/CN.4/SR.3381 (17 August 2017)

ILC, 'Provisional summary record of the 3431st meeting' (17 July 2018) UN Doc A/CN.4/SR.3431 (9 August 2018)

ILC, 'Provisional summary record of the 3434th meeting' (20 July 2018) UN Doc A/CN.4/SR.3434 (21 September 2018)

ILC, 'Provisional summary record of the 3552nd meeting' (28 July 2021) UN Doc A/CN.4/SR.3552 (14 September 2021)

ILC, 'Provisional summary record of the 3583rd meeting' (17 May 2022) UN Doc A/CN.4/3583 (16 June 2022)

ILC, 'Report on the work of its forty-ninth session (12 May–18 July 1997)', UN Doc A/52/10, ILC Yearbook

ILC, 'Report on the work of the seventy-fourth session (2023)', UN Doc A/78/10 (September 2023)

ILC, 'Succession of States in respect of State Responsibility: Statement of the Chair of the Drafting Committee' (28 July 2021) 3–4, <https://legal.un.org/ilc/guide/3_5.shtml#dcommrep> accessed 7 January 2024

ILC, 'Succession of States to multilateral treaties; seventh study prepared by the Secretariat', UN Doc A/CN.4/225 (24 April 1970), ILC Yearbook of the International Law Commission (1970) vol II

ILC, 'Summary record of the 2388th meeting', UN Doc A/CN.4/SR.2388 (24 May 1995)

ILC, 'Summary record of the 2388th meeting', UN Doc A/CN.4/SR.2388 (23 May 1995)

ILC, 'Summary record of the 2389th meeting', UN Doc A/CN.4/SR.2389 (24 May 1995)

380 PRIMARY BIBLIOGRAPHY

ILC, 'Supplement, prepared by the Secretariat, to "Materials on Succession of States"', UN Doc A/CN.4/263 (29 May 1972)

ILC, 2483rd meeting (27 May 1997) UN Doc A/CN.4/2483

ILC, 2484th meeting (29 May 1997) UN Doc A/CN.4/2484

ILC, 2488th meeting (5 June 1997) UN Doc A/CN.4/2488

ILC, Articles on the Responsibility of States for Internationally Wrongful Acts with Commentaries, ILC Yearbook (2001), vol. II, Part Two (ARSIWA)

ILC, Draft Articles on Nationality of Natural Persons in relation to the Succession of States with commentaries, vol II, Part Two, ILC Yearbook (1999)

ILC, Draft articles on Succession of States in respect of Treaties with commentaries 1974, ILC Yearbook, 1974, vol II, Part One

ILC, Guide to Practice on Reservations to Treaties (2011) ILC Yearbook vol II, Part Two

ILC, Summary Record of 1158th Meeting (15 May 1972)

ILC, Summary record of the 2481st Meeting (21 May 1997) UN Doc A/CN.4/SR.2481

ILC, Summary Record of the 2490th Meeting (10 June 1997) UN Doc A/CN.4/SR.2490

ILC, Summary Record of the 2493rd Meeting (13 June 1997) UN Doc A/CN.4/SR.2493

ILC, Summary record of the 2496th Meeting (21 May 1997) UN Doc A/CN.4/SR.2496

ILC, Summary Records of the 1156th Meeting (11 May 1972) and 1157th Meeting (12 May 1972), ILC Yearbook (1972) vol I, 31–41

Koskenniemi M, 'Report of the Study Group of the International Law Commission: Fragmentation of International Law' (13 April 2006) UN Doc A/CN.4/L.682

Mikulka V, 'First report on State succession and its impact on the nationality of natural and legal persons' (17 April 1995) UN Doc A/CN.4/467

Report of the International Law Commission on the Work of its Fifty-Third Session' 23 April to 1 June and 2 July to 10 August 2001, UN Doc A/56/10, 2001, 507, para 177

Report of the Secretary-General: Situation concerning Western Sahara, UN Doc S/2020/938 (23 September 2020)

Report of the Special Committee on the Situation with regard to the Implementation of the Declaration on the Granting of Independence to Colonial Countries and Peoples (30 November 1966) UN Doc A/6300/Rev.1

Report of the Special Committee on the Situation with regard to the Implementation of the Declaration on the Granting of Independence to Colonial Countries and Peoples (23 April 1969) UN Doc A/7200/Add.4 (Part II)

Report of the Sub-Committee on Succession of States and Governments, UN Doc A/5509 (Annex II) II *Yearbook of the International Law Commission* (1963) 260

Tladi D, 'Third report on peremptory norms of general international law (*jus cogens*)' (12 February 2018) UN Doc A/CN.4/714

UN Secretariat, 'Possibilities of participation by the United Nations in international agreements on behalf of a territory – study prepared by the Secretariat', UN Doc A/CN.4/281 (10 June 1974) ILC Yearbook (1974) vol II, Part Two, 26–32

UN Secretariat, 'Succession of States in respect of bilateral treaties: second study – Air transport agreements', UN Doc A/CN.4/253 (24 March 1971) (1971) ILC Yearbook vol II, 111

Waldock H, 'Fifth report on succession in respect of treaties', UN Doc. A/CN.4/256 (10 April, 29 May and 8, 16 and 28 June 1972) ILC Yearbook (1972), vol II

Waldock H, 'First report on the succession of States with respect to treaties' (15 March 1968) UN Doc A/CN.4/202, ILC Yearbook (1968) vol II

Waldock H, 'Second report on succession in respect of treaties' (18 April, 9 June and 22 July 1960) UN Doc A/CN.4/214 ILC Yearbook (1969) vol II

Waldock H, 'Third report on succession in respect of treaties' (22 April and 27 May 1970) UN Doc A/CN.4/224 (1970) ILC Yearbook, vol II, 28 ILC Yearbook (1972) vol I

## PRIMARY BIBLIOGRAPHY

### Organization of African Unity
'Speeches & Statements made at the first Organization of African Unity Summit' (May 1963) <https://au.int/en/speeches/19630508/speeches-and-statements-made-first-organization-african-unity-oau-summit-1963> accessed 1 January 2024

### Collected Courses of The Hague Academy of International Law
Bedjaoui M, 'Problèmes récents de succession d'états dans les états nouveaux' (1970-II) 130 RdC 454

Bentwich N, 'Le système des mandats' (1929-IV) 29 RdC 115

Castañon CGF, 'Les problèmes coloniaux et les classiques espagnols du droit des gens' (1954-II) 86 RdC 557

Castrén EJS, 'Aspects récents de la succession d'états' (1951-I) 78 RdC 379

Crusen G, 'Les servitudes internationales' (1928-II) 22 RdC 1

de Castro F, 'La nationalité, la double nationalité et la supranationalité' (1961-I) 102 RdC 515

Diena G, 'Les mandats internationaux' (1924-IV) 5 RdC 211

Higgins R, 'The Taking of Property by the State: Recent Developments in International Law' (1982-III) 176 RdC

Isay E, 'De la nationalité' (1924-IV) 5 RdC 425

Kunz JL, 'L'Option de Nationalité', 31 RdC 108

Lachs M, 'Le développement et les fonctions des traités multilatéraux' (1957-II) 92 RdC 229

Makarov AN, 'La nationalité de la femme mariée' (1937-II) 60 RdC 111

Makarov AN, 'Règles générales du droit de la nationalité' (1949-I) 74 RdC 269

Makonnen Y, 'State Succession in Africa: Some Selected Problems' (1986) 200 RdC 93

McWhinney E, 'Self-Determination of Peoples and Plural-Ethnic States' (2002) 294 RdC 167

Münch F, 'Les effets d'une nationalisation à l'étranger' (1959-III) 98 RdC 411

O'Connell DP, 'Recent problems of state succession in relation to new states' (1970) 130 RdC 95

Petrén MS, 'La confiscation des biens étrangers et les réclamations internationales' (1963-II) 109 RdC 487

Pillet A, 'La théorie générale des droits acquis' (1925-III) 8 RdC 489

Reid HW, 'Les servitudes internationales' (1933-III) 45 RdC 1

Rezek JF, 'Le droit international de la nationalité' (1986-III) 198 RdC 333

Rolin H, 'La pratique des mandats internationaux' (1927) 4 RdC 497

Sack AN, 'La succession aux dettes publiques d'état' (1928-III) 23 RdC 145

Sánchez Rodríguez L, 'L'*uti possidetis* et les effectivités dans les contentieux territoriaux et frontaliers' (1997) 263 RdC 149

Shawcross H, 'The Problems of Foreign Investment in International Law' (1961-I) 102 RdC 335

Siehr K, 'International Art Trade and Law'(1993) 243 RdC 9

Stern B, 'La succession d'États' (1996) 262 RdC 9

Travers M, 'La nationalité des sociétés commerciales' (1930-III) 33 RdC 1

Udina M, 'La succession des États quant aux obligations internationales autres que les dettes publiques' (1933-II) 44 RdC 665

Vedovato G, 'Les accords de tutelle' (1950-I) 76 RdC 609

Verdross A, 'Les règles internationals concernant le traitement des étrangers' (1931-III) 37 RdC 323

Zacklin R, 'The Problem of Namibia in International Law' (1981-II) 171 RdC 225

Zemanek K, 'State Succession after Decolonization' (1965-III) 116 RdC 186

### Other International Legal Documents
'Application of Eritrea for admission to membership in the United Nations', UN Doc A/47/948-S/25793 (18 May 1993) annex

'Cablegram dated 15 May 1948' (15 April 1948) UN Doc S/747

'Declaration on the Granting of Independence to Colonial Countries and Peoples: information on the implementation of the Declaration', UN Doc A/AC.109/71 (6 May 1964)

382 PRIMARY BIBLIOGRAPHY

'Note verbale from the Secretary-General to the Permanent Representatives of Member States'
(22 May 1990) UN Doc A/44/946
'Progress Report on East Timor' (13 December 1999) UN Doc A/54/654
Application of the FRY for Admission to Membership in the United Nations, UN Doc A/55/528-
S/2000/1043 (30 October 2009)

# Appendix

*Archival material*

France
Archives diplomatiques du Ministère de l'Europe et des Affaires Étrangères de la République
Française. Paris

United States
World Bank Group Archives, Washington DC
International Bank for Reconstruction and Development (IBRD)
International Development Association (IDA), World Bank Group Archives, Washington DC
International Monetary Archives, Washington DC
United Nations Archives, New York

Portugal
Arquivo Nacional da Torre do Tombo, Lisbon

England
The National Archives, London

# Index

*For the benefit of digital users, indexed terms that span two pages (e.g., 52–53) may, on occasion, appear on only one of those pages.*

absorption *see* State succession, classes of

accession to independence *see* State succession, classes of

acquiescence, general principle of 55–56, 64, 87–88, 90, 98, 163, 189–90, 191–92, 214, 329–30, 336

acquired rights, doctrine of 19, 34–35, 58, 291, 325–26, 336
  inapplicability of 292–93, 325

act of State, doctrine of 54–55, 124–25, 214, 294

Afghanistan 77, 112
  succession to territorial obligations and 86, 94
  succession to treaties and 89
  *uti possidetis juris* and 96

Åland Islands *see* Finland, secession of

Alaska, cession of 256

Albania, occupation of 10–11

Alexandretta, cession of
  nationality, succession and 251–52, 265–66
  succession to State property and debt in 129–30

Algeria, secession of 47
  boundaries, succession to 89, 94
  cultural property, succession to 114
  local debt, succession to 117
  localized property, succession to 111–12
  nationality, succession and 245–46, 255, 257–58, 269, 277
  odious debt, succession to 121
  private property, succession and 300–1, 304, 311, 313, 317
  State property and debt, succession to 116, 117, 118–19, 133–34, 203, 225, 233
  treaties, succession to 89

Algiers, absorption of 67

Alsace-Lorraine, cession of
  international claims and responsibility, succession to 238
  nationality, succession and 238
  odious debt, succession to 121

Alsace-Lorraine, retrocession of
  international claims and responsibility, succession to 223, 238
  nationality, succession and 223, 253
  tortious claims, succession to 223, 238

Angola, secession of 28
  State property, succession to 111–12
  territorial obligations, succession to 86, 87

annexation *see* State succession, annexation and

Antigua and Barbuda, secession of
  treaties, succession to 189

Aozou Strip *see* Libya, secession of; Chad, secession of; International Court of Justice

Argentina, Republic of 174–75, 185

Armenia, secession of 9
  boundaries, succession to 98
  nationality, succession and 246–47, 248–49, 250–51, 269, 280, 281
  private property, succession and 303
  State property, succession to 108
  treaties, succession to 186, 192
  *uti possidetis juris* and 75–76

Atacama, cession of 129–30

Australia, Commonwealth of 52, 142, 174–75, 220, 226–27
  succession to international claims and responsibility and 231–32
  succession to private property and 299, 304, 318
  succession to treaties and 173–74

Australia, secession of
  boundaries, succession to 73
  nationality, succession and 270
  treaties, succession to 162–63

Austria, absorption of 10–11, 213
  administrative debt, succession to 118–19
  nationality, succession and 261–62
  private property, succession and 313–14, 322
  retroactive annulment of 11, 313–14
  State property and debt, succession to 124, 125
  treaties, succession to 153–54, 171

Austria-Hungary, dismemberment of 45–46, 330–31
  international claims and responsibility, succession to 217
  nationality, succession and 256
  private property, succession and 309–10
  State property and debt, succession to 113, 114, 126–27

384   INDEX

Austria, Republic of 330–31
   nationality, succession and 246, 248, 261–62
   succession to international claims and
     responsibility and 216, 233
   succession to State property and debt
     and 130–31
   succession to treaties and 91, 165, 172,
     173–75, 188–89
Azerbaijan, secession of
   boundaries, succession to 91–92, 98
   nationality, succession and 246, 269, 280, 281
   treaties, succession to 91–92, 165
   *uti possidetis juris* and 75–76

Bahamas, secession of
   treaties, succession to 162–63, 189, 191
Bahrain, accession to independence of
   boundaries, succession to 70–72, 76
Bangladesh, secession of 29, 48
   general debt, succession to 136–37
   internal law, provisional continuity of 278
   localized debt, succession to 117–18, 136–37
   nationality, succession and 251–52, 253, 256,
     269, 278–79, 301–2
   private property, succession and 301–2, 304,
     322
   State contracts, succession and 314
   State property and debt, succession to 106,
     108–9, 116, 134, 136–37
   territorial claims, succession to 64, 70–72
   tortious debt, succession to 120
   treaties, succession to 177
Barbados, secession of
   administrative debt, succession to 119
   local debt, succession to 116–17
   nationality, succession and 253
   State property and debt, succession to 132
   tortious debt, succession to 120
   treaties, succession to 189
Bedjaoui, Mohammed 17, 18, 22, 102–3, 291
   definition of State succession 19, 21, 34–35
   methodology as Special Rapporteur 3–4, 17,
     36, 103, 325–26
   treatment of State practice by 4–5
   views on provisional continuity of internal
     law 41–42
Belarus, secession of
   nationality, succession and 246, 251–52,
     253–54, 269, 281
   State property, succession to 114
   *uti possidetis juris* and 75
Belbase leases *see* Tanganyika, accession to
   independence of
Belgium, Kingdom of 35, 160

private property, succession and 300, 311–12,
   322
Belgium, secession of
   international claims and responsibility,
     succession to 226
   succession to territorial obligations *see* Congo
     (Independent State of), absorption of
   territorial claims, succession to 65
   territorial obligations, succession to 82
Belize, secession of
   territorial claims, succession to 65–66
   treaties, succession to 189, 191
belligerent occupation 10–11, 18
   State succession as distinguished from 10–11,
     37, 303–4, 313–14, 330
Benin ('Dahomey'), secession of
   boundaries, succession to 73
   local debt, succession to 116–17
borders, internal *see* territorial title, succession to
Bosnia-Herzegovina, independence of
   nationality, succession and 246–47, 254–55,
     263
   State property, succession to 104
   treaties, succession to 157, 164, 166–67, 172
Botswana, secession of
   nationality, succession and 245–46, 248–49
   State property and debt, succession to 132
   territorial claims, succession to 65
   treaties, succession to 93, 186–87, 188–89
boundaries *see* territorial title, succession to
Brazil, secession of
   boundaries, succession to 67, 72–73
   nationality, succession and 269
   private property, succession and 294
   succession to State property and debt 132
   territorial claims, succession to 64
British India *see* India, secession of and Pakistan,
   secession of
Brownlie, Ian 56, 244
Brunei, accession to independence of
   treaties, succession to 189
Bulgaria, secession of
   State property and debt, succession to 106,
     107, 117
Burkina Faso ('Upper Volta'), secession of
   boundaries, succession to 68, 73
   State property and debt, succession
     to 116–17
Burma, absorption of
   international claims and responsibility,
     succession to 203, 211–12, 213, 214
Burundi, accession to independence of
   territorial rights, succession to 80
   treaties, succession to 150, 188, 189

INDEX   385

Cambodia, secession of
  boundaries, succession to 73–74
  cultural property, succession to 114
  legal identity in 49, 147
  nationality, succession and 251–52, 269, 275–76
  territorial obligations, succession to 84
  State property and debt, succession to 106, 133–34, 138
  treaties, succession to 90, 162
Cameroon, secession of
  boundaries, succession to 69–70
  treaties, succession to 161
Cameroons, Trust Territory for 286–87
  treaties, succession to 154, 175
Canada, Dominion of 80–81, 87, 331–32
Canada, secession of
  depositary practice of 160
  succession to nationality and 270
  succession to territorial obligations and 86
  succession to treaties and 173–74
  treaties, succession to 166–67
Carpatho-Ukraine, cession of 296
Central African Republic, secession of
  State property and debt, succession to 116–17, 120
  treaties, succession to 177–78, 188–89
cession see State succession, classes of
Chad, secession of
  boundaries, succession to 69–70
  State property and debt, succession to 116–17, 120
  treaties, succession to 90
  China, People's Republic of
  succession to boundaries and 79, 96–97
  succession to treaties and 152–53, 154, 173–75, 195–96
  uti possidetis juris and 94, 96–97
clean slate (tabula rasa), theory of the see State succession, theories of
Cocos Islands (Keeling Islands), cession of
  private property, succession and 299, 318
Colombia, Union of ('Gran Colombia')
  boundaries, succession to 72–73
  international claims and responsibility, succession to 209, 217–18
  State property and debt, succession to 126–27
colonial protectorates see State succession, classes of
colonies see State succession, classes of
Commission internationale de l'État Civil 160
Congo, Democratic Republic of the ('Belgian Congo'), secession of 35
  administrative debt, succession to 119–20, 135
  cultural property, succession to 114
  local debt, succession to 117

nationality, succession and 246–47, 251–52, 269, 277–78
  private property, succession and 35, 300, 304, 309–10, 311–12, 322
  State property and debt, succession to 133–34, 135–36
  territorial obligations, succession to 86
  territorial rights, succession to 32
  tortious debt, succession to 135–36
  treaties, succession to 150, 177
Congo (Independent State of), absorption of 277–78
  territorial obligations, succession to 84, 86
Congo (Republic of), secession of
  local debt, succession to 116–17
  tortious debt, succession to 120
  treaties, succession to 165, 177–78
Congress of Vienna 82, 213
conquest see State succession
Cook Islands 285
Côte d'Ivoire, secession of
  local debt, succession to 116–17
  treaties, succession to 184, 185
Council of Europe 245, 247
  depositary practice of 160
  studies on State succession of 6, 10
  succession to nationality and 245, 247–48, 253
Crawford, James 28, 37–38, 198
Crete, cession of
  international claims and responsibility, succession to 223–24
Crimea 75–76, 100, 330
Croatia, Republic of
  international claims and responsibility, succession to 203, 220, 237
  investor-State arbitration and 9
  nationality, succession and 246, 252, 263
  private property, succession and 127
  State property and debt, succession to 110, 117–18, 119–20, 127, 128–29
  treaties, succession to 91, 157, 159, 165, 167, 172–73, 188–89
Cuba, secession of 224–25
  odious debt, succession to 121
  succession to military base leases and 80
cultural property see State property, succession to
customary international law 52–55, 62–63, 67–68, 78, 101, 104, 116, 144, 148, 179, 200–1, 213, 294, 303–4
  opinio juris 54–55, 63–64, 66, 67–68, 69, 82, 89, 90, 91–92, 123, 152, 153, 155, 158, 170, 172, 176, 178, 181, 182, 185, 208–9, 211, 219–20, 230, 234, 235–36, 243–44, 311

386 INDEX

customary international law (*cont.*)
  persistent objector rule  73, 87, 94–98
  State practice *see* State practice
Cyprus, Republic of  89, 330
Cyprus, secession of
  nationality, succession and  252, 264–65
  State property and debt, succession to  108–9,
    132–33
  treaties, succession to  89, 162–63, 184
Czechia ('Czech Republic')  92
  nationality, succession and  248–49, 253, 255,
    256
  State property and debt, succession to  106,
    110, 114, 126–27
  treaties, succession to  166–67, 172, 173–74,
    190
Czecho-Slovakia, dismemberment of  43, 45–46
  boundaries, succession to  70–72, 73
  international claims and responsibility,
    succession to  202, 207–8, 217, 218
  nationality, succession and  251–52, 264
  private property, succession and  303
  State property and debt, succession to  106,
    107, 110, 112, 114, 126–27
  treaties, succession to  91, 92–93, 157, 165,
    166–67, 172, 174–75, 190
Czecho-Slovakia, occupation of  10–11

Danzig, absorption of  213
  as international protectorate  51
  private property, succession and  297, 321
  State property and debt, succession to  124
decolonization, law of  300, 329
  definition of  26–27
  definition of State succession and  24, 47
  non-self-governing territories in  25–26
  right of external self-determination
    in  25, 27
  validity of territorial title of predecessors
    in  27–31
Denmark, Kingdom of
  succession to treaties and  173–74
desovietization  2, 103
diplomatic protection, law of  58, 115, 234, 238–
    39, 242–43, 257–58, 292, 294, 315–16, 331
Djibouti, secession of
  territorial claims, succession to  82
  territorial obligations, succession to  82
Dominica, secession of
  treaties, succession to  189
Doumeirah Island *see* Djibouti; Eritrea
Dumberry, Patrick  7–8, 10, 215
Durand Line *see* Afghanistan; Pakistan,
  secession of

East Germany *see* German Democratic Republic
East Pakistan *see* Bangladesh
Egypt, secession of
  boundaries, succession to  98
  as protected State  49–50
  territorial obligations, succession to  85
  treaties, succession to  173–74
Equatorial Guinea, secession of
  boundaries, succession to  70
  nationality, succession and  250–52, 269, 276,
    278
  private property, succession and  301, 322
  State property and debt, succession to  118–
    19, 133–34
  treaties, succession to  93, 155, 177–78
equitable apportionment, principle of  334
  role in succession to international claims and
    responsibility  208–9
  role in succession to State property and
    debt  104, 106–7
equity, principle of  4–5, 102, 103, 122, 130, 131,
    138, 141, 143, 191–92, 213, 322, 334
Eritrea, cession of
  private property, succession and  307
  treaties, succession to  152, 176
Eritrea, secession of  11, 328
  boundaries, succession to  69–72, 73–74, 76
  nationality, succession and  9, 58, 246–47,
    248–49, 250, 252, 253, 265, 281–82
  private property, succession and  303
  State property and debt, succession to  9–10,
    138–39
  territorial claims, succession to  30, 65, 82
  territorial obligations, succession to  82
  treaties, succession to  177–78
Eritrea-Ethiopia Claims Commission  9–10, 58,
    139, 282
Estonia, secession of
  international claims and responsibility,
    succession to  203, 204, 239
estoppel, general principle of  55–56, 87–88,
    99–101, 192–94
Eswatini ('Swaziland'), secession of
  nationality, succession and  245–46
  tortious debt, succession to  120
  treaties, succession to  189, 191, 193
Ethiopia
  occupation of  10–11
  succession to territorial obligations and  87
Eupen-Malmédy
  nationality, succession and  265
European Court of Human Rights  316
  succession to localized debt and  2, 105, 124,
    128

succession to international claims and
responsibility and 228–29, 230
European Court of Justice 115
*ex injuria jus non oritur*, general principle
of 10–11, 37

fair and equitable treatment standard *see* private
property, succession and
Fiji, absorption of
private property, succession and 307–8
State property and debt, succession to 124–25
Fiji, secession of
nationality, succession and 245–46
treaties, succession to 189
Finland, secession of 310
territorial obligations, succession to 77, 82
Florida, cession of 238
nationality, succession and 248–49
territorial obligations, succession and 82
France 108
depositary practice of 160
private property, succession and 309–10
succession to nationality and 275
succession to State property and 108, 112
succession to treaties and 172, 173–74
territorial obligations, succession to 82–83
French India, cession of 60
international claims and responsibility,
succession to 207–8, 222
nationality, succession and 246–47, 248–49,
254–55, 265–66
private property, succession and 296
State property and debt, succession to 107,
112, 117, 129–30
French Indochina 106, 114, 119, 126–27, 138

Gabon, secession of
boundaries, succession to 70
international claims and
responsibility 226–27
private property, succession and 296
State property and debt, succession to 116–
17, 120
treaties, succession to 93
Gambia, secession of
nationality, succession and 245–46
State property and debt, succession to 132
general principles of law 55–58, 244, 335–36
Georgia, secession of
nationality, succession and 246–47, 253, 269, 281
private property, succession and 303
treaties, succession to 91–92, 165
German Democratic Republic (East Germany),
absorption of 331–32

classification of 14, 44
boundaries, succession to 70–72
international claims and responsibility,
succession to 203, 206, 213, 215, 226
nationality, succession and 247, 261–62
private property, succession and 303, 306–7,
314
State property and debt, succession to 118–
19, 124, 328
treaties, succession to 91, 153, 161, 171–72,
192
German Democratic Republic (East Germany),
secession of 82–83
private property, succession and 305–7
State property and debt, succession to 108–9,
111–12, 118
German Empire, creation of 213
as series of absorptions 45
State property and debt, succession to 124–25
Ghana, secession of
boundaries, succession to 68
international claims and responsibility,
succession to 225, 230
nationality, succession and 284
State property and debt, succession to 132
treaties, succession to 151, 180, 187, 192–93
good faith, principle of 103
governments, succession of 10–11, 18
Greece, secession of 107
Grenada, secession of 189
Guatemala, secession of 65–66
Guayana Esequiba *see* Guyana, secession of
Guinea, secession of
boundaries, succession to 69–70
nationality, succession and 246–47, 269
private property, succession and 299
State property and debt, succession to 105,
107, 111, 117, 133–35
Guinea-Bissau, secession of
boundaries, succession to 69–70
treaties, succession to 177
Guyana, secession of
boundaries, succession to 68, 72–73, 97
nationality, succession and 248–49, 253
State property and debt, succession to 132
treaties, succession to 155, 189

Hafner, Gerhard 10
Hawai'i, absorption of
international claims and responsibility,
succession to 213, 215
nationality, succession and 248–49, 261
State property and debt, succession
to 124–25

## 388   INDEX

Hong Kong, retrocession of 223, 330–32
  nationality, succession and 245–46, 250–51,
    253, 265–66, 267–68, 289
  private property, succession and 303, 313–14
  State property and debt, succession to 116–
    17, 129–30
  treaties, succession to 150, 152–53, 154, 176
Hungary, Republic of
  succession to cultural property and 114
  succession to international responsibility
    and 204, 206, 218–19, 222, 236
  succession to treaties and 92–93
Hyderabad, absorption of 213
  nationality, succession and 261
  private property, succession and 307–8
  State property and debt, succession to 108–9,
    124, 307–8

Iceland, accession to independence of
  treaties, succession to 178, 188–89
Iceland, secession of
  as protected State 49–50
  State property and debt, succession to 114,
    137, 138
Ifni, cession of 43, 60, 223
  nationality, succession and 246, 250–51, 255,
    256, 265, 266–67, 278
  private property, succession and 296
  treaties, succession to 176, 184
India, secession of 11
  boundaries, succession to 73, 96–97
  international claims and responsibility,
    succession to 209, 225, 226
  legal identity and 14, 38–39
  nationality, succession and 250–51, 253–54,
    268, 270–71
  private property, succession and 296, 307–8
  State property and debt, succession to 106,
    107, 108–9, 110, 112, 113, 117–19, 122,
    132–33
  territorial claims, succession to 65
  territorial obligations, succession to 83
  treaties, succession to 89–90, 166–67, 168, 183
Indonesia, secession of
  international claims and responsibility,
    succession to 203, 207–8, 225, 226–27,
    230
  nationality, succession and 245–47, 248–50,
    251–52, 253, 254–55, 256, 268, 273–74
  private property, succession and 297–98, 314,
    316, 318, 322
  State property and debt, succession to 106,
    108, 111–12, 114, 115, 118–19, 120, 121,
    133–34

territorial claims, succession to 65
treaties, succession to 168, 177, 184, 185
Institut de droit international 22–23, 327
  methodology of 7–8, 198
  studies on State succession 6–7, 10
  Resolution on State Property and Debt
    2001 6–7, 103, 104, 106, 107, 109, 110–11,
    114, 115, 116–18, 121, 122, 125–26, 128–29,
    130, 143–44
  Resolution on State Succession and State
    Responsibility 2015 7–8, 198, 204–5, 209,
    210, 212, 215, 221, 224, 230, 232–33, 235,
    335
internal law, provisional continuity of 41–43
  as general principle of law 42
  meaning of 'law' 42–43
International Civil Aviation Authority 160
international claims and responsibility,
    succession to
  adoption in 237
  application by class of succession 213, 216,
    217, 222, 224–25, 231, 234
  automaticity in 202, 334
  composite breach in 204–5
  continuing breach in 204
  definition of 197, 205, 206
  diplomatic protection and 238
  equitable apportionment under 209, 217–18
  general rule of succession or non-succession
    in 199, 200, 203, 212–13
  identification of disputing parties in
    consequence of 202
  relations between indirect injury and
    succession to nationality 201, 234
  relations between international claims and
    international responsibility 197, 207,
    224–25
  succession agreements in 235–36
  sufficiency and evaluation of State
    practice 197–98, 201
  third State consent and 235–36
  tortious debt ('municipal torts') and 201, 217,
    226, 232–33, 238, 335
  temporality in 203–4
  territoriality in 207–8
International Court of Justice
  State succession and 6–7, 9–10, 59, 219,
    333–34
  succession to international claims and
    responsibility and 203, 204, 208–9, 218–19,
    220, 228
  succession to territorial obligations and 83
  succession to treaties and 40, 90, 92–93, 147,
    157, 159, 162, 175, 194

INDEX    389

International Law Association  22–23, 201, 327
  studies on State succession  3–4, 6–7, 10, 61,
    143–44, 146, 165, 178
International Law Commission  66, 97–98
  availability and use of empirical data on State
    practice by  2–4, 7, 8, 103, 115–16, 130–31,
    145, 199, 328, 331–32
  codification projects on State succession  1,
    8–10, 17, 36–37, 59, 61, 77, 88, 102–3, 109,
    115–16, 145, 198–201, 210, 212–13, 215,
    221, 327, 336
  definition of State succession by  19–22,
    23–24, 47, 59, 329
  methodologies of  3, 8–9, 18, 102, 288–89
  treatment of decolonization by  30–31, 47–48,
    49, 59, 103, 329
  typology of State succession and  44, 59, 124,
    170, 175, 178, 215, 217
International Law Commission Articles on
    Nationality of Natural Persons in relation
    to the Succession of States 1999  7, 22–23,
    244, 328, 335
  application of  7–8, 245–46, 249, 250–51, 252
  focus on statelessness and human rights of  7,
    244, 328
  reception by the Sixth Committee of  7
International Law Commission Articles on the
    Responsibility of States for Internationally
    Wrongful Acts 2001...  7, 49
  conduct of an insurrectional movement
    under  202–3
  exclusion of State succession from  7–8, 198,
    202, 230
  invocation of an internationally wrongful act
    under  208
  reparation under  320–21
international legal personality *see* legal identity
International Monetary Fund  2–3, 104, 106–7
international organizations, succession of  10–11
international protectorates *see* State succession,
    classes of
intertemporal law, general principle of  55–56
investor-state arbitration
  international claims and responsibility,
    succession to  228
  private property, succession and  304–5
  State succession and  1, 2, 9, 59, 292,
    333–34
  treaties, succession to  165, 195–96
Ionian Islands, cession of  309–10
Iran, Islamic Republic of
  succession to boundaries and  91–92
  succession to territorial obligations and  84
  succession to treaties and  89

Iraq ('Mesopotamia'), accession to independence of
  State debt, succession to  107
  territorial obligations, succession to  84
  treaties, succession to  89, 183
Irish Free State ('Republic of Ireland'), secession
    of  39
  treaties, succession to  177–78
Israel, accession to independence of  330–31
  boundaries, succession to  67–68, 72
  legal identity and  179
  nationality and  43, 246–47, 252, 284, 285–86
  private property, succession and  296, 311, 313
  provisional continuity of internal law and  43
  State contracts, succession and  314
  State property and debt, succession to  107,
    108–9, 111–12, 141
  territorial obligations, succession to  83, 84
  tortious debt, succession to  120
  treaties, succession to  91, 164, 179
Italy, Republic of
  succession to cultural property and  114
  succession to treaties and  91, 167, 168,
    173–74, 177–78
Italy ('Sardinia'), formation of  82–83, 213
  private property, succession and  309–10, 322
  as series of absorptions  45, 124–25
  State property and debt, succession to  107,
    124–25

Jamaica, secession of
  nationality, succession and  245–46
  State property and debt, succession to  132
  treaties, succession to  155, 161, 166, 167, 187
Japan, Empire of  78–79
  private property, succession and  294
  succession to international claims and
    responsibility and  226–27, 237
  succession to treaties and  173–74
Jordan ('Transjordan'), accession to
    independence of
  boundaries, succession to  70–72
  nationality, succession and  285
  State property and debt, succession to  107
  territorial obligations, succession to  86
  treaties, succession to  89, 91, 178, 183, 184
*jus cogens see* peremptory norm of internationl
    law

Kalat (Khanate of), absorption of  261
Kazakhstan, secession of
  boundaries, succession to  91–92
  nationality, succession and  246, 253–54, 269,
    280, 281
  treaties, succession to  163, 166

# 390 INDEX

Kenya, secession of
  nationality, succession and 245–46
  private property, succession and 307–8
  State property and debt, succession to 132
  tortious debt, succession to 120, 121
  treaties, succession to 189
Khuriya Muriya Islands, retrocession of *see*
    Yemen, People's Democratic Republic of
    ('South Yemen'), secession of
Kiribati ('Gilbert Islands'), secession of
  territorial claims, succession to 64
  treaties, succession to 189, 247
Kohen, Marcelo 7–8
Korea (Empire of), absorption of 294
Kuwait, accession to independence of
  boundaries, succession to 67–68
  private property, succession and 310,
    318–19
Kwatung, administrative cession of 46, 78–79
Kyrgyzstan, secession of
  boundaries, succession to 75–76
  nationality, succession and 246–47, 280
  private property, succession and 303

Lachs, Manfred 17
Laos, secession of
  nationality, succession and 246, 251–52, 269,
    275–76
  State property and debt, succession to 106,
    114, 133–34, 138
  territorial obligations, succession to 84
  treaties, succession to 184, 185
League of Nations 82, 118–19, 146, 294–95
  Committee of Jurists 82
  membership criteria of 38–39
  Mandate system of 50, 285
leases *see* territorial obligations
Lebanon, accession to independence of
  boundaries, succession to 62–63
  nationality, succession and 248–49, 253–54,
    255, 284, 285
  private property, succession and 296, 310
  State property and debt, succession to 141
  territorial obligations, succession to 83, 86
  treaties, succession to 89, 179, 182–83
legal identity 37–40
  as question preceding State succession... 13,
    38, 45–46, 147
  limited international legal personality and 44
Lesotho ('Basutoland'), secession of
  State property and debt, succession to 132
  treaties, succession to 189, 191
*lex specialis derogat lege generali*, general
    principle of 51–52

Libya, secession of 27, 68
  nationality, succession and 246–47, 250–52,
    253, 254–55, 268, 274–75
  private property, succession and 296, 306–7,
    310
  State property and debt, succession to 108–9,
    114, 117, 133–34, 138
  territorial claims, succession to 65, 69–70
  territorial obligations, succession to 86
  treaties, succession to 89, 90
Lithuania, secession of
  cultural property, succession to 114
  international claims and responsibility,
    succession to 203
Louisiana, cession of *see* Spain; United States of
    America

Macao, retrocession of 33, 223, 331–32
  investor-State arbitration and 9
  nationality, succession and 252, 265, 268
  private property, succession and 303, 313–14
  State property and debt, succession to 129–30
  treaties, succession to 150, 151, 153, 154, 165,
    176
Madagascar, absorption of 214
  international claims and responsibility,
    succession to 211–12, 213
Madagascar ('Malagasy Republic'),
  nationality, succession and 252, 255, 269,
    276–77
  private property, succession and 299, 304
  State property and debt, succession to 108–9,
    110–11, 117, 124–25, 133–34
  tortious debt, succession to 120
  treaties, succession to 189, 192–93
Malawi ('Nyasaland'), secession of
  boundaries, succession to 99–100
  internal law, provisional continuity of 42–43
  nationality, succession and 252, 254–55, 256
  State property and debt, succession
    to 118–19
  treaties, succession to 167, 186, 187, 189
Malaysia ('Malaya'), secession of 100
  international claims and responsibility,
    succession to 207–8
  nationality, succession and 245–46, 250,
    251–52, 253, 268, 272–73
  private property, succession and 307–8
  State property and debt, succession to 96,
    108–9, 116, 119–20
  territorial claims, succession to 65
  treaties, succession to 150, 153, 163, 184,
    186–87
Mali, Republic of *see* Mali, dismemberment of

Mali (Federation of), dismemberment of
boundaries, succession to  73
State property and debt, succession to  116–
17, 120, 133–34
territorial obligations, succession to  81
treaties, succession to  172, 186–87
Malta, secession of
State property and debt, succession to  132
treaties, succession to  150, 163
Mandatory Territories *see* State succession,
classes of
Marshall Islands, accession to independence of
nationality, succession and  250–52, 284,
287–88
private property, succession and  306
State property and debt, succession to  142–43
Mauritius, secession of  28–29
boundaries, succession to  73–74
localized property, succession to  111–12
nationality, succession and  268
private property, succession and  306
State contracts, succession and  314
State property and debt, succession to  116–
17, 119, 132–34
treaties, succession to  167, 168, 188, 189, 190
McMahon Line *see* India, secession of
Memel Territory, absorption of  51
treaties, succession to  169
merger *see* State succession, classes of
Mexico, secession of
State property and debt, succession to  132
succession to treaties and  173–74
territorial claims, succession to  65
Micronesia, accession to independence of
nationality, succession and  250–52, 256, 284,
287–88
private property, succession and  306
State property and debt, succession to  142–43
treaties, succession to  189
Mikulka, Václavj  244–45
methodology as Special Rapporteur  7
Moldova, secession of
nationality, succession and  246, 253–54, 280
private property, succession and  303
State property and debt, succession to  138–39
*uti possidetis juris* and  75
Montenegro, secession of  44
boundaries, succession to  70–72
international claims and responsibility,
succession to  206, 207–9, 226, 227–29, 230
investor-State arbitration and  9
nationality, succession and  246–49, 250–52,
255, 282–83
private property, succession and  303

State property and debt, succession to  106,
117–18, 139
treaties, succession to  161, 164, 165, 177, 181,
182–83, 186–87, 188–89, 192, 193
Morocco, accession to independence of  49–50,
231–32
boundaries, succession to  73, 94
International Tangier Zone  141
legal identity in  147, 158–59
nationality, succession and  246–47, 284, 286
private property, succession and  298–99,
307–8, 313–14, 322
State contracts, succession and  314
State property and debt, succession to  108–9,
115, 117, 119–20, 141, 307–8
territorial obligations, succession to  81, 86
treaties, succession to  89, 94, 158–59, 178,
179, 184, 185
*uti possidetis juris* and  94
Mozambique, secession of  11
boundaries, succession to  99–100
international claims and responsibility,
succession to  207–8, 225, 230
private property, succession and  310
State property and debt, succession to  111–
12, 133–34
treaties, succession to  177
municipal torts *see* State debt, succession to
Myanmar ('Burma') secession of
boundaries, succession to  72
nationality, succession and  245–47, 249–50,
252, 255, 256, 268, 271–72
private property, succession and  297, 304,
305–6, 316
State property and debt, succession to  111–
12, 117, 119–20, 132–33
territorial obligations, succession to  79
treaties, succession to  89–90, 183, 184, 185,
188–89

Namibia, accession to independence of
international claims and responsibility,
succession to  232–33
nationality, succession and  253–54, 284,
287–88
private property, succession and  303, 313–14
State contracts, succession and  314
State property and debt, succession to  108,
110, 142–43
territorial claims, succession to  65
territorial obligations, succession to  86
treaties, succession to  93, 179
*uti possidetis juris* and  97
Namwan Assigned Tract *see* Myanmar, secession of

## 392 INDEX

nationality, succession and 332–33, 335
  application according to class of
    succession 261–88
  affected body of nationals in 248–50
  automaticity in 245–48, 334
  collective nationalization 242, 246
  definition of 242–43
  dual nationality in 248, 285
  as general principles of law 243–44, 288, 289
  international law versus internal law 242–43,
    288–89
  legal persons in 256–58
  minors and wards in 249–50
  option, rights of 248, 254–56, 270, 271–72, 274
  principle of territoriality in 250–54
  as secondary consequence of succession 242
  statelessness and 247–48, 281, 289
  temporality in 246–47, 289
  types of nationality 242–43
  wives and widows in 249
Nauru, accession to independence of
  international claims and responsibility,
    succession to 231–32
  private property and succession 323
  treaties, succession to 89, 189
*nemo plus juris ad alium transfere potest quam*
  *ipse habet,* general principle of law of 65–
  66, 80, 87
Netherlands, Kingdom of
  depositary practice of 160
  succession to treaties and 173–74
New Zealand, secession of
  nationality, succession and 270
  private property, succession and 307–8
  succession to treaties and 173–74
Newfoundland, cession of 43, 60, 331–32
  nationality, succession and 246, 265
  State property and debt, succession to 129–30
  territorial obligations, succession to 80–81, 87
  treaties, succession to 152, 176
newly independent State *see* State succession,
  classes of
Nice and the Savoy *see* France; Italy
Niger, secession of
  boundaries, succession to 73
Nigeria, secession of
  boundaries, succession to 69–70
  succession to cultural property and 114
  treaties, succession to 166, 185
Non-self-governing Territories *see* State
  succession, classes of
North Borneo, Sarawak and Singapore, cession of
  international claims and responsibility,
    succession to 222–23

nationality, succession and 246, 250, 251–52,
  265, 266
  private property, succession and 310
  State property and debt, succession
    to 129–30
  treaties, succession to 176
North Macedonia, Republic of ('Former
  Yugoslav Republic of Macedonia')
  nationality, succession and 246, 254–55, 263
  State property, succession to 104
  treaties, succession to 172–73, 188–89
Northern Mariana Islands, cession of
  nationality, succession and 250–52, 253–54,
    287–88
  private property, succession and 306
  treaties, succession to 152–53, 175
Norway, secession of 137, 173–74

O'Connell, Daniel Patrick 1, 10, 18, 35–36, 61,
  201, 328, 330
  views on codification of 5, 327, 328
Ogaden region *see* Somalia, merger of
Oman, Sultanate of 95–96
Oregon, cession of 64
Organization for African Unity ('African
  Union')... 68, 73, 94–95
Ottoman Empire *see* Türkiye

Pacific Islands, Trust Territory for the
  nationality, succession and 249–50, 287–88
  tortious debt, succession to 120
Pakistan, secession of 11
  boundaries, succession to 73
  classification of... 14, 38–39, 147
  international claims and responsibility,
    succession to 209, 225, 226
  nationality, succession and 253–54, 268,
    270–71
  private property, succession and 296
  State property, succession to 108–9, 110, 112,
    113, 122
  State property and debt, succession to 106,
    107, 132–33
  territorial claims, succession to 64, 65
  territorial obligations, succession to 86
  treaties, succession to 89, 96, 150, 183
  *uti possidetis juris* and 96
Palau, accession to independence of
  nationality, succession and 250–52, 284,
    287–88
  private property, succession and 306
  State property and debt, succession to 142–43
  treaties, succession to 189
Panama, secession of 226

INDEX 393

State property and debt, succession to
   and... 106, 111–12, 132
   *uti possidetis juris* and 72–73
Papua New Guinea, accession to independence of
   boundaries, succession to 73
   cultural property, succession to 114
   private property, succession and 296
   treaties, succession to 178, 189
patrimonial property *see* State property,
   succession t
Pazartzis, Photini 10
pecuniary debt *see* State debt, succession to
pension debt, civil service *see* State debt,
   succession to
pension debt, social security *see* State debt,
   succession to
peremptory norms of international law 47, 52
Permanent Court of International Justice 40
   international claims and responsibility,
      succession to 204, 239
   nationality, succession and 253–54
   succession and private property 109, 294–95
   succession to territorial obligations and 82–83
   State succession and 58, 333
Peru, secession of 114
Peru-Bolivarian Confederation, dismemberment
   of 217
Philippines, secession of
   nationality, succession and 246, 265, 268,
      269–70
   private property, succession and 296, 310, 316
   State property and debt, succession to 111–
      12, 117, 133–34, 251–52
   territorial claims, succession to 65
   territorial obligations, succession to 79
   treaties, succession to 93, 159–60
Poland ('Congress Kingdom of'), secession of
   depositary practice of 160
   private property, succession and 108–9, 295, 322
   State property and debt, succession to 107,
      108–9, 119–20
   treaties, succession to 173–74
Port Arthur and Talien *see* Kwatung,
   administrative cession of
Portugal, Republic of 173–74
Portuguese India, cession of 330–32
   international claims and responsibility,
      succession to 207–8, 222
   nationality, succession and 246–47, 253–55,
      256, 265–66, 289
   private property, succession and 312, 313
   retroactivity of 10–11, 28–29
   State property and debt, succession to 112,
      116–17, 129–30

primary financial beneficiary principle *see* State
   debt, succession to
private property, succession and
   application to all classes of succession 293
   compensation agreements 293, 297–98, 322
   concessions as 292–93, 308–14
   definition of 305–8
   diplomatic protection and 315–16, 321
   expropriation in 293, 296, 303–4, 316–20
   international minimum standard of treatment
      in 292–93, 294–305, 325
   nationality and 315–16
   nationalization in 293
   reparation and 297–99, 300, 320–25
   valuation in 319–25
protected States and Territories *see* State
   succession, classes of

Qatar, accession to independence
   of 70–72, 76

Reinisch, August 8–9, 10, 200–1
*res judicata,* general principle of 165, 269–70
*res transit cum suo onere,* maxim of 118
responsibility of States for internationally
   wrongful acts, succession to *see*
   international claims and responsibility,
   succession to
Rhodesia and Nyasaland, Federation of 126–27,
   167, 231
Romania, Republic of 173–74
Russian Federation *see* Union of Soviet Socialist
   Republics
Rwanda, accession to independence of
   territorial rights, succession to 32
   treaties, succession to 150, 188, 189

Saar Territory, absorption of
   as international protectorate 51
   legal identity of 13
   treaties, succession to 171
Saint-Gidolph, cession of *see* France
Saint Kitts and Nevis, secession of 189
Saint Lucia, secession of 189
Saint Vincent and the Grenadines, secession
   of 189
Samoa, accession to independence of
   nationality, succession and 285
   State property and debt, succession to 141
Samos, cession of 223–24
Saudi Arabia, secession of
   territorial obligations, succession to 86
   treaties, succession to 89
Senegal, Republic of *see* Mali, dismemberment of

394   INDEX

Serbia, Republic of
   State property and debt, succession to 128–29
   succession to cultural property and 114
   treaties, succession to 172–73
servitudes *see* territorial obligations
set-off, equitable principle of 104, 107
Shantung lease 78–79
Sierra Leone, secession of
   nationality, succession and 245–46, 248–49
   State property and debt, succession to 120,
      132
   treaties, succession to 183
Singapore, secession of
   boundaries, succession to 70–72, 100
   international claims and responsibility,
      succession to 207–8, 225
   nationality, succession and 269
   State property and debt, succession to 108,
      111, 133–34
   territorial obligations, succession to 81
   treaties, succession to 177, 184
Slovakia, Republic of
   international claims and responsibility,
      succession to 202, 204, 206, 207, 218–19,
      236
   State property and debt, succession to 106,
      110, 114
   treaties, succession to 92–93, 157, 165, 172,
      181
Slovenia, Republic of
   nationality, succession and 246, 253, 263
   State property and debt, succession to 114,
      117–18, 128
   treaties, succession to 172–73, 186–87,
      188–89
Solomon Islands, secession of 189
Somalia, accession to independence of *see*
   Somalia, merger of
Somalia, merger of
   boundaries, succession to 73
   international claims and responsibility,
      succession to 211
   nationality, succession and 246–47, 250, 252,
      259–60, 310
   State property and debt, succession to 120, 123
   territorial claims, succession to 2–3
   territorial rights, succession to 87
   treaties, succession to 155, 169, 184
   *uti possidetis juris* and 95
Somaliland, secession of *see* Somalia, merger of
South Africa, secession of
   nationality, succession and 270, 287
   treaties, succession to 188–89
   *uti possidetis juris* and 97

South African Republic, absorption of 213, 214
South Sudan, secession of 2, 11
   boundaries, succession to 69–70, 76, 98
   investor-State arbitration and 9
   nationality, succession and 245–47, 248–49,
      251–52, 253–54, 283–84, 289
   private property, succession and 303, 310
   State property and debt, succession to 105,
      106, 108–9, 110–11, 117–18, 139, 140
   territorial obligations, succession to 85, 86
   treaties, succession to 177
South West Africa, Mandatory Territory
      of 248–49, 253–54, 287
sovereignty 50
   State succession and 32
   meaning of... 23
Soviet Socialist Republics, Union of ('Russian
      Federation') 328
   boundaries, succession to 70–72, 75–76,
      91–92, 100
   claim of Russian Federation to continue legal
      identity of 13, 138–39
   nationality, succession and 254–55, 256, 280
   private property, succession and 303
   State property and debt, succession to 107,
      114, 116–17, 138–39
   treaties, succession to 91–92, 155, 163, 165,
      173–74, 177, 184
Spain, Kingdom of
   succession to treaties and 89, 173–74
   territorial obligations, succession to 84
Spanish Zones of Morocco ('Northern Zones')
      *see* Morocco, accession to independence of
Sri Lanka ('Ceylon'), secession of
   nationality, succession and 252, 268, 270
   succession to State property and debt 132
   treaties, succession to 183
State archives, succession to
   definition of 108, 113
   distinction from cultural property 115
   documents, definition of 112, 113
   presumption of origin in 112
   reproduction of documents 108
   as State property 108, 112
State debt, succession to
   administrative debt 118–19
   clean slate theory and 103
   definition of 115, 116
   general debt 102, 106
   local debt 102, 105, 106, 115–17
   localized debt 117–18
   odious debt 121
   role of specific consent in 104
   secured debt 118

tortious debt 120
transferability of 102
valuation in 107
State practice
availability of empirical data on 2–4, 139, 140,
151, 197–98, 244, 303–4, 328
descriptions of successions in 330–31
diversity of 14
evaluation of 201
exclusion of unlawful 10–11
role of 14, 201, 328, 329–30
significance of decolonization and 60, 132,
291, 300
succession agreements in 51–52, 107, 243, 296
sufficiency of 18
State property, succession to 332–33
automaticity in 102
cultural property as 114–15
debt-claims in 115–16
definition of 102, 107–9, 110
immovable property in 110–11, 112
local property as 109, 111
localized property as 111–12
movable property in 110–11, 112
patrimonial property 108–9, 125, 130, 141
role of specific consent in 104
State archives as 112–14
test of location in 110–11, 112
valuation in 107
types of 107–8
State responsibility, succession to see
international claims and responsibility,
succession to
State succession
annexation and 39, 47, 197–98
codification of 327–28, 333
date of succession 40–43, 107
definition of 1, 13, 19, 31, 59, 61, 329
existence and application of general rules
of... 2, 9–10, 12–13, 18, 201–2, 336
as general international law 1, 18, 36, 51–52
intellectual development of 2, 15, 16, 336
interim ('twilight') period and 104, 146,
156–57, 335
means of effecting in State practice 32–33
nature of 12–13
political narratives concerning 13
process of 87–88, 104, 179–94
prohibition of conquest and 37
scholarship on 2–3, 7–8, 15, 35–36, 145–46
theories of 16–17, 59
typology of 13–14, 43–44, 103, 168–69, 178,
330–32
utility in State practice of 11

State succession, classes of 59, 103
absorption 45, 124–26, 170–72, 216
accession to independence 13, 44, 47–51, 103,
140–43, 178–79, 332
cession 33, 46, 129–32, 175–76, 222, 224–25,
231, 234
colonial protectorates see secession
colonies see secession
disintegration see dismemberment
dismemberment 45–46, 126–29, 172–75, 217, 222
dissolution see dismemberment
distinction between total succession and partial
succession 38, 43–44, 122, 209–10, 331
incorporation see absorption
international protectorates see accession to
independence
Mandatory Territories see accession to
independence
merger 45, 123–24, 169–70, 213, 331–32
newly independent State see accession to
independence
protected States see accession to independence
separation see secession
secession 47, 132–40, 176–78
unification see merger
union see merger
States 37–38
Stern, Brigitte 10
Šturma, Pavel 8, 198–99
methodology as Special Rapporteur 199–201,
212, 215, 221, 232–33
succession agreements see State practice
succession of States see State succession
Sudan (condominium of), secession of
territorial obligations, succession to 85, 86
treaties, succession to 89
Sudetenland, cession of 10–11
nationality, succession and 246–47, 252,
265–66
treaties, succession to 176
Suriname, secession of
boundaries, succession to 70–72
treaties, succession to 177, 189, 191
Switzerland, Confederation of
depositary practice of 161
succession to treaties and 165–66, 193
synchronization, equitable principle of 104
Syria, accession to independence of
nationality, succession and 248–49, 253–54,
255, 284, 285
private property, succession and 296, 310
State property and debt, succession to 141
territorial obligations, succession to 83, 85, 86
treaties, succession to 89, 179

396  INDEX

Syria, secession of  331
  classification of  14
  international claims and responsibility,
    succession to  207–8, 225, 227
  nationality, succession and  269
  treaties, succession to  161, 177, 188–89

Tajikistan, secession of
  nationality, succession and  269, 280
  *uti possidetis juris* and  75–76
Tams, Christian  9
Tanganyika, accession to independence of  270
  boundaries, succession to  99–100
  nationality, succession and  248–49, 250, 284,
    286–87
  private property, succession and  312, 313
  territorial obligations, succession to  79–80, 85
  treaties, succession to  80, 89, 99, 164, 181,
    189, 191
Tanganyika (Mandatory Territory of), creation of
  administrative debt, succession to  118–19
  nationality, succession and  253–54
  tortious debt, succession to  120
Tanzania (Republic of), merger of
  international claims and responsibility,
    succession to  211
  nationality, succession and  246–47, 259, 260
  State property and debt, succession to  123
  treaties, succession to  155, 169, 190
Tarapacá, cession of
  international claims and responsibility,
    succession to  203, 207–8, 223
territorial claims, succession to *see* territorial title
territorial obligations, succession to  77–78, 101
  as customary international law  78
  customs restrictions  82–83
  definition of  77
  fishing and grazing rights  86–87
  leases  78–81
  military base leases  80–81
  navigation and water rights  84–86
  neutralization  82
  rights of passage  83
territorial regimes, succession to *see* territorial
  title, succession to
territorial title, succession to
  acquisition by purchase or donation
  boundaries  63, 66–76
  scope for acquisition of original title  2
  definition of  31–32, 33–35
  descriptions in State practice of  30
  distinction from State property  62–63
  relationship to territorial treaties  61–62, 66,
    84, 86, 88–93, 100–1, 334

  role in the definition of State succession  28
  territorial claims, succession to  62–66, 87, 101
  territorial rights, succession to  63, 336
  territory, definition of  63
territoriality, principle of  33, 329, 330, 334
  relationship to equitable apportionment  105,
    138
  role in succession and nationality  250–51,
    258–59, 289, 290
  role in succession to international claims and
    responsibility  204, 207–8, 227, 230, 237,
    241
  role in succession to State property and
    debt  104, 105, 110–11, 112, 114, 116–17,
    119, 120, 122, 127, 128–29, 132, 134, 137,
    138, 139, 140, 142, 143–44
  test of dominant connection to territory
    in  105, 111
territory *see* territorial title
Tetuan and Nador aeroports *see* Morocco,
  accession to independence of
Texas, absorption of  213
  nationality, succession and  261
  State property and debt, succession to  124–25
Thailand, Kingdom of  129–30, 204
  succession to territorial obligations and  84
  succession to treaties and  89–90, 164, 185, 187
The Hague Academy of International Law
  studies on State succession and  6, 10
  views on codification of State
    succession  30–31
Timor-Leste ('Portuguese Timor'), secession of
  boundaries, succession to  70–72
  nationality, succession and  247, 249–50,
    253–54, 255, 256, 269, 279
  private property, succession and  303–4,
    313–14
  retroactive effect of  313–14
  State property and debt, succession
    to  138–39
Togo (Togolese Republic), secession of  116–17
Togoland, Trust Territory for  286–87
Tonga (Kingdom of), accession to independence
  of  189
treaties, law of  17, 22, 35–36, 145, 146, 162, 167,
    182, 194, 305
  eligibility to succeed to treaties under  147
  fundamental change of circumstances
    under  61–62
  good faith principle under  99
  treaty actions  156–57
  separability of treaty provisions  66, 101
  territorial application rule  150
  third-party principle of  185, 234, 236

INDEX 397

treaties, succession to 332–33
  agreements of provisional application to
    classes of succession 186–87
  ambiguity or silence, interpretation of 146,
    163, 164, 191–92
  amending protocols
  automaticity in 88–93, 146, 147, 155, 171–72,
    175, 178, 334, 335
  automaticity versus clean slate
  bilateral treaties in 162–68
  consent, principle of 146, 147, 334
  constitutive treaties of international
    organizations 149–50
  depositaries and 147, 152, 156–57, 160–62
  devolution agreements in 145, 183–85
  eligibility to 148
  formalities and 180
  general agreements in 183
  general declarations of provisional continuity
    in 189–90, 247
  general declarations of succession in 188–89,
    190
  interim ('twilight') period in 146, 157
  law of treaties and 145, 194, 335
  localization, principle of 154–55
  moving treaty frontiers principle in 151–54
  multilateral treaties in 155–62
  paradigm in 146, 147
  personal versus real or dispositive treaties 61
  provisional treaty actions 180–81
  reservations in 1, 155, 181–82
  succession clauses in 148
  successive treaty actions in 158–59
  successive treaty versions and amending
    protocols in 159–60
  temporality in 147, 156–57, 165
  territorial application in 150
  time-limits in 190–91
Trinidad and Tobago, secession of
  nationality, succession and 248–49
  State property and debt, succession to 132
  territorial obligations, succession to 80–81
  treaties, succession to 155, 162, 166–67,
    187
Trust Territories see State succession, classes of
Tunisia ('Tunis'), accession to independence
    of 49–50
  nationality, succession and 286
  territorial obligations, succession to 86
  treaties, succession to 89, 179
Türkiye ('Turkey', 'Ottoman Empire')
  succession to State debt and 107
  succession to territorial obligations and 86
  succession to treaties and 89

Turkmenistan, secession of
  boundaries, succession to 91–92
  nationality, succession and 246–47, 253–54,
    269, 280
  treaties, succession to 164
Turtle and Mangsee Islands, administrative
    cession of see Philippines, secession of
Tuvalu ('Ellis Islands'), secession of
  treaties, succession to 189, 191
Two Sicilies (Kingdom of), merger of 213,
    309–10

Uganda, secession of
  nationality, succession and 270
  State contracts, succession and 314
  State property and debt, succession to 132
  treaties, succession to 89, 181, 189, 191
Ukraine, Republic of
  cultural property, succession to 114
  nationality, succession and 246, 251–52,
    253–54, 269, 280
  private property, succession and 303
  treaties, succession to 157–58, 165, 182–83,
    188–89, 193
  uti possidetis juris and 100
  Transvaal Republic, absorption of 213
  State property and debt, succession to 108–9,
    124–25
United Arab Emirates ('Trucial States'),
    accession to independence of 76
United Arab Republic, merger of 45, 60, 221
  international claims and responsibility,
    succession to 203, 211
  nationality, succession and 245–47, 249–50, 259
  private property, succession and 296
  State property and debt, succession to 123
  territorial obligations, succession to 83, 85
  treaties, succession to 154, 155, 164, 169, 190
United Kingdom of Great Britain and Northern
    Ireland
  depositary practice of 160
  succession to nationality and 270
  succession to State debt and 115–16
  succession to State property and 109
  succession to treaties and 89, 173–74, 184, 185
United Nations Diplomatic Conference on the
    Succession of States in respect of State
    Property, Archives and Debts see Vienna
    Convention on Succession of States in respect
    of State Property, Archives and Debts 1983
United Nations Diplomatic Conference on the
    Succession of States in respect of Treaties see
    Vienna Convention on Succession of States
    in respect of Treaties 1978

398 INDEX

United Nations General Assembly 7, 24, 25–28, 29, 30–31, 39, 53, 59, 221, 244–45, 247, 287, 295–96, 302, 318–19, 331
United Nations Secretariat 161, 185, 190
United States of America, secession of 11
  depositary practice of 161
  succession to State property and debt 132
  succession to territorial obligations and 80–81
  succession to treaties and 152–53
  territorial claims, succession to 64
unjust enrichment, equitable principle of 104, 107, 209, 335
use of force, prohibition of *see* State succession, annexation and
*uti possidetis, ita possideatis,* customary rule of 74–76
  as general rule of customary international law 69–72, 87–88
  as regional custom in Africa 68, 73, 101
  as regional custom in Spanish Central and South Americas 72–73, 87, 101
  persistent objections to 94–98
Uzbekistan, secession of
  nationality, succession and 246–47, 253–54, 280
  treaties, succession to 155
  *uti possidetis juris* and 75

Vanuatu ('New Hebrides'), secession of 226
  administrative debt, succession to 118–19
  boundaries, succession to 73–74
Venetia-Lombardy, cession of 106, 129–30
Venezuela (Bolivarian Republic of), secession of 97
  succession to State debt and 107
Vienna Convention on the Law of Treaties 1969 66
  succession to treaties, relationship with 88, 145
Vienna Convention on Succession of States in respect of State Property, Archives and Debts 1983 17, 22–23, 44, 328, 332
  adoption of 5, 102–3
  application as customary international law 103, 110–11, 113, 116, 132, 138, 143–44, 148
  reliance in dispute settlement on 9, 140
  role of equity in 4–5, 104, 138, 141, 143
  role of good faith negotiation in 103
  State archives in 108, 113
  State debt in 115–16
  status of 4–5, 22–23, 60, 102–3, 143–44
  typology of 124, 125–26, 129, 130, 137–38, 141–43, 331

Vienna Convention on Succession of States with respect to Treaties 1978 17, 22–23, 44, 145, 327, 328, 332
  application as customary international law 67, 145–46, 149–50, 153–54, 155, 156–58, 162–63, 170, 175, 179, 182–83, 194
  application as treaty law 3–4, 22–23, 60, 62, 145, 194
  automaticity in 92–93, 155, 170, 171–72, 175, 178, 194, 334
  empirical basis of 3–4
  participation in 3–4, 145
  reliance in dispute settlement on 9
  status of 145–46
  territorial regimes and 61–62, 66, 68–69, 77–78, 97–98
Viet Nam (Democratic Republic of), secession of
  nationality, succession of 269
  private property, succession and 298, 304, 313
Viet Nam (Republic of), secession of
  nationality, succession and 245–46, 253–54, 269, 275–76
  private property, succession and 298
  territorial obligations, succession to 84
  State property and debt, succession to 106, 114, 119, 133–34, 138
Viet Nam, merger of
  boundaries, succession to 73–74, 96–97
  international claims and responsibility, succession to 203, 211–12
  nationality, succession and 246–47, 248–49, 259, 260
  State property, succession to 107
  State property and debt, succession to 118–19, 123–24
  territorial claims, succession to 64
  treaties, succession to 169

Waldock, Sir Humphrey 17, 18, 22, 44, 47–48, 61
  definition of State succession by 16, 20, 23
  methodology as Special Rapporteur 3, 17, 36, 145, 194
Walvis Bay, cession of 223
  nationality, succession and 246, 248, 253, 265–66, 267, 289
West Indies, Federation of *see* Antigua and Barbuda; Barbados; Dominica; Grenada; Jamaica; Saint Kitts and Nevis; Saint Lucia; Saint Vincent and the Grenadines; Trinidad and Tobago
West Irian ('West New Guinea'), cession of
  nationality, succession of 265
  private property, succession and 318

Yemen, merger of 328
  international claims and responsibility, succession to 211
  nationality, succession and 246, 250, 259, 261, 273
  private property, succession and 302, 312, 313, 316
  State property and debt, succession to 117–18, 123
  territorial obligations, succession to 86
  treaties, succession to 89, 91, 152, 169, 190
Yemen, People's Democratic Republic of ('South Yemen'), secession of
  nationality, succession and 245–46, 253–54, 268
  State property and debt, succession to 116, 118, 132–33
  treaties, succession to 178, 184
  *uti possidetis juris* and 95–96
Yugoslavia (Socialist Federal Republic of), dismemberment of 32–33, 45–46
Arbitration Commission of the Conference on Yugoslavia ('Badinter Commission') 74–75, 104
  boundaries, succession to 70–72, 74–75
  international claims and responsibility, succession to 217, 219–20
  nationality, succession and 251–52, 254–55
  private property, succession and 303, 309–10

State archives, succession to 112
State property and debt, succession to 104, 105, 106, 107, 108–9, 110, 111–12, 114, 115, 117–18, 120, 126–28
treaties, succession to 91, 159, 160, 172–73
Yugoslavia, Federal Republic of ('State Union of Serbia-Montenegro') 328
  claim to the legal identity of the Socialist Federal Republic of Yugoslavia 13, 32–33, 40, 127, 147, 172–73
  nationality, succession and 246–47, 248–49, 253–54, 255, 263–64
  treaties, succession to 147, 160, 172–73, 181, 186
Yugoslavia, Kingdom of ('Kingdom of Serbia')... 151, 153

Zambia ('Northern Rhodesia'), secession of
  nationality, succession and 253, 284
  private property, succession and 312
  territorial obligations, succession to 87
  treaties, succession to 89, 167, 181, 189, 191
Zanzibar, secession of 270
  nationality, succession and 248–49
  State property and debt, succession to 132
Zimbabwe ('Southern Rhodesia'), secession of 189
Zimmermann, Andreas 10